Mere Irish and Fíor-Ghael

CRITICAL CONDITIONS: FIELD DAY ESSAYS AND MONOGRAPHS

Edited by Seamus Deane

Critical Conditions: Field Day Monographs

Mere Irish and Fíor-Ghael

Studies in the Idea of Irish Nationality,
its Development and Literary Expression
prior to the Nineteenth Century

Joep Leerssen

UNIVERSITY OF NOTRE DAME PRESS
in association with
FIELD DAY

Voor Ann

Published in the United States in 1997 by
UNIVERSITY OF NOTRE DAME PRESS
Notre Dame, Indiana 46556
All Rights Reserved.

and in Ireland by
CORK UNIVERSITY PRESS
University College Cork, Ireland

The paper used in this publication meets the minimum requirements of the
American National Standard for Information Sciences–Permanence of
paper for Printed Library Materials, ANSI Z39.48–1984

Library of Congress Cataloging-in-Publication Data

Leerssen, Joseph Th. (Joseph Theodoor), 1955–
    [Mere Irish & fíor-ghael]
    Mere Irish and fíor-ghael : studies in the idea of Irish
nationality, its development and literary expression prior to the
nineteenth century / Joep Leerssen.
       p. cm. — (Critical conditions : 3)
    Originally published: Mere Irish & fíor-ghael. Amsterdam :
Philadelphia : John Benjamins Pub. Co., 1986.
    Includes bibliographical references and index.
    ISBN 0-268-01427-2 (alk. paper)
    1. National characteristics, Irish—History. 2. English
literature—Irish authors—History and criticism. 3. English
literature—Irish influences. 4. Irish poetry—History and
criticism. 5. Nationalism—Ireland—History. 6. Ireland—
Intellectual life. 7. Ireland—In literature. 8. Ireland—
Civilization. 9. Irish in literature. I. Title. II. Series.
DA925.L44 1997
941.5—dc20

96–42498
CIP

CONTENTS

ACKNOWLEDGEMENTS

The preparations of this study put me under a heavy debt of gratitude to a number of persons and institutions; it is a pleasure to record and acknowledge them here.

In the first place must be mentioned the steady help and the moral and scholarly support of my thesis supervisors, Professors De Deugd and Dyserinck, whose guidance and expertise was an indispensable benefit to me.

Item, the expert and courteous assistance of the librarians and staff of the National Library of Ireland, Dublin, and of the John P. Roberts Research Library at the University of Toronto.

Item, the financial support of the Netherlands Organization for the Advancement of Pure Research (Z.W.O.) which made the initial publication of this study possible.

Item, the scholars who generously aided and inspired me: Dr. Margaret MacCurtain, Professor Doris Edel, Dr. Séamus Ó Mórdha, Professor Seán Ó Tuama, Dr. Alan Titley, Mr. Paul Walsh; and, especially, my dear friend Professor Ann Dooley, for all her advice, help and hospitality.

Item, last but not least: my parents, my parents-in-law – and above all, my wife.

The second edition was prepared during a sabbatical leave of absence granted me by the University of Amsterdam, and spent as a visiting academic at Trinity College Dublin; I am grateful to both these institutions. I was placed under a renewed obligation to the excellent and delightful National Library of Ireland. Dr Máirín Ní Dhonnchadha most kindly offered her collegial and expert assistance in the correction of translations from the Irish. And as always, Ann Rigney was an invaluable support, not only morally as my spouse and companion, but also intellectually as a clear-sighted scholar and sympathetically critical reader.

ABBREVIATIONS

AFM   *Annála rioghachta Éireann. Annals of the kingdom of Ireland, by the Four Masters.* (ed. John O'Donovan). 7 vols. Dublin 1854.

AithDD   *Aithdioghluim Dána. A miscellany of Irish bardic poetry.* (ed. Lambert McKenna). 2 vols. Dublin: Irish Texts Society, 1939–40.

BMCat   *Catalogue of Irish manuscripts in the British Museum.* (eds. S.H. O'Grady & R. Flower) 3 vols. London: The trustees, 1926–53.

5PP   *Five seventeenth-century political poems.* (ed. Cecile O'Rahilly). Dublin: Dublin Institute for Advanced Studies, 1952.

IBP   *Irish bardic poetry.* (ed. Osborn Bergin). Dublin: Dublin Institute for Advanced Studies, 1970.

NDh   *Nua-dhuanaire.* (eds. P. de Brún, B. Ó Buachalla & T. Ó Concheanainn). 3 vols. Dublin: Dublin Institute for Advanced Studies, 1975–81.

NHI   *A new history of Ireland.* (eds. T.W. Moody, F.X. Martin & F.J. Byrne). 10 vols. Oxford: Clarendon, 1976 – (in progress).

RIACat   *Catalogue of Irish manuscripts in the Royal Irish Academy.* Dublin: Royal Irish Academy, 1958.

TD   *The bardic poems of Tadhg Dall Ó Huiginn (1550–1591).* (ed. Eleanor Knott). 2 vols. London: Irish Texts Society, 1922–26.

SPELLING, TYPOGRAPHY, NOMENCLATURE, TRANSLATIONS

Spelling and typography in the quotations correspond to those in the originals. All italicizations are the originals', unless otherwise indicated. Only the following changes have been made:

- Diacritical abbreviations have been spelled out, e.g. y^e to 'the', $th\bar{e}$ to 'them' or 'then'; in Irish, the *seimhiú*-dot has (in accordance with general practice) been spelled out as 'h'; all ampersands appear as '&'.
- 'Long s' has been modernized.
- Capitalization in titles has been rationalized throughout.
- In English and Latin, the usage of u/v and i/j has been normalized: *vniuersall* as 'universall', *maiestie* as 'majestie'.

Page numbers in small roman numerals given in square brackets (with additionally, wherever possible, signature numbers) refer to unnumbered pages in the original; in such cases, I have counted the title page as page [i].

Irish names have been given in their Gaelic or English form depending on the context (Gaelic literature or general history) and on the question as to which form was the better known of the two: O'Flaherty and Ó Maolchonaire rather than Ó Flaithbheartaigh and Conry. A few inconsistencies were unavoidable:

- A Gaelic poet and scholar appears in different contexts both as Hugh MacCurtin and Aodh Mac Cruitín;
- The brothers Ó hEoghusa/O'Hussey have been given different name forms, Eochaidh's name being better known in the Gaelic, that of Maelbrighde (Bonaventura in religion) in the English spelling;
- Both the English and the Irish forms of the name Ó Cléirigh/O'Clery occur.

Many Gaelic names have been left in the old spelling (e.g. Ó Conchobhair rather than Ó Conchúir, Ó Domhnaill rather than Ó Dónaill) so as to maintain consistency between text and quotations. Epithets like *Ruadh* and *Buidhe* have been modernized to *Rua* and *Buí*.

Quotations in other languages than English or French are translated at the foot of the page; wherever editorial translations were available, these have been followed, and indicated as such. Solecisms on my part in translations from the Irish have for this edition been kindly corrected by Dr. Máirín Ní Dhonnchadha, DIAS; I am deeply grateful for her kind and expert assistance.

Therefore, if I know not the meaning of the voice, I shall be unto him that speaketh a barbarian, and he that speaketh shall be a barbarian unto me.

I Cor. XIV: 11

It is computed, that eleven Thousand Persons have, at several times, suffered Death, rather than submit to break their Eggs at the smaller End.

A voyage to Lilliput

        . . . the finest nation,
Wid charming pisantry on a fruitful sod,
Fighting like divils for conciliation,
An' hating each other for the love of God.

Nineteenth-century Dublin street ballad

Talia siquidem mihi dudum proponenti, diuque in animo anxie volventi, vix tandem angulus unus, quasi ab aliis relictis, terrarum scilicet finis Hibernicus orbis occurrit; nec ille omnino intactus; nullius tamen hactenus stile absolute comprehensus.

Sed ad Hibernia potestne aliquid boni esse? Numquid montes illi stillabunt dulcedinem, et valles fluent mel et lac? Sugamus ergo mel de petra, et oleum de saxo.

Topographia Hibernica
(Giraldus Cambrensis)

PREFACE TO THE SECOND EDITION

Ten years have passed since this book was first published, and fifteen years since I started writing it. At the time, I felt that there was a need for such a book: a synthetic, interdisciplinary study of the historical dynamics of Irish literature and of the antagonistic national terms in which that literature and culture have come to be conceptualized. Little of the material covered in this book was new or previously unknown; but the historical study of culture, ideas, attitudes and literature in Ireland seemed fragmented between isolated disciplines, and frequently hamstrung by the essentialist assumption that 'culture' and 'nationality' are extrahistorical, categorical pregivens, permanent throughout history by dint of autonomous self-perpetuation. My ambition, therefore, was to draw comparative material from the various languages of Ireland (Gaelic, Latin, English); to study 'historical' and 'literary' sources from these various linguistic traditions in their mutual interdependence and interconnection rather than as separate spheres; and to draw from that material a historical model concerning the development of an idea of Irish nationality, i.e. as an ideological product of historical developments.

Much work has been done in this field since 1986, and I must ask myself now if there is still a need for such a book as this, or for a new edition. A number of topics I addressed have since been covered by other accomplished scholars, in greater analytical detail than this general survey could hope to offer. The availability of primary source material (I had deliberately given as many and as extensive quotations as possible) has now been guaranteed by the excellent *Field Day anthology of Irish writing*, and an outstanding interdisciplinary compendium and reference work has become available in Welch's *Oxford companion to Irish literature*. Scholars in history and literary history have fruitfully turned to the various interconnections (previously somewhat neglected) between Gaelic and Anglo-Irish Ireland, and in the process they have refined and nuanced to a great extent the manichean historical views of earlier generations. There is now an interdisciplinary notion of 'Irish Studies' which was all but absent in 1980, and crucial but neglected periods and episodes in Irish cultural history (such as the early seventeenth or mid-eighteenth century) have by now been studied very profitably from a variety of perspectives.

Indeed, so numerous are the valuable recent studies in this area that I would almost have to rewrite this book completely if I had to take all of them into account. For eighteenth-century antiquarianism, there is now the excellent Cambridge PhD-thesis by Clare O'Halloran, 'Golden ages and barbarous nations:

1

Antiquarian debate on the Celtic past in Ireland and Scotland in the eighteenth century', the commercial publication of which is eagerly awaited; much work has been done by political and intellectual historians on the Tudor period (Canny, Ellis, Bradshaw), on the seventeenth century (Cunningham, Gillespie) and on the eighteenth century (Barnard, Bartlett, Berman, Connolly, Whelan); the interaction between Ireland's two cultures in Penal times has, moreover, been given fresh interest by the historians and critics associated with the 'Eighteenth-Century Ireland Society' (Carpenter, Harrison, Kelly) who have given us studies of key figures such as Anthony Raymond, John Toland, archbishops King and Molyneux. The study of Irish literature for the early modern period has been steadily profiting from the work of Breandán Ó Buachalla (though published in dispersed form), and has received an enlivening jolt from Michelle O'Riordan's *The Gaelic mind and the collapse of the Gaelic world*; my own work on Irish literary history in the seventeenth and eighteenth centuries would have benefited if I had had the use of O'Riordan's study, of J. Caerwyn Williams & M. Ní Mhuiríosa's *Traidisiún liteartha na nGael* and of Nicholas Williams's study *I bprionta i leabhar*. International contacts and ramifications of literature in Irish have been addressed by scholars like Mícheál Mac Craith and Tadhg Ó Dúshláine, and the late medieval period has been given excellent fresh treatment by Katharine Simms. The beginnings of Anglo-Irish literature, and Irish literary nationalism, in a United Irish context (a lacuna, I confess, in this book) have been admirably charted by Mary Helen Thuente, *The harp re-strung*. Much light on the United Irishmen and their background has also been thrown by the work of Marianne Elliott and of Nancy Curtin; mention should also be made of James Kelly's book on Grattan's parliament, *Prelude to Union*.

Luckily, most of this more recent work proved to be an elaboration and occasional correction of my own work rather than a complete refutation. I have therefore contented myself to rewrite parts of the introduction (which reflected all too woodenly the origin of this book as a doctoral thesis) and the concluding pages – since post-1800 developments are now given fuller treatment in my *Remembrance and imagination*; and I have attempted to clear away such factual, typographical and stylistic errors and solecisms as have come to my notice since the book's first appearance. In the process, I could gratefully profit from the expertise and assistance which was kindly offered to me by Dr. Máirín Ní Dhonnchadha.

On the whole, then, this book must continue to rest on whatever merits it had in 1986. While it is anything but the last word upon the various subjects it deals with, its usefulness for present-day readers will lie mainly (a) in its comparative-synthetic juxtaposition of different cultural spheres, (b) in its attempt to show that the separate, inimical cultural traditions and identities in Irish life did mutually influence and shape each other, and (c) in the trans-insular perspective, which places this interaction against the background of wider European developments. The book's improved index may also enhance its use as a compendium and a cross-disciplinary work of reference.

The emphasis with which I have advanced and argued my contention that culture and nationality are constructs, intellectual artefacts and shared subjectivities rather than objective conditions, seems perhaps a little overstated nowadays: historical constructivism has become a practically self-evident assumption. Studies on nationality and nationalism (Ernest Gellner, Eric Hobsbawm and Benedict Anderson foremost among them) have, whatever their mutual differences of emphasis and political valorization, amply borne out that point which I have tried to argue from an imagological perspective in my introductory chapter; and even within the field of Irish studies practically all scholars have by now abandoned the old habit of national essentialism. Generally, the idea of Irish culture as a historical praxis, and Irish identity as a a reputation and shared self-definition implicated in a historical dynamics, has gained widespread acceptance among scholars whatever their discipline, working period or political stance. This much is exemplified by books as diverse as Cairns/Richards's *Writing Ireland*, the collection *Representing Ireland*, ed. Bradshaw, Hadfield and Mays, and the excellent critical essays and surveys in the *Field Day anthology of Irish writing*. For all that Brian Ború, Eoghan Rua Ó Néill, Wolfe Tone and Patrick Pearse may have had a certain historical role in common, no-one will now seriously contend that their shared anti-foreign championship outweighs the vast historical, cultural and ideological differences between them: a medieval native chief fighting the Danes, a counter-reformation scion to a feudal lordship fighting the Roundheads, a Jacobin democrat fighting the British *ancien régime*, and a Catholic-nationalist poet and educationalist rising against the post-Victorian empire. Nor will the one shared aspect of their anti-foreign protagonism offer us an adequate perspective towards understanding their historical role and position. In other words, a proper historical study of such figures will have to concentrate, not just on what they had in common, but on what made them different.

Perhaps this point is still worth making nowadays, after all the recent revisionism altercations. I still believe that in studying Irish cultural history our task is to study the variability and the dynamics of history rather than to assume and reiterate the received version of its continuity and self-similarity; that it is more rewarding to study the dynamics and variability of the past than to pass judgement upon it by our present-day political standards, or to distill from it some master-plot or invariant formula ('English hegemony and Irish resistance'). It is not that such a view would be wrong; on the contrary, it would be foolish to deny it or to pretend that Irish history took shape in any other conditions than those of hegemony and resistance. (After all, that is also the frame of reference for this book itself.) But this view, while in itself correct, may become reductive. It privileges the similarities and marginalizes the particularities; it invites us to prove general rules rather than to spot the exceptions, to subordinate the recalcitrance of the facts to the neatness of the model. It is a standing invitation to anachronistic projection – and as Paul Veyne has reminded us, the study of history is 'a constant struggle against our tendency towards anachronism'.

I would not like to see this book belatedly brought into the tired and misguided 'revisionism' debate. All historians are by definition revisionists; if they find nothing to improve upon in the history-books of yesteryear, they can take up gardening or biochemistry, and we can contend ourselves with eternally re-reading the old historical classics that have laid down the standard story of the past once and for all. Of course, there is truth and error on both sides of the revisionism debate. Revisionist history is unavoidable and necessary because our inherited versions of the past are often based on superseded or insufficient data, or coloured by attitudes which, as time passes, come to reveal their partiality. Yet on the other hand, it is not enough for the historian to say: 'Contrary to what generations of people have believed heretofore, X, Y or Z was never like this but like that.' That can lead to pedantic one-upmanship. Surely, once such a point has been made, the question immediately following it must be: how was it possible for generations of reasonably sane and reasonably well-informed people to hold such a belief concerning X, Y or Z? And was not that belief, whatever its truth-value, an operative force in historical developments?

Events and facts are in and of themselves meaningless; meaning is something they acquire once humans try to make sense of them. All events and all facts reach us in mediatized form. What we believe or perceive to be: that is what shapes our attitudes and actions; and the historian cannot play off the facts 'as they really were' against the facts as they were seen to be, rightly or wrongly, at the time. In other words, historians must engage critically with the subjectivity of the past, with the way in which events and situations were seen by one's sources. Historians must not slavishly submit themselves to their sources' point of view, as if empathy constituted the sole legitimate basis for historical understanding (which is what some anti-revisionists would seem to think), nor should they discard it as if it were mere bothersome background noise (which is what some revisionists would seem to prefer). It would seem more fruitful instead to register the repercussions which events and conflicts sent through the ranks of participants and onlookers, and to register these shockwaves in all their variety and mutual contradictions and disagreements. History is not just an accumulation of events, but crucially also the human experience of those events.

This book is based on the assumption that the world around us and the past behind us are ineluctably mediatized. The topic of this study is images and ideas, attitudes and mentalities, as seen in their historicity, the extent to which they are different, and fascinating, and enriching if studied in their own context.

Consequently, for all its historicism, this book has little or no room for socio-economic determinism. Many historicist analyses of historical culture appear to treat 'culture' (ideas, letters) as output, to be 'explained' in terms of the underlying socio-economic input (material, political or economic circumstances). Such determinism leaves me dissatisfied. If the fundamental meaning of 'explaining' is to resolve obscurities and to clarify a topic, I am unconvinced that the translation of a topic from one sphere of public life (culture) into the terms of another sphere of public life (politics or socioeconomic relations) necessarily constitutes an 'explanation'. In other words, I am unsure why such a purported 'explanation' should necessarily follow this particular one-track trajectory from mental output to material input. That is not to say that materialist historicism is worthless; far from it. It is only to give my reasons why (even if I have often been inspired, intrigued or instructed by such studies) I have not felt compelled to restrict myself to this unidirectional approach. Cultural and ideological artefacts are not merely secondary epiphenomena; in influencing people and shaping or provoking reactions far beyond the socio-economic or political environment where they originated, their historical function (or 'meaning' or 'importance') is neither circumscribed nor adequately explained by the terms of their societal provenance. The subjectivity of the past leads a life of its own. It is that life, in all its transformations and conflicts, which continues to intrigue.

Accordingly, the texts studied here are usually placed in a double perspective: contextual and intertextual. The attitudes and images expressed at various points in history should be seen, on the one hand, in the context of the ideological and political circumstances, the conditions in which they were uttered, entered the public domain and gained their significance. On the other hand, such attitudes and images are studied in their intertextuality – for part of their significance is derived from conventions, commonplaces and indeed stereotypes, from previous texts and standard patterns of representation and outlook. Whatever is written about Ireland is written in a specific historical/political moment and with a burden of discursive pre-programming, an intertextually established bandwidth of what is sayable and indeed conceivable on the topic of Ireland. The representation of Ireland is a textual fabric in which ideological climate and discursive convention are the warp and the woof. Both dimensions, the contextual and the intertextual, should be taken equally into account when studying Irish literary history.

INTRODUCTION
Aims and Methods

The aim of this investigation is to reconsider the cultural confrontation between England and Ireland from a new methodological perspective, and to trace how this confrontation resulted in a particular notion, literary as well as political, of Irish nationality.

Since the twelfth century, the two countries have found themselves linked in a close and generally painful political involvement that culminated, in 1800, in the passing of the Act of Union between Great Britain and Ireland. Irish resistance to this increasingly confining subordination under the English/British Crown has been frequent in the country's history, and indeed the entire history of Ireland since the middle ages might be written (and has often been written) under the aspect of Irish resistance to English expansionism. The political history of Ireland is to no small extent the history of its confrontation with the neighbouring isle.

My present aim is to investigate the terms in which this confrontation was conceived of. If one speaks of a confrontation between 'England' and 'Ireland', what does one mean by these categories? Under which aspect did 'Ireland' present itself to an English eye, and what was the 'England' whose presence and political control was resisted in Ireland? National names like 'England' and 'Ireland' are generalities whose meaning covers the entire economic, cultural, political life of a country and its inhabitants – its folklore, architecture, legal or educational system, cuisine, agriculture, politics, language, geographic infrastructure, natural resources and so on *ad infinitum*. It is clear, however, that, in this particular confrontation, the national terms had a highly changeable meaning and application over the centuries, and a far more restricted reference. The question what exactly these national denominations did stand for in the context of that confrontation is not merely of academic value – for such national categories, not in their general range of reference, but rather in their more restricted, narrowed-down, politicized, 'confrontational' meaning, form the parameters in which national ideologies with their political terminology or rhetoric take shape.

Some valuable works are already extant which deal with these national attitudes underlying the Irish-English confrontation. M. W. Heslinga's inspiring and ground-breaking study *The Irish border as a cultural divide* (1962) should be mentioned, which offers, as the sub-title puts it, 'A contribution to the study of regionalism in the British Isles'. The work of David B. Quinn on sixteenth-century English colonial attitudes towards Ireland (especially his *The Elizabethans and the Irish*, 1966) has not only sparked off a new and fruitful approach to the troubled and troublesome Elizabethan period in Irish history – exemplified with different emphases in the works of N.P. Canny (e.g. *The Elizabethan conquest of Ireland*, 1976) and of Brendan Bradshaw (*The constitutional revolution of the*

6

Sixteenth Century, 1979) – but has also given a model example of the far-reaching historical and political importance that axiomatic and precritical national attitudes and prejudices can have. Of similar merit, though dealing with a wholly different period, and with the 'other side' of the English-Irish conflict, is Oliver MacDonagh's *States of Mind* (1983) which tills, as the author puts it in his preface, 'the practically unworked field of the history of ideas and mentality in Ireland' with regard to the widespread tendency among Irish nationalists of the nineteenth century to put their political attitude mainly in terms of past history and its claim on the present. This 'Irish habit of historical thought', as MacDonagh calls it, itself stands in a historical relation to, is, in fact, the indirect result of, the earlier English attitudes as investigated by Quinn and Canny.

The aim of my own contribution to this field is, then, to show how one could result from the other: how the various national categorizations, generalizations, characterizations, could interact and develop between the death of Elizabeth and the Act of Union, and how the early attributes that the conflicting parties fastened on each other could come to govern a national conflict repeatedly verging on open war.

That aim is admittedly a highly ambitious one. Merely to register the changing attitudes as expressed in two entire centuries one has to venture deeply both into political and historical discourse of the period, and into the literature of both the countries concerned; one must also take into account such wider intellectual developments as may have influenced the mode and form of the expression of these national attitudes.

This task was greatly facilitated by the fact that I could apply a well-defined methodology to this material, which as a result lost much of its disparateness and amorphousness. The method which I have applied to this topic is that of 'imagology' or 'image studies', originally a specialism in Comparative Literature concerned with the role of cultural perceptions and identity-constructs in international literary and cultural traffic. The theory and methodology of Image Studies were elaborated and refined chiefly in the comparatist programme at Aachen university, headed by Hugo Dyserinck, during the 1960s and 1970s.[1]

Imagology may be loosely defined as the study of the discursive or literary expression of national attitudes. Initially concerned with the literary characterization of 'l'étranger tel qu'on le voit', it has in more recent times developed the realization that national attitudes can govern the very fabric of the discursive or literary activity of a given period: govern both the writers' implicit understanding of themselves as writers in a specific national tradition, and also the reception of their writings. The importance of national attitudes will be noticeable especially in such writings where authors themselves do not confine their subject-matter to native home-grown propria (though that may in its motivation or in its reception obtain its own nationally ideological charge) but address matters which lie beyond the ken of their own cultural tradition. In this case, the writer must come to terms with what Dyserinck has called the 'Fremderfahrung',[2] the experience of the foreign, in the very aspect of its foreignness, i.e. that which distinguishes it from the writer's own position or presuppositions and constitutes it as 'foreign' to begin with. The result of this is an 'image' of the foreign (*l'étranger tel qu'on le voit*), which may, like so many other literary or discursive topoi, enter a textual tradition, become a commonplace, a stereotype.[3]

This implies that national images (of course one might deal with social or gender images as well, should one choose) are to be studied as part of a textual tradition. Indeed it should be kept in mind that the imagologist studies the textual expression of an image, and the historical context of its textual expression, rather than its pretended reference to empirical reality. This position is more or less like that of a historian of witchcraft, who need not enter into the question whether a certain incantation or ceremony could 'really' make one fly through the air on a broomstick: the pretended effectiveness of witchcraft can remain outside his historical endeavour, which instead can concentrate on the social position and impact of the belief in, and practice of, witchcraft. Similarly the imagologist need not be concerned with the referential claim of a given image: we can dispense with the imponderable and ultimately nugatory question whether Spaniards actually *are* proud, or whether the seventeenth-century Irish actually *were* lazy; instead, we can study its development as a discursive topos in a textual tradition, the permutations it underwent in relation to its typological forerunners or successors, the relation in which it stood to political thought and/or literary practice, and so on. In short, we can study a debate without entering it.

Such stereotypes belong at the same time to political and/or literary practice, and to abstract cogitation; they can he regarded as an abstract idea or as the concrete expression of that idea, or, again, as an idea that only exists inasmuch as it is expressed. National images, like elements of a political doctrine or religious dogma, are imponderable in themselves but can be registered unambiguously in their historical impact on empirical reality. The ontology of a Popperian 'world 3' has not unfruitfully been used to describe this quality;[4] alternatively, some imagologists have dealt with imagotypes as 'objets discursifs' (in the terminology of Michel Foucault), textual/discursive expressions of a 'formation discursive', a community of attitudes in which a given tradition of writers shares.[5]

However, neither the philosopher of science Popper, nor the 'historian of systems of thought' Foucault, is primarily concerned with such notions in their concrete textual expression. Rather than pass straight from the textuality of 'objets discursifs' to the matter of the underlying 'formation discursive' with which Foucault is exclusively concerned; and rather than follow Popper in the cognitive, epistemological and methodological concomitants of his useful ontological insights, I, as a literary historian, will concentrate here on the stereotype in its textual expression: stereotypes will be dealt with *in concreto* (as the result of their having been expressed) rather than *in abstracto* (as being capable of being expressed).

National stereotypes can be expressed both in referential (i.e. 'non-fictional') and in fictional texts: they are to be found in travel descriptions and histories as well as in poetry or drama. To some extent the nature of my approach transcends this division of texts into what has traditionally been called the 'literary' field of the critic and the 'non-literary' realm of the historian, much as it also transcends, as Dyserinck has pointed out,[6] the division between the 'intrinsic' and 'extrinsic' study of literature itself. Foucault has questioned the traditional generic divisions between literary, historical and scientific texts, particularly with reference to texts antedating that mode of division which belongs largely to the nineteenth century:

> Il faut aussi s'inquiéter devant ces découpages ou groupements dont nous avons acquis la familiarité. Peut-on admettre, telles quelles, la distinction des grands types de discours, ou celle des formes ou des genres qui opposent les unes aux autres science, littérature, philosophie, religion, histoire, fiction, etc., et qui en font des sortes de grandes individualités historiques? Nous ne sommes pas sûrs nous-mêmes de l'usage de ces distinctions dans le monde de discours qui est le nôtre. A plus forte raison lorsqu'il s'agit d'analyser des ensembles d'énoncés qui étaient, à l'époque de leur formulation, distribués, répartis et caractérisés d'une toute autre manière: après tout la 'littérature' et la 'politique' sont des catégories récentes qu'on ne peut appliquer à la culture médiévale ou même encore à la culture classique que par une hypothèse rétrospective, et par un jeu d'analogies formelles ou de ressemblances sémantiques; mais ni la littérature, ni la politique, ni non plus la philosophie et les sciences n'articulaient le champ du discours, au XVIIe ou au XVIIIe siècle, comme elles l'ont articulé au XIXe siècle. De toute façon, ces découpages – qu'il s'agisse de ceux que nous admettons, ou de ceux qui sont contemporains des discours étudiés – sont toujours eux-mêmes des catégories réflexives, des principes de classement, des régles normatives, des types institu-tionnalisés; ce sont à leur tour des faits de discours qui méritent d'être analysés à côté des autres; ils ont, à coup sûr, avec eux des rapports complexes, mais ils n'en sont pas des caractères intrinsèques, autochtones et universellement reconnaissables.[7]

Foucault's point that a division between 'literary' and 'non-literary' texts (i.e. in the formalist sense: literature as a verbal form of art) is an anachronism both diffractive and restrictive when applied to a seventeenth- or eighteenth-century context, is of capital importance. It means on the one hand that an exclusion of so-called 'non-literary' forms of discourse (travel description, historiography, controversialist pamphlets . . .) would imply a violation of the mind-set of those earlier authors whose work we study; on the other hand it points to the crucial historical importance that 'literary' texts (novels, poems, plays) can have, to the ensuing necessity of taking good note of them, and to the attendant necessity of doing so with methods that do justice to their specific generic character (e.g. their fictionality, the poetical conventions governing them, etc.).

Those conventions and genre-distinctions offer a firmer working ground than the opposition between 'literature' and 'other discourse'. Whereas a writer from the early eighteenth century (be his residence Grub Street or Twickenham) might be at a loss to comprehend our post-romantic differentiation between 'literature-as-art' and 'the rest', he would have little difficulty recognizing a comedy as a comedy, a travel description as a travel description, or an epic poem, a verse satire or a philosophical treatise as precisely that.

In studying national types principally in their literary/discursive expression,[8] this study is, then, primarily a literary one (albeit in a wider sense than the aesthetic definition of 'literature'). Given the fact that it addresses literature as a multinational phenomenon (namely in the confrontation between England and Ireland, as expressed in the respective languages (plus Latin) and in the respective literary traditions of both those countries), and given the fact that it does so from a supranational point of view, it belongs to the field of Comparative Literature, the discipline within which Image Studies was originally developed. The 'supranational point of view' means that the English-Irish imagotypical system is considered relevant, not merely with reference to English, or Irish, or, for that matter, English-Irish developments, but especially with reference to these developments *within their European context*. The English-Irish system is of special interest within this context since its two constituent partners are isolated from the rest of Europe by unambiguous and comparatively stable geographical and political frontiers. We have here, then, to some extent a national confrontation *in vitro* between the North Sea and the Atlantic Ocean, a system whose binate character is less obfuscated by other neighbouring countries than is the case on the Continent – although even here a Scottish-Irish cultural confrontation occasionally plays into the developments which I will try to trace. One of the implications of this isolated character of the English-Irish system is the extraordinary longevity of a confrontation which was only marginally influenced by Continental upheavals such as the Napoleonic wars, the foundation and fall of the Second German Empire or even the two World Wars. Such upheavals altered, and altered radically, the national systems on the Continent, whereas the English-Irish configuration shows some continuity throughout a period dating back as far as the twelfth century. This configuration was, of course, subject to its own changing parameters, such as the Reformation under Henry VIII and Elizabeth; the demise of the Gaelic clan system at the end of the sixteenth century; the Jacobite plantation of Ulster in the early seventeenth century; the civil war, the Confederation of Kilkenny and the policy of Cromwell in the mid-seventeenth century; the Revolution of 1688 and the imposition of the penal laws at the beginning of the eighteenth century, followed by the social decline of Gaelic literature and language, etc. etc. But at the same time the confrontation of later periods was, as I shall try to show, nearly always placed under the auspices of earlier conflicts, and represented as their direct continuation. It was this 'habit of historical thought', as MacDonagh calls it, this pattern of affective continuity, of the retrospective adoption of earlier conflicts as the forerunners of later ones, that gave rise to the cynical and defeatist quip that 'in Ireland there is no future, only the past happening over and over again'. We have here, then, a more or less continuous tradition of English-Irish conflict antedating the rise of nationalistic ideology. Nationalism, as an ideology, is usually considered to have developed around the turn from the eighteenth to the nineteenth century. Indeed it can be observed that, during the nineteenth century, Irish nationalism (especially as from the rise of the Young Irelanders in the 1840s) fell 'into step' with the Continental development of national thought: Italy, Hungary, Poland and

Germany.[9] But the Irish development leading up to this later, nineteenth-century nationalism was extraordinary within the European context.

In all this, it is an imperative necessity not to take the insular framework for granted, not to lose oneself in questions of merely local (or, yes, merely 'national') importance. As Hugo Dyserinck has insistently argued, the field will have to be approached with a non-partisan disinterestedness from a supranational point of view.[10]

Only from this supranational point of view does it become possible (a) to recognize those developments pertinent to the English-Irish confrontation which have a larger, Continental dimension; (b) to avoid the trap of personal complicity or sympathy with either of the conflicting sides; (c) to avoid the pitfall of interpreting Irish developments or Irish situations as somehow 'special' or *sui generis*, for want of trans-Irish comparison.

I have hitherto spoken of unspecified national 'attitudes', 'stereotypes' or 'images', within a 'confrontation'. It is of some consequence to stress that a confrontation is by its nature two-faced; and this binateness extends itself also to its resulting discursive emanations. Such a polarity underlies, also the *Fremderfahrung* of a given writer's experience with, or perception of, the foreign; for the concept of foreignness itself presupposes the polar relationship with its complement, the 'native' or 'familiar' against which it takes shape. One of the main objectives of this study is to illustrate in the case of the English-Irish system how the same binateness is at work at the very core of the idea of nationality, and to offer an illustration of the way in which this realization might be of use in the analysis of a tradition of 'national thought'.

The imagological distinction between *hetero-* and *auto-image* is of particular use here, with respect to the relations and possible interactions between these 'images of the foreign' and 'of the familiar'. Their interactions can be of various kinds. The auto-image is primarily the implied negative counterpart of a given hetero-image, as in Niels Bohr's motto that 'contraria sunt complementa'. The auto-image is thus the embodiment of the ethnocentricity against which the foreign becomes recognizably foreign. In this sense, it is possible to read Tacitus' *Germania* or Mme de Staël's *De l'Allemagne* not just as representations of Germany, but also as implied commentaries, *ex negativo*, on Tacitus' Rome or De Staël's France. However, a different binateness of auto- and hetero-image is also conceivable: one in which De Staël's (hetero-)image of Germany is coupled, not with her auto-image of France, but with the auto-image of Germany as held by her German sources. And this German auto-image (e.g. in A.W. Schlegel) may in turn be seen in relation to the German hetero-image of France. A binate imagotypical system, like France-Germany (and this applies also to England-Ireland) will thus have a doubled polarity, involving two reflexive auto-images (that of France in France and that of Germany in Germany) as related to either of two reflective hetero-images (that of France in Germany or that of Germany in France).

The relationship between auto- and hetero-image is not one of static polarity. As this study hopes to illustrate, the images themselves are subject to extreme vicissitudes (taking place, all the same, within the basic parameters of the under-lying native-foreign polarity) and the relation between them is, if any, a dialectical one, where auto- and hetero-images sometimes polarize in mutual antagonism, sometimes impart certain characteristics to, and mutually influence, each other. It is in this respect that the imagologist must study, not just the substance, but also the mutual interaction and interdependence of the English image of 'Ireland', of the Irish image of 'England' and of the English and Irish auto-images of them-selves as related to both these hetero-images. My investigation of 'the idea of Irish nationality' will thus proceed by a threefold reference: as an English hetero-image, as the Irish auto-image in its relation to the English image of Ireland, and as the Irish auto-image in relation to the Irish image of England.

Images are essentially qualities attributed to a native or 'foreign' nation; yet another duality is at work in this principle. One ought not only to look at the qualifying adjectives or imputations that constitute the stereotypes in themselves, but also to inquire to whom they are attributed: to investigate the demographical distribution which such images implicitly or explicitly outline for those attributes. When studying an image like 'the Irish are lazy', one ought not only to fix on the attribution of laziness, but also on the question to which class that stereotype is attributed. *All* Irish? Toddlers, priests, poor citydwellers and rich landlords? Old women and young men? Catholics and Protestants? Ulstermen, Dubliners, Kerry-men? Gaelic speakers and English speakers? In scrutinizing the categorical dis-tribution of stereotyped attributes one may find interesting patterns of circularity, of self-correction or self-contradiction, and the characterization of a certain group may often be found to serve at the same time as the defining criterion of the member-ship in that group – so that an image like 'the Irish are lazy' may ultimately prove to include its symmetrical counterpart: '. . . but it is the lazy ones who are the real, the genuine Irish', recognizable as such by virtue of their 'typically Irish' laziness.

It is for reasons like these that my title was chosen. *Mere Irish* and *Fíor-Ghael* both mean exactly the same thing: 'the real, the genuine Irish' – but with conno-tations of allegiance that are diametrically opposed to each other. It is the relationship and the interaction between these perspectives which I intend to study here, as well as the relationship between this so-called 'real' Irishman and his implied counterpart: the not-so-real Irishman. In this respect, my investiga-tion of 'the idea of Irish nationality' is also concerned with the origin and development of the national category 'Irish', and with its varying applications throughout the centuries leading up to the nineteenth.

In the nineteenth century, a notion of Irish national identity is universally and self-evidently current (albeit not uncontroversial); its currency was, however, of recent date and had developed out of a slow amalgamation process, where earlier ethnic identities (natives vs. settlers) had slowly, and in continuing sociopolitical enmity, entered into an osmosis of sorts. In the course of the eighteenth century, the settlers had slowly abandoned the intensely cultivated awareness of their English roots and English identity, and had adopted the nation's Gaelic past for their own; it had become customary, by 1800, to speak of Ireland in the first person and of Britain in the third person, even when members of the Protestant elite were discussing history and antiquities; a category 'Irish' and a name like 'Erin' came into circulation which encompassed all inhabitants of Ireland and subsumed them under a historical heritage of ultimately Gaelic origin. This was a new turn, not only for the Anglo-Irish settler and landlord class, but also for the Catholic, Gaelic intellectuals like Charles O'Conor and Sylvester O'Halloran, who were only a generation or two removed from the outlook of Dáibhí Ó Bruadair and his perpetuation of a tribal-religious Milesian consciousness.

This slow process, where a national self-image of sorts slowly developed from earlier ethnic divisions, would not have been possible except for the presence of intermediate or hybrid groups: the Hiberno-Norman noblemen in the middle ages, the Old English in the Tudor period, the Anglo-Irish in the eighteenth century.[11] It is this middle ground that seems to have obfuscated consistently the neatness of the original 'us vs. them' divisions; and it is, remarkably enough, on the middle ground, and among this 'middle nation', as the Anglo-Irish became known, that opposing and interacting images could become the basis of a national, and eventually a nationalistic, idea of Irishness.

This development was to an important degree programmatically literary in orientation, and I hope to show that in various different contexts, be they Gaelic or Anglo-Irish, a literary idea of Irish nationality was formulated before it gained political currency.

In this respect, the findings of this study may also have some value for the early history of Anglo-Irish literature.[12] This is not surprising. Anglo-Irish literature is a perfect example of what is known in Comparative Literature as a *littérature seconde* (which term I will here tentatively translate as 'an outlying literature'): a literary tradition which, as far as the geographic distribution of the language of its expression is concerned, forms a peripheral part of a larger whole, but which is distinct from the larger literature in that language by virtue of non-linguistic, political-geographic, 'secondary' differences. (Other examples being Belgian literature in French, e.g. Verhaeren, or Swiss literature in German, e.g. Frisch). As has been pointed out in some significant instances,[13] such an 'outlying' literature is often distinguished from its 'mainstream' on the basis of its perceived, indeed stereotyped 'national characteristics'.

This study has profited from a number of critical sources both in the literary and in the historical field. Some histories of Irish nationalism proved to be more valuable than others; D.G. Boyce's *Nationalism in Ireland* was by far the most useful among them. Of the histories of Anglo-Irish literature, Patrick Rafroidi's *L'Irlande et le romantisme* was of great value, as was also that older and briefer, but still highly useful book by Russell K. Alspach, *Irish poetry from the English invasion to 1798*. I could profit from a great number of outstanding works in more specialized fields (histories of linguistics, on theatrical and poetical practice in English and in Gaelic literature, on seventeenth- and eighteenth-century anti-quarianism and national theories, etc.); these, too many to be enumerated here, will be acknowledged in their proper context throughout the following chapters.

This book is in the final analysis a pre-history of Irish nationalism. *Nationalism* as an ideology is more specific than what is usually meant by it in everyday parlance, 'resistance to foreign dominance or hegemony'; in its strict sense it means specifically that claims towards sovereignty and autonomy are derived, not so much from arguments of constitutional jurisprudence, economic or political expediency or equity, but from a hypostacized national identity and cultural individuality. The principle of national identity inspires and demands exclusive political loyalty and furnishes the moral legitimation for claims towards independence. Nationalism places culture and politics into a highly specific mutual relationship; it is by definition idealistic rather than materialist or pragmatist, in that it derives political claims (sovereign statehood) from an abstract principle (national identity). The historical presence and influence of nationalism as an active force in constitutional thought is usually dated from the late eighteenth or early nineteenth century; accordingly, Irish cultural nationalism in the strict sense of the term (as what Isaiah Berlin has called 'political romanticism') is studied in my book on the nineteenth century, *Remembrance and imagination*. The present study is concerned with an earlier stage in the political, ethnic and cultural confrontation which has dominated Irish history over the centuries, and is concerned with the pre-1800 emergence of an idea of Irish nationality (as opposed to yet older collective allegiance patterns in ethnic, sectarian, religious, linguistic-cultural or social terms). That slowly-emerging national idea was the main necessary precondition for the emergence of an Irish form of nationalism-proper after the Union; and the idea of Irish nationality was after 1800 to become the main legitimizing principle for subsequent Irish separatists. It is in this sense that I wish the present study to be understood as a pre-history of Irish nationalism.

THE IDEA OF NATIONALITY:
Terminology and Historical Background

Nearly four centuries ago, one of the earliest Irish characters on the English stage (Shakespeare's captain Macmorris in *Henry V*) blurted out a vehement question that has never since lost its urgency: 'What ish my nation?' A plethora of conflicting opinions have been given on that point since Shakespeare's days – so many, so conflicting, that it would merely add to the confusion to give yet another one in the following pages. Instead, it may be more rewarding to scrutinize those answers that have been given, to analyse them in their own right, to investigate the historical tradition of opinions concerning the idea of Irish nationality.

Although nationality in general, and Irish nationality in particular, are, then, at the very core of my topic of investigation, I must stress from the outset that I do not wish to deal with 'nationality' as such; my concern is rather 'the idea of nationality', and that difference, though subtle, is of basic importance to the arguments that I hope to develop and the terminology that I use.

A terminological clarification is obviously called for. Without wishing or pretending to give definitions of general validity (for one thing, the following discussion seems to apply only within the narrower European context), I would like to draw up some explanatory distinctions between terms like 'nation', 'national', 'nationality' and 'nationalism', regarding their usage in the following pages.

To begin with a few exclusions:

(a) The term 'nation' can in common parlance carry programmatic overtones, and be used to denote a political ideal rather than a social concept. As a result of the spread of nationalistic ideologies in the nineteenth and early twentieth century, a 'nation' is often understood (even today) as the marriage of race and land, 'Blut und Boden'; as the spiritual core of human society; as the object of the citizen's most basic allegiance, the governing principle of his or her political existence.

It is *not* this post-Romantic, programmatic sense of 'nation' or 'nationality' (corresponding neither to my own, nor to seventeenth- or eighteenth-century usage) which will be at issue here. Instead, the following pages will make it abundantly clear that my own position stands under the auspices of earlier critiques of nationalism as expressed by, among others, Ernest Renan, Karl Popper, H.L. Koppelmann and Hans Kohn. This critical and anti-essentialist attitude has found a comparatist continuation, not only in the thought of scholars like De Deugd, but also in the imagological method as heralded by the Comparative Literature Programme at Aachen University.[1]

15

(b) Nor do I intend to deal with a far more neutral use of the terms 'national' and 'nationality'; if it is said, for instance, that a country's economy is burdened with the *national* debt, or that, as the holder of a Dutch passport, I have the Dutch *nationality*; then it is obvious that such terms refer to the administrative apparatus of a *state*, and fill the lexical void that is occasioned by the fact that 'state' has few derivations of its own (except for 'statesman' and 'statehood'). In that sense, 'national' and 'nationality' are the adjective and the substantivized adjective of the noun *state*, not of the noun *nation* – regardless of morphological appearance.

In fact, the constructionist, non-essentialist definition of a nation does seem to have close links with the idea of a *politikon*, a state. The Oxford English Dictionary, for example, speaks of 'An extensive aggregate of persons, so closely associated with each other by common descent, language, or history, as to form a distinct race or people, usually organized as a separate political state and occupying a definite territory'. The core of this definition lies in the *close association* which the lexicographer specifies as a *community* of descent, language or history. It would seem, then, that the 'nation' is the community of the state's inhabitants, which is in turn both manifested in, and safeguarded by, that state.

The problem is, of course, that the relation nation–state is not always as ideal as this. The qualifying adverb 'usually' in the lexicographer's definition indicates that the concrete geographical and demographical substance of a 'state' is not always congruent with the social association of the people who constitute the 'nation'. A historical or linguistic 'community' may be divided by state borders, and different, or even hostile 'communities' may find themselves yoked together under the aegis of a common state.

More importantly, it seems that even the 'association' or 'community' that unites a demographic group into a 'nation' is not rigidly determined by the criteria of a common language, history, descent, geographical position or a common set of economic interests. All of these criteria, though they may in certain cases be held up as the common denominator of a self-proclaimed 'nation', can be shown to be immaterial in other cases; one can find religious, linguistic, anthropological or habitational similarities between groups that do not form, or did not form, unified 'nations'; and conversely, one can register divisions of a religious (Germany, Netherlands), linguistic (Switzerland) or any other nature within 'national' communities of long standing. Any number of historical 'nations' can be adduced in evidence to show that the demographic make-up of such national communities (whether they achieved political independence or not) is subject to change. Ulster Presbyterians, for instance, who, at the end of the eighteenth century, belonged in large numbers to the nationalistic vanguard of Ireland, nowadays on the whole support Northern Ireland's appurtenance to the United Kingdom.

What seems to be far more influential in a demographic group's acceptance of a common denominator, in its acceptance of that common denominator as a focus for 'national' community, is, then, the very act of that acceptance.[2] In other words: a demographic group defines itself as a nation, not by the criteria on which that national self-definition is *based*, but by its willingness to perform that self-definition. One ought to remain aware of the fact that a common heritage, interest or 'character' does not cogently constitute a 'nation' unless the people involved are willing to acknowledge it as such. It is equally important to realize that such willingness for national identification may not be universally shared, that the population may not be homogeneously unified in their allegiance to the 'nation'. It is here that the cohesive role of the state, again, becomes obvious. A minority nation such as the Breton one, for example, can only consist of those who actively identify with it. Those inhabitants of Brittany who do not actively and deliberately identify as members of the Breton nation are, by virtue of their citizenship, their identity card, their rights under, and duties towards, the legislative, administrative, economic and political apparatus of the French Republic, implicitly acquiescing in their appurtenance to the nationality which that state claims to embody. The onus of commitment therefore lies less heavily on sovereign nation-states which possess, in their state apparatus, ongoing reinforcements of unity, a perpetuation of identity. In short, the sovereign nation-state pre-empts the citizen's active allegiance by imposing its political realities and pre-givens as the default value.

Part of that status quo is the state's physical outline, its geographic/territorial discreteness. As can be seen from the Oxford English Dictionary's definition quoted above, and from its use of the term 'a definite territory', this geographical cohesion has traditionally been claimed to be proper to the 'nation' as well as to the state – but, as the nation is, in my understanding, the distribution of an allegiance among its members, it follows that a 'nation' need have no clearer geographical outlines than, say, the demographical distribution of vegetarianism or of allegiance to the Jewish faith. Likewise, its political borders will lend to a nation-state an aspect of cohesion which need not by itself be implicit in the demographical pattern of allegiance to that state's national concept: virtually each border will include minorities with national allegiances counter to the state's own, and, conversely, perhaps divide self-proclaiming members of the 'nation' from the nation-state. One can think of the Danish-German, or of the Austrian-Italian borders as examples. The case of Northern Ireland is especially interesting here: a national border was drawn in 1922 which aimed to include a certain demographic group (Ulster loyalists, proclaiming their allegiance to the United Kingdom) into the United Kingdom; in doing so, however, it excluded from the Irish Free State, and included into this newly-defined territory, another demographic group whose national allegiance was Irish and anti-British, and who were (and still are) utterly disaffected with the political situation that was created by this border. The two demographic groups of Northern Ireland are intermingled geographically (if not socially), so that a physical separation of the two is impossible. And indeed the very attempt at separation would need to be questioned as a potentially dangerous one, since on closer scrutiny its motive appears to be the creation of a *state without minorities* – a motive with disconcertingly totalitarian overtones. The desire to obtain a complete congruence between national allegiance and state policy is what I would like to offer as a possible definition of 'nationalism'.

By this definition, nationalism will aim: (a) at political sovereignty for a nationally defined demographic group, by declaring its natural right to constitutional independence; (b) at drawing state borders in such a manner as to exclude no demographic groups considered to share the state's nationality (as in the campaign of Garibaldi, or Hitler's foreign expansionism prior to the Treaty of Munich); (c) to propagate national allegiance as a civic duty among the entire population of the region (e.g. Irish Ireland and Gaelic League activism in pre-1920 Ireland) or state (e.g. official cultural policy in the post-1920 Irish Free State).

The following preliminary terminological distinctions can thus be made. 'Nationalism' is a political doctrine based on the belief that it can supply (as Elie Kedourie puts it)

> a criterion for the determination of the unit of population proper to enjoy a government exclusively its own, for the legitimate exercise of power in the state, and for the right organization of a society of states. Briefly, the doctrine holds that humanity is naturally divided into nations, that nations are known by certain characteristics which can be ascertained, and that the only legitimate type of government is national self-government.[3]

A 'nation', which nationalism considers to be the natural unit of human society, is a group of individuals who distinguish themselves, as a group, by a shared allegiance to what they consider to be their common identity; and 'nationality' can be considered as the focus of a nation's allegiance, the idea (indeed, the self-image) of its common identity, the criterion by which a 'nation' defines itself as such.

Such criteria (descent, language, history, character) claim to be historical constants; however, the most cursory glance at European history will make it clear that national definitions are protean and volatile, and, in fact, so ethereal and ephemeral that one is forced to wonder whether national denominations or identities have any real meaning at all. If one leaves aside the administrative 'passport' nationality excluded from the present argument (above, p. 16) the question as to the exact meaning of national denominations, 'Irish', 'Dutch', 'German', etc., becomes practically unanswerable. This point was made with great force by H. L. Koppelmann, who goes as far as calling such national denominations *leere Worte*, 'empty words' which have no unambiguous reference but merely an emotive quality capable of focusing acritical enthusiasm in whatever ideological direction may be desired; national fervour, according to Koppelmann, directs itself at the mere name of a nation, at the sound of a word (*Wortschall*), rather than at a real, known or knowable phenomenon (*bekannte Realität*).[4] One is reminded of the remarks voiced by Edmund Burke in a letter to his son Richard:

A very great part of the mischiefs that vex the world, arises from words. People soon forget the meaning, but the impression and the passion remain.[5]

But even while I subscribe to Koppelmann's contention that the roots of national thought lie to no small extent in terminological/semantic fallacies, it would be impossible to trace the development of the 'idea of nationality' without having some working definition (if only a terminological one) of the subject at hand.

In order to reach as neutral a model as possible, I shall turn the vexed question of 'national identities' inside out, as it were, and talk of 'national differentiations' instead. Rather than following the definition of the Oxford English Dictionary, one might turn to the definition as given by Dr. Johnson in his Dictionary of 1755, according to which a nation is 'A people distinguished from another people; generally by their language, original, or government'.

What is the difference? – To draw a line around a demographic group is an ambivalent act: to see it solely in terms of its inclusion of certain members within that group is only one side of the coin, and its meaning or even meaningfulness must at the same time also depend on the inverse principle, the fact that by that same line-drawing all other elements outside the group so delineated are excluded from it. A group is defined no less by the exclusion of its non-members than by the inclusion of its members. To put it more strongly: a category or class without an outside limit is as good as nonexistent, and the statement that certain elements be 'included' in such a 'class' is a foregone conclusion, losing all significance.

It may likewise be a cul-de-sac to consider only the internal aspect of a national definition, i.e. the criteria by which members are held to be included in a 'nation'-class. The identification of a group as a nation (i.e. as a characteristically coherent group instead of a loose, random, unrelated collection of individuals) can be regarded as an act of *separation*: a separation from all those who do not share that nation's defining criteria. Breton nationalism is defined largely in terms regarding the difference between the Breton and the French nationality; and if one considers the case of pan-Celtic nationalism (as expressed, for instance, in the magazine *Carn*, published by the Celtic League), it will become understandable why the English language, though demonstrably a larger common denominator, a more widespread medium of intercourse for the people of Scotland, Man, Ireland, Wales, Cornwall and even Brittany, than the respective minority languages (some of them moribund or extinct) of those countries, should be rejected as alien and alienating.

What one should look for when dealing with the concept of 'nationality' would, then, seem to be a pattern of differences or differentiations rather than cohesive characteristics: a pattern of relationships between demographic groups rather than within a given demographic group. To offer a parallel from the field of linguistics, I might point out the now generally accepted Saussurian idea that words and sounds are recognized (semantically and phonetically) not in themselves but by their very difference from other sounds/words; thus language is not made up of discrete meaningful units, but is a signifying system based on the differences between units: the word 'debt' is recognized by its aural dissimilarity from 'bet' or 'get', 'dot', 'doubt', or 'deck'. It is by this structure of differentiation that meaning is achieved, that verbal signs acquire an intersubjectively accepted referential validity, that their inherent randomness is dispelled.

As in this linguistic example, so too in national allegiance. The border that surrounds one group is also the border that separates it from another. To apply this binate character of national identification to captain Macmorris' question will present one with its counterpart, which would run something like 'on what grounds does a demographic group consider itself separate from others?' The possible answers are many, and in them one can recognize the inverted forms of various traditional criteria of national identification: any conflict of interests, any difference of religious, linguistic or historical background may provide the motivation and criterion by virtue of which a demographic group might find itself united in the face of a common opponent. This tallies with the fact that nationalist rhetoric seems to flourish most readily in situations of conflict, e.g. in wartime. It is not, for instance, the community of religion which determines national coalescence (no such process took place between Catholic France and Catholic Spain) but rather religious differentiation which goes hand in hand with the growth of new national ideals (e.g. anti-Continental fervour in England under Elizabeth, or the Dutch rebellion against Spain). Similarly, it is not always the case that a common language entails a common national allegiance; conversely, linguistic divisions may quite easily involve a bifurcation of such allegiances; Belgium is a case in point. And the beginnings of German cultural nationalism, exemplified in the names of Lessing and Herder, did not take place *in vacuo* but in reaction to the strong influence of French classicist culture in Germany; and thus the development of the concept of a 'deutsche Denkungsart', a German mentality, and the notion of a characteristic German nationality, was developed by a contrastive process, namely by opposing it (and its prospective ally, Shakespeare) to the French classicist tendencies of the period.

There is, of course, no telling how old such modes of contrastive nationalization are; the attribution of a radical, characteristic 'differentness' from non-members of the home tribe or *politikon* can be traced back to antiquity and beyond. The Roman concept of *patria*, the Greek appellation *barbaros* were already ideologically charged, and much of the mirth in comedies like Plautus' *Poenulus* or Aristophanes' *Lysistrata* or *Thesmophoriasuzae* consists in poking fun at the uncouth speech of strangers. Even the very names that 'nations' or tribes gave themselves are indicative of friction with, or opposition to, an 'outside'. Émile Benveniste, in his *Le vocabulaire des institutions indo-européennes*, supports his argument that such names reflect 'une différence fondamentale entre l'indigène, en soi-même, et l'étranger'[6] by an interesting discussion of the meaning and usage of the Indo-Iranian *ārya-* (cf. our 'Aryan'), 'd'abord qualification sociale, puis désignation de la communauté'; in the course of that discussion, Benveniste makes the point that

Toute appellation de caractère ethnique, aux époques anciennes, est différentielle et oppositive. Dans le nom qu'un peuple se donne il y a, manifeste ou non, l'intention de se distinguer des peuples voisins, d'affirmer cette superiorité qu'est la possession d'une langue commune et intelligible. De là vient que l'ethnique forme souvent un couple antithétique avec l'ethnique opposé. Cet état de choses tient à une différence, qu'on ne remarque pas assez, entre les sociétés modernes et les sociétés anciennes, quant aux notions de guerre et de paix. Le rapport entre l'état de paix et l'état de guerre est, d'autrefois à aujourd'hui, exactement inverse. La paix est pour nous l'état normal, que vient briser une guerre; pour les anciens, l'état normal est l'état de guerre, auquel vient mettre fin une paix. (p. 368)

Not only in ethnic (tribal or national) appellations, but also on the most basic semantic level of stereotyping statements that assign markers of nationality, an implied contrastiveness or duality can be noticed. If I take, for example, a stylized proposition describing a 'national' characteristic, such as 'Spaniards are proud', it might at first sight pass as a straightforward proposition of the affirmative type, and as such give the impression of a statement logically arguable under that logical aspect. The difference between a genuine affirmative proposition. e.g. 'Spaniards are mortal', or 'Spaniards are monogamous'[7] on the one hand, and the example 'Spaniards are proud' on the other, is, however, undeniable; and when one tries to point out the difference between the two types of proposition, the duality principle at the bottom of national attributes becomes obvious. – It is a matter of elementary logic that, in a proposition of the affirmative type, the subject-term is 'distributed', whereas this need not be the case for the predicate-term; meaning that the proposition 'Spaniards are P' claims validity for all 'Spaniards' but does not claim to have thereby exhausted the entire class 'P'. This is immediately obvious in the examples 'Spaniards are mortal' and 'Spaniards are monogamous': although those propositions implicitly claim to apply to all of (or, in everyday language, to a significant majority of) the class 'Spaniards', they clearly do not claim that all mortal or monogamous beings are subsumed under their particular application. There are many monogamous societies and mortal beings outside Spain.

The proposition 'Spaniards are proud' functions in a different way. It would be made in a context which pretends to impart some item of information specifically concerned with the Spanish people; obviously this statement does not achieve its aim if the predicate-term, 'proud', were as undistributed as the other one, 'mortal': for in that case the characterization does not to any specific or significant extent apply to the Spanish; or better: it does in no manner apply that predicative characterization to a group who are thereby in some way singled out from the rest of humanity. In order for a statement like 'Spaniards are proud' to become meaningful, one has to assume that it implies the predicate-term to be to some degree distributed. What such a statement really means is that 'Spaniards are proud, and more so than non-Spaniards'. Again one sees the contrastive principle at work, which illustrates that even as bald a statement as the example given here does not in fact apply to a single group, but to the relationship between that group and its non-members.

This leads to the (seemingly paradoxical, but crucially important) conclusion that, although it is possible to register cultural *differences*, empirically and unambiguously, it is impossible to translate these into any objective or unambiguous category of cultural *identity*. Cultural discontinuity does not add up to a systematic taxonomy of cultural unit-groups. Differences can be registered on a multitude of different, though mutually compatible, levels; one may regard Western Europe as a 'whole' when comparing it with China, or in dealing with Imperial Roman or medieval history; one can also register differences between extremely narrowly-defined, small population groups in a small area (e.g. the clashes between French- and Netherlandic-speaking inhabitants of the Belgian Voer area). If I may be allowed to adduce my own experience in evidence, I can point out that in social traffic my local background is defined by my home village, Mheer, when I am in the company of people from other, nearby villages; by home province, Limburg, when in the North of the Netherlands; by state citizenship (Dutch) when in Germany or France; and I pass as a European when in America. Similarly, I am a white man in Africa or Asia, a Westerner in Tokyo, and a civilian in an army barracks: none of these identifications are mutually exclusive, and it is the variety of circumstances which in each case determines the choice of criterion by which the act of identification is performed. The individual is, then, unambiguously defined by the sum total of all possible criteria that can compatibly and cumulatively be applied to him or her. This in turn means that the definition of a *group* of individuals is performed by applying certain possible common criteria *whilst disregarding others*. In this sense, a group identity (and this applies also to the 'national' one) is reached by virtue of the agreement to disregard those criteria that exist *within* the group.

Depending on one's choice, which criteria to apply and which to disregard (language, colour of eyes, number of teeth, age, star sign, initial letter of family name, gender, favourite colour, marrying age of paternal grandfather. . . .), the individual can be considered part of a well-nigh infinite number of groups. His/her very membership in all these differently defined groups is a proof that their definitions need not be mutually exclusive.

The range of possible community memberships likewise occupies an entire, continuous, scala between the individual and the totality of humanity, varying from the sub-regional to the supra-national. Virtually any category within this spectrum might under certain circumstances be called a 'national' one; there are no fixed principles known to me by which any particular category within this scala can be cogently defined as the 'national' one. Indeed what some consider a 'nation' is for others only the regional variety within a larger defined 'nation' (e.g. the case of Corsica or of Cornwall). A parallel can be found in the field of dialectology, where the scala idiolect – dialect – dialectical continuum is only definable in its outer poles: the individual and the continuum. Here, too, differences can unambiguously be registered within a dialectical continuum such as the Romance or the Continental West-Germanic one; and those differences can be followed through on an ever more refined level until that of the individual is reached: the idiolect. But these differences do not fix a discrete unit, 'the dialect', on any specific position between idiolect and diasystem. The extent of a 'dialect' can be circumscribed in various ways according to one's particular intent: one can speak of 'the' Huddersfield dialect, or of 'the' Munster dialect, and, in a different context, replace these categories by larger or smaller, subordinate or superimposed categories like 'the' Yorkshire dialect or 'the' West Cork dialect, without denying referential validity to either the larger or the smaller of these. *The choice as to which group-defining criteria to apply and which to disregard is essentially a random, or at least a free one.* Which criterion is 'meaningful' and which is not depends only on the intention of the individual concerned: a speech pathologist and a dialectologist will classify the speakers in a given random group along different criteria, chosen according to the pre-existing motivation which also prompted the very act of classification to be undertaken in the first place; the 'meaningfulness' of one's chosen criteria of group identification (be it a linguistic or a 'national' one) is nothing but the meaningfulness which such criteria acquire in the circumstance of the moment, in the light of the interest they may serve. Any Chinese box is as much a box as the one it contains or the one it is contained in.

But there is another reason why the notion of cultural difference is not translatable into that of national identity. To infer a coherent and discrete national entity from the evidence of demographic differences ignores the fact that, as we have seen, such evidence is often of an attributive nature, couched in terms which are implicitly contrastive in character: registrations of difference. In unifying such attributes into a concept which is inherent in the nation in question, the role of the observer, or of the background against which the difference is registered, is cancelled out, and the attributes, which were originally the result of an implied opposition between the 'nation' and its non-members, become projected wholly into the first of these binate elements. It is as if one were to speak of a magnet with only one pole, or to give a distance X between two points without specifying whether the measurement was made in miles, werst, kilometres, parsecs or Ångström – or even, whether the same scale was used throughout the entire measurement.

This last point is of especial importance since such attributions can be, and have been, made from a variety of different perspectives, different situations of contrast. The concept of a French 'nation' takes shape, not only in its difference from the Low Countries, but also in its difference from (the concept of) an Iberian 'nation', with (the concept of) an Italian 'nation', and with a German, or at least German-speaking, neighbour in the East (not to mention more problematic 'neighbours' – or political/demographic contiguities – such as England and Switzerland, or separatist peripheries like Brittany and the Basque Country). Each of these distinctions from different 'national' groups who are, again, different amongst themselves, and defined also by their contiguity to yet further outlying 'nations', will therefore take place under a different aspect. The notion of 'Frenchness' as opposed to Spain is not identical with 'Frenchness' as opposed to Flanders or to Germany. Different criteria-of-distinction are applied, selected from a much greater number of possible criteria-of-distinction; and it would be highly problematic to subsume them all under a single interiorized criterion-of-identification as an inherent, autonomous and essential *qualitas* of 'Frenchness *tout court*'.

Likewise, the dissimilarity between the different, and differently defined, non-members of any single 'nation' forbids, I think, a straightforward equation whereby the definition of a 'national' entity would be the simple inverse of 'national' distinctions. A 'nation' can be conceived of, not implicitly, in itself, but only in contradistinction to others. I put it then, that it is more fruitful to consider the question of nationality in its relational aspects, to approach it from a strictly supranational, comparative point of view, to consider nationality, not as a discrete, self-contained idea, but as the expression of an international relationship.

To sum up, let me emphasize the following points. To begin with, whenever I use the word 'nation' I do so as a shorthand version for the more correct (i.e. less ambiguous), but certainly more cumbersome, circumlocution 'a group sharing a common culture-political self-definition that distinguishes it from its non-members, and sharing a common allegiance to the criteria by which that self-definition is performed'. I may remind the reader of my particular usage of the term by now and then placing it in inverted commas. The different political embodiments, which such national concepts may at various points in history achieve, I call 'state' or 'nation-state'. When I refer to the existence of a French or German or English 'nation', therefore, I do not mean to offer any opinion whatsoever as to the actual existence, or my belief or disbelief in the actual existence, of such a thing as a distinct group identity for the individuals to whom such a term is claimed to apply; in other words, I do not offer any comment as to the question whether one's allegiance to a 'national' ideal is 'justified' or in any way based on a factual reality. Much like national stereotypes, concepts of nationality are, in their pretended reference in empirical reality, an imponderable. What counts is the belief that is vested in them, at definable and recognizable points in history, and the historical repercussions of that belief.

* * *

Is it not anachronistic to apply such latter-day models to old ideas? Let us consider, briefly, some historical notions concerning nationality, contemporary to the materials I shall be dealing with. First, it should be pointed out that the term 'nation' has been used at times in a far more restricted sense than nowadays. The Sorbonne knew a division into 'nations' in the middle ages; Montesquieu could use the term when referring only to the temporal and spiritual nobility, and even as recently as 1789, the abbé Sieyès could speak of the *tiers état* as being a 'nation'.[8] In the English-Irish context, each Gaelic clan was called a 'nation' in Tudor parlance: a clan chief, when being recognized in his authority by the English, would be called 'chief of his nation'; similarly, a *tuath* or territory under a single sovereign clan chieftain would often be called his *patria*.[9]

A more comprehensive meaning was also current, and seems not to differ too much from the one offered by the Oxford English Dictionary; this usage seems to have closely identified nation and state. Thus, the abbé Sieyès could, besides his socially more restricted usage of the term, answer his own question 'Qu'est-ce qu'une nation?' in more general terms as 'Un corps d'associés vivant sous une loi *commune* et représentés par la même législature, etc'.[10] The *Encyclopédie* of Diderot and D'Alembert had earlier defined *nation* in similarly political terms, as a

> mot collectif dont on fait usage pour exprimer une quantité considérable de peuple, qui habite une certaine étendue de pays, renfermée dans de certaines limites, & qui obéit au même gouvernement.[11]

The same definition was given in 1771 by the *Encyclopædia Britannica*:

> A collective term, used for a considerable number of people inhabiting a certain extent of land, confined within fixed limits, and under the same government.[12]

In the early eighteenth century, too, the nation is primarily defined by the political realities of the state. For Montesquieu, the 'génie d'une nation' consists of 'les mœurs et le caractère d'esprits de différents peuples dirigés par l'influence d'une même cour et d'une même capitale'; and Hume likewise traces nationality back to the principle of 'a number of men . . . united into one political body', occasioning frequent intercourse 'for defence, commerce, and government'.[13]

However, even in these 'neutral', basically political definitions of the terms 'nation' in the works of Hume and Montesquieu and in the *Encyclopédie*, other connotations are at work. The usage of a term like *génie d'une nation* is remarkable, and it should be pointed out that Hume's comment, quoted above, was made in an essay that was concerned with *national characters*. And unlike the *Encyclopædia Britannica*, the *Encyclopédie* expands on its socio-political definition of the 'mot collectif' by adding an extra paragraph which also deals with a nation's *character*. *Génie d'une nation*, national character, *caractère d'une nation* – clearly the idea was not exclusively a socio-political one. Thus, the *Encyclopédie* concludes its entry on 'nation' in the following manner:

> Chaque *nation* a son caractère particulier; c'est une espèce de proverbe que de dire, léger comme un françois, jaloux comme un italien, grave comme un espagnol, méchant comme un anglois, fier comme un écossois, ivrogne comme un allemand, paresseux comme un irlandois, fourbe comme un grec.

One can thus see a shift from the problematic definition of 'nation' towards the wider and vaguer one of 'national character'; this shift is made in a nearly physical sense in the *Encyclopédie* where the article 'Nation' sends the curious reader, via a cross-reference, to the article '*Caractère*'. *Caractère* (in its 'moral' sense, as opposed to typographical and other uses) is defined by the *Encyclopédie* as a 'disposition habituelle de l'âme', which is transposed, in the sub-entry '*Caractère des nations*', to the supra-individual level:

Caractère des nations consiste dans une certaine disposition habituelle de l'âme, qui est plus commune chez une nation que chez une autre, quoique cette disposition ne se rencontre pas dans tous les membres qui composent la nation: ainsi le *caractère* des François est la légèreté, la gaieté, la sociabilité, l'amour de leurs rois & de la monarchie même, &c.

A number of significant elements are contained here. The pious mention of monarchist loyalty as a 'national characteristic' of the French, made practically on the eve of the Revolution, is an anecdotal reminder for the twentieth-century reader that such characteristics (or rather, the self-images that these attributed characteristics stand for) are not quite the historically invariant predisposition they claim to be; and the concessive clause to the effect that not all members of the 'nation' share its 'character' contains the germ of self-contradiction. Even more interesting is the way in which the *Encyclopédie*, as we have seen, lists, *sub verbo 'nation'*, a number of 'national characteristics' as 'une espèce de proverbe'. It seems obvious that the concept of a 'national character' rests largely on such semi-proverbial, traditional stereotypes.

These stereotypes themselves, proverbial already for the compilers of the *Encyclopédie*, date back a long way indeed, and had stratified into systematic schemata in the course of the seventeenth century.[14] We recognize the habit of placing one particular stereotype in a series of others, implicitly contrasting rather than merely enumerating the nationalities that are mentioned. Instances of this instinctive, aprioristical categorization of nationalities by their stereotypical attributes will be further encountered in the course of this study. The idea, however, that such attributes are instances of a 'national character' (much as an individual's traits are instances of his personal character, his 'disposition habituelle de l'âme') seems to be of Enlightenment vintage. Indeed two thinkers mentioned before, Montesquieu and Hume, appear to have been among the first to conceive of an organically unified 'national character' in this way. For the present context, Hume is the more important of the two.

Hume's interest in national characters must be seen in the light of his interest in the human mind in general; he stands in the Lockean tradition of psychological interest, whose attitude is perhaps best summed up in Alexander Pope's dictum 'The proper study of mankind is man'. It was Hume's interest in the human mind, the human understanding, that prompted not only his philosophical investigations, but also his historical work (which aimed at the elucidation of the 'constant and universal principles of human nature', of 'the regular springs of human action and behaviour'[15]), as well as his preoccupation with 'national characters'. Indeed it might be said that, if Hume's philosophy was a theory of the human mind, then his historiography was the diachronic, historical method, and his interest in national characters the synchronic, comparative method, by which he applied his theory to actual practice. Hume's interest in national characters, though publicized only in his essay on that topic, which first appeared in the revised edition of his *Moral and political essays*

(1748), was a long-standing one, as can be seen from Hume's influence in the Edinburgh 'Select Society'. This society was the inner sanctum of the Scottish Enlightenment, and counted Hume, Adam Smith and lord Kames among its members. On Hume's instigation, the society chose for its regular discussions the topic 'Whether the Difference of National Characters be chiefly owing to the Nature of different Climates, or to moral and political causes' no less than three times: at the end of 1754, the beginning of 1755 and in 1757.[16]

This question, as to the 'moral' or the 'physical' (e.g. climatological) determination of national characters, had also been the central issue in Hume's essay on the subject, where he outlined the options in the following manner:

> Different reasons are assigned for these *national characters*; while some account for them from *moral*, others from *physical* causes. By *moral* causes, I mean all circumstances, which are fitted to work on the mind as motives or reasons, and which render a particular set of manners habitual to us. Of this kind are, the nature of the government, the revolutions of public affairs, the plenty or penury in which the people live, the situation of the nation with regard to its neighbours, and such like circumstances. By *physical* causes I mean those qualities of the air and climate, which are supposed to work insensibly on the temper, by altering the tone and habit of the body, and giving a particular complexion, which though reflection and reason may sometimes overcome it, will yet prevail among the generality of mankind, and have an influence on their manners. (vol. 3, 244)

Differences between nations had by some been attributed to different climatological influences, and especially the difference between the Latin South of Europe and the Teutonic North was often explained in climatological terms.

William Temple, the abbé Du Bos and Cheyne had made isolated comments to this effect: Montesquieu, in his *L'esprit des lois*, had been especially influential in endorsing this nascent model, particularly in the twenty-fourth book, 'Des lois dans le rapport qu'elles ont avec la nature du climat', based in turn on his earlier *Essai sur les causes qui peuvent affecter les esprits et les caractères*. Montesquieu's image of the libertarian North as opposed to the absolutist South was supported to no small extent by the then current Whiggish idea of the Germanic (Anglo-Saxon) roots of parliamentary freedom[17] as opposed to the feudal monarchism imported by the Norman-French; this idea could only too easily be fitted into a climatological-geographical opposition of South vs. North, Roman vs. non-Roman Europe.

Hume set himself the goal of exploding such national-climatological determinism, and most of his essay is taken up with a refutation of the idea that national characters can be governed by 'physical' causes. Instead, it is social intercourse, with its underlying political structures, that determines, through man's natural ability for imitation, a 'national character':

> Where a number of men are united into one political body, the occasions of their intercourse must be so frequent, for defence, commerce, and government, that, together with the same speech or language, they must acquire a resemblance in

their manners, and have a common or national character, as well as a personal one, peculiar to each individual. (vol. 3, 248)

The climatological debate did not end with Hume's forceful scepticism. Dr. Johnson, it is true, followed in Hume's footsteps (*mirabile dictu!*) when he wrote in *The idler*, in 1758:

> There are, among the numerous lovers of subtilties and paradoxes, some who derive the civil institutions of every country from its climate, who impute freedom and slavery to the temperature of the air, can fix the meridian of vice and virtue, and tell at what latitude we are to expect courage or timidity, knowledge or ignorance. From these dreams of idle speculation, a slight survey of life, and a little knowledge of history, is sufficient to awaken any enquirer, whose ambition of distinction has not overpowered his love of truth. . . . Nations have changed their characters; slavery is now nowhere more patiently endured, than in countries once inhabited by the zealots of liberty. But national customs can arise only from general agreement; they are not imposed but chosen, and are continued only by the continuance of their cause.[18]

However, two years after that, Oliver Goldsmith was to give renewed testimony in favour of the climate-theory of national characters;[19] and such theories have been voiced repeatedly since then. Its echoes can, for instance, be found in the *Encyclopédie*'s pronouncement, that

> Il y a grand apparence que le climat influe beaucoup sur le *caractère* général; car on ne sauroit l'attribuer à la forme du gouvernement, qui change toujours au bout d'un certain temps: cependant il ne faut pas croire que la forme du gouvernement, lorsqu'elle subsiste long-temps, n'influe aussi à la longue sur le *caractère* d'une nation. (s.v. *Caractère des nations*)

All this does not, however, penetrate to the actual core of Hume's (and Montesquieu's) implicit postulation that there are such things as 'national characters'. We have seen how the *Encyclopédie*, after defining character as a 'disposition habituelle de l'âme', went on to discuss it as the sum total of individual *characteristics*; the same can be said of Hume and Montesquieu. For Hume, 'national character' is a collective noun denoting a nation's 'manners' – indeed, the term 'manners' is used with roughly equal frequency as the term 'character', and no terminological distinction whatsoever is made between the two. With Montesquieu the corresponding term is *mœurs*. Such 'manners' are recognized as modes and conventions of social behaviour rather than as genetic, inborn or hereditary properties of a 'nation'; thus Hume can also recognize a common 'character' in professionally or socially defined groups that do not share a common nationality, e.g. soldiers and priests (vol. 3, 245). In other words, 'character' is not what *actuates* behaviour, but rather what *summarizes* behaviour.

What is remarkable, however, is the ambiguous way in which the attributive nature of such characteristics is (and, at the same time, fails to be) taken into account. In a different context, Hume points out clearly the fact that reports on foreign or alien phenomena are irredeemably embedded in human testimony (the very 'strangeness' of such phenomena consisting in the fact that first-hand knowledge or acquaintance with them is largely unavailable): the well-known treatise on miracles, one of the most famous sections of the *Enquiry concerning human understanding*, is a case in point. Here, Hume formulates the now famous sceptical idea that the credibility of a foreign or unfamiliar phenomenon (e.g. a miracle) stands in direct proportion to the creditableness of the human testimony through which that phenomenon is related: 'If the falsehood of his [the reporter's] testimony would be more miraculous, than the event which he relates; then, and not till then, can he pretend to command my belief or opinion' (vol. 4, 94). Hume then goes on to imply that, in this respect at least, miracles are similar to national characters, which are also embedded in human testimony. He thus points out, in the same section,

> With what greediness are the miraculous accounts of travellers received, their descriptions of sea and land monsters, their relations of wonderful adventures, strange men, and uncouth manners? But if the spirit of religion join itself to the love of wonder, there is an end of common sense; and human testimony, in these circumstances, loses all pretensions to authority. (vol. 4, 95)

And elsewhere, Hume also remarked wryly that 'Men run with great Avidity to give their Evidence in favour of what flatters their Passions, and their national Prejudices.'[20]

It is all the more puzzling that these cautions are largely ignored in the essay on national characters, where Hume relies with a-critical confidence on traditional 'descriptions . . . of uncouth manners' in order to glean his evidence. Although he bears down on climatological determinism with the full force of his sceptical acumen, he does not extend this scepticism to the nature of his own evidence – generalizations based on hearsay concerning the most distant countries. As an example I give two of Hume's anti-climatological arguments:

> Where any accident, as a difference in language or religion, keeps two nations inhabiting the same country, from mixing with each other, they will preserve. during several centuries, a distinct and even opposite set of manners. The integrity, gravity, and bravery of the TURKS, form an exact contrast to the deceit, levity, and cowardice of the modern GREEKS.

> The FRENCH, GREEKS, EGYPTIANS, and PERSIANS are remarkable for gaiety. The SPANIARDS, TURKS and CHINESE are noted for gravity and a serious deportment, without any such difference of climate as to produce this difference of temper. (vol.3, 253)

The reader will have noticed that the individual traits (indeed, commonplaces) are all temperamental attributes: 'integrity', 'gravity', 'bravery', 'deceit', 'levity', 'cowardice', 'gaiety' – Hume seems to take all these vague imputations at face value. ˙

From these examples it also transpires that the inherent contrastiveness of national attributes is present (albeit in a disguised form) without being recognized. The fact that a national attribute refers to a perceived relationship between one nation and another (usually the observer's/reporter's own) rather then to a perceived *proprium* of a nation *tout court*, is here disguised by the way in which national characteristics tend to be described *quasi* in their own right, but really in a tacit comparison to another nation. The opening paragraph of Hume's essay is another example of the way in which national attributes are given as relative rather than absolute phenomena, and of limited applicability at that:

> THE vulgar are apt to carry all *national characters* to extremes; and having once established it as a principle, that any people are knavish, or cowardly, or ignorant. they will admit of no exception, but comprehend every individual under the same censure. Men of sense condemn these undistinguishing judgements: Though at the same time, they allow, that each nation has a peculiar set of manners, and that some particular qualities are more frequently to be met with among one people than among their neighbours. The common people in SWITZERLAND have probably more honesty than those of the same rank in IRELAND; and every prudent man will, from that circumstance alone, make a difference in the trust which he reposes in each. We have reason to expect greater wit and gaiety in a FRENCHMAN than in a SPANIARD; though CERVANTES was born in SPAIN. An ENGLISHMAN will naturally be supposed to have more knowledge than a DANE; though TYCHO BRAHE was a native of DENMARK. (vol. 3, 244)

At the same time, however, Hume can gather all these comparative differentiations (be it repeated, these being of very obscure provenance) and subsume them all as elements of a 'national character'. In doing so, he implicitly rules out the crucial subjectivity of the observer/reporter and vests the attributes of a binary relation (observer-observed, or one nation – another nation) exclusively and quasi-objectively in the second element. The existence of national attributes thus becomes independent of the act of observing or registering them and gains the appearance of an objective phenomenon (i.e. one which exists independently of its being observed or registered), a fixed property inherent in the nation itself. This was the most incisive change to occur in the concept of a 'nation' during the centuries under survey here: whereas it may be said that, until the early eighteenth century, 'nations' were generally considered to have certain *reputations*, the later eighteenth century can begin to conceive of nations in terms of their *characters* – and though a 'nation's' outlines are still political or linguistic demarcations, the way is thus paved towards the deployment of such conceived 'characters' as the defining criteria of national identity and the motivating mainspring of historical and political action. The nation can henceforth develop into a humanoid supra-individual with a 'characteristic' humanoid identity; and the relations with or between nations can shift from a political to a temperamental frame of reference.[21]

Such a thumbnail sketch must raise more questions than it could confidently undertake to answer within the present context. Indeed, though some promising incursions have been made into this largely uncharted field,[22] a more thorough and comprehensive investigation of the conceptual or ideological developments of national thought in the seventeenth and eighteenth centuries remains as yet an endeavour for the future. It can only be hoped that, if the foregoing pages may serve as a useful prolegomenon for what follows in the next chapters, these may in turn yield evidence and point out source materials from which such future endeavours can benefit.

IRELAND IN ENGLISH REPRESENTATIONS

Early and medieval descriptions

From very early times the reputation of Ireland has been marked by ambiguity. The instrumentality of Irish monastic scholars in keeping alive the flame of Christian religion and classical learning through the dark centuries following the ruin of the Western Roman empire, and in helping to re-establish Christian religion and classical learning in merovingian and karolingian Europe, had earned Ireland an enviable reputation for piety and civility. On the other hand, the classical literary tradition thus salvaged from the turmoil following the great migration of peoples included the geographical works of authors such as Strabo, Pomponius Mela, Solinus and others, whose references to Ireland were less than complimentary.

To Strabo, whose Geography dates from the early first century AD, Ireland (which he calls Ierne) is a half-mythical country beyond barbarous Britain, at the edge of the inhabitable world. The inhabitants are wild and primitive (ἀγθρίων τελέως ἀνθρώπων καὶ κακῶς οἰκούντων δὶα ψῦχος, 'men who are complete savages and lead a miserable existence because of the cold': vol. 1, 442). The inhabitants surpass even the British in barbarity, in that

* ἀνθρωποφάγοιτε ὄντες καὶ πολυφάγοι, τούς τε πατέρας τελευτήσαντας
κατεσθίειν ἐν καλῷ τιθέμενοι καὶ φανερῶς μίσγεσθαι ταῖς τε ἄλλαις
γυναιξὶ καὶ μητράσι καὶ ἀδελφαῖς. (vol. 2, 258)

References to sexual amorality and cannibalism are also to be found in later works.

A little later, the Roman Andalusian Pomponius Mela, in his work *De situ orbis* (also known as *De chorographia*), proffered a similar mixture of the weird and the horrible concerning Ireland:

° Super Britanniam Iuverna est paene par spatio, sed utrimque aequalis tractu litorum oblonga, caeli ad maturanda semina iniqui, verum adeo luxuriosa herbis non laetis modo sed etiam dulcibus, ut se exigua parte diei pecora

---

* they are man-eaters as well as heavy eaters, and since, further, they count it an honourable thing, when their fathers die, to devour them, and openly to have intercourse, not only with the other women, but also with their mothers and sisters (ed.'s trl.)

° Beyond Britain lies Ireland, nearly as large in size, but on both sides oblong along a similar coastline; the climate does not favour the ripening of seedcrops, but then again the country is

impleant, et nisi pabulo prohibeantur, diutius pasta dissiliant. Cultoris eius
inconditi sunt et omnium virtutum ignari magis quam aliae gentes, pietatis
admodum expertes. (p. 68)

Solinus embellished his account still further, and in his third-century *De
mirabilibus mundi* (a.k.a. *Polyhistor*) wrote:

* Illic nullus anguis, avis rara, gens inhospita, & bellicosa. Sanguine interemp-
  torum hausto prius victores vultus suos oblinunt. Fas ac nefas eodem loco
  ducunt. Puerpera siquando marem edidit, primos cibos gladio imponit mariti,
  inque os parvuli summo mucrone auspicium alimentorum leviter infert, &
  gentilibus votis optat, non aliter quàm in bello, & inter arma mortem oppetat.
  Qui student cultui, dentibus marinantium beluarum insigniunt ensium
  capulos. Candicant enim ad eburneam claritatem. Nam praecipua viris gloria
  est in armorum nitela. Apis nusquam. Advectum inde pulverem, seu lapillos
  siquis sparserit inter alvearia, examina favos deserunt. (p. 70f.)

There is a fluid border between the genres of geography and fantasy. Solinus'
work was, like the later one by Mandeville, a book of wonders full of the most
fabulous monsters and miraculous phenomena. However, Solinus, like his two
predecessors, enjoyed a tenacious reputation throughout the middle ages, and
the descriptions of Ireland that these authors gave did not go unheeded in later
times. An interesting development is sparked off by Solinus' assertion that
Ireland not only lacked snakes (which is an ecological fact) but also bees (which
is a figment of the author's fertile imagination). Later authors, e.g. Giraldus
Cambrensis and Edmund Campion, repeatedly pointed out that notwithstanding Solinus' claim, there were, in fact, bees in Ireland – which ultimately
led subsequent authors (Camden, Moryson) to assert that Ireland harboured
extraordinary quantities of bees.

When the first subjects of the king of England entered Ireland in arms, in the
year 1169 – marking the beginning of that long and painful confrontation which
to this day is claiming its victims – a vague and contradictory notion concerning
the nature of the country and the character of its inhabitants may have already
been at work. Beda had spoken in laudatory terms of the civility of the neigh-

---

abundant in grass that is juicy and even sweet; with the result that the cattle is fully replenished
after only a small part of the day, and, if one were not to keep them from grazing further, would
burst from continued eating. The peasants of this island are uncivilized, more ignorant of all
decency than other nations, wholly lacking in good faith.

* There are no snakes at all there, only few birds, and an inhospitable and bellicose race of people.
  Those who are victorious in battle paint their faces with the blood shed by their victims: custom
  and aberration amount to the same thing. When a mother gives birth to a male child, she puts
  his first food on her husband's sword, and gently feeds it into the little one's mouth on the
  swordtip; and does so with heathen prayers that he may not meet his death but in battle and in
  arms. Those who aspire to refinement adorn their swordhilts with the teeth of sea animals, for
  these are of an ivory-white brightness – and the greatest boast of man is to 'shine forth' in battle
  prowess. There are no bees there. If one throws sand or pebbles brought over from there
  between their beehives, they desert their combs in swarms.

bouring isle, which could also boast luminaries such as John Scotus Erigena. Such positive aspects had become dulled with age, however; a more critical attitude towards Ireland had come into being, and was intensively drawn on by various forces wishing to establish their influence there. The foremost among these was the papacy, which had, since the Cluny reforms, been involved in a drive to establish its effective ecclesiastical control in Western Europe. This had incurred some delay in the more monastically oriented Irish church, and it was not until the reforms of St. Malachi that archbishoprics under Roman control were established in Ireland. St. Bernard of Clairvaux had, in his biography of his friend Malachi, sought to highlight his friend's achievements by dwelling on the difficulties he had had to overcome, and had drawn up a rather negative picture of the state of affairs in Christian Ireland.

It was this type of attitude that pope Adrian IV could draw on when he issued the bull *Laudabiliter* in 1155, placing a desired reform of Irish morals and of church affairs under the responsibility of the king of England, Henry II, whom he authorized

> * ut pro dilatandis ecclesie terminis, pro viciorum restringendo decursu, pro corrigendis moribus et virtutibus inserendis, pro Christiane religionis augmento, insulam ille ingrediaris.[1]

In this bull, Adrian stated that in this point he acceded to Henry's own stated desire ('Significasti siquidem nobis, fili in Christo carissime, te Hibernie insulam . . . velle intrare', p. 144); this, and the fact that pope Adrian himself was an Englishman, may indicate the possibility that the strategic or territorial design of the king of England on the neighbouring island was, if not in orchestrated concord, at least compatible with the policy of the Holy See. However, it was not until Henry's hand was forced by his more adventurous Cambro-Norman barons, that Adrian's privilege, which proclaimed Henry *dominus* of Ireland, was called on to justify an actual political claim.

Adrian's bull expressly condoned English presence in Ireland with the argument that a moral, religious, ecclesiastical and cultural reform was called for in that island. This attitude was reinforced in the work of an author who was related to many of the Cambro-Norman invaders of Ireland, who moved in English court circles and accompanied Henry's son John to Ireland: Gerald de Barri, archdeacon of St. David's, commonly called Giraldus Cambrensis. He wrote his *Topographia Hibernica* and his *Expugnatio Hibernica* in the late 1180s; though these may have been conceived of as parts of an intended, grander *Topographia Britannica* (for he also wrote a *Descriptio Kambriae*), the *Expugnatio* seems predominantly intended to vindicate the actions of the Cambro-Normans (more specifically those of his closer relatives) and of the English Crown in

---

> * that you should enter that island for the purpose of enlarging the boundaries of the church, checking the descent into wickedness, correcting morals and implanting virtues, and encouraging the growth of the faith of Christ. (eds.' trl.)

Ireland. Cambrensis is also the main authority for the bull *Laudabiliter*, which he quotes (and was often unjustly accused of having forged) in full.

The undercurrent of criticism on Irish life and manners, which runs throughout *Laudabiliter*, is also present in Giraldus' works – if anything more strongly so, even if at first sight the *Topographia* is a semi-fabulous description of the Mandevillesque curiosities of Ireland, and the *Expugnatio* a history of contemporary affairs in that country. It is, for Cambrensis, a self-evident fact that the Irish are primitives or, as he calls it, 'barbari';[2] he implicitly and explicitly asserts the moral and cultural superiority of the Anglo-Normans and sees the subjection of Ireland as a necessary and laudable act of civilization. Ireland is accordingly made out to be a wild, strange place full of weird and outlandish sights, and Irish society is, as far as Giraldus is concerned, a pool of blackest ignorance, barbarity and superstition. Giraldus does, it is true, have a few positive comments on the Irish clergy, but criticizes the importance of monasticism – which, again, conforms to the papal interests in a subjection of Ireland.[3]

Ireland's primitive rudeness, according to Giraldus, is most obvious in the fact that the Irish have not yet developed an urban society. They are semi-nomadic forest-dwellers, a *gens silvestris*:

> * Est autem gens haec gens silvestris, gens inhospita; gens ex bestiis et bestialiter vivens; gens a primo pastoralis vitae vivendi modo non recedens. Cum enim a silvis ad agros, ab agris ad villas, civiumque convictus, humani generis ordo processerit, gens haec, agriculturae labores aspernans, et civiles gazas parum affectans, civiumque jura multum detrectans, in silvis et pascuis vitam quam hactenus assueverat nec desuescere novit nec descire. (Lib. III cap. 10; p. 151)

This very barbarism constitutes at the same time the radical inferiority of the Irish as compared to the English. Only their treachery and dishonesty is to be feared:

> ° Est igitur longe fortius timenda eorum ars, quam Mars; eorum pax, quam fax; eorum mel, quam fel; malitia quam militia; proditio quam expeditio; amicitia defucata quam inmicitia despicata. (Lib. III cap. 21; p. 166)

---

* This people then is one of forest-dwellers and inhospitable; a people living off beasts and like beasts; a people that yet adheres to the most primitive way of pastoral living. For as humanity progresses from the forest to the arable fields, and thence towards village life and civil society, this people, spurning agricultural exertions, having all too little regard for material comfort and a positive dislike of the rules and legalities of civil intercourse, has been able neither to give up nor to abandon the life of forests and pastures which it has hitherto been living.

° Therefore one must fear their craftiness far more than their warfare; their quietude more than their fieriness; their sweet talk more than their invective; malice rather than pugnacity; treason more than open war; hypocritical friendliness rather than contemptible enmity. (Giraldus was obviously so pleased with this little passage that he repeated it in the *Expugnatio:* p. 250)

This little passage is a most interesting example of Giraldus' self-consciously polished style, with its multitude of puns, paradoxes and little rhymes. It may also serve as a first indication that the fabrication of a national image does not depend solely on the author's observations and opinions, but also on the literary, stylistic qualities of the medium of his expression. Something similar is at work when Giraldus take a side-sweep at contemporary court fashions:

> * Gens igitur haec gens barbara, et vere barbara. Quia non tantum barbaro vestium ritu, verum etiam comis et barbis luxuriantibus, juxta modernas novitates, incultissima; et omnes eorum mores barbarissimi sunt. (Lib. III cap. 10; p. 152f.)

The passage pivots around the pun on *barba – barbarus*, 'bearded' – 'barbarous': it aims at the *modernas novitates* of wearing beards rather than at the Irish themselves. In the process, however, Giraldus draws up a picture of a wild, nomadic society beyond the pale of civilization and true humanity.[4]

English intercourse with Ireland was so restricted during the middle ages (when Crown policy was too preoccupied with dynastic rivalries and the wars with France to occupy itself more extensively with Irish politics) that Giraldus' initial observations remained unchallenged and gained nearly universal acceptance. Moreover, Giraldus may have been the spokesman for an attitude which was generally current in his day, for two near-contemporaries, William of Newburgh and William of Malmesbury, refer to Ireland in terms that closely resemble Giraldus' stance.[5] It was mainly the non-urban, noncentralized life of the Irish that seems to have fixed on them the attributes of barbarism and laziness. Ralph Higden's *Polychronicon* did much to disseminate Giraldus' views. Higden based himself wholly on Giraldus in his references to Ireland (with a few additional references to Solinus) and his chronicle was printed (in Trevisa's English translation of 1387) both by Caxton (in 1482) and by Wynkyn de Worde (in 1495). It was soon found necessary to distinguish between these native Irish and the population group (nowadays called the 'Old English') that moved in after Henry's recognition as *dominus Hiberniae*: the Hiberno-Norman barons scattered over the countryside, and the inhabitants of the cities loyal to the English Crown. Malmesbury in particular, in his *De rebus gestis Anglorum*, sees Ireland as a country that is wholly dependent on an English presence for whatever progress is being accomplished, and in this context distinguishes between native/rural backwardness and urban/English progress:

> ° Quanti enim valeret Hibernia si non adnavigarent merces ex Anglia? Ita pro peniuria, immo pro inscientia cultorum, ieiunum omnium bonorum solum, agrestem et squalidam multitudinem Hibernensium extra urbes producit:

---

* Thus this people is a barbarous, a truly barbarous one: because it is most rude, not only in its barbarous mode of dressing, but also in its abundant hairdos and beards, much like those newfangled modern fashions; and all their customs are most barbarous.

° For what would Ireland be good for if it did not have the trade that comes to it from England? Both for the poverty and for the ignorance of the peasants, its soil, barren of all good produce;

Angli vero et Franci, cultiori genere vitae, urbes nundinarum commercio inhabitant. (vol. 2; p. 485)

In contrast to the city-dwellers, the Gaelic Irish did not *de facto* recognize the king's authority and were hence habitually called 'the king's Irish enemies' – as opposed to the king's English subjects dwelling in Ireland. This term 'Irish enemy' was obviously considered the equivalent of a less opprobrious Latin term recalling Giraldus: *sylvestri Hiberni*, or 'the Irish inhabiting the wild countryside'. This, again, was often translated as 'wild Irish', with the connotation 'not yet subdued into submission to the law'. Thus, Richard II wrote, in early 1395, to the duke of York that

en nostre terre Dirland sont trois maners des gentz., cestassavoir Irrois savages nos enemis. Irroix rebelx et Engleis obbeissantz.[6]

And a gloss from 1401 equates 'Wildehirissheman' with the Latin 'Hibernicus et inimicus noster' (ibid.). In this manner, the very nomenclature perpetuated an initial political attitude and reinforced early accusations of savagery, barbarism and cultural inferiority. The later use of the term *meere Irish* for the Gaelic Irish, though it meant nothing stronger than 'pure', 'unmixed' (as in the Latin *merus*) could also become loaded with the more supercilious connotation of its homonym, and be interpreted as 'those who are only Irish and nothing better'.

Although a statute of 1331 admitted free Irishmen, Gaelic and English, to English law, the effective political division of the inhabitants of Ireland into those who were the king's subjects and those who were the king's enemies was manifested again at the parliament of 1366 held at Kilkenny, where statutes were passed forbidding the king's English subjects in Ireland to adopt Gaelic customs, and limiting the intercourse between the two population groups as much as possible. It was an attempt to stem the tide of Gaelicization among the Hiberno-Norman nobles (the 'irroix rebelx' whom Richard II referred to), and it is interesting in that it obviously regards Gaelic barbarism as a debauching force rather than a mere lack of civility. Even more interesting is the fact that the national division of Ireland is *defined by* (rather than *defining*) the adoption of cultural patterns and of a political stance. A pattern of societal behaviour is the defining criterion of nationality: the king's obedient subjects are, *ipso facto*, called 'Englishmen', 'without taking into consideration that they be born in England or in Ireland',[7] those who follow a Gaelic life-style are therefore 'Irishmen'.

The differentiation between 'subjects' and 'Irish enemies' was formally dropped when Henry VIII was declared *king* of Ireland (instead of *lord*, the title of his predecessors since Henry II).[8] From this moment, the king of Ireland exacts dutiful loyalty from all Irishmen, the 'mere' Irish included; and so the segregated, not-so-peaceful coexistence of the middle ages ended, and the English-Irish confrontation entered a new phase.

brings forth only the boorish and squalid crowd of non-urban Irish, but the more civilized English and French inhabit the trading market towns.

The Tudor period

Henry's elevation from 'lord' to 'king' of Ireland took place at the behest of his Irish council on the grounds that the former title was considered to be a papal benefice which implied that Henry only held Ireland by the grace of the Holy See; moreover, N.P. Canny argues that the change was advocated and instigated by those pro-English citydwellers of Ireland (more particularly the Palesmen of Dublin) as part of their aim to pacify the unruly Gaelic Irish and strengthen their own position in Ireland.[9] But even if the title was 'thrusted' on Henry, even if Henry was 'none too enthusiastic about this new commitment in Ireland' (ibid.), the act did fit into his general policy which aimed at reinforcing the central authority of the Crown, more particularly of the Tudor dynasty wearing that Crown. All allegiance to others than the monarch (be it in religious or secular matters) was suppressed, and the medieval bifurcation between religious and civic loyalty was subsumed into one's joint appurtenance to the realm and the church of England. Henry's assumption of the kingship of Ireland was likewise a matter of national 'Gleichschaltung' after the earlier division between Englishry and Irishry.[10] It was extended in its natural consequence: Henry's policy of 'surrender and re-grant', by which Gaelic chieftains were pressed to hold their lands by enfeoffment, and with a title in the peerage, rather than in their own right and under the native Gaelic laws. In fact this boiled down to an enforcement of English modes of tenure and succession in lieu of the old Gaelic ones.

On the religious level, too, this centralizing (which in the case of Ireland meant: Anglicizing) policy was at work; as early as 1537, well before Henry's elevation to the kingship, a number of acts had been passed implementing his reformation policy in Ireland: 'An act authorizing the king, his heirs and successors, to be supreme head of the Church of Ireland', 'An act against the authority of the bishop of Rome', 'An act for the suppression of abbyes', etc. (28 Henry VIII *c.* 5,13,16). What is the most interesting aspect of these acts is the fact that a deliberate cultural Anglicization was also envisaged: for in that same session of parliament, a number of laws were passed of an overtly cultural-political nature. The most important of these was the 'Act for the English order, habite and language' (28 Henry VIII *c.* 15) which equated political and religious loyalty with cultural assimilation. Thus, the preamble states:

> The king's majestie . . . prepending and waying . . . how much it doth more conferre to the induction of rude and ignorant people to the knowledge of Almighty God, and of the good and vertuous obedience, which by his most holy precepts and commandements, they owe to their princes and superiours, then a good instruction in his most blessed laws, with a conformitie, concordance, and familiarity in language, tongue, in maners, order, and apparel, with them that be civil people . . . as his Grace's subjects of this part of this his land of Ireland, that is called the English pale, doth; and most graciously considering . . . that there is againe nothing which doth more conteyne and keep many of his subjects of this his said land, in a certaine savage and wilde kind and maner of living, then the diversitie that is betwixt them in tongue, language, order, and habite, . . . doth

. . . desire . . . that the said English tongue, habite, and order, may be from
henceforth continually (and without ceasing or returning at any time to Irish
habite and language) used by all men that will knowledge themselves according to
their duties of allegiance, to be his Highness true and faithfull subjects . . .
whosoever shall . . . not . . . use . . . the English tongue, his Majestie will
repute them in his most noble heart as persons that esteeme not his most dread
lawes and commandements . . .[11]

In Henry VIII's policy it becomes apparent that the medieval, ethnocentric arroga-
tion of cultural superiority over an alien, and therefore barbarous, country, could
eventually lead into the more elitist and supremacist attitude of sixteenth-century
European colonialism:[12] divergence from English cultural standards is regarded not
only as barbarism but even as a subversion of legal authority, and while the natives
are considered subject to English law, their barbarism precludes them from enjoy-
ing civic rights under that law. Any persecution, no matter how severe, is justified,
to 'allure and bring in that rude and barbarous nation to civility and acknowledg-
ing of their duty to God and to [the Crown]'.[13] It follows that the imputed
barbarism of the natives is the main excuse for whatever ruthless policy may be
deemed expedient. Accordingly, a number of colonialist pamphlets and policy
outlines were written, of which Spenser's *View of the present state of Ireland* is the
best-known example. A common element in such writings was the tendency to
deny civility, be it in religious or in socio-cultural terms, to the natives – to the
point of accusing them of cannibalism or incest, or equating them with animals.
As the sixteenth century passed, the charge of moral/religious laxity gradually
merged into a religious polarity between Protestantism (English, moral, civilized)
and Catholicism (Irish, immoral, benighted).

From an early date onwards, anti-English forces in Ireland (that is to say,
those opposing Tudor centralization) argued their opposition or resistance with
religious objections. The excommunication of Elizabeth by Pius V in 1570 was
a contributing factor in the politicization of religious allegiance.

It is striking that the Elizabethan authors who dealt with Ireland in the light
of these more modern developments – the Reformation, the rise of colonialism
– could still fall back on classical and medieval authors for their purposes. This
continuity is exemplified in one of the earliest Tudor descriptions of Ireland:
Andrew Borde's geography, the *Introduction of knowledge*, of 1552. His chapter on
Ireland follows a number of medieval points (e.g. lack of (agri)culture, laziness,
loose sexual mores, irascibility), most prominent of which is the emphasis laid
on the loyalty and civility amongst the Englishmen of the Pale. At the same time,
Irish swiftness, their use of mantles and darts, as well as some more traditional
attributes, will be encountered repeatedly in later times, both in descriptive texts
and in fiction:

Ireland is a kingdomship longing to the kinge of England. It is in the west parte of
the world, & is devyded in ii. partes .i. is the english pale. & the other, the wyld
Iryshe. The English pale is a good countrey, plentye of fishe, flesh wildfoule & corne.

> There be good townes & cities as Dublin & Waterford, wher the english fashion is, as in meat, drinke, other fare & lodging. The people of the english pale be metely well manered, using the english tunge but naturally, they be testy, specially yf they be vexed yet there be many well disposed people as wel in the english pale, as in the wyld Irish, & vertuous creatures whan grace worketh above nature. The other parte of Irland is called the wild Irysh, and the Redshankes be among them. That countrey is wylde, wast & vast, full of marryces & mountains, & lytle corne, but they have flesh sufficient, & litle bread or none and none ale. For the people ther be slouthful, not regarding to sow & tille theyr landes, nor caring for riches. For in many places thei care not for pot, pan, kettil, nor for mattrys, fether bed, nor such implementes of houshold. Wherfore it is presuppose that they lak maners & honesti, & be untaught & rude, the which rudenes with theyr meloncoli complexion causeth them to be angry and testy without a cause. . . . . In such places men and women wyl ly together in mantles and straw. There be many the which be swift of fote, & can cast a dart perilousli, I did never finde more amite and love than I have found of Irishe men the whiche was borne within the english pale. An in my lyfe I dyd never know more faythfuller men & parfyt lyvers than I have knowen of them. (2nd and 3rd pages of chapter 3; no page or signature number)

Another indication of the continuity between medieval and colonial attitudes is the fact that two of the most important sixteenth-century writers to fix the image of Ireland were themselves Catholic: Edmund Campion and Richard Stanyhurst. The Jesuit Edmond Campion is revered as a martyr in the Roman Catholic church, owing to the fact that he was executed as a traitor by the Protestant English authorities. He had earlier been forced to leave England (1569), and lived in Dublin for a while, where he stayed with his erstwhile Oxford acquaintance Richard Stanyhurst. The result of this sojourn was a history of Ireland, rather hastily finished in manuscript; the author did not find any later opportunity to revise the initial version of 1571. Campion's manuscript was published in 1633 by Sir James Ware, but had at that time already obtained a greater indirect influence in that Stanyhurst's description of Ireland was largely based upon it. This description appeared in Holinshed's well-known *Chronicles* of 1577 and repeatedly echoes Campion's history verbatim.

How important the impact of these combined descriptions of Ireland was for later attitudes and writings regarding the country and its inhabitants may be gathered from a small detail which can be traced, like a radioactive isotope, from text to text: it is Campion's short description of the Irish eau-de-vie, whiskey (then called 'usquebaugh', fr. Gaelic *uisce beatha*, 'aqua vitae'), which, the Jesuit thought, 'dryeth more, and inflameth lesse' than the distilled cordials known in England (p. 14). This particular little characterization became a formula that can be found in virtually all English descriptions of Ireland up to (and even into) the eighteenth century. And this fact may in turn serve as an indication that such descriptions were often as indebted to earlier descriptions as they were to the individual author's personal observations; or, in other words: that such descriptions may be regarded as belonging to a textual tradition with its own intertextual cohesion.

Campion, being the ardent recusant that he was, takes a less derogatory stance towards the Catholic native Irish and their life-style than did most Tudor writers, who were, as a rule, strongly anti-Catholic. Campion can thus praise the Gaelic Irish for their industriousness, which is quite the opposite of the traditional imputation of sloth, current since Giraldus' day; remarkably enough, even Stanyhurst does not follow Campion's original text in this instance. Likewise a passing remark such as

> They are sharpe witted, lovers of learning, capable of any studie, whereunto they bend themselves, constant in travailes. (Campion p. 19)

is suppressed in Stanyhurst's description.

Both Campion and Stanyhurst follow Cambrensis in regarding the Irish as an amoral people, too little civilized to keep their passions under control. Cambrensis' statement that 'Quod igitur in his naturae, illud optimum; quicquid fere industriae, illud pessimum' was often repeated by later authors, and a similar gap between instinct and civility is hinted at by Campion:

> The lewder sorte, both clearkes and lay men are sensuall & over loose in livying. The same being vertuously bred up or reformed, are such myrrors of holynes and austeritie, that other nations retain but a shadow of devotion in comparison of them. (p. 19)

The tacit understanding is that a task is to be performed in civilizing the Irish: even without sharing the more vehement outlook of some Elizabethan writers like Spenser or Churchyard, and notwithstanding the fact that there was no religious antipathy at work in these Catholic authors, the ethnocentric axiom of English cultural and moral superiority is operative. Colm Lennon, in his biography of Stanyhurst, has rightly pointed out that Stanyhurst's attitude to the Gaelic Irish ameliorated appreciably from his description in Holinshed's *Chronicles* to a later work that he published in Antwerp in 1584, *De rebus in Hibernia gestis*. The difference between the two works may be reduced to the formula that, in the earlier, the author spoke as a Palesman, one of those loyal subjects who had in Henry VIII's reign cherished the hope of re-shaping all Ireland in their own image, loyal to the Crown and to English law[14] – whereas in the later work, Stanyhurst spoke primarily as a recusant; for *De rebus in Hibernia gestis* was written in exile, when Stanyhurst, suspected of plotting against the government, had been arrested and interrogated, and had subsequently fled to the Continent.

As a result, Stanyhurst's contribution to Holinshed's *Chronicles* is less tolerant in tone than either Campion's history or his own later work. It may also be that it was the framework of publication, Holinshed's proud epitome of the Great British heritage, which caused the description of Ireland to adopt a more pointedly anti-Gaelic tone. Of course, Stanyhurst, as a Palesman, may have had grievances overruling the community of religion: he must have known of the cattle-raids and robbing incursions of the adjacent clans into the Pale, and may to some extent have shared in the bitterness engendered thereby – a bitterness more clearly noticeable in other urban Irish writers of the period like Smythe, Good, and John Derricke. Derricke, for instance, wrote a long and extremely vengeful rhyming tract concerning the raids of Irish soldiers ('kerns') on the Pale, describing their barbarous manners and ending with their utter destruction at the hands of the English authorities. The poem, called *The image of Irelande*, was printed in 1581. Derricke saw the Irish aggression as born of primitive barbarism inflamed by the wicked machinations of poets and priests. Of the Irish poets and reciters, he said:

> This Barde he doeth report, the noble conquestes done,
> And eke in Rhymes shewes forthe at large, their glorie thereby wonne.
> Thus he at randome ronneth, he pricks the Rebells on:
> And shewes by suche externall deeds, their honour lyes upon.
> And more to stirre them up, to prosecute their ill:
> What great renowne their fathers gotte, thei shewe by Rimying skill. (fol. vii r.f.)

At the same time, he explains in the marginal note:

> The Barde by his Rimes hath as great force amongst Woodkarne to perswade, as the elloquent oration of a learned Oratour amongst the civill people. The pollicie of the Barde to encense the Rebelles to doe mischiefe, by repeating their fore-fathers actes. O craftie Apostle as holie as a Devill. (ibid.)

And of the priest, it is said:

> The Frier of his councells vile, to Rebelles doth imparte.
> Affirmyng that it is, an almose deede to God,
> To make the English subjectes taste, the Irishe Rebells rodde.
> To spoile, to kill, to burne, this Friers councell is:
> And for the doyng of the same, he warrantes heavenlie blisse. (fol. vii v.)

And again, in the margin:

> The Frier perswades the Rebels that it is an high worke of charitie, to kill loyall Subjects, which thyng they beleeve though never founde on scripture, O ghostly Frier as innocent as Judas. Beholde the plaguy counsell of a pockie Frier, the very fruite of Papistrie. (ibid.)

Later on, Derricke again finds occasion to lash out against priest-craft:

> The Friers in Irelande, are chiefest instrumentes of Irishe disturbaunce, they are the onely spurre to pricke them onward to rebell against the Queene, procurying the meanes of their utter destruction, beyng the hed welspring of all sinne and wickednesse. (fol. ix r., margin)

Stanyhurst's own, Palesman-like, attitude lacks this Protestant dimension, but crops up repeatedly in the additions he makes to Campion's original discourse, e.g. in his caveat to the reader not to impute any barbarous custome that shall be here layde downe, to the citizens, townsmen, and the inhabitants of the english pale, in that they differ little or nothyng from the auncient customes and dispositions of their progenitors, the English and Walshmen. (fol. 17 v.)

Another addition made by Stanyhurst shows the implicit tendency to regard the Anglicized Pale as an ideal model for the reform of Ireland, and to urge a conformation of Gaelic Ireland to the English model; contending that

a conquest draweth, or at the least wise ought to drawe to it, three things, to witte, law, apparayle, and languague [sic]. For where the countrye is subdued, there the inhabitants ought to be ruled by the same law that the conqueror is governed, to weare the same fashion of attyre, wherewith the victour is vested, & speake the same language, that the vanquisher parleth. And if anye of them lacke, doubtlesse the conquest limpeth. (fol. 3 r.)

Conversely, Stanyhurst argues most strenuously against any form of Gaelicization or of tolerance of things Gaelic among the English colonists, describing it nearly as a fall from grace:

And truely as long as these empaled dwellers did sunder themselves as wel in land as in language, from the Irishe: rudenes was day by day in the countrey supplanted, civilitie engrassed, good lawes established, loyaltie observed, rebellion suppressed, and in fine the cyone of a yong England was lyke to shoote in Ireland. But when their posteritie became not all togither so wary in keeping, as their auncestors were valiant in conquering, and the Irish language was free dennized in the English pale: this canker tooke such deepe roote, as the body that before was whole and sounde, was by little and little festered, and in maner wholy putrified. (fol. 2 v.)

And the end of Stanyhurst's description is particularly 'English' in its outlook, even to the point of seeming to endorse a religious conformation (i.e. reformation) after the English model:

God with the beames of hys grace, clarifie the eyes of that rude people that at length they may see theyr miserable estate: and also that such, as are deputed to the government thereof, bend their industry with concionable pollicye to reduce them from rudenesse to knowledge, from rebellion to obedience, from trechery to honesty, from savagenesse to civilitie, from idlenes to labour, from wickednesse to godlynesse, wherby they may the sooner espy their blyndenesse, acknowledge their loosenesse, amende their lives, frame themselves plyable to the lawes and ordinaunces of hir Majestie, whom God with his gracious assistance preserve, as wel as to the prosperous government of hir realme of England, as to the happye reformation of hir realme of Ireland. Finis. (fol. 28 v.)

But even though Stanyhurst's anti-Gaelic, Palesman-like attitudes in this description may have been, in a sense, *impar sibi*, the fact that they did conform to the prevalent outlook on Irish affairs in England at the time, as well as the fact that they were published in Holinshed's highly successful *Chronicles*, made them far more influential than either Campion's or his own, later, history. The following, more general, description of the Gaelic national character (in which Stanyhurst follows Campion) became standard fare in most subsequent writings about Ireland:

> The people are thus enclined, religious, franke, amorous, irefull, sufferable of infinite paynes, very glorious, many sorcerers, excellent horsemen, delighted with wars, great almesgivers, passing in hospitality. (fol. 28 r.; cf. Campion p. 19)

Some other traits that are emphasized are Irish martial pride, which makes the chieftains susceptible to the inflammatory encomia of their bards, and the uncouth diet. Customs unknown in England are related as matters of slightly distasteful curiosity, e.g. the usage of fostering and the 'keen' (fr. Gaelic *caoineadh*, to weep), the ritual protestation of grief at a funeral. This trait was later to be represented as an instance of falseness, of a tendency to dissemble one's true feelings under histrionic behaviour. Popular beliefs and customs are cited at great length, ostensibly as an example of 'Irish superstition', but in so much detail that the author himself must have found some entertainment or interest in them. Nevertheless the point is used to illustrate the assertion that the Irish have adopted the mere semblance of Christianity and are still little better than heathens; similar opinions, though far more stridently expressed, can be found in Spenser and other Protestant Elizabethans.[15]

The most important author to draw on Campion/Stanyhurst's description was the great historian William Camden, who published his geographical *Britannia* in 1586.[16] An authorized translation, by Philemon Holland, followed in 1610. Camden's *Britannia*, which was to maintain its fame for centuries as one of the classic geographical/historical descriptions of the British Isles, thus deals with Ireland only in the British context that Holinshed had also used. Nevertheless Camden's description could become as influential in its own right as Stanyhurst's in the *Chronicles*, and references to Camden can be found in most later writings on Ireland.

The author himself largely depended on Pomponius Mela and on Giraldus Cambrensis; but in his description of whiskey ('Aquam vite optimam habent, quae multo minus, quam nostra, inflammat, & magis exsiccat', p. 567) the influence of Campion/Stanyhurst comes to the surface. Camden himself is reticent in his descriptions, limiting himself largely to historical and geographical data; in dealing with the present disposition of the country, he quotes at some length an inhabitant of Ireland who, though not mentioned by name in the first Latin edition, is identified in the English edition as a teacher from Limerick, Joseph Good – what is not mentioned is the fact that Good was a Jesuit with an obvious interest in the counter-reformatory improvement of the Roman Catholic church in his country. Good is more explicit in his denunciations of the Gaelic Irish than Camden himself, who is of the opinion that they

* alicubi sunt incultiores, qui mira naturac divertate, & inertiam amant, & quietum oderunt, quique in praeproperam Venerum sunt effusiores. (1586 ed., p. 492)

He also calls them 'bellicosi' and 'ingeniosi' (p. 492).

For Good, however, the Irish are pure evil; though well-built and musically talented, they are rotten to the core: dirty in dress and behaviour, nauseating in their cuisine and eating habits, dastardly in the cattle raids on the Old English settlements, and most particularly foul in their desecration of religion:

° & in caussa est turpissima sacrificulorum vita, qui è templis domos prophanas constituunt, & in meretricibus indulgent, quae illis quocunque concedunt, subsequuntur, abdicatae verò per veneficia nocendi artes quaerunt. Sacrificulorùmque horum fili, qui studia non consectantur, plerumque latrocinio sunt insignes. (p. 520)

This criticism is stressed and expanded in the later English version,[17] which also included the following additional passage:

The Priests Lemmons and their bastards, abide within the circuit of a Church, drinke until they be drunke, lie together, shed bloud, and keepe up their cattel there. Among those wild Irish, there is neither divine service; nor any forme of Chappell but outwardly: no Altars at all, or else they be filthily polluted: the image of the Rood or Crosse defaced, if there be any at all. The sacred vestiments are so foule and nasty that they would make one to cast up his stomacke: The Altar portable without any crosses emprinted upon it, and by some abuse or other polluted. The Missal or Masse booke all torne, and bereft of the Canon: yet the same is tendred to all othes and perjuries; the Chalice of lead without a cover to it, the small vessels for wine made of a horne. The Priests minde nothing but gathering of goods and getting of children. (1610 ed. p. 144)

Camden explicitly endorses Good's description, but takes care to exclude the Old English from the opprobrium contained therein:

† Hoc solummodo pro illo praefabor, nihil eum ad calumniam, sed omnia ad veritatem collinare, & tantùm de inconditis illis, & merè Hibernicis loqui, qui in extremis delitescunt, & humaniores mores nondum induêrunt. (1586 ed. p. 518)

And, again, Camden stresses at the conclusion:

* . . . are uncivilized in some areas; who, by a remarkable freak of nature, both love idleness and hate quietude; and who are only too indulgent in headlong amorousness.

° and the reason for this is the filthy life of their clergy, who turn their churches into profane households and make use of unchaste women; these follow them wherever they can and, when rejected, try to harm them with artful spells and potions. The sons of these clerics will, if they do not follow a career in learning, mostly become criminals.

† I only make the prefatory remark that he (Good), so far from wanting to spread calumny, has aimed only at truthfulness, and that he speaks only of those rude and 'mere' Irish who skulk in the most distant corners of the country and have not yet adopted a more civilized life-style.

> * Hi sunt sylvestrium Hibernicorum mores, ex autore nostro, in reliquis qui
> Anglicam, quam dicunt, provinciam incolunt, nihil abest quod in cultu, &
> humanitate requiratur. (p. 524)

If one compares this closing statement to the one in the later English edition, the
intensification of anti-Gaelic matter again becomes obvious; for here, Camden
adds:

> and for much more might the whole island be beholden unto it [i.e. the English
> conquest], in case upon a certain peevish and obstinate love they beare unto their
> owne country fashions, they had not stopped their eares and shut up their hearts
> against better governance. For, the Irishry are so stiffly settled in observing of the
> old rites of their country, that not only they cannot be with-drawn from them, but
> also are able easily to draw the English unto the same. . . (1610 ed. p. 148)

Since this first English translation was authorized, the changes cannot be simply
attributed to Philemon Holland; the likelihood is rather that Camden's own attitude had become more negative during the 1590s and early 1600s, possibly as a
consequence of the Tyrone rebellion which evoked strong feeling in Elizabethan
circles. Such sudden spells of deterioration in the English image of Ireland can be
seen to appear with dreary regularity in the wake of active hostility or warfare:
after the Tyrone rebellion, the Ulster rising of 1641, the Jacobite war of 1690, the
uprising of 1798, the agitation of O'Connell, etc. Periods of comparative quiet,
such as the years after 1620, the reign of Charles II, and most of the eighteenth
century, show a gradual amelioration of English attitudes – a pattern which is
obviously in keeping with the long-standing idea that Ireland could improve only
by submitting to a process of civilization/ Anglicization, and by the implied
acquiescence in English superiority; it is as if English authors tend to interpret the
quietude of those calmer periods as resulting from the beneficial influence of
spreading English civility (thus linking a more positive image of Ireland to an
attitude of self-congratulation). Conversely, disruptions of such political lulls in
periods of crisis are often interpreted as native Irish wildness and rebelliousness
perversely reasserting itself.

Thus, the year 1589 could witness the publication of a surprisingly positive
Briefe description of Ireland by Robert Payne, obviously aiming to attract potential
undertakers for the plantation of Munster which was then in progress. Payne is
most emphatic in his division of the population. The lowest class consists of
indigents, the next lowest of the wild and warlike 'kerns', the outlaw Gaelic
warriors who were the bogeymen of the Elizabethans. Payne soothingly adds
that 'most of that sorte were slayne in the late warres' (p. 4). The best Gaels are
cattle-farmers who, although they may not be all that clean or civil, are certainly
hospitable (p. 3) and law-abiding (p. 4). They are also eager to Anglicize themselves (the true hallmark of an honest disposition): they speak English, or at

---

* This is the life-style of the woodland Irish, taken from our informant; in the others, who inhabit
  what is called the English Pale, not a single requirement of civility and humanity is lacking.

least teach their children to speak English, and 'reforme them selves dayly more and more after the English manners' (p. 4) – in short, a colonist's ideal native. Payne also points out that Irish loyalty lies with England, not with England's main enemy, Catholic Spain. However, such complacency was bitterly disappointed in the following decade.

Payne's claim that national unity with England outweighed the religious differences between Catholic natives and the Crown, was proved wrong. The identification of the colonial English interest in Ireland with Protestantism, and that of its native opponents with Catholicism, was to become all-pervading during the course of the seventeenth century. What was at work was perhaps the following: Anglocentric policies of national unification were introduced hand in hand with a religious reformation policy – into a country whose natives had not known an effective central monarchy, or a national political consensus or a recognized common national interest, a country based on a de-centralized clan system with a multitude of rivaling sovereign nobles whose political interests were at variance, and whose strongest common links were those of bardic culture and the Catholic religion. A national – i.e. nation-wide, concerted – opposition (in a political sense) against English national centralization efforts was by and large unthinkable in this politically de-central context. Counter-policies therefore tended to react against English expansionism mainly in its religious aspects, i.e. as an anti-Reformation, recusant stance. To put the matter in simplified terms: English national ideology was fought, not in its political manifestation (since that would have presupposed a common national interest in what was a decentralized clan society) but in its religious manifestation (since that appealed to a religion and a centralized church organization which was well established throughout the land). Even more crudely simplified: Gaelic or Old English political opposition against English expansionism tended to fasten on what was, for them, the most easily recognizable as well as the most generally objectionable tenet implied in that expansionism: the claim to a nationally English religious allegiance. The rebellion of 'Silken' Thomas Fitzgerald of 1534, though inspired mostly by dynastic motives (namely to protect the near-royal stature of the Geraldines in Ireland) quoted Henry VIII's breach with the papacy as its ostensible motive; James Fitzmaurice's rebellion of 1579 was supported actively (with men and with indulgences) by pope Gregory XIII, and his proclamation on landing in Ireland stated that

> This war is undertaken for the defence of the Catholic religion against the heretics . . . we fight not against the lawful sceptre and honourable throne of England, but against a tyrant which refuseth to hear Christ speaking by his vicar.[18]

Again, in 1599, the foremost war aims of Hugh O'Neill's rebellion were concerned with the status of Catholicism in Ireland.[19]

It may be said that English expansionism was, on the Irish side, by and large, translated into religious or ecclesiastical terms. This point was also reinforced by the fact that most important ambassadors of the anti-English cause on the

Continent tended to be churchmen – Irish Catholic bishops living in exile, who attempted to obtain military or diplomatic support from the Catholic powers abroad: Edmund Magauran, archbishop of Armagh († 1593) and Owen Mac Egan, bishop of Ross († 1603) in Spain, Peter Lombard, archbishop of Armagh († 1625) and St. Oliver Plunket, archbishop of Armagh (†1681) in Rome.

In contrast to this tendency on the Irish side to see the confrontation mainly in religious terms, the earlier colonialist writers such as Thomas Churchyard and Edmund Spenser took a broader and more politically-oriented stance – though later writers like Rich were to let Protestant feelings take pride of place. Men like Spenser or Churchyard, and, later, Sir John Davies, saw the conflict mainly as an effort to subdue unruly subjects who refused to recognize the proper authorities; anti-Catholic attitudes surfaced mainly in the notion that perfidious priests, ever intent on weakening the Protestant cause, inflamed the natural hot temper of the Irish. As in the representation of John Derricke, the priest's role was often considered as working in conjunction with the equally inflammatory Irish poets and reciters. It was the political subjugation of Ireland that really mattered, and a cultural Anglicization was considered no less necessary towards this end than a religious reformation; it will be remembered that even the Catholic English in Ireland, like Stanyhurst and the Jesuit Good, could advocate a religious reformation, albeit presumably one in counter-reformation terms. Stanyhurst's appeal for Irish submission to the triune aspects of English culture (apparel, law, and language) is a case in point. Spenser had also argued that the Irish language was subversive, being in itself a constant reminder of separateness:

> the wordes are the Image of the mynde, so as they proceding from the mynde, the mynde must bee needes affected with the wordes: So that the speech beinge Irish, the harte must needes bee Irishe, for out of the aboundance of the heart the tonge speaketh. (p. 88)

Spenser can in like manner argue for the suppression of Gaelic clan appellations, instead of which the Irishman

> should take unto him self a severall surname eyther of his trade or facultie or of some quallitie of his bodye or mynde, or of the place where he dwelte, so as everie one should bee distinguished from other or from the most parte whereby they shall not onely not depend upon the head of their sept as now they doe, but also shall in shorte tyme learne quite to forgette his Irishe nation and herewithall would I also wishe, all the Oes and the mackes which the heades of septes have taken to theire names to bee utterlye forbydden and extinguished, for that same beinge an old manner (as some sayth) first made by Obrin for the strengtheninge of the Irishe, the abrogating thereof will as much enfeeble them. (p. 201)

– Again, the continuity from earlier, medieval attitudes is noteworthy, for Spenser explicitly refers back to Edward IV's act requesting Irishmen to take English surnames (cf. p. 387 n. 8).

Stanyhurst likewise objected to the use of Irish, at least within the Pale; however, both in his *Description* and in his later Latin work he emphasized that he did not mean to denigrate the Irish language as such, but rather to object to its currency within the Pale, which he denounces at some length. Haynes, too, a late Elizabethan colonialist pamphleteer with views comparable to Spenser's, considered the subversiveness of the Irish language to be proved by the earlier corruption/Gaelicization of the Hiberno-Normans: 'It hath beene observed that the Irishe language beinge permitted to be used of the Englishe hath beene noe small question to draw them into their [i.e. 'meer Irish'] manners' (p. 55).

A number of highly explicit condemnations of Gaelic poets are extant, most of them fastening (like Derricke) on the subversive and inflammatory influence of their poetry on the unruly chieftains, in whose praise they would say (as Spenser puts it),

> that he was none of those Idle milke-sopps that was brought upp by the fyer syde, but that most of his dayes he spent in armes and valiant enterprises, that he did never eate his meate before he had wonne yt with his sworde, that he laye not slug-ginge all night in a Cabben under his mantle, but used commonlie to kepe others wakinge, to defende theire lyves, and did light his candle at the flame of theire howses, to leade him in the darkenesse, that the daye was his night and the night his daye, that he loved not to lye longe woinge of wentches to yeild to him, but where he came he tooke by force the spoyle of other mens love, and left but lamentacion to theire lovers: that his musicke was not the harpe nor layes of love, but the cryes of people, and Clashinge of armor, and that fynallie he dyed not bewayled of manye, but made manye wayle when he dyed, that dearelie bought his death. (p. 97)

This war-like type of Gaelic bardic encomium was known also to another English inhabitant of Ireland, and likewise used in a denunciation of the intolerable peril that these poets were to the English cause in Ireland: the Dublin apothecary Thomas Smythe had written in 1561:

> these people be very hurtfull to the commonwhealle, for they chifflie mayntayne the rebells; and, further, they do cause them that would be true, to be rebellious theves, extorcioners, mutherers, ravners, yea and worse if it were possible. Their furst practisse is, if they se anye younge man discended of the septs of *Ose* or *Max*, and have half a dowsen aboute him, then will they make him a Rime, wherein they will commend his father and his aunchetours, nowmbrying howe many heades they have cut of, howe many townes they have burned, and howe many virgins they have defloured, howe many notable murthers they have done, and in the ende they will compare them to Aniball, or Scipio, or Hercules, or some other famous person; wherewithall the pore foole runs madde, and thinkes indede it is so.[20]

Thus, the English view of the English-Gaelic confrontation encompassed not only the political and ecclesiastical points of friction, but contained also an awareness of the linguistic and literary forces at work.

The seventeenth century

The repression of the Tyrone rebellion brought many of English gentlemen-officers to Ireland, some of whom committed their reminiscenccs and opinions of the country and its inhabitants to writing: John Dymmok, John Harington, Fynes Moryson and the less noteworthy Josias Bodley.[21] Dymmok, who attributes most Irish problems to the stubborn pride of the clan chieftains, is traditional enough in his estimate of the Irish national character:

> The people are of nature very glorious, francke, irefull, good horsemen, able to endure great paynes, delighted in warr, great hospitallitye, of religion for the most parte Papists, great gluttons, and of a sensuall and vitious lyfe, deepe dissemblers, secret in displeasure, of a crewell revenging minde, and irreconsiliable. Of witt they are quick and capable, kinde harted where they take, and of exceedinge love towardes their foster bretheren. Of complexion they are cleare, and welfavoured, both men and weomen, tall and corpulent bodies, and of hemselves [sic] careles and bestiall. (p. 6)

Such a description closely recalls that of Campion/Stanyhurst in places, and the tell-tale 'whiskey formula' is also to be found (p. 5). Dymmok has a particular tendency to emphasize the treacherousness of the Irish – which leads to a curiously contradictory usage of the epithets 'francke' and 'deepe dissemblers'. He divides the population into four categories: 'English Irish, meer Irish, degenerate English, and wilde Scots' (p. 7), but concentrates on the second of these, as being by far the most picturesque.

Sir John Harington is an exceptional figure. He was a godson of queen Elizabeth, and a typical example of the witty, elegant courtier of her reign; a celebrated writer of epigrams, he was also the first English translator of Ariosto's *Orlando Furioso*; he accompanied Essex on his ill-fated expedition. Harington is surprisingly positive concerning Ireland and the Irish: apart from his criticism that the Irish are 'much given to whoredome' and 'abusive in their discourse', he has little but praise for the country, especially its hospitality: 'I was well usede, and therefore am in dutie bounde to speake well of the Irishrie'.[22] At one point, Harington contemplated an Irish career, and applied for the post of Irish lord high chancellor and of archbishop of Dublin – jointly! – in a letter which seems so outrageously shameless that it may even have been written in jest, but which is obviously sincere in its positive comments on Ireland:

> I never fownd in the remote sheers of England or Walls eyther the gentry more kynde in theyr fashion of intertaynment, or the marchawnts and townsmen and women more cyvill in behaveowr, or the mean sort and peasants more lovyng and servisable whear they are honestly used, throwgh all the fyve provinces; but they are so seldome used to soch usage, and so grosly abused, sometyme by the soldyer in war, sometyme by the offycer in peace, that yt ys no wonder yf they take revenge. . . . Neyther ys the Country withowt rare examples of fidelyty in servants, of love and chastytye in matrons, howsomer some pens have taxed the one with trechery, the other with incontynency.[23]

The main difference between Harington and his contemporaries is that, here, a social rather than a 'national' distinction is made. It is not a national Irish group which is compared to the English nation, but rather a comparison of the Irish upper class with its English counterpart, of the Irish peasantry with that of the rural shires of England. In short, Harington's view of Ireland does not employ a national but rather a social matrix; and, in further distinction from his fellow-travellers, he is as willing to see *similarities* between the two countries, as he is to register differences. It was rather the strangeness of Gaelic Ireland which gave it its interest to contemporary, more Anglocentric, observers; Harington takes a less ethnocentrist point of view, and is less predisposed to concentrate on those points which make Ireland un-English (and therefore inferior).

It may also be noted in passing that Harington ameliorated a short but negative reference to Ireland in his translation of *Orlando Furioso*. Ariosto had called Ireland an 'Isola del pianto', continuing,

> che l'Isola del pianto era nomata
> quella che da crudele e fiera tanto
> et inumana gente era abitata. (X, 93; p. 286)

Harrington's translation regarding the 'Isle of woe' is less negative towards the inhabitants:

> For Ile of wo it may be justly called,
> Where peerlesse peeces are abused so;
> By monster vile to be devourd and thralled:
> Where pyrats still by land and sea do go
> Assalting forts that are but weakly walled.[24]

A year or so after Dymmok and Harington, Fynes Moryson arrived in Ireland as private secretary to Mountjoy. Moryson was a well-to-do and widely travelled young gentleman: he had ventured as far as Poland and Turkey in the years 1591–97. He was later (1617) to publish the memoirs of these travels, which to no small extent are concerned with his Irish sojourn, from which he remembers, above all, the bad cuisine and dirty bedclothes. He quotes Mela (p. 191) and incorporates the standard description of whiskey as well as a comment on the plentiful occurrence of bees. He also continues the colonial view of regarding any divergence from the English ethos as an instance of moral inferiority combined with a deliberate act of political disobedience – e.g. in the following reference to the (by now traditional) attribute of laziness:

> the mountaines would yeeld abundance of Mettals, if this publike good were not hindred by the inhabitants barbarousness, making them apt to seditions, and so unwilling to inrich their Prince & Country, and by their slothfulnesse, which is so singular, as they hold it basenesse to labour. . .[25]

Laziness is, in Moryson's view, the root cause of all Irish characteristics, good or bad: it is their sloth which makes them 'love liberty above all things, and

likewise naturally . . . delight in musick, so as the Irish Harpers are excelent'
(p. 483). And, again, the accompanying shadow of rebelliousness is also present:
for the bards

> in their songs used to extoll the most bloudy licentious men, and no others, and
> to allure the hearers, not to the love of religion and Civill manners, but to outrages
> Robberies living as outlawes, and Contempt of the Magistrates and the kings
> lawes. (p. 199)

The picture is completed with a dose of dirty vermin in three forms, lice, wolves
and Catholic priests – all three being 'fruites of their idlenes, slovenlynes, and
superstition':

> * Quatuor hybernas vexant animalia, turpes
> Corpora vermiculi, sorices per tecta rapaces,
> Carnivori vastantque lupi crudeliter agros,
> Haec tria nequitia superas Romane sacerdos. (p. 193)

Their utter lack of civility can even degrade the Irish from the position of human
beings to that of animals:

> To conclude, not onely in lodging passengers, not at all or most rudely, but even in
> their inhospitality towards them, these wild Irish are not much unlike wild beasts,
> in whose caves a beast passing that way might perhaps finde meate, but not
> without danger to be ill entertained, perhaps devoured of his insatiable Host.
> (*Itinerary*, p. 203)

Such dehumanization had been hinted at even as early as in Giraldus' days
('gens ex bestiis et bestialiter vivens') and was to reappear again to indicate the
most complete absence of anything that was considered to constitute civilization.
Later in that century, Thomas Dineley described the Irish as

> sitting upon their hams, like greyhounds in the sun, neer their cabin, they'll work
> not one jott, but steal, which is . . . an inseperable vice to them . . .[26]

Later examples are given in a great number of nineteenth-century anti-Irish
political cartoons, which tended to give the Irish simian, prognathous, features.[27]

At the same time, however, Moryson (and other Englishmen after him) can
be of the opinion that the Irish possess a certain astuteness, mostly employed in
prevarication: they are 'subtill temporisers' (*Itinerary*, p. 486) and

---

* Four species vex the Irish: disgusting lice their bodies, rapacious mice their dwellings, and
carnivorous wolves cruelly despoil their fields. And, worse than these three in perniciousness,
the Roman priest. (Moryson himself gives the following English version ibid.:) 'For four vile
beasts Ireland hath no fence,/ their bodyes lice, their houses Rats possesse,/ Most wicked Preists
governe their conscience,/ and ravening Woolves do waste their feilds no lesse.'

> They are by nature very Clamorous, upon every small occasion raising the houbou (that is a dolefull outcrye) which they take one from anothers mouthe till they putt the whole towne in tumult. And theyr complaynts to magistrates are commonly strayned to the highest points of Calamity, sometyes [*sic*] in hyperbolicall tearmes, as many upon small violences offered them, have Petitioned the lord Deputy for Justice against men for murthering them while they stoode before him sounde and not so much as wounded. (*Itinerary*, p. 484)

The incident mentioned here was to become a favourite joke and may lie at the root of the later 'Irish bull' – for most of Moryson's unusual description, indicating that the Irish may be *amusing* in their uncouth behaviour, foreshadows the later treatment of comical Irish characters on the English stage. The 'hyperbole' of using the verb 'to murder' is no more than a linguistic confusion: Gaelic *marbhadh* can mean anything from 'to kill' to 'to wound, upset deeply'; the Hiberno-English dialect vests this entire spectrum of meanings in the English verbs 'to kill' or 'to murder'.

Barnaby Rich was an army officer who also wrote romances in the style of Lyly: his *Riche his farewell to military profession* (1581) – a premature title – is known for its influence on Shakespeare's *Twelfth Night*. Besides, he lived in Dublin, had met Stanyhurst when serving in the Netherlands under Leicester, and was eventually appointed lord deputy in Ireland. Rich is the first English author to regard the Irish situation primarily from a religious point of view: this strenuous Protestant, who had drawn up a memorandum for the suppression of recusancy in Ireland as early as 1591, published various pamphlets castigating a number of human weaknesses, such as the use of tobacco, female vanity, and, especially, Catholicism. It is this last frailty which, in his view, dominates the Irish character. A typical example from 1609 may be outlined by quoting its own full title: *A short survey of Ireland. Truely discovering who it is that hath so armed the hearts of that people with disobedience to their Prince. With a description of the countrey, and the condition of the people. No less necessarie and needfull to be respected by the English, then requisite and behoovefull to be reformed in the Irish.* Of the 56 pages in 25 chapters, 51(24 chapters) deal exclusively with the contention that the pope of Rome is the Antichrist, and with a denunciation of the vileness of popery and its ministers. Only the last chapter in the *Short survey of Ireland* deals with that country and exhorts the Irish to abandon their misguided trust in Catholicism:

> And who are the inducers of these and many other mischiefes but your Jesuites, your seminaries, & your ungodly massing Priests? these are they that are the common disturbers of the Countries quiet, that have stirred up and set on foote many rebellions: these are they that have blinded your understanding, abused your zeale, and led you into ignorance, under a counterfeit pretence of holinesse. (p. 53 f.)

This pamphlet, like sundry others (e.g. his dialogue *A catholicke conference betweene Syr Tady Mac. Mareall a popish priest of Waterforde, and Patricke Plaine a young student of Trinity College by Dubline in Ireland*, 1612) is different from earlier denunciations of Irish Catholicism (e.g. in Derricke) in that religion is no longer just another problematic factor in the general unruliness of a rude people, but a governing factor in the national confrontation. Only in isolated instances does Rich give a national characterization of the Irish which is not determined by the paradigm of religion, e.g. in his opinion that they are

> more uncivill, more uncleanly, more barbarous, and more brutish in their customes and demeanures, then in any other part of the world that is knowne. (*Short Survey*, p. 2)

Generally, Rich explains Irish national temperament in religious terms (much as Moryson had explained it in terms of laziness): the Irish are 'wild' to the extent that they are Catholic.

> the people are daily seduced, infected and perverted by Jesuites, Seminaries & other runnagate Priests the ministers of Antichrist, wherwith the Country doth swarme, and have so mightily prevailed, that they have wrought a generall contempt, as well against his Majestie himselfe, as against his godly proceedings. (ibid., p. [iv])

Again, in his longer *New description of Ireland, wherein is described the disposition of the Irish whereunto they are inclined* (1610), Rich may describe the Irish as

> rude, uncleanlie, and uncivill, so they are very cruell, bloudie minded, apt and ready to commit any kind of mischiefe (p. 15)

– but he will add that this is on account of their religion rather than their 'naturall inclination' (ibid.). Nevertheless, the fifth chapter has as its title 'That the Irish by nature are inclined unto cruelty' (p. 17); in such a discussion of fixed, autonomous (i.e. not religiously or otherwise ideologically determined) national traits, Rich draws on a contrastive listing of nationalities and their ('respective'?) characteristics: a frequently used device to defer the onus of proof into a telescoping, quasi-proverbial list of national characters and thereby authorize the individual characterization – or at least obscure the tree by planting a whole forest:

> All the Countries that are knowne (especiallie in *Europe*) have their severall inclinations aswel to vertue as vice: We say, the *Frenchmen* are politike and deceitfull, and not so valiant in conquering, as provident in keeping. The *Spaniard* is said to bee proud and tyrannious. The *Italian* full of curtesie, and full of craft. The *Dutch* are more wise when they be in their Cups, then when they bee in their Clossets; the *English* are reputed to be more wise to look after, then they are to foresee: and the *Englishman* (indeede) doth then thinke himselfe to bee best in fashion, when he is most out of fashion. (p. 14f.)

Such contrastive enumerations are apt to crop up wherever a certain national character is being described – we have seen, and will see, several other instances. Indeed, the early seventeenth century witnessed an increasing tendency to systematize the ethnic-cultural differences of the European landscape into contrastive 'tables' and schemata.[28]

Rich's *New description of Ireland* is filled with a detailed analysis of Irish nastiness, itemized under headings such as cruelty (p. 17 ff.), ingratitude (p. 21 ff.) and incivility (p. 24 ff.). All this leads, of course, to a denunciation of the ultimate villain, the pope.

For all that this new type of description is religiously dominated, Rich can still draw on earlier sources. Though he sharply denounces earlier authors such as Cambrensis, Campion and Stanyhurst (who, being papists themselves, were far too benevolent in their estimate of the Irish), he can adopt Stanyhurst's contention when claiming 'That a conquest should draw after it *Lawe, Language,* and *Habit*' (heading to chapter 9, p. 32).

Rich had been so caustic towards Ireland and its inhabitants that his popularity in Dublin suffered. In order to assuage hurt feelings, he published another pamphlet in 1612, which added some sugar to the acid, sporting the mellow title *A true and kinde excuse written in defense of that booke, intituled, A newe description of Irelande . . . pleasant and pleasing both to English, and Irish.* Rich is forced to acknowledge that his earlier description of Irish dirt and lack of hygiene was based on the manners of the rural poor, who were equally backwards on the other side of St. George's Channel (p. 8) – another instance, as in the case of Harington, that national attributes may find credit only by the grace of overlooking those social divisions which are cross-national as well as intra-national. Moreover, the underlying principle seems to be that the 'meere Irish' and their life-style are to be considered representative for the entire population of Ireland – for Rich no less than for Moryson of Dymmok. The frequent parenthetical additions to the effect that the proffered descriptions do not apply to the civilized and urban population of Ireland, is in itself an affirmation that, unless otherwise specified, the 'meere Irish' (that is, those most unlike Englishmen) are the 'real' Irish – which is nearly, but not quite, a tautology. The mechanism is typical for the discourse of exoticism and ethnocentrism: those aspects of a given country are present as 'representative' which are most unusual and deviant, most remarkable and most unlike the author's domestic frame of reference. What is remarkable is considered by the same token to be typical, what is different is therefore characteristically representative. This 'typicality effect', with its tendency to foreground striking and strange elements, will push exoticist representations into the direction of caricature: England is reduced to bowler hats and umbrellas, Holland to wooden shoes and windmills, France to berets and stick-shaped loaves of bread.

Rich's emphasis on religiously determined barbarity was reinforced by the Scottish traveller William Lithgow, who passed through Ireland in 1619. Lithgow was an aggressively anti-Catholic Presbyterian; his travel description, which appeared in 1622, is full of hateful remarks against the 'snakish Papists,' 'that snarling Crew' – an attitude perhaps partly explained by (or else partly explaining) the fact that Lightgow has been held prisoner by the Inquisition in

Malaga. He sees 'Ignorance and Sluggishnesse' (p. 428) as the most important Irish national characteristics. Here, too, a contrastive procedure is apparent, e.g. in his unfavourable comparison of the Irish to 'the *Barbarian moore*, the *Moorish Spaniard*, the *Turke*', to 'the undaunted, or untamed *Arabian*, the Divelish-idolatrous *Turcoman*, or the moone-worshipping *Caramines*' (p. 429). In a further similarity to Rich, Lithgow's denunciation of 'Theeves and Woodcarnes' is performed under the religious aspect: they are

> but the Hounds of their hunting Priests, against what faction soever, their malicious malignity is intended. (p. 432)

The explanation of a national character as the result of external influences can even bring Lithgow to the point of adopting a less denunciatory attitude, and seeing the poorer Irish as victims rather than authors of iniquity. They are, he says, labouring under a threefold oppression: that of the landlords, of the established clergy exacting tithes (for whom the Presbyterian Scotsman had little sympathy) and of the Catholic priests:

> O! what a slavish servitude doe these silly wretches indure, the most part of whom in all their lives, have neither third part food, Natures clothing, nor a secure shelter for the Winter cold. The miserable sight whereof, and their sad sounding groanes, have often drawne a sorrowful remorse from my humane compassion. (p. 430)

Perhaps this even reflects, to some extent, the slightly more complacent and less defensive attitude to Irish problems that began to be adopted in early Stuart times. The last throes of rebellion in Ulster had been subdued, the last rebellious nobles had fled to the Continent, and Ireland was, if not yet wholly pacified, at least reduced to obedience to an effectively authoritative Crown. Sir John Davies, architect of the plantation of Ulster, devised an English policy whereby all Irish would come under the effective administration of English common law, and published his ideas in 1612 as *A discoverie of the true causes, why Ireland was never entirely subdued*. Although the government was still firmly committed to the Protestant cause (and Catholic enmity as expressed in the Gunpowder Plot of 1605 did little to change that), the larger European context seems to have effected a slight relaxation in the enforcement of anti-Catholic policy; in 1604, a peace was made between England and Spain, followed by the Twelve Years' Truce between Spain and the United Provinces in 1609. The last years of James I's reign saw the negotiations for a projected marriage between his son Charles and the Infanta Maria, daughter of Philip III of Spain; as it turned out, Charles was to marry another Catholic princess, Louis XIII's sister Henrietta Maria. To this background, it is not such a surprise to see some monastic establishments tolerated in Ireland during Charles' reign.

In those years, Sir James Ware began his labours in the investigation of Irish antiquity; his mentor, archbishop Ussher, had in his historical works repeatedly addressed matters of Irish ecclesiastical history, but Ware himself, a Dubliner born and bred, scion of an established family there, can claim pride of place as the first important historian of Ireland from a non-Gaelic background. He edited and published older texts such as the manuscript works of Campion, Spenser and Giraldus Cambrensis, and made use of the services of a Gaelic antiquary, Duald Mac Firbis, whom he employed as a scribe, translator and amanuensis. At the same time, he was aware of the philological and antiquarian investigations that were undertaken by Continental scholars, e.g. the Frenchman Samuel Bochart. Ware became close friends with Bochart during his stay in Paris, where his monarchist sympathies had forced him to flee during the interregnum; after his return to Dublin, he donated Bochart's *Hierozoicon* to the library of Trinity College. It was Ware, too, who definitively exploded the long-standing authority of Giraldus' descriptions of Ireland, when he wrote in his *De Hibernia et antiquitatibus eius*:

> * Admonendus est etenim lector, Topographiam eam cautè legendam, id quod ipse Giraldus quodammodò fatetur, in apologia quam habemus in prima sua praefatione in librum Expugnationis Hibernicae, cum ob fabolosa, iam dicta Topographia inserta, insimularetur . . . Atqui non possum non mirari viros aliquos huius seculi, alioqui graves & doctos, figmenta ea Giraldi, mundo iterùm pro veris, obtrusisse. Plurimi addi possent ex aliis authoribus, quae aliorum etiam industriis relinquimus. (p. 99 f.)

A more positive attitude towards Ireland was also present in some early Stuart writing that remained unpublished – e.g. *A discourse of the present state of Ireland* (1614) by one S.C., who was ready to believe that the native Irish 'are civilized, grown to be disciplined soldiers, scholars, politicians, and further instructed in points of religion, then accustomed' (p. 431); similarly Luke Gernon, an attorney living in Limerick, set out, in his *Discourse of Ireland* (1620), to contradict whatever negative ideas his readers might have concerning the Gaelic Irish:

> Lett us converse with the people. Lord, what makes you so squeamish – be not affrayd. The Irishman is no Canniball to eate you up nor no lowsy Jack to offend you. The man of Ireland is of a strong constitution, tall and big limbed, but seldome fatt, patient of heate and colde, but impatient of labour. Of nature he is prompt and ingenious, but servile crafty and inquisitive after newes, the simptomes of a conquered nation. Their speach hath been accused to be a whyning language, but that is among the beggars. I take it to be a smooth language, well commixt of vouells and of consonants, and hath a pleasing cadence. The better sorte are apparelled at all poynts like the English onely they retayne theyr mantle . . .[29]

---

* The reader should be warned that that Topography is to be read with caution, as Giraldus himself somehow states in an apology which we find in his first preface to the book of the Conquest of Ireland, where he refers to charges of having inserted fabulous material in his aforementioned Topography. . . . And all the greater is my amazement to see some men of the present day and age, otherwise grave and scholarly, again obtrude those fictions of Giraldus on the world as if they were facts. Many more examples to the same effect could be added from other authors, but that I leave to the industry of others.

This increasing relaxation of anti-Irish mistrust is, as it were, summed up in Thomas Stafford's *Pacata Hibernia, Ireland appeased and reduced* (1633). This book optimistically treats of the definitive establishment of Crown authority in Ireland, and smugly refers to 'the loyall fidelitie of the greater part [i. e. of the Irish] to their lawful Prince' (p. vi). A few years later, at the end of 1641, the Ulster Irish rose in arms, and such complacency was violently disrupted.

Puritan distrust of an overwhelmingly Catholic people had not, of course, ceased completely. Rich's and Lithgow's ideas were continued, for instance, in Edward Cecil's *Government of Ireland under Sir John Perrot* (1626), whose idea of good historiography was mainly to denounce the fact that

> . . . the Romish and Spanish practises (those ambitious States affecting universall Supremacie, the one in over-ruling Religion, the other in coveting absolute Monarchy) had taken holde of the revolting disposition & nature of the *Irish* (now wearier of the *English* yoke of obedience then ever: in respect of their contrariety in Religion, which (through their wildenesse and barbarisme) they would not have beene so sensible of, but by the stirring up of the Romance Locusts: the instruments of strife, bloud, and dissension) . . .'[30]

Until the political decline of king Charles I, such Puritan authors were outweighed by moderate monarchists like Ware and Stafford; after the Ulster rising of 1641, however, they could freely vent the anti-Irish, anti-Catholic emotions stirred up by that revolution, in which a sizable number of Protestant settlers were driven from their homes, severely maltreated, and even killed. The reports that reached Dublin, and then England, swelled the numbers and exacerbated the afflictions of the victims, and were believed only too readily by the more extreme anti-Catholics. A deluge of pamphlets (the seventeenth-century equivalent of the newspaper article) was published, which repeated, and added to, the previous reports of atrocities committed, offering the curious reader an unsavoury combination of sadistic practices described in relentless detail, and violent hate propaganda against the perpetrators: the papist Irish.[31] Such propaganda had, of course, its added importance in the context of the civil frictions within England. It contributed to keep the memory of '1641' alive as a symbol of the blind genocidal ferocity of the Catholic Irish. Sir John Temple contributed his share with his vehemently anti-Catholic history *The Irish rebellion of 1647* – one of the few lengthier works on the subject in this period, and repeatedly re-issued. Its aim, as stated in the sub-title, was less to give a historical analysis of the events, than to describe 'the barbarous cruelties, and bloody massacres, which ensued thereupon.'

For the rest of the century, historians would usually reaffirm the more extreme anti-Catholic point of view. A weary silence is kept during the early restoration period, but from the later 1670s onwards, when the Titus Oates plot, and, later, the imprudent policy of James II helped to fan anti-Catholic prejudice and political paranoia into renewed frenzy, old memories of '1641' are brought up again. The title of an anonymous pamphlet of the year 1678 may serve as an illustration: *An account of the bloody massacre in Ireland, acted by the instigation of Jesuits, priests, and friars, who were the promoters of those horrible murthers, prodigious cruelties, barbarous villainies, and inhumane practices executed by the Irish papists upon the English Protestants in the year 1642.* Edmund Borlase, son of the Sir John Borlase who was lord Justice in Dublin during the Irish civil war, brought out a *History of the execrable Irish rebellion* in 1680, which also adopted a strongly anti-Gaelic/Catholic tone – similar to that of Sir John Temple, though probably written in reaction to a later edition (1674) of Temple's *The Irish rebellion*. Later that century, after the revolution of 1688, two historians who had the unwarranted temerity to call their works 'true' and 'impartial' (namely John Shirley,[32] with his *The true impartial history and wars of the kingdom of Ireland,* 1691, and George Story, with his *The true and impartial history of the most material occurrences in the kingdom of Ireland,* 1691) once more reiterated a strongly negative verdict on the character of the Irish. More deserving of its title was John Nalson's An *impartial collection of the great affairs of state* of 1682, which is equally anti-Puritan and anti-Catholic – on its frontispiece, Catholicism and Puritanism are symbolically amalgamated into the figure of 'Janus Bifrons'. Nalson's strongly royalist work attempts, if not to exonerate, at least to lighten the guilt of 1641, mainly in its criticism of the anti-Catholic historians like Temple and Borlase, whom Nalson accuses of parliamentarian partiality:

> There is not any one particular which hath heen Exaggerated with more vehe-mence then the Cruelty of the Rebels, by Sir *John Temple*, Dr. *Borlase*, and others; and doubtless their Cruelty was strange and barbarous; but then on the other side there is not the least mention of any Cruelty exercised upon the *Irish*, or of the hard measure they received from some of the board in *Ireland*, who were of the Parliamentarian Faction, and *Scottish* Religion, which rendred them desperate, and made the Rebellion Universal; they take no notice of the Severities of the Provost Martials, nor of the Barbarism of the Soldiers to the *Irish*. . . . And certainly as to acknowledge an undeniable Truth, does in no manner Excuse the barbarous Cruelty of the Rebels; so to deny or smother Matters of Fact, so easily to be proved, even by many Protestants still alive, has given the Papists the advantage to bring into Question, especially in Foreign Courts and Countries, the truth of all those inhuman Cruelties, which are charged upon them by such Writers as are found Guilty of such manifest Partiality. (vol. II, vii)

Accordingly, Nalson finds the opportunity to praise the generosity of some Irish rebels as well as to expose the general ferocity of most (II, 633–4). The fact that such a moderate stance was not of immediate effect on the generality of public opinion is perhaps illustrated by Clarendon's *Short view of the state and condition of the kingdom of Ireland.* This little treatise in defence of Ormond was written in 1659 and held, like Nalson's later work, the royalist middle ground between Catholics and Puritans. It was used by Nalson as an important source, and is especially moderate in its evaluation of the Irish conduct in the rebellion:

> It is not the purpose of this discourse to lay any imputations of this rebellion and
> savage cruelty upon the Irish nation, and the catholics of that kingdom, of whom
> many persons of honour were never in the least degree tainted with that
> corruption . . .[33]

Nevertheless, such a moderate description could, in its first printed edition
(1720), be given a preface which showed, in its anti-Irish and anti-Catholic bigotry, far more the influence of Borlase and Story than of Nalson and of Clarendon
himself (p. 3 ff.). And none other than David Hume, no matter how hard he tried
to suppress his own Whiggish sympathies when writing history, was to be less
tolerant in his treatment of the Irish conduct in 1641 than either Nalson or
Clarendon.

Many characteristics attributed to the Irish in these more Whiggish histories
are echoes of the older tradition, e.g. the propensity to laziness and dirt. Again
and again, a statement to the effect that the Irish account idleness their most
cherished boon crops up, even in slightly earlier works like Richard Blome's
geograpy *Britannia* of 1673:

> They accounted *Ease* and *Idleness* their greatest *liberty* and riches, not coveting
> worldly possessions, contenting themselves with mean *Cottages, Hovels*, or *Cabens*.
> (p. 303 f.)

Like the description of the drying and non-inflammatory qualities of Irish
whiskey, this was to become a near-formulaic commonplace. Shirley, again,
follows an older, Morysonesque model in explaining such laziness as a
recalcitrant refusal to co-operate with the authorities:

> the People of the ancient Stock not accustoming themselves to Labour, but rather
> to Spoil and War, desirous to live idly upon the Product of the Country, and
> Manufacture of the industrious *English*, by such unlawful ways as opportunity has
> put into their hands, have in a great measure neglected their own Patrimonies, and
> suffered them in many places to become of no considerable Value, as being eaten
> up by the encroachment of Boggs, and overgrown with such excrements of nature
> as hinder Fertility; and this mainly out of not altogether so much sloth and
> neglect, as their irreconcilable hatred to those of the *British* nation that inhabit
> amongst them, that they should get nothing by their Lands. (p. [v.] f.)

Here as elsewhere a certain convenient polarity seems to be at work, blaming all
negative aspects of life in Ireland on native wickedness, while ascribing the more
positive developments to English presence. Blome mentions with apparent self-
congratulation that many of the native Irish 'ridiculous and absurd customs,
since the English are settled amongst them, are forgotten' (p. 304); Story, too,
can describe the Irish as 'perfect *Barbarians*', 'till at length they were partly
civilized by the English Conquest of that Country' (p. 159), and a nearly literal
echo of that sentiment can be found in Robert Morden's *Geography rectified* of
1680 (p. 45). And Sir William Petty, author of the important *Political anatomy of
Ireland*, had made a satisfied comment on the fact that

there is much superstition among them, but formerly much more than is now; forasmuch as by the conversation of Protestants, they become ashamed of their ridiculous practices, which are not de fide. (p. 66)

Such glimmers of intelligence in the Irish natives were (naturally enough) often represented as a type of animal cunning, which also began to characterize the Stage Irishman of those years. Story, in his *Continuation of the impartial history* (1693) put it as follows:

it has become a Proverb in *England*, to call a dull unthinking Fellow, a Man of an *Irish* Understanding, yet for anything appears to the contrary, they have acted a prudent part for at least these Five Hundred Years; nor is their crafty insinuating wheedling way as yet any thing abated; and whosoever will look amongst the Natives of that Countrey at this juncture, will probably find some Knaves, but as few Fools as in any other Kingdom of the World. (p. 307)

The final summing-up of this stereotyped tradition is perhaps best exemplified in a description by one baron Ronsele from the year 1692, which shows the cumulative results of all these descriptions, repetitions and variations on the ground bass of Irish inferiority:

Those that have described the humours of the natives would speak of the Irish in this manner. They are naturally strong, very nimble, haughty of spirit, silly in their discourse, careless of their lives, great admirers of their foolish and superstitious religion, which they neither understand nor follow, according to the canons of the Church of Rome: they are patient in cold and hunger, implacable in enmity, constant in love, light in belief, greedy of glory, great flatterers and dissemblers, stubborn as mules, great cheats in their dealings, ready to take an oath on all occasions, commonly great thieves, very barbarous when they have the upper hand, of a bloody temper, very unjust to their neighbours, breakers of their trust, mortal enemies to all those that are not of the Romish religion, and ready to rebel against the English on all occasions. A fine description indeed of a nation.[34]

The eighteenth century

'A fine description indeed' – one that we may consider war propaganda rather than mere observation: the texts mentioned in the last pages all dealt with the enmities that racked Ireland in the preceding decades, and were all written under the shadow of the struggle between Jacobite and Williamite forces bringing back memories of the civil war.

As the political situation was stabilized under the reign of William and Mary, the English attitude to the Gaelic Irish seems, if not to have improved, at least to have relaxed somewhat. To be sure, fear of Jacobite upheavals still prejudiced the Anglo-Irish political attitude in Ireland – not unreasonably so, since the disaffected Catholic population (by far the majority of the country's inhabitants) had strong Stuart sympathies; but the political status quo (i.e. what has become known as the 'Protestant Ascendancy') was maintained with a number of severely repressive anti-Catholic laws aimed at destroying the Catholic landed interest, and at making the Catholic Irishman a politically powerless (and thus harmless) second-class citizen. It was only after the Jacobite rising of 1745, which in Ireland had no repercussion whatsoever (though it stirred the muse of a good few Gaelic poets), that the fears for Catholic treachery and subversion began to abate somewhat.

English descriptions from the early part of the eighteenth century are largely a slightly toned-down continuation of the earlier tradition; there are rather fewer political or historical works dealing explicitly with the country, and most extensive references to it are to be found in travel descriptions. Guy Miège's influential geography *The present state of Great Britain,* published in the wake of the English-Scottish parliamentary union of 1707, included in its second edition (1711) a description of Ireland. It was taken from Laurence Eachard's *Exact description of Ireland* (1691), which includes the laziness formula ('they . . . count it the greatest riches to take no pains, and the most pleasure to enjoy their liberty', p. 19) and may generally be recognized as wholly traditional:

> they excell in nimbleness and flexibility of all parts of the body; they are reckoned of a quick Wit (tho' besotted to many follies) prodigal and careless of their Lives, enduring Travel, Cold, and Hunger; given to fleshly lusts, light of belief, kind and courteous to strangers, constant in love, impatient of abuse and injury, in enmity implacable, and in all affections most vehement and implacable. They are very much delighted with Musick . . . (p. 15, cf. Miège p. 4)

Miège's highly successful work did much to reassert and confirm this view, which remained in evidence throughout the century, especially in the Stage Irishman who was indeed 'in all affections most vehement'.

Not even the changes in English historiography instigated by David Hume would perceptibly alter this traditional view. The philosopher's great *History of England from the invasion of Julius Caesar to the revolution in 1688* appeared between 1754 and 1761, and eventually in a revised, definitive edition in 1788; although it initially came under attack from both ends of the political spectrum, it was to become the lodestar of a new historiographical attitude, the foremost example of that kind of 'philosophical history' of which Edward Gibbon's *Decline and fall of the Roman empire* is perhaps the best-known example today.

Until Hume's time, historiographical practice had largely consisted of the retrojection of contemporary political debate, an investigation of the past to find arguments to bolster one's stance in whatever debate was at issue. What Hume's important fellow-worker in the development of 'philosophical history', William Robertson, wrote of the party-bound views on the Scottish past may well be taken to have a more general application:

> The transactions of Mary's reign gave rise to two parties, which were animated against each other with the fiercest political hatred, embittered by religious zeal. Each of these produced Historians of considerable merit, who adopted all their sentiments, and defended all their actions. Truth, however, was not the sole object

of these Authors. Blinded by prejudices, and heated by the part which they themselves had acted in the scenes they describe, they wrote an apology for a faction, rather than the history of their country.[35]

Similarly, the Irish histories of men like Story and Borlase were little more than conflicting personal interpretations (each determined by the author's political or religious attitude) regarding past events in which Story and Borlase themselves had been involved. All the same, the frequent use of the word 'impartial' in the titles of their respective works may indicate that the notion of trans-partizan objectivity existed as a historiographical ideal at least – the problem was only that each individual author considered his own opinion to be the impartial truth, the whole truth and nothing but the truth.

It was mainly the applicablity of past events to present-day politics that fomented strong conflict between historians. The question whether the early christianization of the British Isles had, or had not, taken place under the auspices of the bishop of Rome was of direct importance in the conflict between the Church of England and Roman Catholicism; the question whether matters of church policy in early Christian Britain were decided by councils of clerics or by an episcopal authority was of direct import to the differences between the Presbyterian Church of Scotland and the Episcopalian Church of England; the evaluation of transactions and personalities in the civil war and the interregnum were of direct and explosive relevance to the ongoing debate between Whigs and Tories, as were questions concerning parliamentary institutions and their power relative to the kingship in pre-Norman England; and the revolution of 1688 (prudently chosen by Hume as the *nec plus ultra* of his own history) was the very foundation of eighteenth-century party po... :cs. In this traditional, faction-ridden historiographical imbroglio, only an uncertain 'centre' in the political spectrum – that of moderate Protestants and monarchists s·1ch as Clarendon and Nalson – could to some extent justify their claim to 'imparuality' by pointing at the fools to their right and the knaves to their left: Catholic disloyalty on the one hand, Puritan republicanism on the other.

In his new, 'philosophical' approach, Hume to a degree followed this moderate tradition; however, his intentions in investigating the past were aimed at elucidating matters, not of contemporary, but of timeless, importance. It was an attitude which had been indicated earlier in Bolingbroke's well-known dictum that 'history is philosophy teaching by example'.

Much like his interest in national characters, Hume's historiographical attitude can be explained from the philosopher's general preoccupation with the workings of the human personality in its physical environment – hence, also, the importance of character sketches in his history. In this respect, one might regard Hume's interest in the past as the diachronic or historical, and his interest in national characters as the synchronic or comparative method in his investigation of human nature: Hume himself, like Bolingbroke, regarded historiography as an approach to the philosophical analysis of man. As he himself put it, in the *Enquiry concerning human understanding*:

> Its [i.e. history's] chief use is only to discover the constant and universal principles of human nature, by shewing men in all varieties of circumstances and situations, and furnishing us with materials, from which we may form our observations and become acquainted with the regular springs of human action and behaviour. These records of war intrigues, factions, and revolutions, are so many collections of experiments by which the politician or moral philosopher fixes the principles of his science; in the same manner as the physician or natural philosopher becomes acquainted with the nature of plants, minerals, and other external objects by the experiments, which he forms concerning them.[36]

Hume could thus strive for impartiality, not as the middle ground between the political extremes, but rather by taking up a new position outside the arena of political factionism: that of his individual scepticism, which brought on him the execration of Whigs and Tories alike; and when Hume described the Protestant-Catholic division of the Reformation as a conflict between 'enthusiasm' and 'superstition', he could count on outrage from both parties – and thus, perhaps, be vindicated against each of them.

There were, however, a few key events in modern British history which had been so overlaid with claims, counter-claims and conflicting interpretations that their immediate, contemporary impact had never diminished; which had from the outset been a matter of political conviction, where no 'neutral' description was possible; where, in Gibbon's words, 'every character is a problem, and every reader a friend or enemy, where a writer is supposed to hoist a flag of party, and is devoted to damnation by the adverse faction'.[37] The reign and end of Mary, queen of Scots was, as can be gathered from Robertson's above-quoted reference, one of these; the revolution of 1688 (preceded by the polarization of political attitudes as a result of the Titus Oates affair) was another one; and the Ulster rebellion of 1641, which had become the affective foundation for the anti-Catholic penal laws in Ireland, was a third one. Hume, too, found it impossible to deal with these events without in some measure condoning or rejecting some of the conflicting interpretations with which they had been vested. In these instances, he found himself forced to define *his own position* as the 'impartial' one (on the strength of its being based upon a disinterested research of the available records) while rejecting conflicting opinions as hopelessly prejudiced by party bigotry:

> There are, indeed, three events in our history, which may be regarded as touchstones of party-men. An English Whig, who asserts the reality of the popish plot; an Irish Catholic, who denies the massacre of 1641; and a Scotch Jacobite, who maintains the innocence of queen Mary, must be considered as men beyond the reach of argument or reason, and must be left to their prejudices.[38]

Hume's stance here is axiomatic and essentially non-arguable; it has some of the circularity of an *ex cathedra* pronouncement of one's own infallibility; it is, in fact, a relapse into the pretended, subjective 'impartiality' of earlier historians, who were mainly 'impartial' because they said so. This does not materially flaw

Hume's history as a whole; but it did much to confirm the old abhorrence of the genocidal Irish who had performed the massacre of 1641. Hume's own image of Ireland seems to have been traditional enough; the following description of Irish antiquity owes something to the Jacobean colonialist view of Sir John Davies:

> The Irish, from the beginning of time, had been buried in the most profound barbarism and ignorance; and as they were never conquered, or even invaded by the Romans, from whom all the Western world derived its civility, they continued still in the most rude state of society, and were distinguished by those vices alone, to which human nature, not tamed by education, or restrained by laws, is for ever subject. The small principalities, into which they were divided, exercised perpetual rapine and violence against each other; the uncertain succession of their Princes was a continual source of domestic convulsions; the usual title of each petty Sovereign was the murder of his predecessor; courage and force, though exercised in the commission of crimes, were more honoured than any pacific virtues; and the most simple arts of life, even tillage and agriculture, were almost wholly unknown to them. (vol. I, 424 f.)

Davies' influence is also noticeable in Hume's description of the plantation of Ulster under James I (designed by Davies) as introducing 'humanity and justice among a people, who had ever been buried in the most profound barbarism' (vol. vi, 60 f.). And, like Davies, Hume sees the earlier omission to extend English common law to the native Irish as a grave error:

> Being treated like wild beasts, they became such; and joining the ardour of revenge to their yet untamed barbarity, they grew every day more intractable and more dangerous. (vol. vi, 396)

Hume's own estimate of the Gaelic character is equally traditional. He explains the atrocities of 1641 from 'the sloth and barbarism to which they ['that turbulent people', i.e. the Gaelic Irish] had ever been subject', and from their 'habitual sloth and ignorance' (vol. vi, 429 & 544) – in accordance with his basic tendency to see human nature as the mainspring of history. His long and detailed description of these atrocities was largely based on the not always reliable depositions made by survivors at the time; the enumerations of those acts which he calls 'memorable in the annals of human kind, and worthy to be held in perpetual detestation and abhorrence' (vol. VI, 439) threw the full weight of the author's prestige and 'impartial' philosophical approach on the side of the more strenuously anti-Gaelic version; though it provoked some reaction among Irishmen and was criticized by Adam Smith,[39] Hume's version of the 1641 rebellion was tacitly accepted at face value in England, and probably accounts for the fact that the English historical treatments of Ireland (e.g. in the histories of Smollett, Wynne and Barnard) were markedly 'cooler' towards their subject than the more sympathetic Anglo-Irish ones later that century.

Travellers to Ireland, however, began to disseminate a different attitude to the country. Apart from William Brereton in 1635, no English tourist had given a description of Ireland since Lithgow and Moryson until 1698, when the eccentric London publisher and bookseller John Dunton undertook a business trip to Dublin. The scurrilous and somewhat vague controversy that developed between him and his Irish colleagues led to the publication of his chaotic apologia *The Dublin scuffle* in 1699, which also contains the account of Dunton's subsequent journey into the West of Ireland. Although some Anglo-Irishmen would soon begin to venture into the as yet wholly non-Anglicized wilds of Connemara (e.g. Thomas Molyneux, who was lured there in 1709 by the fame of the Gaelic antiquary Roderic O'Flaherty), intrepid Dunton must have been among the very first Englishmen journeying into those parts for other than professional reasons – even later travellers such as Bush (1769) and Twiss (1772) were deterred by the hardships of travelling in Connacht. Dunton's main motive was to observe 'Irish savages' in the flesh and, as a matter of course, he went looking for them in the West. This is in itself a most remarkable fact: that certain parts of Ireland might be considered to be more genuinely Irish than others – a direct consequence of the old division of Ireland in 'mere' and 'civil' inhabitants, and in a way a type of circular feedback: those Irish are the genuine, 'typical' ones, who correspond to the descriptions that are extant of them. Dunton obviously had an idea of what 'Irish savages' should be like – be it from stage characters or from earlier descriptions: he refers to Eachard, Story, Moryson and Camden;[40] and his observation of Ireland is, in a literal sense, a quest for the confirmation of that preconceived idea; thus he can describe Connemara as

> a wild mountainous country in which the old barbarities of the Irish are so many and so common, that until I came hither, I looked for Ireland in itself to no purpose. (MacLysaght, p. 329)

– in other words: Ireland, the real Ireland, is only to be found in those parts (suitably 'wild' and mountainous) where the 'old barbarities' are still current. These 'old barbarities' are, of course, 'old' because they have long been a tradition in the English image of Ireland. The geographic entity known by the name of 'Ireland' does not entirely correspond to its image as conjured up by a tradition of English descriptions; but it is 'Ireland' which is adapted to the image (in restricting it to a 'real' Ireland of mountains and barbarities) rather than vice versa.

It is, accordingly, no surprise to find that Dunton's descriptions of the country are a confirmation of current attitudes. What is new, however, is his comic treatment of the Irish – an indication how influential comic Stage Irishmen and Irish jokes were becoming. Dunton, in the description in the *Dublin scuffle,* is trying to amuse his readership:

> And here I shall give ye a glimpse of the Country; or, as it were, *a general view of my Irish rambles.* And, as an Irishman is a living Jest, 'twill be merry and pleasant. (*Dublin scuffle*, p. 398)

Accordingly, he will try to phrase his observations as wittily as possible:

such things as *Chastity, Wit, and good Nature*, are only heard of here; such Vertues as *Temperance, Modesty, and strict Justice* . . . have the same Credit with the *Beaus* of *Ireland*, which the Travels of Mandevil find with us. (*ibid.*, p. 399)

Indeed, many of the sketches Dunton gives read like a Stage Irish scene in contemporary comedy, e.g. the scurrilous sermon preached by a Connemara priest.[41] And the first faint glimmers of a more sentimental image can be discerned in Dunton's praise of Irish music:

The music was no way disagreeable, but most of their airs were melancholy and doleful as suiting the humours of a people always in subjection. (MacLysaght, p. 344)

The Irish barbarity, or alienness, is no longer an object of loathing or a desire to reform; instead, a nearly benevolent interest, a willingness to be entertained or amused by Irish peculiarities, becomes noticeable. At the same time it is obvious that a preconceived expectation can actually overshadow firsthand experience. The image is the yardstick by which reality is measured, and even positive experiences counter to that image will be described in terms of it: a certain reception accorded to Dunton was 'fuller of humanity than I could hope from persons appearing so barbarous' (MacLysaght, p. 330).

Such trends were noticeably influenced by a new appreciation of the Irish landscape. Wild and mountainous country was the natural stronghold of 'old barbarities' – and as the aesthetic appreciation of the one grew, so did the political attitude to the other ameliorate. As roads improved and a certain amount of law and order was established even in the remoter districts, those aspects of the landscape which would previously have inspired a traveller with unease – forests, mountains – could now be viewed from a less apprehensive state of mind.[42] Furthermore, the concept of the 'sublime' was now beginning to create a matrix for the aesthetic appreciation of such landscapes.[43] Boileau's translation of Longinus had become influential in England through the mediation of John Dryden; in the British aesthetic tradition which attempted to deal with the 'sublime' in the terms of the empiricist, sensationalist psychology of John Locke, meanwhile comparing it to related concepts such as the 'pathetic' or the 'beautiful', sublimity gradually became invested with traits that were gloomier than anything in the original, then generally attributed to Longinus. Especially Edmund Burke's milestone *An enquiry into the origin of our ideas of the sublime and beautiful* (written around 1750, published in 1757) linked the sublime definitively to notions like 'terror', 'obscurity', 'power', 'vastness' and 'infinity' (chapter headings). It is obvious that 'wild mountainous regions' could thus, from the traveller's half-admiring, half-disconcerted point of view, easily become examples of sublimity. John Dennis, author of critical and aesthetic works like *The advancement and reformation of modern poetry* (1710) and himself an important theoretician of the sublime,[44] could describe his crossing of the Alps as having been marked by 'a delightful Horrour, a terrible Joy, and at the same time that I was infinitely pleas'd, I trembled'; similarly, archbishop Herring's journey through Wales of 1738 spoke of the prelate's 'pleasure, mixed with horror'.[45] Links with notions of the 'picturesque' were laid by frequent references to the 'sublime' landscapes in the paintings of Salvator Rosa, Claude 'le Lorrain' and others. In view of the fact that the word 'picturesque' retained, throughout the eighteenth century, its basic meaning 'as in a painting'[46] (much as 'romantic' kept its meaning 'as in romance') one may here perhaps recognize the same tendency to measure first-hand experience by anterior, preconceived, secondary standards (literary or aesthetic) concerning representations of reality – much as in Dunton's search for an Ireland that corresponded to his image of that country.

The more peripheral parts of the British Isles (like, for instance, the Wales that archbishop Herring visited), being, on the whole, of a higher elevation than the Home Counties of England, they could be given the new attraction of being aesthetically pleasing in their wildness; Ireland was one of these parts. The theatre-manager and -historian William Rufus Chetwood, who had employment in Dublin for a while, published A *tour through Ireland in several entertaining letters* in 1746, which presents a wholly new, positive enthusiasm towards the country, its landscape and its inhabitants. Chetwood sets out to refute 'the strange Stories delivered in several old geographers, viz. *Strabo, Solinus, Mela,* and *G. Cambrensis*' (p. 74); his book accordingly gives 'many curious and entertaining Particulars of a kingdom, which, to my certain Knowledge, has been grossly misrepresented' (p. 3). Chetwood describes an English servant as the embodiment of stupid anti-Irish prejudice, and has him say:

> Wauns, Measter, they tolden me in *Hampshire* the Fowkes here had gutten long Tayles, but I canno foind but they are like hus; and that they had gutten nothing to yeate but Buttermilk and Purtatoses; (but yet I thowt if they had Buttermilk, they mun have gutten Cows among 'em too) but I found they have as good Victals here as we have, and the Fowkes speak English too: Adad I thowt we mun have maade Signs to um. (p. 133)

Chetwood, like Dunton before him, is pleased by native music, and its melancholy character; 'for, by the way, the *Irish* Musick has something peculiarly sweet and melancholy, and the whole Nation seem to have a Turn that way' (p. 76) – a remarkable contrast to the more picaresque view of Irish national character, as found in Moryson and Dunton. It may be well to remember that Chetwood's account was written after the highly successful career of Carolan, and at a time when a surfeit of buffoonish Stage Irishmen (with which Chetwood, as a theatre man, must have been familiar) began to provoke a more sentimental reaction in the theatre treatment of Irish characters. Chetwood is struck deeply by the sublime landscape of the Golden Vale (p. 145) and by some picturesque caves (p. 193 f.). Even more impressed with the Irish landscape was Richard Pococke, bishop of Meath and a dedicated traveller, who made a journey along the Atlantic coast in 1752 and who described repeatedly the mountainous areas there (and in Wicklow) as 'romantick' (pp. 42, 57, 60, 85, 162).

The appreciation of the landscape seems to have gone hand in hand with a more positive interest in its Gaelic inhabitants and their history and position. John Loveday, a tourist who visited Ireland in 1732, had gone to the trouble of reading up on Irish linguistics and antiquity – he refers to Edward Lhuyd and Sir James Ware (pp. 28, 49); Chetwood himself defended the often ridiculed Irish claim to ancient civilization when he gives his opinion that a Gaelic royal court

> was much on the same footing as her Neighbours, and indeed the State of the whole Nation: What do our Barons and their Feuds differ from the petty Princes of *Ireland*, except in Title? We can gather from their Antiquaries, that each Monarch always entertained the following ten Officers in his Court, which (by the way) does not savour greatly of Barbarity, *viz*. a lord or Prime Minister, a Judge, an Augur or Druid, a Physician, a Poet, an Antiquary or Herald, a chief Musician, and three Stewards of the Household. (p. 74)

Such attitudes must appear like an odd novelty within the context of the tradition outlined so far, and can only be understood as the result of a long counter-tradition maintained by those Gaelic 'antiquaries' mentioned by Chetwood. The activities and influence of those native scholars will be dealt with at greater length below.

The growing popularity of the more sublime, picturesque or otherwise 'scenic' spots of Ireland, e.g. that of the lakes of Killarney, can be registered consistently in the travel descriptions of the eighteenth century. Samuel Derrick, the Irish-born successor to Beau Nash as Master of Ceremonies in Bath, published a description of various places in 1767 – though the letters pertaining to Ireland were not by him, but by one William Ockenden – and here, Killarney already counts as 'one of the most beautiful and romantic spots in this kingdom' (II, 66), warranting a long and detailed description (II, 57 ff. and 79–99). At the same time, a more positive attitude towards the rural Irish makes itself felt. Although Ockenden can evince a more old-fashioned disdain in his contention that they 'prefer beggary and wretchedness to the sweets of industry and labour' (II, 48), a change is apparent in a sketch like this:

> This couple were remarkably civil; and indeed their countenances bespoke good-nature, resignation, and content: perhaps they had never known any different scenes: they were not perplexed with compound or comparative ideas. (II, 47)

As the century wore on, such sympathies could become even stronger; whereas Ockenden can still express satisfaction at the fact,

> that a man has it in his power to punish, with his own hand, the insolence of the lower class of people, without being afraid of a Crown-office, or a process at law. (II, 35)

the same fact could be described by Arthur Young, in 1780, with indignation:

> Disrespect or any thing tending towards sauciness he [i.e. the landlord] may punish with his cane or his horsewhip with the most perfect security, a poor man would have his bones broke if he offered to lift his hand in his own defence. Knocking down is spoken of in the country in a manner that makes an English man stare. (vol. 2, pt. 2, p. 40f.)

Instrumental in this development was *Hibernia curiosa* by John Bush, which appeared in 1769. It was highly successful and generally recognized (even on the Continent) as a counter-stroke against the 'onbillyken afkeer', the 'unreasonable dislike'

> * welken die, anderszins zoo verstandige, Engelschen tegen Ierland en deszelfs inwooners, voeden. Al had de Heer *Bush* door zyne edelmoedige poogingen alleenlyk deezen afkeer gemaatigd, en zyne Medeburgers hierdoor eenen weg tot gewigtiger ontdekkingen aangewezen, men zou aan hem geene geringe verpligting hebben . . .[47]

Once again, appreciation of the landscape and the inhabitants go together. If one must fear the 'wildness' of the latter, this ought to be attributed, according to Bush, to the iniquities of the prevailing social system rather than to a native disposition:

> If in any part of the kingdom there are any wild Irish to be found, it is in the western parts of this province [i.e. Connacht], for they have the least sense of law and government of any people in Ireland, I believe, except that of their haughty and tyrannic landlords, who, in a literal sense, indeed, are absolute sovereigns over their respective towns and clans . . . Their imperious and oppressive measures, indeed, have almost depopulated this province of Ireland. The will and pleasure of these chiefs is absolute law to the poor inhabitants that are connected with them, and under whom the miserable wretches live in the vilest and most abject state of dependance. (p. 28 f.)

Bush goes to such lengths in describing, and denouncing, the squalor of the poor – not as the result of native sloth and 'cynical content in dirt and beggary', but as a result of social injustice – that his travel description at times comes close to social pamphleteering. He denounces absenteeism, rackrents, middlemen, religious tithes, etc., and identifies, not with the representatives of his own social class, but with the rural poor,

> who live in huts . . . of such shocking materials and construction, that through hundreds of them you may see the smoak ascending from every inch of the roof, for scarce one in twenty of them have any chimney, and through every inch of which defenceless coverings, the rain, of course, will make its way to drip upon the half naked, shivering, and almost starved inhabitants within. (p. 30)

* which the English, otherwise so rational, harbour against Ireland and its inhabitants. Even if Mr. Bush's noble undertaking were but to contribute towards the moderation of that dislike, thus showing his fellow citizens the way to more important discoveries, the public would on this account alone be greatly indebted to him.

Instead, it is the upper class, hitherto the object of English sympathy as the representatives of 'civility' in Ireland, who are now blamed for these shocking conditions:

> And the case of the lower class of farmers, indeed, which is the greatest number, is little better than a state of slavery, while the priest and subordinate landlords, in ease and affluence, live in haughty contempt of their poverty and oppression, of which the first proprietors are but too seldom, indeed, for the interest of this kingdom [sic], spectators. (ibid.)

Obviously, Bush's attitude – or rather, this new attitude, of which Bush is an early and outspoken representative – continues the old distinction between Catholic natives and Protestant colonists, but inverts the earlier values which saw the former as uninstructed primitives and the latter as the harbingers of civilization. We have seen how Palesmen, 'civil Irish', etc. tended to be excepted explicitly from the opprobrium heaped on the country by English authors. Henceforth, however, the mere Irish (though that term had by now fallen into disuse) are described as the innocent, hapless victims of an irresponsible and inhumane class of fast-living parasites who gamble, duel, ravish and carouse, and to whose callousness and covetousness the instability of the political situation (e.g. the agrarian troubles around the Whiteboys and similar organizations) are to be attributed. The ostentatiousnes and recklessness of these landlords and middlemen, and more particularly their hot-headed propensity to quarrel and duel, are generally condemned.[48] Here, an echo of earlier denunciations levelled by early Anglo-Irish Patriots at absenteeism, excessive wine imports, irresponsible indulgence in luxury and the lack of a sense of responsibility in the management of Irish estates becomes noticeable. Generally, the political ideas of such Anglo-Irish Patriots are represented with sympathy in these travel books – though not in a party-political frame of reference. The efforts of the Dublin Society meet with general approval, and even the central Patriot issue of the time, the lifting of restrictions on Irish external trade, is advocated.

Again, the appreciation of Ireland's natural beauty comes as part and parcel of this new attitude. Bush is deeply impressed by spots like the Giant's Causeway, the Salmon Leap at Leixlip, or the Wicklow Mountains, where he describes the Powerscourt waterfall with epithets like 'lofty' and 'sublime', in terms of 'grandeur' and 'sublimity' (p. 74). But the acme of his enthusiasm is reached in Killarney, that 'aquaeo-insular paradise' (p. 103), to which he dedicates a thirty-five page, lyrical description of which the following excerpt may be a representative example:

> The immense declivities and hollow bosoms of [the mountains around the lake], over-spread with woods of various kinds, from the verge of the lake or bay almost to their very tops, present a prospect that affects the mind of the spectator in a manner unspeakable, and possesses the imagination with the highest conceptions of natural sublimity. You may laugh at my rhapsody, if you please, but to add to the effect of such a supereminent landscape, what will carry his imaginations to the highest pitch

of frantic enthusiasm, is the melodious echoing of the horn, resounding with ineffable sweetness from the lofty circulating bosom of the mountains. (p. 98)

Such eulogies were echoed in later productions, e.g. the plagiaristic *Tour through Ireland* of 1780, collected by Philip Luckombe from the descriptions of Bush, Twiss and Campbell.

Arthur Young, the most important theoretician of agriculture of his day, undertook his journey largely from professional motives. Although he describes the Killarney area extensively in its sublime impressiveness (v. 2, pt. 2, pp. 92–113), his main aim is to take stock of Irish agriculture. His attitude is close to that of those Patriots in Ireland who were agriculturally inclined, e.g. around the Dublin Society, for which institution he has unmixed praise and commendation. His report is replete with criticism of the middleman-ridden Irish landlordism (he calls the middlemen 'the most oppressive species of tyrant that ever lent assistance to the destruction of a country', v. 2, pt. 2, p. 18). He is likewise scathing in his comments on absenteeism and on the Penal laws, regarding which he quotes the radical criticism of Edmund Burke.[49] His attitude to the 'common Irish', though in some respects echoing older English attributions, is benevolent:

> The circumstances which struck me most in the common Irish were, vivacity and a great and eloquent volubility of speech, one would think they could take snuff and talk without tiring till doomsday. They are infinitely more chearful and lively than any thing we commonly see in England, having nothing of that incivility of sullen silence, with which so many Englishmen seem to wrap themselves up, as if retiring within their own importance. Lazy to an excess at *work*, but so spiritedly active at *play*, that at *hurling*, which is the cricket of savages, they shew the greatest feats of agility. Their love of society is as remarkable as their curiosity is insatiable; and their hospitality to all comers, be their own poverty ever so pinching, has too much merit to be forgotten. Pleased to enjoyment with a joke, or witty repartee, they will repeat it with such expression, that the laugh will be universal. Warm friends and revengeful enemies; they are inviolable in their secrecy, and inevitable in their resentment; with such a notion of honour, that neither threat nor reward would induce them to betray the secret or person of a man, though an oppressor, whose property they would plunder without ceremony. Hard drinkers and quarrelsome; great liars, but civil, submissive and obedient. (v. 2, pt. 2, p. 106f.)

It is remarkable how the negative import of the earlier English image of the Irish is now changed to a positive one, without changing the constitutent ingredients of that image: individual phrases in Young's description will be recognized as dating back to earlier, seventeenth-century descriptions. Similarly, like earlier English commentators, Young still regards these 'common Irish' as the genuine representatives of the 'real' Ireland:

> The manners, habits and customs of people of considerable fortune, are much the same every where, at least there is very little difference between England and Ireland, it is among the common people one must look for those traits by which we discriminate a national character. (v. 2, pt. 2, p. 106)

But far less benevolence is accorded to the 'luxury and extravagance' (p. 107) of the higher classes – especially the middlemen and larger tenants,

> who drink their claret by means of profit rents; jobbers in farms; bucks; your fellows with round hats, edged with gold, who hunt in the day, get drunk in the evening, and fight the next morning. I shall not dwell on a subject so perfectly disagreeable, but remark that these are the men among whom drinking, wrangling, quarreling, fighting, ravishing, &c. &c. &c. are found as in their native soil. (v. 2, pt. 2, p. 113)

It is owing to the likes of these, 'that the character of the nation has not that lustre abroad, which I dare assert, it will soon generally merit' (ibid.).

A similar stance was taken by Charles Topham Bowden, who published his *Tour through Ireland* in 1791. Again, the landscape: Ireland is 'the most romantic island in the world' (p. 249), exemplified in the usual beauty spots, the Giant's Causeway, the Wicklow Mountains, Killarney. Again: the more positive attitude to the inhabitants of those parts, of whom it is said: 'more hospitality, attention, or civility, I never experienced than I did amongst them' (p. 251). It is remarkable that Bowden even identifies with their geographical position, speaking of England in trans- rather than cismarine terms:

> However prejudice may represent the Irish, certain it is human nature is much the same here are in England. The common people are far removed from the semi-barbarous state, which is the general opinion on the other side of the water. (p. 250)

And, again, the sympathy for the Irish poor is counterbalanced by denunciations of middlemen and other parasites on the Irish economy (p. 165). What is, however, remarkable in Bowden's descriptions is that he discusses the Catholic poor not only in social terms, as the victims of unjust and ill-managed landlordism, but also in cultural terms: as the inheritors of a fascinating Celtic past and a romantic Celtic language, which is characterized in a sentimental fashion combining Rousseauesque and Ossianic traits:

> Amidst the unspeakable miseries of those half-fed wretches, they enjoy in a very exalted degree poetry and song. It would seem that Providence, to cheer them in the vale of calamity – their only inheritance – had given them the talent of soothing woe. For my part, I am totally ignorant of the Irish language; I have read the opinions of the learned Ballet of Paris, relative to it, but cannot discriminate whether it be his *pure Celtic*, the *Carthaginian* tongue of Vallancey, or the Erse of my friend McPherson. All that is necessary for me to remark is, that there is a sympathy in the Irish language and the Irish airs, so sweetly plaintive, as to appear the operation of the Deity in giving charms to a state of poverty and sorrow. I have sat under a hedge and listened to the rustic songs of those peasants, while at labour, with a pleasure that transcended any I had ever felt at Vauxhall. (p. 165 f.)

This may to some extent echo Dunton's and Chetwood's enjoyment of the melancholy Irish music; but the reference to the antiquarian Charles Vallancey – bracketed by references to the French 'Celtomane' Jean-Baptiste Bullet (Bowden's spelling must be a misprint) and to James Macpherson – puts it in a wholly different context. Whereas a tourist like Dunton would, in his travel description, betray the preparatory readings for his journey by references to authors like Camden, Moryson, Story and Eachard – i.e. English authors with a 'colonial' outlook on Irish affairs – the preparatory reading referred to in Bowden's description is wholly of Irish provenance, with Patriot Irish antiquarians like Vallancey, O'Halloran, O'Flanagan and Charles O'Conor – men who, since the 1760s, had advanced the claims of Ireland to a great and ancient native Gaelic civilization. Bowden's book is a first indication of the possible influence that such researches had on the image of Gaelic Ireland in Anglo-Irish and in English circles. The immediate result is that one of the most tenuous and widespread traits attributed to the Irish – that of cultural barbarity – is subverted. Thus, the two connected aspects of a more appreciative attitude towards Ireland (the appreciation of the landscape and the social compassion with the rural poor) are joined by a third trend: a new interest in the native Gaelic culture of Ireland.

Such developments are determined by the literary and critical background of the descriptions themselves – as discourse, as a textual tradition, rather than as registrations of a political and social situation; they are changes in the literary tradition of English books dealing with Ireland, rather than in the political configuration in which English people deal with Ireland. The individual ingredients composing the image of Ireland changed little; what changed was their treatment at the hands of the travellers/authors. It is a telling fact that such changes in national imagery as encountered in the genre of the travel descriptions have no corresponding changes in the historiographical treatment of Ireland. The travel books' treatment of the country was, then, dictated in turn by matters of literary taste and convention. A similar trend can be observed in a new, sentimental estimate of 'the typical Irishman': this stereotype was now coming under the influence of a dramatic tradition, which, though originally based on the images as fixed by earlier descriptions of Ireland (like those described in the preceding pages), had from the mid-century onwards developed in a different direction – a direction which was autonomously dramatic, no longer influenced by non-fictional descriptions of the country, dictated only by the need for theatrical effectiveness rather than by any considerations of supposed reference to the actual, off-stage 'Ireland'. This later development of the Stage Irishman, non-realistic as opposed to the purportedly-realistic earlier tradition, will be considered in the next chapter as the sentimentalized 'counter-Stage-Irishman'; although it was a mere literary convention without any pretended referentiality, it could influence one's approach to the actual country as much as a landscape by Rosa or Claude could determine the rise to popularity of the lakes of Killarney.

Take, for instance, the following sentimental description of an Irish person – an Irish 'type' whom the author claims to encounter for the first time in the flesh after having been appraised of him only in theatrical representations until then. This little sketch (which is also remarkable for its idealization of the Irish language as a naturally lyrical medium of expression, and for its sentimentalization of Irish people and their manners) is set in the stage coach between Athlone and Dublin; the two protagonists hail, not insignificantly, from what was since Dunton the most Irish part of Ireland, Connacht; they are 'a young buxom lass from Roscommon, and a country squire from Galway':

> The girl could not be above eighteen. She was dressed in a plain riding-habit, with a hat and feather. You would rather praise the neatness than the richness of her dress. But for her person, that indeed was rich in all the gifts of nature; it was of the middle size, but of shape the most correct. Her face had the rosy virgin tint of innocence and health. It was that florid bloom which the painted Dolls, who haunt our scenes, affect, but can never acquire: or rather, it was that young and purple light of love, which Reynolds may conceive, but cannot paint. Her features were all turned to the softest harmony. And though embarrassed, she was never awkward. If a *mauvaise honte* sometimes suffused her cheeks, her sensibility added grace to her blushes. Our squire, you may suppose, was not without feelings, but he was devoid of sentiment. He was that very Hibernian I had so often heard of, but never noticed before. They were utter strangers to each other; and her loveliness excited his curiosity to know her connections. He asked her a thousand questions to exact the secret: I suppose, Madam, says he, you know such and such people, &c. &c. . . . What most evidently prevailed, *absit invidia*, and what betrayed her into all the *Chesterfieldian* indecorums of laughter, was his addressing her in Irish. And when he had a mind to be tender beyond expression in plain prose, he would accost her with an Irish song; which he sang with great softness. The gentleman was perfectly good-humoured, and had a high flow of animal spirits. You could not have been displeased with the display of this native character. I was delighted with it, for it was the original, and I had hitherto seen only the copy.[50]

A few things here may be stressed. Though the girl's natural beauty is idealized as superior to anything artificial, she is nevertheless described with epithets like 'the most correct' and with a pictorial reference to the portraits of Sir Joshua Reynolds; the use of a term like 'Chesterfieldian' is a derivation from the letter-writing nobleman; and in the young squire, too, experience is described by reference to earlier representations: he is the 'original' of which the author 'had so often heard-' and 'seen hitherto only the copy' – presumably a reference to Irish stage characters, who from the mid-century onwards had been represented as full of natural gallantry, stealing kisses from giggling chambermaids and venting their amorous feelings with outbursts of unaffected lyricism.

In the light of what will be said in the next chapter concerning the national background of the authors who created such sentimental Irish characters for the London stage, it is fitting to find that the anonymous author of the little sketch quoted here, though pretending to be an English gentleman, was in fact the northern Irish Protestant minister Thomas Campbell, a not unimportant antiquary in his day, whose historical interests are also represented in the *Philosophical survey of the south of Ireland* (1777) from which the above excerpt is taken. One doubt that springs to mind on finding out the real nationality of the purportedly English author is, whether the little sketch, pretending to be a *first* and a *real* experience of the dispositions of the native Irish, may not have been as fictitious as the earlier, second-hand representations that the author refers to. Ultimately, this problem (whether Campbell 'really' witnessed the scene he describes, or whether, like the earlier descriptions of Irish scenes to which his own refers here, it is the embodiment of a literary commonplace rather than the account of an experience) is insignificant. The anecdote works on the recognizability of the scene, and the mere pretence that this scene had any basis in factual real-life experience is enough to lend the description a spurious yet effective air of veracity and plausibility. More importantly, this pretence can only work if the author obscures his own Irish identity and national background: to represent this 'experience' convincingly, the Irish author has to adopt an English attitude, an English persona – the image can only work in an English, rather than Irish, representation, and cannot be lifted from it. A good few examples of this same mechanism will be encountered in Anglo-Irish authors creating Irish characters for the London stage. Similarly, Irish-born Oliver Goldsmith had, in 1759, contributed an anonymous 'Description of the manners and customs of the native Irish' to the *Weekly magazine* – specified in the subtitle as having been communicated 'In a letter from an English gentleman'. This little piece foreshadows Bush and later travellers in preferring the character of the 'natives' to that of the 'Protestants', who share in the traditional shortcomings of the Irish without having their 'national virtues to recompence these defects'.[51] Goldsmith includes a sentimental anecdote of the hospitality accorded to the narrator in a poor cottage, among poor but upright peasant labourers. The author is also strongly attracted by the charms of a comely daughter, but pretends (with some inconsistency) to be agreeably surprised by her chastity. As in Campbell's later sketch, the representation claims to refer to the author's actual experience; as in Campbell's case, the claim may now safely be considered false, for Goldsmith never returned to Ireland after he left it in 1752, at the age of twenty-six. And, as in Campbell's case, the assumed nationality of the author is a necessary contrivance for the plausibility of this purportedly real (though actually invented) anecdote.

The English image of Ireland is precisely that: English. Even when created, perpetuated or influenced by Anglo-Irish authors, it is ultimately determined by the pre-expectations of its English audience, dealing with those aspects which are considered 'unusual' or 'interesting', i.e. defined negatively by their non-Englishness. And those Irish authors who thought to combat the negative import of that image in fact agreed with its most basic point: the fact that the 'real' Ireland is that which differs most from England.

THE FICTIONAL IRISHMAN IN
ENGLISH LITERATURE

Introduction

Most fictional Irish characters in English literature, especially in the seventeenth and eighteenth century, appear in drama. Indeed the 'Stage Irishman' is a ubiquitous and long-standing stock character in the English theatre, and a number of studies have discussed the traits in which he was characterized.[1] My aim here, however, goes beyond a typology. I intend not only to point out the stereotyped characterization with which the Stage Irishman is vested, but also to discuss his position within the play in which he appears, and to compare this position with the political situation of Ireland and the Irish vis-à-vis English opinion (the discursive expression of which formed the subject of the previous chapter). The assumption underlying such a comparison is, of course, that the relationship between Irish characters and the English theatre is no less governed by 'ideology' than is that between the natives of the kingdom of Ireland and English observers; an explanation of this assumption may be in order.

The point can be made that the very conventions on which drama, as a literary genre, is based, have 'ideological' implications (I use the term 'ideology' in the same sense as Gérard Genette, whose definition of the term I shall have occasion to quote shortly). The conventions of drama do not allow a straightforward enactment or re-enactment of reality on the stage, in all its amorphous, bewildering, disparate, contradictory variety; they require that a representation be given of a 'reality' that is selected and refined, ordered, and, to some extent, discrete and self-explanatory within its spatial and temporal limits.[2] This not only applies in the Aristotelian Unities, but also in the psychology of the characters – especially those characters who, like the Stage Irishman and other 'stock' characters, occupy only minor roles which do not present much opportunity for psychological elaboration. In the conventions of fictional drama, characters ought not to be inconsistent with what the audience is led to expect from them, unless such inconsistency can be justified or explained – that is to say, unless it can be shown to be only *seemingly* inconsistent. This point was made as early as 1640 by La Mesnardière, who, in his *La poétique,* pointed out that

> le poète doit considérer qu'il ne faut jamais introduire sans nécessité absolue ni une fille vaillante, ni une femme savante, ni un valet judicieux. . . . Mettre au théâtre ces trois espèces de personnes avec ces nobles conditions, c'est choquer directement la vraisemblance ordinaire. . . .[3]

The same exhortation – not to contradict, without good reason, the 'vraisemblance ordinaire', i.e. the audience's pre-expectations of a character's attributes – is also given with explicit application to nationally stereotyped pre-expectations: La Mesnardière gives the playwright the advice

> qu'il ne fasse jamais un guerrier d'un Asiatique, un fidèle d'un Africain, un impie d'un Persien, un véritable d'un Grec, un généreux d'un Thracien, un subtil d'un Allemand, un modeste d'un Espagnol, ni un incivil d'un Français. (p. 73)

Gerard Genette has pointed out how transgressions against this rule of the 'vraisemblable' often caused *moral* as well as aesthetic dissatisfaction in the public; an example in English literature will be encountered at the end of this chapter, in the umbrage that was taken at Sir Lucius O'Trigger, the Irishman in Sheridan's *The rivals*. From this indication that a mimetic law can obtain its own moral value, that the need for *vraisemblance* can involve *bienséance,* Genette concludes:

> En fait, vraisemblance et bienséance se rejoignent sous un meme critère, à savoir, 'tout ce qui est conforme à l'opinion du public'. Cette 'opinion', réelle ou supposée, c'est assez précisément ce que l'on nommerait aujourd'hui une idéologie, c'est-à-dire un corps de maximes et de préjugés qui constitue tout à la fois une vision du monde et un système de valeurs. (p. 73)

It is here that the 'ideology' that underlies the conventions of dramatic representation meets the political ideology underlying English public opinion regarding Ireland and the Irish. –

As a character, the Stage Irishman is caught in the pre-determined set of personality traits that current opinion and a long-standing discursive tradition have fixed on him. Owing to geographical proximity and political involvement between England and Ireland, the Stage Irishman was, more than any other character except, perhaps, the Stage Welshman and the Stage Scotsman, fixed as a 'type' from a very early date, a matter of general consensus, of commonplace even, verging on the proverbial.[4] Like any stock character, he is therefore a two-edged instrument for the playwright to use. On the one hand, he does not stand in need of much elaboration on the part of the playwright; as such, he is a handy addition to the cast, a ready-made cheville, a labour-saving device. On the other hand, however, the playwright will have to take him fairly much on his own terms – that is to say, on the highly stratified pre-expectations in the audience. Hence, his deployment in a play will be, in a way, problematic: he cannot be moulded as other characters can, his clownishness precludes him from taking a constructive part in the plot development, he can only with great difficulty be characterized in terms other than the current stereotype, and therefore must be treated with some deftness in order to 'fit' into the play, between the other characters. The 'ungovernability' of the Irishman as a stock character matches, and is perhaps exacerbated by, the very traits attributed to his nationality:

wildness and unreliability. Thus, both political and mimetic ideology meet and co-operate to make the Stage Irishman, in more ways than one, a troublesome presence in the theatre – a presence which, if the stage mimesis of reality is to remain harmonious, is to avoid self-contradiction, must be accommodated into the mimetic stage conventions.[5] If the Stage Irishman may, like a court jester, challenge the audience's superiority (involving both their national, English superiority over his Irishness, and their supremacy as the theatre's ultimate authority), he must, like a court jester, ultimately confirm it, be made to acknowledge the hierarchical order of things. In this manner, his presence may in fact serve to defuse or sublimate the ongoing political conflict of which his nationality is a reminder.

It is this twofold accommodation of the Irish presence (as a character taking part in a fictional contrivance, and as an Irish character in front of an English theatre audience) which I intend to follow through the theatrical practice of the seventeenth and eighteenth centuries. A preliminary outline of that development may be of use.

One of the more noticeable ways in which the act of accommodation could be performed, especially in seventeenth-century tradition, is the introduction of pretend-Irish characters who later turn out to be English. Many instances of this deployment-at-one-remove will be encountered, and it helps to displace the responsibility for the Irishman's characterization onto the character who dons the disguise (and who is, at the same time, an umbilical link between the Irishman and the main action of the play). What is shown does not purport to represent 'an Irishman', but rather a character's idea (subject to, and sanctioned by, the audience's recognition of their own idea) of what an Irishman is like.

Towards the end of the seventeenth century, the deterioration of the Irish image in England, encountered in discursive prose (e.g. Story's history), is also noticeable in dramatic or pseudodramatic literature. Here, Irishmen of unmitigated loathsomeness are represented, whilst at the same time a claim to realism is raised – i.e. the claim that these characters correspond to their real-life counterparts – and the 'disguise'-motif (aiming at accommodation) is abandoned in favour of straightforward exorcism. This negative treatment persisted longer in non-dramatic, than in dramatic, literature.

In the post-Farquhar century of English comedy, with its ceaseless ambiguities on 'true' and 'false' identity (involving multiple impersonations, disguises, dissemblings and stratagems), the Irishman is more easily absorbed. The negative aspects attributed to his national character recede into the background, and a more burlesque, comic treatment (hinted at by some precursors in the seventeenth century) reasserts itself.

It is around the middle of the eighteenth century that a development takes place which is peculiar to stage practice and has no immediate counterpart in Irish representations in other genres, let alone in non-fictional discourse: the Stage Irishman is given a more appreciative treatment, which inverts or reinterprets the attributes given to him previously. No longer a craven, heartless, dissembling enemy, he becomes a noble, sentimental, forthright hero, whose loyalty to England is only rendered more striking by his Irish accent and other markers of non-Englishness. Although this development – possibly a little 'Rousseauesque' – was influenced to no small degree by *Irish* rather than *English* playwrights, it nevertheless took place on the London stage, before a London audience, and seems to have been dictated largely by the sentimentalization that affected the entire genre of comedy in the later half of the eighteenth century.

This imputation of pro-English loyalty is the more remarkable since it had repercussions far beyond the theatre, within whose conventions it had originated.[6] An early, and somehow typical, example (and, as such, perhaps a good starting point for the discussion of the source material) of this idealization of the Irish-English relationship is given in Ben Jonson's *Irish masque at court,* performed at the end of 1613. It begins as a Jonsonian 'antimasque', a comic counterpiece to the elevated symbolism of the masque proper, in that four 'mere Irish' are brought on, all in a bustle. A slapstick dialogue between these four (Dennis, Donnell, Dermock and Patrick) develops, and the rumbustious bumpkins vie with each other to address the king, wholly disregarding court formalities. They are nationalized as Irishmen by their apparel (cloaks), by the dancing of an Irish dance, by dietary references (usquebaugh, 'bonny clabber', i.e. *bainne clabair,* curdled milk), but mainly by their 'brogue' or Irish accent, which Jonson observes in great detail – even to the point of letting them address the king as 'Yamish', as in the Gaelic vocative for James, 'a Shéamuis'. Notwithstanding these strongly non-'civiliz'd' characteristics, the Irishmen avoid all possible political discord by explicitly dissociating themselves from 'te villanous vild Irish',[7] and by stressing Irish loyalty to the throne; after a garbled protestation of loyalty ('Tey be honesht men' 'And goot men: tine owne shubshecks' 'Tou hast very goot shubshecks in Ireland', etc.), it is said:

> Don. Be not angry vit te honesht men, for the few rebelsh, & knavesh.
> Pat. Nor beleeve no tayles, king Yamish.
> Der. For, by got, tey love tee in Ireland.
> Don. Pray tee, bid 'hem velcome, and got make 'hem rish for tee.
> Der. Tey vill make tem shelves honesht. (pp. 402–3)

No matter how alien and exotic these mere Irish are, they are content to be under British guidance and full of loyalty. Then, an Anglo-Irishman ('a civill gentleman of the nation') comes in, accompanied by a 'bard', and interrupts the gaggle of the rustics. What follows then is a legitimation of James' sovereignty over Ireland by the representative of Gaelic culture, the bard, who is presented to James by the 'civill gentleman' in the following way:

> Advance, immortall Bard, come up and view
> The gladding face of that great king, in whom
> So many prophecies of thine are knit.
> This is that JAMES of which long since thou sung'st,

Should end our countryes most unnaturall broyles;
And if her eare, then deafned with the drum,
Would stoupe but to the musique of his peace,
Shee need not with the spheares change harmony.
This is the man thou promis'd should redeeme,
If she would love his counsels as his lawes,
Her head from servitude, her feete from fall,
Her fame from barbarisme, her state from want,
And in her all the fruits of blessing plant.
Sing then some charme, made from his present lookes,
That may assure thy former prophecies,
And firme the hopes of these obedient spirits,
Whose love no lesse, than dutie, hath cald forth
Their willing powers: who, if they had much more,
Would doe their All, and thinke they could not move
Enough to honour that, which he doth love. (p. 404)

However, even here, another, more properly 'dramatic' treatment is present, since it turns out that the four bumpkins are not what they appear to be. Whilst the bard sings two songs, accompanied by harps, the masquers who play the 'mere' Irishmen let fall their Irish cloaks and 'discover their masquing apparell' (p. 405). Thus the antimasque becomes a masque proper: by symbolically divesting the mere Irish of their barbarism and fitting them into the courtly order of things. Their divergence from courtly standards is neutralized, and those whose differences make them uncouth are shown to be, at least in essence if not in appearance, good subjects. This is a form of political optimism that belongs to the years after the Flight of the Earls, the years of the Ulster plantations, the time of Sir John Davies. The alienness of Gaelic Ireland has lost its sting, has become a tickle. It had not always been so.

Pre-restoration drama

The Tudor plays in which Irishmen appear are naturally concerned with the political/religious conflict of the period, culminating in the Tyrone rebellion. Two interesting plays concern the historical figure of captain Thomas Stukeley, whose extraordinary career as an adventurer and soldier of fortune is well known. At one point in his eventful life, he had plans to support the anti-reformatory forces in Ireland (possibly with a view to establishing himself as a power in that country) and undertook, with support from Rome, an expedition which was, however, waylaid at Lisbon – Stukeley being prevailed upon to enter the service of king Sebastian of Portugal.

The earlier of the two plays concerning Stukeley is *The battell of Aleazar*, presumed to be by George Peele and printed in 1594. An Irish Catholic bishop participates in Stukeley's expedition; his utter perfidy is used as a contrast to Stukeley's blunt valour, which will not stoop to the bigotry and equivocation of

Papists. The bishop's aim is 'Conquering the land [Ireland] for his holynesse,/ And to restore it to the Romane faith' (ll. 440–1) – at which the governor of Lisbon, though presumably himself of the Romane faith, points out (no doubt with full approval of the audience):

> Under correction, are ye not all Englishmen,
> And longs not Ireland to that kingdome Lords?
> Then may I speake my conscience in the cause,
> Sance scandall to the holy sea of Rome,
> Unhonorable is this expedition,
> And misbeseeming yoo to meddle in. (ll. 445–50)

Stukeley states that he does not hold himself determined in his political allegiance by the accident of birth. At this, the bishop unctuously rejoins with a remarkable statement on the moral duty to love one's country:

> Yet captaine give me leave to speake,
> We must affect our countrie as our parents,
> And if at anie time we alianate
> Our love and industrie from doing it honor,
> It must respect effects and touch the soule,
> Matter of conscience and religion,
> And not desire of rule or benefite (ll. 466–72)

– but Stukeley only sneers at the bishop's duplicity. The question of national allegiance is raised (as a moral one), and the ambiguity of the Irish position (whether loyal to England or to Catholicism) is hinted at – but nothing more. English national pride does, however, come out in a speech laid into the mouth of king Sebastian, who, in trying to dissuade Stukeley from his expedition, is obviously 'playing to the gallery' and flattering Elizabeth:

> I tell thee, Stukeley, they [his shipsl are farre too weake
> To violate the Queene of Ireland's right,
> For Irelands Queene commandeth Englands force,
> Were everie ship ten thousand on the seas,
> Mand with the strength of all the Easterne kings,
> Convaying all the monarchs of the world,
> To invade the Iland where her highnes raignes,
> Twere all in vaine, for heavens and destinies
> Attend and wait upon her Maiestie,
> Sacred, imperiall, and holy is her seate,
> Shining with wisdom, love and mightines (etc.; ll. 724–36)

Stukeley's decision to follow Sebastian's advice is, similarly, a re-assertion of his national loyalty:

> Saint George for England, and Irelande nowe adue,
> For here Tom Stukley shapes his course anue.

The other play concerned with this man, the anonymous *Famous historye of the life and death of captaine Thomas Stukeley,* was printed in 1605. This play is of especial interest since it brings the bogeymen of the period, the rebellious Irish kerns, on stage with some pretence to realism: one of the scenes is laid among Shane O'Neill and his followers, who plan to take the city of Dundalk by stealth. The dialogue (printed, curiously, in two versions – one in prose representing the Hiberno-English dialect, one in standard English blank verse) limits itself to the obvious points that the Irish are alien, barbarous, cunning and ruthless if not very redoubtable enemies. More interesting is the scorn concerning them, that is evinced by the English characters:

> *Stuk.*   What Enemie lies there nere about this towne?
> *Gains.* The Rebell Shane Oneale and all his power.
> *Stuk.*   Why doe ye not beat them home into their dens?
> *Gains.* We have enough to do to keepe the Towne.
> *Stuk.*   To keepe the towne? dare they beleager it?
> *Gains.* I and assaulte it.
> *Stuk.*   Hang them savage slaves,
> Belike they know you dare not issue out. (ll. 1060–7)

The scorn reflects partly on Stukeley's own character, which lends the play considerable dramatic interest; he is imperious, flamboyant, egoistic and proud. On the other hand, the political message seems to be an endorsement of the ruthless repressive state policy that Spenser had advocated in his *View*:

> *Har.*   Who would have thought these naked savages,
> These Northerne Irish durst have beene so bold,
> T'have given assault unto a warlike towne?
> *Gains.* Our suffrance and remissenes gives them hart,
> We make them proud by meuring up our selves,
> In walled towns, whilst they triumph abroad
> And Rebell in the countrey as they please. (ll. 1179–85)

This attitude is further borne out by a very unrealistic scene, where the defeated O'Neill (who until then is depicted as an arrogant, overweening man) voluntarily dons a halter and humbly submits to the English, having been made sensible of the error of his ways; thus, he contritely says to one of his retainers:

> Therefore I beare this hatefull cord in signe
> of true Repentance, of my treasons past,
> and at the Deputies feete on humble knees
> will sue for pardon from her majesties:
> Whose Clemencie I grieve to have abus,
> what sayest thou: is it not my safest course. (ll. 1286–91)

This, again, is flattery – aimed, not at the amour-propre of anybody in particular, but at the political smugness of all those who would like to think that breaking military resistance is tantamount to obtaining loyalty – a view which is now 'confirmed' by witnessing this very process taking place in the character of O'Neill. Thus the audience is reassured of English superiority, of the propriety of English policy in Ireland, notwithstanding the enmity of the misguided dissenting Irishmen.

One of the outstanding Elizabethan plays cashing in on national sentiment is Shakespeare's *Henry V*, which repeated for the audience the glory of Harfleur and Agincourt. It was written under the shadow of the Tyrone rebellion, whilst Elizabeth's favourite, Essex, was campaigning in Ireland. Thus, the opening chorus to Act V draws a parallel between the triumphant return of Henry after his French expedition, Caesar's triumph in Rome, and the imminent, equally triumphant return that Shakespeare optimistically predicted for Elizabeth's general in Ireland:

> But now behold,
> In the quick Forge and working-house of Thought,
> How London doth poure out her Citizens,
> The Maior and all his Brethren in best sort,
> Like to the Senatours of th'antique Rome,
> With the Plebeians swarming at their heeles,
> Goe forth and fetch their Conqu'ring *Caesar* in:
> As by a lower, but by loving likelihood,
> Were now the Generall of our gracious Empresse,
> As in good time he may, from Ireland comming,
> Bringing Rebellion broached on his Sword;
> How many would the peacefull Citie quit,
> To welcome him? much more, and much more cause,
> Did they this *Harry*.[8]

Thus Elizabeth's Irish wars are placed in the great national tradition of the Hundred Years War with France.

An interesting stratagem here is the use of four characters, each representing one of the British nations: the Welshman Fluellen, the Englishman Gower, the Scotsman Jamy and the Irishman Macmorris. Of these four, Fluellen is certainly the foremost, not least because of Henry's (and, for that matter, the Tudors') own strong links with Wales. The deployment of these four representatives most probably was intended to underscore the ideal of intra-British co-operation under a beloved monarch; this reading seems to be supported rather than contradicted by the presence of the Scotsman, representative of a kingdom that was politically separate from the English-Welsh-Irish conglomerate until James VI's accession to the English throne as Elizabeth's successor: captain Jamy has a very slight, unassuming part and his role seems largely contrived in order to complete the numbers, without stressing his presence (possibly awkward politically) too much. The play was written at a time when James' and Elizabeth's common Protestant interests had already made the (historically doubtful) participation of a Scots officer at Agincourt a possibly shrewd dramatic ploy.

Among these four, Macmorris is usually regarded as one of the earliest typical 'Stage Irishman' types, viz. that of the firebrand soldier. Bartley speculates that he was modelled on Hiberno-Norman officers in Elizabeth's army (Macmorris, or in Shakespeare's spelling, Mackmorrice, as the Gaelicized form of Fitzmaurice), and finds in his 'few speeches . . . excitability, enthusiasm, touchy national pride, and a certain extravagant quarrelsomeness'. Duggan believes that Shakespeare appreciated the bravery of Irish officers like Macmorris whom he regards as a realistic character, and Truninger reads in Macmorris's speeches 'a valiant but pitiless warrior,' 'the merciless Irish cut-throat, who has no other ambition beyond war'.[9]

In my opinion, Shakespeare's treatment is not all that appreciative of the character's martial qualities. He is first mentioned as the one who is responsible for an important setback in the siege, namely the fact that the mines dug under his supervision have been undermined themselves by French countersappings. Fluellen is far from satisfied with the way the mines have been dug, and roundly abuses Macmorris for his part in this: 'By *Cheshu* he is an Asse, and in the World, I will verifie as much in his Beard' (fol. 78). When the two captains meet, however, Fluellen is not quite as forthright as he boasted, and gingerly prefaces his criticism with some of his hobby-horse observations on strategic practice in classical antiquity. It is at this point that Macmorris interrupts the Welshman with his first short speech:

> It is no time to discourse, so Chrish save me: the day is hot, and the Weather, and the Warres, and the King, and the Dukes: it is no time to discourse, the Town is beseech'd and the Trumpet call us to the breech, and we talke, and be Chrish do nothing, tis shame for us all: so God sa'me tis shame to stand still, it is shame by my hand: and there is Throats to be cut, and Workes to be done, and there ish nothing done, so Christ sa'me law. (fol. 78)

All this impetuosity seems less a call to action than a way of forestalling the criticism that the self-conscious Macmorris feels is coming to him – a way of preventing Fluellen from impugning him. And when Fluellen persists in probing Macmorris's doubtful knowledge of warfare, the Irishman bursts out in a wholly unreasonable *non-sequitur* effectively prohibiting Fluellen from coming to the point.

> *Welch.*   Captaine *Mackmorrice*, I thinke, looke you, under your correction, there is not many of your Nation. . . .
>
> *Irish.*   Of my Nation? What ish my Nation? Ish a Villaine, and a Basterd, and a Knave, and a Rascall. What ish my Nation? Who talks of my Nation? (fol. 78)

Again, Macmorris is vehemently trying to change the subject, and Fluellen accordingly complains that 'you take the matter otherwise than is meant'. Macmorris thereupon seizes the advantage and states his intention to cut off Fluellen's head, at which point he is placated by Gower and Jamy, and the action is interrupted. Macmorris seems to me an irascible and bullying soldier whose knowledge in the art of war is questionable and who hides his ineptitude behind a blustering volubility. Communication with him is impossible, and he is, if any-thing, a discordant note in the British foursome of Gower, Jamy, Fluellen and himself.

In the more stable Stuart reigns, Irish officers become less threatening or aggressive – on the contrary: they often carry the style of 'captain' without being in actual service or, for that matter, possessing any valour at all. Thus the characters of 'Captain Whit' in Jonson's *Bartholomew Fair,* and 'Captain Albo' in *A faire quarrel,* by Thomas Middleton and William Rawley, are little more than panders. The latter play makes it quite obvious that 'captain' Albo is not a real officer; when the prostitute Meg asks him 'how thou camest to be a captain', Albo answers.

> As thou camest to be a bawd, and Priss to be a whore; every one by his deserts
> (p. 246)

Albo is merely a comic foil for the two swaggering heroes of the play, Chough and his servant Trimtram. The latter, finding that Albo is Irish, concludes that he can therefore abide nothing venomous, and accordingly overwhelms him by dint of flatulence. The traditional view that no venomous beast can live in Ireland is often played upon in this manner, making for broad jests, e.g. in the second part of *The honest whore* by Dekker.

Similarly, the Irishman in *The Welsh ambassador,* when describing his national tastes, is confronted with a typical rejoinder from his English interlocutor:

> Yfaat la I love shamrocks, bonny clabbo . . . cleene trouses and a dart.
> *Clown.* But not a fart.

The Welsh ambassador is of central importance regarding its treatment of Irish national attributes. It is the first continuation of Shakespeare's device to have various British national characters confront and complement each other, and is at the same time a good example of the no less important dramatic tradition in which Irish characters appear as the assumed disguise of English characters.

The play, which dates from the early 1620s, can with some certainty be ascribed to Thomas Dekker. As part of its tortuous plot the brothers Eldred and Edmund, Anglo-Saxon princes, return to court in the disguise of, respectively, a Welsh servant and an Irish footman. Here, they meet with the 'Anglo-Saxon' (English) court jester, and between the three a lively and humorous debate concerning the merits and defaults of the three nations is kept up. The clown has the quickest wit of the three and usually has the punchline in these dialogues – e.g. when the 'Welshman' knocks and announces himself as 'Reece ap meredith, ap shon, ap Vaughan, ap lewellins ap morris' (a joke on what was held to be a Welsh obsession with genealogy); the clown retorts: 'So many of you? Come all in'. He similarly gets the better of both by volubly and earnestly agreeing with Eldred on Welsh, over against Irish, and with Edmund on Irish, over against Welsh, superiority. Irish and Welsh claims to antiquity and early civilization are matters which are obviously not to be taken seriously. Ultimately, however, such quarrels and quibbles are defused as good-humoured banter, and such scenes end with moments of reconciliation that seem intended to represent an ideal of British unity and harmony. Some scenes of this kind lead up to a comical dance by way of an entr'acte:

Edm.	Crees sa me if I heare the pipes goe I cannot forebeare to daunce an Irish hay.
Eld.	As good hay in *Wales; Rees ap Meredith* was daunce too.
Clowne.	Hey then for *England;* if my leggs stand still, hange mee.

Then, after cracking a few national jokes, they dance, under the motto:

Edm.	Hey for St. *Patricks* honour.
Eld.	St. *Tavy* for *Wales.*
Clowne.	St. *George* for *England.* (Act V, sc. ii)

The 'music-hall' style of these interludes is suggested even more strongly when the three prepare a song for a masque to be held at court that evening; again, a jolly statement of harmony and mutual good-humour.

Edm.	Tree merry men, and tree merry men.
Eld.	And tree merry men was wee a.
Clowne.	English
Edm.	Irish
Eld.	And prave Welse
Clowne.	And turne about knaves all three a. *(Exeunt.)*

The most ironic part is, however, that the national distinction which gives rise to all this horseplay and joke-cracking is utterly spurious: for underneath their disguise, Edmund and Eldred are as much natives of England as the clown himself. The fact that the Irish and Welsh characters are only disguises stands, in a way, in direct contradiction to all the fun that is made of them; it even undercuts the very foundation of all this mirth. The implication is, as in Jonson's Irish masque, that in each non-English bumpkin slumbers a courtier, and that the crust of uncouthness only has to be stripped away in order to reveal the 'real' man, that is to say, the man of English culture. Thus the national alienness of non-English subjects is accommodated smoothly.

   This dramatic ploy is, in a way, an extension of the basic theatrical process of representing an invented 'reality' on the stage. The actor is not required to face an Irish role immediately; instead he plays someone playing an Irishman, which is a form of type-casting that sidesteps all issues of believability or realism in the part which might otherwise be raised. What is represented on the stage is not the purported portrait of an Irishman as such, but a representation of what an

Irishman was popularly supposed to be like. It is this a priori consensus between playwright and audience on 'what an Irishman is supposed to be like' which accounts for the highly formulaic, stratified typology of early Stage Irishmen, who in repeated instances represent only a limited number of traits: the soldier, the costermonger, the footman, brogue, irascibility, naivety, shamrocks, unusual forms of swearing, bonny clabber, shaggy hair, narrow trousers, cloaks and darts are the ingredients for practically all Irish appearances on the Tudor and early Stuart stage.

Another play by Dekker, *Old Fortunatus,* again uses the disguise ploy: in act IV, sc. II, Andelocra and his servant Shadow play a prank on the courtiers by posing as Irish costermongers. This particular instance of an English-character-disguised-as-Irish is the more interesting since it is followed through by the two pranksters in that Andelocra subsequently disguises himself as a French quack doctor, in order to cure the evil after-effects that his apples had on the courtiers. It is a remarkable, early instance of what was to become another longstanding casting trick: the combined usage of two different, wholly opposite Stage Aliens, the uncivilized Irishman and the overcivilized Frenchman. Many later examples will be encountered. In both Irish and French roles, Andelocra's assumed nationality is driven home by speech mannerism and accent: a thick brogue for the Irish character, and the usual type of Maurice Chevalier-English for the Frenchman. In this way, a contrastive nationalization (or national peculiarization) is acted out, which otherwise is made mainly in throwaway references such as the one spoken by the bawd Birdlime in Dekker's *Westward ho:*

> I see, that as Frenchmen love to be bold, Flemings to be drunke, Welchmen to be cald *Brittons,* and Irishmen to be Costermongers, so Cocknyes, (especially Shee-Cocknies) love not *Aqua-vite* when tis good for them.[10]

Yet another instance of Dekker's use of Irish characters is the second part of the *Honest whore,* where the blundering efforts of well-intentioned but inept Bryan, the Irish footman, figure prominently. Although the play is set in Italy, the Irish servant's relationship with his Italian master is in no way differentiated from one where the master would be English – indeed, Bartolino's attitude to his Irish servant (he tells Irish jokes about St. Patrick, costermongers and chimney-sweeps) sacrifices Italian local colour to the obviously popular Irish joke.

Beaumont and Fletcher, too, introduced an Irish character into their works, namely in the comedy *The coxcomb,* which dates from 1609. Here, too, the Irish character is an assumed one: it is really the coxcomb himself, Antonio, who puts his wife to the test by disguising himself as an Irish footman delivering a billet-doux to her. The Irish character is, again, an assumed one, typified by the usual trappings of narrow trousers, shaggy hair, and a brogue. This last point is emphasized for the benefit of the audience by Antonio's aside, where he denounces Hiberno-English as an uncouth gaggle:

this rebell tonge sticks in my teeth worse than a tough Hen, sure it was ne'er
known at Babel, for they sold no Apples, and this was made for certain at the first
planting of Orchards, 'tis so crabbed. (vol. 8, 334)

Antonio doesn't do too badly, though, for although his wife sees through his
ploy, she nevertheless allows, in an aside:

By my faith he speaks as well as if he had been lousy for the language a year or
two. (p. 335)

It will be noticed that neither reference to Irish accent, both of which, being
voiced in asides, are obviously meant to be taken as sincere, is particularly
complimentary. Still, Irish characters are objects of fun rather than loathing –
much has changed between Stukeley and the reign of James.

The transition from loathing to comic indulgence in the treatment of Irish
characters can perhaps be located around the turn of the century. A play from the
year 1600, the anonymous Sir John Oldcastle (dealing with Sir John, lord Cobham's
persecution for heresy in Catholic England) features yet another Irish servant who,
though faithless and the murderer of his master, is yet the occasion for some
amusement. An interesting aspect of the Irishman's character is his capacity for
double-think: he can at one moment, with apparent sincerity, profess love for the
master whom he has just murdered; as he searches his victim's pockets, he says,

Alas poe mester, S. Rishard Lee, be saint Patricke is rob and cut thy trote, for dee
shaine, and dy money, and dee gold ring, be me truly is love thee well, bee shitten
kanave.

A similarly paradoxical attitude is represented in Dekker's Old Fortunatus, where
Andelocra, in his Irish disguise, defends the Irish against the imputation of
being dissemblers:

By my trot, and by Saint Patrickes hand, and as Creez save me la, tis no dissembler:
de Irish man now and den cut di countrie-mans throate, but yet in fayt hee love di
countrie-man, tis no dissembler.

The figure of this Mack Shane in Sir John Oldcastle, murderer and robber though
he be, tempers the audience's loathing with perplexity; anyway, a depraved
English priest soon manages, in a humorous display of the superiority of English
wit over Irish dimness, to despoil the ex-servant of his ill-gotten gains. This play,
too, plays on the uncertainty of Irish stage identity, though in a different way
from the disguise-theme used elsewhere. Here, Mack Shane and lord Cobham's
servant Harpoole (sought for heresy, like his master) exchange clothes, so that
the hapless Irishman faces the judge, not as the Irish murderer he is, but as a
supposed English heretic. The usual disguise-ploy is inverted, and the judge
believes Mack Shane to be Harpoole trying to pass for an Irishman:

> *Bishop.*　What intricate confusion have we heere?
> Not two houres since we apprehended one,
> In habite Irish, but in speech, not so:
> And now you bring another, that in speech
> Is altogether Irish, but in habite
> Seems to be English: yea and more than so,
> The servant of that heretike Lord Cobham.
> *Irishman.*　Fait me be no servant of the Lord Cobhams,
> Me be Mack Shane of Ulster.
> *Bishop.*　Otherwise called Harpoole of Kent, go to sir,
> You cannot blinde us with your broken Irish (11. 2508 ff.)

Other, and more straightforward, examples of Irish identities being assumed by way of disguise are Nathan Field's *Amends for ladies* (1618), in which Maid Honour appears as an Irish footman with a dart, and Ben Jonson's *The new inne* (1631). Here, Lady Frampul disguises herself as a low-class Irish nurse – a disguise so well maintained that she even mutters Gaelic phrases (to wit, of a nature indicating some alcoholic predilection) in her sleep ('Er grae Chreest. . . Tower een Cuppan D'usque bagh doone', ll. 475, which is ungrammatical but intelligible Irish: *Ar grá Críost, tabhair aon cupán d'uisce beatha dúinn:* 'for the love of Christ, give us one cup of whiskey'); she speaks with a brogue and affects a great interest for matters of genealogy which is taken as lightly here as it was by the clown in Dekker's *The Welsh ambassador:*

> I did tell him of *Seely*
> Was a great family come out of *Ireland*
> Descended of *O Neale, Mac Con, Mac Dermot,*
> *Mac Murragh,* but he marked not. (ll. 6)

From nearly all the examples of this period one can gather that an Irish presence on the stage tends to be linked to a relativization of the idea of a 'true' identity. The Stage Irishman tends to make his appearance there where the opposition between what one seems to be and what one really is (an opposition which is at the very root of dramatic stagecraft and art) becomes troubled.

The later seventeenth century: Howard, Crowne, Shadwell

The attitude of Stuart plays towards Irish characters does not seem to have been influenced appreciably by the parliamentary war and Cromwellian interregnum – possibly, because the theatre had its roots in a courtly, i.e. royalistic background which shared its anti-Roundhead feelings with the Irish. The most explicit example is Sir Robert Howard's *The committee,* which, though not divulged until after the Restoration, was probably written in Cromwellian times. It is strongly anti-Roundhead and pro-Cavalier, describing the efforts of gallant captain Careless to hold on to his lands without signing the obnoxious Covenant. In a side-action, he picks up the destitute Irishman Teg who provides the note of low comedy. Indeed Teg was such a successful and obviously popular creation that the play, in its fourth edition, received the subtitle *The faithful Irishman*. As Bartley quite rightly points out, 'the Catholic royalist Irishman naturally finds a niche in this strongly royalist and anti-Puritan play'.[11] Although Teg's naivety and dim wit at times disturb his master's stratagems, his loyalty is never in doubt. Indeed the calling of servitude seems a natural one to him, since he was previously a servant to Careless's friend.

Teg is truly a seminal Stage Irishman, who was revived repeatedly and also starred in a later, farcical version of the play, Thomas Knight's *The honest thieves*. A new comical trait is his propensity to make verbal blunders, that is, statements which, though their intended meaning is clear and straightforward, are so infelicitously expressed as to be self-contradictory. When ascribed to Irishmen, such blunders became known as 'Irish Bulls' and came to occupy a place alongside the brogue as standard markers of an Irish character's nationality. For instance, Teg's answer to Careless's inquiry 'How long hast thou been in *England?*' runs: 'Ever since I came hither, i'faith' (p. 76). This particular 'bull' was taken up practically literally in nearly a dozen eighteenth-century comedies with Irish characters. In a dramatic context, such bulls are, in a sense, boomeranging punchlines. Whereas, in earlier plays, Irish fun would receive its capping punchline from the mouth of an English interlocutor (e.g. the clown in *The Welsh ambassador)*, they are now provided by the stooge himself – a handy elimination of the middleman in the provision of laughs to the audience. Again, the fun is to be had only by those who are superior enough to recognize the logical fallacies in the Irishman's quirky speech habits. Generally it is to his superiors (like Careless and the audience) that characters like Teg can have a positive appeal. Careless's own reaction is typical:

> Poor fellow, I pity him; I fancy he's simply honest: Hast thou any trade?
> *Teg.* Bo, bub bub bo, a trade, a trade! an Irishman a trade! an Irish man scorns a trade, that he does; I will run for thee forty mile; but I scorn t'have a trade.
> *Blunt.* Alas, poor simple fellow.
> *Careless.* I pity him. . . (p. 77)

Even after one of Teg's stupidities, Careless's friend Blunt reiterates:

> I am pleased yet, with the poor fellows mistaken kindeness; I dare warrant him honest to the best of his understanding. (p. 86)

On the other hand, Teg's strange manners seem threatening only to those who, like the Puritans Mrs. Day and Abel, are themselves miserable upstarts. Mrs. Day is an ex-kitchenmaid, which gives Teg the giggles when he delivers a message from Careless to her. Her reaction to what is indeed a lack of respect in the Irish servant is significantly different from that of noble Careless or Blunt:

> *Mrs. Day.* . . . This is some Irish Traytor.
> *Teg.* I am no traitor, that I am not; I am an Irish Rebel; You are couzen'd now.

> *Mrs. Day.* Sirrah, Sirrah, I will make you know who I am, an impudent Irish rascal.
> *Abel.* He seemeth a dangerous fellow, and of a bold and Seditious spirit.
> *Mrs. Day.* You are a bloody rascal, I warrant ye.
> *Teg.* You are a foolish, brable brible woman, that you are. (p. 100)

Similarly, a conflict is sparked off between Teg and a bookseller who sells printed copies of the Covenant. Here again, national hatred takes the place of Cavalier *sprezzatura* and organic master-to-servant authority:

> *Book.* You shall pay dearly for the blows you struck me, my wilde Irish, by St. *Patrick* you shall.
> *Teg.* What have you now to do with St. *Patrick?* he will Scorn your Covenant.
> *Book.* I'le put you, Sir, where you shall have worse liquor, Then your Bonny-Clabber.
> *Teg.* Bonny-Clabber? by my goship's hand now you are a rascal if you do not love Bonny-Clabber, and I will break your pate if you will not let me go to my Master. (p. 121)

The underlying idea seems to be that the Irish are only considered dangerous or inimical by those who have no true superiority over them – a notion which becomes widespread in the eighteenth century, when the Stage Irishman grew more sympathetic and sentimental in direct proportion to the extent in which political fears for Gaelic Jacobitism dwindled after 1745. Conversely, one can see a period of acute deterioration in the Stage Irishman during the deepening conflicts preceding and following the revolution of 1688. Possibly the last playwright of the seventeenth century to present a non-negative reference to Ireland is Thomas Otway, whose *Friendship in fashion* has the characters approving unequivocally of the beauties of an Irish song, performed onstage by one of the cast. Here, again, the Irish reference provides the occasion for a blatant break through the dramatic fiction, a startling pointer to the play's theatricality; the song is commented upon:

> I'll assure your Ladiship I learnt it of an *Irish* Musician, that's lately come over, and intend to present it to an Author of my Acquaintance, to put it in his next Play. (vol. 2, 39)

A self-fulfilling prophecy if ever there was one.

During the turmoil around Titus Oates's pretended Popish Plot (a true 'plot', in a piece of real, off-stage drama that far surpassed most theatrical productions in startling revelations, intrigues, cliffhangers and *coups de théâtre*), and in the ensuing exacerbation of religious friction, the figure of the Catholic Irishman took a sharp turn for the worse: Puritans found Irish Catholicism anathema, and the fact that some perjured witnesses in the Plot happened to be of Irish origin did little to improve the creditableness of Irishmen in England.

Many of the references to Irishmen in plays from the last quarter of the seventeenth century contain allegations of mendacity. In John Crowne's *City politiques* (1683), which dealt with the split between whiggish London and the

Cavalier court, false witnesses are brought in to testify that a plot of high treason is being hatched. The witnesses' nationality is Irish, their religion Catholic – and from the way both these negative traits are presented, it is obvious that the two had become indissolubly linked:

> *Governor.* What countrymen are they?
> *First Witness.* I am an Irishman; I'm not ashamed o' my country.
> *Governor.* What religion are you of?
> *First Witness.* Hubbubbow! Ask an Irishman what religion he is of? Shertainly if I be an Irishman I'm a good Catholic. (p. 138)

It is precisely the witness's Irishness that is his undoing and makes him, if not less reprehensible in the play's ideological terms, at least less dangerous: the 'typical', bull-type blunder is a self-contradicting flaw in the Irishman's concocted evidence.

> *Florio.* I'll swear I never saw this fellow's face before in my life.
> *First Witness.* Hubbubbow, tou hasht drunk above a tousand times usquebaugh wi'me, to de carrying on of tish plot.
> *Florio.* Usquebaugh? What's that?
> *First Witness.* A brave liquor tat we have in Ireland. Ter'sh no such here, I never shaw any here.
> *Florio.* How could I drink it then? (p. 139)

> *Governor.* You Irishman, which do you say is the true Florio?
> *First Witness.* Tish is de man I was bid to shwear against.
> *Governor.* Bid to swear against! Who bid you? Confess, or the rack shall make you. (p. 141)

Ten years later, the idea that evidence is untrustworthy if it comes from an Irish source, still holds, e.g. in George Powell's comedy A *very good wife,* where it is combined with the disguise-motif: the rogue Venture dresses up as an Irish doctor called 'Sir Feezil Mackafarty', and denounces Squeezewit to his fiancée Carroll as having contracted syphilis from a prostitute; at this, the offended Squeezewit bursts out:

> Oh wicked and abominable, my patience can hold no longer, as I'me a true Christian Man, Madam, this abominable bogtrotting Rogue, is a perfect Irish Evidence, a Poultroon, a Scoundrel, a Cheat, and a Vagabond. (p. 42)

He also offers to fight the matter out by the sword, at which Venture/ Mackafarty's remarkable reaction is:

> Feeght, the Eerish Man and de Physitian Feeght! by my Shoule it neither belong to my Country nor my Profession to Feeght; but I will do better then Feeghting, for I will take my Corporal Ote upon the 4 Apostle, dat every Sillable I have spoken be all Trute dear Joy. (p. 42)

Squeezewit is not impressed with this prevarication ('Trute, I'll trute you in the Devil's name') and draws his sword. This, it is implied, is the proper way to expose Irish lies: in the ensuing fight, Venture loses his false moustache and beard, and is thereby shown for what he really is.

Again, a national attribute is thus represented at one remove. Powell does not present Irish mendacity as such in Mackafarty, but rather Venture's (and, for that matter, Squeezewit's) belief in Irish mendacity. He repeats and reinforces a commonplace without himself actually endorsing it, presents the Irish liar as a type created, not by him, but by his characters who share to some extent the prejudices of the audience. Only in his stratagem to bring out the truth (in his instance, Venture's 'true' identity) does he imply his own participation in this outlook. In contrast to Jonson and Dekker, who showed Irish disguises to hide a genteel core, the core of Powell's Irishman is a rogue.

By far the most fascinating Irish character created during these years is the Irish priest Tegue O'Divelly, who figures in two plays by Thomas Shadwell, the poet laureate: *The Lancashire witches* (1682) and *The amorous bigotte* (1690).

The Lancashire witches, which has not attracted all the critical attention it so richly deserves, is a most curious play. What makes it of especial importance for my present purposes is the relationship between the main plot, the exploits of witches in seventeenth-century Lancashire, and the sub-plot which is (somewhat anachronistically) brought into it: the pretended 'Popish Plot' which had been denounced in 1678 by Titus Oates. The Titus Oates 'plot' caused a fatal alienation between more Puritan Protestants who chose to believe Oates' paranoid depositions, and the more tolerant Court party. Shadwell's position between the two is uneasy. Himself a staunch low-church Protestant, Shadwell professes (in the preface to the play's printed version) his scepticism concerning the real existence of witchcraft; but he does not extend that scepticism to the political witchery of the Popish Plot. This is all the more contradictory since he repeatedly equates the two, witchcraft and popery: he calls witchcraft a 'Religion to the Devil', 'attended with as many Ceremonies as the Popish religion is' (p. 101); and witchcraft and popery, both hatching pernicious plots, meet in the person of the Catholic villain-priest. His name is, remarkably enough, Tegue O'Divelly, also spelled Tegue O'Devilly,[12] and his elaborate exorcisms lead one of the characters to observe:

> I do not know what to think of his Popish way, his words, his Charms, and Holy Water, and Relicks, methinks he is guilty of Witchcraft too, and you should send him to Gaol for it. (p. 162)

The priest's real crime is, however, that he is an agent of the Popish Plot. The dilemma is, then, that Shadwell consistently equates Plot and Witchcraft, whilst believing in one and not believing in the other. The dilemma is glossed over by the fact that Shadwell to some extent actually dissembles his own disbelief in witchcraft (much as the priest dissembles his participation in the Plot). Although Shadwell expresses his own scepticism towards witchcraft in the play's preface, and although he gives similarly sceptical lines to the play's most positive character,[13] he nevertheless attempts a 'realistic' stage representation of witches' performances: flying broomsticks, sudden materializations or disappearances etc., thereby implicitly showing a witchcraft that 'really works'. Shadwell's own justification for this indulgent representation of 'real' witchcraft is of transcendent flimsiness, boiling down to the point that (a) it makes for an entertaining spectacle, and (b) it was necessary in order to palliate his enemies. Those enemies (who, elsewhere in the preface and in the play, are treated with something less than consideration) thus make handy scapegoats for Shadwell's own inconsistency:

> For the Actions, if I had not represented them as those of real Witches, but had sho'd the ignorance, fear, melancholy, malice, confederacy, and imposture that contribute to the belief of Witchcraft, the people had wanted diversion, and there had been another clamor against it, it would have been call'd Atheistical, By a prevailing party who take it ill that the power of the Devil should be lessened, and attribute more Miracles to a silly old Woman, than ever they did to the greatest of Prophets, and by this means the Play might have been Silenced. (p. 101)

As this passage may show, Shadwell's position, though firm in its low-church convictions, has ambiguous implications. The diabolical priest O'Divelly, the Puritan arch-enemy, Father of Lies, becomes the figure into which all the author's unease is projected. He stands for everything that his creator abhors; discredits, like a true 'Geist der stets verneint', all that Shadwell believes in, and the contradictions in his position are the exact inverse of Shadwell's own. And, like a true devil, the priest must be exorcized from the play; and exorcized he is, by the crudest of dramatic contrivances, a *deus ex machina*. Towards the end, a messenger arrives from the capital and arrests O'Divelly for complicity in the Popish Plot.

The point can be made, of course, that, in this low-church whiggish play, any priest could have performed that diabolical function. Why, then, an *Irish* priest? It is an ironic point in literary history that Shadwell's main claim to fame is the fact that he was the subject-victim of one of the most damning and devastating verse satires in the English language: John Dryden's *Mac Flecknoe* (*c.* 1678). Here, Dryden sarcastically hailed Shadwell as the true successor of the proverbially boring writer Richard Flecknoe, the inheritor of the mantle of Dullness. The title of Dryden's satire gives a Gaelic twist to Shadwell's successorship to Flecknoe, namely by using the patronymic 'Mac', which, though equally common in Scotland and in Ireland, was interpreted by Shadwell as an unambiguous imputation of Irishness. He defended himself against this charge of Irishness (if such it was) even though Dryden probably did not even intend it to be taken literally; it is only one of many barbs in Dryden's long and manifold attack on the 'True Blue Protestant's' witlessness, slowness, careerism, corpulence, etc., etc. Shadwell's limp and not very spirited disavowal of Irishness which, if anything, shows that he was no match for Dryden's mind or pen, makes clear that, of all taunts and insults, the throwaway patronymic had cut deepest. It was contained in the dedication to his *Tenth Satyr of Juvenal* (1687), where he peevishly protests against Dryden's

> . . . giving me the *Irish* name of *Mack*, when he knows I never saw *Ireland* till I was three and twenty years old, and was there but four months.[14]

The fact is that Shadwell's father, who, unlike his whiggish son, was presumably a royalist, was rewarded after the Restoration by being made recorder of the City of Galway, and that he later entered the service of Inchiquin. The links with Ireland ran a little deeper than Shadwell cared to admit. It is therefore most appropriate that, apart from all the other anathema focused in O'Divelly, that character is also, as an Irishman, the opposite of Shadwell's eager and not invulnerable Englishness. Although O'Divelly's priesthood contains all the elements which are required for his part in the play's occurrences, he is nevertheless persistently specified as being Irish: by a highly detailed brogue and an unintermittent rash of Irish catchphrases (St. Patrick, fait and trot, joy, gra, etc. etc., to the point of overkill). It is not only Catholicism, or one's subliminal doubts in one's beliefs, but also the taint of Irishness, that is exorcized at the end of the play.

Indeed it is not only within the framework of the play that Shadwell tries to do away with the Irish anti-Shadwell he has conjured up – in the epilogue, he points out to the audience how his desire to have an Irish character represented as realistically as possible necessitates the reminder not to mistake the actor for his part, not to bear him any ill-will that might have been generated by O'Divelly's perfidy. This exhortation is typical of Shadwell's inconsistent eagerness to keep O'Divelly safely fictional, whilst at the same time striving for 'realism' in the representation of his figment – much as in the case of his realistic representation of witchery.

This claim to realism is, by the way, a startling one, or at least one which stands in a marked contrast to the guarded attitude of previous playwrights who, when it came to Irish characters, usually covered Irishness with an extra layer of impersonation. Unlike those who presented Stage Irishmen as 'what people believe Irishmen are like', Shadwell presents O'Divelly as what he himself believes Irishmen (here, Irish priests) are like. The older forms of accommodation are dropped in favour of a new mode of dealing with Irish presence: that of exorcizing him from the stage.

The actor in O'Divelly's part was Antony Leigh, who had some success on the London stage.[15] He must have been quite successful as O'Divelly, because Shadwell later resuscitated the character, and Leigh again played the part. This time, the play was *The amorous bigotte,* which in its subtitle already stated to include 'the second part of Tegue O'Divelly' . It was produced after William III's takeover, which had paved the way for Shadwell's poet-laureateship – in which he was, ironically, successor to Dryden. Shadwell's literary position was, by his time, as secure as the larger political one was for the Protestant interest, and the playwright could obviously handle the priest with increased relaxation and confidence. Still, there is, in this later play, one reference to the Plot-ridden anxiety of *The Lancashire witches,* in which Shadwell makes O'Divelly state outright that, yes, forsooth, he *did* participate in a *real* Popish Plot:

> Have I Converted sho many Heretick dogs and was sho deep in our braave Plott, and had like to have bin after being slain uppon a Gibbet, and been a great Martyr for de Plott, and dosht dou require a Reason of mee? (p. 21)

The Plot is no longer a matter of debate in this play, which was produced under a programmatically low-church Protestant government that had also rehabilitated Titus Oates himself.

The play is set in Spain, and O'Divelly tries to keep a rich widow, who has declared her intention to bequeath her estate to the church, from re-marrying. Shadwell again makes his priest as unsympathetic as possible: he used to be a pimp with the Spanish army in Flanders, he tries to rape a girl during her confessional and dispenses a doubtful morality of equivocation and hypocrisy.[16]

O'Divelly's Irish nationality has no bearing whatsoever on character or events; O'Divelly is the puritan bugbear-priest *tout court* and presumably only made Irish because the earlier successful part of O'Divelly suited Leigh so well. The priest now moves (instead of in Protestant England) in the convivially debauched and hypocritical milieu of upper-class, Catholic Madrid, and consequently stands out far less than he did in the earlier play. No longer a dangerous, surreptitious intruder, he is identified for what he is, and has gone where he belongs.

This fact indicates how O'Divelly's Irishness in *The Lancashire witches* depended on the English context against which it could be highlighted. *The amorous bigotte* thus, retrospectively, underscores the fact that O'Divelly is an instance of a binary, antithetical treatment of England and Ireland, the two countries being conceived of as polar opposites identified with a corresponding polarity Protestant-Catholic.

Anti-Irish dramatic pamphlets

An anti-Catholic, whiggish approach to Irish characters in the wake of Shadwell (involving a claim to 'realism' and exorcismal stage treatment) can be observed in a number of anonymous, mutually related plays, all of them printed in 1690, that deal with the ousting of James II by William III, and the ensuing campaigns in Ireland. They are all written from a Williamite point of view and are as negative towards Ireland as are the contemporary Histories by Protestant authors like Borlase and Story. Thus, three 'Teagueland witnesses' in *The bloody duke* (whose author is also responsible for a similar product entitled *The abdicated prince*) are the typical perjured frauds that Irish witnesses were supposed to be, and one of the 'good' characters describes them as follows:

> This is a pack of rare Villains of the right Stamp and Breed; a Generation that suck in Villany with their Milk, whose *Native* Language is a compound of *Oaths,* and

Lying their only *Inheritance;* who have Courage enough only to render 'em *Ruffians,* and who have no other Sence or Honour than *Impudence.* Now, there are *good Caligula's* Creatures and Favourites, the Darlings of His heart, and his only true Friends, that are prepare'd to comfort and discountenance the *Plot* and to *Hector* people out of their *Belief,* or their *Lives.* (p. 47; Caligula is, in this play, the name used to represent James duke of York, the later James II)

A well-nigh-hysterical pitch of xenophobia, disguised as national pride, is directed at two Irish soldiers, Mac Donald and Teague, in *The late revolution.* Philanax and Misopapas (described in the dramatis personae as 'Two noble Lords, true Protestants and good English-men', p. iv) decide to rid England of this foreign, papist vermin in words that are best left to speak for themselves:

Phil. What reptile Vermin,
What worse than *Egypts* Torments, Frogs and Locusts
Still croke, ill bodeing, round the *Court and Throne,*
With inarticulate, hoarse hollow Murmurs.
. . . . . .
what cou'd lost England do so base
To merit punishment from such a Brutal Race?
Misopap. 'Tis for their own, not ours they hither came
. . . . . .
The nations rage to hunt'em thence employed,
Like Toads and Serpents *made to be destroy'd.*
Phil. But were it in the Traytors gore embre'wd [sic]
An *English* Sword would *blush,* if stain'd with *Irish* Blood.
If they their Ancient Masters dare withstand
The Slaves deserv'd not Death from such a Hand:
From Ages past to Servitude inur'd
Born with a Clog, and in the Womb secur'd,
Like other Captive Beasts, they shake their Chain,
And bite the Links, and gnash their Teeth, and rave in vain.
Misopap. Yes, I could almost all but this forgive:
Have Gratitude, have Faith and Oaths bin broken:
So many solemn Obligations snapp'd,
And all that Men call Sacred, violated
And trampled under Foot. *Why this is their Religion:*
This they are bound in Conscience to perform,
. . . . . .
I swear I never can, ne'er will forgive it:
Till all these Vermin from our Fields are swept,
Broken and lost, and *crumbled into Atoms;*
Scatter'd i'th' Air, or drown'd in deep Oblivion.
Phil. Nor I –
1. Citizen. Nor we my Lords! Might we presume
To offer Aid in such a *Noble Cause.*
2. Citizen. Not all the Methods yet of Tyranny
Contriv'd t'enslave, to soften and to ruine us,

Have yet so far emasculated all
That breathe within our once renown'd City,
To make us quite forget *we're Englishmen*. (p. 11–12)

Similarly, *The royal flight*, too, though not in quite as repulsive a genocidal frenzy, fervently wishes to rid England of all Irish, wondering

'Tis strange what Nature made these Irish for,
They're neither good in Peace, nor fit for War;
The highest Office they are fit for most,
Is to be Trotters in the Penny Post. (p. 58)

This last play, whose Puritan attitude is also evinced by its depiction of a band of perfectly loathsome, whoring, pimping and pederastic priests, was presumably a continuation of *The royal voyage*, which owes its considerable interest to the fact that it deals specifically with James' efforts to establish a power base on Irish loyalty. The anonymous playwright accordingly pours forth all his spleen and hatred of the Irish; he himself announces, in a lengthy preface,

that the *End* of this Play is chiefly to expose the Perfidious, Base, Cowardly, Bloody Nature of the Irish, both in this and all past Ages, especially to give as lively a Scheme as will consist with what's past, so far of the worse than Heathenish Barbarities committed by them on their Peaceable British Neighbours, in that Bloody and Detestable Massacre and Rebellion of Forty One, which will make the Nation stink as long as there's one Bog or Bogtrotter left in it (p. [iii])

Already, as in the contemporary whig histories, the 1641 rebellion is becoming a cornerstone in the stereotypical structure of Irish perfidy and cruelty. The author vouches for the historical accuracy of the descriptions he gives, even to the point of forswearing the fictional character of his medium: 'though every one knows this way of writing allows great Liberty; I protest 'twas impossible to invent more dreadful things than I found ready to my Hand' (p. [iii]).

In this sense, *The royal voyage* is a perfect example of Allardyce Nicholl's point that plays such as these were not productions for theatrical use but rather political pamphlets, whose authors

put forward their ideas and their satire in the form of plays which, even from their incipience, were probably never intended to be acted.[17]

– as can also be seen from the fact that such plays 'deal entirely with political and religious questions' (p. 225).

In this manner, the creator of fictional Irishmen can claim authority for their 'realism' by linking his 'play' firmly to non-fictional source-texts:

After all, let any Man take the pains but to read the Irish Histories, Foreigners as well as others, nay their own too, if he has any patience, into the bargain, and if he does not confess that I have not, nay cannot misrepresent the *Irish*, when I speak

> any thing ill of 'em, I'll be content to be sent over into that blessed Island, and live there 'till I've forgot my Mother Tongue, and grow as Irish as *O Hanlan's* &c (as their mannerly Proverb has it). (p. [iv])

And, as in so many non-fictional texts, the generalization is no sooner made than the need for a safeguarding restriction makes itself felt:

> Tho on t'other side, so far is this piece from any Reflection on the British there, that one main end thereof is to give 'em their due Encomiums, and just Honour. (p. [iv])

No time is lost at the beginning of the play to confirm the author's views by an obliging self-characterization of the Catholic Irish army leaders, one of whom (Nugent) proposes:

> Let's o'er to *England*,
> That golden Land, where Palms and Laurels wait us,
> Delicious Murthers, and sweet Massacres:
> *Hang, Drown, Stab, Burn, Broil, Eat, Damn* our proud Conquerors
> *Neagle.* That will do well; 'tis excellently motion'd;
> What brave *Milesian* wou'd not stake his Soul
> On the Design? (pp. 3–4)

Amidst the blank verse, the appearance of 'mere' Irish speaking prose comes as a note which, though comic, is no less full of savagery; for example, the 'revealing' chat of Irishmen after a cattle-raid is given as follows:

> 1. Rare times, by Saint Patrick; the best that *Ireland* ever saw, by my Soul Joy; why who would be at the Trouble to raise and breed Cattle of their own, when the *Heretick Dogs* can do't to our Hands, without any pain?
> 2. Right neighbour Teague; and besides they are all our *Tenants*, not we Theirs; for I heard *Father Dominick, our Priest,* make a Swear, that this was all our Country, Five Thousand Years before the *New-Moon* was made, and the *English* Thieves never came hither to rob us of our own till the next year after the Flood was over.
> 3. Well, See what 'tis to have learning; they must talk what they will, but if I know any thing, there's ne'er a Clergy, in Christendom to compare with the *Irish;* . . . since they have so kindly prov'd the Lawfulness and Necessity of our plundering the *English.* . . . (pp. 7–8)

The unhallowed amalgam of Gaelic barbarity and Popish perfidy is laid on with a trowel, and becomes even worse when the characters merrily, and with sadistic enjoyment, fall to exchanging reminiscences of the 1641 massacre, expressing their hope for another one ere long (thus echoing the intentions of Nugent and Neagle). It will be obvious that the author's hatred is aimed at an image he has conjured up himself, and put into the mouths of characters created and animated by himself, rather than at real political occurrences.

Another interlude is provided by the masque-like representation of an Irish funeral (pp. 38–9) at which 'two fat Friars' sing a scurrilous song, and the company lament the deceased 'with unsufferable Howlings, as their manner is' (p. 38):

> Ah Brother Teague! Why didst thou go?
> *Whillilla lilla lilla lilla lilla lilla loo!*
> And leave thy Friends in grief and wo,
> *aboo aboo aboo aboo aboo aboo aboo!* (etc.; p. 39)

It is remarkable that the author seems to be unable to bring Irish on stage without wreaking, as it were, his own vengeance on them. In both scenes, as well as in all others involving mere Irish, the Irish invariably exit in a headlong flight from the English. The funeral ends, according to the stage directions:

> While they are in the midst of their Harmony comes a Shot from the Town, and kills the two Fryars and several others –, all the rest start up and run away. (p. 39)

The cattle-raiders likewise see their gleeful gluttony (in which even the bovine victim is given its propagandistic nationality) similarly interrupted:

> They sing an *Irish* Song, Dancing round a fat *English Ox*, tied to a stake; and as soon as that was over, fall all together upon it, cutting out pieces of them alive, and broiling it upon the Coals. In the mean while, a small party of *English*, surprize, and fall upon 'em; on which, all the Rabble set up the *Irish* yell, and run away without striking a stroke.
> *1st Englishman.* A soul-less heap of Animals! that Nobler Beast
> They here torment, has infinite more Valour,
> Than all their Rascal Nation, piled together (pp. 9–10)

This treatment in a way echoes the exorcism of Tegue O'Divelly at the end of Shadwell's play. The play's treatment of the Irish is carried to the point that their very presence on the stage becomes a usurpatory intrusion, and must therefore be balanced by their expulsion at the hands of the English. In comparison to the similar anxiety to 'get rid of the Irish' as expressed in *The late revolution* and *The royal flight*, it becomes clear that, on the microcosm of the imaginary stage, the author is acting out his larger political hopes – accordingly, he describes the course of political events as 'the Drama really acted'; compare also the peroration of his preface announcing the 'happy end' both of the war and of his play:

> That the desirable work of their entire Conquest may soon be accomplished, which all *Europe* as well as *England* groans for, the Second part of the Drama really acted, and our glorious king *William* there conquering all our Enemies, I am sure every honest Man wishes as heartily as I do; – for those who hope the contrary, tho' their own Countries, *Europe's*, and Religion's implacable Enemies, I'd wish 'em no greater plague, than possessed with all the Rage, Malice, and defeated desperate Wickedness of an Irish-man, to stand by and see our great victorious Prince enter Triumphantly into his Royal City of Dublin – which a few Weeks may in all fair probability produce, and a few more the *Second Part* of the *Royal Voyage,* or *Irish Expedition.* (p. [v])

Again, then, the Stage Irishman evokes both apprehension and reassurance. He incorporates not only the enemies' viciousness, but also their weakness and utter inferiority.

The early eighteenth century: Farquhar

In the century after the Revolution of 1688, a slow but steady amelioration of the Ireland-image as expressed in the fictional Irishman can be noticed. A vogue of 'paddy jokes' had begun to sweep the country; a well-known printed collection is the anonymous *Bogg-witticisms, or, Dear Joy's common-places* of ca. 1690 which, for its fun, often depended on ludicrous imitations of the brogue and on a liberal sprinkling of 'bulls' – verbal blunders considered to be typical of the muddled thought and speech of the Irish. The vogue continued in pieces like *The Irish Hudibras* and various broad-sheets (see Bliss texts nos. 16, 17, 21), and influenced the character writings of later vintage, such as the vignettes by Ned Ward in his *London spy* (1703). Ward, one of the more colourful Grub Street writers, also published (anonymously) a fictitious Irish travel description entitled *A trip to Ireland, with a description of the country* (1699) . The intention of this pretended travel description is 'to give such a Description of *Ireland,* as should make my Reader laugh at its inhabitants' (p. [iv]) – a phraseology that is reminiscent of John Dunton, whose *Dublin Scuffle* appeared in the same year (cf. above, p. 66). Ward's sense of humour is broadly scatological, and draws on the traditional imagery of dirty, cowardly and dim-witted Irishmen, whose only virtue seems to exist in providing laughing-stock for English wits. A later production in the same vein appeared as *The comical pilgrim* in 1722 (anonymous, sometimes attributed to Defoe) which contained, as the subtitle explains, *Travels of a cynick philosopher, thro' the most wicked parts of the world, namely England, Wales, Scotland, Ireland and Holland.* Here, too, standard images are repeated in a pseudo-travel-book with comical intent. The extreme ludicrousness and stupidity attributed to the Irish in this type of writing may have helped to lighten the opprobrium of infernal wickedness that Protestant whigs had heaped on the anti-Williamite Irishman. The tradition of anonymous Williamite play-pamphlets found a late continuation in two plays from 1705 concerning the siege of Derry, by John Michelburne. But even though Michelburne has claims to an excuse for whatever bitterness he might express (in that he himself lived through the ordeal of that siege, and in it lost his wife and his children), it is remarkable that his tone is far less hysterical or viciously bigoted than in the earlier plays. Nevertheless, the Irishman was to remain a rather nasty character for a few decades to come; as is illustrated, for example, by 'Macsteer, Captain-general of the rapparees', who plays a bullying part in John Dennis's *A plot and no plot* (1697).

The early eighteenth-century treatment of the Stage Irishman is first exemplified by George Farquhar. The topos of Irish mendacity, dating from the Plot, is still alive here: in *The twin rivals* (1702), the attorney Subtleman is in need of false witnesses for his client's claims, and confidently states: 'I expect a cargo of witnesses and usquebaugh by the first fair wind' (p. 41). This particular trait seems, however, to be cancelled out by the stronger one of Irish stupidity (comparable to the treatment in *City politiques*) which involves a naive honesty; else, this mendacity is subsumed under the general falseness inherent in a new type, that of the Irish fortune-hunter who comes over to England to win (under false pretenses, of course) rich heiresses or widows. One of these is Farquhar's character Macahone (in whose name might lurk a scatological Gaelic connotation), in *The stage-coach* (1704), his adaptation from Jean de la Chapelle's *Les carosses d'Orleans*. Macahone, called by one of his fellow-travellers 'that *Irish Booby*' (p. 4), is Farquhar's equivalent of what, in the French original, was a Dutch fortune-hunter with a faulty command of French. Macahone is thus primarily 'a stranger with a funny accent and bad manners', and only in the second instance specified as an Irishman. This particular choice of nationality for the stranger was perhaps partly made because of the success of the actor Bowen in Irish parts. Bowen himself was an Irishman whose main success was Teg in four revived versions of Howard's *The committee*. He also played in two other plays by Farquhar: the aforementioned *The twin rivals* and *The beaux' stratagem*. Macahone's introduction already sets the tone: a mixture of insolence, pretence, brogue, silly nomenclature, and a bull:

> *Capt.* May I crave your Name, Sir?
> *Mac.* My name is Torlough Rauwer Macahone, of the Parish of *Curough a Begely*, in the County of Tiperary, Eshquire; where is my Mansion-House, for me and my Predecessors after me. (pp. 4–5)

Macahone's pecuniary designs on the womanhood of England are, however, hoodwinked – as are all plots of Irish fortune-hunters in the comedies of the century – in this particular instance, by a prostitute, who out-pretends his pretence and makes the fortune-hunter believe she is a rich lady.

Farquhar's earliest play, *Love and a bottle*, gave an atypical representative of this type: Roebuck, who, though at the time penniless and enamoured of a London lady, is in fact a gentleman (wearing, significantly, an English-sounding name rather than one with an O- or Mac-) who had to leave his native Dublin suddenly in order to avoid having to marry a woman he did not love. Roebuck, an Anglo-Irish inhabitant of the capital, is a denial of the pre-expectations that would be generated on hearing of a person's Irish nationality. As in so many Anglo-Irish political writings of the time, great pains are taken to dissociate the Protestant gentlemen of Ireland from the country's Gaelic aspects, to identify them with English religion, culture, political loyalty. Thus, when Roebuck introduces himself to Lucinda as 'an Irishman', the following exchanges are sparked off:

> *Luc.* Oh, horrible! an Irishman! a mere wolf-dog, I protest!
> *Roe.* Ben't surprised, child; the wolf-dog is as well-natured an animal as any of your country bull-dogs, and a much more fawning creature, let me tell ye. (*Lays hold of her*)

> *Luc.* . . . Tell us some news of your country; I have heard the strangest stories –
> that the people wear horns and hoofs!
> *Roe.* Yes, faith, a great many wear horns: but we had that, among other laudable
> fashions, from London . . .
> *Luc.* Then you have ladies among you?
> *Roe.* Yes, yes, we have ladies, and whores, colleges and playhouses, churches and
> taverns, fine houses and bawdy-houses, in short, everything you can boast of, but
> fops, poets, toads, and adders. (pp. 14–15)

– fops and poets belong to the venomous creatures not found in Ireland.

Other stock characters besides the Stage Irishman enjoy an undiminished popularity throughout the eighteenth century: apart from types like The Martial Soldier (or Sailor), or The Cunning Priest (now obsolescing), two of the most important are the Stage Frenchman and the Stage Attorney. The Frenchman we have already encountered in Andelocra's impersonation in Dekker's *Old Fortunatus,* as well as in Venture's disguise in Powell's *A very good wife;* Bartolino, in Crowne's *City politiques*, is an early example of the Attorney. Either character is often combined with a Stage Irishman – it seems to be a general tendency to compound stock characters into Irish priests, Irish soldiers, French doctors and sometimes even Irish Frenchmen, etc. The various stock characters are also frequently pitted against each other (as also happened in Hollywood horror films of the 'Frankenstein meets Dracula' type); thus, the aforementioned attorney Subtleman in *The twin rivals* attempts to seduce the play's Stage Irishman, Teague, to give perjured evidence so as to advance the claims of Mr. Would-be the younger. Subtleman's plans misfire, though, since Teague happens to be the footman of Mr. Would-be the elder.

The character of Teague is obviously inspired on Teg in Howard's *The committee* – an assumption strengthened by the fact that Farquhar himself, as a young actor, played Captain Careless in that piece.[18] Like his namesake in *The committee,* Farquhar's Teague is an uncouth and rough-hewn chap. He is given to lying (p. 57), his style of combat is sneaky, consisting of grabbing people from the back (p. 108) and choking them (p. 78), and his frisking of a female prisoner is less than courteous (pp. 99–100). All this can, however, be excused, and redound to the character's credit, since Teague's motivation is wholly one of loyalty to his master, the hero of the piece. Thus, it is the information that Teague rudely snatches from the woman-prisoner's handbag that brings about the happy denouement. It takes a comparison with a later, sentimentalized, version of the same play (Henry Brooke's *The contending brothers* of 1762) to see how much more polished the Noble Savage was, compared to this Tamed Barbarian.

Farquhar's best-known play, *The beaux' stratagem,* presents us with what is, in national terms, the most complex of his Stage Irishmen. It is in this play that the Stage Irishman passes through a number of permutations that effectively place him on the breach between the seventeenth-century, Protestant treatment and the eighteenth-century, comical treatment, of Irish nationality. The play's Irish character is called Mack Shane, and, like Teague O'Divelly, he is a priest who has assumed a false (French) nationality. What determines his character most of all is his priesthood, which is full of the usual imputations of jesuitical equivocation and sanctimonious amorality. Thus, he involves a servant in a scheme to corrupt a woman's virtue with the following type of argument:

> Gip. But should I put the count into the closet –
> Priest. Vel, is dere any shin for a man's being in a closhet?
> Gip. But if the lady should come into her chamber, and go to bed?
> Pr. Vel, and is dere any shin in going to bed, joy?
> Gip. Ay, but if the parties should meet, doctor?
> Pr. Vel den – the parties must be responsible. (pp. 311–12)

Apart from the priestcraft, it is the brogue that stands out most strongly as Mack Shane's characteristic trait. The priest's disguise is all the more flimsy as he passes himself off as a French, or at least a French-speaking priest, called Foigard; in this way, he is not subject to the anti-Catholic laws of England, where the action takes place. The notion of a French speaker with a brogue is, naturally, ludicrous enough:

> F. Och, dear joy, I am your most faithful shervant, and yours alsho.
> Gib. Doctor, you talk very good English. but you have a mighty twang of the foreigner. . . .
> Aimwell (aside). A foreigner! A downright Teague, by this light! – (p. 283)

The denouement, in which his true, Irish, identity is revealed, becomes a veritable Babel: the stratagem used to expose the Irish priest's *alias* of a Francophone Fleming involves the Englishman Archer passing himself off as an Irish acquaintance of Mack Shane:

> Aim. Sir, I arrest you as a traitor against the government; you're a subject of England, and this morning showed me a commission, by which you served as chaplain in the French army. This is death by our law, and your reverence must hang for't.
> Foi. Upon my shoule, noble friend, dis is strange news you tell me! Fader Foigard a subject of England! de son of a burgomaster of Brussels a subject of England! ubooboo! –
> Aim. The son of a bog-trotter in Ireland! Sir, your tongue will condemn you before any bench in the kingdom.
> . . . (Re-enter Archer)
> You know this fellow?
> Arch. (In a brogue) Saave you, my dear cussen, how does your health?
> Foi. (Aside) Ah! upon my shoule dere is my countryman, and his brogue will hang mine. – (To Archer) Mynheer, Ick wet neat watt hey zacht. Ick universton ewe neat, sacramant! (pp. 321–2)

On the surface, the merciless confrontation of duplicity with Justice (here, a threatened arrest on the count of treason) reminds one of the similar fate of the priest O'Divelly in *The Lancashire witches*. The difference is, however, considerable: Justice here is, in Archer's impersonation, scarcely less duplicitous than the Irishman himself. Whereas O'Divelly's arrest was a crude contrivance without any bearing on the main action of the play, Foigard's exposure is a supporting sub-plot in the main 'Stratagem'. The priest is not removed from the action to have harsh justice meted out to him, but is blackmailed by Aimwell and Archer to support them in their devious plans: an agreement can be reached to the satisfaction of both parties.

In this respect, Farquhar not only closes the earlier, anti-Irish, propagandistic tradition; he can at the same time be considered as the beginning of a new type of dramatic treatment of the Stage Irishman, one which is essentially comical. One of the more generally valid observations that can made of eighteenth-century English comedy (and, indeed, of most other comedy besides) is that most of the dramatic energy (both in terms of 'fun' and of plot development) is generated by a discrepancy between appearances and realities. Misunderstandings, misapprehensions and specifically mistaken identities are at the core of a comedy, much like the hero's 'tragic flaw' is at that of a tragedy. Penniless young officers woo heiresses in disguise, or turn out to be of unexpectedly noble background; young ladies dress up in men's clothes for the slightest of reasons (one of which was probably to show the audience a pair of shapely thighs in narrow breeches); unsuspected family relationships are hushed up and/or exposed, etc., etc. Nowhere is a personal identity such a protean commodity as in these comic conventions, and the above-quoted scene with its conflicting impersonations is a good example of this practice. The appeal of the Irishman's personality can now become less destructive or subversive to the dramatic conventions in which he is placed, and the 'threatening' or dangerous part of his character progressively dwindles whilst he increasingly becomes a figure of good-humoured fun.

A later, lesser author than Farquhar called John Breval used a similar ploy to deal with his stage Irishman, Macahone (the same name as in Farquhar's *Stage coach*) in his play called, interestingly, *The play is the plot* (1718). Here, Captain Carbine's servant Jeremy impersonates an Irishman (Maghloghan Moor) who can win Macahone's confidence, and extract the sensitive information that he deserted from the army. At this point, Captain Carbine comes in and accuses him:

> *Mac.* By St. Patrick, and I did confess nothing and you have no Evidensh here, but this Gentleman, and he will not be after hanging his countryman.
> *Jer.* Faith but I will, my dear Friend.
> *Mac.* Arra! Is not the Brogue upon your Tongue Joy – but, my Shoul it is upon your face, tho' – arrah (p. 26)

The nationality is mainly vested in the brogue, and the fact that Jeremy is capable of putting on this accent is explained beforehand:

> *Car.* Wer't thou ever in Ireland?
> *Jer.* Three Years, an't please your Honour.

Car. Thou hast the Brogue then a little sure?
Jer. As well as any Teague of 'em all, Sir, if that can do your Honour any Kindness.
(p. 7)

As in Farquhar's play, the threat of capital punishment is merely used as a way of forcing the Irishman to comply with the captain's plot – abducting his beloved. Carbine later on even returns the favour by protecting Macahone from the wrath of the maiden's miserly father. At the denouement, where all true identities are extricated from the various deceits, stratagems and plots, a general reconciliation follows, which includes the Irishman. A shorter version of this comedy was produced as a farce called *The strollers* in 1723, proving successful enough for later revivals.

Another Teague-servant of the early eighteenth century was created by Mrs. Centlivre, in her farce *A wife well-managed* (1715). The action is set in the depraved hypocrisy of upper-class Madrid, so that the incongruous dim-witted naivety of the Irishman is presented as an exception to his surroundings – a difference from the previous combination of Spanish background and Stage Irishman in *The amorous bigotte*, even though a number of correspondences (most notably the presence of a lecherous priest) between the two plays exist. It is Teague's lack of intelligence that causes a billet-doux from a lady to her confessor, of whom she is enamoured, to fall into the husband's hands. The husband, in thinking up a counter-scheme (naturally involving disguise and impersonation) naturally realizes that Teague's stupidity and lack of dissimulation is, in these intriguing circles, a handy commodity: 'Ha! A lucky Thought comes into my Head, and this Fellow's Simplicity is of some Use' – a different approach from the earlier Teagues, whose simplicity was only 'of use' if made up for by a large dose of good intentions.

Mrs. Centlivre, like Farquhar, had links with Ireland. Farquhar's Irish background is well known, Mrs. Centlivre was born in Ireland and grew up there. In fact, many of the playwrights who created Irish characters in the eighteenth century were themselves linked to Ireland. Men like Macklin, the Sheridans, O'Keeffe and Macready, as well as numerous minor playwrights who will be mentioned in passing (Kelly, Jackman, Oulton, Molloy), were Irish, and Richard Cumberland was Ulster Secretary during the Irish viceregency of his protector Halifax (1761–2); Halifax also appointed Cumberland's father, Denison Cumberland, to the Irish episcopal see of Clonfert, whence he was transferred to that of Kilmore in 1773. It was during a visit to his father at Clonfert that Cumberland composed, in 1769, *The West Indian,* and with it created Major O'Flaherty.[19] It appears that, both quantitatively and in terms of significance, the Stage Irishman in the mid-eighteenth century was, to an important degree, the product of playwrights with Irish connections or a first-hand experience of the country. One must be careful, however, in treating the eighteenth-century Stage Irishman as an Irish creation: for the audience to whom he was presented was that of London. Such plays as were specifically Irish in orientation will be discussed in another context (pp. 325–9, 368–72) below.

The fortune-hunter

Fortune-hunters are further attested in farces such as John Mottley's *The craftsman* (1728) and Moses Mendez' *The double disappointment* (1746). In the latter play, the Irishman, who carries the programmatic name of O'Blunder (and a great many members of that clan were to tread the London stage) is made to sing an Irish song, without, for all that, making the slightest headway with the heroine:

> *Isabel.* Your musick is as harmonious as your language is polite and your Person agreeable. (*aside*) Odious Blockhead!

As in most farces, the asides are the moments when characters' genuine feelings can reach the audience's (if not the fellow-characters') ears. Thus, O'Blunder utters a surprizingly self-condemnatory 'aside' at the entrance of another of Isabel's wooers, a Frenchman:

> If this Frenchman should be as great a Rogue as myself, now, upon my soul, it would be very comical.

Indeed, the Frenchman, too, is a fortune-hunter, and the two Stage Foreigners deceive each other's deceptions no more and no less than they manage to deceive the fair Isabel.

The fortune-hunter in Mottley's *craftsman* is called Mac Tawdry. He plots to marry a widow under false pretenses but is in turn out-witted by the fact that the parson who performs the wedding service turns out to be a layman in disguise. Again, in *The double disappointment,* as in so many other farces and comedies, the 'happy end' coincides with the re-establishment of true identities. The most interesting aspect of *The craftsman* is that the type of the Irish fortune-hunter is explicitly treated as a stage convention rather than as an extra-theatrically existing, 'real' type. A certain reserve concerning the validity of the play's Stage Irishman is expressed by its hero, the journalist D'Anvers:

> I believe, Sir, this Letter will convince you, that there's nothing left for you but to withdraw: The least Part of your Crime is your Attempt upon this Lady; since such as you are too often the Occasion of National Reflections, which are always unjust. (p. 22)

However, MacTawdry's retort buries such serious high-mindedness under another stage-Irishism:

> Uboo, upon my Shoul, now I think it is a National Reflection upon an *Irishman,* to lose a great Fortune after he has got her.

It was especially in the novel that the Irish fortune-hunter led his most tenacious existence. Smollett introduces no less than four of them, two in *Humphry Clinker* (Sir Ulick Mackilligut in Bath, and the footman Oneale near the Scottish border) and two more in *Roderick Random:* Captain Odonnell and Captain Oregan.

Fitzpatrick, in Fielding's *Tom Jones,* is another example, in which novel semi-proverbial side-remarks occur such as '(he had) more Satisfaction of Mind than ever any *Irishman* felt in carrying off a Fortune of Fifty Thousand Pounds' (p. 828).

A contradiction makes itself felt, however: If the Irish are as stupid and obnoxious as they are made out to be, how can they be represented as any way successful with that paragon of virtue and clearsightedness, English Womanhood? The issue is skirted in the comedies of the period, where all fortune-hunters are eminently unsuccessful, but Steele had addressed the matter earlier in the *Spectator* for 23 March 1711 (nr. 20). In dealing with impudence towards ladies, he distinguishes between English/Scottish disregard for good manners and Irish ignorance of them. The advantage of Irish womanizers is that their flatteries are not only amusing, but also obviously sincere – notwithstanding their uncouth way of expression. Impudence, according to Steele,

> exerts it self in a different Manner, according to the different Soils wherein such Subjects of these Dominions, as are Masters of it, were born. Impudence in an *English-man is* sullen and insolent; in a *Scotch-man* it is untractable and rapacious; in an *Irish-man* absurd and fawning: As the Course of the World now runs, the impudent *English-man* behaves like a surly Landlord, the *Scot* like an ill-received Guest, and the *Irish-man* like a Stranger who knows he is not welcome. There is seldom any thing entertaining either in the Impudence of a *South* or *North Briton;* but that of an *Irish-man is* always Comick: A true and genuine Impudence is ever the Effect of Ignorance, without the least Sense of it.
>
> . . .
>
> I cannot tell how to account for it, but these people have usually the Preference to our own Fools, in the Opinion of the sillier Part of Womankind. Perhaps it is that an *English* Coxcomb is seldom so obsequious as an *Irish* one; and when the Design of pleasing is visible, an Absurdity in the Way toward it is easily forgiven. (p. 77)

In this distinction, Steele not only announces the amelioration of the bull into a vehicle for sympathetic utterances, but also indicates the notion that opposes Irish artlessness to the foppish dissimulation current in England. I hope to show further on how important this distinction was to become in later, sentimental treatments of the Stage Irishman.

The contradiction between Irish boorishness and Irish success with English ladies is resolved in a different way in Fielding's *Tom Jones,* where the deluded victim of the Irish fortune-hunter Fitzpatrick explains:

> He was handsome, dégagé, extremely gallant, and in his Dress exceeded most others. In short, my Dear, if you was unluckily to see him now, I could describe him no better than by telling you he was the very Reverse of every Thing which he is: For he hath rusticated himself so long, that he is become an absolute wild Irishman. (vol. 2, 582)

At the same time, Fielding is sensible of the fact that he is dealing with a received type, with popular generalizations, rather than with real characters; and, like Mottley in his *Craftsman,* he adds a reminder of the fact, cautioning the reader that not all Irish are odious; as Mrs. Fitzpatrick concludes her story, Sophy reacts: 'Indeed, Harriet, I pity you from my Soul; – But what could you expect? Why, why, would you marry an *Irishman?*' (p. 601). Sadder and wiser Mrs. Fitzpatrick gives the answer:

> Upon my word . . . your Censure is unjust. There are, among the *Irish,* Men of such Worth and Honour, as any among the *English:* Nay, to speak the Truth, Generosity of Spirit is rather more common among them. I have known some examples there too of good Husbands; and, I believe, these are not very plenty in *England.* Ask me, rather, what I could expect when I married a Fool. . . . (p. 602)

Fielding had expressed a similar view, in his paper *The champion:*

> There is nothing so unjustifiable as the general Abuse of any Nation or Body of Men: For which Reason, I have always disliked those Sarcasms we are too apt to cast on a particular Part of His Majesty's Dominions, whose Natives have been commonly censured by the *English* Mob for Blundering and Assurance, tho' it is notorious that several of our greatest Wits and best-bred Men have come to us from that Quarter. (Sat. 29 March 1740, p. 45)

In the two Irishmen of Smollett's *Roderick Random,* captain Oregan and captain Odonnell, the character of the mercenary suitor merges with a fourth type of Stock Irishman (after priest, servant and fortune-hunter): that of the officer. Odonnell is a wholly despicable character, as is another Irishman, the gruesome ship surgeon Mack Shane, in the same novel; the latter, however, is not portrayed primarily as an Irishman, i.e. in his national attributes, but mainly as a vehicle for *Roderick Random's* scathing attack on the lamentable conditions in the British Navy. Oregan is more interesting. He meets the hero under the most disadvantageous of circumstances: as his opponent in a duel, his rival for the affection (and fortune) of a lady. Oregan, a pathetically dishevelled character, is equally inept in both capacities, and, as Roderick's superiority on the duelling ground and in the amorous pursuit is clearly established, a basis for a more sympathetic understanding between the two men becomes possible.

> I took notice of his deshabille, and professing sorrow at seeing a gentleman reduced, slipt two guineas into his hand, at the sight of which, he threw away his pistols, and hugging me in his arms, cried, 'Arrah, by Jesus, now, you are the best friend I have met with these seven long years.' (p. 292)

At this point Oregan's shabbiness is explained as being due to causes wholly outside his own control, and Roderick, 'well convinced of this poor man's honesty and courage' (p. 293) undertakes to help him. He takes Oregan to his lodgings,

> where he was fitted with decent cloaths from my wardrobe, so much to his satisfaction, that he swore eternal gratitude and friendship to me, and at my request, recounted all the adventures of his life. (p. 294)

A patronizing tone is noticeable, and is confirmed when Roderick and the beloved maiden make themselves merry 'at the expense of this poor admirer', viz. by reading his blundering loveletters. Understanding between Irishman and Englishman is obviously only possible when the Irishman disclaims his presumption to be the Englishman's rival – the amorous rivalry being interpreted as including a social claim to rivalry. English displeasure at the 'impudence' of the Irish fortune-hunter is not just vicariously felt on behalf of the courted woman, but also directly as a refusal on the Irishman's behalf to acquiesce in his inferiority which, to the Englishman, seems axiomatic. This is shown in Oregan's counterpart, captain Odonnell, who attacks Roderick in a more vicious and dangerous way, but who, as a revenge, gets whipped with nettles and laughed out of town: a revenge aimed primarily at the Irishman's personal dignity. Similarly, when (in real life) the duchess of Manchester married an Irish commoner, Edward Hussey (speedily created lord Beaulieu), the verse satires composed on the occasion tended to express the outrage at the flouted *class* distinctions primarily in *national* terms, in lines like

> Nature, indeed, denies them [the Irish] sense,
> But gives them legs and impudence,
> That beats all understanding.

– though lines like 'How slight the diff'rence is between / The Duchess and the Hussey'[20] hint at the deeper cause of dismay. Impudence, lack of reverence, is also the sin of an Irish officer appearing in Richardson's *Sir Charles Grandison*. It is Major O-Hara who is initially introduced as being

> pert, bold, vain, and . . . particularly fond of his new scarlet coat and laced waistcoat. . . . His bad and straggling teeth are shewn continually by an affected laugh, and his empty discourse is interlarded with oaths. (vol. 2, 21)

He is married to, or at least living with, the depraved mother of Sir Charles's innocent ward Emily, Mrs. Jervois. Grandison, intended by Richardson as a character uniformly motivated by all that is noble, gentlemanlike and correct, protects poor Emily from the distress of being exposed to this fallen woman – in other words, he refuses to let Mrs. Jervois see her daughter. She, accompanied by her husband/protector and his brother-in-law, comes to seek an explanation, and the confrontation between Grandison and O-Hara takes the following course:

> 'I am called Major O-Hara, Sir: I am the Husband of the Lady in the next room, as she told you.'
> 'And what, pray, Sir, have I to do either with you, or your marriage? I pay that Lady, as the widow of Mr. Jervois, 200*l.* a year: I am not obliged to pay her more than one. She has no demands upon me; much less has her husband.'
> The men had so much the air of bullies, and the woman is so very wicked, that . . . I had too little command of my temper.

'Look ye, Sir Charles Grandison, I would have you to know – '
And he put his left hand upon his sword-handle, pressing it down, which tilted up the point with an air extremely insolent.
'What am I to understand by that motion, Sir?'
'Nothing at all, Sir Charles – D – n me, if I mean anything by it – '
'You are called *Major,* you say, Sir – Do you bear the king's commission, Sir?'
'*I have* borne it, Sir, if I do not now.'
'That, and the house you are in, give you a title to civility. But, Sir, I cannot allow, that your marriage with the Lady in the next room gives you pretense to business with me. If you have, on any other account, pray let me know what it is?'
The man seemed at a loss what to say; but not from bashfulness. He looked about him, as if for his woman; set his teeth; bit his lip; and took snuff, with an air so like defiance, that, for fear I should not be able to forbear taking notice of it, I turned to the other.

. . . . . .

'But Mr. O-Hara, what are your pretentions?'
'Why look-ye, Sir Charles Grandison' (throwing open his coat, and sticking one hand in his side, the other thrown out with a flourish) 'Look ye, Sir,' repeated he – I found my choler rising, I was afraid of myself.
(vol. 2, 64–5)

The scene then culminates in a duel, easily won by the inimitable Grandison, and the ignominious expulsion of the loathsome threesome.

I have quoted this altercation so extensively since it illustrates very clearly that there is little in O-Hara's words or behaviour that is allowed to reach the stage of actual impudence: all he does is take snuff, open his coat, and begin sentences in which he gets interrupted by the overbearing Sir Charles. The 'impertinence' of the Irish officer is practically wholly of Grandison's own construction. It is a neatly symbolic example of how Irish stock characters tend to be the mere focusing points of English imputations: contorted looking-glasses for English expectations. And again, the result is a dilemma – as in Fielding's treatment of Fitzpatrick, the irresistable booby. Grandison, being the perfect specimen of a gentleman, cannot put up with Irish impertinence – but, on the other hand, Richardson's moral outlook certainly included a complete condemnation of Grandison's retaliatory measure: the duel. The perfect gentleman finds himself in a 'catch-22', and is accordingly only to be excused on the grounds of a quick temper getting the better of him, and being suitably contrite after his splenetic honour has been vindicated by a show of arms. The letter in which he relates the incident accordingly begins:

> I am very much dissatisfied with myself, my dear Dr. Bartlett. What pains have I taken, to conquer those sudden gusts of passion, to which, from my early youth, I have been subject, as you have often heard me confess! (vol. 2, 63)

Major O-Hara is afterwards reconciled (i.e. made to recognize Sir Charles's ineffable moral superiority) and leaves the action of the novel in a positive manner, in a scene of typically Richardsonesque sentiment and mawkishness.[21]

The mid-century amelioration

As far as stage practice is concerned, Irish officers (those untainted by the trait of fortune-hunting) are by far the most positive Irishmen to appear in the post-Farquhar English theatre; in two examples from the earlier eighteenth century, they are part of the usual British three- or foursome already encountered in *Henry V* and *The Welsh ambassador*. One of these plays, Charles Molloy's *The half-pay officers* (1720) even goes as far as to draw directly on Shakespeare's characters Fluellen and Macmorris. Many lines, speeches and incidents are culled from Shakespeare's play, mostly those of a comical nature. The English officer completing the British spectrum is captain Bellayr, and the three are boon companions. The implication of national solidarity is brought out when Bellayr says of his friends:

> they are honest brave Fellows; and tho' they can't make fine Speeches, they can break Heads: They are gallant before an Enemy, and so generous, they'll injure nothing, except good *English*. (p. 8)

In order to reach this positive stage, Macmorris had to be changed thoroughly – as Bartley observes, the author 'found it necessary to modernize Fluellen much less than Mackmorrice'.[22] Whatever negative hints were present in Shakespeare's original, are replaced here by the innocuous trappings of brogue and bull.

Another play with an Irish officer is Charles Shadwell's *The humours of the army* (1713) which is set in Portugal. The author, son of Thomas Shadwell, also had plays performed in Dublin, one of which deals with Irish history in a heroic manner and will be considered separately. *The humours of the army*, again, has representatives from all four British nations, loyally co-operating for the British cause. Brigadier Bloodmore, English, is Commander-in-Chief. There is a Scottish colonel, Hyland, and a Welsh major, Cadwallader. The Irish angle is, interestingly, represented by two men. One of them is major Outside, who is mainly characterized by a broad brogue; the other Irish major, called 'Young Fox' and described in the dramatis personae as 'a gay airy young fellow' speaks standard English. He provides the occasion for some satire on contemporary London life, since he has just returned from the capital and gives his fellow-officers an ironic account of the state of affairs there.

Shadwell goes to some length to emphasize the harmony between the two Irish officers, e.g. in a scene where Outside claims to have the same nationality and the same local background as Young Fox, concluding:

> by St. Patrick, he only speaks his vords one way, and I do speak them an oder vay, but we do mean de same ting.
> *Young Fox.* Exactly my dear Country-man. (p. 49)

Also, Young Fox at one stage affectionately adopts Outside's brogue which the latter takes in good humour:

> Out. (To Young Fox.) By my Shoul, my dear Major, I was very glad to see you,
> before I did hear you was come from *England.*
> Young Fox. (Mimicking of him) Arrah, my dear Country-man, I will be after kissing
> of you, for your Friendships. (p.52)

The ideal of overcoming national divisions is an undercurrent in the play. After
a scene where the Scotsman Hyland takes the position that Scottish blood is
thicker than British water, Bloodmore concludes with a conciliatory remark –
whilst turning this conciliation into a typically 'English' virtue!

> That's the Indiscretion of being National Abroad; the honest *Englishman* makes a
> Friendship with all Mankind, never supports the Villain of his own Country, and
> always stands by the honest Man, be he *Turk, Jew* or *Infidel.* (p. 13)

Plays in a military setting would remain an important sub-genre during the rest of
the century, and even in other plays a military character often played an important
part. Such plays, such characters, became the vehicle of increasingly anti-French
declarations of British military glory, courage, invincibility etc. The process took
place simultaneously to the decline of Stuart pretensions and the growing colonial
hostility with France. As is already hinted at in these earlier plays by Molloy and
Charles Shadwell, the Irish soldier becomes a whole-hearted British loyalist in this
development, and is accordingly treated in increasingly positive terms. The mirth
generated by his funny speech and expressions is no longer a redemptive
counterweight for his disconcerting alienness, but becomes a focus of benevolent,
if somewhat patronizing, interest – as can already be gathered from captain
Bellayr's remarks, in *The half-pay officers*, quoted on the previous page.

A decisive step in this direction is taken in Smollett's comedy *The reprisal*
(1757) which, though now overshadowed by the author's novels, was highly
successful in its day and often revived. Its patriotic fervour is already hinted at in
its subtitle, *The tars of Old England*, and leads to a rousing finale with, for a
chorus:

> While British oak beneath us rolls,
> And English courage fires our souls;
> To crown our toils, the fates decree
> The wealth and empire of the sea.[23]

The play is concerned with the escape of an English party who have been ruthlessly
and illegally captured by a French man o' war, commanded by its Stage-French
captain De Champignon. Two British (presumably Jacobite) officers serve on the
French ship, the Irish lieutenant Oclabber and the Scottish ensign Maclaymore. But
although their military and political loyalty is clearly anti-English, they disapprove
of De Champignon's perfidy and help the English prisoners, some of whom
Oclabber had previously met as tourists in Paris. In opposing De Champignon's
plans, Oclabber and Maclaymore become the English party's protectors, and
accordingly become proportionately more sympathetic as characters. Oclabber's

reminiscences of his Irish sweetheart can thus become a mixture of comic and sentimental elements; and it is this a-political, positive treatment of the Irishman that entails the one unquestionably positive national Irish trait, music: after reminiscing on 'my own honey, dear Sheelah O'Shannaghan, whom I left big with child in the county of Fermanaghan, grammachree' (p. 126), Oclabber relates how he

> composed a lamentation in the Irish tongue – and sung it to the tune of Drimmendoo; but a friend of mine, of the order of St. Francis, has made a relation of it into English, and it goes very well to the words of Elen-a-Roon. (p. 126)

The titles belong to two of the more famous Gaelic songs of the period, which must evidently have had some recognition value for the London audiences: *Eibhlín a rún* and *Droimeann donn dílis*, the latter being a Jacobite song. Smollett also referred to this 'Drimmendoo' as the typically Irish song in *Humphry Clinker*, and the air of 'Ellen a Roon' is used in an Irish adaptation of Gay's *The beggar's opera* set in Dublin, namely Charles Coffey's *The beggar's wedding* (1729, p. 63).

A dilemma lurks in the fact that this positive character Oclabber should be in the service of the enemy. It is part of his positive characterization that he should be brave (unlike the craven crew consisting of Frenchmen, p. 156) – but his valour is aimed against the play's own nationality. Thus, Oclabber addresses De Champignon at the approach of an English man o'war:

> Faith and troth! my dear, the contradiction is all over; you have nothing to do but to station your men; and as for Mr. Maclaymore and my own self, the English cannon may make our legs and arms play loggerhead in the air, honey, but we'll stand by you for the glory of France, in spite of the devil and all his works, gra.   (p. 154)

Maclaymore, too, defends the ship so bravely against the English attack that he is in danger of coming to blows with a close friend of the captive party, of whom one member anxiously says:

> O Lord! Mr. Oclabber, your ensign is playing the devil – hacking and hewing about him like a fury; for the love of God interpose; my master is come aboard, and if they should meet, there will be murder!

How is this dilemma of conflicting loyalties to be resolved? Smollett sidesteps the issue neatly by taking verbal refuge in a 'bull' of the Irish character, thus deflecting the potentially tragic problem; Oclabber answers light-heartedly:

> By my saoul! I know he has a regard for Mr. Heartly, and if he kills him, it will be in the way of friendship, honey; howsomever, if there's any mischief done, I'll go and prevent it. (p. 156)

Thus the two demi-Britons can preserve both their courage and their sympathy with the English audience. This is also expressed in the prisoners' gratitude, after the English have captured the ship:

Heartly (embracing Ocl. and Macl.) Gentlemen, I'm heartily glad of having an opportunity to return, in some measure, the civilities you have shown to this young lady. Mr. Lyon, I beg you'll order their swords to be restored; they were in no shape accessory to our grievances. (p. 157)

Smollett's own Scottish national pride (expressed at its most forceful in *Humphry Clinker*) and his Tory sympathies may in some way have contributed to this deliberate amelioration of non-English, pro-Stuart expatriates.

'Deliberate amelioration' also in social terms: Oclabber can unite traditional Gaelic characteristics with the undoubted quality of a gentleman – a combination that was unthinkable earlier. Social standing had presupposed Anglicization (at least under the penal laws, in religion and in political loyalty), and the recognizably Gaelic Stage Irishman was usually given the humbler employment of footman, servant, or, at best, fortune-hunter.

'Deliberate amelioration' may also be the key term for the treatment of the Irishman in the comedy of Thomas Sheridan – father of Richard Brinsley Sheridan, son of Swift's intimate friend. The Stage Irishman had, by the mid-eighteenth century, obviously become so stratified that *counter*-Stage Irishmen could be conceived of. The earliest example of such a conscious contradiction of traditional Stage Irish attributes is Thomas Sheridan's title hero in *The brave Irishman*, going by the style of Captain O'Blunder. The dating of this play is difficult. The version known to us was performed in England in early 1746 and first printed in 1754, largely from the actors' memories; the positive and deliberately non-standard treatment of O'Blunder would seem to tally with these dates. However, an earlier version of the play was acted while Sheridan was still at Trinity College, Dublin, in 1737. The title of this earlier version, *The honest Irishman*, likewise indicates a positive attitude to the play's hero. However, in the final reckoning it is impossible to know what and how much alteration took place between 1737 and 1754.

The brave Irishman is less about O'Blunder's Irishness in itself than about the reception it meets with in England. To be sure, O'Blunder is abundantly furnished with 'typically' Irish characteristics: a brogue, bulls, a shillelagh, a predilection for stealing kisses from handsome servant girls, a tendency to burst into song. By this time, the potato has also become a national marker; O'Blunder forces his counterpart, the insulting cowardly Frenchman (and of course the Irishman has an insulting cowardly Frenchman for a counterpart) to eat a potato (p. 24). This is, of course, an overt reminder of *Henry V*, where Fluellen forces Pistol to eat the national leek of Wales. O'Blunder is also made out to be most fond of his native Gaelic language, and eager to meet other Gaelic speakers (cf. p. 16).

All this Irish nationality is not in itself the substance of the play. Sheridan is concerned rather with the fortunes of the brave Irishman *in England*. English pre-expectations of what the Irish are like are no less remarkable than the characteristics vested in O'Blunder. His bride, Lucy, on hearing of his arrival, asks her servant girl:

I hear he's a strange animal of a brute. – Pray had he his wings on? I suppose they sav'd him his passage.

Betty. Oh ! Mem, you mistakes the Irishmen, I am told they are as gentle as doves to our sex, with as much politeness and sincerity as if born in our own country. (p. 4)

At this, Lucy is already half won over, for, in an aside, she confesses a little later: 'I long to see him; and Irishmen, I hear, are not so despicable; besides the captain may be misrepresented'.

It is the misrepresentation of the Irishman that is at the core of the play. O'Blunder, an equal mixture of naive honesty and irascible courage, is gazed at as a two-headed monster by the rabble, and is, in a practical joke, 'misrepresented' by the aptly-named rival Cheatwell, who hands him over as a madman to a pair of doctors whom in turn he represents to O'Blunder as innkeepers. Most of the fun in this farce centres around this mutual misapprehension between O'Blunder and the two physicians; but at least half the laughs are on the doctors who, in their excessive professionalism, are apt to see pathological symptoms in the slightest things. Indeed, as soon as the spell of misap- prehension is lifted, and O'Blunder becomes sensible of the real profession of his interlocutors, he settles the situation in no uncertain terms: by forcefully battling his way out of the consulting room. The question of imputed insanity sums up Sheridan's treatment of the confrontation of Irish and English nationality: the madness that the Englishman imputes to the Irishman, and that he sees confirmed in each national or personal peculiarity deviating from English pre-expectations, is in the end shown to lie in the misunderstanding *between* the parties rather than *within* either of the parties concerned.

The most explicit amelioration that is attempted in this farce centres around the rivalry of O'Blunder and Cheatwell for the hand of the rich heiress Lucy. In the conventions of the time, the Irish suitor must invariably be a fortune-hunter, wooing the lady from merely pecuniary motives. This convention is here neatly inverted: when it turns out that Lucy's father has gone bankrupt, all suitors drop their suit, implicitly admitting their base motives, with the exception of noble O'Blunder to whom money matters are of no consequence. A general reconciliation takes place, in which Cheatwell is relegated to a position of inferiority: he is married off to the servant girl and provided for with a farm on O'Blunder's estate. The play then concludes with a reassertion of Irish decency, now properly appreciated by the play's English characters.

> *Capt.* Well then, without compliment, I am glad I have made one poor man happy; and since we have made a double match, hey for Ireland, where we will live like Irish kings.
> *Lucy.* This generosity amazes me, and greatly prejudices me in the honesty and goodness of the Irish.
> *Capt.* Oagh my dear little charmer, I've another song, just *a propos*,
> Of all the husbands living, an Irishman's the best,
> With my fal, lal, &c.

No nation on the globe like him can stand the test.
With my fal, lal, &c.
The English they are drones as plainly you can see,
But we're all brisk and airy, and lively as a bee.
With my fal, lal, &c. (p. 28)

The positive Stage Irishman: Macklin, Cumberland

The very same vindication of Irish suitors, as being quite the opposite of fortune hunters, was undertaken by Charles Macklin who, like Sheridan, came from an Irish background. Macklin's comedy *Love à la mode* was performed at Drury Lane in late 1759, and is concerned with the rivalry of four suitors aspiring to the hand of witty, wealthy Charlotte. The four – another instance of a 'British foursome', albeit with a Jew substituted for the earlier Welshman – are the horsecrazed Squire Groom, the would-be wit Mordecai, the caustic proud Scotsman Sir Archibald MacSarcasm and an Irish army captain in Prussian service, Sir Callaghan O'Brallaghan, who, next to his Irish characteristics, also embodies those of the all too soldierly soldier. Like his colleague O'Blunder, O'Brallaghan's national characterization depends in part on the pre-expectations of other, British, characters. Charlotte and her guardian Sir Theodore discuss him in a dialogue of some interest:

> *Sir Theodore*: Well, well, notwithstanding your mirth, madam, I assure you he [O' Brallaghan] has gained the highest esteem in his profession. But what can you expect, my dear, from a soldier, a mere rough-hewn soldier, who, at the age of fifteen, would leave Ireland, his friends, and every other pursuit, to go a volunteer into the Prussian service . . . But he ever had, from a child, a kind of military madness.
> *Charlotte*: O, I am in love with his warlike humour – I think it highly entertaining.
> . . .
> One cannot possibly do without Sir Callaghan Brall – Bra-Brall. Pray, guardian, teach me to pronounce my lover's name.
> *Sir Theodore*: Thou art a mad creature! Well madam, I will indulge your wicked mirth. His name is Callaghan O'Brallaghan
> *Charlotte*: O shocking! Calligan O'Bralligan! – why, it is enough to choak one . . .
> *Sir Theodore*: You may laugh, madam but he is as proud of that name as any of your lovers are of their title. (pp. 46–7)

From the outset, the Irish character is placed between the opposite poles of ridicule and admiration, and the play's explicit intention is to vindicate O'Brallaghan. When Mordecai and Sir Archy try to provoke Sir Callaghan's militariness in as ridiculous a light as possible, their attempts are stymied by the Irishman's refusal to be funny. His serious rejoinder takes the form of patriotic praise of the British army in Quebec – an early instance of the mechanism by which Irish ridicule is replaced by Irish loyalty, and Irish loyalty is proportionate to English-French enmity. Such elevated and wholly commendable feelings cannot, of course, be mocked or ridiculed, and Charlotte concurs with sudden gravity:

> You are right, Sir Callaghan, his virtues [i.e. those of gen. Wolfe and of his soldiers]
> in that action – aye, and of those that planned it too – will be remembered by their
> country, while Britain or British gratitude has a being.

Here is no more room for petty anti-military or anti-Irish feelings: the two have
become linked with British national pride. A new and stronger emotion has
been conjured up that will not be laughed at with impunity. Such national
sentiments are essentially non-comical and must have functioned as a sort of
'show-stopper'. The only thing left for Sir Archy to do is to add that the High-
landers contributed their share to British glory in the Quebec campaign;
O'Brallaghan agrees, again to Charlotte's unexpected approval:

> *Sir Callaghan:* I dare say they were not idle, for they are tight fellows. Give me your
> hand, Sir Archy; I assure you your countrymen are good soldiers – aye, and so are
> ours too.
> *Charlotte:* Well, Sir Callaghan, I assure you, I am charmed with your heroism, and
> greatly obliged to you for your account. (p. 57)

Thus, the general expectation that an Irish presence on the stage must entail
farcical blunders and ridiculousness is disappointed – to the surprise of the
characters and, presumably, to the intended surprise of the audience. The other
prejudice (the Irishman must be after Charlotte's money) is likewise debunked: as
the (spurious) word is spread that a bankruptcy has eliminated Charlotte's wealth,
Groom, Mordecai and MacSarcasm all ignominiously withdraw their suit. Only
Sir Callaghan's intentions shine forth in all their honesty. The play's conclusion is a
pointed reference (delivered by the Irishman) at its own fictionality:

> The whole business is something like the catastrophe of a stage play; where knaves
> and fools are disappointed, and honest men rewarded. (p. 77)

Thus the didactic intent of the comedy finally asserts itself, and the comedy in
the end stands out primarily as a moral lesson on the need for honesty, on the
nature of prejudice overcome by honesty.

This same concern, and the same conflict between forthright manliness and the
hypocrisy of social appearances is worked out in another play by Macklin, with
the interesting title *The true-born Irishman*. The piece is set, and was initially
produced, in Dublin, where it obtained considerable success in 1761: an indication that its patriotically Irish sentiments had become successful with the theatre-
going public of Ireland. It failed, however, when staged in London in 1767. There,
it was presented explicitly as an attempt to correct the popular view of Irish characters as traditionally represented on the stage. This becomes apparent from the
prologue that was added for the occasion – a prologue which, being of considerable interest and not having been printed earlier, I quote here at some length:

> Hibernia's Sons from earliest days have been,
> The jest and Scandal of the Comic Scene;

For Dullness gave her Bards this modest Rule,
'To Irish Tones associate Knave and Fool
'Let these, and Nonsense deck'd with Bull and Brogue,
'Be native marks and means to Comic Vogue.'
Peculiar Case, that they alone should stand
Proscrib'd for Tones that mark a Native Land.
As if wise Nature, at her own Expense,
Had drop'd them here, devoid, of Truth, and Sense.
A lovely Bard this partial Law reviews,
When social Justice fires his Feeble Muse.
A homebred Character he vows to draw
In fair defiance of this Gothic Law.
Milesian sprung, confess'd in every part
Hibernia's Seal impress'd on Tongue, and Heart.
Nay more, our Bard still rises in Offence,
And dares give Irish Tones a sterling Sense.
But what is stranger still, indeed a wonder,
He hopes to make him please without a Blunder.
A Prodigy, you'll own, on Britain's Stage,
And may excite the Hypercritics Rage!
To him he weds a Belle with follies fraught
By Nature good, by Fashion almost naught.
Some months refin'd in Londons polish'd School
Return'd – just ripe for wholesome ridicule.
    . . .
In her he shows, what Taste and Fashion make us
When common Sense and Decency forsake us.
This is his Plan, on this you must decide,
He's on his Country fairly to be tried.[24]

The moralistic intent is then elaborated on (the play is in 'Virtue's Cause'). Macklin's self-conscious deviation from traditional Stage Irish characterizations is stated programmatically, as is his contrast between instinctive, native honesty and the acquired fripperies of fashion. This last polarization is embodied in the play's two central characters, Mr. O'Dogherty and his wife. Mrs. O'Dogherty has been in London to see the coronation of George III, and has come back full of anglicized ideals. But whereas earlier writers would represent the anglicization of the Irish as a process of cultivation, the tendency here is to regard it as a fall from grace. Mrs. O'Dogherty has not become cultured, but snobbish, frivolous and pedantic. The old polarity between Ireland and England as equating one between barbarism vs. cultured humanity is reinterpreted as one of natural, artless forthrightness vs. fashionable affectation. The early stirrings of a Rousseauesque elevation of the primitive are perhaps not far off, and the play certainly endorses plain middle-class honesty against aristocratic pretence.

Macklin's characteristic inversion of the values concerning Stage Irish typology entails a few interesting 'inverted' Stage Irish characteristics for the Anglicized Mrs. O'Dogherty. Whereas the main trait of the Stage Irishman was his brogue,

Mrs. O'Dogherty's deliberate suppression of her native accent here becomes, among the other Irish characters, a similar type of deviant speech peculiarity in its own right. The husband puts it as follows:

> then such a phrenzy of admiration for every thing in England – and, among the rest of her madness, she has brought over a new language with her.
> *Counsellor.* What do you mean by a new language?
> *O'Dogh.* Why a new kind of London English, that's no more like our Irish English, than a coxcomb's fine gilded chariot like a Glassmanogue noddy – (p. 85)

Likewise, Mr. O'Dogherty later exhorts his wife:

> And as to yourself, my dear Nancy, I hope I shall never have any more of your London English; none of your this here's, your that there's, your winegars, your weals, your vindors, your toastesses, and your stone postesses; but let me have our good, plain, old Irish English, which I insist is better than all the English English that ever coquets and coxcombs brought into the land. (p. 111)

To cap this foolish denial of her Irish nationality, Mrs. O'Dogherty even changes her name. She drops the Irish patronymic 'O' and calls herself (and her suffering husband) 'Diggerty'. The husband does not much like the change from 'plain, modest, good-natured, domestic, obedient Irish Mrs. O'Dogherty' to 'the travelled, rampant, high-lifed, prancing English Mrs. Diggerty': 'Ay, ridiculous indeed! to change her name – was there ever such impertinence?' (p. 85). However, he is quick to confront her snobbish prattle with blunt facts – to be met only by a scandalous lack of uxorial obedience:

> *Mrs. D.* Mr. Diggerty, what do you think? Hav'n't the dogs of this here country the brogue?
> *O'D.* Indeed and that they have, my dear, and the cows too, and the sheep, and the bullocks, and that is as strong as ever your own mother had it, who was an O'Gallagher.
> *Mrs. D.* Oh!
> *O'D.* Not two of whose ancestors could ever speak three words of English to be understood.
> *Mrs. D.* You are a strange rude man, Mr. Diggerty, to tell me of my mother's family – you know I always despised my mother's family – I hate the very name of Gallagher, and all the old Irish whatever.
> *Counsellor.* The present company excepted, sister – your husband, you know –
> *Mrs. D.* O, I never think of him.
> *Counsellor.* Ha, that's polite indeed. (pp. 95–6)

Mrs. Diggerty's eventual repentance correspondingly involves a return to wifely submission, to her husband's name and nationality.

> *O'Dogh.* Ogh, that 's right, Nancy – O'Dogherty for ever – O'Dogherty ! – there's a sound for you – why they have not such name in all England as O'Dogherty – nor as any of our fine sounding Milesian names – what are your Jones and your

Stones, your Rice and your Price, your Heads and your Foots, and Hands, and your Wills, and Hills and Mills, and Sands, and a parcel of little pimping names that a man would not pick out of the street, compared to the O'Donovans, O'Callaghans, O'Sullivans, O'Brallaghans, O'Shaghnesses, O'Flahertys, O'Gallaghers, and O'Doghertys – Ogh, they have courage in the very sound of them, for they come out of the mouth like a storm; and are as old and as stout as the oak at the bottom of the bog of Allen, which was there before the flood – and though they have been dispossessed by upstarts and foreigners, buddoughs and sassenoughs, yet I hope they will flourish in the Island of Saints, while grass grows or water runs. (pp. 111–12)

The importance attached to names enumerated and contrasted in this manner intriguingly recalls a long-standing similar practice in Gaelic poetry, of opposing English and Irish nationality by a long enumeration of 'representative' family names (see below p. 245). The scornful reference to dispossession by upstarts and foreigners, buddoughs (*bódach,* boor) and sassenoughs (*Sasanach,* Englishman) belongs also in the same poetic genre. The emphasis on names is all the more remarkable since Macklin himself was guilty of Mrs. Diggerty's sin: he had changed his original Gaelic name, MacLaughlin, to Macklin so as not to hamper his London stage career by the type of name praised so highly by Mr. O'Dogherty, but all too unpronounceable for an English audience. ('Sir Callaghan Brall- Bra- Brall – '). It is as if Macklin is making up for his own fickleness in the creation of a True Born Irishman, Mr. O'Dogherty – *not,* no, never, to be called Diggerty.

Another remarkable aspect of this play is that Mr. O'Dogherty's national pride is linked to an early Patriot-style political stance: a combination of Patriot attitudes (i.e. a denunciation of Tory-Whig factionism, a call for 'virtue' in public affairs and an advocation of the political liberties and responsibilities of the citizen) and national pride was then by no means as self-evident as the later meaning of the term 'patriotism' would lead one to think.[25] O'Dogherty's Patriot hackles are raised by Mrs. Diggerty's desire to have her husband created a peer. Mr. O'Dogherty scorns the idea, for the usual way to obtain such a government favour is to sell one's political leverage to the Crown interest. Such corrupt (and therefore anti-Patriot) practice is denounced roundly:

O'Dogherty. Why, you must know, we are to have an election shortly for the county that I live in, which young Lord Turnabout wants to carry for one of his own gang; and as the election in a great measure depends upon my interest, the young fox, knowing the conceit and vanity of my wife, has taken her by her favourite foible, and tickled it up, by telling her that if I direct my interest properly, it would not be difficult to procure me a title . . . she would have me desert my friends, and sell myself, my honour, and my country, as several others have done before me, merely for a title, only that she may take place of a parcel of foolish idle women, and sink the ancient name of Dogherty in the upstart title of Lady Thingum, my Lady Fiddle Faddle, or some such ridiculous nonsense.

. . . When I was there before [i.e. in parliament] I was stigmatised as a singular blockhead, an impracticable fellow, only because I would not consent to sit like an image, and when the master of the puppets pulled the string of my jaw on one side, to say aye, and on t'other side, to say no, and to leap over a stick backwards and forwards, just as the faction of party and jobbers, and leaders, and political adventurers directed – ah, brother, brother, I have done with them all – O, I have done with them all. (p. 86)

The gouty, irritable O'Dogherty follows up this condemnation with equally caustic remarks concerning the fickleness of 'patriots' who betray their political idealism. The denunciation of title-hunting and political corruption thus avoids a party-political slant; instead, it is seen in the polarity of English decadence vs. Irish honesty. For when Mrs. Diggerty throws a tantrum at her husband's stubborn refusal of peerage aspirations, the dialogue takes the following turn:

> Mrs. D. . . . O fie, fie, fie – but you are true Irish to the very bone of you.
> O'D. Indeed I am, and to the marrow within the bone too; and what is more, I hope I shall never be otherwise.
>
> . . . . .
>
> O my dear, I tell you again and again, that the English can never be precedent to us. They, by their genius and constitution, must always run mad about something or other. . . . But, my dear, they can afford to run mad after such nonsense . . . stay till we are as rich as they are, and then we may be allowed to run mad after absurdities as well as they. (pp. 101–2)

O'Dogherty's own political ideals can, notwithstanding his denunciation of dishonest patriots, be placed in a patriot-libertarian tradition:

> take this judgment from me then, and remember that an honest quiet country gentleman who out of policy and humanity establishes manufactories, or that contrives employment for the idle and the industrious, or that makes but a blade of corn grow where there was none before, is of more use to this poor country than all the courtiers, and patriots, and politicians, and prodigals that are unhanged – (p. 87)

This sentiment is highly reminiscent of the aims and ideals of anti-partisan, early Patriot organizations such as the Dublin Society, and echoes nearly verbatim the great patron-saint of Irish Patriot thought, Swift, who had described, in *Gulliver's Travels,* the opinion of the wise king of Brobdingnag,

> that whoever could make two Ears of Corn, or two Blades of Grass to grow upon a Spot of Ground, where only one grew before; would deserve better of Mankind, and do more essential Service to his Country, than the whole Race of Politicians put together.[26]

The true-born Irishman also contains a denunciation of absenteeism, middle-manship and extortionate farm rents – even though it is spoken by the play's most odious character, the English nobleman Mushroom; O'Dogherty grumpily concurs: 'Faith, count, there's many a true word spoken in jest' (p. 91).

The basic mechanism of the play is an inversion of the traditional English-Irish stereotypes under a Patriot Irish aspect. An example *in nuce* of this mechanism is given when O'Dogherty denounces Mushroom's adulterous intentions, as well as British mercantilist restrictions on the Irish economy, by playing on the traditional image of Irish fortune-hunting:

> an impudent rascal! make a cuckold of an Irishman – What, take our own trade out of our hands – and a branch of business we value ourselves so much upon too – why, sure that and the linen manufacture are the only free trade we have – (p. 113)

In Macklin's play, a character's Irishness becomes directly commensurate to his likeability. Irishness is the gauge of a character's 'goodness' – an acute, and obviously partly deliberate, change from the completely opposite values adhering to Irish nationality in the plays of the late seventeenth century, prepared though it was by earlier attempts at a cautious amelioration of the Stage Irishman as performed in Smollett's and Thomas Sheridan's plays. After Macklin, one can see the Stage Irishman undergo a sentimentalization, a revaluation, which in fact created a new type based on the inverted or re-valued typology of the older Stage Irishman. This development of what may be called the *counter*-Stage Irishman will be discussed under various headings. First the influential character of Major Dennis O'Flaherty, who appeared in George Cumberland's sentimental comedies *The West Indian* and *The natural son,* will be considered, and the revaluation of the brogue; then, the treatment of Irish characters as loyal friends to England and its imperial interests; finally, the general investment of noble motives and sentiments in Irish characters.

As from the 1760s, virtually all Irish characters on the British stage are sympathetically characterized, and their Irishness seems to be meant to contribute to their positive nature. Although Macklin's Irish-Patriot tendencies were not fully adopted in London (we have already seen that the play failed there after having been successful in Dublin), his influence can be registered in a number of later plays – understandably so, since his stature was, for a while, second only to Garrick himself. Generally, English audiences' feelings towards Stage Irishmen seem to have become more sympathetic; Churchill, for instance, in his *Rosciad,* addressed the popular Irish actor Moody in 1761 in lines that strongly resemble the sentiments expressed by Macklin's prologue to the London version of *The true-born Irishman:*

> Long, from a nation ever hardly us'd,
> At random censur'd, wantonly abus'd,
> Have BRITONS drawn their sport, with partial view
> Form'd gen'ral notions from the rascal few;
> Condemn'd a people, as for vices known,
> Which, from their country banish'd, seek our own.
> At length, howe'er, the slavish chain is broke,

And Sense awaken'd, scorns her ancient yoke:
Taught by thee, MOODY, we now learn to raise
Mirth from their foibles; from their virtues, praise.[27]

This development could even reach the point where serious exception was taken
to a negative representation of Irish characters: hisses and disturbances were
caused, for instance, by George Colman's *The Oxonians in town* of 1769[28] and R. B.
Sheridan's *The rivals* of 1775. A good many playwrights followed Macklin's example in writing deliberately non-traditional Irish parts; most important among
these was Richard Cumberland, who, in Major Dennis O'Flaherty, created one of
the most successful Irish characters since Howard's 'Teg' – a star role for such
famous actors of Irish parts as Moody and Owenson. O'Flaherty first appeared in
Cumberland's *The West Indian* where the prologue introduced him as follows:

Another hero your excuse implores,
Sent by your sister kingdom to your shores
Doom'd by Religion's too severe command,
To fight for bread against his native land.
A brave, unthinking, animated rogue,
With here and there a touch upon the brogue.
Laugh, but despise him not, for on his lip
His errors lie; his heart can never trip. (p. iii)

Elsewhere, Cumberland explicitly states that his intention was to depart from
the standard Stage Irishman, believing

this was an opportunity for some originality, and an opportunity for shewing at
least my good will to mankind, if I introduced the characters of persons, who had
been usually exhibited on the stage, as the butts for ridicule and abuse, and
endeavoured to present them in such lights, as might tend to reconcile the world
to them, and them to the world.[29]

It is obvious, however, that in this departure Cumberland already follows a new
anti-tradition instigated by characters like Smollett's Oclabber and Macklin's
O'Brallaghan. It is no surprise to find that contemporaries also noticed the
parallel, which they interpreted as the result of direct borrowing on Cumberland's
part: 'this part was no invention of the author; Sir Callachan O'Brallachan is the
model from which he took the Irish Major' (p. 176). The similarities seem rather
to result, however, from the common tradition against which both O'Flaherty and
O'Brallaghan were to pose an alternative. Thus, Cumberland conceives of
O'Flaherty in the following terms:

I put him into the Austrian service, and exhibited him in the livery of a foreign
master, to impress upon the audience the melancholy and impolitic alternative, to
which his religious disqualification had reduced a gallant and a loyal subject of his
natural king: I gave him courage, for it belongs to his nation; I endowed him with
honour, for it belongs to his profession, and I made him proud, jealous,

susceptible, for such the exiled veteran will be, who lives by the earnings of his sword, and is not allowed to draw it in the service of that country which gave him birth, and which of course he was bound to defend: for his phraseology I had the glossary ready at my hand. (p. 174)

A number of characteristics of the old Stage Irishman can still be observed in O'Flaherty – albeit presented under a different aspect. Thus, the echoes of Irish fortune-hunting are still present in the major's financially-motivated wooing of rich lady Rusport. All this is, however, forgotten when O'Flaherty's honesty is outraged by lady Rusport's stinginess towards young Dudley:

> O'Fla. You refused him!
> L. Rus. Most undoubtedly.
> O'Fla. You sent him nothing!
> L. Rus. Not a shilling.
> O'Fla. Good morning to you – Your servant – (*going*)
> L. Rus. Hey-day! what ails the man? where are you going?
> O'Fla. Out of your house, before the roof falls on my head – to poor Dudley, to share the little modicum that thirty years hard service has left me; I wish it was more, for his sake.
> L. Rus. Very well, Sir; take your course; I sha'n't attempt to stop you; I shall survive it; it will not break my heart if I never see you more.
> O'Fla. Break your heart! No, o' my conscience will it not – You preach, and you pray, and you turn up your eyes, and all the while you're as hardhearted as an hyena – (p. 52)

– What is more, this bedrock of honourable honesty is explicitly presented as a *national* characteristic:

> An honest man! look at me, friend, I am a soldier, this is not the livery of a knave; I am an Irishman, honey, mine is not the country of dishonour. (p. 97)

Another traditional stage Irishism to be retained is that of the brogue – which includes, as we have seen, a propensity to verbal blunders. This trait, too, is presented under a more positive aspect: as the result of an honest, eager heart thwarted by a somewhat awkward tongue. In Cumberland's own words:

> When his imagination is warmed, and his ideas rush upon him in a cluster, 'tis then the Irishman will sometimes blunder; his fancy having supplied more words than his tongue can well dispose of, it will occasionally trip. But the imitation [on the stage] must be delicately conducted; his meaning is clear, he conceives rightly, though in delivery he is confused; and the art, as I conceive it, of finding language for the Irish character on the stage consists not in making him foolish, vulgar or absurd, but on the contrary, whilst you furnish him with expressions, that excite laughter, you must graft upon them sentiments, that deserve applause. (p. 175)

Cumberland's characters agree with their author; witness, for instance, an exchange like this:

Dudley. . . . now, major, if you are the generous man I take you for, grant me one favour.

O'Fla. Faith will I, and not think much of my generosity neither; for, though it may not be in my power to do the favour you ask, it can never be in my heart to refuse it.

Dud. Cou'd this man's tongue do justice to his thoughts, how eloquent would he be! *(aside)* (pp. 91–2)

To sum up, Major O'Flaherty presents an adaptation of, rather than a change from, the traditional Stage Irishman. The most important new aspect is that all his 'national' peculiarities are presented as positive, likeable traits.

Likeable O'Flaherty was revived for a later, equally sentimental comedy by the same author: *The natural son* (1784). Here as in the earlier play it is he who effects the happy end; again he is presented as an amorous man; again, the lurking charge of fortune-hunting is nipped in the bud: 'I prize the friendship of the fair sex too well to raise money upon them' (p. 38). O'Flaherty's gallantry becomes positively cloying, as in the scene where he claims a kiss due to him by a wager:

> May the blessing of blessings light upon your generous heart! *(Salutes her respectfully.)* May the cheek which I have touched be unstained with a tear! And may your lips, which I had not the boldness to approach, be the sacred treasure of your husband! Mrs. Phoebe Latimer, I hope I shall not offend if I offer at the same presumption. – Be confident, dear madam, that you have not in the world a more faithful humble servant than myself! *(aside to her).* (p. 81)

Another remarkable parallel between the two plays is the fact that O'Flaherty's reward at the end of both consists of the wherewithal to retire to his beloved fatherland. When Young Dudley (in *The West Indian*) offers O'Flaherty 'an asylum in the bosom of your country', the sturdy major reacts endearingly:

> And upon my soul, my dear, 'tis high time I was there; for 'tis now thirty long years since I sat foot in my native country – and by the power of St. Patrick I swear I think it's worth all the rest of the world put together. (p. 116)

Even more endearingly, in the second play:

> . . . with a rood of potatoes in my front, and an acre of bog at my back, I can sit chirping like an old cricket in my chimney-corner, and ruminate on the occurrences of this happy day. (p. 86)

– one wonders what went wrong the first time. Such a reduplication (especially given its intertextual incongruity) makes it appear as if the happiest end involves a certain dismissal or segregation: here as in other plays (we have encountered the example of Thomas Sheridan's *The brave Irishman*) the Irish character, no matter how sympathetic, obligingly leaves England and goes back where he belongs.

'Sentiments that deserve applause':
Irish characters and English chauvinism

The most interesting aspect of the idealized Stage Irishman is implied in the positive approach to the brogue and to the bull. Whereas these were mere instances of Irish ridiculousness earlier on, they are now vindicated by the sterling uprightness (or, in the vocabulary of the time, 'artlessness') that they convey. We have seen Macklin's attack on Mrs. Diggerty, and Cumberland's pro-brogue feeling. Other instances become numerous, as, for instance, in Isaac Jackman's comic opera *The Milesian,* whose Captain Cornelius O'Gollagher is described in the following terms:

> Certainly an indifferent orator, and yet his expressions come so truly from the heart that he makes his auditors feel, altho' they smile at him. (p. 25)

There is a strong echo from *Love à la mode* here, by the way, in that the Irishman's tongue-twisting name is the cause of some initial mirth (as was Sir Callaghan O'Brallaghan's) overcome by his military dignity.

> *Mr. Belfield.* I long to see this worthy Hibernian; your account of him has charmed me.
> *George.* Indeed, Sir, he is a most deserving officer, and if any thing exceeds his conduct and resolution, it is his humanity; but there is one thing I must particularly mention to you, we must all take care to pronounce his name properly;   I never saw him out of humour but once, and that was when a gentleman call'd him Gallager; you must endeavour to pronounce it as they do in Ireland – Gallagher.
> *Belfield.* It's a very difficult name, but no matter, I will call him Captain, and that will answer the purpose as well. (Enter *Richard.*)
> *Richard.* Sir, there is one captain Gol-Gollgager below stairs. (p. 9)

Thus the captain's status as a British officer overrides the impossibility of pronouncing his name properly. His service under the British flag is one additional advantage on earlier Irish officers like Oclabber, O'Brallaghan and O'Flaherty, who served abroad.

Again, W.C. Oulton's farce *Botheration* (1798) ends with the trusty Irish servant pointing out that '[his] tongue may blunder, but [his] heart ne'er can' (p. 46). Playwrights express sympathy for the brogue also through the mouths of their English characters. In Charles Dibdin's sentimental *opéra comique, Harvest home* (1787), two farm labourers appreciatively discuss the voice of Unah, an Irish girl:

> *Goody* . . . Lord, lord, how I do love to hear her chaunt her wild Irish notes! and then her comical brogue –
> *Muzzy* . . . I like her Lango-lee's and her Gramacree's, and her Lilly Lilly Loo's as well as thee dost.[30]

And fifteen years after the *True-born Irishman*, Mrs. Diggerty's foible is balanced out in the national pride that Irish-born lady Fallal takes in her brogue, in Richard Griffith's *Variety* (1782):

> What's that you're saying, Sir Frederick? Soften off a little of my brogue – Then indeed you may spare yourself the trouble . . . for I would not part with anything I brought from my own dear country upon any account whatever; and I'd have you to know, that I think my brogue, as you call it, the prettiest feather in my cap; because it tells every body, without their asking, that I am an Irish woman; and I assure you, I am prouder of that title, than I am of being called my lady Fallal. For I don't believe there's a Fallal to be found in all Ireland, except myself, and I'm out of it. (p. 18)

A number of elements in the new treatment of the Stage Irishman are closely connected with this changed attitude to the brogue. One of them is that a larger amount of national self-esteem, national pride, is benevolently accorded to Irish characters (as in the case of lady Fallal), another is that the bull, inevitable concomitant of the brogue, changes its nature. Whereas the brogue-as-a-laughable-deviation-from-standard-English was the medium for stupid blunders, the brogue-as-an-endearing-peculiarity-of-artless-people can become the vehicle for what Cumberland called 'sentiments, that deserve applause' – in other words, claptrap: clumsily phrased statements of clearsightedness, loyalty, pathos or even wit. We have already seen how Captain O'Brallaghan and Major O'Flaherty play to the gallery in flights of gallant sentiment, and I shall give more examples of a similar nature. They are especially remarkable in their quality of 'playing to the gallery' – that is: leaving the self-confined universe of fiction created and enacted on the stage and, in an interruption of action and plot development, turning directly to the audience. A clear example is the aforementioned servant in Oulton's *Botheration*, whose concluding lines to the play (in a type of epilogue) mark the end of the plot/fiction and the return to everyday reality where the stage is just a stage. The character steps back and the actor re-emerges: the servant of play characters becomes the servant of the theatre-going public:

> And Thady O'Blarney's ambition shall be, to serve faithfully and honestly those kind Masters and Mistresses before whom he has now the honour to stand.
> They will, he hopes, take pleasure in their man,
> Whose tongue may blunder, but whose heart ne'er can. (p. 46)

This is true to Thady O'Blarney's function throughout the play. He has previously played up to the public in a patriotic toast ('the two Sisters, England and Ireland, joined in a body, with Majesty for the Head and our brave Tars and Soldiers for the arms!', pp. 30–1) and by exhorting his mistress to pray, not for her pet animals, but rather for 'Prosperity to our Country, Confusion to our Enemies, and Long life to the King!' (p. 7). He also performs an equally patriotic, show-stopping song which has not the slightest function in the play's action; it ends:

> Oh, the devil burn them all that would the dear sweet sisters, England and
>   Ireland, sever!
> And may we, great and small, both one and all, sing 'God save the King,' and
>   'Rule, Britannia,' for ever!
> And may Old England, as before, for ever 'Rule the Main,'
> And teach invaders, should they come, their rafts are all in vain.
> Her loyal sons as Volunteers shall joyfully attend.
> For who would not a soldier be, his country to defend? (p. 28)

It is obvious that such sentiments must redound to Thady's popularity with the
London public of the year 1798. Indeed it had almost become *de rigueur* to have
Irishmen proclaim their affinity to England; the audiences obviously loved to
hear English-Irish concord asserted in a brogue.

A typical bull aiming at applause rather than laughter is one made by the
clerk Connolly, in Hugh Kelly's *School for wives* (1774):

> An Englishman's very lodging, ay, and an Irishman's too, I hope, is his castle; – an
> Irishman is an Englishman all the world over. (p. 107)

But, as in the case of Messrs. O'Brallaghan and O'Flaherty, it is mainly those of
the military profession who are most given to protestations of Great-British
loyalty. Thus, Captain Mullinahack, in O'Keeffe's *The world in a village* (1793):

> Madam, let me he blown into chops and griskins from the mouth of a cannon,
> when I turn my face as an enemy against George my belov'd King, and Ireland my
> honour'd country! (pp. 61–2)

The old ploy of having a 'British threesome' is often combined with all this
national fervour. F. Pilon's *The siege of Gibraltar* (1780), a propagandistic national
piece full of martial valour and love of the fatherland, has an Irish and a Scottish
sergeant in the besieged garrison: boisterous O'Bradley and prudent, upright
Trumbull. The Quebec campaign, which occasioned some patriotic dialogue in
Love à la mode, is the subject of George Cockings' *Conquest of Canada,* in suitably
heroic blank verse with a liberal dressing of exclamation marks and lofty sentiments on the valour of Great Britain and its army. Here, too, Scotsmen and
Irishmen complement the English soldiery; one of the Irishmen is called Peyton
and is as good as English. When chasing Indians in the French service, he can,
for instance, say:

> They ne'er could face th' uplifted glitt'ring Steel,
> Nor stand the light'ning of an *English* eye. (p. 46)

James Cobb's comic opera *Ramah Droog* (1800) is set in the fort of a rebelling
Indian rajah, where an Irish sergeant has introduced himself disguised as a
physician. When he meets the Rajah, the following exchange takes place:

> *R.* . . . You are an Englishman, I think?
> *Lif.* I am an Irishman, which is the same thing.
> *R.* The same thing! How is that?
> *L* An Irishman is an Englishman with another name. Why now, for instance, there
> is my brother Tady; his name is Tady, and I am Barney; my name is Barney; but
> then our interests are the same; and we are like my two arms, when one needs
> defence, the other naturally comes to his assistance. (p. 46)

Sergeant O'Liffey's sop to English national feelings is rewarded when the author
has him characterized by his wife in the following way:

> Sir, I have the honor to be a serjeant's lady – Nay, more, he is a serjeant of
> grenadiers, and an Irishman – Need I add, that he is a man of courage? (p. 6)

Again, in J.S. Dodd's *Gallic gratitude* (1779), set in the Maledives, an upright
sailor, boatswain Derby O'Rudder, stresses English–Irish concord – with just the
barest hint of sarcasm:

> O yes, we do belong to England sure enough; we are sisters – we send her our
> beef, and our pork, and our linen, and our soldiers and sailors; and she sends us
> Bishops, and Deans, and Judges – so there we are even, you know. (p. 27)

In J.C. Cross's *British fortitude,* a Captain O'Leary concludes his gallant efforts
with the rousing cry 'So huzza, my honey, for true Liberty and Old England' (p.
30), and in William Pearce's *Netley Abbey,* Oakland and his Irish music/ dancing
master McScrape discuss the glory of the British fleet as follows:

> *Oakland.* Aye, aye, our true security is our fleet: and when an Englishman resorts
> to his ships, 'tis like putting on his armour.
> . . . . .
> Indeed it may be said, England is itself, a sort of man of war – a three decker.
> *McScrape.* . . . And stop – Ireland is a sort of a stout frigate, cruizing by her side!
> *Oakland.* You are right; so she is. (p. 5)

An interesting example of how such patriotic asides and audience-cheerers on
Irish loyalty to England can be worked into the fabric of a play's plot is given by
Joseph Holman's comic opera *What a blunder!* (1800), which describes the
adventures of two Britons, the Englishman Dashington and the Irishman Sir
Sturdy O'Tremor, in Spain. The main (and quite successful) point of fun in the
Irish character is the fact that herculean Sir Sturdy is a hypochondriac and
believes himself to be in a terminal decline.

The Spanish background is presented with all its traditional attributes of
arrogant indigents, prison-like convents, perfidious friars and the threat of the
Inquisition. Against this overwhelmingly non-British exoticism, the differences
between English and Irish nationality dwindle into insignificance, and are
presented from a Spanish point of view, as Lopez explains to Diego:

> Mark me – You are of the kingdom of Valencia, I of Castille – yet we are both
> Spaniards. – So one of these strangers is of England, the other of Ireland; which
> though different islands, yet the natives of both own one country – one king – and
> (this in your ear, Diego) will, with one heart, defend their country and king
> against all the rest of the world.

And in the same breath, the alienness of Spain is further contrasted with
English-Irish concord, as Lopez continues:

> – Here come two miserable-looking Hidalgos – fellows, that live in dirt and
> poverty, from the fear of debasing their noble descent, by honestly earning a whole
> coat and a good meal. (s.d.) Two Hidalgos enter with great stateliness, and the
> appearance of extreme poverty. (p. 3)

One may well ask why one Spaniard should have to explain to another Spaniard
what a 'Hidalgo' is. The point is, of course, that Lopez is really addressing an
English audience over Diego's shoulder: for all his 'Spanishness', he is really the
mouthpiece for a narrowly English attitude. In giving what pretends to be a
'Spanish' outlook on Irish-English solidarity, Lopez is catering to the audience's
national complacency. To hear one's own opinions repeated from a completely
different standpoint must flatter one's claims to be objectively correct in one's
assumptions; it is in this way that all these remarks 'aimed at the gallery'
function: whether spoken by an 'Irish' or by a 'Spanish' character, they all repeat
from a non-English point of view the gallery's own, English, political ideals, thus
making it seem as if these ideals are current also in a non-English context, and
are not dependent on their Englishness. The audience is to be gratified with the
pretence that all the world thinks as they do.

It can be concluded from this, that the emotion catered for by this frequent
stratagem is not necessarily a sympathy for Ireland, but rather the need to feel
that Ireland is sympathetic to oneself. English audiences, in the aggressively
patriotic decades surrounding American independence and the growing
conflicts with France, obviously wanted to feel that the Irish would cleave to
them – and this need was catered for by the London stage at least. Whatever
positive characterization stage Irish characters would receive, was really a trade-
off against this Anglocentric imputation of loyalty, aimed, simultaneously, at
giving the protestations of that loyalty the additional credit of being spoken by a
'nice' character.

Holman's way of placing an Irish character in a context even more exotic for
an English audience is not new: Spanish settings had been used by Thomas
Shadwell and Mrs. Centlivre, and Dekker's Bryan had been in Italian service.
What is new, however, is the fact that this confrontation of the Irishman with
'real' foreigners is now used to show how little he, after all, differs from
Englishmen .

Similarly, John O'Keeffe's comic opera *Fontainbleau* (1790) features an Irish
innkeeper in France, who lures English tourists to her establishment (called 'The

British lion' or elsewhere 'The Lion of England') by serving roast beef and other English fare, and trumping up the Englishness (or, at least, non-Frenchness) of her Irish birth:

> *Sir John:* So this is your house, eh! And you are English?
> *Mrs. Casey:* English! that's what I am. I was born in Dublin. (p. 11)

Simultaneous with, and proportional to, the process by which the Irishman is given a more English and pro-English character, his traditional fellow-foreigner, the Stage Frenchman, becomes more negative. This is most strongly noticeable in those plays referring to Anglo-French colonial and political enmity, e.g. Cockings' *The conquest of Canada,* Cross's *British fortitude,* with its revealing double subtitle *and Hibernian friendship; or, an escape from France,* or Pearce's *Netley Abbey.* Dodd's *Gallic gratitude, or, the Frenchman in India* contrasts the loyalty of boatswain O'Rudder with the treachery of the French valet La Bronze, and is introduced by a prologue, spoken by 'Britannia', which begins:

> France, from my first existence, well I know,
> Hath ever been my most invet'rate foe.

The piece's main political drift is an attack on the employment of French servants by English masters. Derby O'Rudder can at one point burst out:

> Your faithful servant, d'ye call him! you might expect faithfulness from an Irishman, or an Englishman, or a Scotchman, and not be disappointed neither: but, you might put all the fidelity of a Frenchman into a ballast basket, and it wou'd not sink it. (pp. 23–4)

He is in this respect backed by 'Britannia' herself, who puts it more loftily in the prologue:

> Hence French quacks, tutors, cooks, and valets came
> To enervate those brave hearts she ne'er could tame.
> To spy our motions, and the news convey
> To gain our confidence, and then betray.
> Thinking th'occasion apt, once more she dares
> To interfere in our domestic wars;
> Widens the breach in this unhappy broil,
> And hopes to share, of our distress the spoil. (unpaged)

And the play's hero, Sir Thomas, in the end regrets:

> There were honest men enough of my own country who I might have taken, and not have employ'd a subject of our natural enemies. And I hope, from my example, Gentlemen will see the folly of giving employment to Frenchmen, in preference to our more honest, though less servile, countrymen. (p. 34)

Thomas Hurlstone's comic opera *Just in time* (1792) puts more anti-French sentiment in the mouth of an Irish servant (in this case, Melville's trusted Barney O'Liffy) who, in return, is endowed with 'ingenuity and fidelity' (p. 2), as well as a diverting sense of (presumably brogue-ridden) rhetoric:

> Notwithstanding the many hair-breadth scrapes that I have experienced in your honor's service, and as the good-looking stars have destined that I should dedicate the remainder of my unbroken bones to your generosity, my name-sake the Liffey, shall run backwards before I'll cease to push forwards to assist you. (p. 5)

True to his kidney, O'Liffy has the lowest of opinions of the valet Le Frizz, a Francophone Swiss: 'I never heard such a howling as the outlandish brute made, in all my born days before' (p. 46). And Captain Gallagher in Jackman's *Milesian* has this to say to the French valet he catches wooing one of the maids:

> I'll tell you what, Mr. Monsieur, if you marry in this island, I will apply for leave to smother the issue. I am sure, if our forefathers were living, they would deny the relationship. They were men and Britons, and deserv'd the fair; but as to you, ha, ha, ha! (pp. 38–9)

Mrs. Griffith had in the earlier *The platonic wife* (1765) contrasted the loyalty of the Irish servant, Patrick, with the perfidy of the French chambermaid Fontange. This play is of a rigidly symmetrical construction: Patrick serves Mr. Frankland, Fontange serves Emilia. Mr. Frankland harbours impure desires for Emilia; Fontange shamelessly tries to seduce Patrick (p. 50). Fontange betrays her mistress to Mr. Frankland, who offers her a reward, but Patrick betrays his master's evil plans to Emilia, and is likewise offered a reward:

> *Emilia.* As for you, honest Patrick, I think the best return I can make you, for saving my life and honour, is to present you with the same sum that Fontange was to have had for destroying both. (p. 96)

The polarity between Irishness and Frenchness is thus reinforced in moral and, especially, sexual terms. And Patrick in the end foresees (like Cumberland's Major O'Flaherty) a joyful repatriation, in a statement holding a barb against absenteeism and economic colonialism:

> Heaven bless and prosper your ladyship, for that. Patrick will carry it into his own country, and that itself would be a help to poor Ireland, for every one has a pluck at it, and would be glad to take all they can get from it, and no body never gives it nothing at all. (p. 96)

The enmity between Irish and French servants becomes almost a standard device, introduced even when the action does not call for it. Thus, in Waldron's *Maid of Kent* (1778), the honest Irish captain Brian O'Connor not only thwarts a craven lord's evil designs on the title-heroine, but for good measure also beats up the lord's *valet de chambre* ('walley-de-chaver'), the Frenchman La Poudre.[31]

Again, what is at issue in all this Irish-French enmity is really a projection of the English audience's anti-French attitude onto Irish characters – a projection which liberates the audience's own anti-French attitude from its English subjectivity. English values thus become universal values, shared by all the good (e.g. Irish) characters, denied by the bad (e.g. French) ones; in the process, Englishness can become a positive value in itself. This model is acted out most consistently in *The South Briton,* by 'A Lady' (1774). The dedication (dated, by the way, from Dublin) already remarks that

> Too much have national distinctions prevailed through the empire, and foreign fripperies sullied the genuine British lustre.

Accordingly, the play is full of little pointers to the effect that nothing can beat Good Old English standards. A few examples:

> Her father and his were neighbours, Old English gentlemen; they venerated the laws, lived hospitably, and dispensed universal benevolence around them. (p. 11)

Or again, when a chambermaid remonstrates against the heroine's

> old English dress, which your father so much admired, and which you will thus partly continue in spite of a body.
> *Miss A.* And what so calculated for comfort and ease? When these were worn, noble virtue and dignity graced our sex, domestic happiness formed the pleasures of life, and valour and integrity marked their offspring. (p. 13)

The ease with which 'Old *English'* ideals are used to replace the 'national distinctions' prevailing 'through the empire', i.e. Great Britain and Ireland, will be noted.

The action is occasioned by the return of young Mowbray from the Grand Tour. This exposure to foreign, Continental culture has tainted him with affectation and snobbery (though he is not a bad fellow at heart) and it is only after a long confrontation with the play's positive forces that he comes to see the errors of his ways and reverts to homely British ('Old English') values. These are embodied in three sterling gentlemen of the old school, another manifestation of the British Threesome: the English Admiral, the Scotsman Leslie and the Irish baronet Sir Terence O'Shaughnessy. Young Mowbray fatuously jokes on this last man's Irish name ('he shou'd be a *Calmuck* by the name') but is rebuked for this by Leslie (p. 19) – an echo of the jokes on Sir Callaghan O'Brallaghan's name. Another echo from Macklin's *Love à la mode* is contained in the rivalry that flares up (as in the quarrel between MacSarcasm and O'Brallaghan) when Sir Terence and Leslie discuss the relative antiquity of the Irish and the Scottish past. Mowbray teasingly voices the supercilious English view which makes light of both, but quickly retreats into a more non-national position when Leslie is stirred up to deliver a strong statement:

> *Mow.* What is your plaguey antiquity; the present is the age which exhibits a very different picture from your feudal times of barbarism; Scotland and Ireland, are the Crim Tartary and Siberia of Britain, man!
>
> *Leslie.* Hold your hand, Mr. Mowbray; tho' distant from the centre, we will still help to support the ballance, and have I trust, in common with our fellow subjects, hearts well affected to our king, and glowing with the generous warmth of liberty.
>
> *Mow.* Ha, ha, ha! I only touched the key, which always raises you Caledonians, just to see if even in a man used to the world, it cou'd be eradicated. Believe me, Leslie, nobody more detests national distinctions; they are the produce of knaves or fools, the instruments of interest or vanity! We are all children of the same empire, and that empire only a citizen of the world. . . . (p. 57)

It is in statements such as these that Mowbray's sound character comes to the fore. Conversely, disdain for things British is the disease that he has incurred abroad and from which he must be cured:

> *Mow.* . . . the ocean is not sometimes more ungovernable, than our British multitude.
>
> *Leslie.* Does not the lion roar when provoked, and so do they, when they behold enemies preferred to their own sons, their arts despised, and their manufactures neglected, for the light the flimsy baubles of southern climates. (p. 17)

It is on this note, too, that the play finds its happy end, when Mowbray has forsworn all alien trumpery:

> *Admiral.* Why now you speak like a Briton: you were as unlike one before, as one of the exotics at Kew, to an Oak in Whittlebury.
>
> *Sir Terence.* So it is, faith! – The devil take their exotics, they'll banish all our sound timber at last! But here is an Englishman, an Irishman, and a Scotch man, agreed upon one point together; and if they'd take my advice now, they'd always endeavour to do so; for we have enemies enough abroad, and not to be disputing among ourselves at home!
>
> *Mow.* If that opinion was generally adopted, it wou'd remove these idle distinctions, which are a disgrace to us; we shou'd then see the national glory shine with double splendor, supported by an united phalanx of the empire! Public duty would revive private virtue; we shou'd see glorious Patriots and good citizens; find our wives preferred to other women! and our country to the rest of the globe. (p. 79)

A nastier note amidst all this British harmony is the fact that, as a new non-British outsider focusing the play's antipathies, the villain is a Jew, the rich Issacher, to whom all the others refer with unrestrained bigotry. Macklin's Jew Mordecai, in *Love à la mode,* was not necessarily more ridiculous (let alone villainous) than his rivals MacSarcasm and Groom; but Issacher is a most disconcerting instance of anti-semitism. Another manifestation of racism taking over where anti-Irish national prejudice leaves off, is provided by Jackman's *The divorce* (1781), in which a 'Sambo' commits the ultimate sacrilege of wanting to marry a white woman, and is kicked down the stairs by the attorney, no doubt to the heartfelt satisfaction of the audience.

Respect and self-respect

The positive attitude of the Irishman towards England also makes his attachment to his native country an acceptable emotion – no disaffection being supposed to lurk underneath it. We have seen how expressions of loyalty to England and to Ireland often go together and, in a number of cases, the Irishman's reward consists of the opportunity to return to Ireland. Often Irish characters' sympathy for England is reciprocated by English characters' sympathy for Ireland:

> *Doctor.* By my shoul, captain, you talk as well as if you'd been brought up in the shitty of Dublin.
> *Captain.* I'm a well-wisher of the place, tho' not a native. . . .[32]

Again, in *The natural son,* O'Flaherty introduces himself:

> Dennis O'Flaherty is my name, I hope you like it; it has been a pretty while in the family, and I should be loth to change it.
> *Sir Jeff.* I shall love your name and your nation as long as I have breath. (p. 38)

In R.B. Sheridan's *St. Patrick's Day,* Lieutenant O'Connor bravely stands up for the honour of his profession and his country, and by so doing wins the hand of the justice's daughter as well as, presumably, a hand from the gallery:

> *Just.* You're an Irishman and an officer, ar'n't you?
> *Lieut.* I am, and proud of both.
> *Just.* The two things in the world I hate most – so mark me – Forswear your Country, and quit the Army – and I'll receive you as my Son in law.
> *Lieut.* You, Mr. Justice, if you were not the father of your Daughter here, I'd pull your nose for mentioning the first, and break your bones for proposing the latter.
> *Doctor.* You're right, Lieutenant.
> *Just.* Is he? – why then I must be wrong – (p. 192)

This native pride often takes the form of family pride. Irish claims to a direct, unbroken link with a known ancestry of fabulous, antediluvian antiquity had obviously become well known enough to make them a standard stage trapping. They are, again, presented as endearing aspects of the quaint Irishman: a little harebrained, but harmless really, and in a way quite colourful. Sir Terence O'Shaughnessy in *The South Briton,* for example, is a true blue Gael, for he holds his lands under the Treaty of Limerick (i.e. dating back to pre-Ascendancy ownership) and

> I love my name, and can trace our pedigree back as far as the flood, and I don't find we have fallen off much. (p. 20)

And Waldron, in his *Maid of Kent,* makes Captain Brian O'Connor steal the audience's hearts with the following words:

> Saint Patrick be thankful, I'm never afraid of doing what's right! – for tho' I'm but a menial man of low degree, I am sprung from a very great offspring, and have got the thick blood of the kings of Ireland bubbling in my veins, joy! (p. 94)

Apart from national pride (be it loyally English or British, or harmlessly Irish), the brogue has also become a vehicle for other kinds of 'sentiments that deserve applause'. Unah, in Dibdin's *Harvest home,* for example, wards off the amorous Trim:

> Ah! now don't be too much in a hurry! – Nobody gets my love but Patrick: when I have two hearts, you shall have one of them; but, you see, as I never had but one, and he stole it, how can I give you the other?
> *Trim.* Why, then, I must wear the willow!
> *Unah.* I'll tell you what wear – Wear a heart that rejoices in the happiness of others; and that's a willow that might grow in the garden of a prince. (pp. 23–4)

She follows this up with a song of which the opening lines may give a sufficient impression: 'Though I am humble, mean, and poor,/ Yet, faith, am I desarning'.

Such idealization of the peasantry helps to strengthen the sympathy with which the menial Irish (as opposed to the officers and baronets mainly discussed so far) are represented on the English stage. This sympathy with the Irish peasant is all the more interesting when it appears in plays dealing with their plight under rack-rents, absenteeism and the penal laws. Apart from isolated digs against the penal laws which we have encountered already (above p. 125 and 131), there are two plays to be mentioned which deal more extensively with these problems: Cumberland's *The note of hand* and O'Keeffe's *The prisoner at large.*

Cumberland's play of 1774 is a moral lesson against racing and gambling. Young Rivers has gambled away his Irish estate – albeit only to his disguised uncle who wants to teach him a lesson. The lesson of responsibility is also driven home by Rivers' Irish tenant, O'Connor MacCormuck, who has sought out his young landlord in order to talk business with him. The blunt, rough-hewn Irishman is a touchstone against which vapid pretence is immediately exposed; his clear untroubled eye passes stern judgement on the vanities of the upper class.

> We, that are his poor tenants in Ireland, have taken full as much offence at him, as he can at us; – rack, rack, – drain, drain – and here's the gulph that swallows it; *(looking into the gaming room)* damnation! there's a room full of 'em yonder, hard at work. Oh, you're a precious set. . . .
> *Rivers.* You are not aware, perhaps, that you are railing against some of the first people in the kingdom.
> *MacCormuck.* Ay, but in faith they are the last I shou'd wish Mr. Rivers to be found with. (pp. 33–4)

MacCormuck explains, too, that it is absenteeism and rackrenting that breed agrarian discontent:

> *MacC.* Faith, . . . hitherto we have been favour'd with little else from your hands, I think, but receipts for our rents, and regulations for raising them.
> *Rivers.* That's true enough, but others have done the same; others, as well as I, have rais'd their Irish rent.
> *MacC.* Ay, have they, and their Irish riots at the same time. (p. 36)

However, at Rivers' proposal to return to Ireland and mend his ways, MacCormuck is immediately reconciled into tear-jerking loyalty:

> *Rivers.* Will you bear me company?
> *MacC.* All the world thro', so you come to little Ireland at the end of it, by the soul of me; and you shall be as welcome as St. Patrick's day, every hair of your head (p. 37)

The happy end again drives the lesson home, not only to reformed Rivers, but also to the audience.

> *Rivers.* . . . since you think our demands have been too heavy, take it rent-free for your life, and in return administer my interests with more humanity and better fortune than your predecessor: – tell my needy tenants, they shall no longer be rack'd to pamper the carcase of a race-horse, and support the profligate excesses of a gaming table.
> *MacC.* Now you are a noble genius! and were all absentees of your mind, we would leave their estates untax'd for ever. (pp. 47–8)

In terms of plot construction, MacCormuck is primarily the instrument by which falseness or subterfuge is discovered, the embodiment of honesty over-coming pretence. He sees through the false practices (p. 20) of card-sharpers and, in a sub-plot, through the Pippin-alley clerk Sapling. This person, who vainly wants to pass himself off as a gentleman, is rudely interrupted in his imposture by the thundering MacCormuck:

> *Sapling.* . . . methinks 'tis a very snug, convenient apartment this of mine; quite private, and free from noise or interruption. (*s.d.*) violent noise is heard without, and the door is burst open, and O'CONNOR MAC CORMUCK, enters the room.
> *MacCormuck.* Oh! is it there that you are? (p. 10)

– naturally, MacCormuck does not believe Sapling's genteel claims ('A gentleman! I should as soon take your mother for one', p. 11), and in the end Sapling is forced to rescind his dreams of glory:

> Well, Sir, I was born in Pippin Alley, I was bred in Pippin Alley, and to Pippin Alley must return. There is more fatigue than I dream'd of in the character of a gentleman. (p. 27)

Here as in his relation with Rivers, MacCormuck serves to correct the upset social balance – be it in the agrarian riots of rackrented tenantry, or in the pretensions of an upstart clerk. He thus assuages all possible apprehensions that might be caused by the play's social criticism.

O'Keeffe's *The prisoner at large,* performed at the Newmarket theatre in 1778, is set near the Lakes of Killarney – a region whose picturesque interest had, as we have seen, become popular through numerous travel descriptions. Here, as well as in those travel descriptions, it is remarkable that an appreciation of the beauties of the countryside goes hand in hand with a defence of the deprived Irish peasants. The setting in O'Keeffe's play is referred to in connection with a horn being played there in order to bring out the lake's acoustic qualities – a practice mentioned likewise in contemporary travel descriptions, and indicative of O'Keeffe's playing up to 'tourist' value:

> They may talk of fine views, and vistas, and beauties of nature; but 'tis to hear the divine echos of my horn, that brings the gentlefolks all the way from Cork, and even Dublin, down here to the lake of Killarney (p. 9)

The play takes place amongst the honest rustics on the estate of lord Esmond. However, the lord is absent, and has been for a long time; meanwhile, the tenants are being racked by the extortionate rents imposed by the middleman Dowdle. The reason for Esmond's absence is that, while on the Grand Tour, he fell into the clutches of Parisian card-sharpers and has been held in a French debtors' prison ever since. In Dowdle's words:

> They never saw their landlord, Lord Esmond, since he was a boy. No, he spent his time and money flying over Italy and Germany, like a wild goose, till he's got himself now cooped up in a prison at Paris! (p. 3)

Now, however, while the evil French count Fripon (one of the sharpers) is endeavouring to collect Esmond's rents, the rightful lord returns, and, with the help of honest Jack Connor (a tenant drawn with the symptoms of the most sentimental loyalty to his 'poor master'), they overthrow the schemes of middleman and parasite: a wholesome alliance of landlord and tenant. The play ends with lord Esmond, restored to his estate, concluding:

> My ruin, I hope, will teach our nobility, instead of travelling to become the dupes of foreign sharpers, to stay at home and spend their fortunes amongst their honest tenants, who support their splendour. (p. 35)

Earlier sympathy for the menial Irish is evinced by the fact that Irish servants are sympathetically described as having feelings, too. The end of the older, more arrogant disdain for Irish coachmen and footmen can be observed in Vaughan's *The hotel* (1766), where the Irish coachman Timsey, whom Neville kicks for his insolence, is given the opportunity at least to complain of his inability to revenge himself:

> *Tirnsey.* O, my jewels, that little Timsey was but a Jontleman, to return the civility!
> *(Exit)*
> *Neville.* The impositions of these fellows are intolerable. (p. 21)

In O'Keeffe's play of the following year, *The she-gallant,* the Irish servant Thady Mac Brogue is already shown as both the physical and the moral superior of an insolent gentleman.

> (s.d.) Sir *Geofry* strikes him twice with the pole.
> *Thady* closes with him, trips up his heels, wrests the pole out of his hand, and is going to strike, but stops his hand.
> *Thady.* . . . No – I'd scorn to strike you, and you down – Get up, you rascal you – (p. 24)

Later on, the gentleman is even forced to admit this himself:

> I that was never over valiant, must make a trial of my prowess, on an *Irishman,* a fellow with muscles, firm as his country oak; but, indeed, I must do him the justice to own, that he exercis'd some of the generosity of an *Irishman,* by not pounding me to mummy, when he got me down, which I can't deny but I deserv'd (p. 26).

Even towards their own masters, Irish servants begin to display a modicum of *amour propre:* their loyalty towards the master never sinks them into abject servility. In Holcroft's *The school for arrogance* (1791), the sham-Irish nobleman Count Connolly Villars[33] is driven, in his arrogance, to strike his loyal servant MacDermot, who then morally obliges the aristocrat to apologize:

> *MacD.* Viry well, my Lord – *(Throwing down the letter)* I humbly thank your Lordship! – By Jasus! But I'll rimember the favour –
> *Count (more coolly)* Read, Sir.
> . . . . . .
> *MacD.* No, my Lord! – Mac Dermot is a man! – An Englishman! – Or an Irishman, by Jasus, which is better still ! And by the holy poker, if but that your Lordship was not a Lord now! – *(Pulling down his sleeves, and clenching his fist with great agony)*

The count then tries to mollify him with a gift of money:

> *MacD.* What! – I touch it! – No, my Lord! – Don't you think it! – I despise your guineas! – An Irishman is not to be paid for a blow! (pp. 33–4)

It is the *national* pride in the servant that is shown as the strongest operative emotion at work here: MacDermot makes continual references to his Irishness. After Villars has brought himself to apologize, the servant can find himself in a position to give his master a moral pat on the shoulder:

> There is many an upstart Lord has the courage to strike, whin they know their poor starving dependants hands are chained to their sides, by writchedness and oppression: but few indeed have the courage to own the injury! (p. 34)

Again, in William Macready's play *The bank note,* Killeavy is the fearless but pacific Irish servant; he, too, can give his 'bulls' (in this case, on the double meaning of 'diet': parliament and nourishment) a loyally pro-English twist: 'There's Ratsbone diet, and there's Polish diet; but the devil a morsel I cou'd find equal to our good old English diet' (p. 87). Killeavy, when called a 'scoundrel' by his quick-tempered master, coolly leaves his service – showing native pride and magnanimity in refusing to claim the back pay due to him. The master later apologizes and finds his apologies accepted, but Killeavy will not come back into his service.

Macready, later to become one of the foremost English dramatists, created another likeable Irish servant, morally the superior of his master, with Murtagh Delany, servant to Mr. Connoolly, in his *The Irishman in London* (1793). Mr. Connoolly, an inveterate snob, is the male counterpart of Macklin's earlier Mrs. Diggerty. He genteelly despises his Irishness and foppishly emulates the London *bon ton* even to the point of, like Mrs. Diggerty, hypercorrecting his brogue into a sillier anti-brogue. His silly pretence is constantly exploded by his blunt, honest, Irish servant:

> *Conn.* Why, you scoundrel, do you want to bring a mob about us? hold your tongue about Ireland, I say – Go wait at home for me, and don't be exposing –
> *Murl.* Exposing to talk of Ireland! Faith, Sir, begging your pardon, I think a man does not desarve to belong to any country, that's ashamed to own it. (*Exit*)

The following dialogue offers an example, not only of Connoolly's anti-brogue (*prating, great* etc. hypercorrected to *preeting, greet* etc.) but also of a bull which in the end redounds to the Irish servant's credit rather than to his ridicule:

> *Frost.* . . . you did not tell me what sort of passage you had.
> *Conn.* Why, Sir, they said it was a good one, but I was sick of it.
> *Murt.* Sick ! Arrah, Ladies, we were kilt, myself was quite dead, I was all-a-. . .
> *Conn.* Your [the English] manufactories are so astonishingly greet, they prove at once the wonderful industry and wealth of your nation.
> *Murt.* Ax your pardon, Ladies; I tell you: I could see three times as much as Maister Pat, for I slept all the way on the outside of the coach, and the devil a manufactory I saw equal to our own. Och! if you could only look at the oyster beds in Poolbeg, the Foundling or the lying-in Hospital at Dublin, they are the right sort of manufactories.
> *All.* Ha, ha, ha!
> *Murt.* Faith you may laugh, but I am sure there can't be better *manufactrys* in the world, than those that provides comfortable lodgings, and every other sort of bread and meat, for poor craters that can't provide for themselves.
> *Conn.* Hold your preeting, sirrah; Leedies, I hope you'll excuse him. (pp. 30–1)

The duel and Sir Lucius O'Trigger

It should be remembered that all these positive changes in the sentimental treatment of the Irishman were strictly a theatrical affair, taking place within the context of a large sentimentalization of the comic genre as a whole.

Outside the theatre, some opprobrium still stuck to the Irish character, particularly that of a fondness for fast life and the duel. As late as 1754, a pamphlet had appeared in London, which perpetuated the old charge of imposture and fortune-hunting and which complained about the large presence of Irish beggars in London. It sported the telling title A *candid enquiry why the natives of Ireland, which are in London, are more addicted to vice than the people of any other nation; even to the dread and terror of the inhabitants of this metropolis.*

However, it was the propensity for duelling (witness Captain Oregan in Smollett's *Roderick Random*) that was, it seems, the most persistent attribute. As Bartley points out,[34] the practice of duelling was on the decline in the 1770s and positively frowned upon, whereas the custom seems to have led a slightly more tenacious existence in Ireland. Hence the fact that this slower rate of decline of duelling in Ireland could, during the 1770s, acquire the dimension of a 'national' characteristic. A few comedies are extant which deal with pugnacious Irishmen. One of these was William O'Brien's *The duel* of 1772, featuring the trigger-happy Sir Dermot O'Leinster and his son. However, two years later, Hugh Kelly undertook to invert the current image, and wrote a play called *The school for wives*, in order

> to remove the imputation of barbarous ferocity, which dramatic writers, even meaning to compliment the Irish nation, have connected with their idea of that gallant people. (p. iv)

He discusses the previous stage treatments of the Irish as follows:

> With respect to the gentlemen of Ireland, where even an absolute attempt is manifested to place them in a favourable point of view, they are drawn with a brutal promptitude to quarrel, which is a disgrace to the well-known humanity of the country. – The gentlemen of Ireland have doubtless a quick sense of honour; and, like the gentlemen of England, as well as like gentlemen of every other high-spirited nation, are perhaps unhappily too ready to draw the sword, where they conceive themselves injured. – But to make them proud of a barbarous propensity to duelling, to make them actually delight in the effusion of blood, is to fasten a very unjust reproach upon their general character, and to render them universally obnoxious to society. The author of the SCHOOL FOR WIVES, therefore, has given a different picture of Irish manners, though in humble life; and flatters himself, that those who are really acquainted with the original, will acknowledge it to be at least a tolerable resemblance. (p. v)

As it is, however, Kelly performs two inversions on the traditional image, rather than one, and these in a way cancel each other out: after having placed the supposed love for the duel among the Irish firmly in the gentry, in upper-class circles, he vests Irish dislike of the duel in a middle-class protagonist, the clerk Connolly. What he achieves therefore is a subcontrary to, rather than a contradiction of, the traditional view: the Irish gentleman with a predilection for the duel is not contradicted by a differently inclined Irish gentleman, but counterbalanced by a middle-class Irishman. It is easy to see that the two subcontraries can exist side by side, are not mutually exclusive; indeed Kelly's view, rather than being a novel one, is part of a more general tradition attested in, for instance, contemporary travel description: namely, that there is a temperamental difference between the hard-living, rakish squireens and landlords of Ireland, and the decent hard-working poorer peasants and cottagers.

This is in fact a continuation of the differentiation between 'mere' and 'civil' Irish, one having become more sympathetic to the English observer as the other dropped off in goodwill. In the end, then, Kelly's counter-Stage Irishman is but a slightly modified continuation of an older tradition, much as Cumberland's Major O'Flaherty was. The following excerpt may illustrate that Kelly's Irish clerk Connolly fits the typology of the later eighteenth-century Stage Irishman effortlessly: by his way of vindicating his dignity after having incurred English laughter at one of his bulls, by attesting to the loyalty and concord between England and Ireland, and by obtaining English sympathy in the end:

> Con. Faith, you may laugh, gintlemin, but tho' I am a foolish Irishman, and come about a foolish piece of business, I'd prefer a snug birth in this world, bad as it is, to the finest coffin in all Christendom.
>
> . . . . . .
>
> Capt. 'Tis not very customary, sir, with gentlemen of Ireland to oppose an affair of honour.
> Con. They are like the gintlemin of England, sir, they are brave to a fault; yet I hope to see the day that it will be infamous to draw the swords of either, against any body but the enemies of their country. (Exit)
> Bel. I am quite charmed with this honest Hibernian, and would almost fight a duel for the pleasure of his acquaintance. (pp. 45–6)

However, an Irish duellist was to reappear with a vengeance in the following year, 1775; it was Sir Lucius O'Trigger, the Irish character in what is perhaps the most enduring comedy of those under review here: R.B. Sheridan's The Rivals. The outrage with which the aptly-named O'Trigger was greeted has gone down in theatre history; it caused the play to be withdrawn after the first night and to be revised thoroughly before it returned to the stage. Some of the press reactions are worth quoting here, since they show that O'Trigger's role was considered a national libel on Ireland. Thus, the Morning chronicle, 18 Jan. 1775:

> This representation of Sir Lucius is indeed an affront to the common sense of an audience, and is so far from giving the manners of our brave and worthy neighbours, that it scarce equals the picture of a respectable Hotentot. . . .[35]

And the Morning post, three days later:

> Sir Lucius O'Trigger was so ungenerous an attack upon a nation, that one must justify any severity with which the piece will hereafter be treated: it is the first time I ever remember to have seen so villainous a portrait of an Irish Gentleman, permitted so openly to insult the country upon the boards of an English theatre. (p. 47. The author subscribed himself 'A Briton')

What was it in O'Trigger's part that caused all this revulsion? Surely not his brogue, nor his bulls; for these remained standard practice throughout the century without causing the same dismay – and as it is, such bulls as are put into Sir Lucius's mouth are far outweighed by the blunders of the famous Mrs. Malaprop, whose 'malapropisms' are nothing else than bulls spoken in a genteel English accent:

> Well, Sir Anthony, since *you* desire it, we will not anticipate the past; – so mind young people – our retrospection will now be all to the future. (p. 124)

Nor is Sir Lucius put into ludicrous or undignified situations like Captain O'Blunder, in Thomas Sheridan's play. True, he is under the misapprehension that the billets-doux written to him come from the fair Lydia; but as the real authoress turns out to be Mrs. Malaprop he extricates himself from the awkward situation with quite unruffled dignity. Whatever ridicule is present here must fall on Mrs. Malaprop's shoulders.

It is obvious, then, that public outrage cannot have fastened on a degrading treatment of Sir Lucius's traditionally 'Irish' attributes. The attacks were *not* led, as seems sometimes to be believed or implied, by London Irishmen whose national pride was outraged, but, on the contrary, by the respected London media and 'sentimental blockheads', as the *Morning post* called them (p. 51), among the theatre audience who were insulted by the duellist rather than by the Irishman. Sheridan justified himself in the preface to the printed version:

> It is not without pleasure that I catch at an opportunity of justifying myself from the charge of intending any national reflection in the character of Sir *Lucius O'Trigger*. If any Gentlemen opposed the Piece from that idea, I thank them sincerely for their opposition; and if the condemnation of this Comedy (however misconceived the provocation) could have added one spark to the decaying flame of national attachment to the country supposed to be reflected on, I should have been happy in its fate; and might with truth have boasted, that it had done more real service in its failure, than the successful morality of a thousand stage-novels will ever effect. (p. 71)

Lee's performance in the part, it seems, is to a great extent to be blamed for Sir Lucius's initial unpopularity. However, the changes made by Sheridan were not merely in the casting (Lee being replaced by Clinch and by Moody) but also in the characterization – and these latter changes seem to have been aimed mainly at making the Irishman not only less contrived, but especially less wantonly bloodthirsty.[36] This last change was the one which was applauded most particularly. The *Morning post* for 17 January puts it tellingly: 'Mr. Moody *O'Flahertized* Sir *Lucius O'Trigger* very laughably' (p. 52). Moody was, it will be remembered, the actor whom Churchill had addressed as the vindicator of Ireland's character on the London stage, and his star role (or, at least, one of his more important star roles) was Cumberland's Major O'Flaherty, whom he had played in 1771, 1772, and 1773, and whom he was to play again for eight more productions between 1782 and 1788.[37] In what a contemporary journalist recognized as an 'O'Flahertization' of the part, some of the more idealized, sentimentally noble treats of Cumberland's officer must therefore have been introduced in the acting. The *London evening post* recognized an O'Flahertizing influence *à la* Moody also in the part as played by Clinch:

> Mr. Lee (who in another line is a very respectable actor) was on the first night so obviously embarrassed in the part of Sir Lucius O'Trigger, that it was rather difficult to define the character. Mr. Clinch has very fortunately brought it more to sight, and by a very gentlemanly brogue, and naiveté of manner, made Sir Lucius so agreeable to the audience, that the part is likely to be as fortunate to him as that of Major O'Flaherty was to Mr. Moody. (pp. 50–1)

The 'gentlemanly brogue, and naiveté of manner' are interesting descriptions of the Stage Irishman's positive qualities. The *Morning chronicle*, too, pronounced its satisfaction with the new O'Trigger, for similar reasons of added sentimental interest:

> the sentiments thrown into the mouth of Sir Lucius O'Trigger produce a good effect, at the same time that they take away every possible idea of the character's being designed as an insult on our neighbours on the other side of St. George's channel. (p. 50)

What can be concluded from this? In the decades after the 1745 rising, a remarkable amelioration of the Irish stage characters becomes noticeable. Instead of being a threatening or despicable figure, the Irishman becomes a harmonious fixture on the English stage, endearing, loyal, prepossessing. The genteel, feline bloodthirst of O'Trigger is a disconcerting exception to all this. As we have seen that harmlessness and loyalty were deliberately projected onto Irish characters in order to flatter English national feelings, it may become understandable why English newspapers should have felt such vicarious outrage on behalf of their Irish fellow-subjects. In presenting a dangerous Irishman, Sheridan indirectly hurt the fabric of accommodation and pretended harmony that was woven in the interest, and to the amusement, of the English audience.

O'Trigger's threatening qualities can be observed in the larger structure of the play as well as in his own speeches. For instance, the gentle, likeable fop Archer is presented *solus* in a situation of contentment: he is practising a cotillion. In his little soliloquy, his placidity, his (anti-French) Englishness and homeliness, are stressed to a considerable degree:

> Confound the first inventors of cotillons! say I – they are as bad as algebra to us country gentlemen – I can walk a Minuet easy enough when I'm forced! – and I have been accounted a good stick in a Country-dance. – Odd's jigs and tabors! . . . but these outlandish heathen Allemandes and Cotillons are quite beyond me! – I shall never prosper at 'em, that's sure – mine are true-born English legs – they don't understand their curst French lingo! – their *Pas* this, and *Pas* that, and *Pas*

t'other! – d – n me, my feet don't like to be called Paws! no, 'tis certain I have most Antigallican Toes! (pp. 114–15)

It is at this point that a servant enters and announces 'Here is Sir Lucius O'Trigger to wait on you, Sir.' O'Trigger comes in and, in the ensuing scene, works Archer's feelings up to the pitch at which he, helped (or rather steered) by the Irishman, delivers the challenge for a duel that he is to regret so bitterly for the rest of the play. Sir Lucius is thus presented as a dangerous intrusion in, and disruption of, English placidity; the more disturbingly so, as no motives are assigned to his bloodthirst. He coldly relishes duelling for the sake of duelling, and Archer's servant's outburst 'I hate such bloodthirsty cormorants' (p. 118) is quite understandable.

It is, accordingly, this lack of 'proper' motivation (even Sir Charles Grandison could indulge in a bit of a duel with that modicum of motivation) which Sheridan tried to remedy in his revision of the part. Whereas O'Trigger originally picks a fight with Captain Absolute (who also goes under the assumed identity of Ensign Beverly) for no other reason than the sheer pleasure of it, a grievance is assigned to him in the revised version – but in so perfunctory a manner that it glaringly stands out as the flimsiest of patching jobs. When Absolute demands (understandably) to know why O'Trigger seeks to quarrel, the Irishman answers:

> the quarrel is a very pretty quarrel as it stands – we should only spoil it, by trying to explain it. – However, your memory is very short – or you could not have forgot an affront you pass'd on me within this week. – So no more, but name your time and place. (p. 129)

The 'affront' referred to so vaguely is not specified; only in one other place O'Trigger, equally perfunctorily, loosely mentions that 'There is a gay captain here, who put a jest on me lately, at the expense of my country, and I only want to fall in with the gentleman, to call him out' (p. 117). That is surely a very flimsy foundation on which to rear the important sub-plot resulting from it. But what is truly marvellous is the eagerness with which the contemporary audience accepted this weak excuse for a motive in what remained a questionable pursuit. Thus, the *Morning post*:

> Sir *Lucius O'Trigger* being retouched, has now the appearance of a character; and his assigning Beverley's reflection on his country as the grounds for his desire to quarrel with him is a reasonable pretense, and wipes off the former stigma undeservedly thrown on the sister kingdom. . . . (p. 49)

The *Morning post*'s mistake in referring to Absolute (whom O'Trigger addresses *in propria sua persona*, as 'Captain') by his alias, Beverly, only underscores the eagerness of the audience to hear O'Trigger's motives rather than to assess them in the context of the play, the willingness to overlook the weakness of the excuse. The only reason I can think of to account for this sudden appreciation of the new O'Trigger is the fact that he has become recognizable as an Irishman. Instead of a strange and disquieting individual, foiling the audience's attempts to recognize in him what they had come to expect from an Irish play character, he has become a character with motives that fit him satisfactorily into the existing English preconceptions of what an Irishman ought to be like: touchy pride, and, especially, touchy national pride belong to the accepted, honourable characteristics of 'the' Irishman as far as the audience is concerned. O'Trigger is at his most dangerous to the comfort of the audience when he is not easily recognizable or classifiable in his national traits; be that as it may, it remains disconcerting and, one feels, somehow symbolic that, by 1775, meaningless bloodthirst could, quite literally 'overnight', become excusable and even honourable by the merest reference to national honour.

Conclusion

Sir Lucius' vicissitudes make it clear that the Stage Irishman was not the mere creature of the playwright, but rather subject to the audience's recognition and approval. O'Trigger, whose motives were unfathomable, unrecognizable, unclassifiable in the first version of *The rivals,* had sinned against the requirement of *vraisemblance,* which, as Genette has pointed out, entailed an outrage against the audience's sense of *bienséance* as well (above, p. 78), and which could provoke (and did, as we have seen, provoke) moral indignation as well as aesthetic dissatisfaction.

Even the great sentimentalization of the Stage Irishman, stimulated by the changing taste of the time, took the form of a mere modification of the received type, a reinterpretation of characteristics within the received terms of reference: cowardice changed into its antonym, valour; mendacity into its antonym, honesty; perfidy into loyalty; stupidity could be revalued into naivety, artlessness, lack of dissimulation or of social veneer; all such changes, however, are determined by the original trait that they set out to contradict. One is reminded of the same mechanism taking place in the hypercorrection of Solinus' assertion that Ireland harboured no bees: from statements contradicting Solinus by asserting that bees definitely did exist in Ireland, a tradition emerged which stressed that extraordinary quantities of bees were to be found in Ireland. An initial statement on the remarkableness of the apiary population will, under the pressure of falsification, be modified or even inverted (from being remarkable in its paucity to being remarkable in its plenitude) rather than dropped as being inconclusive or irrelevant; likewise, the traditional Stage Irishman, once established, will be modified or contradicted (within its original terms of reference), rather than forgotten or ignored. The extraordinary dismay of the London audience and press at dangerous, dangerously unfamiliar Sir Lucius O'Trigger is a case in point. An audience will, *nolens volens,* relate to a given (re-)presentation of a stock character in terms of earlier (re-)presentations, in those 'received terms of reference' which form the parameters of whatever treatment the Stage Irishman might receive. Sir Lucius did not fit into those terms, did not 'make sense' in them. Sheridan found himself forced, like so many playwrights before him, to provide a mode of accommodation for his Irishman. As we have seen, this need to accommodate the Irishman, to make him agreeable to a London audience (be it by ridicule or denigration, be it, on the contrary, by exorcism, be it by devices intended to obscure or complicate the notion of his identity,[38] be it by sentimentalization) governed his stage presence from the beginning. From Ben Jonson's ploy to hide court masquers under Irish garb, to Shadwell's exorcism of an anti-Shadwell in the priest O'Divelly, to the vicarious outrage of the so-called 'sentimental blockheads' at the anti-Irish insult which they felt Sir Lucius to contain, the Stage Irishman seems to have been consistently determined by the attitudes governing the London stage, rather than by his so-called national traits.

This makes the most thoroughly theatrical of all these Irish denizens of the stage, the sentimentalized anti-Stage-Irishman of the later eighteenth century, all the more remarkable. Unlike earlier Irishmen in English fiction, he seems to have no basis whatsoever in the non-fictional discourse regarding Ireland. Whereas earlier developments in Stage Irish typology follow those in English discursive prose (e.g. the deterioration of the 1680s), this sentimentalization (implying, or implied by, a corresponding change in the audience's attitude) seems to have been dictated by literary or theatrical taste, rather than by political/discursive developments. And it was the image thus created in a purely *literary* development, which was in turn to have repercussions in the discursive, extra-theatrical approach to Ireland that became noticeable shortly afterwards: in the travel descriptions of Bush and his successors, and in the sketches of men like Campbell, which appeared in the decades immediately following the plays of Thomas Sheridan, Tobias Smollett and Charles Macklin.

The political influence of this literary sentimentalization is twofold. First, it may (if those travel descriptions are anything to go by) have materially assisted the Patriot shift in attitude towards the Catholic Irish – from the distrust towards a traditionally hostile nation – to a sensibility of their rights as sentient compatriots; second, by creating an 'Irishman' whose nationality is no longer subject to the manifold divisions running through Irish society. Although plebeian 'mere Irish' servants (albeit with increasingly noble souls) remain in evidence throughout the century, the sentimentalization process creates a social hybrid who partakes both of Gaelic Irish and of Ascendancy characteristics, while belonging to neither class, and it is he who is held up as the 'typical' Irishman. All these men with brogues and interjections indicating the native speaker of Gaelic, with Milesian patronymics and Milesian family-pride in the ancient roots of the O'Blunders, O'Tremors, O'Triggers, O'Brallaghans *et hoc genus omne,* at the same time seem to belong to the upper classes: they are commissioned officers, and a disproportionate number of them are either knights or baronets: Sir Callaghan, Sir Lucius, Sir Sturdy, Sir Terence. . . . Even Macklin's 'True-born Irishman', O'Dogherty, moves in gentry and aristocratic circles, and obviously has enough landed interest to buy himself a seat in parliament or a peerage, should he so wish. And especially the love of the duel seems to reflect an aristocratic rather than a middle-class outlook and life-style.

All these hybrids, these 'Gaelic Ascendancy'-men, are, then, in themselves an instance of a process by which an Irish nationality was to spring from a disregard for cultural, economic, political and religious divisions within Irish society – a process which stands at the beginning of Irish nationalism proper, and which will be the substance of the closing chapter.

GAELIC POETRY AND THE IDEA OF IRISH NATIONALITY

Bardic poetry and clan society, 1200–1600

One of the more widely used textbooks of Irish literary history, Aodh De Blácam's *Gaelic literature surveyed* (1929), describes the reign of Cormac mac Airt, in the third century AD, as follows:

> The nation which had come into being in Cormac's day was a nation comparable to antique Greece or Fascist Italy. It must have abounded with energies that it drew from an intense excitement of racial consciousness. The sense of nationality in the Old Irish period was unparalleled elsewhere in the contemporary Europe. (p. 23)

Such a passage says more about De Blácam's attitudes than about the legendary Cormac mac Airt and the equally legendary Ireland of his day, of course; and with the work of more scientific celtologists and historians of early Irish history and literature, much has been done in the last decades to correct such unfortunate anachronisms as the one quoted here. Nevertheless, the danger of reading earlier Irish poetry from a post-Romantic perspective, itself under the shadow of nineteenth- and twentieth-century national thought, is still present: in 1973, De Blácam's book was (*faute de mieux?*) reprinted successfully, including the appreciative invocation of Mussolini, unaltered but for the addition of an extra chapter on twentieth-century literature, and enjoys the reputation of what the 'blurb' called an 'invaluable and indispensable reference work'.

In attempting to trace the development, in Irish political poetry, of a national outlook – that is to say: an expression of national images distinguishing Irish Gaels from Foreigners – I may, I hope, safely dispense with the 'intense excitement of racial consciousness' *à la* Mussolini which De Blácam found as early as the third century. The problem remains, however, that much Irish poetry, even that of late medieval times, has been traditionally subjected to readings in *national* terms, with a tendency to attribute latter-day attitudes to bardic poets. Even in recent years, bardic poems like those of Fearghal Óg Mac an Bhaird have been discussed (by no less an authority than Professor Tomás Ó Concheanainn) in a frame of reference largely based on the axiom of that poet's 'patriotism'; even in recent years, scholars of undisputed merit such as Brendan Bradshaw and T.J. Dunne have crossed swords on the issue of national motivation in certain sixteenth-century poems. Though scholars dealing with pre-Norman Ireland have done much to put the Gaelic traditions, institutions and attitudes of their period into a proper light, a reassessment of the political attitude of the bardic poet *vis-à-vis* the English-Irish confrontation is still needed. Granted that an unmistakably 'national' stance, composed of amalgamated Jacobite, Catholic and post-bardic attitudes, is expressed forcefully in the 'us vs. them' of eighteenth-century Irish poetry, the question must still be settled how far this stance can be traced back, when exactly political poetry in Irish began to address the English-Irish confrontation as one taking place between 'nations', i.e. demographic groups united into political cohesion by a common 'character', by common differences from other such groups.

I shall, in the following pages, offer a reconsideration of the practice of political bardic poetry in the later middle ages – not, indeed, to deny it explicitly and categorically all sense of Gaelic nationality, but to advance a verdict of 'not proven'; to call into doubt, rather than to prove wrong, the all-too-easy reading of bardic poetry as being nationally motivated or inspired; to indicate that such a reading must still labour under the onus of proof and cannot continue to don a complacent air of self-evidence; to suggest that the poetry which was the direct expression, not of a feudal society or of a nation-state, but of a 'clan society', ought to be read accordingly. National thought is the desire to see cultural identity incorporated into political sovereignty, and the justification of political aspirations in terms of cultural identity. That link between culture and politics seems so obvious to latter-day readers that it is habitually read into older Gaelic sources. It seems necessary to undo that heritage of anachronism and to re-assess, to which extent Irish poetry formulated or implied such a connection between cultural self-awareness and anti-English (political or religious) resistance.

'Bardic poetry'[1] was, to begin with, neither 'bardic' (in that the classical Gaelic scholar-poet, the *file,* was the 'bards'' hierarchical superior), nor quite 'poetry' in any modern sense. The ceremonial 'metrical discourse' that these *filí* composed between *c.* 1200 and 1600, fulfilled a nearly journalistic social function, in a prosody and vocabulary of awesome refinement and complexity – as if *Debrett's Peerage* were written in the stanzaic pattern of 'The wreck of the Deutschland'. Nevertheless I hope to show that the non-fictional, discursive quality of bardic poetry does not negate its importance as poetry: that, owing to formal requirements ('formal' both in a social and in a literary, textual sense) significant differences can be registered between the treatment of national stereotypes in bardic poetry and in the historiographical, religious and linguistic discourse which will be dealt with in the next chapter. It should also be remembered that bardic poetry cannot be accommodated within traditional literary periodization, which progresses from the middle ages through the renaissance into the seventeenth century; such period concepts have little sense in the context of this highly static, archaizing poetic tradition. Most of the characteristics I shall outline here follow directly from this isolated insularity.

It should be understood, moreover, that the social and literary system under discussion here is that of the later, i.e. post-Viking middle ages: a system which had begun to stratify, systematize and even reinterpret its own origins and source-traditions in what was often a distortion of the older strata of Gaelic cultural and political practice as elucidated by scholars like Binchy, Byrne, Mac Cana, Mac Niocaill and Ó Corráin. Historical – or rather, pseudo-historical – interpretations were at work after 1200 which do not necessarily reflect the earlier Gaelic tradition itself, but rather a wishful retrospection on a golden, pre-Norman or pre-Viking past – as it ought to have been, rather than as it was.

The best point of access into an understanding of the poetry which reflected these attitudes, into an understanding of its conventions and social position, lies probably in the men who wrote it: *the filí*, the professional poets and their social role within the Gaelic clan system. Their social position was one of great importance and can perhaps best be described as a combination between a censor in the Roman republic, a member of the Académie française, a minister of culture, and a representative of the modern media. His professional qualifications included (apart from his descent from a family of established bardic renown) a command over the highly complex rules of Gaelic prosody and a vast store of historical, genealogical and mythological knowledge. All this knowledge was transmitted orally and part of it can be traced back into the pre-Christian era; the poet is originally a *seer* who, until the arrival of Christianity, had been vested with pontifical powers. A remnant of these seems to persist in the fact that he composes his poetry in darkness and on a bed of rushes, or in the fact that a satire (or curse, *aor*) by a fully qualified poet was considered capable of blighting the face of its subject-victim by causing boils and sores to erupt.

Bardic poetry is only in the third instance a written one and only in the second a spoken one: the poet would not recite his own poetry, but would leave that task to one of his retinue, a reciter-harpist. The poet did not aim at providing entertainment, but rather at applying his lore and his craftmanship with language to a celebration of the events of his day, thereby establishing a link between the past and the present. The poet was the cultural guardian of the Gaelic heritage, whose task it was to guarantee historical continuity, to legitimize the present in terms of past history. It is significant that the skills of the poet, the historian and the judge to some extent overlapped: the highest degree for all three callings was that of *ollamh*, 'scholar, professor', and the poet would as often call himself *saoi*, 'sage', as *file*, 'poet'; other terms were *fear dána* or *éigeas*, both meaning 'a man of learning'.

As the guardian of culture, it was his task to praise the chieftain on his accession to power by recounting his genealogy and his ancestral greatness, and by voicing the flattering expectation that he will increase the fame of his lineage; a similar function was implied in his delivery of a formal elegy on the chieftain's death; and with the ever-present threat of a possible satire in case the chieftain would fall short of his obligations, the poet exercised a kind of mentorship. The suzerainty of the independent chieftain (whom one might call a petty prince, or, indeed, a king) was the fundamental concept of the Gaelic *politeia*. Each ruler of a *tuath*[2] was, theoretically at least, sovereign. His 'kingship' is not to be confused with the overlordship of a provincial king or a high-king, superimposed on these sovereign chieftains. As Mac Cana puts it:

> Overkings there were, and provincial kings, but the king *tout court* was the king of the petty or tribal kingdom, the *tuath*, and he and his kingdom constituted the central nexus, both ritual and political, in Irish society. One's *tuath* was one's *patrie* and beyond its boundaries one became an outlander, a foreigner (Old Irish *deoraid*, Welsh *alltud*), and however this definition may have been blurred by political

expansionism in the historical period the conceptual and indeed the practical autonomy of the *tuath* long remained a basic feature of Irish social organisation.[3]

In a parallel to other early European social systems, the king, or, in clan terms, the chieftain, would be regarded primarily as the source of prosperity and nobility: he would bestow gifts and confer honour. The provenance of both would lie in the agricultural produce of his own territory and in raids on enemy territory. Accordingly, the kingly qualities most central to the poet's critical control would be his chieftain's warlike prowess, his munificence and the fertility of his territory; as regards this last point, we can find echoes of an extremely archaic view of the king as his country's husband: not only does his country do the king honour by bending down her fruit- and nut-laden tree boughs as in a curtsey (a recurring literary topos), but the accession to power is even regarded as a form of marriage between the king and his bride/country. The country's fertility is the natural consequence of this matrimony.

One initial property of bardic poetry to which I shall therefore pay special attention is the traditional personalization or anthropomorphization of the country as a woman. Again, the origins of this topos recede into prehistoric antiquity. The most important geographical denominations for the country of Ireland are, in fact, the names of the Celtic (or perhaps pre-Celtic) tutelary goddesses of the land: Fodla, Banbha and Éire (Ériu). The country is thus the chieftain's bride (at his accession), his wife or (after his death) his widow. The nature of this personification is especially noteworthy since it coincides with the poet's own relationship with his chieftain: more than a mere retainer, but not quite the king's equal, the poet saw his allegiance to his patron largely in terms of a marriage ('to love, honour, and obey', as it were), as that of a wife to her husband. The relationship king–*ollamh* thus matches that between the king and his land; this has been explored fruitfully in the well-documented case of the renowned poet Eochaidh Ó hEoghusa and his relations with his patron Aodh, the Mág Uidhir chieftain of Fermanagh, by James Carney, who remarks

> There is a close and mystic bond between the prince and his ollav, and this may have something to do with the fact that the ollav or druid was the prince's only possible approach to the earth goddess whose husband he was. This may explain the idea, basic to Irish thinking, that prince and ollav are in a symbolic sense husband and wife. Ó hEoghusa gives strong expression to what he regards as the legal right of the ollav to share the prince's bed and it is obviously a right upon which he sets considerable value.[4]

Another expression of this matrimonial view of the relationship poet–patron can be found in the topos current in elegiac poems: the poet's position after the king's death is that of an unprotected widow. He has lavished all his esteem and praise on his deceased patron, without bothering to curry favour with anyone else; he is therefore left without protection, and unlikely to find any. Thus, Tadhg Óg Ó hUiginn wrote in his elegy to Tadhg Ó Conchobhair († 1403):

> * Re linn Taidhg – truagh an mealladh! –
> cách 'n-ar gceann do chuireamar;
> gan toirrthim ar m'aire ann
> ní ráibhe a n-oirchill agam.
>
> Liaide do lucht ar n-ionnlaigh
> mo threise ar Ó dToirrdhealbhaigh;
> is uaimhneach a fhear dána
> ón tseal uaibhreach anára.
>
> Uadha a-táthar ag teacht ruinn
> mé a ollamh 's a fhear cumuinn;
> nír shaoil mé nachar mhaith dhamh
> ar chaith sé d'aoibh re a ollamh. (AithDD vol. I, 18)

Again, a similar image can be seen to apply in the relationship between the king and his land: 250 years later, an elegy to the Confederation's general Eoghan Rua Ó Neill would begin with the line 'Do chaill Éire a céile fíre', 'Ireland has lost her true husband'.[5] We shall see in later years a proliferation of this topos of Ireland as an unprotected widow. Conversely, Gofraidh Fionn Ó Dálaigh, in the mid-fourteenth century, depicted Éire as a blushing, eager young bride, anxiously awaiting marriage to (i.e. the royal accession of) Tadhg, heir to the chieftainship of Clann Cárthaigh: 'Fuirig go foill a Éire / gearr go bhfuighe fír-chéile', 'Patience a while, O Eire! Soon shalt thou get a true spouse'.[6] The expressions are remarkably parallel, notwithstanding the three eventful centuries separating the two poems. Here, then, is a literary link between the wholly dissimilar political situations of 1403 and 1649, the respective years of these poems to Tadhg Mac Cárthaigh and Eoghan Rua Ó Néill. A closer scrutiny of the problems underlying this parallel depiction of Éire and her *fír-chéile* across the intervening centuries may help us towards discerning possible patterns in the emergence of a national image and ideology in Gaelic poetry.

The Gaelic order and bardic conventions

To begin with, we should realize that Ó Dálaigh's poem was staking such far-fetched claims for young Tadhg Mac Cárthaigh as to be hyperbolical to the point of vacuousness. He does not merely anticipate Tadhg's accession to the McCarthy chieftainship (whose territory was confined to the southern and inland parts of the province of Munster), but expands his expectations to the idea that this bold young chieftain will go on to become high-king of all

---

* In Tadhg's day – what a fool I was! – I made many foes; I thought not of this disaster coming, and made no preparation against my foes.

My favour with Toirdhealbhach's grandson only increased the number of my illwishers; terrible the sight of his poet fallen after a proud spell of honour.

I was his *ollamh* and friend, and therefore am attacked; little did I dream his favour would come against me in the end. (ed.'s trl.)

Ireland: for it is a marriage to Éire that is alluded to. Again, such high-pitched expectations were common fare in encomiastic bardic poetry and need by no means reflect the realistic political expectations of the poet. Indeed the formulaic speciousness of his flattering strains lies at the very core of the hope he expresses: Gofraidh Fionn Ó Dálaigh evokes the idea of a king of All Ireland, residing at Tara and holding the ancient national assemblies that fell into abeyance at the coming of the Foreigners; and though he presents this idea of such a high-kingship as a past reality, a Gaelic institution from earlier times which since the twelfth century has given way to foreign pressure, such a view is essentially a mere conceit, a literary formula expressing contemporary nostalgia rather than historical tradition. The Feis Temro, for instance, one of the national institutions traditionally referred to as corollary to a functioning high-kingship,[7] was in fact a fertility rite culminating in the installation of a sacred king as spouse or consort of the sovereignty goddess. This ritual had been discontinued as a pagan rite as early as the sixth century, and was resurrected only in later times by pseudo-historians in the form of a 'constitutional "organ" of the "high-kingship"'. Even in the later medieval context, the notion of a high-kingship was based, not on present or past political institutions, but rather on a fanciful reinterpretation of an imaginary past. Such notions represent essentially a construct superimposed by post-Viking pseudo-historians on the half-forgotten, much distorted traditions surviving or remembered from older days; post-Viking political ideals are thus draped around the skeleton of an imperfectly remembered, glorified and anachronistically idealized past. Therefore, to state one's patron's rights, his likelihood to succeed to a semi-legendary supreme monarchy, was in fact nothing more than a flattering way of expressing confidence in his royal qualities and qualifications, and in the strength and nobility of his clan. Only in this way can we explain the fact that a relatively small band of poets could unflinchingly hail a great many prospective high-kings, advance royal claims to the see of Tara which stood in blatant mutual incompatibility. The high-kingship – or rather, the poetical topos of the high-kingship – was little more than a literary ideal legitimizing the internecine rivalries and spoliations of the individual clans.

Éire is, in these terms, the outermost frame of reference for Gaelic society and can often mean something like 'the whole world'.[8] Éire is not defined through any juxtaposition with other countries or 'nations'; it is the ultimate societal horizon for Gaelic political thought. To be high-king is, *tout court,* to reign supreme.

The native political unit is, then, the clan and its dependencies; it is between clans that rivalries, jealousies and claims to greatness take shape. However, clans stand in different degrees of closer or remoter kinship, all of which are recorded in the storehouse of bardic knowledge. The aforementioned Clann Cárthaigh, for instance, were divided into three main branches, residing in Kerry (McCarthy More), West Cork (McCarthy Reagh) and Muskerry. They could command the allegiance of lesser families in their territories such as the O'Callaghans, MacAuliffes or the O'Donoghues of Cashel. Indeed, they could trace a common descent linking them genealogically to these families: after their common ancestor Eoghan Mór, this cluster of vaguely related families would be called the Eoghanacht – Eoghan himself being the mythical son of mythical Oilill Olum, who was believed to have been king of Munster in the third century AD. Another cluster of families also settled in Munster descended from a different son of Oilill Olum, namely Cormac Cas, after whom they were called the Dál gCais; the most important family of this lineage was that of O'Brien, Í Bhriain. From a third son of Oilill Olum, Cian, descended the Cianacht, whose most important representatives were the O'Carrolls, Í Chearbhaill.

Although the sense of kinship or common blood between McCarthy and O'Brien (or McCarthy and O'Carroll) was thus far less than that between McCarthy and MacAuliffe, it was, again, greater (owing to all these families' descent from Oilill Olum) than their sense of consanguinity with, for instance, the O'Driscolls, a Munster family whose pedigree bypassed Oilill Olum completely. Again, there was an ultimate, outer frame of reference, namely that of the Gaelic race (with the eponymous ancestor Gaedheal Glas). Or, to put it differently: all Gaelic inhabitants of Ireland traced their descent from a common family, that of Míl who settled in Ireland before the dawn of history. Míl came from Spain with his sons and nephew who thus became the fountain heads of the four main branches of the Gaels; their names were Eber, Eremon, Ir and Ith. The Eoghanacht, Dál gCais and Cianacht were all considered descendants of Eber, the aforementioned O'Driscolls of Ith. Together they were the southern septs (the stature of the Ithians being altogether subordinate), those of the north being the Eremonians and the less important Irians. The opposition between north and south, reflecting a long rivalry between Munster and Midland kings, was thus couched sometimes in territorial, sometimes in genealogical terms. These frames of reference do not tally completely, and it should be kept in mind that the system outlined here is, again, a post-Viking pseudo-historical construct, consisting of genealogical square pegs violently forced into the round holes of earlier tribal-territorial relations.

In this post-Viking bardic view, then, a man like young Tadhg Mac Cárthaigh would thus have a set of concentric spheres of political allegiance: there would be, first, his own branch of the Clann Cárthaigh, then the Clann Cárthaigh as a whole, then the Eoghanacht as opposed to Dál gCais and Cianacht, then the descendants of Oilill Olum as a whole, which category would in its turn be comprised within the totality of the descendants of Eber. And only in the ultimate instance would the opposition to, and rivalry with, the Eremonians be subsumed under the common name of 'Gael'. This neat and, be it repeated, pseudo-histori-cally and poetically contrived, concentricity of allegiances is, however, disturbed by the fact that relatively closely related clans would often persist in traditional enmity owing to their territorial contiguity and the conflicts arising therefrom (cf. the conflicts between the Í Néill and Í Dhomhnaill).

A poet's concern would, then, be twofold: to be the censor of the chieftain's ritual position, privileges and obligations, within the clan, and to be the arbiter of the clan's territorial and racial/genealogical position within the clan system. The interdependent prestige of chieftain and clan was his to formulate.

With such fundamental and grave responsibilities attendant upon the poet's office, one need not be surprised to find that the poet's social prestige was second only to that of the king himself. Indeed, the relation between chieftain and poet was often problematic owing to the latter's jealous defence of his own privileges. His encomium on a patron would always include blatant references to the royal practice of liberality towards the poet, and sometimes reads like unabashed extortion. On the other hand, a poet was not restricted in his choice of patrons: although he would frequently have a special relationship with a certain family or chief, he might also bestow praise on (and in return expect rewards from) other chieftains. A poet's ultimate allegiance was to his own class and its social privileges – or, to put it in a friendlier way, to Gaelic culture of which he was the guardian and which was largely transmitted through the medium of verse written under royal patronage. In this sense, the poet himself *was*, to some extent, one of the few cohesive factors combining various clans into a vague 'Gaeldom': he could pass from clan to clan without ever being considered a stranger; he could cross the Eremonian/Eberian divide, and remain a constant feature amidst all these variables of Gaelic society. The poet's aristocratic and professional pride could even clash with his duty of subservience to the chieftain: the examples are numerous of poems irritably or even threateningly exhorting a chief to honour the poet's claims or privileges, and no less numerous are poems trying to mend a rupture between the poet and a patron with whom he has obviously gone too far. An extreme example of bardic arrogance is given by the eminent Muireadach 'Albanach' Ó Dálaigh (fl. early thirteenth century) who was eventually chased out of Ireland by the irate Ó Domhnaill for having killed that chieftain's steward – who had, Ó Dalaigh thought, spoken to him in a disrespectful manner. In the poet's own lofty words:

> * Beag ar bhfala risin bhfear,
> bachlach do bheith dom cháineadh,
> mé do mharbhadh an mhoghadh –
> a Dhé, an adhbhar anfholadh? (IBP p. 90)

Such frictions were, however, mostly transitory. On the whole, the balance of nobility (emanating from the king but subject to the poet's praise and approval) was kept to the satisfaction of both parties. The clan system was thus based on the reciprocity of inter clan rivalry, and on the clan-transcending impartiality of the guardians of history and of culture, the poets. The situation has been aptly described by Proinsias Mac Cana as a 'spiritual unity and political disunity . . . both encompassed within a common, universally acknowledged ideology'.[9] This whole system of internecine rivalry, family pride, aristocratic and professional pride was placed under a shadow, however, by the intrusion of non-Gaelic contenders for supremacy: the new Hiberno-Norman aristocracy.

---

* Trifling is our difference with the man: that a churl was abusing me and that I killed the serf – O God! is this a ground for enmity? (ed.'s trl.)

The Hiberno-Norman presence

It is indicative of the complete absence of anything resembling a politically effective 'national' or 'common Gaelic' political perspective that the Hiberno-Norman barons who settled in Ireland were not, in the bardic view, specifically linked to England and to the English king whose vassals they were. They are either called *Gall* (pl. *Goill),* meaning 'foreigner' and applicable to anyone hailing from outside Ireland (whether from Continental Gaul, as the root of the word indicates, or from Scandinavia, as its application to the various waves of Vikings shows), or *Danar.* The latter expression is interesting in that it tends to identify the Hiberno-Normans with the successive waves of Vikings/Norsemen in the preceding centuries. The English conquest of Ireland seems, then, to have at the time been regarded as a new wave of Viking incursion arriving by way of Normandy and England: irksome to say the least, but peripheral to the affairs of Gaelic Ireland, much as if the first squalls of the deluge were taken for just another spell of bad weather. It also seems that a far more cataclysmic development was at the time considered to lie in the abeyance of the 'high-kingship', which was attributed mostly to intra-Gaelic causes (the usurpation of Brian Ború, the internecine rivalry which precluded a consensus of loyalty to the overkings after him). There seems to have been a natural reluctance to recognize the relativity of the Gaelic frame of reference, to recognize that the Gaels might have to share Ireland with Foreigners,[10] outsiders insinuating themselves into a country whose society they did not 'fit' – upsetting, perhaps, though certainly not supplanting the tacit, implicit Gaelic claim to a homogeneously Gaelic Ireland.

As these new *Danair* turned out to lay more permanent and far-reaching claims to the ownership of Ireland, Gaelic unease grew. The erection of feudal Norman castles in particular was a visible and forcible disruption, and their blatantly solid and lapidary architecture imposed on the landscape an unnerving aspect of 'j'y suis, j'y reste'. Accordingly, it is no surprise to find foreign castles referred to frequently in bardic poetry in highly inimical terms. It was recognized that a second Brian Ború would be needed to expel these newfangled and unexpectedly troublesome intruders; as a result, 'prophecies' begin to be produced which link the expulsion of these new *Danair* or *Goill* to a restoration of the high-kingship.[11]

Such prophecies exhibit a pattern that has some significance in the literary evolution of a sense of nationality. They describe the present quasiprophetically from a spuriously 'past' point of view; in doing so, they describe the present also as the fulfillment of a past prophecy, that is to say, as proof positive of the prophecy's reliability. In this manner, the prophecy can go on to present its hopes for the future in similar and all the more 'convincing' terms. Both the arrival of usurping Foreigners (by now a political reality) and the fact that they will eventually be driven out of Ireland (as yet a mere wish) are 'foretold' in the purportedly 'ancient' prophecy.

Such pseudo-prophetic modes of literary propaganda, which retrodate the present into the time-warp of a vision of the future seen from the past, and which constantly fanned hopes for a future that will return to the *status quo ante expugnationem*, were to persist for more than six hundred years without ever being either materialized or abandoned. This fact is in itself remarkable and stands in need of closer scrutiny.

Prophecies of this kind were bolstered by dint of repetition; frequently a poet would allude to earlier foretellings and speculate optimistically that the time for their fulfillment was at last drawing nigh.[12] An early example is contained in a poem by Giolla Brighde Mac Con Midhe, from the early fourteenth century:

  *   Táinig tairngire na n-éarlamh –
uaisle Fódla feirrde dháibh;
ní cian go bhfóirthear a bhformod –
fóirfear ar fhiadh bhfonnbhog bhFáil.

Amharas fa fhad go dtáinig
ar dhá dtrian ar thairngir siad;
briathra na gcéadbhuileadh creididh –
nír bréagnuigheadh eidir iad.

Nír chreid Dá Thí ar thairngir Finnéan:
Fódla ag Gallaibh, gníomh nár cheil;
Goill do theacht i ngoire Ghaoidheal,
reacht oile nár saoileadh sein.[13]

Roughly half a century later, the poet Sean Mór Ó Clumhain began an encomium in the following way:

  °   (An) deimhin a-nos teacht don tairnngire?
neart ainbhfine ó 'd-chlos ar choillMhidhe
Gaoidhil go seanshruth mbraonach mBreaghmhuighe;
ar meanmuine ar aonach Teamhrach toinnghile.

Uaisle Gaoidheal gan rígh dá roileagadh
aoinfhear d'oireagar dhíbh nír dhligheadar;
cur ris, a Dhé, do b'ard an anobar
gur thoghadar é i mbalg fhis 's nír ibheadar.

---

  *   The prophecy of the saints has come to pass – the nobles of Fódla will be the better for it; it is not long till their dissensions are healed – the soft-earthed land of Fál will be saved.

    For a long time until he came there was doubt about two thirds of what they prophesied; believe the early prophetic visions – they have not been shown to be false at all.

    Dá Thí did not believe what Finnéan predicted, that Fódla would be in possession of the Foreigners – a deed he did not conceal; the Foreigners coming near the Irish, that was another jurisdiction that was not expected. (ed.'s trl.)

  °   Is this a proof that the Prophecy is coming to pass? After hearing of the foreign opposition on wooded Midhe, the Gaoidhil, marching to the storied swelling stream of the Breagha's plain, are our hope for another Fair on bright-surfaced Teamhair.

    The nobles of the Gaoidhil, kingless and crushed, were not free to set up (as king) one of themselves – 'twere a dread thing, O God, to attempt it – till they had chosen him after prophetic inspiration, and they got it not (?).

Gluaisis mac Ruaidhrí an ruathair iolbhuadhaigh
sluaighrí fionnLuaraigh go Cruachain gcomhdhálaigh;
forfhógra Thaidhg i mBreaghmhuigh bhailbhéanaigh
(failmhéaghaidh) gach aird go Teamhraigh dtromdhámhaigh;
ón tSionuinn bhreacdhuinn uaine eidhnéanaigh
teinnghéabhaidh go seanTuinn dTuaidhe dtormánaigh.

Luaidhe gach mhúir Ghallda tré ghoirmtheinidh
roinnfidhir dúin uaine arda d'orchoraibh;
clocha aoil an mhachaire millfidhir
le cathaidhe bhfinnchinidh chaoimh Conchobhair. (Aith DD vol. I, 9–10)

This anti-Foreign incentive was not presented as a pan-Gaelic ideal based on interclan solidarity; rather, the Foreigners were to be expelled mainly as part of the chieftain's campaign to seize the high-kingship of Tara for himself; in presenting the expulsion of the Goill as a precondition for the seizure of the high-kingship, Foreign presence in Ireland could thus find its expression in terms of the internecine Gaelic rivalry inherent in the clan system. The afore-mentioned Muireadach Albanach hints at this as early as *c.* 1215–20, in a poem to Cathal 'Croibhdhearg' ('Redhand') Ó Conchobhair, in which he asks for patronage and protection against the wrath of Ó Domhnaill and which contains the optimistic stanza:

* As é an Croibhdhearg chuirfios soir
   na Gulla do ghabh Theamhraigh:
   an duine ní diombáidh linn
   'ga ttiomáin uile a hÉirinn. (IBP p. 106)

As T.J. Dunne points out,[14] it should be taken into account that these lines are addressed to a brother of the last chief to claim the actual title of high-king of Ireland, whose 'reign' was interrupted by the Anglo-Norman takeover – hence also the description of the Foreigners as the seizers of Tara, seat of the high-king. Far from being a call for a nation-wide anti-Foreign crusade, the poem is rather a standard encomiastic exhortation to a chief to stand up for his personal and dynastic rights, and to prove his excellence over all rivals. The same observation applies to all other productions in this vein, which exhort a chief to expel the Foreigner and claim the high-kingship.[15]

Ruaidhri's triumphant charging son, captain of fair Luarach, has marched on crowded Cruacha; Tadhg's proclamation will empty (of troops) every height in Breagha's bird-whispering plain even to poet-burdened Teamhair; from the green ivy-bordered Sionna he will seize all land up to the old resounding Wave of Tuaidh.

   Ashes of every foreign castle rising in blue flame, the high green strongholds will be broken in pieces by shots; the limestone forts of the plain will be destroyed by the battler of courteous Conchobhar's fair race. (ed.'s trl.)

* It is the Redhand that will drive eastwards the Foreigners who have seized Tara: it were no grief to me that he should banish them all from Ireland. (ed.'s trl.)

Generally, however, the poet would carefully maintain, for all his flattering exultation, a diplomatically non-committal attitude in his encomia: no matter how fancifully he would describe his patron's superiority, he would never state precisely 'over whom' he was superior. Explicit comparisons with other clans or other chiefs were always carefully avoided, so as not to incur the displeasure or the jealousy of one who might turn out to be a prospective patron.[16] The poet would, in fact, be far more realistic in his effusions when he would actually instill some pieces of political advice into his poems – as he was fully qualified to do, given his prestige in the Gaelic order. It is in such a context that the actual reality of the day, and the bardic attitude regarding it, is more clearly recognizable.

Let us return, for example, to Giolla Brighde Mac Con Midhe's poem to Aodh Ó Domhnaill, 'Tainig tairngire na n-earlamh', of which I have quoted the first three stanzas above. Much of this poem is taken up by personal praise and by arguments as to how Ulster chieftains can also command the allegiance of Connacht and Munster clans (presumably also regarding a possible high-kingship). This rather vacuous flattery gradually subsides into plain cautionary advice when the poet comes to deal with the enmity of the Foreigners; the dead weight of seriousness is then lifted by a new twist of flattery, but the point has been made, and forcefully so:

> * Budh leat Muimhnigh i measg Connacht;
> im chúirtibh clach cleachtaid gleo;
> do-bheir duinne i ndath na nglaschlach
> clach 'na buinne lasrach leo.
>
> Leat Conall is cungnamh Gaoidheal;
> Goill it aghaidh aithnidh daoibh;
> druid ort re himreasain ngallda
> olc d'fhinnleasaibh arda aoil.
>
> Do budh é gliocas Gall nÉireann
> iarraidh do shíthe ó sho a-mach;
> ar mbuain re hallmharchaibh úicfe
> 'na ndamhdhabhchaibh cúirte clach.

---

* Yours will be the men of Munster among the Connachta; about the courts of stone they practise battle; fiery redness caused by them in the colour of the grey stones makes the stone turn to a flaming sea.

Yours are the Kindred of Conall and the assistance of the Irish; you know the Foreigners oppose you; to press against you with foreign battle is grim for the white, high castles of limestone.

It would be wisdom on the part of the Foreigners of Ireland to sue you for peace from now on; when you have dealt with the Foreigners, you will raze the courts of stone to their very floors.

Cionnus choiseonas cíos Gaoidheal –
Goill do léim ní lag an snaidhm –
gan bhéim ort, a Aodh Í Dhomhnaill?
ná taobh tocht a horlainn airm.

A Aodh í Éigneacháin Uisnigh,
urchar id lurg ní lamh tóir;
ní fhéach oraibh cách do chnocaibh;
sgáth romhaibh ní docair dhóibh.

Mór anocht – aidhbhseach i lúirigh –
lorg an ghaoi nach gabhdaois uird;
iongnadh linn líne do chleithe,
míne a cinn is leithe a luirg.

Is tú is treise thairngeas bogha
dá mbí i ndeabhaidh re dáil fras;
do chrann arna bhéin id bhiodhbhaidh,
ní léir barr a fhiodhraidh as.

A Aodh mhic Dhomhnaill Í Dhomhnaill,
déana longphort ós Loch Rí;
do ríghe ina síodh ní seachmhaidh:
díon na síne ar fhearthain í.[17]

This is admirable diplomacy as well as accomplished poetical craftmanship. The first stanza describes an attack on a foreign castle by those whom Aodh's winsome personality has united, thus introducing the heinous topic (the Foreigners and their castles) in an inoffensive manner. The next stanza elaborates on the idea that the main point of conflict between Aodh and the Gall lies in the latter's entrenched position in his stronghold. Of course, the Goill know Aodh's superiority as well as the poet does, says the next stanza reassuringly, but that is exactly why they will want to sue for peace and meanwhile fortify themselves with their odious castles. The conclusion, offered in the fourth stanza: Aodh must give the Goill no rest, their entrenchment is a serious threat to his position and must be dealt with immediately. This warning is turned into flattery again as the poet

How can it maintain the tribute of the Irish – the attack of the Foreigners is no mean oppression – without causing you reproach, O Aodh Ó Domhnaill? Do not trust repose from the butt of your weapon.

O Aodh, descendant of Éigneachán of Uisneach, no troop dares to attack you from the rear; no-one thinks to attack you from the hills; it is not difficult for them to be afraid of you. Many now are the marks of a spear – huge in a breastplate – that hammers could not repair; remarkable I find the length of your spear, the smoothness of its head and the width of its shaft.

You are the mightiest man that draws a bow of all who are wont to be in battle at the scattering of showers of arrows; when your spear has been struck into your foe, the end of its shaft cannot be seen protruding from him.

O Aodh, son of Domhnall Ó Domhnaill, make a fort above Loch Rí; no superfluous matter that your kingdom is at peace: it is the guarantee of good weather rather than rain. (ed.'s trl.)

interprets the Foreign fortifications as a tacit recognition that they dare not meet Aodh in the field; the next stanzas make suggestive comparisons between the relative degrees of usefulness of offensive weaponry and defensive armour. This circumspect argument is then summed up when the poet openly exhorts Aodh to build a fort for himself, too – to wit, in a position considerably extending his own territory.

Other, later examples of the more cautionary and realistic references to foreign presence in bardic poetry can be found in the poems of Tuathal Ó hUiginn to various Connacht chieftains.[18] Of especial interest is the ode to Eoghan Ó Raghallaigh, lord of Breifne († 1449), which falls into two halves. The first is of the traditional incentive/encomiastic kind, working on the patron's pride; Connacht, the poet says, the ancient kingdom of Ailill and Medb with its capital at Cruacha, is now divided into three parts, one of which (rightfully belonging to the Í Raghallaigh) is under the sway of the Foreigners. This situation is intolerable and shameful to anyone with a sense of honour.

> * Ar Ghaoidhealaibh is guth linn
> an chríoch do chosain Oilill
> mar léagar le cloinn Chréidhe
> Goill d'fhéagadh a heichréidhe. (AithDD vol. 1, 119)

Then comes the flattery: there is one, at least, who will not put up with this outrageous state of affairs – it is the lord of Breifne, whose present territory is but a pitiful corner of what is his by rights. This barbed reference to Ó Raghallaigh's honour is elaborated pointedly, goading him on to take action:

> ° Dúthaigh fhíre hí don fhior,
> Cruacha caithir a sinnsior,
> ní ghairfe mé acht deoradh dhe
> Eoghan dá mbé sa Bhréifne.
>
> D'Ó Raighilligh a-tá a tháir
> a theach i dTulaigh Modháin
> gé do-ní sa tulaigh thoir
> ní badh chubhaidh i gCruachoin.
>
> Fian Gall do ghabháil treise
> ar mínleach na Midheise
> doibhinn an fáth fa bhfuirigh
> gan ráth Oilill d'ionnsuighidh. (pp. 120–1)

* This land once held by Oilill is a standing reproach to the Gaoidhil, seeing that Créidhe's race let the Goill enjoy the sight of their plains. (ed.'s trl.)

° The true country of the hero is Cruacha, his ancestor's fort; if Eoghan remains in Breifne I can only call him an exile. That his home should be in Tulach Modhain is a shame for Ó Raghallaigh, even though in that hill to the East he is conducting affairs which he should conduct at Cruacha. The seizing of power by the Goill over the plain of Midhe is the reason – a lamentable reason! – why he delays in making for Oilill's fort. (ed.'s trl.)

It is at this point that a new theme is introduced: the contrast between the ancestral claim of Ó Raghallaigh to the territory, and the claims of the Goill which are founded on chartered grants from the English king. The very mention of these claims is a recognition of the fact that the Hiberno-Normans might after all be more than a merely transitory presence in Ireland. Moreover, it implies that the poet is becoming aware of a clash, not just of different territorial claims, but also of different legal and social systems: the clan system with its tanistry and warlordism, and the feudal system hased on primogeniture and fiefdom/vassalage. Seen in this light, the poet's exhortations to reconquer Connacht from the Goill take on a deeper meaning: beyond the physical reappropriation of lands and produce, it also implies a refusal to recognize the validity of feudal law, English law, in Gaelic Ireland.

> * Cairt ainbhfine ar Inis Fáil
> cá meisde do mhac Sea-áin?
> sa chartaigh má déaghthar dhi
> léaghthar 'n-a hacraibh Éire.
>
> Gach Gall aca lenab áil
> sealbh an oiléinse d'fhagháil
> cairt ó rígh Shaghsan do shir
> le a ngabhsan tír Airt Éinfhir.
>
> Ná héisdeadh re cáir dá gcluin
> earroidheacht Tuathail Teachtmhair;
> fa ráidh an rulla fallsa
> dáibh ní hurra an t-Eoghansa. (p. 121)

This argument is developed in the poet's statement that the idea of feudal landownership through royal grant is a blow at the very root of the Gael's claim to Ireland:

> ° Sliocht na gcéidfhear dá bhfuil féin
> ní leanann – is lorg soiléir –
> rádh cairte dá gcuire i seadh
> duine do mhaicne Míleadh. (p. 121)

---

* What matters it to Seaán that there is a foreign charter to Inis Fail? If you look at Éire herself she and all her acres are to be found named in that charter.
   Every Gall who wants possession of the island asks a charter for it from the King of the Saxons, and with it takes over the land of Art Aoinfhear.
   Let the native folk of Tuathal Teachtmhar not listen to the claims they hear advanced for their possession; according to what the false document says Eoghan is not their lord. (ed.'s trl.)
° No man of the race of Mil is to be successor to the race of the ancients of whose blood he is – this is clear – if he pays heed to the language of the charter. (ed.'s trl.)

The Gaels themselves came as conquerors, and took possession of the land by right of conquest; charters had nothing to do with it and therefore should not be recognized: the Gael's charter is his sword and his spear.

> * Cairt eile ní iarrfa sibh
>   acht tú ar thoradh do ghaisgidh;
>   léim fa ghaoibh géara dod ghuin
>   séala dhaoibh ar do dhúthaigh.
>
>   An chraoiseach leathan sa láimh
>   's an colg a ceardcha Bholcáin
>   madh faigse hí budh hí an tsleagh
>   is í do chairtse an cloidheamh.
>
>   Sróll uaine ler éirigh séan
>   ar inneall biadhta brainéan,
>   cairt ar nar sireadh séala,
>   do chineadh Airt fhoisgéala.
>
>   Cairt eile thoghbhus tusa
>   dá dtig táth do dhúthchasa
>   tógbha sgiath i nglotain gháidh;
>   docair dá thriath a thógbhail. (pp. 122–3)

In the course of this forceful exhortation, with its relentless harping on that jarring loanword *cairt,* charter, the poet is led back to his main point: that Ó Raghallaigh should do honour to himself and his lineage by going forth and conquering. And in typically encomiastic style, the final stanza reminds him that he might keep a higher kingship than that of Connacht in mind. . .

> ° A mhic inghine Í Fhearghail
>   an gcuimhnighe ar chlaoinTeamhraigh
>   d'fhios tighe Dá Thí an dtiocfa,
>   nó an bhfoile ar tí thoighiochta. (p. 123)

As Tuathal's poem so cleverly indicates, the feudal and the Gaelic systems of nobility were in some respects polar opposites: in the feudal system, the fixed

---

* Thou shalt seek no other charter except thy own reliance on thy gallantry; to charge against the sharp spears that pierce thee is thy true charter to thy land.

    The sharp spear in thy hand, the blade from Vulcan's smithy, the spear if it be nearer thee, thy sword – those are thy charter.

    The green satin banner. which good fortune attends and which promises to feed the ravens – that is the charter, a charter requiring no seal, which thou shalt show to Art's race.

    Another charter shalt thou raise aloft, a charter that will unite all thy native land – thou shalt raise up thy spear in face of danger – even its lord can hardly lift it. (ed.'s trl.)

° O son of the daughter of Ó Fearghail, art thou mindful of sloping Teamhair? Wilt thou come to Dá Thí's house? or rather, art thou on the point of coming to it? (ed.'s trl.)

point is the overlord, the monarch, and all nobility emanates from him and by his grace; in the Gaelic system, it is the local sovereign chieftain who defines aristocracy in its various degrees of excellence, and it is by the acquiescence or submission of the local chiefs and their competitors that the office of overlord can be filled. Whereas the Gaelic overking exerts vassalage from his lesser peers, the feudal king bestows it on his subjects. The notion expressed by Tuathal Ó hUiginn, that warlike prowess is the Gaelic chieftain's charter, is therefore far more than a poetic conceit – a chieftain's position would in actual fact be founded wholly on his superiority over his rivals, and Ó hUiginn makes this point with as much professional interest as a herald-at-arms would have in assessing the relative order of succession between claimants to a title in the peerage. Hence also the extent of bardic dismay when the poets were later to find that the Gaelic chieftains were succumbing to Tudor expansionism; in bardic terms, the decrease in martial valour implied in this trend would be, quite literally, a constitutional crisis. The implication seems to be that the recognition of a *political* (rather than cultural) pan-Gaelic interest and identity had come hand in hand with a gradual recognition of the enmity of the Foreigners as a fixed element in Irish society.[19] It is no surprise to find, then, that a poet's praise for his chieftain's valour would often be couched in descriptions of his fight against the Foreigners: thus, Giolla Brighde Mac Con Midhe sprinkles laudatory hints at an anti-Foreign stalwartness through his odes, for instance when he praises Giolla Pádraig Ó hAnnluain:

> * Do hairgeadh leis thoir is thiar
> puirt Ghall Uladh is Oirghiall;
> puirt Ghall Midhe 's a margadh,
> barr Line arna lomargadh.[20]

And Tadhg Óg Ó hUiginn apostrophizes numerous chieftains with chevilles largely based on their enmity towards the Goill.[21] However, the aforementioned poem by Mac Con Midhe to Ó hAnnluain, as well as various others, can also contain references to raids against neighbouring Gaelic clans, sometimes even mentioned in one breath with the references to anti-Foreign battles. In the stanza from Mac Con Midhe's poem quoted here, for instance, the chief of Line mentioned in the last line is not, like Ó hAnnluain's victims in the rest of the stanza, a Foreigner, but a Gael: the Ó Thuirtrí territory of Line, in Ulster, was held by the Í Fhloinn.[22] And this trend, again, seems to imply that Gaelic-Foreign enmity came to be regarded increasingly in the same light as intra-Gaelic internecine rivalry. A parallel development took shape among the Hiberno-Normans. Inherent in the feudal system is a tendency to emancipate one's power from the vassalage under one's liege, to rule in one's own right rather than as a mere

---

* East and west the settlements of the Foreigners of Ulster and Oriel were plundered by him; the settlements of the Foreigners of Midhe and their market, the chief of Line were utterly plundered. (ed.'s trl.)

instrument of the monarch. The Hiberno-Normans were not exempt from this; but in the Irish context, isolated as they were from their English peers and liege, surrounded on all sides by Gaelic lordships, they underwent this tendency in an intensified form which in fact amounted to an estrangement from their original culture and an adaptation to their Gaelic surroundings. This well-known process, giving rise to the oft-repeated quip that some of the Hiberno-Normans became 'Hiberniores Hibernis ipsis', did not necessarily change their enmity with the Gaelic lords into friendship – but perhaps more importantly, it wove this enmity into the existing web of interclan strife which, paradoxically, was one of the main cohesive forces of the clan society. The main Hiberno-Norman families became cordially accepted as fellow rivals in the time-honoured infighting for prestige, an infusion rather than an intrusion into the Gaelic system.[23] One might use the simile of a soccer league, in which the individual clans would be the competing clubs, linked by the very principle of their mutual rivalry, and with the poets as referees – unabashed 'home referees', of course. In this view, the 'acceptance' of new clubs into the league – Hiberno-Norman ones – would be marked by the fact that a similar rivalry would be extended to them.

A great problem for the traditional division between Gael and Gall was the question of intermarriage, which began to facilitate the absorption of the Hiberno-Normans into their Gaelic environment at a remarkably early period.[24] How was one to address a chieftain whose mother, for instance, was a Foreigner? Aonghus Ó Dalaigh's address to Art Mor Ó Maoilsheachlainn, king of Meath (†1344), managed to wangle a way out of this dilemma, but it is obvious that he evaded rather than resolved the problem:

> *   Dlighi a mhic na mná gallda
>   goill a hUisniuch d'innarba;
>   ginn de féin a boigcnes bán
>   sgoiltes go léir in lemán. (BMCat vol. I, 362)

Notwithstanding all their formulaic anti-Foreign protestations, the poets, when accepting new prospective patrons, do not seem to have had any exorbitant scruples merely on account of these patrons' non-Gaelic descent. Muireadach Albanach must again be mentioned as an early example: when he was forced to flee from Ó Domhnaill (cf. p. 158 above), his first destination was the arch-enemy – in this case, the foremost Norman settled in Connacht, Richard FitzWilliam De Burgo. The poet announced himself at his doorstep with a poem of remarkable condescension, more or less implying that he was honouring De Burgo by his visit, which was to be understood as an acknowledgement of the Norman's nobility and social acceptability; it began:

---

*   Thou (above all), O Englishwoman's son! art bound to hunt the English out of Uisnech: a wedge of his own self it is, O soft and white of skin! that utterly rends the elm. (ed.'s trl.)

*   Créd agaibh aoidhigh a gcéin,
a ghiolla gusan ngaillsgéimh,
a dhream ghaoidhealta ghallda,
naoidheanta sheang shaorchlannda? (IBP p. 88)

By the mid-fourteenth century, this process of Gaelicization among the Hiberno-Norman nobles was practically completed, and the descendants of Richard Fitzwilliam de Burgo had taken Gaelic styles like Mac Uilliam Uachtar (or Clann Riocaird) and Mac Uilliam Íochtar. The Statutes of Kilkenny, passed by the Kilkenny Parliament of 1366 as a last-ditch attempt to reverse this trend, have already been mentioned; how effective they were in practice can be gathered from the fact that the king's justiciar in Ireland, who convoked the next Kilkenny parliament in 1367, was none other than Gerald, third earl of Desmond – the same Desmond, Gearóid Iarla, who was himself a poet of merit in the Irish language: we have a poem of great elegance and sardonic wit by him, in which he explains to the Gaelic chieftains that he is forced to implement some of the king's anti-Gaelic policy, but ventures to express the hope that this will not be taken as an act of personal ill-will against his beloved compatriots . . .

°   Fuilngim tír na nÉireannach
nach rachainn i gceann Ghaoidheal
mina tíosadh éigeantas
ó ríogh Shaxan dom laoideadh.[25]

The terminology is especially interesting in its use of the term *Éireannach*: the idea is that Desmond swears by a country which is possessed co-jointly by the Gaels and by Goill like himself, and he brings these two groups (which in the Gaelic frame of mind were more like manichean opposite halves of the human race) together under the term *Éireannach*, derived from the country they both inhabit, and defined as against yet another group: the Saxons with their king in London, those of the neighbouring island. This terminology not only begins to dissociate the Gaelicized Goill of Ireland from their English fellow-subjects, but in fact almost amounts to a geographical view of 'nationality', as distinct from the racial/genealogical one employed in the bardic system. It is, I think, by no means a coincidence that this view, which was later to prove an exact anticipation of seventeenth-century terminological and ideological developments, should be expressed by one in Desmond's hybrid position, by a non-Gaelic Irishman. As we shall see in the next chapter, a similar usage of *Éireannach* reappears later in the work of another non-Gaelic Irishman, Geoffrey Keating, where both *Gaedheal* and *Sean-Ghall* ('Old Foreigner') are subsumed under the common term *Éireannach*, from which the *Nua-Ghall* ('New Foreigners') are explicitly excluded.[26]

---

*   Whence comes it that ye have guests from afar, O youth of foreign beauty, O ye who are become Gaelic, yet foreign, young, graceful and highborn? (ed.'s trl.)

°   I swear by the land of the Irish that I would not move against the Gaels, if it were not that a command had come from the Saxons' king to spur me on.

In the rest of this poem, Desmond whimsically describes his problematic position in having ties with both warring parties, in having friends who are each other's enemies; he states his preference for the Gaels – notwithstanding their incurable feuds or his own dependence on the English crown.

> * Fearr liom bheith 'gam bráithreachaibh
> giodh [créad] a n-inntinn umainn
> ná beith a gcoir bhráighdeanais
> ag ríogh Shaxan i Lunainn.[27]

The sardonic opposition of two allegiances – or, conversely, of two enmities, which, for someone in Desmond's position, amounted to much the same thing – is greatly enhanced by the use of assonance as prescribed by the metre. The phonetic resemblance between the rhyming terms 'braithreachaibh' – 'bhraigh-deanais' neatly offsets the semantic divergence ('brothers', albeit in a non-uterine sense – 'imprisonment') between them, much as the intervening second line helps to point out that the opposition between *bráthar* and *bráighdeanas* may not, after all, be much greater than that between Scylla and Charybdis.

Not only in his poetry did Desmond attest to his love for Ireland[28] and for Gaelic culture: he was also patron to one of the foremost bardic poets of his century, Gofraidh Fionn Ó Dálaigh. Ó Dálaigh had written a poem to Desmond around the middle of the fourteenth century, asking him to be his advocate with his father Maurice, second earl of Desmond.

This poem, 'A Ghearóid deana mo dhail'[29] in which Ó Dálaigh addressed Gearóid as 'a naoidhe gheal-fhóid Gaoidheal', 'O child of the Gaoidhil's fair land' (p. 513), was probably occasioned by Maurice's irritation at what he must have considered to be Ó Dálaigh's fickleness: the *file's* 'double-talk' in indiscriminately awarding supremacy to any patron he could address; Ó Dálaigh's patrons, incidentally, also included the De Burgos in Connacht, and we may recall that it was also Ó Dalaigh who hailed young Tadhg Mac Cárthaigh as Eire's prospective *fír-chéile* in the ode mentioned above on p. 155. It should be understood, of course, that what might at first sight seem like bardic 'duplicity' can in fact be explained either from the formulaic conventions of the praise-poem as a genre, or from the poet's social position which transcended the clannish allegiances that divided Gaelic society; hence, the quarrel between Desmond senior and Ó Dálaigh was essentially a cross-cultural misunderstanding. Maurice must have taken bardic rhetorical flourishes at face value; he must have taken flattering strains seriously which had in their proper context become mere formulaic patterns of praise. Ó Dálaigh went as far as to explain this divergence of poetical norms in the following remarkable and well-known, if often misinterpreted, stanzas:

---

* I would rather be among my own folk – whatever be their feeling towards me – than to find myself imprisoned at the hands of the Saxons' king in London.

* Flaitheas nach gabhaid Gaoidhil
  geallmaoid dóibh i nduan-laoidhibh
  a ráthughadh dhúibh níor dhluigh
  gnáthughadh dhúin a dhéanaimh.

  Dá chineadh dá gcumthar dán
  i gcrích Éireann na n-uarán
  na Gaoidhil-se ag boing re bladh
  is Goill bhraoin-inse Breatan.

  I ndán na nGall gealltar linn
  Gaoidhil d'ionnarbhadh a hÉirinn
  Goill do shraoineadh tar sál sair
  i ndán na nGaoidheal gealltair. (p. 513)

These stanzas have in later centuries gained some notoriety for the cynicism they are seen to embody: a shameless admission that the poet would abandon all principles of honesty, veracity and loyalty in order to flatter his patron of the day. One might, of course, with equal propriety impugn an Augustan poet for describing the sun as 'Phoebus' which, after all, is heinous blasphemy for a Christian and a dangerous revival of paganism. To impose principles of honesty, veracity and loyalty on a bardic praise-poem is, in a belated way, the same sort of shortsightedness that Maurice, second earl of Desmond, seems to have fallen victim to. What Ó Dálaigh is arguing in all sincerity is that one should not confuse the language of formal poetry with that of political reality – he is, in fact, deigning to explain some of the conventions of the bardic encomium to one on whom they were obviously lost. Nevertheless, the poem's language, formalized and non-realistic as it may claim to be, does reflect some of the political aspects of the Geraldines' situation – the polished chiasm in the third quoted stanza, for example, crosses through the binary opposition Gael-Gall with great smoothness and felicity, and anticipates the skillful dialectics that young Gearóid himself was to weave into his own, later poem. Indeed, the stanza following the excerpt quoted above resolves the tension between parallel and chiastic opposition in a conclusion similar to that of Gearóid: a statement of the extraordinary, aloof position of the Geraldines with respect to these clashing interests:

° Na Goill is Gaoidhil Bhanbha
  fa seach re hucht th-agallmha
  is tú ceann an dá chineadh
  geall red chlú ní chuirfidhear. (p. 513)

* In our poems we promise the Gaoidhil a kingdom they never get. You should not pay attention to it, 'tis our custom!
  Two races to whom poems are sung are in cool-streamed Eire, the Goidheal known to fame and the Goill of Britain, isle of varied beauty.
  In poems to the Goill we promise the driving of the Gaoidhil from Eire; in those to the Gaoidhil we promise the driving of the Goill East overseas! (ed.'s trl.)

° Goill and Gaoidhil of Banbha both in turn seek thy converse. Thou art head of both races; thy fame shall not be equalled. (ed.'s trl.)

Many more such examples of a bardic acceptance of the Normans' participation in the Gaelic way of life can be found; suffice it is here to point out the case of Tadhg Óg Ó hUiginn, who wrote numerous poems to Hiberno-Norman patrons besides the ones he addressed to Gaelic chieftains; and even in his Gaelic-oriented poems it is obvious that the division of alliance or enmity is wholly dependent on the vicissitude of political interest, and on the mutually contradictory interests of the individual clans, rather than on the criterion of appurtenance to the Gaelic race. Thus in one case Goill and Í Néill are the common enemies of the Í Dhomhnaill, whereas in another poem the Goill are incited to wrest Ulster from the Í Néill.[30]

Many bardic poems addressed to Hiberno-Norman patrons overtly refer to strong racial enmity which is only neutralized by the transcendent qualities of the patron. An example is Tadhg Óg's ode to Seamus Buitillear (James Butler), fourth earl of Ormond, which skillfully weaves a complicated argument that may be epitomized as follows: the magical signs of Éire's benevolence and acceptance have made Ormond the uncontested leader of the country; his stature transcends the enmity between Gael and Gall; but to whom should he entrust the country during his absence? Tadhg Óg exhorts Ormond to put a Gael in charge of Ireland whenever he himself leaves the country: he himself or a Gall of his own greatness is needed to keep the Goill in their proper place and to defend them against the natural jealousy of the dispossessed Gael; therefore let him trust no inferior Foreigner (for his equal is not to be found) to maintain the status quo. (AithDD vol. 1, 139–43)

A similar idea – only the patron's personal excellence can transcend and subdue the natural enmity between Gael and Gall – is contained in Tadhg Óg's poem to Uilleog Rua Mac Uilliam Uachtar, which combines this idea with the more traditional motif that the poet's favour with his patron creates jealousy and envy among the less fortunate retainers. The resulting argument is that Ó hUiginn feels afraid of the enmity of the Goill among whom he finds himself and therefore turns to Mac Uilliam for protection (AithDD vol. 1, 163–6).

A similar integration of Hiberno-Norman patrons into the bardic view of society took place on the level of poetic idiom. So much of bardic poetry was imbued with genealogical lore that even the simplest territorial designations were almost always rooted in the name of an earlier ruler or ancestor. We have encountered chevilles for Ireland such as 'Art's Plain' or 'Laoghaire's Land', etc. Likewise the smaller territories would, more often than not, be called after an ancient sovereign who had ruled over them: Cathaoir Mór in the case of Leinster; Mugh, Corc or Oilill Olum in the case of Munster; Guaire, Ailill or queen Medb in the case of Connacht.[31] Such epithets abound and served a double function: both as reinforcement of the link between the clan and their territory, and as ready-made chevilles to fit the requirements of metre and assonance. The literal applicability of these tags was disturbed by the intrusive settlement of the Hiberno-Normans – but poetical language, formalized as it was, declined to adapt to the new political realities. Thus the position of the Foreigner could be assessed wholly in a Gaelic frame of reference: Tadhg Óg Ó hUiginn bewails Uilleog lord of Clanrickard's death as a blow to the northern half, Leath Chuinn, Conn's Half, of Ireland: 'Fuilgnidh bhur léan, a Leath Chuinn !' – notwithstanding the fact that the term can by no means be taken literally, for the actual descendants of Conn might not be in any way aggrieved by their usurper's demise.

Moreover, although the poet would oblige Norman family pride by reference to their supposed descent from Charlemagne or from ancient Greece, he would more often have recourse to the more familiar field of Milesian ancestry – if not a biological, matrilinear one, then at least a rhetorical, metaphorical one: a Norman's prowess may equal that of Conn, his hospitality that of Guaire, his beauty that of Naoise. . . . Such a process would blur the division between Gael and Gall, and indeed such a blurring could only be in the poet's interest, since it was only through the Gaelicization of the Normans that the threat they posed to the Gaelic order could be defused, or, in practical terms, that the poet would be able still to find patronage in all of Ireland, including the Norman castles. It is, then, no coincidence to find the difference between Gael and Gall stressed in poems to Gaelic patrons, glossed over in poems to the Hiberno-Norman nobility.

Even in later times, these relations with the important Hiberno-Norman families remained largely unaffected by such frictions as resulted from the Tudor drive against non-English Ireland. Even in the sixteenth century, the Norman families of the west are treated much like the poets' Gaelic patrons. It is nothing exceptional to find, in the midst of intense Gaelic-English enmity, poets comparing Hiberno-Norman lords favourably to their Gaelic peers – an indication of the extent to which the old dichotomy between Gael and Gall had in their case lost its political edge.

In true encomiastic style, it is mostly the military valour and the hospitality of such a patron that is praised – or, in other words, such encomia attest to the patron's worthiness as a successor to the great Gaelic tradition of nobility. When addressed to a Foreign patron, such odes therefore reaffirm the cultural identification between Hiberno-Normans and Gaels. This identification is reinforced by the Gaelic terms in which a Hiberno-Norman lord is referred to. The hospitality of Theobald Butler's castle at Cahir, for instance, is celebrated in the following terms:

> * Triall gach einfhir gu cúirt tTeabóid,
> ceann na ndamhsgol,
> brugh fairsiong fíal fleadhach fionmhor,
> teisd gan trághadh.
>
> Rioghbhrugh orrdhraic na bhfleadh bhfoirfe,
> iosdadh flatha,
> Teamhair Chuinn as choir 'na chonchlann
> nó Ard Macha;[32]

---

* Each man comes to Theobald's castle, chiefest of the poets' gatherings, castle extensive, lively and cheerful, with wine a-plenty; an undiminishing reputation.

   The celebrated royal castle of the perfect banquets, abode of a prince: it rivals Conn's Tara and Ard Macha.

– the poem then goes on to compare Theobald's castle with all the other legendary royal halls of Gaelic antiquity. Theobald himself is like Naoise, 'Fear mar Naoisi mór mac Uisneach', and has an appearance like Guaire, 'gnuis mar Guaire'. He is 'cre chúil Ghall is Ghaoidheal/'s a mer meadhoin': 'a protective parados for Gall and Gael, and their middle finger', i.e. he occupies the central and most eminent position (p. 25). His like cannot be found among the descendants of Conn, Niall, Eoghan Mór, Brian or Carrthach (pp. 25–6); only Guaire, the seventh-century king of Connacht, famous for hospitality and liberality towards poets, can be compared to Theobald.

The Connacht Burkes, too, remained on good terms with bardic culture well into the sixteenth century: a poet like Tadhg Dall Ó hUiginn, one of the more prolific sixteenth-century poets, repeatedly addressed them in terms which wholly identify them with the Gaelic order, and incite them to resist Tudor rule, much as he might have incited his Gaelic patrons like Ó Domhnaill, Ó Néill or Ó Ruairc. Tadhg Dall urges Riocaird Óg Mac Uilliam (Burke), for instance, to desist from using his English title (presumably that of sheriff or seneschal[33]): to go by an English style or dignity would, in one of his elevated rank in the Gaelic order, be an odious dissonance. Mac Uilliam should rather, Tadhg Dall says, value his Gaelic style – presumably his tanistry to the chieftainship of Mac Uilliam Uachtar or Íochtar.

> *   A mheic Riocaird, a rún tais,
> an t-ainm iasachta uarais,
> níor thárraidh tú dá tharbha
> nár sháraigh clú an chéadanma.
>
> Dá bhaghthá ceannus Chláir Fhlionn,
> niorbh fhiú dhuit, a dhreach shéaghoinn,
> ainm allmhardha dá rádh ruibh
> fa chlár ndaghBhanbha id dhúthaigh.
>
> . . .
>
> Mairg fhuair an t-aoighidh anma,
> nó an reacht uathmhar allmhardha,
> fá bhfuil sionn éadána ort,
> a mhionn céaddhála Connocht. (TD vol. 1, 161)

The bold tone of this poem is striking: the poet is not asking a favour, but sternly berating Burke's shortcomings in the upkeep of his Gaelic heritage. The attitude of authority in matters of cultural import becomes apparent in a stanza like:

*   O son of Richard, gentle of heart, as for the foreign title thou hast got, never didst thou gain any advantage from it that the fame of the former title did not outdo.

Didst thou get the headship of Flann's Plain it would not advantage thee, thou gallant form, in thy native place, to reign over Banbha by a foreign title . . . .

Not happily didst thou obtain the strange title, or the horrid outlandish right, about which I make bold against thee, thou diadem of Connacht's first assembly. (ed.'s trl.)

*   Crosmaoidne h'iomlaoid anma
    ort a hucht na healadhna;
    cóir car an athanma ar ais
    suil rabh h'athardha it éagmais. (p. 162)

Such aversion to English titles is not particular only to Tadhg Dall. A poem like that by Uaithne Ó Cobhthaigh addressed to James Butler, ninth earl of Ormond, repeatedly insists that Butler's own name (in its Gaelic form: Séamus) is a higher mark of nobility, belonging exclusively to himself, than Butler's title of earl (*iarla*), which is held by other noblemen of lesser stature. Ó Cobhthaigh also insists that Butler has his own valour, rather than the king's grace, to thank for his pre-eminence: he came and conquered by his own might.

°   Don leith do-ríghne rogha,
    leath an mhílidh gur mheala;
    gan chur ccroinn ar chró Logha
    roinn Logha dhó fa deara.³⁴

The conclusion remains unspoken but is unavoidable: although the Normans came as vassals of the English king, they should, in the worsening friction of the Tudor period, no longer consider themselves as such, but rather hold their own by right of conquest, and in defiance of the Tudor policy which aimed to centralize and reinforce crown supremacy. One of the most explicit expressions of this idea is contained in a remarkable poem by Tadhg Dall Ó hUiginn, addressing Seán, the Mac Uilliam Íochtar, in terms highly reminiscent of those which Tuathal Ó hUiginn had used in his above-quoted (pp. 164 ff.) poem to Ó Raghallaigh, a century and a half earlier.

†   Fearann cloidhimh críoch Bhanbha,
    bíoth slán cháich fá chomhardha
    go bhfuil d'oighreacht ar Fhiadh bhFáil
    acht foirneart gliadh dá gabháil.

    Ní fhuil cóir uirre ag aoinfhear –
    críoch shuaitheanta sheanGhaoidheal,
    bheith fa neart an té is treise –
    is é ceart na críchese.

---

*   In the name of poetry we forbid thee to change thy title; thou shouldst renounce the new appellation rather than thy patrimony. (ed.'s trl.)
°   This warrior chose a half (of Éire), long may he enjoy it! his refusal to lay down his spear on Lugh's Steading (i.e. Mumha) caused that share of Éire to be his. (ed.'s trl.)
†   The land of *Banbha* is but swordland: let all be defied to show that there is any inheritance to the Land of *Fál* save that of conquest by force of battle!
    No one man has any lawful claim to the shining land of the ancient Gaels. The law of this territory is that it shall be subjugate to him who is strongest.

Ní fhagaibh athair ag mac
Inis Fhódla na bhfionnshlat;
sí le héigean go n-aghar
ní héidear í d'átaghadh.

Ní fhuil do cheart ar chrích bhFáil
ag Macaibh Míleadh Easbáin,
's ní bhí ag gach gabháil dár gheabh,
acht sí d'fhagháil ar éigean. (TD vol. I, 120)

Tadhg Dall subsequently recounts how Ireland was conquered by successive
waves of invaders: various mythological pre-Gaelic settlements, then the Gaels
themselves, and finally the Hiberno-Normans. The conclusion:

* Gi bé adéaradh gur deóraidh
Búrcaigh na mbeart n-inleóghain –
faghar d'fhuil Ghaoidhil nó Ghoill
nách fuil 'na aoighidh agoinn.

Gi bé adeir nách dleaghar dháibh
a gcuid féin d'Éirinn d'fhagháil –
cia san ghurt bhraonnuaidhe bhinn
nách lucht aonuaire d'Éirinn?

Gé adeirdís sliocht Ghaoidhil Ghlais
coimhighthe le cloinn Séarlais –
clocha toinighthe bheann mBreagh –
coimhighthe an dream adeireadh. (pp. 122–3)

The poem goes on to sing Mac Uilliam's personal praise, which (as in other
instances given earlier) puts him in an extra-partizan position ensuring
concord between Gael and Gall: Ireland under his rule is

° Gan adhbhar le a mbiodhgfadh bean,
gan leattrom Ghoill ag Gaoidheal;
gan éadáil Ghaoidhil ag Gall,
gan éagáir aoinfhir d'fhulang. (p. 131)

The father does not bequeath to the son *Fódla's* Isle of noble scions; until it be obtained by
force it cannot be occupied.
    Neither the sons of *Míl* of Spain nor any who have conquered her have any claim to the
land of *Fál* save that of taking her by force. (ed.'s trl.)
*   Should any say that the Burkes of lion-like prowess are strangers – let one of the blood of
Gael or Gall be found who is not a sojourner amongst us.
    Should any say they deserve not to receive their share of Ireland – who in the sweet, dew-
glistening field are more than visitors to the land?
    Though the descendants of *Gaedheal Glas* used speak of the race of Charles, set stones of
Banbha's hills, as foreigners – foreigners were they who spoke thus. (ed.'s trl.)
°   [without anything] which might make a woman tremble, no Gael committing injustice against any
Englishman, nor any Englishman despoiling a Gael, no wrong of any man permitted. (ed.'s trl.)

I would like to situate this poem firmly in a context of cultural fraternization between the Hiberno-Normans and Gaelic culture as represented, and presided over, by the poets: a fraternization which was additionally stimulated by the appearance of Tudor policy as a common danger to both. This is not the way in which this poem has traditionally been read. An indicative marginal note on a manuscript copy made by Charles O'Conor of Belanagar reads: 'mo mallacht ort a thaidhg is naireach an dan é so do dhiaidh', 'Curse you, Tadhg. This is a shameful poem you have left' (TD vol. 1, 120n. and vol. 2, 255). Understandably enough, the poem has often, and, I think, somewhat anachronistically, been interpreted as a cynical betrayal of the Gaelic cause in favour of patronage from the Foreigner.[35] Such a reading, it should be pointed out, must necessarily identify a man like Mac Uilliam Burke with the later enemies of the Gaelic order – i.e. the Tudor undertakers and later English colonists – which runs, I think, directly counter to the position of the Connacht Burkes after the proclamation of Henry VIII's regality in Ireland, and counter also to the intention of the poet, who sought rather to accommodate the Hiberno-Normans inside the Gaelic order.

The Old English presence and Tudor expansionism

While such Hiberno-Norman families as the western Butlers or the Burkes were assimilated into the Gaelic order, that order was coming under attack from the east, through a new Anglicization drive which used, for its bridgehead in Ireland, the Pale around Dublin.

As the Old English of the Pale were more loyally pro-English and, what is more, strongly anti-bardic in their attitude (and we have seen a few examples to this effect, above pp. 42, 49, from Smythe, Derricke and Stanyhurst), so too did the bardic poems addressed to those clans closer to the Pale show considerably more anti-Foreign feeling when compared to the situation in the western part of the country. Tadhg Óg Ó hUiginn, for example, addressed one of the Midland septs, the Eberian Í Chearbhaill of Ely, in a poem that began, characteristically:

* Déanaidh comhaonta, a chlann Éibhir
  budh iomdha i n-aghaidh bhur gclann
  náir gan bhur gcungnamh re chéile
  urlamh mbáigh an ghléire Gall. (AithDD vol. 1, 100)

Tadhg Óg gives stern warning that the Foreigners are encroaching on Gaelic land:

° Fada a-táid fa thoraibh aolta
  iath Mumhan na maoilionn dte
  an Mhidhe ar dtreabhadh a tulach;
  dleaghar cridhe dubhach dhe.

* Be ye united, O children of Éibhear; many are your foes; shame on you not to help each other; the bravest of the Goill are ever ready to attack you. (ed.'s trl.)
° For long past Mumha with its warm-clothed hills and Midhe with its ploughed slopes have been held down by white-gleaming castles; any heart would mourn the sight.

Fear a cosanta a gcloinn Eoghain
ná agaibh féin – féachaidh sin –
ó nach faicim, a chlann Cháirthinn,
aicill Gall do ráidhfinn ribh.

Cíos na dtuath i dtimcheall Chaisil
do chath eachtrann is é as lón;
nár do thaisibh na ríogh romhaibh
fíon Caisil oraibh ga ól.

A-tá ag Gallaibh an glas céadna
ar chloinn Táil – gá truaighe ceas!
ní fhuil acht deoraidh i ndaoirse
d'fhuil Eoghain don taoibhse theas. (p. 101)

The emphasis in this poem lies on the dispossession of the Gaels at the hands of the Foreigners; we may recall that similar rhetoric was used by Tuathal Ó hUiginn when he addressed expropriated Connacht chiefs like Ó Raghallaigh. It was in this respect indeed that the enmity between Gael and Gall could differ from that between the different clans of the Gael: what was at stake was not the booty of a raiding party, cattle, farm produce, and prestige or loss of face, but rather the ownership of the land itself. Hence, perhaps, the insistence on the part of the poets that such land was held by right of conquest, not by enfeoffment. In this light we should note that it is in poems to the weaker and more exposed clans (Ó Raghallaigh and Ó Cearbhaill rather than Ó Néill or Ó Briain) that we can find these bitter references to expropriation; and also that the confrontational setting was different in various parts of Ireland. Whereas territories like that of Desmond or of De Burgo were islands in a Gaelic sea, clans like the Í Chearbhaill found themselves adjacent to a massive block of territory subject to English law: the Pale on the east coast and the large palatinates of the Butlers and Fitzgeralds occupying Kilkenny and Kildare. Other clans adjacent to this more solid and threatening, and less easily Gaelicized, Foreign presence were the Í Thuathail and junior Í Bhroin of Wicklow, the Í Chonchobhair Fhailghe of Offaly and the Í Mhaoilsheachlainn of Meath; and it is not surprising that we find these names among the patrons of the more genuinely and exclusively anti-English poetry that is extant.[36]

It should be kept in mind, however, that such poems, although they may represent Foreign encroachment as a threat common to all Gaels,[37] in the final analysis are addressed to particular chieftains. If they counsel inter-clan co-operation, it is always in the traditional encomiastic mode, proclaiming that the

As I see not in Eoghan Mór's race any man able to save Éire or among you either, O race of Cairtheann – you see it yourselves – I can only tell you to look out for the Goill!

The cess of the lands around Caiseal now goes to support the foreign bands; that Caiseal's wine be there drunk to their health is an insult to the relics of your kings.

The Goill, alas! have fixed their chains on the race of Tál; also the race of Eoghan in the South are exiles in bonds (ed.'s trl.)

stature of the chieftain addressed is so pre-eminent that he will unite other clans under his leadership. Although the horizon may be broadened to include other Gaelic septs, the ultimate political interest is that of the individual clan.

This point might easily be overlooked. Tadhg Óg Ó hUiginn's above quoted poem to Ó Cearbhaill, 'Deanaidh comhaonta a chlann Éibhir', has been translated by its editor under the title 'Let *Éire* be united';[38] however, after some reflection it will become clear that, although 'Clann Éibhir' are apostrophized (that is to say: not Éire at large, but still the second largest of the four main branches of the Gael) it is not to all of them that the poem is addressed. A political bardic encomium has to have a patron, a well-defined individual to whom it is specifically addressed and by whom the poet expects to be remunerated; Tadhg Óg does not address the Eberians as Kipling might address 'the English', *in abstracto*, at large: the idea would be to him like someone making a dinner-speech alone on a mountain top. This poem is addressed to Maolruanaidh Ó Cearbhaill, lord of Ely, who is Eberian by virtue of the Í Chearbhaill's descent from Cian son of Oilill Olum, king of Munster and scion of Eber. There is no telling how wide or how narrow the intended reference of the 'clann Éibhir' in the opening line may be: the term might apply to as narrow a group as the Í Chearbhaill, who deserve the appellation 'clann Éibhir' as much as they deserve other genealogical epithets used by Tadhg Óg, e.g. 'síol Cein' (Cian's race), 'clann Cairthinn' (Cairtheann's descendants) or even 'fuil Gaoidheal' (Gaoidheal's blood) – or, for that matter the Í *Chearbhaill* (offspring of Cearbhall) that we now read as a mere family name. The drift of this poem may indeed be 'Let Éire be united' – but with the definite addition of '. . . under the leadership of Ó Cearbhaill'. The poet's prime concern is not Éire in general, but Ó Cearbhaill's leadership; it is, in this respect, similar to Gofraidh Fionn Ó Dálaigh's poem promising Éire a *fír-chéile* in the person of Tadhg Mag Cárthaigh (above, p. 155), Likewise, the enumeration of Gaelic defeats is clearly intended to goad the pride of one particular man: Maolruanaidh Ó Cearbhaill.

The designation of the 'other camp' is equally indeterminate. *Gall*, 'Foreigner', can, according to the context, mean Hiberno-Norman, or Old English, or English. Although *Sacsan, Sean-* or *Nua-Ghall* could specify which sort of Foreigner was meant, the shorter root form in itself provided such a good assonance with its counterpart *Gael* (*Gaedheal, Gaoidheal*) that it remained in poetic use long after its political meaning had become so diffuse as to designate different groups which were mutual enemies.

* * *

The presence of vaguely-defined 'Foreigners' was not in itself of grave concern to the poet; indeed their presence might be useful, either to swell the number of prospective patrons, or else for the seizing of cattle and the gaining of martial glory.[39] What was of far graver concern was the introduction of a Foreign legal system, by which land was owned by charter, and passed on by primogeniture instead of tanistry; a legal system also, by which land could be the object, not only of raids and isolated incursions, but even of capture and expansionist covetousness.

Such concerns were greatly exacerbated by the Tudor initiative, which constituted a far more radical disturbance than any Hiberno-Norman presence had been before. The often enforced policy of 'surrender and regrant', for instance, whereby a chieftain would be required to surrender his territorial rights to the king, who would then reinstate him in his rights as a vassal and with a title in the peerage, implied an obtrusion of exactly those customs of tenure which Tuathal Ó hUiginn had so eloquently rejected as being alien to, and invalid within, Gaelic Ireland; and as can be seen from this example, the Tudor offensive was a cultural as well as a strategic or political one, involving points of law and custom as much as questions of land ownership or political allegiance. The most obvious point of divergence lay in the mode of succession: the Gaelic system proceeded by way of tanistry, i.e. the chieftain would appoint his successor during his own lifetime from the circle of his sons, brothers, and paternal first and second cousins and nephews – an appointment ultimately subject to the clan's effective support for such a chieftain-designate (*tanaiste*). This custom was obviously irreconcilable with the straightforward primogeniture applying in English law, which the chieftain would be expected to adopt when accepting enfeoffment at the hands of the king; frictions were bound to result – for instance, in the succession to the Ó Neill leadership after the death of Conn Bacach Ó Neill.[40] It will be remembered how emphatically Tadhg Dall Ó hUiginn, in his poem to Burke quoted above on pp. 175–76, had made the case that, in *crioch Banbha*, 'the father does not leave the land of Fódla to his son'.

It is small wonder that a poet should be apprehensive at this development. The Hiberno-Normans had only swelled the ranks of his eligible patrons; but here was a threat to the entire cultural tradition of which he was *ex officio* the keeper. And so we see the poet ply his trade in defence of that culture that kept him alive, which it was his task to keep alive.

The poet's main task was to be the arbitrator of nobility, of honour: not only in contemporary terms, in praising or exhorting the chieftain – his martial valour, his raids, his liberality and hospitality – but especially in historical terms, in holding up the chieftain's conduct to the great examples of the glorious past, to the great deeds of the historical or mythical rulers who were his ancestors. The encroachment of Tudor colonization was a complete disruption of this fabric of honour and nobility which, as far as the poet was concerned, was the main unifying, cohesive force both of (synchronically) Gaeldom, the Gaelic order, and of (diachronically) Gaelic history, the continuity of the Gaelic tradition. The practice of 'surrender and re-grant' had begun to turn many Gaelic chiefs into liegemen of the king; the process of anglicization had begun to gnaw at the very core of the Gaelic order: the sovereignty of the chieftain. The poets must have felt that it was time to voice a warning, to remind the chiefs of their responsibilities. We have, for instance, an ironic poem by that refined poet Laoiseach Mac an Bhaird, which contrasts the effete silliness of one 'who adopted foreign ways', 'ghlacas an ghalldacht' (IBP p. 49), in cutting his hair and clothes according to the English fashion, with the rugged manliness of one Eoghan Bán son of Donnchadh, who persists in traditional values, martial valour and rebellion against the Goill:

> *   Bró mharc-shluagh ar bhrú mbeirne,
>   troid gharbh, comhlann ceitheirne,
>   cuid do mhianuibh meic Donnchaidh,
>   's gleic d'iarraidh ar allmhurchaibh. (IBP p. 50)

A better known, indeed a famous example along the same lines, is the anonymous poem 'Fúbún fúibh, a shluagh Gaoidheal', which seems to date from the very opening years of the Tudor initiative and which berates the Gaelic chiefs for their supine acceptance of a new dishonourable station.[41] The opening and closing stanzas run:

> °   Fúbún fúibh, a shluagh Gaoidheal,
>   ní mhaireann aoinneach agaibh;
>   Goill ag comhroinn bhur gcríche;
>   re sluagh síthe bhur samhail.
>
>   . . . . .
>
>   . . . . .
>   A uaisle Inse seanAirt,
>   neamhmhaith bhur gcéim ar gclaochlúdh,
>   a shluagh míthreórach meata,
>   ná habraidh feasta acht 'faobun'. (pp. 272–3)

And between these two stanzas, the various chieftains who have sued for, or accepted, English re-grants of their ancient nobility, are scornfully exposed: the Clann Cárthaigh and other septs, including even Ó Néill – 'tugsad ar iarlacht Uladh rioghacht go humhal aimhghlic' '[who] has exchanged in foolish submission his kingship for the Ulster earldom' – and Ó Domhnaill, who also failed Éire 'to her great distress'. And the poet heaps deprecations on these newfangled ways in political, cultural and religious alliance:

> †   Fúbún fán ngunna ngallghlas,
>   fúbún fán slabhra mbuidhe,
>   fúbun fán gcúirt gan Bhéarla,
>   fúbún séana Mheic Mhuire. (p. 273)

---

*   A troop of horse at the brink of a gap, a fierce fight, a struggle with foot-soldiers, these are some of the desires of Donnchadh's son – and seeking battle against the foreigners! (ed.'s trl.)

°   Shameful is your course of action, O men of the Gaeil, not one of you has life in him; the foreigners are dividing your land among themselves; you are like a phantom host . . . .

O nobles of the Island of Art of yore, unworthy is your altered rank, you weak degenerate crowd. Henceforth say nothing but 'faobún'. (ed.'s trl.)

†   Shame on the grey foreign gun, shame on the golden chain, shame on the court without *poetic language [Irish law?]*, shameful is the denial of Mary's Son.[42]

Although I do not deny that this poem comes very close to a national Gaelic stance in its anti-Foreignness, urging a common opposition to the encroachment of English legal customs, I also think that it is nevertheless possible to misread it, to see it as a national, or even nationalistic, incitement to rebellion. I think that there is a subtle, but radical, difference between reading this poem as an incitement or as an indictment. At first sight, it certainly seems an invective aimed at goading and shaming the renegade Irish chiefs into dropping their dishonourable anglicization; such a reading would tether the significance of the poet's exclamation of disgust to his ulterior motive in goading the chieftain's *amour propre* and influencing his political behaviour. In this view, political behaviour and royal honour are thus interdependent entities, the former being actuated by the latter.

I would rather argue that the two, behaviour and honour, were, in the bardic frame of reference, identical. The chieftain does not fill his position by the grace of a third party (God or liege), but by the grace of his own superiority over his rivals, by the grace of his own nobility as evinced through his behaviour. It is not his mere descent, but also his personal honour, which makes him acceptable as an heir to his predecessors; and this honour is to be assessed primarily by the poet. This poem is thus far more than a mere paedagogical attempt at influencing the chief's behaviour obliquely, indirectly, by goading his personal sense of honour: it is an overt threat of impeachment and only one step removed from the dreaded *aor,* or satire-curse, harping as it does on the ominously blunt imprecation 'fúbún'. Rather than a scornful vehicle of political advice, the poem is a menacing observation. It bluntly registers that the Irish chieftains are forfeiting the right to be accounted heirs to the glorious past. They are betraying their cultural heritage, their claim to bardic appreciation, praise, and, yes, recognition; they are falling short of the obligations of their station and are accordingly branded by their cultural mentor, the poet. The poet must feel this indeed as a cataclysmic change – ranking equal in importance with the 'séana Mheic Mhuire', the stunning godlessness of the Reformation. It is as if history itself is coming under threat, now that the present can no longer provide a proper continuation of the past.

In the tradition of a common allegiance to Gaelic honour and nobility on the part both of the poet and of the chieftain, the latter is now failing to perform his duty; as a result, the Gaelic cause henceforth can be seen to be defined increasingly in bardic, rather than merely political/military terms. Whereas the standard of political relations used to be the prestige of the sovereign chieftain, this standard now seems to default and is accordingly replaced by a professionally bardic ideal: the Gaelic order is no longer defined according to the parameters of the chieftain's synchronic and diachronic relations with all other, contemporary and historical, chiefs, but rather in terms of the social position of the poet and the importance accorded to his calling and to the heritage he guards and embodies. In short: the Gaelic order is henceforth to be defined as that set of circumstances in which bardic learning can be maintained; all other activity is considered subservient to this main criterion. Thus, submission to English rule is seen primarily as the abandonment of the custom of patronage towards the bards; conversely, the honour of those resisting foreign custom lies primarily in keeping up this royal tradition of poetic patronage. Seán Ó hUiginn, for instance, in a sarcastically 'naive' phraseology, favourably compares Aodh Ó Broin of Wicklow to all other chiefs:

> *   Cia cheannchus adhmad naoi rann,
>   dá bhfaghadh cunnradh ann súd?
>   ar Laighnibh ciarbh ard a tteisd
>   dom aithne is cruaidh an cheisd úd.
>
> Is é freagra Branach oirn:
>   ná cluintior ocht roinn ná naoi;
>   go dul Sagsanach tar sál
>   ní dhíolfam dán iná laoidh
>
> . . .
>
> (four more cowardly, reluctant clans are named)
>
> . . .
>
> Fear nach umhal do nós Gall
>   Aodh mac Seaáin is ard gnaoi,
>   ós air do chuirios mo chrann
>   le hadhmad ocht rann nó naoi.[43]

These junior Í Bhroin were among the clans who challenged English encroachment most strenuously and persistently; they are therefore continuously exalted by numerous visiting poets and very often endowed with the quality of *uaisle*, 'nobility'; a quality expressly denied by the poets to all other clans who did not put up so valiant a resistance; a quality, therefore, which seems to be largely defined as a function of anti-English resistance. Doighre Ó Dalaigh, for instance, asks in a poem to the same Aodh Ó Broin: 'Cia as uaisle do Laighneachuibh?', 'Who is noblest of the Leinstermen?', and the term recurs with obsessive insistence no less than eighteen times in a poem of twenty-one stanzas.[44] 'Uaisle' is personified as a woman cast out by all great families except the Í Bhroin – 'An uaisle ní dhíbiortach as sliocht Cathaoir Mhóir Laighnigh':

> °   An uaisle do thréigiodar
>   Gaoidhil Fhódla acht a aicme;
>   a n-aimsir an éigiontuis
>   gnáth an fíorchara d'aithne.

---

*   Who buyeth a piece of nine verses, even though he get the purchase thereof? To the men of Leinster, though high their repute, I know that is a difficult question.

The answer the O'Byrnes [i.e. the senior branch, as opposed to the more rebellious junior branch to which Aodh Ó Broin belonged, J.L.] make us is: 'Let not verses, eight or nine, be heard; until the Sasanachs have retired oversea we shall pay for neither poem nor lay.'. . .

He who never bowed to Foreigners' custom, Hugh mac Shane, or comeliness renowned: it is with him I have tried my fortune with a piece in verses eight or nine.[43]

°   The Gaels of Fódla have abandoned nobility, except for his [Aodh's] people; in time of distress the true friend is wont to become recognized.

   *   Mac Seaáin as fíorchara
       don uaisle a n-am na héigne;
       lé do ghabh an ríoghmhac-sa
       's fir Éirionn d'éis a tréigthe. (p. 21)

The personification of Nobility as a woman in need of protection is a parallel to the traditional motif of Éire in need of a monarch, and also to the view of the poet in need of a patron; indeed, the final stanza describes Aodh's shelter much as a wandering poet in dire need of patronage might have seen it:

   °   An uaisle is bean roiligthe
       d'éis a n-uair d'fhearaibh maithe;
       dénadh ar mhac Doirinne,
       cá fearr áirighthe aice? (p. 23)

I have elsewhere given some examples of the increasingly hostile attitude towards poets among English officials and Old English writers (cf. pp. 48–9, 254–5). As the situation of bardic poets in Tudor Ireland became increasingly precarious, the extension of patronage towards them became correspondingly more important, not only in terms of clannish *mores,* but also in a more concrete sense. As can be gathered from English ordinances as quoted in the fifth chapter, it became imperative for the poet to be able to give a patron's name, to be accounted part of the retinue of a specific lord; otherwise his life might be in danger. The situation is brought home forcefully in a poem by Tadhg Dall Ó hUiginn, dating from the mid-1580s, when Sir John Perrot's 'Composition of Connacht' had begun to establish English control over that province. Tadhg Dall sued one of the Gaelic signatories of the Composition, Cormac Ó hEadhra, for protection in the following way:

   †   Atáid dlighthe nuaidhe aniogh
       dá gcur ar Mhacaibh Miliodh
       ag slógh nár ghlacnuaidhe Ghall
       fa chlár bhfaltuaine bhFréamhann.

       Goirid na críocha 'na gceann,
       iarraid ar chách go coitcheann –
       go dtig a sgrios uile as –
       fios gach duine 'sa dhúthchas.

       D'éis na dtíreadh do thionól,
       sgríobhaid Goil Ghuirt Éiriomhón

---

 * The son of Seán is a true friend of nobility in the time of need; this royal youth took its part when the men of Ireland had abandoned it.

 ° Nobility is a woman wholly forsaken by noble men, each in turn; to turn to the son of Doireann – what greater assurance exists for her?

 † To-day new laws are being imposed on the Sons of *Míl* by the noble, bright-handed English host, throughout the green-maned land of Frewen.
     They summon the territories to them, and require from all in general, until they are all ascertained (?), a knowledge of every man, and of his native place.

anmonna a slógh, druim ar dhruim,
i nglanrolla mhór mheamruim.

D'éis a gcruinnighthe 'na gceann
is éigean d'fhearaibh Éireann,
a ghríobh fhirfheardha ó Thigh Tháil,
tighearna gach fhir d'admháil.

Ní ghabhaid ó neach fa nimh
gan bheith dó ag urraidh éiginn –
truagh an cás do cumadh dáibh –
nó bás go hullamh d'fhagháil.

Gá dtú ris, a rí Luighne? –
ort chuirim mo chomuirghe;
feadh mo ré, mar dhleaghar dhamh
budh é ar leabhar do leabhar.

Ní ar mo bháigh do bheith ruibh,
ní ar bheith im' ollamh aguibh,
a chnú do chrobhuing Eaghra,
thoghuim thú mar thighearna.

Do aomhsad Gaoidhil is Goill –
bheith agad is as toghoim –
rí fíréanda do rádh ribh,
a ríréadla ó chlár Chaisil. (TD vol. 1, 216–17)

Chiefs like Ó hEadhra could be worthy patrons within the Gaelic frame of reference, and at the same time provide effective protection against English persecution; this last point did not apply to rebellious chiefs like the Glenmalure Í Bhroin, who, as enemies of the English authorities, were not much use as a poet's guarantor.

Notwithstanding this forced acceptance among the poets of the patron's acceptance among the English, the ultimate aim of patronage remained: to provide shelter in which the bardic tradition can be perpetuated; accordingly, the

Having assembled the territories the English of Eremon's field write the names of their hosts, one after another, in a large, clean roll of parchment.

And when they have been assembled before them, each of the men of Ireland, thou warrior of *Tál's* Dwelling, with manly following, must acknowledge an overlord.

They require that everyone under heaven have a guarantor, or else – piteous the strait which has been wrought for them – die forthwith.

In brief, thou king of Leyney, on thee I set my security, in all my days, as is meet, thy book shall be my book.

Not because my inclination is towards thee, or because I am thy poet, thou fruit of *Eaghra's* cluster, do I choose thee as lord.

For this have I chosen to be with thee, thou royal star of Cashel's plain, both Gaels and English have agreed to give thee the title of righteous king. (ed.'s trl.)

second half of Tadhg Dall's poem comes around again to reaffirm Ó hEadhra's stature in Gaelic, i.e. bardic terms. This shift is foreshadowed earlier in the poem by the remarkable line 'budh é ár leabhar do leabhar', 'our book shall be your book' – with its royal plural in the first person possessive pronoun that is all the more striking because it is juxtaposed with the singular of the second person possessive pronoun (though the poem vacillates between second person plural and singular generally, the metre does not impose a use of *do* to the exclusion the the plural *bhur*); and there is also, two lines previously, the more homely singular in the first person possessive pronoun, *mo chomuirghe,* 'my security'. The result of all this oscillation is here that the poet appears as a representative of his class, though in personal danger, and that Ó hEadhra is addressed particularly in his personal responsibility for safeguarding the Gaelic order. The relationship between poet and patron is then further elaborated upon:

> * Do-ghéan an laoidh ngréasaigh ngloin,
> do-ghéan duit an duain shaothoir,
> 's do-ghéan aonrann uair oile,
> a shaorbharr bhruaigh Bhóroimhe.
>
> Do-bhéaram dhuit, mar dhleaghair,
> eólas do ghéag ngeinealaigh;
> cíos do shean ar fhiadh nÉireann,
> rian a gcean 'sa gcaithréimeann.
>
> Do-bhéaram dhuit, a dhreach sheang,
> fios t'uaisle ós fhearaibh Éireann,
> 's dá gach urraim budh dual duit –
> luagh ar gcumainn, a Chormuic.
>
> Do-bhéara mé, a mheic Úna,
> ar chách do chur iomthnúdha,
> an ceann bhus fhearr dhuid dom dhán,
> 'san chuid bhus fhearr dom iomrádh.
>
> Ní fuláir dhuit 'na dhíol sin
> go dtiobhra tú, a thuir Chaisil,
> h'anam 's do chorp tar mo cheann,
> dá bhfagham tocht 'nar dtimcheall.

* I shall compose for thee the artistic, well-wrought lay, the laboriously wrought (?) poem, and another time the single stanza, thou noble chief of *Bóromha's* shore.

I shall give thee, as is due, knowledge of thy genealogical branches, of the tribute taken by thy forbears from the plains of Ireland, the course of their triumphs and their exploits.

I shall tell thee, thou slender form, of thy nobility transcending that of the rest of the men of Ireland, and of every homage that were due to thee – the price of our friendship, Cormac.

In order to raise the envy of the rest, to thee, thou son of *Úna,* I shall devote the best portion of my poesy, and the best part of my converse.

In requital thereof, thou chief of Cashel, it is not too much for me that thou offer thy life and body on my behalf if I be captured.

*   Giodh cúis bháis do bheith ar neach
    i dtigh cúirte is é ar h'eineach –
    níor chorruighthe dho ioná dhuit,
    ag so an chomuirche, a Chormuic. (TD vol. 1, 218)

With this closing line (which, as is the formal requirement of this sort of poetry, echoes the opening line) and the elegant twist of the meaning of 'guarantee' – both needed and offered by the poet – the symbiosis of nobility between poet and patron is reaffirmed; their complicity will yet shelter the Gaelic order from outside interference. And again we see that the notion of nobility (or better, 'honour', *éineach,* rather than *uaisle*) has finally been placed in a cardinal position. It is in effect the opposite of the oppressive bureaucracy of the English, which is mentioned at the beginning of the poem as the danger against which Ó hEadhra's protection is needed – 'smacht ríogh glaininse Ghall', 'the [oppressive] law of the king of the bright isle of the English'.

As the appeal for complicity-as-protection may indicate, the changes that are registered are external to the actual bardic practice. The poet's position is becoming more precarious, the number of his enemies is growing and the number of suitable employers is diminishing; but within those strongholds of the Gaelic order that yet withstood Henry VIII's and Elizabeth's aggression, bardic poetry kept running on in much the same vein as before. Thus, the later sixteenth century could, in the more strongly Gaelic north-west of Ireland, witness the flourishing or the beginning of the activities of poets who may rank as the equals of men like Gofraidh Fionn Ó Dálaigh, Giolla Brighde Mac Con Midhe or Tadhg Óg hUiginn: namely, Tadhg Dall Ó hUiginn, Eoghan Rua Mac an Bhaird and Fearghal Óg Mac an Bhaird, and Eochaidh Ó hEoghusa (a brother of the Bonaventura O'Hussey whom we shall later encounter as a grammarian in the Franciscan college in Louvain). Ó hEoghusa was *ollamh* to the Maguire chief of Fermanagh, Aodh Mag Uidhir, and pursued an important career which externally seemed by and large untroubled by the changes of the sixteenth century. In his poetry a more strident anti-Foreign tone does indeed make itself heard, and chieftains are no longer incited against other clans, but exclusively against the adjacent Foreigners; but that can at least partly be explained from the fact that Gaelic rivals were becoming a little thin on the ground.

There were also those visiting poets who addressed the rebel chieftain Fiacha Ó Broin, on the very edge of the English Pale; Aonghus Ó Dálaigh praised a raid on the Pale in his well-known poem 'Dia libh a laochraidh Gaoidhil', 'God with you, O war-band of the Gaels'. Niall Ó Ruanadha, Fearghal Óg Mac an Bhaird, Aithios Ó Lorcain, Domhnall Ó hUiginn: they all say, in their different ways, that the stoutness of the Í Bhroin has earned them

---

*   Even were one on trial for his life in a courthouse, while depending on thy honor neither he
nor thou need tremble; here, Cormac, is the guarantee. (ed.'s tr.)

the general recognition of their superiority over all other Gaels. To attest to such a 'fact' was, as we have seen, standard practice for bardic encomia; and indeed these poems read much like earlier odes.[45] However, this praise was now becoming less and less unrealistic – less through any particular change in Í Bhroin habits than through the decline of all their rivals, of all other Gaels.

As usual, a more realistic picture is given in a poem that dispenses cautionary advice rather than praise: for instance, Tuileagna Ó Maolchonaire's 'Fuath gach fir fuidheall a thuaighe', which makes very clear that Ó Broin is the noblest Gael because he is practically the only unvanquished Gael left alive:

*   Fuath gach fir fuidheall a thuaighe;
    tuig, a Fhiacha, duit is dual,
    má tá nach binn libh mo labhra,
    ós cionn do chinn tarla an tuagh.

    Ní chluinim gan chlaoi ó Ghalluibh
    a ngné threisi acht tusa a-mháin
    d'fhéin Gaoidhiol (gá ttáim dá thuiriomh?)
    aoinfhear amh-áin d'fhuidheal áir.

    Leó do múchadh meadhair Gaoidhiol,
    ní gníomh aoinfhir righe rú,
    scél náir re thuiriomh is truaighe,
    fuidheal áir na tuaighe thú. (p. 147)

In the West, the same idea is expressed in an otherwise traditional incitement by Tadhg Dall Ó hUiginn to Brian 'na Múrtha' Ó Ruairc, which paints a picture of the Gael in utter disarray, unable to withstand the routing Saxon. It then describes Ó Ruairc as the one person capable of recapturing the initiative, of forcing his own terms on the English; it is not Foreign tolerance that Ó Ruairc should seek, Tadhg Dall says, on the contrary: the Foreigners' enmity is a sign of how dangerous they feel Ó Ruairc to be.

°   Méad a fhuatha ag ógbhaidh danar
    dhó féin bhíos do bharamhail;
    cách dhó dá fográ re fada –
    Fódla aga ar aradhain. (TD vol. 1, 115)

---

*   Each man hates him who escaped his hatchet. Take good notice, Fiacha, of this, if you set any store by my words at all: the hatchet is hanging over your head.
    Except for you I have not heard of anyone who has been left undefeated by the Goill. Of the warriors of the Gael (why go into enumerating them?), only a single man is the survivor of the slaughter.
    The pleasures of the Gaels were extinguished by them, not a single chieftain withstood them – a tale of shame it is, sad to relate. You are (the only one) who escaped the hatchet's slaughter.
°   The hatred of the foreigners for him is his testimony (?); all have been proclaiming for long that she is his – he holds *Fódla* by the bridle. (ed.'s trl.)

Then the poem slips into the usual encomiastic vein of foretelling how all other clans will rally around Ó Ruairc's leadership, and how, after an apocalyptic battle,

> *   Muidhfidh ainnséin ar fhóir Saxan
> ré síol Ghaoidhil ghéirreannaigh,
> nách bia do shíor ón ágh d'fhógra
> ós chlár Fhódla acht Éireannaigh. (p. 118)

Putting the patron in a pre-eminent position, as the mainstay and prince of the Gaels – that is, after all, no great change from earlier bardic practice. We have seen that there was a wide divergence between the actual stature of rivalling chiefs and the hyperbolic claims advanced for them in bardic poetry. This divergence was now, however, beginning to narrow down – not, as we have seen, by any change in poetical practice, but by a decrease in the number of rivalling chieftains who still defied English rule. What we have, then, is a picture of political reality slowly conforming to bardic rhetoric.

I sum up:

The sixteenth century offers us the image of the Gaelic order carefully, consciously guarded and shepherded by the poets – all the more carefully and consciously so, since that order had come under attack and many chieftains proved themselves unequal to the task of defending it.

Whereas, in pre-Tudor times, the Gaelic order was conceived of largely in terms of the chieftain's prowess amongst his rivals, we see here a new perspective placing a stronger emphasis on the position of the poet as the defining point of reference. A more deliberately professional-bardic view of the Gaelic order is professed in later poems.[46] The 'Gaelic order' is defined, not as a *politikon* opposing the political advance of English expansionism, but as a set of cultural values, an economy of honour and nobility which guaranteed a historical continuity from the olden days down to the present; characterized, not by political structures of government, administration, geographical integrity or constitutional sovereignty, nor even by national attitudes like a perceived common character linking all Gaels *qua* Gaels and determining their fundamental non-Englishness, but rather by a set of bardic, aristocratic values such as genealogical commitment to clan, sept or lineage; cultivation of the old histories of the exploits of the ancestral Gaels; liberality to poets and their craft.

This, of course, is the raw material from which cultural nationalism is made; but to make such a statement is more far reaching than it may seem at first sight. We can indeed call the bardic, professional ideal of the Gaelic order the raw material of cultural nationalism, much as loose words are the raw material of a proposition. What is needed to make a coherent construct out of these materials is, then, a syntax: a mode of defining the interrelations between the different constituent units. Certainly, bardic poetry in itself did not contain such a 'syntax'

---

*   Then will the Saxon tribe be vanquished by the seed of keen-weaponed *Gaedheal, so* that from the proclamation of war there will never be any save Irishmen over the land of *Fódla.* (ed.'s trl.)

of national thought; it might have, if there had been a central *political* point of reference to the Gaelic order – a common Gaelic political ideal to oppose the proto-colonialist ideology of Tudor expansionism. But such a cohesive force was absent, and the professional bardic ideal of a Gaelic culture remained without a central political focus.

If we compare, by way of contrast, an English statement from the same period, we can see that here a definitely 'national' view was taken of the conflict between Gael and Gall – i.e. that the conflict was seen to take place, not between usurpers and dispossessed, but between groups defined in their national appurtenance: thus, lord Roche sent an appeal from Cork in 1568, when raided by the earl of Clancarty (thus was an English title re-granted to the chief of Clann Cárthaigh), MacDonough, O'Keeffe, MacAuliffe, O'Donoghue More and O'Sullivan More,

> to showe your honors [i.e. the Council at Dublin] howe all the said yrishe nacyons [i.e. clans] have Joyned them together agaynste me being nexte to them of all the englyshe nacyons of these partes. (BMCat vol. 1, 378n.)

As my treatment of their writings in this period may have indicated, Tudor Protestants did indeed develop a strong 'national' awareness in these conflicts – even to the point of imputing similar feelings to the native raiders. The real origins of Aodh De Blácam's sentiments as quoted at the outset of the present chapter can be found with men like lord Roche rather than with Cormac mac Airt.

The breakdown of the bardic order

There was, however, a moment in time when the Gaelic order had indeed become a single political unit: this was at the critical period when it had shrunk to contain only the alliance between the last two independent Gaelic princes, Ó Néill and Ó Domhnaill, with their client chiefs such as Mag Uidhir and Ó Dochartaigh. During the period of the Tyrone rebellion, it can be said that the Gaelic order, with uncontested leaders in the persons of Aodh Ó Néill and Aodh Rua Ó Domhnaill, had at last been given a unified unambiguous political focus; and poetical claims that Ó Néill and Ó Domhnaill, as chiefs of their septs, were the leaders of the Gaelic cause had, at last, obtained a literal, political validity of sorts. To put matters in this way may help to explain the literary impact of the defeat of the earls O'Neill and O'Donnell, their flight from Ireland, their death abroad, and the subsequent Jacobite plantation, as well as the extraordinary popularity of the poems of this period among a later audience.

The Flight of the Earls (1607) was immediately recognized for the catastrophe it was, and drew laments from nearly all the poets in the country. And these laments, much as they employed the rhetoric and circumlocutions of traditional elegy, were, for once, more than the ritual elegies of tradition. At the vanishing point of the bardic order we can finally witness a perfect coincidence and congruence of bardic language, private emotion and political reference: their patrons, last vestiges of a Gaelic social structure, irretrievably lost, the bardic heritage left in a political vacuum, the poets themselves at the mercy of an alien, hostile, Protestant government . . . it is no wonder that under these circumstances they left us a number of poems in which political despair, professional uncertainty and personal anguish merge into one. It is perhaps in this outburst of deeply felt, elegiac poetry that a self-image of bardic Ireland was most forcefully and effectively expressed. In the fall of O'Neill and O'Donnell, the fall of the entire Gaelic order is lamented – and again we can see that, in the final analysis, 'the Gaelic order' is to be understood in cultural terms, i.e. as the medium of bardic learning.

Eoghan Rua Mac and Bhaird, the O'Donnell's *ollamh,* followed the events especially closely. He wrote a valedictory poem for Aodh Rua on that chief's ill-fated mission to Spain in 1602, which builds up to the statement that the fate of the entire Gaelic order is entrusted to Aodh's ship (IBP pp. 31–4). After the Flight, Eoghan Rua urged Ó Néill to return speedily to his imperilled country; a figure is used here, which was to become standard practice for the next three hundred years: that of Ireland as a young woman, left without protection and exposed to the advances of dishonourable men.

> * Frith an uainsi ar Inis Fáil,
>   buime mac Mileadh Easpáin;
>   rugadh a neart, frith a bhfaill,
>   gach crích ag teacht fá a tuairim.
>
>   Tugadh slán gach fir impe,
>   iomdha a huilc 'sa héigcinnte,
>   a neamghlóir as saobh re seal –
>   senróimh na naomh 's na neimheadh.
>
>   Ní thuit cara tar a ceann,
>   ní faghthar troid na timcheall,
>   mo thruaighe mar tarla dhi –
>   labhra uaithe ní héisdthi.
>
>   Atáid a gceann a chéile
>   a haos cumtha, a coigéile,
>   ar ndul a séana a seisi
>   méla cor na gcricheisi.

* Now is Inisfail, nurse of the children of Mil of Spain, taken at disadvantage: her strength is reft, she is caught unwarded; denizens of all strange countries flock towards her.

All men have challenged her for their own, her evils and uncertainties are many; her 'unglory' for a while past is evidence of her derangement that was the old home of saints and of sanctuaries.

No friend falls now for her sake, for her no fight is fought; woe is me for the plight in which she is today: no utterance is heard from her.

All her poets and companions are together on the decline of her prosperity and of her pleasure: sad is the plight of the land.

> Do díoghladh cneadha cath nGall,
> fuaradar ógbhaidh eachtronn
> a n-algas don eing re headh,
> tangas re grian na nGaoidheal.

> Dá mbeith compán nó cara
> do chloinn Néill anallana,
> do chídhfeadh mar tharla an tír,
> do chífeadh damhna a deimbríogh.[47]

This poem also contains two other topoi destined to remain in use for a long time: the comparison between the sufferings of the Gaels and those of the children of Israel, and the injunction to trust to God's mercy towards the righteous – indications of the growing tendency to regard the Gaelic-English conflict in religious terms, foreshadowing the trend among many men of letters to take refuge in the Church now that no more worldly patrons were left (cf. generally the next chapter).

The figure of the desolate, defenceless and dishonoured woman is, however, by far the most important, probably because of its implied correspondence to the personal situation of the poet in a society bereft of its cultural integrity. Ainnrias Mac Marcuis struck the same note when he described the desolation of Ireland after the Flight of the Earls – a cultural rather than a social or political upheaval, it seems:

> *   Anocht is uaigneach Éire,
> do-bheir fógra a fírfhréimhe
> gruaidhe a fear 'sa fionnbhan flioch,
> treabh is iongnadh go huaignioch.

> Uaigneach anocht clár Connla,
> gé lán d'fhoirinn allmhardha;
> sáith an chláir fhionnacraigh fhéil –
> don Sbáin ionnarbthair iadséin.
>   . . .

> Gan gháire fa ghníomhradh leinb,
> cosc ar cheól, glas ar ghaoidheilg,
> meic ríogh, mar nár dhual don dreim,
> gan luadh ar fhíon nó ar aifrinn.

The wounds of the English battalions are avenged: the young men of the foreigners have for a time their wicked will of the land, and the Gaels' hold (on Ireland) hath been assailed succesfully.

Were there but a comrade or a friend (a member of the Clann Neill of old) that should see how the realm lies now, he would weep for the cause of its debility. (ed.'s trl.)

* To-night Ireland is desolate, the banishment of her true race hath left wet-cheeked her men and fair women; strange that such a dwelling-place should be desolate.

Desolate to-night is the Plain of Connla, though swarming with a foreign host; those who sufficed the generous, bright-acred land – they have been banished to Spain . . . .

There is no laughter at the children's play, music is checked, speech is fettered; the sons of kings, such was not their nature, care neither for feasting nor mass.

<pre>
*   Gan imirt, gan ól fleidhe,
    gan aithghearradh aimsire,
    gan mhalairt, gan ghraifne greagh,
    gan tabhairt aighthe i n-éigean.

    Gan rádha rithlearg molta,
    gan sgaoileadh sgeól gcodalta;
    gan úidh a fhaixin leabhair,
    gan chlaisdin nglúin gheinealaigh.⁴⁸
</pre>

The nadir of the poets' hopes after the Flight of the Earls must have come with the chieftains' deaths in exile. The elegy which Eoghan Rua Mac an Bhaird composed on the death of Rudhraighe Ó Domhnaill in Rome (1608) is obviously intended as an elegy on Gaelic Ireland as well as on the individual chief: he depicts, over ninety-one stanzas, the glory and the tragedy of the Gaels, their history of three thousand years, and the violent disruption brought by the Goill. He describes how Gaelic Ireland shrank to its last stronghold, the O'Donnell territory, and follows the gradual diminution of the Gaelic order down to its last sovereign, independent chieftain, slowly closing in on his actual subject, Rudhraighe Ó Domhnaill, the last hero of the Gaels. Then the sorrow of bereaved Éire is described, and the poem concludes as an epitaph – with one of the most felicitous, most poignant 'closure'-echoes of the opening line in all Gaelic literary history – not only on Ó Domhnaill, but on Gaelic history as a whole:

<pre>
°   Ocht mbliadhna sé chéad gan cheilt,
    míle ó ghein Iosa oirdheirc
    go madhmadh don Chlár Chuinnsi
    ag ládh talmhan toruibhsi.

    Truagh nach mar Thadhg Ó nDálaigh
    tugas cúl dom chompánaibh
    lá ar gceiliobhruidh maraon ruibh
    do seinfhionnmhuigh chaomh Chriomhthuin.

    Tug an toice maraon ribh
    cúl don chrichsi Chlann Mhilidh,
    gach maith uaibh ag dearadh dhi,
    maith an sealadh fuair Eiri.⁴⁹
</pre>

<pre>
*   No gaming, no banqueting, no pastime; no commerce or horse-racing or deeds of daring.
        No reciting of poems of praise, no relating of stories at sleeping time, no interest in
    consulting books, no hearkening to genealogies. (ed.'s trl.)
°   Eight years and six hundred without denial and a thousand from the birth of Most Excellent
    Christ to the defeat of Ireland – to thy burial.
        Alas that I didn't bid farewell to my companions after the manner of Tadhg O'Daly; to bid
    farewell in your company to the old fair level Plain of Criomthan.
        Fortune in thy company turned its back upon this territory of the children of Mil, every
    good from thee deserting her. Ireland was prosperous for a long time. (ed.'s trl.)
</pre>

It is this identification of public loss and private grief, this mixture of the grand historical scale and the intimacy of the *ollamh*'s own mourning, which elevates these lines above the level of the formal, formulaic elegy – the traditional 'metrical discourse' of the bards with their ritual protestations of affliction.

This harmonious marriage of the elevated bardic language of political poetry with the sense of real personal emotion thus occurs at the very point where the bardic order breaks down and its age-old mould is violently torn apart. Perhaps this is one of the reasons why the poetry of these years should have become so popular later on. One of Eoghan Rua's most famous poems is that addressed to Nuala Ní Dhomhnaill, 'A bhean fuair faill ar an bhfeart',[50] in which she is depicted as a lonely mourner at the family tomb of the exiled O'Donnells in Rome. The poem works mainly by the great forcefulness of its central image: the lonely woman at the abandoned tomb, alone and friendless in a strange country in the face of death, helplessness and utter defeat. This strangely evocative picture certainly implies a similar bereavement of other 'women' (that is: metaphors or metonyms in female guise) left helpless by the death of their protector: Éire as well as the poet himself, Ó Domhnaill's chief *ollamh*, who looked to his chief as to a husband. Indeed, these symbolic connotations in the person of Nuala Ní Dhomhnaill, and in her situation as depicted by Eoghan Rua's poem, may have inspired, or were at least made explicit by, a later political *aisling*, 'An Síogaí Rómhánach', where Éire herself appears in a vision as weeping on the tomb of the earl.

We need only think of Mangan's 'translation' of this poem (O, Woman of the Piercing Wail etc.) to realize how such poetry could later be subjected to a national or even nationalistic reading. That no *political* commitment as such was present in the intentions of these latter-day bardic poets becomes obvious, not only in their tendency to see the political upheavals of their time exclusively in their cultural (and, by implication, professional) impact, but also in the fact that many of them showed little compunction in shifting their allegiance to the incoming power – that is to say, to James I who, they thought, might as a Scotsman and as successor to an originally Gaelic throne be sympathetic to their cause – their professional cause, that is: the maintenance of Gaelic learning. The existence of such bardic endorsement of James's royal title was apparently even appreciatively registered at court, if Jonson's Irish masque is anything to go by (above, pp. 80–1). Thus, Eochaidh Ó hEoghusa described James' accession as an unexpected turn for the better, a political metamorphosis worthy of Ovid's pen:

> * An ghrian loinneardha do las;
>   sgaoileadh gach ceo Cing Séamas;
>   tug 'na glóir comhorchra cháigh:
>   móir na comhortha claochláidh.[51]

---

* The brilliant sun lit up: king James is the dispersal of all mist; the joint mourning of all he changed to glory; great the signs of change. (ed.'s trl.)

And Fearghal Óg Mac an Bhaird wrote an ode extolling James' claim to no less than three royal styles, Scotland, England and Ireland: 'Trí coróna i gcairt Shéamuis'.

The dating of this poem is problematic but highly relevant, and deserves closer scrutiny – if only for the sake of illustrating how later political attitudes can interfere with the reading of a bardic poem. Both Eleanor Knott and Paul Walsh read this ode as an attempt to curry favour with the incoming powers – 'not indeed with the intention of decrying his former master, but rather to conciliate a new patron in place of those he felt he was losing in Ireland'.[52] The poem's editor, Lambert McKenna, also implies that this was an inaugural ode addressed to James on or after his accession to the English throne.

This view is challenged, however, by Tomas Ó Concheanainn who suggests that Walsh was 'probably relying on his memory' when he gave his opinion; he himself holds that the poem was written before James' accession to the English throne – presumably sometime during Fearghal Óg's Scottish sojourn which Ó Concheanainn places 'sometime between 1577 and 1595' (p. 249). Ó Concheanainn's motive for this redating seems to lie in the fact that he sees Mac an Bhaird *a priori* as a patriotic poet: 'Some of his best poems . . . reflect in a depth of patriotic feeling the hopes and fears of his race during a very troubled period in Irish history' (p. 235).

Against this background, an inaugural ode to the King of England would indeed seem incongruous; but even if written well before James' accession to the English throne, 'Trí coróna . . .' seems to lack that required depth of patriotic feeling, for Ó Concheanainn calls it a 'mediocre poem' (without elaborating on his critical criteria) and deals with it, not in the context of Fearghal Óg's other poems, but in an appendix, which concludes in characteristic fashion:

> Although eulogistic bardic poetry is notorious for its insincere and exaggerative modes of expression, we should nonetheless be disappointed if *Trí Coróna i gcairt Shéamuis* was composed after Brian na Múrtha, who had taken refuge in Scotland, had been handed over by James to Elizabeth (1591). (p. 250)

Ó Concheanainn thus seems to date the poem before 1591 mainly in order to spare himself the disappointment of the patriotic feeling which he has projected into Fearghal Óg . . . feelings which seem to divide the universe in a manichean split between Gaels and anti-Gaels, with Fearghal Óg belonging to the former and king James to the latter – at least, as from 1591. In such a view this poem obviously presents a problem – a problem that can not, unfortunately, be solved by calling the poem 'mediocre' or by relegating it to an appendix.

Nor am I convinced by the textual evidence offered by Ó Concheanainn, which boils down to the statement that two stanzas indicate that queen Elizabeth was still alive when the poem was composed. The stanzas in question are nos. eighteen and nineteen, and they read:

* Críoch Sagsan na gcoll gcorcra
gan innte d'fhuil ríoghochta
acht éinríoghan dá gclaon coill,
craobh ler léirlíonadh Lonndoinn.

Ó ló na mnásoin a-mach
a-tá id chairtse go cosgrach
triath ríoLunndan do rádh ruibh
rádh na bhfíorughdar fíorthair. (AithDD vol. 1, 179)

To begin with, these stanzas, lacking definite verbs, do not cogently represent a living queen. But what is more, I think it a misreading to apply both of these stanzas to Elizabeth, whether alive or dead, a misreading partly occasioned by their forced isolation from their context. If we look at the preceding stanza, no. seventeen, we read:

° Bhar seanseanmháthair – seol glan –
(inghean) airdríogh fhóid Sagsan
críoch a sgéal linn gá leanmhain
do fhéagh sinn i seinleabhraibh. (ibid.)

The queen referred to here is James' great-grandmother: Margaret, wife of James IV of Scotland and eldest daughter of Henry VII of England. She is James' link with the Tudor dynasty, she is the reason why he is senior claimant to the English throne, as have been the Stuarts ever since her time – 'Ó ló na mnasoin amach'. The reference to Elizabeth in stanza eighteen is thus bracketed by two references to Margaret Tudor (1489–1541) in stanzas seventeen and nineteen. These lines offer as much or as little evidence on either queen's life or death at the time of composition. They describe merely the timeless validity of James' claim to the Tudor succession, i.e. Margaret's parentage and marriage, and Elizabeth's childlessness. That is also the drift of the next stanza (no. twenty), which concludes the portion of the poem dealing with James' English royalty:

† Ag so ar Lonndain na learg dtais
ciall do chairte, a Ching Shéamais,
rádh seinleabhar ar bhur son
fa chlár seingleabhar Sagsan. (ibid.)

---

* That Saxons' land of purple hazels had only one queen of royal blood, the princess for whom London was thronged, the queen whom hazels salute.
   After that princess – it stands in triumph in thy charter – the truthful authorities all assert that thou art lord of royal London. (ed.'s trl.)
° Following up the story which I have read in the ancient books, I find that thy great-grandmother – noble her descent! – was daughter of the king of the Saxons' land. (ed.'s trl.)
† O King James, the true force of thy charter to gently-sloping London is that the ancient books assert thy claim to the Saxons' beauteous land. (ed.'s trl.)

James' right to the Scottish throne, by the way, is described in terms that are not at all differentiated from the statement of his right to the English (and Irish) regality: nothing in the poem indicates that one is actual, the other possible, one present and the other future.

There is not even any contradiction between the reading of this poem as an inaugural ode and Fearghal Óg's loyalty to the Gaelic cause. If we accept it as an inaugural ode, then it could well be seen as an expression of hope that O'Neill and O'Donnell, who were at this time submitting and suing for peace, would fare better under a Scottish king than under an English queen.

Problems such as these are by no means rare in the history of bardic and post-bardic literature. There is, for example, an earlier eulogy by Flann Mág Craith addressed to queen Elizabeth, which was interpreted by Standish O'Grady (BMCat vol. 1, 544) as a mock-laudatory satire *per antiphrasin* (i.e. using incongruously laudatory terms in order to mock its subject), notwithstanding the fact that another poet, Dáibhí Ó Bruadair, had taken it seriously enough to attack it in one of his own poems.[53] Indeed, the fact that Mág Craith's poem elicited Ó Bruadair's response seems to have been the sole cause for its very survival among a later, nationalistically Gaelic audience, to whom its subject-matter and import were repugnant. Ó Bruadair's editor, John Mac Erlean, offers as his own 'excuse for printing the poem' (!) a quotation from the scribe and poet Seán na Ráithíneach:

> *   ní fheadar cia hé [the poem's author, Mág Craith; J.L.] et ní mó scríobhfainn an aisti si mar ghraidh dhi acht go bhfuil a freagra ag Dáibhidh ó Bruadair (ibid.)

This example illustrates how the very availability and accessibility of these poems is part of a political tradition, and that its reception can politicize a poem in a way that would have been unthinkable at the time of its creation.

Such poems prove that a nationalistic intent cannot be proved to have been operative at the time, despite *ex posteriori* imputations of men like Seán na Ráithíneach, Dáibhí Ó Bruadair, Standish O'Grady, John Mac Erlean or Tomás Ó Concheanainn. In fact, most poems of this period make it abundantly clear that the breakdown of the bardic order was lamented in purely professional terms; let us survey a sample.

Fearghal Óg Mac an Bhaird himself began to address a prince of the Church after the Gaelic princes had disappeared over the political horizon: he wrote poems to Flaithrí Ó Maolchonaire, the archbishop of Tuam living in exile, who was himself the scion of an established scholarly family. Mac an Bhaird's complaints refer, not to the 'Gaelic cause' as a whole, but merely to his own fallen station in the new social order. The feeling that actuates this poetry is the bitterly wounded aristocratic pride of the *ollamh*:

*   I do not know who he is, nor would I copy this production for the love of it, except that there is a response to it by David Ó Bruadair. (ed.'s trl.)

    * Fúarus iongnadh, a fhir chumainn,
cádhus úatha ní fhúair mé,
na dáoine dar dhúal ar n-ionramh,
as úar náoidhe an t-iongnadh é.

Meisi folamh, féch na diongna,
's dáoine dáora ar nár dhúal gean
sunna ón Spáin ag agháil ionnmhuis
a n-anáir chláir bhionnghlais Bhreagh.

Mná anúaisle buirb is bathluigh
a mbeartaibh óir san aird thall
atáid trá agus sinn gan édáil,
dar linn atá égáir ann.

Re foluibh ísli fhuinn Luighdheach
dár las um chorp crithir thnúidh,
a mhic Fíthil ó íadh Énna,
grían do dhíchil déna dhúin.[54]

Such humiliation must have been especially bitter for those whose appointed task it was to be the arbitrators of nobility and merit; and it is interesting that the poet's scorn is directed against his fellow-Gaels – that is, the vulgar Gaels, now coming to the fore after the removal of the Gaelic aristocracy – rather than against the English usurpers. A similar and, if anything, more extreme example to the same effect is furnished by an anonymous prose work of the period, *Pairlement Chloinne Tomáis*,[55] a rather gross satire mocking the social pretensions of the lower-class Irish. Until the Jacobean upheaval, these had been little better than serfs; the minor improvements and their new self-awareness are bitterly and scornfully contrasted with their churlish life-style, the author's allegiance being clearly with the old aristocracy. We may, for instance, safely regard the following words (spoken by the sages attending the chieftain Ó Madagáin) as reflecting the author's own attitude:

    ° ní dhlighionn aonneach d'fhuil uasail ar bith measgadh ar fhuil anuasail; óir dá
      mhéid macnais & foghluim, onóir agas ughdarrás do-gheibhid an aois anuasal,

---

  * I have found a marvel, my friend – no reverence have I found from people to whom it were
     fitting to wait upon me; it is a cold new marvel.
        That I am empty – see whether this be not a thing to mark, while base folk, unworthy of
     regard, are here receiving riches from Spain in honour of the sweet green plain of Bregha.
        Vulgar wives of churl and clown are yonder in golden raiment, while I lack wealth – I
     deem it unjust.
        Against the low-born families of Lughaidh's land, which have caused a spark of envy to
     kindle within me, O son of Fitheal from Enna's land, show unto me the sunlight of thy earnest
     care. (ed.'s trl .)
  ° and no-one of any noble blood at all should mix with ignoble blood; for however great the
     luxury and learning, honour and position the lower orders acquire, they do not accordingly

ní bhí modh ná measardhacht ionnta dhá réir, mar adeirid na heolaigh, *ut dixit poeta: Rustica progenies nescit habere modum.* Agas is dearbh dá réir sin, nach cóir duitse go deogh ná go deireadh an domhain t'fhuil do shalcha le fuil mho-ghuidh ná dhaoirsig, óir ní miannach maith iad, agas ní bhfuil cruth dá aoirde ionna rachaid, nó oifig nó ughdarrás dogheabhuid, nach é budh mian leo fola uaisle do mhaslughadh agus do mhilleadh, dá dtíosadh leo a dhéanamh. (p. 7)

It is interesting to note how far the social upheaval resulted, for many writers of a professionally 'bardic' turn of mind, in an equation between the two parties inimical to their old aristocratic values: namely the Gaelic churls and the English settlers. Thus, in *Pairlement Chloinne Tomáis,* one of the churls is represented as addressing an English tobacco-merchant in (broken or macaronic) English full of mutual flattery and courteous phrases. Similarly, the climax of the churls' pretensions is remarkably apposite in that it combines English (foreign) influence and upstart (democratic/anti-aristocratic) arrogance: they decide to hold a Parliament, an institution both anti-aristocratic and English.

Fearflatha Ó Gnímh's 'Mo thruaighe mar táid Gaoidhil'[56] similarly despairs of degenerate Gaels and usurping English alike, and his poem 'Mairg do-chuaidh re ceird ndúthchais' makes the sardonic point that there is no future left in the business of poetry:

    *   Tairnig onóir na héigse
        teasta cion an choimhéidse,
        'na gcriadhairibh oir gurbh fhearr
        do sgoil fhiadhoirir Éireann.

        Ná gabhaid chuca seach cách
        dísbeagadh a ndréacht neamhghnáth:
        ní dóibh a-bháin do-bhearair
        táir, acht don ghlóir Ghaoidhealaigh. (IBP p. 121)

A similar theme was developed by one of the most sardonic wits of this lost generation, Mathghamhain Ó hIfearnáin, who wrote a bitter injunction to his son ('A mhic ná meabhruigh éigse': 'My son, cultivate not the poetic art', cf. BMCat vol. 1, 392–3) *not* to become a poet. The same Ó hIfearnáin sarcastically begins to use the language of market vendors, hawking his poetry now that no more patrons or persons of literary taste can be found:

exhibit breeding or moderation, as the learned say, *ut dixit poeta: Rustica progenies nescit habere modum.* It is obvious therefore that you should never until the end of the world sully your blood with the blood of serf or churl, for they are not a good breed, and it does not matter how high they reach, nor what office or standing they attain, they always desire to pollute and corrupt high-born kindreds, if only they are able. (ed.'s trl.)

    *   The honour of poesy is departed; the credit of this guardianship is gone, so that the school of Ireland's land were better as husbandmen of the ploughland.

      Let them not take to themselves beyond others the scorn of their choice verses; not they alone, but the glory of the Gael is despised. (ed.'s trl.)

* Ceist! cia do cheinneóchadh dán?
  a chiall is ceirteólas suadh:
  an ngéabhadh, nó an áil le haon
  dán saor do-bhéaradh go buan?

  Gé dán sin go snadhmadh bhfis,
  gach margadh ó chrois go crois
  do shiobhail mé an Mhumhain leis –
  ní breis é a-nuraidh ná a-nois.

  D'éirneist gémadh beag an bonn,
  níor chuir fear ná éinbhean ann,
  níor luaidh aoinfhear créad dá chionn,
  níor fhéagh liom Gaoidheal ná Gall. (IBP p. 145)

One can note once again, in the final line quoted, the brotherly conjunction of Gael and Gall, and conclude that Ó hIfearnáin's regrets were not of a national, but of a professional or 'class' nature. The same goes for Ó Gnímh himself. His melodious dirges on the ruin of Gaelic Ireland, e.g. 'Beannacht ar anmain Éireann' or 'Tairnig éigse fhuinn Gaoidheal', always culminate in a mournful description of the low esteem into which poetry and learning have fallen;[57] and yet, while he was mourning the downfall of the Gael, he tried to make a shift in the new dispensation by turning towards the Gaels' old enemies, the incoming powers. The ex-*ollamh* to the Clandeboy O'Neills began to address, for instance, an Ulster Scottish family who had remained in the good graces of the government, and wrote a poem to Randall MacDonnell, first earl of Antrim, praising him (and justifying himself?) by stating that 'Éireannaigh féin Fionn-Lochlannaigh', 'Indeed the Fair Danes are Irish'.[58]

The sheer concentration and number of such bardic complaints helped to set the tone for later Gaelic poetry dealing with the status of Gaelic learning and culture in an English-dominated Ireland. The opposition was that between culture and boorishness, aristocracy and rudeness, venerable tradition and upstarts, intellectual achievement and brute physical force. Later on, we shall see how the two principal external advertisements of cultural allegiance, namely language and religion, were also grouped into this opposition.

But as these oppositions were created by the bards, they were as often distributed along social divisions, class divisions, as along national lines. The national division was blurred by the bardic esteem for certain non-Gaelic aristo-crats, as well as by their loathing for the lower-class Gaels.[59] Indeed the Gaelic image of the English settlers as bumpkins and upstarts unable to appreciate

---

* Question ! who will buy a poem? Its meaning is genuine learning of scholars. Will any take, or does any lack, a noble poem that shall make him immortal?

   Though this is a poem with close-knit science, I have walked all Munster with it, every market from cross to cross – nothing gained from last year to this time.

   Though a groat were a small earnest, not one man or woman offered it: no man mentioned the reason; neither Gael nor Gall gave heed to me. (ed.'s trl.)

culture and wit (an image central to the work of later poets like Dáibhí Ó Bruadair and his successors) seems, as can be gauged from the writings of this period, to have been coined originally by the bardic-aristocratic *mépris* for the now enfranchised, more assertive, lower-class Gaels. This equation between Gaelic and Foreign boors can even lead (for instance in *Pairlement Chloinne Tomáis*) to *Gaelic* descriptions of (lower-class) Gaelic repulsiveness that resemble, if anything, the writings of Englishmen like Fynes Moryson and Barnaby Rich:

> *   Agas go madh é budh biadh agas budh beatha dhóibh .i. féitheach ceann & cosa beathadhach, fuil & follracht & ionathar na n-ainmhighthe n-éigcialluighe, & fós go madh é bhus arán & bhus annlann dóibh .i. arán omh úrgharbh eorna, agas praiseacha práipeamhla prácáis, bun bainne, & bréaním ruibeach cuasghorm gabhar & caorach . . . go madh iad a gcoilceacha codulta, eadhon cnámhlach agas cosa pise agas pónaire & gaosadán, & comhgháir deargshor agas dreancadaighe fana gcroicionnuibh cruadha cróna croisfhéitheacha . . .[60]

Similarly, though less coarsely and vindictively, Geoffrey Keating was to defend Ireland's reputation in his *Foras feasa ar Éirinn* of 1629, not by refuting English denigrations, but by restricting their application to the mere lower classes (cf. below p. 275)

Whereas a recognizable and characteristic attitude is taken towards the lower-class Gaels, only the barest hints of a distinctive character attributed specifically to the Foreigners emerge from bardic texts. Here and there, notions of Gaelic nimbleness as opposed to Foreign cumbersomeness can be found, mainly dating from Tudor times. An Ó Cléirigh poet described the Foreigners as 'Goill gan meanma on mallfaicsin', 'spiritless strangers of the sluggish eye',[61] and Mathghamhain Ó hUiginn said to Feidhlim Ó Broin: 'Níor saoileadh go tteacht as-teagh/fosaidh Gall re gort Gaoidheal' (Let it not be imagined that the inertia of the Goill could spread over the land of the Gaels[62]). Other references are more concerned with their boorish inelegance – Lochlainn Ó Dálaigh, in his poem on the Ulster plantations[63] calls the settlers 'dírim uaibhreach eisiodhan/d'fhuil Ghall, do ghasraidh Mhonaidh' (an arrogant, impure crowd of Foreign stock, of Monadh's lineage[64]); a favourite epithet with many poets, e.g. Fearfasa Ón Chainte, is *garbh,* 'rough'.

There is not much matter of characterological interest here – in fact, its very dearth stands out as the more interesting feature and seems to indicate, once again, a lack of national categorization: the Foreigners are merely seen as irksome and disagreeable, even evil intruders and usurpers[65] – but this seems to apply to their status as 'enemies of the Gaels' rather than as 'representatives of England'.

---

*   And these were to be their food and nourishment: the head-gristle and trotters of cattle, and the blood, gore and entrails of dumb animals; and furthermore these were to be their bread and condiment: coarse, half-baked barley-bread, messy mish-mashes of gruel, skimmed milk, and the butter of goats and sheep, rancid, full of hairs and blue pock-marks . . . these were to be their bed-clothes: vegetable refuse, the stalks of peas, beans and ragweed, and multitudes of red lice and fleas about their hard swarthy skins with their tangled sinews. (ed.'s trl.)

The Foreigners are not considered as members of a 'nation' differing by certain characteristics from the Irish 'nation' – such categories with their attendant character traits and attributes do not seem to have been current in bardic poetry, the poetry of the Gaelic clan society. The breakdown of that society and of the bardic order was to clear the way for new developments.

Themes and issues in seventeenth-century poetry

The social and political developments of the seventeenth and eighteenth centuries are mirrored in a number of ways in Irish poetry. As Catholic land ownership decreased steadily and land was reassigned to a new, Protestant, class of landlords (usually colonists from Britain), the old nobility as well as their erstwhile dependants were put under a new system whose policies and representatives (middlemen, sheriffs, bailiffs, courts of assizes etc.) were much resented. The economic policies which were implemented by the colonist-landlord and the penal legislation of the eighteenth century reduced the Catholic population to poverty and servitude. The poet-class partook fully of these developments. Whereas the seventeenth century still produced proud individualists of an aristocratic turn of mind, e.g. Dáibhí Ó Bruadair, the poets of the eighteenth century became part of a more popular tradition, their poetry gradually becoming less distinguishable from the oral folk-tradition of anonymous poetry and song. One poet straddles the divide between the earlier, aristocratic tradition, and the later, more communitarian one: Aogán Ó Rathaille (c. 1675–1729).

Long before Ó Rathaille, however, the impact of social upheaval made itself felt in a number of basic trends that began to affect the literary practice of the seventeenth century, trends that distinguish it sharply from the previous bardic tradition. One of these is the emergence of members of non-bardic, even non-Gaelic families. To be sure, occasional Hiberno-Norman names do crop up even in medieval and sixteenth-century Irish poetry: e.g. Gearóid Iarla and William Nugent; but such names now become more frequent and even take pride of place in the canon of leading literary figures, e.g. Keating, Hackett and Ferriter.

Another novelty is the abandonment of the old syllabic prosody of bardic 'school'-poetry. Accentual metres begin to be used – that is to say, they had most probably been used long before, but not in the learned, 'official', tradition that we know from the manuscripts. The syllabic and accentual continue side by side for a while throughout the seventeenth century, often even combined into compound verse-forms like *trí rann agus amhrán* (three syllabic stanzas and one in accentual 'song'-metre). Command over the intricacies of syllabic metre became more and more slipshod over the decades, however, as the poets preferred to cultivate the elaborate vowel-patterns of the *amhrán* metres; and the few examples of *deibhí* verse from the eighteenth century read like poor imitations.

Yet another basic change in poetical practice was the abeyance of patronage. I have quoted a number of well-known bardic poems to illustrate how traumatic this development was for the professional poet, whose livelihood was thereby placed under a sentence of death. Accordingly, the later poets found themselves forced to engage in other forms of employment, or faced destitution. They had no more official, panegyrical or elegiac poetry to compose *ex officio* (though some vestiges of official 'family'-links remained, even if only emotional ones, e.g. Ó Rathaille – Mac Cárthaigh, or Mac Cruitín – Ó Briain). The poet did continue to speak on issues of general importance as his predecessors had done (much as he did continue to write occasional verse, e.g. epithalamia), and with the same implicit claim to make his opinion heard and hearkened to – but there were fewer and fewer persons of consequence left to listen to him. His audience was sliding down the social scale as much as he was.

This shift in the social status of the poet and of his audience was neither performed nor acknowledged willingly, and a nostalgia for the old, aristocratic ways can often be noticed. Especially in the seventeenth-century tradition, of which Ó Bruadair is the bitter and cantankerous closing figure, a number of attitudes and stylistic devices survived which were a deliberate echo of bardic aristocratic pride. Indeed many of the earlier post-bardic poets still enjoyed privileged social positions: Ferriter belonged to Hiberno-Norman nobility which was not uprooted until after Cromwell, and poets like Hackett, Keating and Mac Giolla Phádraig were priests who, especially in the upswing of the Confederation of Kilkenny, could exercise considerable authority in public affairs. Mac Giolla Phádraig's poem 'Faisean Chláir Éibhir' is in many respects a straightforward continuation of bardic anti-boorish invective. The one notable change is that the metre is *amhrán*:

> * Och! mo chreachsa faisean chláir Éibhir:
> loca cas ar mhac gach mná déarca,
> cufa geal 'ma ghlaic is fáinne aerach
> mar gach flaith d'fhuil Chais dár ghnáth Éire.
>
> 'S gach mogh nó a mhac go stairs go hard lé smig,
> cor tar ais dá scairf is gáirtéar air,
> a stoc tobac 'na chlab dá lántséideadh,
> 's a chrobh ó alt go halt fá bhráisléidibh.
>
> Is cor do leag mé cleas an phlás-tsaoilse:
> mogh in gach teach ag fear an smáilBhéarla
> 's gan scot ag neach le fear den dáimh éigse
> ach 'hob amach 's beir leat do shárGhaelgsa'. (NDh vol. 1, 11)

* O how woeful this new fashion in Eber's plain: each beggarwoman's son has curled locks, bright cuffs around his paws and a golden ring like any prince of the blood of Cas that used to be established in Éire.

Each churl or his son is starched up around the chin, scarf thrown around him and a garter on him, his tobacco-pipe in his gob and he puffing away at it, and his hand from joint to joint bedecked with bracelets.

The situation that brought me down is a trick of this deceitful world, with a churl in each house that is owned by a speaker of nasty English, and no-one paying any heed to a man of the poetic company, save for 'Get out and take your precious Gaelic with you'.

Another new feature in this poem is the emphasis on the political and cultural significance of one's choice of language. The last line is especially noteworthy: a deliberately coarse, vulgar and colloquial clang to end the sonorous invective of the preceding lines. The effect is all the more studied since, by an extreme application of the assonantial *amhrán*-scheme, literally every vowel rhymes with its corresponding syllable in the penultimate line. A double twist is involved. On the one hand, through the opposition of the two prefixes, the *smáilBhéarla*, 'nasty English', despised by the poet, is contrasted with the *sárGhaeilge*, 'noble Irish', cast out by the boors; and the literal meaning of these prefixes is contrasted with the actual situation described (the 'nasty' finds acceptance while the 'noble' is rejected), the two terms being made to rhyme moreover with their corresponding social backgrounds: *plás-tsaol*, 'false world' going with the English, the man of the *dámh-éigse* 'noble literati' rhyming with the Gaelic. All this leads up to the poem's 'punch line', the sneering imitation of vulgar Irish which is allowed to intrude into the poem's lofty eloquence in a deliberate destruction of its rhetorical harmony.

Time and again in seventeenth- and eighteenth-century Gaelic poetry, the point is made both on the aural and on the semantic level, that the inner harmony of Gaelic Ireland has been jarred by the intrusion of foreign elements. This is usually done by introducing English words, names or phrases into the text. An earlier example is contained in the bardic poem by Laoiseach Mac an Bhaird referred to above on p. 181: the alien fripperies of the renegade are designated by uncouth loanwords which serve to drive home how silly and foreign the articles in question are: *clóca*, 'cloak'; *cóta*, 'coat'; *sbuir*, 'spurs'; *buat*, 'boot'; *sdocaidhe*, 'stockings'; *locaidhe*, 'curls'; *ráipéar*, 'rapier' (derisively qualified as being 'too blunt to kill a fly'); and *sgarfa*, 'scarf' (IBP pp. 49–50). Similar sartorial loanwords are used in this poem by Mac Giolla Phádraig: besides *scarf* and *loca* we see *cufa*, 'cuffs'; *gáirtéar*, 'garter' and *bráisléid*, 'bracelets'. One has to keep in mind how extraordinary sensitive these poets were to the material of their art, the Irish language in all its aural patterns, in order to realize that such words were not introduced fortuitously as signs for unaccustomed new objects or situations, but, on the contrary, as deliberately as a composer would use a strongly dissonant chord. No time had been lost in Gaelicizing names like Fitzgerald and Butler – but such a process was conspicuously refrained from in the case of men with names like 'Dawson', anti-Gaelic representatives of English rule and English culture.

The Irish language can thus in itself be used to express an Irish identity; accordingly, one can observe that a great deal of what can only be called 'national' pride later on came to be vested in the Irish language. The following short verse, traditionally attributed to Geoffrey Keating, is well known, and contains the remarkable claim that the Irish language is free from loanwords – another indication that the poetic usage of terms like the ones mentioned above was undertaken deliberately:

*   Milis an teanga an Ghaedhealg,
     Guth gan chabhair choigcríche,
     Glór géar-chaoin glé glinn gasta,
     Suaire séimhidhe sult-bhlasta.

     Gidh Eabhra teanga is seanda
     Gidh Laidean is leigheanta,
     Uatha uirthi níor fríth linn
     Fuaim nó focal do chomaoinn.[66]

The linguistic commitment expressed in such poetry gains even more interest when it is realized that, around the same time (i.e. the second quarter of the seventeenth century), similar concern for the language's heritage and future began to actuate the discursive activities of Irish priests and monks living in exile on the Continent. That activity, which will be dealt with more closely in the following chapter, was to culminate in the production of a seminal Irish grammar written in Latin by the theologian Francis O'Molloy and printed on the presses of the *Congregatio de Propaganda Fide* at Rome in 1677. Here, too, the poetic tradition of language enthusiasm was continued: a long poem was appended which linked the decline of the old nobility and the decline of literacy, learning, and the language in general:

°   Truagh daoine ar dhíth litri.
    iar cclaoidhe dfuath aibghitri.
    An aincheas as lor do lan.
    Ainbhféas as mor ar mhoran.

    Fodla liu do chraidhman ccioth
    An aghaidh sluaigh a sinsior.
    Nir an oirfideadh an fhuinn
    Foirchideal glan no foghluim.

    Ni thuig Gaoidhil gaoidhealg fein
    Ni labhraid í gan aoinbheim.
    Ni leighid le cágaidh coir.
    Treighid ni fhaghaid onoir.

---

*   So sweet a language is Irish, a voice untainted by foreign aid, a speech brightly pealing, clear, pure and sprightly, pleasant, mild and sensuous in the mouth.
      Though Hebrew be the oldest language, though Latin be the most learned, I have not found that it [Irish] is indebted to [either of] them for [as much as] a sound or a loanword.
°   Pity the people for want of literacy after the destruction of their letters; the doubt that is trouble some to many, the ignorance that is great to more.
      Ireland has fallen under the shower against the host of its ancestors. The music of tunes has not remained, nor proper instruction, nor learning.
      The Irish do not even understand the Irish language, they speak it carelessly, they do not read it with any propriety; they abandon it, and leave honour behind.

* Beag a luadh ar na leabhruibh.
Ar ghlor cheart a cceileabhruibh.
Ni breath dhaor dhfianuibh fail.
An riaghuil chlaon do chongbhail.

Leughadh rainn da niarr orra
Na tteangaidh mhin mhathardha.
Diomhaoin och ar easbadh iad.
Déasgadh na Sgot on Scitia.[67]

This linguistic and language-political preoccupation remained strong throughout these centuries. Another poem from the later seventeenth century, addressed to Gordon O'Neill, complains of the fact 'go bhfuilid uaisle Eiriond/ mon-uar ag treigin a gceirst/san nGaedhilg na nuam noirrdheirc' ('that Ireland's nobles, alas! give up their right to the melodious Irish'[68]); the same poem then continues:

° Níor thréigthe dhóibh í ile
air bhéurla chríoch gcoigríchthe
teangaidh aerdha bhlada bhinn
béurla do bheannaidh na tailginn

Dá dtuigmís (sní tuigthior linn)
milteanga mhuighe Féidhlim
níl ceól ná comhrádh bá binde
lomlán deól is dfhírinne

Sgoith gach béurla táinig ón tur
a ghoirios gach deaghughdar
(is faghluim sgagtha mar sin)
do thaghluim ghartha Ghaoidhil

Tá an dán san diadhacht innte
san ríghréim go róichinnte
bí an tsuirghe shaor sna treathain
sgach ní sduilghe dealathain (p. 90)

Here as elsewhere, then, the language is presented as the natural medium of, and point of access to, Gaelic literature, culture and history; at the same time,

---

* Little is now said about books. or the celebration of good speech. It is no longer a severe judgement on the people of Ireland that they keep the crooked rules.
   If you ask them to read verses in their own sweet mother tongue it is a waste of time, because they cannot. This is what happened to the Irish from Ireland.[67]

° It never should be laid aside for the speech of foreign lands, the merry, tasteful, sweet tongue, the language the shavelings blessed.
   If we understood the honeyed tongue of Fédhlim's plain – and we do not – no music or discourse were sweeter, full of truth and knowledge.
   The flower of every speech that from the Tower came – it is thus perfected lore itself – which every writer adopts to garner the Gael's generosity.
   In it there is poetry and piety, accurate successions of kings, courtship, the Triads, and every difficult composition. (ed.'s trl.)

the point is made that it is the heirloom of a certain class of Irishmen, who are now abandoning it owing to social pressure:

   *   Ní hí an teanga do chuaidh ó chion
       acht an dream dár dhual a dídion
       (mon-uar) dár bhéigin a ndán
       sa nduan do thréigin go tiomlán.

       Dlighidh siadsan dhá dhruim sin
       firiasma [sic] ghléire Gaoidhil
       dán a dtíre bá trom teist
       do ládh go lonn a láincheist. (p. 91)

Much the same point is made in a poem by none other than Aodh Mac Cruitín, the historian/grammarian/lexicographer from the early eighteenth century, whose importance will be indicated more properly in the closing chapter. In a long poem that also mentions his own philological investigations, Mac Cruitín (anglice: MacCurtin) emphatically represents the Irish language as being that of the Gaelic nobility, as being the very medium of, or even charter to, Gaelic nobility, since it contains the records of the Gaels' ancestral greatness. Thus the bardic attitude that Gaelic nobility consisted mainly in a continuity between the greatness of the past and its present inheritors is ushered into the new context of the eighteenth century, with its philological and antiquarian interest:

   °   A uaisle Éireann áilne
       A chrú na gcéimeann gcombáidhe,
       Tréigidh bhur dtromshuan gan on,
       Céimidh lom-luadh bhur leabhor.

       Trom an téidhm-se thárlaidh dhaoibh
       Idir mhnáibh agus mhacaoimh,
       Ar séanadh seanrádh bhur sean,
       Comhrádh soluis bhur sinsear.

       Nír dhealbh an domhan uile
       Teanga as milse mór-thuile
       De bhriathraibh as briocht-shnuite blas
       Caint as cian-tuilte cúntas.

---

*   It is not the language which has come into disesteem but those who should defend it, they who have been, alas! obliged to abandon their poems and verses all.
    The true remnant of the best of the Gaedhil should, then, strongly support their country's poetry, in value great (ed.'s trl.)

°   Ye nobles of lovely Ireland, race of high parentage, abandon your heavy unremittant sleep, delineate the pure discourse of your books.
    Heavy is this disease that has befallen you, between women and striplings, following the denial of the old speech of your elders, the bright talk of your forefathers.

> * Má tráightear tiobruid an fhis,
> Leabhair uama as iris –
> Falach bhur scéal ní scrios gann
> Gan fios bhur gcéimeann gcomhthrom.
>
> Na dréachta druadh nír léig brat
> Ar ghéig dar geinadh romhat,
> 'S gidh marbh ar n-uaisle aniogh
> D'ár nguais-ne nír dháil deiriodh.[69]

How tenacious this commitment to the Irish language was may also be judged from a scribal commentary that was made on this poem as late as 1820, by one Seamus Bunbury:

> The last Poem was written by Hugh McCurtin as an Address to Irishmen, recommending the study of the Irish Language to them, with which Poem I conclude this Book, warmly recommending the same to my Countrymen and to all well-wishers of their Country, rouse up your thoughts O Friends of Erin and take Example when you see all Nations around you open their Eyes (in this enlightened age) to Patriotism. and Dont let your Noble language go to decay and which you may easily obtain by very little trouble.[70]

Also, additional evidence of a preoccupation with language as a common cultural-political cause can be found in poems by Mac Cruitín's contemporaries who began to hail the antiquarians and philologists of the age: Seán na Ráithíneach, Roderick O'Flaherty and others addressed eulogies to Edward Lhuyd; Seán Ó Gadhra addressed O'Flaherty in a poem of praise and also wrote a dirge on the decline of the Irish language, 'Tuireamh na Gaedhilge', which bestowed praise on the efforts of antiquarians like Sir James Ware, John Colgan, Peter Walsh, Roderick O' Flaherty and Thady Roddy, and proudly maintains, 'Is fíor gur teanga aosta an Ghaedhilg/Ó aimsir an Tuir', 'it is certain that Irish is an ancient language from the time of the Tower of Babel'.[71] Tadhg Ó Neachtain's celebration of the presence of Gaelic scholars in Dublin in the 1720s, which will be dealt with in the final chapter, can also be seen in the context of an affirmation of the importance of Gaelic culture, Gaelic lore.

In all these endeavours the main value of the language is seen to lie in the fact that it represents a link with the golden past; thus the poet's concern for his language echoes the older bardic concern for the continuity of history, for the historical continuity of culture.

---

* The entire world has not produced a language more sweet in regard to great flow of statements of the most well-honed sound, a speech which has long had full description.

 If the well of knowledge be left to dry up, the verse-books and chronicles – the eclipsing of your histories and the lack of knowledge of your just grades will be no small destruction.

 The mythical tales never lacked patronage at the hands of preceding generations, and though our nobles are dead today, our enterprise has not yet seen its last.

The old prophetic mode of writing underwent a revival that may partly be explained by this urgently-felt need to remain in touch with history. New pseudo-ancient 'prophecies' were made (or reiterated – which amounts to much the same thing), 'foretelling' the past, 'foretelling' the present, foretelling a future from a single unifying temporal perspective; past, present and future are all combined into a pseudo-future, foretold in a fictitious prophecy that is itself retrojected back into pre-Conquest days. Breandán Ó Buachalla, who sees this phenomenon as a manifestation of messianism, puts it as follows:

> *   Mar shampla: bhí sé sa tairngreacht go dtiocfadh Naomh Pádraig, go dtiocfadh na Lochlannaigh, go dtiocfadh na Normannaigh, go dtiocfadh na Sasanaigh: b'in í an stáir a haithinsint, ach faoin 16ú haois bhí sé sa tairngreacht freisin go ruaigfí na Sasanaigh: 'Cuirfidh Sacsanaigh tar sáil,/scarfaidh iad da ngabháil; /maith liom a ndul tar a n-ais,/i leabhar na sean fuaras. . . . Biadh Éire go suthain sáimh/do réir thairngire Bhearcháin;/ag fine Gaedheal gan glas/is ansa tsaltair fuaras'.[72]

It is the retrospective displacement of prophecy, its treatment of the present as a pseudo-future, which adds to its credibility. What is more, the future foretold often seems more a return to the past. In O'Molloy's poem, for instance, a revival of Irish is prophecied which amounts to nothing less than a reinstatement of the bardic order:

> °   Fill a nos a aos mhanma.
> Na bi go dían dogarmtha.
> S nach cian o chathsaoirlios chuinn.
> Go mbia an tathaoibhnios aguinn.
>
> Biaidh na bruigne na mbotha
> Na bhfionta biaidh banshrotha.
> Cnuic ura na ngealfhonn nglan
> A bhfearonn duna dealgan.
>
> Biadh an ghaoidhealg fa mheas mhor
> An Ath cliath na bhfleasg bhfianol.
> Budh math a fian budh gaoth grinn.
> S gach laoch ag triall fa tuairim.[73]

---

*   For instance: it was in the prophecy that St. Patrick would come, that the Vikings would come; that the Normans would come; that the English would come; history was to be recognized in it, but as from the sixteenth century it was also in the prophecy that the English would be expelled: 'The English will retreat overseas, fall back from their aggression; it makes me happy that they shall leave again, I read it in a book of the elders . . . . Éire will be at peace for ever, according to Bearcan's prophecy, belonging to the Gaelic stock without fetters; in the psalter I read it.

°   Return now you people of hope, do not be stubborn and unheeding and it will not be long for the royal land of Conn, before we have the Renaissance.
     The crowds of poets will be in their huts surrounded by streams of ladies, the fresh mountains of the bright clean land in the region of Dundalk.
     The Irish language will be greatly honoured in Dublin of the brave young warriors, the hosts will be great, the talk sharp and every hero giving his opinion.[73]

Before tracing the development of this particular mode of prophetic poetry into the eighteenth century, however, it may be in order to begin with a short look at seventeenth-century post-bardic political poetry, a representative selection of which has been provided by Cecile O'Rahilly's collection of *Five seventeenth-century political poems*.

The tendency, inherent in the prophetic mode, to replace the present by a future perfect and to contrast the transitoriness of the dire English presence with the great once and future Gaelic order, was one of the most prominent features of the post-bardic tradition, which was spurred into heightened activity by the early successes and the eventual breakdown of Catholic Ireland's last hope of independence: the Confederation of Kilkenny of the 1640s. A seminal poem was Donncha Mac an Chaoilfhiaclaigh's 'Do frith, monuar, an uain si ar Éirinn', 'Ireland, alas, had to labour under adversity', which dates from the eve of the Confederate war. In the past, the poem says, Ireland was under the protection of the great heroes of yore – and a long enumeration of these heroes is nostalgically given:

> * Ba díobh Fionn mac Cumhaill na Féine,
> Oisín mac Fínn, Caoilte is Caol Glas,
> Goll is Usgar, Cuireall is Daolgas,
> is trí sáirmhic Aoinchéarda Béara
> Donn is Coinnche is Colla is na hAodha,
> na trí gairbhmhic, Cairbre is Céadach,
> Smeig ar Drúcht is Mac Lúighidh na ngéarlann,
> Brian Ó Biorrainn, Conn Crithir is Faolan.
> Is na gaisgíg i ngleacuíocht ba thréine:
> an Chú do thuit ar Mhuigh Mhuirthéimhne,
> Conall Ceárnach an t-ársa léidmheach
> is Laoghaire gruaigheal Buadhach na mbéimeann. (5PP p. 6)

The present is then depicted in contrast to this past which lasted

> ° go teacht iona rí do rí Séamus
> is dá mhac 'na dhiaig do riar Rí Séarlas.
> Atáid ó shoin 'na dtocht fá dhaorsmacht
> nach míne tréad le taobh na faolchon.
> 'S an mhéid aca nár ceangladh i ngéibhinn,
> do díbreadh iad i n-iathaibh céana,

---

* Among them were Fionn mac Cumhaill of the *fian*, Oisín Finn's son, Caoilte and Caol Glas, Goll and Osgur, Cuireall and Daolglas, and the three noble sons of Aoincheard: Béarra, Donn, Coinche, Colla and the Hughs, the three Gairbh-sons, Cairbre, Ceadach, 'Dewdrop' Smeig and Mac Lughach of the sharp blades, Brian Ó Biorainn, Conn Crithir and Faolan, and those heroes who in contention were most mighty, the Hound that fell on Muirthemhne's Plain, Conall Cearnach the audacious veteran and the bright-cheeked Victorious Laoghaire of the slashes.

° ... until the time king James became king and that of his son who ruled in succession to him, king Charles. Ever since, they are mute in dire oppression which is not kinder than that of the flock subject to a wolf. And those of them that weren't bound in fetters were banished into far-

's i gcrích Eachaidh a maireann dá n-éis sin,
Court of Wards is cách dá léirsgrios;
meirse is cíos is fis *Exchéquer;*
ciorrú stóir san tSeómra Réaltach,
san *King's Bench* a bhfuil dá séide,
is Cúirt na nEasbog dá n-argain d'aonghuth.
Assizes aca 'na gceannaibh conntaethe
ag cur talaimh is fearainn fá chéile. (5PP p. 8)

Two points of similarity link this poem to the long, anonymous complaint 'Tuireamh na hÉireann': both depict the evils of subjection to English law enforcement by means of introducing loanwords from English legalese; and both describe the English impact through a contrastive enumeration of the many Gaelic chieftains who were brought to grief. From 'Tuireamh na hÉireann':

*   Is docht na dlithe do rinneadh dár ngéarghoin:
     Siosóin cúirte is téarmaí daora,
     wardship livery is Cúirt *Exchéquer,*
     cíos coláisde *in nomine poenae;*
     greenwax, capias, writ, replévin,
     bannaí, fineáil, diotáil éigcirt,
     provost, soffré, portré, méara,
     sirriaim, sionascáil, marascáil chlaona.
     Dlí beag eile do rinneadh do Ghaeulaibh,
     surrender ar a gceart do dhéanamh.
     Do chuir sin Leath Chuinn trí na chéile,
     glacaid a n-airm gé cailleadh iad féin leis.
     An t-iarla Ó Néill fuair bárr féile
     's an tighearna Ó Domhnaill ba mhór géille,
     Ó Catháin na n-each mbán is na n-éide
     is Ó Ruairc uasal, tiarna Bréifne,
     Mág Uidhir Gallda is Mág Uidhir Gaeulach,
     Ó Ceallaigh, Ó Buídhill is Ó Raghallaigh [etc.] (5PP pp. 73–4)

off lands, and in the land of Eachaidh those that survive them find only *Court of Wards*, amercement and cess and *Exchequer* fees and the ruination of all and sundry; the diminution of wealth in the Star Chamber, their despoliation in the *King's Bench*, and the *Bishops' Court* plundering them. *Assizes* in the capitals of their counties upturning land and estate.

*   Harsh were the laws which were framed to persecute us: court sessions and harsh legal terms, wardship, livery and the Court of the Exchequer, college tax in *nomine poenae, greenwax, capias, writ, replevy,* bans, *fines,* unjust indictments, *provost,* sovereign, portreeve, mayor, sheriff, seneschal, deceitful marshal; yet another small law which was imposed on the Gaels: to make *surrender* of what was theirs by right.

    This put Leath Chuinn into turmoil, they take up arms though they met their death thereby; Ó Néill, earl, who received the greatest bounty; Ó Domhnaill, lord, to whom many submitted; Ó Catháin of the white steeds and the armours, noble Ó Ruairc, lord of Breifne, Foreign Mág Uidhir and Gaelic Mág Uidhir, Ó Ceallaigh, Ó Buidhill and Ó Raghallaigh . . .

'Tuireamh na hÉirann' takes an explicitly positive stance towards the old Hiberno-Normans and sees them, like Keating, as virtually identical with the Gaels: 'Do shíolraigh a bhfuil trí na chéile,/do bhí an Gaeul Gallda 's an Gall Gaeulach': 'They mixed their blood together, the Gael became Gall and the Gall Gaelic' (p. 72): the names of Hiberno-Normans are also enumerated at length (pp. 76–7).

The clearest example of the introduction of hateful English is perhaps to be found in Éamonn an Dúna's 'Mo lá leóin go deó go n-éagad', 'My eternal Day of Sorrow', which renders the poet's *meabhair ar Bhéarla*, his 'memories of English', as follows:

> *Transport, transplant,* mo mheabhair ar Bhéarla.
> *Shoot him, kill him, strip him, tear him,*
> *A Tory, hack him, hang him, rebel,*
> *a rogue, a thief, a priest, a papist.* (5PP p. 90)

But by far the most interesting poem from the mid-seventeenth century is *An Síogaí Rómhánach*, the anonymous vision-poem sometimes attributed to a Mac an Bhaird. It describes an allegorical spirit-woman weeping at the tombs of O'Neill and O'Donnell in Rome – a close parallel, as I have remarked before, to Eoghan Rua Mac an Bhaird's poem to Nuala Ní Dhomhnaill. The interplay between past and future, kept apart by the dire present but linked by the promises of the prophecies of bygone days, is especially subtle here. As an elegy on the Confederate general Eoghan Rua Ó Neill, the poem bewails the fact that the old prophecies, the high hopes which he inspired, have not come true – but 'on the rebound', as it were, new hopes are born from the ashes of the old ones, and bright promises are projected into the future; a future, to wit, in which the scions of the great Gaelic past will be conquerors:

> * Gidheadh'fós, mo dhóigh níor thréigeas,
> 's ní bhiaidh mise gan misneach éigin.
> Is treise Dia ná fian an Bhéarla.
> Mairidh fós do phór Mhilésius
> an t-Aodh Buidhe se d'fhuigheall na nGaolfhear
> an fear do thárrngair fáidh nach bréagach
> chuirfeas Gallaibh i ndeireadh na péice,
> Mairidh an ruaidhfhear gruaidhgheal Féilim,
> is Colonel Fearghail, an gaisgidheach éachtach,
> is Aodh Ó Broin le dtuitfeadh céadta.
> Mairidh an chóip nach dóigh d'éinneach:

* Yet nevertheless I did not abandon hope and I shall not be without some little courage. God is mightier than the English-speaking *fian*. Of Míl's stock there still lives Aodh Buí of the remnant of Gaelic men, the man whom a true seer foretold, he who will reduce the foreigners to their dying gasp. The red-haired bright-countenanced Féilim still lives, and Colonel Fearghal, the valiant hero, and Aodh Ó Broin by whom hundreds might fall. The company yet lives which is not to be trifled with by anyone: Uí Ruairc, Uí Raghallaigh, Branaigh all combining, the resolute, steed-

Ruarcaigh, Raghallaigh is Branaigh le chéile,
is Síol gConchubhair sturrumhail stéadmhar,
Siol gCeallaigh nár fionnadh bheith tréithlag,

. . .

(eleven more clans are enumerated)

. . .

Do-dhéanaid an dáimh si go gearr aonchorp
is do-bhéaraid lámh i láimh a chéile.
Bualadh ar Ghallaibh i Saingeal do-bhéaraid,
i Mullach Maistean ar Danaraibh réabfaid.
Ní bhiaidh ceangal le Gallaibh ag éinneach,
ní bhiaidh caidreamh le hAlbanaigh mhaola,
ní bhiaidh marthain ar eachtrannaigh i n-Éirinn.
Biaidh céad cómharc i dtóin lucht Bhéarla
is Chailbhin chleasaigh bhradaigh bhréagaigh.
Biaidh gáir fá tholl i dtoll Luitéarus.
Biaidh an buadh ag sluagh na nGaol so.
Biaidh a n-uaisle i n-uachtar éirceach.
Biaidh a gcreideamh gan mhilleadh gan éclips.
Biaidh a n-eaglais ag teagasg an tréada,
bráithre is easbuig, saguirt is cléir mhaith. (5PP pp. 29–31)

Thus the glorious future is depicted as a return to the ways of the glorious, Gaelic past.

However, it is not just the 'Foreigners' that are to be expelled, as in the earlier bardic tradition; the spiteful references to these Foreigners' Protestant religion indicate that a new attitude was at work in the political poetry of this period, namely a religious one. This new attitude becomes especially obvious in the now popular motif that present distress must be seen as punishment for sins committed in the past – an argument repeatedly encountered in the poems of Ferriter and Keating. To be sure, a similar motif had been expressed repeatedly in the political poetry of Renaissance France, e.g. Alain Chartier's 'Quadrilogue invectif'.[75] In this seventeenth-century context it should be specified, however, that in the usage of this motif in Gaelic, the notion of 'sin' is not just an abstract one, but unambiguously the sin of dissent and strife, the lack of unity. Thus it is often little more than a rephrasing of the well-known maxim 'united we stand, divided we fall' in moral-religious terms: the sin of dissent brings its own retribution with it. Poets like Keating and Hackett, who both addressed poems to

---

riding Síol gConchubhair, Síol gCeallaigh who were not found to be weak . . . Soon will the heroes combine, and give their hand to each other. They will vanquish the strangers at Singland and rout the foreigners at Mullaghmast. Then none shall leage with the stranger, nor with the bare-headed Scotsman. Then shall Erin be freed from settlers, then shall hundredfold retribution be wreaked on the rear end of those English-speakers and of the crafty, thieving, false sect of Calvin. From one Lutheran backside to another the whacks will resound. The Gaels in arms shall triumph, their nobles shall bear sway over unbelievers, their faith will be without blight or eclipse. Their church, brothers and bishops, priests and good clergy, will be teaching the flock.[74]

the Confederation urging greater unity and denouncing internal division, were obviously aware of this fact, and the breakdown of the Confederation was largely, and not unjustly, blamed on the split between the Rinuccini and the Ormond factions. As we shall see, a general recrimination was triggered off between these parties after the ruin of the Confederation (below, p. 257); and *An Síogaí Rómhánach* may be considered a poetical contribution to that debate, which largely consisted of both parties mutually accusing each other of factionism and 'bad politics'. The elevation of the notion of 'bad politics' to the moral status of 'sin' can be attributed to the fact that, by now, the common cause was defined mostly in religious terms. It was a fight of Catholics against the English heretics (so that one can already see the merger of two different criteria, that of geographical or demographic background and that of religious affiliation) and, from a counter-reformatory perspective, dissent was indeed tantamount to a betrayal of God and his church. It is by models such as these that the extreme identification between 'the Irish cause' and 'the Catholic cause' was achieved – and it is not to be forgotten that most of the Gaelic-writing, anti-English literati (Keating, Hackett, Mac Giolla Phádraig and many exiled scholars on the Continent) had become part of 'the Catholic cause' by the most explicit form of identification possible: the taking of holy orders. This concept of a national cause defined in religious terms is clearly expressed in the following, anti-Ormondite lines in *An Síogaí Rómhánach*:

> *   Do bhí cuid líonta dhíobh do bhréagaibh,
>   cuid nó dhó le pór na n-éirceach
>   is dá chuid eile do Ghallaibh ag géilleadh.
>   Cuid le cleasaibh ag mealladh na nGaol so,
>   cuid ós árd i bpáirt na hÉireann
>   is iad go bráth fá láimh dá tréigean.
>   Cuid ag seasamh le Saxaibh don taobh 'muigh
>   is iadsan leó fá thóin na méise.
>   Biaidh mo mhallacht ag fearadh ar an gcléir sin
>   is ar a gcuaine go Luan an tsléibhe,
>   lucht gan dísle chroidhe dá chéile,
>   lucht na bhfeall, na meang 's na n-éigceart,
>   do thug náire do Chlár Éibhir
>   's do chuir suas d'uaislibh Gaodhal,
>   ar ar thuit cunntracht an Nuncio dhéidheanaigh,
>   Eóin Baisde, ardeasbog Féarmo,
>   aonfhear áite an Phápa i n-Éirinn,

---

*   Some abounded in falsehood, some aided the heretic horde, many submitted to the strangers, some craftily deceived the Gaels, some affected to espouse the cause of Erin while in secret they ever deserted her. Some feigned to oppose the strangers to whom they secretly adhered. My curses shall ever rain on such clerics and on their people till the judgement day; on those who did not love each other, the men of deceit, of guile and injustice who brought grief to Eber's plain, who rejected the noble Gaels and on whom fell the curse of the last Nuncio, John Baptista Rinuccini, archbishop of Fermo, sole legate of the pope in Erin; this is the cause of

Ag so an chúis is cúis dom dhéaraibh
ag so an cás do chráidh go léir mé,
do chuir folach ar sholas na gréine,
do chuir buaire is gruaim ar spéiribh,
's do chuir an Eóraip fá cheó éclips. (5PP pp. 28–9)

Of course, the exact mirror-image of this attitude is reflected in comtemporary English (Cromwellian) ideology, which saw the rising of 1641 as inspired by Popish subversion and which saw the extirpation of anti-English resistance largely as a religious crusade. Cromwell's enemies were 'Papists' as much as they were 'Irish'; the above-quoted line 'a rogue, a thief, a priest, a papist' (p. 212) contains a significant combination of Puritan bogeymen. Again, from the Irish point of view, the Cromwellian Gall had likewise become characterized in cultural, religious, political and legal terms. A characteristic quatrain from the period runs:

  * Cúis m'osnadh mo dhúithche fa mhoghsain fá dhubhbhroid
     ag cosmhar clamh prútach gan chreidiomh gan chóir;
     An lucht leanta so Cromwell lér teasgadh ár bprionnsa
     inár ngealbhrugha ag damhsadh 's ag imirt 's ag ól. (BMCat vol. 1, 30)

What all this means, in fact, is that the old bardic polarity Gael–Gall, which had already accrued the additional polarity bardic culture–foreign boars, and Gaelic language–English language, now becomes further spccified by the addition of the opposition Catholic–Protestant. This means, on the one hand, an increase in the number of marginals to whom not all of these criteria apply congruently; besides Gaelic Protestants like Lord Inchiquin, a growing number of non-Gaelic Catholics must in poetical practice be accommodated into his binary polarity. On the other hand, those who shared the various common denominators had, in their common opposition to English colonialism, not only a cultural (linguistic, literary, legal) focus of identification, but also a religious one. The terms were fixed, and were to remain fixed. From the Confederation to the present day, Irish national aspirations have most often tended to define themselves in anti-English as well as anti-Protestant terms, superimposed on the older bardic view that the real Ireland was that which supported Gaelic culture.

Accordingly, a critic like T.J. Dunne speaks of the works of Hackett and Keating in terms of 'a specific form of patriotism and Catholicism rather than "nationalism"', and draws attention to the fact that Hackett's poetic-political exhortations were 'party political, and Counter-Reformation, rather than "nationalist"';[76] and the same could be said of the poems of Keating. Such poems, like the above-mentioned ones as edited by Cecile O'Rahilly in her *Five seventeenth-century*

---

my tears, this is the cause which has truly grieved me; this has cast a shadow over the sun's light; this has clouded the sky with gloom and terror; this has cast Europe under an eclipse.[74]

  * My mourning's cause is that my country is ground down by a mangy brutish clown, devoid of religion or of justice: that these followers of Cromwell, by whom our prince was cropped, should now in our fair dwellings dance and gamble and drink away. (ed.'s trl.)

political poems, are written from a partizan anti-Ormondite, pro-Rinuccini point of view. The point still remains, however, that the 'Irish' stance, from being so all-pervasive as to be hardly noticeable in the middle ages, is becoming more and more explicit, defined by an increasing number of cumulative criteria which distinguish it from the 'English' interest. Accordingly, Ó Buachalla concludes his discussion of seventeenth-century political messianism as follows:

> * Faoin 17ú haois is í an tairngreacht pholaitiúil, arbh í an buntéama *na Gaill d'ionnarbadh agus Banba a shaoradh,* amháin a bhí cumadh ach san aois sin tugadh diminsean sochreiligiúnach agus diminsean soch-chultúrtha araon don bhfráma polaitiúil. Ní Danair, Gaill ná Sacsanaigh a bhí le ruagadh anois, de réir na tairngreachta (bíodh gur mhair na hainmneacha sin i gcónaí agus nár éirigh na filí riamh as a n-úsáid) ach sliocht Liútair agus bodaigh na Bhéarla . . .
>
> Is casadh fíorthábhachtach é seo agus bhí an dá eilimint sin – an reiligiún agus an cultúr – mar bhuneilimint feasta i ráiteachas na tairngreachta.[77]

It may be added that, especially in the poetry written by the exiles on the Continent, the concept *Éire* undergoes a certain shift away from the older bardic usage. Though more conservative poets like Mac Giolla Phádraig can still use bardic territorial terminology like *Leath Chuinn* or *Clár Éibhir,* more comprehensive names embracing the entire island seem to be on the increase (Éire, Inis Fáil, Inis Ealga, etc.). The poet's *Heimweh* concerns Ireland as a whole, not the dynastic/territorial divisions that were so central to bardic thought. As Dunne has noted (pp. 17–18), Hackett's exile poetry is an example of this development, which can also be noticed in poems by Keating (e.g. 'Om sceol ar ardmhagh Fáil', 'Mo bheannacht leat, a scríbhinn') and even in William Nugent's earlier 'Triall ó Dhealbhna' (cf. NDh vol. 1, nos. 4,14, 17,19). It seems more than a coincidence that this Éire, this affective homeland, defined geographically rather than territorially, should be loved so comprehensively by these poets with their Norman names, who stood largely outside the hothouse of traditional bardic school-lore. Gearóid Iarla's phraseology replacing 'Gaedhil' by 'Éireannaigh' had perhaps been a (very early!) straw in the wind.

This new, more comprehensive view of 'Ireland' as an undivided, undifferentiated fatherland of all Irish (these being so defined by their cultural, religious and political stance) was one of the most important preconditions for the meteoric rise of the *aisling* genre in these 150 years.

---

* From the seventeenth century it is the political prophecy, with as its main theme *to banish the Foreigners and liberate Banba,* which is the only one to be composed, but in that century, both a socio-religious and a socio-cultural dimension are imposed on the political frame. It is not the Danair, Foreigners or English that are to be expelled according to the prophecy (although these names remained in use and the poets never came to abandon them), but Luther's tribe and the English-speaking churls . . .

This is a truly important shift, and henceforth those two elements – religion and culture – were basic elements in the prophecy's message.

The *aisling* genre can be traced back in a number of different directions; all these 'roots' may have contributed something to its growing appeal and importance, which eventually made the *aisling* the dominant form of political literature in Irish. A general European tradition, found especially in France, of dream-like visions that poets have of comely allegorical maidens, is indicated by Murphy and by Ó Tuama,[78] Ó Tuama highlighting the importance of certain *complaintes* for the political dimension of such visions. Another source tradition consists in vision poetry which is amatory in nature, i.e. the maiden in the dream-vision is not the incarnation of the country, but an ideal of feminine beauty. The overlap between the political and the amatory *aisling* is, as we shall see, considerable, and Ó Tuama's pointer at the *reverdie* as a source-tradition for the latter type is therefore not without interest even in the consideration of the political *aisling*. Moreover, there are the many visions (e.g. *fís Adamnáin*) in earlier Irish literature itself, including also those poems, e.g. by Gearóid Iarla, which describe mystical-religious visions and which go by the very name of *aisling*.

But the most important source-tradition at the roots of the seventeenth- and eighteenth-century *aisling*, especially with respect to its combination of political and sexual interest, is the topos of the *puella senilis*, the old hag who will be rejuvenated if a hero gives her his love. This topos is itself rooted in the highly archaic tradition which sees kingship as the ruler's espousal of the land; the *puella senilis*, hence, is less a symbolically or allegorically created figure than a reference to common mythological knowledge: the sovereignty-goddess or territorial deity. This poetic figure was adapted in sixteenth-century political poetry to a parable form;[79] after the Flight of the Earls, Ireland begins to be identified metonymically as a woman who, according to the altered circumstances, is either a fallen woman or a dishonoured widow; I have already noted a similar usage of the anthropomorphized *uaisle* (above p. 183). In the post-bardic tradition, Keating's 'Mo thruaighe mar tá Éire', 'Ireland has aroused my pity', is a highly explicit example, which recurs later in Donncha Mac an Chaoilfhiaclaigh's 'Do frith, monuar, an uain si ar Éirinn' and in Dáibhí Ó Bruadair's 'Créacht do dháil mé im árthach galair'.[80] The traditional reading of such poems as a *reproach* to Ireland for being 'a fickle and faithless woman, no better than a *meirdreach* who gives her love to every foreign adventurer', 'a mother who has shamefully disowned her children and suckles instead a foreign brood'[81] may, however, be a little oversimplified: Keating and Ó Bruadair, at least, pity rather than condemn Éire's inability to withstand dishonour; Ireland is forsaken by her kin as much as vice versa; a victim as much as a hussy, she may be 'more sinned against than sinning', and to see the poet's complaints as a straightforward reproach (whereas pity is also undeniably involved) seems somehow a Victorian confusion of 'shame' and 'guilt'. Poems like those by Keating and Ó Bruadair seem to me to draw their very strength from their hesitation to assign any blame in this shameful situation; Foreigner, Gael and Éire stand in a triangular relationship in which no-one is wholly free from blame and in which, conversely, no-one is exclusively guilty.[82]

The first poem in which a mystical experience, mythological symbolism and feminine attractiveness co-operate in presenting an allegory of the poet's political hopes and fears (which may count as a provisional definition of the *aisling* of this period) is, again, *An Síogaí Rómhánach*. Here, the vision-woman, at the graves of the Ulster earls, does not address her grievances directly to the poet, but voices them in a long prayer to God, full of rhetorical questions as to why the Gaels are made to suffer, although they are the moral superiors of their tormentors, the English heretics. The opposition between suffering righteousness and triumphant wickedness runs throughout the poem; finally, after a description of Tudor and Stuart rule in Ireland, a eulogy on Eoghan Rua Ó Néill and a denunciation of discord, the maiden ends with the following prayer:

> * Guidhimse Dia, más mian leis m'éisteacht,
> guidhim Íosa do-chí an mhéid se,
> is an Spiorad naomhtha arís d'aontoil,
> Muire mháthair is Pádraig naomhtha,
> Colum croidhe is Bríghid déidgheal,
> go ndaingnighid sin Gaoil da chéile
> is go dtigidh dhíobh an gníomh so 'dhéanamh:
> Gaill d'ionnarbadh is Banba 'shaoradh. (5PP pp. 31–2)

Given the indeterminate quality of the Foreigners who are to be expelled (they are only loosely described as 'Protestants' or as 'Speakers of the English language'), one cannot go as far as to call this a downright nationalistic poem; but even so, it provides us with a startling instance of how the co-operation of cultural and religious criteria can give rise to a proto-nationalistic stance.

It will be recognized that such allegory makes for very effective rhetoric. It harks back to the oldest poetical conventions and sovereignty myths and instills into them, and into the political issues that are dealt with, all the attractiveness that a beautiful maiden can provide. Love of the fatherland is thus explicitly yoked to love between the sexes; and the fact that the poet is stricken by regular lovesickness when the vision leaves him may go to show that he beheld the maiden not only as a spokeswoman for a political cause, but also saw her as a woman with a considerable amount of sex appeal:

> ° An tráth do chríochnaigh an tsíbhean phéacach,
> mar adubhras ar dtúis san méid sin,
> ar mbualadh a bas go prap fá chéile,

---

* I pray God – may he deign to hear – I pray Jesus – who sees all – and the Holy Spirit – with one accord – Mary, our mother, and holy Patrick, Colum of the heart and ivory-fair Brigid, that the Gaels may band together and achieve the great exploit: to drive out the Foreigners and set Banba free.[74]

° When the beauteous maiden had finished, as I recounted at first in the above, after clapping her hands together suddenly, she ascended swiftly into the clouds and left me on the flagstone alone, without voice, vigour, movement or motion, prostrate on a tomb on that grave of the Gaels. The age of the Lord this year I shall declare: 1650. Thus ends my story to you. Farewell to the maiden who

do-chuaidh sí suas do ruaig go néallaibh,
is d'fhág sí mise ar an lic am aonar
gan ghlór, gan tapadh, gan spreacadh, gan aonchor,
sínte ar thuama ar uaigh na nGaol san.
Aois an Tighearna i mbliadhna 'déarad:
míle go leith, cúig deich is céad leis.
Ag sin díbhse críoch mo sgéil se.

Slán don mhnaoi bhí araoir ar uaigh Uí Néill,
le crádh croidhe ag caoine uaisle Gaol.
Gidh d'fhág sí mo chlí go suaite tréith,
mo ghrá í 's gach ní dá gcualaidh mé. (p. 32)

Such *aisling* poetry could combine the messianic prophecy that better times were ahead with another important motif: the personification of the country as a (supernatural) woman. This latter motif is linked inextricably to the non-rational, nearly occult encounter with fairy females, often explicitly *sí*-women with the gift of prophecy; it links 'Ireland' furthermore with liminal settings such as tombs, darkness, lakeshores or river-banks, mountain tops, crossroads and solitude, and she invariably appears when the poet is isolated from human company and in a troubled frame of mind. Her appearance upsets his emotional state still further, leaving him weak and exhausted by the encounter. A very interesting and early example, though not an *aisling* proper, is the well-known quatrain by Pádraigín Hackett:

* Isan bhFrainc im dhúscadh dhamh
  in Éirinn Chuinn im chodladh;
  beag ar ngrádh uaidh don fhaire –
  do thál suain ar síorfhaire. (NDh vol. 1, 19)

The poet contrasts waking reality (France) with his dreams, and resolves the contradiction through a pun on *faire* (watchfulness: being awake or being intent) which leads up to the statement that all the poet's wakefulness is that of sleep (i.e. that all his waking endeavour is a mere interval between the dreams he yearns for, or that he only lives fully when he dreams of Éire). Ireland, in this elegant and conceit-like polarity, is bracketed with the oneiric side of the poet's existence. In this respect, it becomes significant that the poem has as its title 'Isan bhFraingc, iar bhfaicsin aislinge', 'In France, after having had a dream-vision'.

Another implication of the *aisling*'s personification of Ireland as a dream-woman, is that the present is measured against the past – the past remaining, as we have seen, the constant yardstick for political evaluations. By such a comparison, however, the very notion of a unified, homogeneous entity 'Ireland' is

last night stood on the grave of Ó Néill, with anguished heart, keening the nobility of the Gaels; though she left my heart tormented and despondent, dear to me is she and all I heard from her.
* Awake I find myself in France, asleep in Conn's Ireland; because of that, I have no love for being awake; I keep constant vigil for the suckling of sleep.

retrojected into the past; indeed, 'the past' becomes the projecting screen for present ideals: what Ireland ought to be is equated with what Ireland used to be. The past becomes the standard of dissatisfaction rather than the object of historical observation. A popular anonymous quatrain from the period runs:

> * Ní hí an Éire-seo an Éire do bhí anall-ód ann
> Ach Éire lucht Béarla agus anstró Gall,
> Éire gan éifeacht, 's í i n-anró fann,
> Éire gan Ghaelig, 's is searbh leó rann.[83]

An Síogaí Rómhánach contains a mixture of all those features. The lovely fairy-woman is not merely the bearer of a prophecy; she is also a keening-woman for Eoghan Rua Ó Néill and a reminder of Nuala Ní Dhomhnaill. Thus the break-down of the Confederation is represented as an echo of the Flight of the Earls, and the similarity between these two catastrophes is underscored by the family relationship between Eoghan Rua and Hugh O'Neill. Like Keating's *aisling*-elegy on John Fitzgerald,[84] *An Síogaí Rómhánach* is essentially an elegy in vision-form. This elegiac mode can be followed further in the *aisling* tradition until Aogan Ó Rathaille's time; only the new Jacobite hopes of the eighteenth century gave a more optimistic turn to the communications of the vision-woman.

Dáibhí Ó Bruadair and his time

The most important poet straddling the reigns of James II and William III was Dáibhí Ó Bruadair, whose work offers a cross-section of all those post-bardic, proto-national attitudes I have outlined so far. His life (*c.* 1630–1691) made him a witness of nearly all the great upheavals of the seventeenth century: the Con-federation, the Cromwellian age, the Restoration, the pretended Popish Plot, the revolution of 1688 and the beginnings of Ascendancy Ireland. His long decline into ever deeper poverty epitomizes the fate of the Gaelic population in general, and his complaints and invectives thus have a particular relevance, providing a commentary from a Gaelic point of view on the developments of the time.

Ó Bruadair's earlier poetry shows that he still retained the old bardic pride in his literary calling. Thus his main grievances concerned the spread of the English language, and the implications of this trend for poetry; Ó Bruadair castigates anglicized fellow-Gaels in a stanza like:

> ° Nach ait an nós so ag mórchuid d'fhearaibh Éireann,
> d'at go nó le mórtus maingléiseach,
> giodh tais a dtreoir ar chódaibh gallachléire,
> ní chanaid glór acht gósta garbhbhéarla.[85]

---

* This is not the Ireland that we used to have in the old days but an Ireland of English speakers and Foreign vexation; an Ireland without sense, weak in distress; an Ireland without Gaelic where the stanza is scorned.

° How queer this mode assumed by many men of Erin, with haughty, upstart ostentation lately swollen; though codes of foreign clerks they fondly strive to master, they utter nothing but a ghost of strident English. (ed.'s trl.)

Likewise, he can lash out against (presumably Gaelic) servants who do not treat him with the respect due to him: a coarse invective like 'Seirbhiseach seirgthe íogair srónach seas' can be seen as an echo of the older bardic *aor*, or satire-curse. And when his social decline slowly made him a part of those lower classes whose respect he demanded, the poet expressed his haughty distaste in a poem that begins:

> *   Is mairg nach fuil 'na dhubhthuata,
> cé holc duine 'na thuata,
> ionnás go mbeinn mágcuarda
> idir na daoinibh duarca. (vol. 1, 130)

Ó Bruadair then goes on to voice sardonic regrets for his now-worthless accomplishments as a poet, similar to those we have encountered in the poetry of the expiring bardic order, e.g. in the poems of Mathghamhain Ó hIfearnáin.

Another example of Ó Bruadair's tendency to view the political situation from a professionally literary point of view is contained in one of his fascinating nonsense poems, 'Guagán gliog', 'A jingling trifle', which ends on a disconcerting note of seriousness:

> °   An uair nach cluinim cion ar chéill i nduain
> 's an uair sultmhar rith do réir na suadh,
> an uair nach fuilid fir na féinne suas
> is guagán gliog dom thuigse an dreácht is dual. (vol. 1, 78)

Ó Bruadair expressed similar sentiments in a number of other poems, such as 'Is urchra cléibh':

> †   Is urchra cléibh gan éigse chothrom ar bun
> is fuireann gan scléip dobhéaradh oirthisi cion
> tar imioll is méala spéir a crotha do dhul
> sa bhfuilid gan ghléas gach ré ar a lorg a bhus.
>
> Geadh trudaireacht gléir a bhféadaid forgla a bhfuil
> ag spriongar re déanamh dréacht i bhfocalaibh Scuit
> is fusaide féire i bhféith na fochaille fis
> nach tuigthear acht sméirlis éigse i bhforba Chuirc.

---

*   Woe to those who are not gloomy boors; though bad it be for one to be a boor, yet better were it than that I should live with sullen men around on every side. (ed.'s trl.)

°   When I see how people set no value on poetic wit, and when to run in steps of sages brings to no-one any joy, when the heroes of the Fenians stand no longer up erect, an empty jingle is the only poetry which suits my mind. (ed.'s trl.)

†   My heart is broken at the absence of correctly written verse and of the gentleminded folk who would bestow its due on it; 'tis sad the beauty of its form has vanished from the reach of sight, while many here, though ill-equipped, are searching for it all the time.

Nothing but the merest mumbling can the best of those attain who are striving now to fashion poems in the speech of Scot; 'tis easy for their muse to blunder, knowledge is now so corrupt that in Corc's land nought but vulgar poetry is understood.

* Dá dtigeadh le héinneach gréas i gcosmhalacht chirt
  i gcunnail i gcéim 's i réimibh scoile do chur
  iar dtuireamh an scéil do adearadh scoturra glic
  ionnus a chéille air féin nach doirche *Dutch*. (vol. 3, 194)

Ó Bruadair can thus maintain, to a degree, the old bardic view which saw the triumph of English aggression primarily as a class upheaval. When he lashes out against boors and churls, he does not (and need not) specify whether these are Gaelic or English. Ó Bruadair, though living nearly a century after the battle of Kinsale, was not the only one to hold on to this aristocratic view at such a late stage. Other works from the 1670s share in his outlook, e.g. the poetry of Séafra Ó Donnchadha 'an Ghleanna', who saw the pernicious influence of the Foreigners above all in class terms.[86] An even more explicit example from this same period is the second part of *Pairlement Chloinne Tomáis*, which maliciously imputes pro-Cromwellian feelings to the Gaelic lower classes and thus identifies the English and the Gaelic rabble. It attributes to lowly Gaels a poem which begins:

° Treise leat, a Chromuil,
  a rígh chroinic na sgulóg,
  as red linn fuaramuir suaimhnios,
  mil, uachtar agus onóir.

  Mar do choisg Pádruig an bó-ár
  do chloinn Ádhaimh an Éirinn,
  do choisg tú dhínne lá seachtmhuine
  is mórán dliosdionuis éigcirt.

  Iarruim gan Caomhánach ná Branach,
  Nuallánach ná Cinnsiolach,
  Raoisioch ná Róisteach
  d'fhagháil fóid do chuid a sinnsior.[87]

In some respects, however, Ó Bruadair's attitude differs from the old bardic outlook. A poem like his 'A shaoi re gliogar gibé thusa', 'Sir, you who blabbed, whoever you are', for instance, contains a retort against an unknown poet who had flattered the duke of Ormond by encomiastically exalting him over Conn, Niall, Goll, Brian and Fionn mac Cumhail; and another retort of the same kind is

---

* If anyone could write a piece of poetry correct in form, prudently embroidered in the style and metres of the school, when the tale was told, a clever Scottic yeoman would assert that its sense to him was such that Dutch could not be more obscure. (ed.'s trl.)

° More power to you, Cromwell, you king in rustics' chronicles; during your reign we got peace, honey, cream and honour.

  Just as St. Patrick removed murrain from the race of Adam in Ireland, so you removed our one day-a-week service, and many unjust ordinances.

  I pray that no Kavanagh, O'Byrne, O'Nolan, O'Kinsella, Rice nor Roche [the latter two being Hiberno-Norman names, J.L.] may get a sod of his ancestral land. (ed.'s trl.)

to be found in his poem against the old *file* Flann Mag Craith who had written a poem in praise of queen Elizabeth (cf. above, p. 197). We have seen that, for the bardic poet, the choice of patron was in no way indicative of a real political allegiance; however, Ó Bruadair's criticism of what he interprets as a betrayal must presuppose the notion of an allegiance to the cause he considers betrayed. Unlike the earlier poets, Ó Bruadair makes the choice of a poem's dedicatee a matter of conscious choice, a matter of conscience rather than of mere expedience – a choice also, for which the poet can be held accountable by his fellow-Gaels; a choice therefore which must be both morally and politically correct:

> * A chluanaire aindeis nó a amail gan faobhar fis,
> nach tuarann lasair id leacain más d'Éirinn sibh
> an tuairim tharcuisne ar cheapaibh a craobh do shil,
> ód bhuain an abalach aiste gan ghaol re glic. (vol. 1, 206)

The reproach levelled here is, in fact, a *national* one, resulting from a combination of moral ('your course of action was shameful') and political ('especially considering your Irishness') motives.

Ó Bruadair's retort to Flann Mág Craith is especially interesting in that it illustrates the importance of the reign of James II for the development of a national feeling among Irish Catholics. The Stuarts had been able, from the beginning, to count on a cautious sympathy among the Gaelic poets, owing, perhaps, to the fact that their lineage could be traced back to Gaelic roots; we have seen, for example, Fearghal Óg Mac an Bhaird's ode to James I. Given the Stuarts' implementation of Protestant policy (though it was often deemed insufficient by the Puritans), this embryonic goodwill had no opportunity for development; but Charles I could still be called *ár bprionnsa,* could still be the ideological figurehead of the Confederation of Kilkenny. All this reached a new stage with the accession of James II, the first Catholic on the throne since Tudor times, who inspired high hopes among the Catholic population for a redress of their long-standing grievances. Gaelic hopes were fanned by James' pro-Catholic policy in Ireland, especially under his lord lieutenant Tyrconnell. James was thus the first monarch to unite both criteria for Gaelic sympathy, descent and religion, and as such he could count on the allegiance even of Ó Bruadair, who had lashed out against the thought of praising the English queen Elizabeth.

It may not be exaggerated to say that James' reign provided the political focus which united Catholic, post-bardic and anti-colonial views into a *nationally* Gaelic ideology. Ó Buachalla refers to the fact that it was James II who was regarded as the final avatar of the prophesied Liberator of the Gaels:

---

* O despicable flatterer. thou fool, devoid of keen-edged wit; should thy check not blush for shame, if thou be an Irishman, at that slanderous attack thou madest on the branching stocks, when thou essayedst that putrid verse, which hath no kin to cleverness. (ed.'s trl.)

* Ag deireadh an 17ú haois is é an duine is gradamúla agus is comhachtaí de na huaisle a bhí thar lear Séamus Stíobhart, Séamus II, agus is eisean seachas aon duine eile d'uaisle na linne a tharraing chuige féin an chonsaeit fhileata agus an ról meisiasach.[88]

It is true that T.J. Dunne can see Ó Bruadair's enthusiasm for the Stuart monarchy as 'committed Royalism [underlying] the class rather than the national basis of his outlook'[89] – but it seems to me that the more optimistic poems Ó Bruadair wrote during the Tyrconnell viceregency see the benefits of James' rule in what might be called 'national' terms, transcending traditional professionally-poetic or aristocratic interests. One indication is that a new form of allegorical personification finds its way into Ó Bruadair's poetry at this time: it is no longer the identification of the land of Ireland as a woman; instead, the inhabitants, as a group, are symbolized as a man, the Catholics receiving the Gaelic name 'Tadhg',[90] the colonists receiving the English names 'Raif' (Ralph) or 'Seón' (John, later also: 'Seón Buí': 'Yellow John' or 'John Bull'). We shall also see that in Ó Bruadair's poetry, imagotypical characterizations for these groups abound as never before.

Nor is Ó Bruadair an isolated case. A contemporary of his, Diarmaid (mac Seáin Bhuí) Mac Cárthaigh also celebrated Catholic-Gaelic optimism in his poem 'Céad buidhe le Dia', 'A hundred thanks to God'. Here as in Ó Bruadair's 'Caithréim Taidhg', 'The triumph of Tadhg' (which was inspired by 'Céad buidhe le Dia'), the names 'Tadhg' and 'Diarmaid' stand for 'the Gael', whereas the Protestant colonists are symbolized as 'Seón' or 'Ráif'. Both Mac Cárthaigh's and Ó Bruadair's poems exult over the fact that Tadhg and Diarmaid have gained the upper hand under James' beneficial rule, and (a little vindictively) that the colonists have lost their pride and their overbearing manners. A sample from Mac Cárthaigh's poem:

° Sin iad Gaedhil go léir i n-armaibh
gunnaoi is púdar púirt is bailte aca
Presbyterians féach gur treascaradh
is braidhm an diabhail i ndiaidh na bhfanatics.

Cá ngabhann *Seon* níl cóta dearg air
ná '*Who's there?*' re taobh an gheata aige
ag iarraidh slighe atá luighead go sparrainneach
mo chur fá chíos ist oidhche i n-acharann.

* At the end of the seventeenth century, the most honoured and authoritative person among the nobles oversea was James Stuart, James II, and it is he rather than any other of the nobles of the time who attracted to himself this poetical conceit [i.e. his being the saviour foretold, J.L.] and messianic role.

° Behold there the Gaedhil in arms, every one of them; they have powder and guns, hold the cities and fortresses; the Presbyterians, lo, have been overthrown, and the Fanatics have left an infernal smell after them.

    Whither shall John turn? He has no red coat on him, nor 'Who's there?' on his lips when standing beside the gate, seeking on the slightest excuse by provoking me to have me amerced for nocturnal contentiousness.

* Cá ngabhann Ráif sa ghárda mhalluighthe
  prinntísigh dhíoblaidhe na cathrach
  do stiall gach aontaobh séipéil bheannuighthe
  ag díbírt cléire dé sdá n-argain.

  'You Popish rogue' ní leomhaid a labhairt rinn
  acht 'Cromwellian dog' is focal faire againn
  nó 'cia súd thall' go teann gan eagla
  'Mise Tadhg' géadh teinn an t-agallamh.[91]

It is even stated explicitly that James' reign is the long-awaited fulfilment of the old prophecies:

° Naoimh is fáidhe a lán do tharrangair
  go bhfaghadh Éire cabhair san am do ghealladar
  do t'fheartaibhsi a Chríost le guidhe do bhanaltrann
  tiucfa i gcrích gach ní do mheasadar.[92]

Similarly, James' lord lieutenant Tyrconnell is identified with one of the most popular incarnations of prophetic messianism, Ball Dearg Ó Domhnaill: '*Tyrconnell* na lann mo bhall dearg sa', 'the swordsman Tyrconnell, my Ball Dearg of prophecy' (ibid.). The strengthening of religious into national feeling which has resulted from these political revolutions then finds its most explicit expression in the stanza –

† Agus gach aon is Éireannach dearbhtha
  is tá gan cheist don chreidiomh chatoilce
  d'éis gur scannradh fann bhar n-aithreacha
  atá dia buidheach don líon so mhaireann díobh. (ibid.)

I think that in this context one may regard the term *Éirannach* in much the same light as the phrase *d'Éirinn* which was used by Ó Bruadair in the above-quoted fragment of 'A shaoi re gliogar gibé thusa' (cf. above, p. 222): a shorthand denomination for the common ground shared by all those who were at odds with English rule – those who wear Gaelic names, who hold

---

* Whither shall they turn? – Ralph and his cursed guard, formed of the devilish city apprentices, who pillaged and wrecked holy chapels on every side, and plundered and drove into exile the clerks of God.
   'You Popish rogue' they won't dare to say to us; but 'Cromwellian dog' is the watchword we have for them, or 'Cia sud thall' ['Who goes there', J L.] said sternly and fearlessly, 'Mise Tadhg' ['I am Tadhg', J.L.], though galling the dialogue [may be].
° Prophets and saints in great numbers have prophesied that Erin would surely get help at the promised time; by Thy wonderful power, O Christ, and Thy nurse's prayer, everything they predicted shall certainly come to pass.[92]
† And everyone known as a tried and proven Irishman, and who is in faith without question a Catholic, after your ancestors' terror and feebleness, God is well pleased with all who survive of them.[92]

their heroic chiefs of yore dearer than Elizabeth or Ormond, those who were persecuted by the colonists, who speak Gaelic, dance the sword-dance, hate the Foreigners and are, above all, Catholic. In short: the 'standard model Irishman', whom the English had called 'mere Irish', and whose description as gleaned here from the poems of the Jacobite reign could equally well have been taken from the pages of later nationalists like Pearse, Corkery or De Blácam.

Ó Bruadair's poem 'Caithréim Tadhg', 'The triumph of Tadhg', was written 'ar haithris', in imitation on hearing Mac Cárthaigh's poem; it too uses the term *Éireannach* in a very emphatic way, namely as its closing word:

> * Na bearta sin do mhalartuigh an saoghal clis
> gan aireachtain go hathchumhair le braon dod chith
> athchuingim ort a fhairge na daonnachta
> go ndeachaidh sin chum maitheasa na n-Éireannach (vol. 3, 140)

Ó Bruadair's poem concentrates particularly on 'Tadhg's' newly-won right to hold rank in the army, and depicts this new development mainly by enumerating a number of Gaelic names and juxtaposing them with the hapless Protestants. It is typical of Ó Bruadair, too, that he should concentrate more than Mac Cárthaigh on the Gaelic *cultural* identity (in language, pastimes etc.) of his exemplary 'Irishman':

> ° Cuid dá ranncaibh Flann is Fearadhach
> is Muireadhach ó Duibhdhiorma an scafaire
> bíth a séis le chéile ag reaicearacht
> i gcanmhain nach taigiuir le Sacsanaibh.
>
> I dtigh na gárda is gnáth gér bh'annamh san
> sórdán nach sólás le geamaraibh
> fianuigheacht ar fhialríoghraidh Banbha
> píp trí mbeann is damhsa an ghadaraigh.
> . . .
> . . .
> Mac Órlaithe móire is Mhangartaigh
> mac Murrainne is Tumaltaigh uí Shlatara
> mac Méidhbhe is Féidhlimthe uí Chathasaigh
> ag coimhéad cuanta is gual ar ghéadfaraibh. (vol. 3, 130)

---

* May the deeds that have changed, without being observed, this world of deceit with a rain-drop of grace in a brief space of time, to the profit redound of the Irish, o ocean of kindness, I pray. (ed.'s trl.)

° In their ranks amongst others are Flann, too, and Fearadhach, and Muireadhach Ó Duibh-dhiorma, the gay-hearted warrior, there they are talking and chatting among themselves in a language that soundeth not pleasant to Saxon ears.

In the guardhouse now often, though rarely in former times, a humming is heard about Banbha's noble kings, the dance of the withe and the strains of the three-droned pipe. . . .

The son of Órlaithe Mhór and Mangartach, the son of Murrann and Tumultach Ó Slatara. the son of Meadhbh and Féithlim Ó Cathasaigh on guard at the ports, and the gaffers in black despair. (ed.'s trl.)

And the reinstatement of the great Gaelic past is predicted in the following terms:

> *   A bhuidhe re dia atáid triatha Carrathach
> Clanna Táil is ársaidh Gearaltach
> Clanna Néill is Chéin is Charoluis
> i gcóir an daoiste mhaoil ó Bhearabhuic.[93]

In much the same vein as this 'Caithréim Tadhg' runs Ó Bruadair's 'Caithréim an dara Séamuis', 'the triumph of James II', which is the retort against Mág Craith's eulogy to Elizabeth mentioned earlier. Here, Ó Bruadair's main cause for joy is the return of Catholic (Gaelic and Hiberno-Norman) judges to the benches and, again, the recognition of the Gaelic language as a legally valid vernacular:

> °   Atáid ar bínnse Dálaigh Rísigh
> sdá n-áileadh saoi do Nóglachaibh
> re héisteacht agartha an té nach labhrann
> béarla breaganta beoiltirim. (vol. 3, 88)

The Catholic army under James can accordingly be eulogized in terms that derive wholly from a heroic Gaelic Ireland of bardic vintage:

> †   Go Luaimneach ag ruathar ón Máigh go Bóinn
> sag fuanscar fá chuan chloinne Mhághach mhóir
> badh uamhan ar fuaid oirear Phárthalóin
> nach suanaid i dTuadhmhumhain ó dTáil sa shlóigh. (vol. 3, 124)

It seems, then, as if Ó Bruadair is witnessing the final fulfilment of the old prophecies. The oppression of the present has been overthrown, history is liberated from its stagnation, and the Gaelic past has once again found a legitimate continuation. The poet's description of the contemporary political situation in old bardic terms is thus nothing less than a recognition of the present as a worthy successor to the great Gaelic heritage; and the lone upholder of that heritage, the aristocratic poet, can thus express his allegiance to a new Jacobite, Catholic kingdom of Ireland.

Accordingly, it can be noted that Ó Bruadair and his contemporaries (including Eoghan Ó Caoimh, who may also be the author of the foregoing quatrain) reverted to a highly personal outlook on the defeat of the Jacobite monarchy at

---

*   Thanks be to God! the chieftains of Cárthach's clan, the descendants of Tál and the Geraldine veterans, the clansmen of Nial and of Cian and of Carolus are ready to meet the bald bumpkin from Berwick town. (ed.'s trl.)

°   On the Bench now are seated the Dalys and Rices, and a sage of the Nagles is urging them to listen to the plea of the man who can't speak the lip-dry and simpering English tongue. (ed.'s trl.)

†   Driving all his foes before him rapidly from Máigh to Bóinn, and pitching his tents among the people of the clan of Mágha Mór, it will cause alarm and terror through the lands of Parthalón if he rests not with his hosts in Thomond of the tribes of Tál. (ed.'s trl.)

the hands of Parliament and William III: the tone of his swansongs 'An long-bhriseadh', 'The shipwreck', and 'Is urchrá chléibh', 'My heart's death pang', are a reversal to his bitter poems of earlier decades, gauging the upheaval of society by the measuring-rod of his own lack of patronage and social standing. A similar outlook is expressed in Ó Caoimh's description of the defeat at Aughrim (1692), which reverts half-way through to considering the poet's own destitution as the main consequence of that catastrophe (BMCat vol. 1, 527–8).

James' defeat and his exile, though considered cowardly by some, did not end his popularity among the Irish poets. As far as they were concerned, the Stuarts remained the rightful kings of Ireland – de iure if not de facto – and, as Ó Buachalla points out, the Stuarts exerted the royal prerogative to appoint bishops (Roman Catholic ones, of course) up to 1765. The Stuart king who resided at the exile court in France, under the protection of the powerful Louis XIV, was still the rí ceart of the Gaels. It is no surprise to find that the messianic prophecies henceforth vested all political hopes in a return of the rightful king – a hope which was not wholly unrealistic until Charles Edward's defeat at Culloden in early 1746. Particularly through the mediation of the 'wild geese'-émigrés, and because of the complete conflict of interests with the new Protestant Ascendancy, which was founded on expropriation and on the institutionalized bigotry of the penal laws, the Jacobite persuasion continued to give a political focus to a Gaelic/Catholic allegiance, which may as a result be called, I think, national. It is a tendency which became noticeable only briefly in Ó Bruadair's poetry, and which is only subliminally present in his great successor, Ó Rathaille, who shared the older poet's aristocratic pride. But the indications figure clearly in Ó Rathaille's minor contemporaries and in his successors. Ó Rathaille's own achievement, which cast its shadow over the entire following century, lay on a different plane: it was the conciliation of the political and the lyrical as compatible poetic modes, or, in T.J. Dunne's words, 'the ability to infuse tradition with a personal and subjective response to tragedy. This makes him a vital transitional figure, in literary terms, helping the transformation of poetry from public ritual to personal statement'.[94]

Aogán Ó Rathaille and the *aisling*

Aogán Ó Rathaille (c. 1675–1729) had a more comprehensive outlook on contemporary affairs than Ó Bruadair, even though he expressed it in more intimately personal terms. It is true that a perspicacious critic like T.J. Dunne has argued that Ó Rathaille's outlook was 'aristocratic, not 'national', his major concern being conventional praise poetry, whether for Gaelic Irish, Old English or even New English patrons' (p. 26); this, however, I take mainly as a reaction against the overly nationalistic scheme of interpretation imposed on the poet by an earlier Gaelic League readership (e.g. his editors, Dinneen and Ó Donnchadha, and, later, Daniel Corkery[95]). Certainly, Ó Rathaille was not the nationalistic poet that the Gaelic League made him out to be – a kind of Gaelic Kipling. But the fact that Ó

Rathaille offered 'no real hope for the reversal of the revolution which had destroyed his world and no articulation of Gaelic or Catholic solidarity which might achieve it', can, I think, be seen in terms of what Dunne calls the poet's 'profound fatalism'; at best, it merely proves the fact that Ó Rathaille did not, in the opening years of the eighteenth century, formulate a nationalistic ideology that would more properly belong to the later nineteenth century. Even so, Ó Rathaille evinces a more *national* awareness (and, *pace* Dunne, an awareness, if not always an explicit articulation, of 'Gaelic or Catholic solidarity') than his predecessor Ó Bruadair.

Whereas the stance of Ó Bruadair's political poems before and after the reign of James II was adopted from a predominantly private, or, at best, professional point of view, Ó Rathaille's identification with those who shared his language, culture, religion and political hopes stood in marked contrast to Ó Bruadair's self-centred grievances. Furthermore Ó Rathaille prefaces his complaints for Ireland, as a matter of course, with an expression of regret at the absence of a unifying political leadership. It is under this governing factor of the lack of political centralization that all other woes are subsequently enumerated; not as private and individual grievances, but as related instances of a single collective oppression or dispossession:

> *   Monuar-sa an Chárrth'-fhuil tráighte, tréith-lag
>   Gan rígh ar an gcóip ná treorach tréan-mhear
>   Gan fear cosnaimh ná eochair chum réitigh
>   Is gan sciath dín ar thír na saor-fhlaith.
>
> Tír gan triath de ghrian-fhuil Éibhir,
> Tír fá ansmacht Gall do traochadh,
> Tír do doirteadh fá chosaibh na méirleach
> Tír na ngaibhne – is treighid go héag liom.
>
> Tír bhocht bhuaidheartha, is uaigneach céasta,
> Tír gan fear, gan mac, gan chéile,
> Tír gan lúth, gan fonn, gan éisteacht,
> Tír gan chomhthrom do bhochtaibh le déanamh.
>
> Tír gan eaglais chneasta ná cléirigh,
> Tír le mioscais, noch d'itheadar faolchoin,

---

*   Woe is me! weak and exhausted is the race of Carthach, without a prince over the hosts, or a strong, nimble leader; without a man to defend, without a key to liberate; without a shield of protection for the land of noble chieftains.

A land without a prince of the sun-bright race of Eibhear; a land made helpless beneath the oppression of the stranger; and a land poured out beneath the feet of miscreants; a land of fetters – it is sickness to me unto death.

A land poor, afflicted, lonely and tortured; a land without a husband, without a son, without a spouse; a land without vigour, or spirit, or hearing; a land in which is no justice to be done to the poor.

A land without a meek church or clergy; a land which wolves have spitefully devoured; a land placed in misfortune and subjection beneath the tyranny of enemies and mercenaries

Tír do cuireadh go tubaisteach, traochta
Fá smacht namhad is amhas is méirleach.

Tír gan tartha gan tairbhe i nÉirinn,
Tír gan turadh gan buinne gan réiltean,
Tír do nochtadh gan fothain gan géaga,
Tír do briseadh le fuirinn an Bhéarla.[96]

Dunne writes of this particular poem that it 'concentrated on the Cárrth-fhuil
. . . in particular' (p. 26); but that is not very evident after the first line. The one
iarla mentioned in passing in line 46 is not referred to by name, and the last
stanzas before the *ceangal*-envoi take, instead, an extremely widesweeping view of
'the Gaels' (among whom the poet includes some Hiberno-Norman families)
culminating in the *dalta na hÉireann*, 'Ireland's darling child': the Pretender.

      *   Ní'l Ua Dotharta i gcomhthrom ná a chaomh-shliocht;
Ní'l Síol Mórdha treon ba thréanmhar;
Ní'l Ua Flaithbheartaigh i gceannas ná a ghaolta
Síol mBriain dearbh n-a nGallaibh le tréimhse.

Ar Ua Ruairc ní'l luadh, mo ghéar-ghoin;
ná ar Ua Domhnaill fós i nÉirinn;
Na Gearaltaigh táid gan tapa gan sméideadh,
Búrcaigh, Barraigh, is Breathnaigh na gcaol-bharc.

Guidhim an Tríonóid fhíor-mhór naomhtha
An ceo so do dhíochur díobh le chéile,
De shleachtaibh Ír is Chuinn is Éibhir
Is aiseag do thabhairt n-a mbeatha do Ghaedhealaibh.

Aiseag do Ghaedhealaibh déin, a Chríost, i n-am
N-a mbeatha go léir ó dhaor-bhruid daoithe Gall.
Smachtuigh na méirligh, féach ár gcríoch go fann!
Is dalta na hÉireann faon lag claoidhte thall. (p. 10)

and robbers. A land without produce or thing of worth of any kind; a land without dry
weather, without a stream, without a star; a land stripped naked, without shelter or boughs; a
land broken down by the English-prating band.[96]

  * O'Doherty is not holding sway, nor his noble race, the O'Moores are not strong, that once
were brave; O'Flaherty is not in power, nor his kinsfolk, and sooth to say, the O'Briens have
long since become English.

    Of O'Rourke there is no mention – my sharp wounding! Nor yet of O'Donnell in Erin; the
Geraldines, they are without vigour, without a nod, and the Burkes, the Barrys, the Walshes of
the slender ships.

    I beseech the Trinity, most august, holy, to banish this sorrow from them altogether – from
the descendants of Ir, of Conn, of Eibhear – and to restore the Gaels to their estates.

    O Christ, restore betimes to the Gaels all their estates, rescued from the dire bondage of
foreign churls; chastise the vile hords, behold, our country is faint, and Erin's nursling, weak,
feeble, subdued, beyond the sea! (ed.s' trl.)

A similar more 'comprehensive' view of 'the Gaels' as a coherent group with congruent religious and political grievances and needs, and with whom the poet identifies without any professional or aristocratic reservations, is contained in another of Ó Rathaille's political poems, 'Créachta crích Fódla' 'The wounds of Fódla's land', which indeed begins in a traditional post-bardic fashion ('Fódla' and 'Banbha' for Ireland, personified as a dishonoured woman) but which shifts its focus in the end from the land/woman to the inhabitants:

   *   Ó chailleamar Éire, is méid ár mí-chómhthruim,
       Is treascairt na laoch mear, tréan, nár mhí-threorach,
       Ar Arad-Mhac Dé 's ar thréan na Tríonóide
       Go mairidh dá n-éis an méid seo dhíobh beo aguinn.

       Chailleadar Gaedhil a dtréithe caoin córach,
       Carthannacht, féile, béasa, is binn-cheolta;
       Alla-thuirc chlaon do thraoch sinn fí mhór-smacht
       Agallaim Aon-Mhac Dé ar Ghaoidhil d'fhóirthin. (p. 4)

Also, whenever Ó Rathaille made use of the old prophetic mode of poetry, he placed such prophecies under the aegis of the Jacobite cause: the return of the rightful king. Thus it is a political ideal (to wit, the very ideal which had earlier begun to focus the disparate anti-colonial attitudes into a common allegiance) which governs the poet's cultural, linguistic, social and religious concerns:

    °   An truagh libh-se faolchoin an éithigh 's an fhill duibh
       Ag ruagairt na cléire as dá léirchur fá dhaoirse?
       Monuar-sa go tréithlag mac Shéarluis ba rí aguinn,
       I n-uagh curtha in' aonar, 's a shaordhalta ar díbirt!

       Is truaillighthe, claonmhar, 's is tréason don droing uile,
       Cruadhmhionna bréige fá shéala 's fá scríbhinn,
       'Ga mbualadh le béalaibh ar gcléire is ar saoithe,
       'S nár dhual do chloinn tSéamuis coróin tsaor na dtrí ríoghachta.

---

   *   Since we have lost Erin, and because of the extent of our misfortunes, and because of the overthrow of the nimble, strong warriors who were not wanting in vigour, we entreat the noble Son of God and the Might of the Trinity, that those of them who are alive with us may thrive after them.

       The Gaels have lost their gentle, comely qualities: charity, hospitality, manners, and sweet music; wicked, alien boors it was that forced us under great oppression; I beseech the only Son of God to grant relief to the Gaels. (ed.'s trl.)

    °   Are ye moved with pity because the lying wolves of black treachery are scattering the clergy and bringing them to complete servitude? Oh woe is me! the son of Charles who was our king is lifeless, buried in a grave alone, while his noble son is banished;

       It is foul and evil, it is treason in that wicked race, to brandish audacious perjuries, sealed, and in writing, before the faces of our clergy and our nobles, that the children of James have no hereditary title to the noble crown of the three kingdoms.

> * Stadfaidh an toirneach le fóirneart na gréine,
>   Is scaipfidh an ceo so de phórshleachtaibh Éibhir;
>   An tImpre beidh deorach is Flóndras fá dhaorsmacht,
>   'S an 'bricléir' go modhmharach i seomra ríogh Séamus.
>
> Beidh Éire go súgach 's a dúnta go haerach
>   Is Gaedhilg 'gá scrúdadh n-a múraibh ag éigsibh;
>   Béarla na mbúr ndubh go cúthail fá néaltaibh,
>   Is Séamus n-a chúirt ghil ag tabhairt chonganta do Ghaedhealaibh.
>
> Beidh an Bíobla sin Liútair 's a dhubhtheagasc éithigh,
>   'S an bhuidhean so tá cionntach ná humhluigheann don gcléir chirt,
>   'Gá ndibirt tar triúchaibh go Neuuland ó Éirinn;
>   An Laoiseach 's an Prionnsa beidh cúirt aca is aonach! (p. 166)

Paradoxically, Ó Rathaille was able to draw the strength for his proud individualism from this very sense of common-Gaelic solidarity, as can be seen from the famous poem that he composed on his death-bed, 'Cabhair ní ghairfead', 'I shall not call for help'.

This poem is highly typical of the tension in Ó Rathaille's work between traditional aristocratic-poetic pride and a more 'modern' tendency to consider one's position as part of a larger social complex, to measure one's own plight by the standard of political disruption rather than vice versa. Thus, the poet employs a traditional identification between himself and the land, but couches it in terms that are quite the opposite of the proud, hieratic stance of tradition: instead, there is a link of fever and suffering between the poet, ravaged by illness, with tears and sweat streaming down his face, and the country, so ravaged by injustice that even its gore-stained rivers emit muffled groans. Again, the parallel that Ó Rathaille draws between Ireland's bereavement (at having her crowned king wrested from her) and his own (having lost his Mac Cárthaigh patron), though it may at first sight seem a bardic echo, is, in this context, a deliberate subordination of the poet's personal plight to that of the country; Ó Rathaille sees himself as part of the collectivity of the Gaels rather than pretending to subsume the entire tragedy of the Gaels in his personal situation. A similar relation between the poet and the generality of Gaeldom is set up in this poem's second stanza, with its sudden shift from first person singular to first person plural:

---

* The thunder will be silenced by the strength of the sunlight, and this sorrow will depart from the true descendants of Eibhear: the Emperor will shed tears, and Flanders will be in dire bondage, while the 'Bricklayer' will be in pride in the halls of King James.

Erin will be joyful, and her strongholds will be merry; and the learned will cultivate Gaelic in their schools; the language of the black boors will be humbled and put beneath a cloud, and James in his bright court will lend his aid to the Gaels.

Luther's Bible and his false dark teaching, and his guilty tribe that yields not to the true clergy, shall be transported across countries to New Land from Erin, and Louis and the Prince shall hold court and assembly. (eds.' trl.)

> * Do thonnchrith m'inchinn, d'imthigh mo phríomhdhóthchas,
> Poll im ionathar, biorranaibh trim dhrólainn,
> Ar bhfonn, ar bhfoithin, ar monga 's ar míonchomhgair,
> I ngeall le pinginn ag fuirinn ó chrích Dhóbher. (p. 114)

Ó Rathaille's outlook never fails to place his private woes into a larger social context; and this outlook is ruled by an ideal that is more properly 'political' than anything in his predecessors. That political ideal one might describe as 'having a 'true' leader present'. The 'true' leader is, in local and personal terms, a good landlord and a good patron, and in a wider and more properly 'national' sense, the *de iure* king, the exiled Stuart. The 'true' leader's hallmark is his social grace, the fact that he spreads and inspires social harmony.

Seán Ó Tuama has shown that allegiance to traditional Gaelic lords continued well into the penal days, when their social position had been taken over by Protestant landlords and they themselves continued on as 'gentlemen-tenants', poor peasant-princes among poorer peasants.[97] Thus a semblance of traditional values was perpetuated within the Gaelic peasant-class, even though that class as a whole was weighed down by that of the colonists which had been superimposed on it. Indeed, Ó Rathaille seems to have been eager enough to welcome any opportunity of assimilating these new landlords into the old pattern of traditional values, showing a compound sympathy similar to that of the medieval court-poets: his basic professional affection belonged to the traditional MacCarthy patrons, but when and if new lords like Warner or Brown could prove themselves 'true leaders' – i.e. spread the social harmony and cheerfulness that was one of the charms remembered of the good old days and that included, of course, their munificence towards the *file* – then Ó Rathaille, for one, was willing enough to acknowledge their eminence, much as he seems to have accepted James II's claims to his allegiance. The very bitterness of his denunciation of Valentine Brown indicates that Ó Rathaille had cherished hopes that were disappointed, and the poet is as angry about his own misguided hopefulness as about Brown's way of disappointing him. On the other hand, a man like Warner is presented explicitly as the continuation of a Gaelic tradition of hospitality, as a kind of 'honorary Gael': the description of the hospitality and merriment at Warner's house (which used to belong to a Mac Cárthaigh!) follows the same pattern as other poems that describe the cheer of bygone days when the Gaelic lords were still in their proper station.[98] And, again, Ó Rathaille is at his most caustic when it comes to those who disrupt this last vestige of the harmony which the poet seeks in his social environment: Valentine Brown, who after all behaved no better than could have been expected from one of his ilk, but more especially the petty instruments of landlordism, e.g. sheriffs and bailiffs, be they of English or of Gaelic descent. Against such he lashed out with a bitterness reminiscent of Ó Bruadair, though in much more harmonious verse:

> * My brain trembles as a wave, my chief hope is gone; my entrails are pierced through, venomous darts penetrate my heart; our land, our shelter, our woods, our fair neighbourhood in pledge for a penny to a band from the land of Dover! (eds.' trl.)

* Caiseal gan chliar, fiailteach, ná marcraidhe ar dtúis,
Is beanna-bhruigh Bhriain ciar-thuilte 'mhadraidhibh úisc,
Ealla gan triair triaithe de mhacaibh ríogh Mumhan
Fá ndeara dham triall riamh ort, a Bhailintín Brún.

D'aistrigh fiadh an fial-chruith do chleachtadh sí ar dtúis,
Ó neaduigh an fiach iasachta i ndaingean-choill Rúis,
Seachnaid iasc grian-tsruith is caise caoin ciúin,
Fá ndeara dham triall riamh ort a Bhailintín Brún.

Dairinis tiar Iarla ní'l aici 'en chloinn úir,
I Hamburg, mo chiach! Iarla na seabhac síodhach súbhach;
Seana-rosc liath ag dian-ghol fá cheachtar dhíobh súd
Fá ndeara dham triall riamh ort a Bhailintín Brún. (pp. 30–2)

For all its personal bitterness, this poem indicates that Ó Rathaille's concerns were not just with his own position, but with the human fabric of society – and in that view the responsibility for social harmony lay at the top. This ultimately political view (defining the poet's attitude largely in a broader political context) is, however, expressed through the intimate, lyrical mediation of the poet's verse: his 'old grey eye crying bitterly' at the dispossession of the old order. This essentially *lyrical* treatment of political issues is what separates Ó Rathaille from his predecessors. The poet's personal plight is never treated in absolute terms, but as the subordinate part of a wider disruption; the opposite was true of a man like Ó Bruadair, who would address the larger topic of public affairs exclusively in terms of their effect on his own situation. Ó Bruadair registered social upheaval *in,* Ó Rathaille registered it *through* his personal plight.

In Ó Rathaille's view, one's principal duty in the context of the disrupted social order was to remain true to one's own ideals, or, more particularly, to those who shared those ideals. It is again an attempt to maintain some form of social harmony, a kind of moral solidarity. Thus Ó Rathaille addressed a poem to Donncha Ó hIcidhe 'ag fágáil Luimnigh i mí October, 1709, ag dul go Sasana, ag teiceadh roimh mhóidibh "Abpribasion"' – on leaving Limerick, in the month of October, 1709, for England, in order to escape from 'Approbation' oaths:

° Tréig do thalamh duthchais,
Déin ar choiste Lundain,
Ag seachaint móide an amhgair
Do chuir do thír fá bhrón.

---

* First, Cashel without society, guest-house, or horsemen, and Brian's turreted mansions black-flooded with otters, Ealla without the government of a chief descended from the Kings of Munster; it is this which has made me ever to have recourse to thee, Valentine Brown.
    The wild deer has lost the noble shape that was her wont before, since the foreign raven nestled in the thick wood of Ross; the fishes shun the sun-lit stream and the calm, delightful rivulet; it is this that caused me ever to have recourse to thee, Valentine Brown.
    Dairinis in the west – it has no lord of the noble race; woe is me! in Hamburg is the lord of the gentle merry heroes; aged, grey-browed eyes bitterly weeping for each of these, have caused me ever to have recourse to thee, Valentine Brown. (eds.' trl.)
° Quit thy native land, approach the London jury to shun the oaths of trouble that have brought sorrow on thy country.

  * Cuir do dhóthchas coimseach
     I gCríost, do Thighearna dílis,
     Ná tabhair ar bheatha as tsaoighil seo
     An tríoraidheacht tá it chomhair.

     Fillfidh Dia do dhíbirt
     Tar éis gach iompódh tíre,
     Is leagfaidh se do naimhde
     Do chuir tú as do chóir. (p. 140)

Ó hIcidhe may not, perhaps, expect much material gain from his loyalty to his religion – but in moral terms the loyalty that brings about his social undoing will guarantee him the unbroken pride that Ó Rathaille himself could muster on his death-bed when he uttered his 'Cabhair ní ghairfead'. The same 'terrible beauty' of a defeat more glorious than victory[99] is evoked in a poem that Ó Rathaille addressed to Eoghan Mac Cárthaigh on the forfeiture of his estate. In part it is traditional enough, regretting the rape and contumely of the great lineage of Clann Cárthaigh; but a large part of the poem is also, in a way, a celebration of this tragedy: Ó Rathaille describes at great length how all the sí lament, how the rivers scream, and even Sol, Luna and Boreas add their condolences. All this echoes the medieval bardic rhetoric employed at the death of a king, heightened by the few classical references, and all co-operating to show that Mac Cárthaigh was never greater than in his ruin. At the climax of this description, the mythical signs of Ireland's grief become literally identical with those of supreme victory: the *Lia Fáil*, 'stone of destiny', roars (as it is supposed to do when a true king stands on it), though this time out of grief rather than as the hailing of a new monarch – and this parallel between the greatness of a tragic downfall and that of victory is underscored by the erroneous dismay of the English, who interpret the stone's roar as an announcement of their overthrow:

  ° Do ghlac fanntais dream an Bhéarla,
     Do shaoileadar go bhfillfeadh arís chughainn Séamus,
     An tan do scread an leac fát scéalaibh
     An Lia Fáil n-a lár ag géimnigh. (p. 224)

Then, after an *aisling*-like interlude in which the poet tells the news to Fionscoth the sí-woman, Mac Cárthaigh's fate is, again, placed in its larger context:

---

  * Put thy deliberate hope in Christ, thy beloved Lord; do not give for this mortal life the eternity that is in store for thee.
     God will restore thee from banishment after thou hast gone round every land, and will overthrow thine enemies who put thee from thy right. (eds.' trl.)

  ° The tribe of the English speech fell into a fainting fit; they thought that James would return to us again, when the Stone screamed at the tiding of thee – the Lia Fail moaning in its centre. (eds.' trl.)

* Is brónach anois le cur i nGaedhilg,
  An ceo so thuit 'n-a chioth ar Ghaedhalaibh,
  Is ar gach aicme de chlannaibh Mhilésius
  An méid díobh d'iompuigh le Liútar a n-éide;

  Mar d'imthigh tar sruíll anonn ar gcléir mhaith,
  Mar do cuireadh ar díbirt choidhche Séamus,
  Do chuireadh fá smacht ar mhair den tréada,
  Is do cuireadh Eoghan fá bhrón, mo ghéarghoin. (p. 228)

Ó Rathaille thus creates a vision of the unity of men within society, man as part of society; a society, with which the individual is linked by deliberate mutual sympathy and solidarity, yes, which is defined even by this very interplay of affective connections: for the society of Mac Cárthaigh, Ó hIcidhe and Ó Rathaille most explicitly includes those who are willing to share in, and extend, its harmony (e.g. a 'good' landlord like Warner), but excludes men like Valentine Brown. It is this *chosen allegiance* to a certain demographic group (a group defined, but not determined, by the criteria of culture, religion and political stance) which is more 'national' than anything in Ó Bruadair or in Ó Rathaille's other predecessors.

The most important instances of Ó Rathaille's power to create genuinely lyrical poetry from the bitterness of political circumstance are his *aislingí*, which may be said to have given all subsequent poets in the Irish language a generic prototype to emulate. This is not the place to perform yet another critical genuflection to the formal gorgeousness of 'Gile na gile's' word- and sound-patterns. What I would like to do instead is to draw up a rough typology of Ó Rathaille's *aislingí* in order to show that they not only create an erotically charged approach to the personified 'nation', but also proclaim the poet as the nation's natural spokesman.

Ó Rathaille follows the tendency of earlier poems like *An Síogaí Rómhánach* to instill a great amount of feminine attractiveness in his personifications of Ireland. His *aislingí* claim that the poet has seen a figure who first and foremost presents herself in human shape, and only in the second instance reveals her non-human characteristics. Not a *puella senilis* or a dishonoured woman, the first impression she makes is one of feminine beauty. In 'Mac an cheannaí' she is *ainnir shéimh* with *súile glas, cúl tiubh casta, com* and *mailí gheal, beol bhinn* and *glór caoin, cneas mhín* (a 'wild maiden' with green eyes, curled and thick hair, fair waist and brow, sweet mouth, mild voice and sweet cheek); in short, she is a *buídhbhean míonla* – small wonder that 'is ró-shearc linn an cailín', 'I was exceedingly charmed by the young lady' (p. 12). In 'An aisling', the poet encounters 'scaoth bhruinneal soilbhir suairc',

---

* Sad it is to record in Gaelic, this trouble that has fallen as a shower on the Gaels, and on every band of the descendants of Milesius, now so many of them became turncoats with Luther.

  How our good clergy have gone over across the waves, how James was sent for ever into banishment, how all that survived of the company were put beneath the yoke, and Eoghan was afflicted with sorrow – my sharp wounding! (eds.' trl.)

a band of maidens merry and gay. Subordinate to this initial description is, in both poems, the non-human aspect of these women: the name of the *ainnir shéimh* in 'Mac an cheannaí' is given as Éire; the young girls in 'An aisling' are identified as *sí*-women of the court of the fairy-queen Aoibheall. 'Gile na gile' never affixes a name to the apparition, whose nature is only revealed indirectly: from the fact that she cannot withstand the poet's invocation of Christ and seeks refuge in a *ráth*, a fairy-fort. The opening stanzas only gradually work towards the revelation of her superhuman (but at the same time wholly feminine) beauty:

> *   Gile na gile do chonnarc ar slighe i n-uaigneas;
>   Criostal an chriostail a guirm-ruisc rinn-uaine;
>   Binneas an bhinnis a friotal nár chríon-ghruamdha;
>   Deirge is finne do fionnadh n-a gríos-ghruadhnaibh.
>
>   Caise na caise i ngach ruibe dá buidhe-chuachaibh,
>   [Bhuineas an cruinneac don rinneac le rinn-sguaba]
>   Iorradh ba ghlaine 'ná gloine ar a bruinn bhuacaigh,
>   Do geineadh ar gheineamhain di-se 'san tír uachtraigh.[100]

The amatory element – albeit of the sublimated *amour courtois* style – is not far away, especially in the keenness of the poet's disgust and (purportedly vicarious) jealousy when he sees the dream-maiden pawed and importuned by an ugly goblin; and the intensity of that feeling works in complete independence of the possibility of reading the 'goblin' politically as the English usurper:

> °   Mo threighid! mo thubaist! mo thurrain! mo bhrón! mo dhíth!
>   An soillseach muirneach miochair-gheal beol-tais caoin
>   Ag adharcach fuireann-dubh mioscaiseach cóirneach buidhe;
>   'S gan leigheas n-a goire go bhfillid na leoghain tar tuinn. (p. 20)

Ó Rathaille's *aisling* is thus characterized by the fact that it can instill the *amour courtois* idiom of a poet stricken and stunned by a sudden access of love for the perfectly beautiful woman, into the metonymy 'Ireland as a woman'; the genre can thus begin to draw on the tradition of the French (Provençal) *reverdie* or *pastourelle*, which, as Seán Ó Tuama has authoritatively shown, made its way into Ireland in the wake of the Hiberno-Norman barons; the medieval *dánta grá* show this courtly influence, and we have seen similarly amatory overtones in *An Síogaí Rómhánach*.

---

*   The Brightness of Brightness I saw in a lonely path, crystal of crystal, her blue eyes tinged with green, melody of melody her speech not morose with age, the ruddy and white appeared in her glowing cheeks.
   Plaiting of plaiting in every hair of her yellow locks [which wipe the dew from the grass in her sweeping] an ornament brighter than glass on her swelling breast, which was fashioned at her creation in the world above. (eds.' trl.)

°   O my sickness, my misfortune, my fall, my sorrow, my loss! The bright fond, kind, fair, soft-lipped, gentle maiden, held by a horned, malicious, croaking, yellow clown, with a black troop! While no relief can reach her until the heroes come back across the main. (eds.' trl.)

Equally traditional is the motif that the poet is left exhausted and broken after his vision; though in Ó Rathaille's *aislingí*, this motif seems to be expressed with an unprecedented intensity. The last stanza of 'An Aisling' sees the poet 'nervous, dejected and sad'; a mood of pessimism and dejection seems to suffuse 'Mac an Cheannaí' throughout, while the mood of 'Gile na gile' is one of frenzy, feverish fear and horror. It is, of course, possible to read this emotional disturbance as an echo of the *amour courtois* idiom representing love as a wasting illness leaving the afflicted swain without appetite or energy; within the *aisling* context, however, it takes on a different meaning from that which one could expect in analogy to *reverdie* or *pastourelle*. Nor would the explanation that the poet is saddened to hear of the maiden's tribulations stand up to closer scrutiny: for both in 'Aisling meabhuil' and in 'An aisling', hope, not grief, is imparted, without rescuing the poet from incurring a severely melancholic hangover. This reference is maintained even in those later *aislingí* of the eighteenth century which are scarcely more than poetic pep-talks for the Jacobite hopes of Gaelic Ireland. How is this 'hangover' motif to be regarded?

The most basic common trait of all *aisling* poetry lies not within the description of the poet's vision as such, but in a preliminary statement which is so foregrounded that it runs the risk of being overlooked. The most basic statement of an *aisling* concerns the fact that the poet has seen a vision. If readers or listeners want to take cognizance of the poem, they must, if not lend credence to this claim, at least let it pass unchallenged; it is the *conditio sine qua non* in the contract between poet and audience, and it is under this aspect that the rest of the poem is entered into. It marks the shift from reality (in which a poet presents a poem to an audience) into fiction (in which supernatural females and their prophecies can be seen and heard).

'The rest of the poem' concerns the exchange of information between the *spéirbhean* and the poet (usually from the former to the latter). The substance of this information, again, regards political realities: its reference is not to the fictitious or allegorical world of *sí*-maidens, but to the situation of the poet and of his audience.

Within these conventions, then, the poet enters into contact with the spirit world, gains information there, and re-creates this information transfer in the transaction between himself and his audience. The *aisling* as a poem is thus a direct reconstruction, a repetition, of the *aisling* as a vision, and it places the poet in a mediating position between the spirit-world of *sí* and of mythical phenomena, and the rest of humanity who have no access to that world. This process of mediation finds its concrete expression in the literary artefact, the poem; thus, the poet's visionary activity is, to some extent at least, a form of literary inspiration – and this during the lifetime of Dryden and Pope, and nearly a century before Blake, or Coleridge's opium poems. The poet's emotional exhaustion would seem, in this way, to be the exhaustion of the Pythia or of the shaman after their delivery of the trance-induced oracles, the exhaustion of the mortal who has ventured beyond human limitations.[101] In this sense one can see the obligatory reference to the poet's emotional exhaustion in *aisling* poetry, not necessarily as a consequence of any ingredients of the vision itself, but primarily of the simple fact that he has had a vision.

The *aisling* therefore has a dual function. It makes the abstract political notion of 'the land' or 'the nation' comprehensible and lovable by anthropomorphizing it into a human, and most attractively human, shape; and it places the poet in a uniquely close relationship with this personified nation – he being the one who can see her 'in the flesh', share her griefs and hopes, and divulge them to his fellow-mortals. Thus one can find, even at this late date, an echo of the archaic, hieratic position of the *file*, who was originally a *seer* as much as a 'rimer' or 'maker' (ποιητής) of verse, who composed in darkness and could blight a prince's face by pronouncing a satire-curse.

In the *aisling*, therefore, the nascent national ideal becomes inextricably linked to the medium of poetry as its natural form of expression: at this early period in its development, the sense of 'nationality' is a field between the poles of literature and politics, a political form of literary inspiration and the literary expression of a political ideal .

This phenomenon is illustrated particularly clearly in one of the most outstanding *aislingí* of the genre, 'Úr-chill an Chreagáin', 'The church-yard of Creggan', composed by Ó Rathaille's younger contemporary from South Ulster, Art Mac Cumhaigh. Typical *aisling*-features are the liminal nature of its setting, a borderland between reality and the spirit-world (the churchyard where the poet sleeps) and the obligatory reference to the poet's emotional trouble (he sleeps *faoi bhrón*, weighed down by sorrow). His initial doubt concerning the identity of the apparition (a *sí*, not Helen of Troy) and her bitter reference to the injustice of the rule of 'clann Bhullaí' (the Williamites) are also standard procedure. What is unusual, however, is the fact that she tries to lure the poet away with her to a paradise in the west:

> *   A fhialfhir charthanaigh ná caithtear tusa i ndealramh bróin
>   ach éirigh 'do sheasamh agus aistrigh liom siar sa ród,
>   go tír dheas na meala nach bhfuair Gallaibh ann cead réim go fóill,
>   mar bhfaighir aoibhneas ar hallaíbh do do mhealladh le siansa ceoil.

– and the poet objects by referring to his obligations to his wife, kin and friends. It would be irresponsible to leave them behind in sorrow:

> °   Cha dhiúltfainn do chuireadh ar a gcruinníonn siad na ríthe d'ór,
>   ach gur cladharta liom scarúint le mo charaid tá sa tír go fóill;
>   an céile úd a mheallas le mo ghealladh tráth bhí sí óg,
>   dá dtréigfinn anois í gur fiosach domh go mbeadh sí i mbrón.

---

*   Good generous sir, don't let yourself be thrown into sad oppression, but stand up and go westward with me on the road to that sweet honey-land of which the foreigners have not yet taken any possession, where we may take pleasure in halls, enticed by music.

°   I would not turn you down even for royal gold-hoards, but it would be wrong to abandon my friends who are still in this land; there is my spouse whom I won in her youth with promises; I am sure it would leave her in sadness if I were to leave her now.

The reiteration of the *spéirbhean's* seductive invitation confronts the poet with the following choice:

> * nach mb'fhearr dhuitse imeacht le hainnir na maothchrobh meor,
> ná an tír so bheith ag fonóid faoi gach rabhán dá ndéan tú a cheol?[102]

It will be obvious that this *aisling* contains an unusually overt expression of some of the underlying tensions of the genre: the poet is presented with the option of allying himself either with the mythical, aristocratic past and the literary tradition that are accessible to him by virtue of his poetic talent, or with the drab reality of the Gaels' oppression and misery. In this context, it is anything but illogical that the poet should venture the guess that his temptress might be one of the Muses: 'an de naoi mná deasa thú ó Pharnassus bhí déanta i gcló?', 'are you one of the nine Parnassian women so shapely in form?'. The choice goes between the old aristocratic poetical attitude on the one hand, and a new, humbler, communitarian one on the other, one which involves a more complete identification between poet and Gaelic peasant. The *aisling* is thus not only a vision of political hope, but also of literary desire/temptation. Another indication that the *spéirbhean* may to some extent be symbolic also of the poet's own visionary faculty of literary inspiration is contained in the folklore version of how the blind Ulster poet Séamas Mac Cuarta (*c.* 1645–*c.* 1720) obtained his literary gift, which was given to him as an indemnity for his lost eyesight by a vision-woman:

> When a young boy he went up the country as it was customary in that time to work with farmers. He stopped at a place named Kellystown in the Barroney of Slane in County Meath, where he was accustomed to be sitting out at night, taking care of horses, and, by getting cold in his head became blind. In a short time after he dreamed at night that the most beautiful woman in the world came to him which induced him to folow her through all the Kingdom: but when he awoke she vanished away but lift him the gift of poetry. This is all we can obtain of him by tradition but wheather it was a dream or, as the people thell, a familiar spirit, it is sure anoff, that in this kingdom or aney other, in the opinion there never was any man had such flow of eloquence in his native language. [*sic* throughout][103]

The poetical tradition following Ó Rathaille does indeed become far more community-oriented: the poets seem to have accepted their reduced status (as small farmers, peddlers, innkeepers or schoolmasters) among the common Gaelic populace, and function as the spokesmen of their peers. The only vestiges of earlier poetic pride can be observed in the 'Courts of Poetry' in Munster, where poets would gather and enjoy the company of fellow-poets; or perhaps also in the fact that poets would tend to indulge in a rather irregular lifestyle (though picaresque rather than Byronic!) as if it were the privilege of their literary talent (e.g. Eoghan Rua Ó Súilleabháin, Mac Conmara, An Mangaire Sugach, Mac

---

* Wouldn't leaving with this maiden of soft-fingered hands be better for you than [to be in] this land that sneers at you for every bit of song you make?

Giolla Ghunna) – but in the poems of these men, none of the earlier literary-aristocratic disdain for ignorant boors and churls (in the style of *Pairlement Chloinne Tomáis* or of Ó Bruadair) can be noticed.[104]

The poetry of the eighteenth century, in the wake of Ó Rathaille, is indicative of an outlook on the English-Gaelic confrontation in which religious, linguistic or more broadly cultural aspects, economic and legal factors and a well-defined political stance (Jacobitism) have been welded into a coherently structured ideology which, I think, may be called *national* in that it brings cultural identity and political aspiration together in an interlocking relationship. In a way, the very fact that these successors of Ó Rathaille had accepted their appurtenance, no longer to a specific caste or social class, but to the totality of Gaeldom, religiously and socially defined by the penal laws, culturally by the Irish language, and politically by their Jacobitism: this fact constitutes in itself the act of allegiance by which a 'national' group creates its own self-recognition as such. All these elements, language, religion, economic and political position, had merged into a criterion of national co-appurtenance.

The waning of Gaelic literature and the growth of a national stance

By this time, the very use of the Irish language seems to have undergone a certain revaluation and politicization: we have seen how Ó Rathaille emphasized in his elegy on Mac Cárthaigh's dispossession that it was sad to record these things 'in Gaelic' (above, p. 236), implying that the language itself vouchsafed a continuity between past and present, and was therefore unsuitable to record the disruptions that began to intervene between the two.

There are other indications that, in the context of contemporary politics, the use of Irish was becoming a form of complicity, a medium for communication between Gaels but hermetically inaccessible to the outsider. An early but highly typical example is a traditional anecdote involving Ó Rathaille himself – an anecdote which is no less significant *se non è vero:* The story goes that the son of a Protestant clergyman in Killarney accidentally hanged himself while thinning out the crown of a tree; the occurrence, and the father's anguish at seeing his son suspended lifeless by the neck in a forked branch, are related with evident satisfaction and little compassion, and Aogán Ó Rathaille, being present at the scene, improvises the following stanza:

> *   Is maith do thoradh a chrainn,
>   Rath do thoraidh ar gach aon chraoibh,
>   Mo chreach! gan crainn Inse Fáil
>   Lán det thoradh gach aon lá. (p. 264)

---

*   Good is thy fruit, O tree, may every branch bear such good fruit.
    Alas! that the trees of Inisfail are not full of thy fruit each day (eds.' trl.)

The minister, obviously without knowledge of Irish, then reacts:

> * 'What is the poor wild Irish devil saying?' ar an ministir.
> 'He is lamenting your darling son,' ar gaige bhí láimh leis.
> 'Here is two pence for you to buy tobacco,' ar an méithbhroc ministreach.
> 'Thank 'ee, a mhinistir an Mhic Mhallachtan' (i.e., an diabhal), ar Aodhagán,
> agus do chan an laoidh: –
>> 'Hurú, a mhinistir a thug do dhá phinginn dam
>> I dtaobh do leinbh a chaoineadh!
>> Oidheadh an leinbh sin ar an gcuid eile aca
>> Siar go hearball timcheall.' (p. 264)

The medium of Gaelic gains a new significance here: not only in its intelligibility, as a medium of intercourse between Gaels (both in the present, and between the past and the present), but also in its unintelligibility to English speakers, as a medium for anti-English complicity. Another interesting instance of this new awareness is contained in a bilingual poem by Donncha Rua Mac Conmara, with alternate distychs in Gaelic and in English – the English ones being perfectly respectable and innocuous, the Gaelic ones highly caustic and subversive. The anecdotal *Entstehungsgeschichte* of this poem, as handed down in folklore, states that Mac Conmara sang the song to a mixed company in an inn (Gaelic locals and visiting English sailors), 'to the great amusement of the Irish present, and indeed to that of the English, though the latter understood but one part of it, while the former chuckled in comprehending the entire';[105] one stanza as an example:

> ° Come, drink a health, boys, to Royal George,
> our chief commander – nár órduigh Críost
> Is aithchimís ar Mhuire Mháthair
> É féin 's a ghardai do leagadh síos;
> We'll fear no cannon nor loud alarms
> While noble George shall be our guide –
> 'S a Chríost go bhfaiceadsa iad dá gcárnadh
> Ag an mac so ar fán uainn ag dul don bhFraingc.

---

* 'What is the poor wild Irish devil saying?' said the minister. 'He is lamenting your darling son,' said a wag who stood beside him, 'Here is two pence for you to buy tobacco,' said the sleek badger of a minister.

'Thank 'ee, Minister of the Son of Malediction' (i.e., the devil), replied Egan; and he spoke his lay:

'Huroo! O minister, who didst give me thy two pence for chanting a lament for thy child; may the fate of this child attend the rest of them, all, even unto the last.' (eds.' trl.)

° Come drink a health, boys, to Royal George, our chief commander – not appointed by Christ; and let us beseech Mother Mary to scuttle himself and all his guards. We'll fear no concern nor loud alarms while noble George shall be our guide – and Christ that I may see them kicked aside by him who left us on his exile to France.

Gaelic and English are thus, as languages, placed in the same polarity of opposite interests that is at work in politics, religion, and social-economic affairs. This polarity finds an apt expression in Art Mac Cumhaigh's 'Tagra an dá theampall', 'The dispute of the two churches', which describes allegorically a conversation between the Protestant church and the Catholic chapel, the edifices renewing and perpetuating the old debates. Although cardinal Ó Fiaich's edition of Mac Cumhaigh's poems gives an all-Gaelic version, a bilingual version also exists, with, in alternating stanzas, the Catholic chapel speaking in Irish and the Protestant church in English.[106]

The same poet Mac Cumhaigh also introduced the linguistic division into the subject-matter of his *aislingí*: his 'Ag cuan Bhinn Éadair ar bhruach na hÉireann' has the vision-woman identify herself in racial terms ('bean de'n Ghaedhealtacht is do thréibh Mhilesius', 'a woman of Gaeldom and from the stock of Milesius'), which leads into a joint treatment of legal and linguistic dispossession:

> * Tá mo chroi-se réabtha 'na mhíle céad cuid,
> Agus balsam féin nach bhfóireann mo phian,
> Nuair a chluinim an Ghaelig uilig dá tréigbheáil,
> Agus caismirt Bhéarla i mbeol gach aoin,
> Bhullaigh *is Jane* ag glacadh léagsaí
> Ar dhúichibh Éireann na n-ór-bhall caoin,
> 'S nuair a fhiafraím scéala 'sé freagra ghéibhim:
> *'You're a Papist, I know not thee'.*[107]

Likewise Eoghan 'an Mhéirín' Mac Cárthaigh, a Munster poet, identifies the *spéir-bhean* by the very fact that 'Do fhreagar an bhéith mé gan mhoill i nGaedhilg', 'the being answered me straightways in Irish'; also, in Eoghan Rua Ó Súilleabháin's *aisling* 'Cois na Siúire', the poet states 'gur labhair sí go cneasda caoin, gan tslás, i nGaedhilg', 'that she spoke gently, tenderly, flawlessly in Irish'.[108] The later *aislingí* of Pádraig Cúndún, from the period 1812–1834, are all specified as speaking Irish.

The most interesting area of linguistic interpenetration lies in the poets' adoption of English legal jargon. It is in part a sarcastic imitation of foreign impositions, much like the last line of the foregoing quotation, and as such stands in a long tradition which I have already discussed. The adoption of legal English has, however, a more particular function here: it indicates humourously the inflexible formality that Catholics had come to expect from English and penal jurisdiction. An unusual, but poetically highly effective, example is given by the astringently lyrical Ulster poet Cathal Buí Mac Giolla Ghunna, who wrote a few poems in worried anticipation of the judgement of his soul before God's throne (as well he might, considering his scandalous reputation for rakishness). One of these is a poetical act of contrition, ending with the stanza:

> * My heart is rent into a hundred thousands pieces, and not even balsam can stop my pain, when I hear every least bit of Irish being abandoned and the aggressive English speech in every one's mouth. Willie and Jane grabbing leases on the homelands of Ireland of the golden-smooth localities; and when I ask a question the answer I get is: *'You're Papist, I know not thee.'*

* Nach trua mé lá an tsléibhe is mé ar thosach an tsló
is gur measa mé féin nó an té rinne brath leis an bpóig,
cuirfidh mé cré an dáréag agus glacfar é, dar ndóigh,
ar an dúil is go ndéarfaí i láthair Dé, '*He's not guilty my Lord*'.[109]

The shift from homely Irish to alien, stark, bureaucratic English is used with great effect – an aural chill intensifying the poet's vacillation between optimism and apprehension. Legal English was used much more lightheartedly by the Munster poets who convoked the Courts of Poetry in a mockery of English judiciary court sessions. The example had been given in one of Ó Rathaille's lighter poems which issued a warrant against a man who had stolen a cock from a priest and which used the English legalese of 'whereas', 'wheresoever', 'for so doing' – ironically pointing, in the process, at the gap between Justice and legal practice, and at the poet's own inability to reconcile the two.[110]

Ó Rathaille's successors in Munster, such as Seán Clárach Mac Domhnaill, Eoghan Rua Ó Súilleabháin and Seán Ó Tuama 'an Ghrinn' continued to use this device in their poetical convocations to the Courts of Poetry – in fact they created thus a new genre called the *Barantas* or 'warrant' which began with the English preambular 'Whereas' (though sometimes the Irish equivalent *De bhrigh* was also used). All this was not exclusively a matter of mere 'fun', however, as soubriquets like 'an Ghrinn', 'of the merriment', or 'An Mangaire Súgach', 'the jolly peddler', may seem to indicate: Seán Ó Tuama's warrant for the first Court after the death of Seán Clárach Mac Domhnaill addresses matters of a cultural-political nature which indicate that these poets were keenly aware of an appointed task to keep Irish literature alive amidst repression and pauperization, and that a national interest was felt here, no less than in their Jacobitism or in their social and economic conflict of interests with the landlord class:

° Ag seo reamh-rabhadh nó príomh-fhógra do gach aon lér mian athnuadhadh na sean-nós nÉireannach ar feadh na gcríoch reamh-ráidhte, go bith-chinnte, do gach n-aon ainmnighthe 'san leathanach so, le cómhchruinniughadh go toirteamhail trom-thionóil go teaghlach an bhreithimh reamh-ráidhte i gCroma an tSubhachais an t-aonmhadh lá fichead den ochtmhadh miosa is neasa, dá ngairmthear ('san mbéalrádh Gallda) *October*, chun an lae sin d'onórughadh re iarchruinniughadh aith-bheodhadh agus síor-aithris na saor-ghníomha saidhbhre sochar-mhianda do chleacht ár bhforas feasa, ár gcoinneal adhanta, ár gceap craoibhe, ár stoc stiúrthaighe agus ár mbile buacach buadh-fhoclach .i. Seán geal

* Am I not be pitied on the Day of Doom, when I stand before the multitude, I who am worse than the one who committed betrayal with a kiss; I'll say the Apostles' Creed and it shall, I trust, be accepted, in the hope that it may be said in God's presence, 'He's not guilty, my Lord'.

° This is a ᶜ᷄rewarning or first notice to whomever wishes to renew the old Irish customs throughout the said land [i.e. Limerick and Leath Mogha], most particularly to all those named hereinafter, to gather together in large and great numbers to the house of the said Judge [i.e. Ó Tuama] in Croom-of-the-Merriment, on the twenty-first day of the eighth month instanter, which is designated (in the Foreign parlance) October, in order to honour that day by collecting and reviving and rehearsing the rich, beneficial, noble deeds practised by our support of knowledge, our burning candle, our branch-leader, our stock of guidance, our

Clárach Mac Domhnaill, árd-ollamh Inse iath-ghlaise oileánaighe Éireann i n-a chómh-aimsir, chum cuidiughadh go cáirdeamhail ria aroile le greann agus glé-mhian do chothughadh agus do shíor-choiméad diaidh i ndiaidh fá chomhair ár lucht leanamhna féin, amhail do rinne an t-éigeas iolbhuadhach adubhramar agus mórán eile dár sinsearaibh rómhainn ó aimsir go haimsir. Óir dá laighead mhaireas anois dár dteangain ghaois-bhriathraigh Gaedhilge gan dul i mbáthadh agus i mór-dhearmad tré gach doilgheas tré n-ar hionnarbadh í go nuige seo, rachaidh go comair go neimhnídh muna bhféacham meodhán dícheallach le cuidiughadh go caoin caomhchumainn le chéile go toileamhail re n-a coiméad ar bun.

Ag sin bunadhas cúise an tsuaidh-thionóil nó na scol-gharma so. Dá dhearbhadh sin, gach aon ghabhas air féin bheith i rith re héigse nó le glé-mhian ár seanGhaedheal agus ná tiocfaidh san gcómhdháil seo mar adubhramar thuas, beidh deighilte ris an éigse agus gearrtha go hiomlán as comhluadar gach aon díobh go fuin a shaoghail.

Toirbheartha fám láimh an *23° die 7bris 1754*. Seán Ó Tuama.[111]

At the same time, these poets also continued to write verse that eagerly anticipated the overthrow of the oppressive Ascendancy and the return of the Stuart; poets not only wrote *aislingí*, they also exchanged them in a point-counter-point play; such productions show how entangled the various ideological manifestations of the Gael-Gall conflict (religious, literary, linguistic, social, economical, political) had become. The enumeration of English names, for instance, had by now become a recurrent fixture in Gaelic poetry, linking the English presence with an uncouth disturbance of Gaelic harmony. Thus, Seán Clárach Mac Domhnaill foretells a brighter future by affirming that the Gaels will be in the ascendant again, and by drawing up the following contrast:

> *   Beidh Tadhg gan ghruaim ar bínse thuas
>   'na ghiúistís mhórdha mhaiseach tréan,
> Beidh Wilkes is Jones is Speed is Owens,
>   Reed is Groves is Grant is Lane
> Fé haistí daora daingeana in anaithe 's i ndaorbhroid. . .[112]

lofty, high-spoken leader, good Seán Clárach Mac Domhnaill, arch-doctor of the green-meadowed sea-girt Island of Ireland in his lifetime, so that we may help each other in friendly fashion to nourish and preserve humour and clear intelligence for evermore to our own followers, as did this aforementioned versatile poet and many another of our ancestors before us from one era to the next. For however little survives today of our wise-worded Gaelic language, still uneclipsed or unobliterated by any of the torments which caused its destruction hitherto, it will shortly be altogether reduced to nothing if we do not seek out an effective means of friendly assistance and deliberate association with each other to guard it.

That is the fundamental motive of this sage-gathering or school-summons. In witness of which, anyone who undertakes to engage with poetry and with the clear intelligence of the old Gaels and who does not present himself in the assembly as aforementioned, he shall be cut off from poetry and marked off wholly from the society of all of them until the end of his life.

Delivered under my hand this 23rd day of September 1754. Seán Ó Tuama.

*   Tadhg will be gaily seated high on the bench, a stately, handsome, firm judge; Wilkes and Jones and Speed and Owens, Reed and Groves and Grant and Lane will all be under cruel, binding locks, in terror and dread bondage.

This type of device remained popular throughout the century and can be encountered in the works of virtually all Irish poets of the period.[113] Apart from the older use as an aural illustration of English uncouthness, an additional function (particularly in the prophetic mode) of such enumerations may have been the reinforcement of the prophecy's claim to realism, validity, believability: names like Wilkes and Jones obviously cannot belong to the world of fairies, of Gaelic myth, but they refer to real political circumstance. They thus reinforce the claim of the poetical construct to political validity, and point to the community existing between the poet and his audience sharing a common oppression.

Something similar was at work in the degree of intertextuality between the individual poems, in the fact that a large amount of sharing, borrowing and mutual reference went on between them, which was quite distinct from the common idioms and formulas of medieval bardic poetry. One can see this new form of intertextuality as an indication that post-bardic poetry was performing a slow, gradual shift from aristocratic individualism towards the less individualist outlook and the 'shared ownership' of folk poetry; in such a reading one might regard the conventional forms and commonplaces that surface in poem after poem, decade after decade, in the same light as one would register the recurrence of certain motifs in folktales.[114]

But such a reading might lose sight of the strongly political nature of the poetry of this period. In a politicized context, intertextual recurrences may serve the distinct purpose of creating a typological generic canon by which the individual poem can easily establish its credentials and draw on a common 'pool' of rhetorical tropes and symbols; meaning by this that generic patterns can thus be evoked by subtle signals, recognizable from received usage and intertextual analogies, which afford immediate recognition value and familiarity – much like the characteristic chord progressions that immediately identify a certain type of North American folk song as a 'blues' (which might also be achieved on the textual level by a formulaic opening-line like 'Woke up this morning', or by the stanzaic pattern that typically repeats the first distych).

This point is of special interest if one bears in mind the basic generic ambiguity of the *aisling*, with its characteristic mixture of amatory and national enthusiasm. The attractions of the *spéirbhean* are partly political, partly sexual (witness also the fact that she is often thought at first sight to be a classical *femme* (or *déesse*) *fatale* like Venus or Helen of Troy); the ambiguity between the social and the amatory is expressed quite forcefully by a poet who devoted himself to both fields with equal enthusiasm, Eoghan Rua Ó Súilleabháin:

> *   Gur fhreagair mé an spéir-bhean cé nár shíleas;
>   i labharthaibh Gaedhilge séimh gan coimhightheacht
>   Gur bhlaiseas a béal beag éadtrom ioghartha,
>   Gan séanadh óm chroidhe le táinte póg.[115]

*   . . . when the vision answered me (though I did not expect that) in words of Irish, tender and intimate, so that I followed the dictate of my heart and kissed her dainty little well-shaped mouth with a multitude of kisses.

Eoghan Rua seems to kiss the woman's mouth, not just for its sensual appeal, but also for the sweet language it enunciates. A similar ambivalence lies at the bottom of another typical feature of the political-amatory poem: the unwillingness to give the name of the subject. The Pretender especially has many nicknames like *an seabhac siubhal* (the roving falcon, or hero), *mac an bricléir* (the bricklayer's son), *an buachall bán* (the fair lad), *Cormac Spáinneach* (Spanish Cormac). There are also numerous instances of rebuses where 'six' and 'mouse' spell the true king's name (*sé + mus* = Seamus, James). Seán Ó Tuama has traced the erotic dimension in this deliberate suppression of names back to an *amour courtois* convention, which must thus be considered as an additional motive in adopting the political expedient of never being too explicit in one's subversiveness.[116]

Against this background, it becomes apparent that the clue as to the 'real' nature of a poem or song (love poem or national-political poem?) is often furnished by intertextual pointers. This means that a poem or song can shift between genres by minute changes. There is, for instance, an ambiguous poem by one of the Mac Coitir brothers extolling what is either a beloved woman or Ireland, under the name of *Móirín Ní Luineacháin;* however, there are also later versions of this same poem in the manuscript tradition, which change that name to *Móirín Ní Chuilleanáin* (which is also the title of an air to which that poem can be sung). That small change turns the poem into an unambiguously political one, makes a political reading (as opposed to an amatory one) unavoidable: for Seán Ó Tuama an Ghrinn had previously patented the soubriquet *Ní Chuilleanáin* as the name for a straightforward personification of Ireland; and another instance of the same usage of *Ní Chuilleanáin* is found in an anonymous *aisling* ('Tá sgamal dubh i ceó draoidheach') whose political nature is in turn indicated by the fact that it uses the 'magic mist' motif introduced by Eoghan Rua Ó Súilleabháin in his famous *aisling* of that name, 'Ceó draoidheachta'.[117] Another example is the well-known figure of *Roisín dubh* who, in some poems, is a very human subject and, in others, a personification of Ireland.[118] Again, various versions of the equally well-known 'Fáinne geal an lae', 'the bright dawn of the day', vacillate between the amorous *pastourelle* and the political *aisling*. Finally, it is often the tune to which a poem is set which can betray its political nature – especially if it is a well-known Jacobite party tune such as 'An cnóta bán' ('the white cockade'), 'An seabhac siubhal' or 'Seán Buí'.

Thus, political significance can be created by reference to other poems. Such intertextual cross-references and covert signalling devices play a large part in the creation of a poetic code in which female names like *Clíona na carraige* (from Ó Rathaille to Uilliam Dall Ó hIfearnáin), *Caitlín Ní Uallacháin* (from Ó hIfearnáin to Yeats), *Grainne Mhaol* (from the original Grainne O'Malley via Seán Clárach to the broadsheets of the mid-nineteenth century), *Síle Ní Ghadhra, Cait Ní Dhuibhir, Méidhbhín Ní Shúilleabháin*, etc. etc. become the signifiers of an unambiguous, political ideal.

An interesting case is that of *Caitlín Tiriall*, or Kathleen Tyrrell. She began her career as the beloved in a beautiful, rapturous love poem dating back as far perhaps as the seventeenth century.[119] The air to which this poem was set was accordingly called 'Caitlín Tiriall' and served as the melody for a number of other love songs, as well as for some political *aislingí* – for example, one as late as *c.* 1828, by Eoghan Caomhánach.[120] By that time, however, some mis-understanding must have arisen over the Hiberno-Norman name of Tyrrell/Tiriall, for we find that the name was reinterpreted in the folk tradition as *Caitlín Tiaráil* or 'Kathleen the slave', and the beloved maiden of the original thus becomes yet another metonymy for Ireland – as can be seen in Crofton Croker's testimony from the 1820s:

> Of about four hundred popular ballads (chiefly printed at Limerick) which I purchased without selection, in 1821, more than one-third were of a rebellious tendency, particularly a song entitled 'Cathaleen Trail' (Catherine the Slave), so is Ireland allegorically styled.[121]

As becomes obvious from this last example, the *aisling* (perhaps by virtue of its generic ambiguity) was a very long-lived genre, managing to survive not only the complete abandonment of Jacobite hopes, but even the linguistic shift from Gaelic towards English: Zimmermann's collection of *Irish political ballads and rebel songs 1780–1900* gives two nineteenth-century broadsides which, though in English and in the broadsheet idiom, exhibit all the typological traits of a traditional *aisling* (nrs. 27 and 28). Máire Bhuí Ní Laoghaire's *aisling* 'Ar leacain na gréine i ndé' is another example of the literary formula outliving the circum-stances which gave rise to it, since, as L.M. Cullen points out, 'there is reference in the manner of the *aisling* to help from the Spaniards, despite the fact that the help expected was coming from republican France'.[122]

The same tenacity is at work in the *aisling's* centuries-old corollary, the prophecy. Máire Bhuí herself falls back on the old, oft-repeated prophecy of St. John:

> * Go raibh deire an cháirde caithte leo [i.e. the English. J.L.]
>   'S go dtiocfadh *slaughter* ar gach piara másach
>   Nár ghéill don Phais is do chaith an phóit.'[123]

Many more examples gleaned from broadsides of the period 1780–1860 can be found in Zimmermann's collection, one of them foretelling that 'Young Bony [i.e. Bonaparte, J.L.] and O'Connell will free old Ireland' (pp. 29–30).

Especially in these later examples it becomes clear that such political poetry is directly influenced by the very decline of an autonomously 'Gaelic' cause: the shift from *Caitlín Tiriall* to *Caitlín Tiaráil* is illustrative of the decline of the Irish language which made such diffraction of meanings possible.[124] The issues which in the early and mid-eighteenth century defined a Gaelic cause are receding: both Jacobitism and the Irish language are on the wane and the English language

---

*   That the limit of the respite given to them had expired, and that slaughter would befall each fat-buttocked peer who disbelieved the Passion and drank to excess.

begins to take over as the vehicle for political poetry; the political issues become broader, less exclusively pertaining to the Catholic, Gaelic-speaking part of the population, whose hermetic complicity under the Ascendancy yoke was celebrated by earlier poets. Poems are now addressed to United Irishmen, e.g. by Micheál Óg Ó Longáin and the Ulster poets, or to Daniel O'Connell. Tomas Rua Ó Súilleabháin, for instance, wrote a poem beginning 'Sé Domhnall binn Ó Cónaill caoin', 'It's dear Daniel, that sweet O'Connell', and introduces English terms, not as an alienating device, but as loanwords borrowed from a British political vocabulary current both in Westminster and in West Munster: he looks forward to the time 'Nuair bheidh an dlighe fúinn féin arís/Ar theacht EMANCIPA-TION', 'When we shall be our own masters again, at the coming of EMANCIPA-TION'.[125] Even more apt as an illustration of this process is Peadar Dubh Ó Dálaigh's bilingual *aisling* which combines Gaelic and English in alternating lines, and which combines the Gaelic folk-heroine Granuaile (a female pirate captain from Elizabethan times) with the contemporary Irish national politician Daniel O'Connell. The refrain runs:

> Agus éirigh, 'Ghrainne Mhaol
> [so rise up, Granuaile]
> And exterminate this heresy;
> Tabhair lámh le Domhnall cléibh
> [join hands with darling Daniel]
> To gain Erin's sons their liberty.[126]

At the same time, the actual rhetorical scheme of these ever-topical effusions remained fixed: the foretelling of a bright future (the more imminent the better) which will retrieve the glorious past from the gloomy present. In such a scheme it is indeed appropriate that Granuaile and O'Connell join hands, and that Emancipation (albeit within the United Kingdom of Great Britain and Ireland) is seen as the return to a pre-penal paradise. An English-language broadside from the mid-1820s:

> Three hundred years and better, as plainly you may see,
> Poor Granua's sons were bound in chains, and never since got free,
> But look into the prophecy that's written most sublime,
> That Granua Uile would break her chains in the year of twenty-nine.[127]

This conciliation of the dire present with a future which recaptures the past is one of the most basic and changeless characteristics of the prophecies and *aislingí* throughout the eighteenth century. A telling example is to be had from An Mangaire Súgach (Aindrias Mac Craith) who, in 1745, joyfully announced the Jacobite Restoration. This poem is, significantly, known in two different versions, one employing the future tense ('Béidh Prussia 'gus Póland fós ar mearbhall', 'Prussia and Poland will yet be in turmoil'), the other using the present tense ('Tá Pruise agus Póland fós ar mearathall', 'Prussia and Poland are already in tur-moil'), but both in unison when declaring 'scartha *go deó* le Seóirse Hanobher', 'the defeat *for ever* (my italics) of Hannover George'.[128] Thus *aisling* and prophecy are, as it were, an escape, not into the future (or, for that matter, into the past which will be recaptured), but into the extra-temporal sanctuary of literary timelessness, which D.-H. Pageaux calls 'le temps reversible, cyclique, de l'image', 'une sorte de temps mythique, en dehors de toutes limites precises: le 'in illo tempore' propre au mythe'.[129]

Such a deliberate shift from mere political topicality to the more 'timeless' values of literary convention helped to create the sort of intertextual cohesion that defines a 'tradition' – a unified perspective on occurrences which is governed by the established modes of perspective and evaluation rather than by the changing nature of the occurrences themselves. No matter whether it is Ball Dearg Ó Domhnaill, king James or Daniel O'Connell who figures in the prophetic promises, the prophetic mode as such remains an unchanging fixture. True: the Jacobite cause, that catalyst which had triggered the combination of legal, social, religious, linguistic and cultural frictions into what can be called a *national* Gaelic awareness, had gradually receded over the political horizon. But it is, at the same time, a telling fact that Gaelic political poetry took a very long time indeed to reflect this decline of Stuart hopes; and the dismissive tag of 'Charlie-over-the-waterism' is a rather simplistic explanation for the tenacity of poetical Jacobitism, its extended existence in the timelessness of poetry and prophecy. P.S. Dinneen was truly insightful when he described this non-realistic, literary Jacobitism as a 'poetic dream, convenient for poetic purposes and for the unification of history'.[130]

The political unification of religious, linguistic and racial criteria which had been brought about by Jacobitism survived the demise of its provider; and throughout eighteenth-century poetical practice one can register any combination of these various criteria for national identification. A 'Gaelic' identity is no longer racially or genealogically determined, but is defined by a socio-political and/or cultural act of allegiance. This is illustrated in Éamonn de bhFál's retort to Liam Mac Cartain's eulogy on three Munster bishops (1733) as 'Princes of the true noble stock of Eoghan', 'trí phrionnsa d'úr-fhuil cheannasaigh Eoghain': de bhFál only admits two of the three to this honour and excepts from praise the bishop of Kerry, who had opposed the Fitzgerald earl of Desmond, and whom he dismisses as 'mac Eoghain an Bhéarla chaim', 'Eoghan's son with his crooked English'. In the work of later poets, the different overlaps between racial, religious, political and cultural identification are so multifarious as to defy classification: various links between Jacobitism, anti-Protestantism, professional poetic pride, language concerns, historical interest and social hatred against the landlords can be found in any possible combination in the work of almost any eighteenth-century poet.

Conclusion

The process is one of crystallization, both on a synchronic and on a diachronic axis: diachronically, the 'unification of history' into the literary timelessness of an ideal Gaeldom whose eternal cause actuates the national aspirations of the leaders of the Gaels and of their poets at any given moment in time; and synchronically, a crystallization of various elements into a coherent structure of group identification, leading to the emergence of a national self-image of non-British Ireland, to which a specifically 'Gaelic' identity was attributed, an identity which was to remain as immune to historical change as the poetic genre in which it had been formulated.

The reader will already have gained a general impression of the nature of the stereotyped terms of the division Gael – Gall (or native – colonist) which takes shape in the poetry of these two centuries. One can disregard the mere invective that was employed in the heat of the conflict and say generally that the English-Gaelic opposition was largely one of newfangled roughness versus old nobility. Earlier bardic attitudes remain operative in the view that the English are without respect for, or even tolerance of, learning:

> * Ní fhulaingid Goill dúinn síothughadh i nÉirinn seal.
> Ar gcroidhthe gan ghimhliughadh is ísliughadh fé n-a smacht
> Ar gcumas do luigheadughadh is díthiughad ar gcléir ar fad
> Is fuirm a mío-rún críochnughadh ar saoghail as.[131]

Notions similar to the one expressed here by Séafra Ó Donnchadha are current throughout the period: in the poetry of eighteenth-century Séan Ó Tuama no less than in the earlier reproach of Dáibhí Cúndún against 'scum na Sacsan', from the Cromwellian period:

> ° Ní fhoidhnid teagasg ar Laidin ná ar Gaelge
> Ná d'aon bheith gasda 'sa healadhnaibh saora. (5PP p. 48)

The English are generally represented as upstarts, without culture or good manners, the crassest of *nouveaux riches,* boors with all the intolerance of crass ignorance. Their abject morals are exposed in their shameless profession of heresy; but it is his language more than anything else that is the heinous marker of an Englishman's identity. Though other traits (like their opulent eating habits) are also mentioned, the landlords and colonists are most commonly identified as 'speakers of English'.

In fact the most interesting characteristics attributed to the English are directly related to the language they employ. Their speech (both in its contents and in its linguistic medium) stamps them as uncouth, blubbering, simpering, stupid blockheads and bullies – this in complete contrast to the mellifluous and harmonious *Gaeilge ghlic* and the clever speakers of that well-wrought language. This, again, makes the poet the natural champion of his country, since the beauty and harmony of the Irish language are his particular province.

> *   The Foreigners will not suffer us ever peace in Erin without enslaving our hearts, and humbling them under their sway, to reduce our power, and destroy our clergy altogether, the aim of their evil plan is to expel us from it entirely. (ed.'s trl.)
> °   They do not tolerate the proper knowledge of Latin or of Irish, nor that anyone should be well-versed in the liberal arts.

Indeed many factors co-operated to impose literary rather than any other terms on the Gaelic-English polarity:[132] the ancient tradition of the poet as a 'seer' as well as a mentor of his nation's cultural interest; the fact that (with isolated exceptions like *Foras feasa ar Éirinn* or *Pairlement Chloinne Tomáis*) nearly all political literature written within the Gaelic tradition of these centuries was poetry rather than prose discourse or prose fiction; the fact that the literary tradition was the only unbroken link with the great Gaelic past, of which little else than its myths and its poems remained.

The implied concomitant of the Gaelic treatment of the English colonists in their poetry (that is to say: the corollary self-image) is that of a Gaelic Ireland as the heirs to bardic culture, pious true Christians and rightful owners of the country, now oppressed by alien intruders whose foreignness is commensurate with their rudeness and falseness. It was this equation between 'Gaelic' and 'genuine' Ireland that was to be passed on to the late eighteenth-century Patriots and early nineteenth-century nationalists: to the English-speaking part of the population of Ireland which at this period was going through the process of cultural-political osmosis that will be the subject of the closing chapter. A glimpse of the Gaelic outlook on this process is afforded to us by a letter which An Mangaire Súgach wrote, in 1787, to Richard McElligott (later a member of the Gaelic Society of Dublin), in which the researches of contemporary antiquaries like J.C. Walker are mentioned, and in which he reverts to a traditionally bardic idiom when explaining the paucity of surviving manuscripts:

> there were so many severe & penal laws Instituted & enacted against them, their Authors patrons, & other Encouragers; by which means they were expellced, & oblig'd to quit their Country, Family. Friends, & other protectors; so that there are hardly any fotsteps [sic] of them to be traced till now that by the lenity of the present Government, they begin to breath, & hope to be encouraged, & redressed; yet it will take up a great deal of Time & labour to collect specimens of their work & anec-dotes of their lives, & [here is a blot of sealing wax, J.L.] translations, and that by traversing a great part of the country far & near & by Improving an acquaintance with many distant Correspondents.[133]

The combination of historical pride with both cultural and political grievances is as strong here as it is in An Mangaire's poems, and his reference to the enlightened policy of Grattan and his party may thus be regarded as more than mere obsequiousness. Similar sentiments about the history and the present situation of the Gael found their way into Walker's and McElligott's own disquisitions and served to fortify the link between nascent nationalism and the Gaelicization of the anti-British stance.

Thus, a self-image of a Gaelic Ireland of ancient civilization and cultural refinement (implying as its obverse the un-Irish foreignness and cultural disrup-tion introduced by the anti-Gaelic forces) was transmitted from the bardic poets into middle-class Dublin of the late eighteenth century. A polarity is thus created and perpetuated in which 'England' and 'Ireland' are made to coincide with 'foreign barbarism' vs. 'native civilization', and with 'disruption' vs. 'continuity'.

A few questions remain to be asked. How, for instance, could it have become possible by 1780 for the Anglo-Irish to evince interest in, even to have established channels of communication with, the learned tradition that belonged to a wholly alien language and cultural outlook, and which traditionally stood in the most strident political enmity with the colonists' Protestant interests?

That question in turn raises another. Before dealing with the Anglo-Irish attitude, it will be necessary to see how bardic lore and the Gaelic heritage, the inheritance and shibboleth of a pauperized peasantry oppressed into hermetic complicity, could have been made accessible to 'outsiders' ignorant of Gaelic and unconcerned in the Catholics' plight. In order to do so, we must briefly turn our attention to the Continent and to the exiled Irishmen who dwelt there.

THE VINDICATION OF IRISH CIVILITY IN THE SEVENTEENTH CENTURY

Persecution and exile of the learned classes

The preceding survey of English and of Gaelic literature has brought up a number of similarities, symmetries in the national imagery of both parties concerned. Yet it should be kept in mind that the relationship between England and Ireland is 'asymmetrical' in one important aspect: namely, that there was a strong, encroaching English presence within Ireland without a corresponding Irish presence in England. As a result, Irish attitudes can sometimes give the impression of being more 'defensive' than English ones, pondering the effects of the English presence, themselves profoundly concerned with English attitudes; whereas on the other hand, English observations rarely go beyond the first physical impression, evince no interest in the Irish estimates of themselves, and only seldom (an isolated instance being Spenser) attempt to obtain, let alone to impart, information concerning native culture and native attitudes. The inner workings of Gaelic culture seem to have remained a closed book to English observers, as is evinced by their wholesale denigrations of the Gaelic Irish as uncivilized barbarians – a judgement wholly disregarding the long poetical and scholarly traditions that have been outlined in the preceding chapter. True, some aspects of bardic lore and Gaelic mythography had found their way into Giraldus Cambrensis's works – but, like other medieval fabulations of national ancestry (e.g. Geoffrey of Monmouth), these were discredited in the more modern climate of the seventeenth century; the more easily so, since the modern Gaels presented, to the colonial English eye, only a picture of unrelieved barbarity and ignorance, incompatible with claims to an unbroken cultural heritage stretching back into the most venerable antiquity.

As we have seen, the social pre-eminence of the Gaelic intelligentsia had been threatened by the policy of Anglicization pursued intermittently during the middle ages, at first in areas bordering on the Pale, and which had become more consistent and more widespread in Tudor times. The strident condemnation (by Smythe, Derricke, Spenser and others) of the subversive influence of Gaelic poets (and the line between poetry and other forms of learning in the 'humanities' is nearly impossible to draw in the Gaelic system) found its counterpart in an active suppression policy on the part of the English authorities against native poets and sages. The Statutes of Kilkenny had already contained a clause against 'tympanours, fferdanes, skelaghes, bablers, rymours, clarsaghers',[1] and as early as 1415 (cf. AFM sub anno) references are found to the harassment of bards by English officials. The Dublin parliament of 1435 expelled Irish poets and musicians from English-held areas, and other ordinances to this effect came out in 1534 (NHI v. 3 520, v. 8 96). The enforcement of such anti-bardic rules increased sharply in the sixteenth century; the seneschal of O'Byrne's Country, Sir Henry Harrington, was instructed in 1579 that

> he shall make proclamation that no idle person, vagabond or masterless man, *bard, rymor, or other notorious malefactor*, remain within the district on pain of whipping after eight days, and *of death* after twenty days. He shall apprehend who support such, and seize their goods, certifying the same to the lord deputy.

Likewise, lands were granted with the specific provision

> to prosecute, banish, and punish by all means malefactors, rebels, vagabonds, *rymors, Irish harpers, bards*, bentules, carrowes, idlemen, and women, and those who assist such.[2]

Such formulas seem to have been standard usage in the granting of seneschalships or sheriffships, and similarly phrased provisions were part of the martial law imposed on Co. Kildare in 1571.[3]

When the last vestiges of the Gaelic order were broken in the defeat of O'Neill and O'Donnell, and with the earls' subsequent flight to the Continent in 1607, the social framework that had sustained the Gaelic men of learning crumbled; we have seen how those who stayed in Ireland began a long slide down the social scale, ending in the general pauperism of the rural Catholic population in the eighteenth century. Many others, however, followed their exiled patrons to the Continent, where, accordingly, a disproportionate amount of representatives of the bardic families of the north-west of Ireland (the last region to succumb to English expansion) is to be found in the subsequent decades among the Gaelic intellectuals living in exile.

Now that traditional social patronage was no longer possible, most of these men of learning took holy orders, and, in a sense, took the Roman Catholic church as their new patroness. An immense increase in Continental Irish intellectual activity can be observed at this period. Irish colleges, mostly affiliated with the local university, were founded at an early date in Paris, Salamanca, Lisbon, Douai; then in Sevilla, Rouen and Bordeaux, and (the most important among these) in Louvain and Rome; then, around 1630, at Madrid and Prague; and later foundations include those at Poitiers (1654), Toulouse (1659), and Nantes (1680).[4] Some of these foundations belonged to the Jesuit or Dominican order (Sevilla, Salamanca, Douai, Lisbon); but by far the most important order was that of St. Francis.

This emigration of Irish intellectuals had two immediate consequences: first, the cloistering of scholarly minds into the 'think tanks' of the monastic colleges; second, the fact that these men, who until then had worked in a tradition that was an oral, or at best a manuscript one, now obtained access to the vast material propaganda resources of the counter-reformation, with, as one of its most formidable weapons, the printing press. The monasticized Irish exiles participated vigorously in the recusant enterprise, and developed a broad spectrum of activities involving religious, historical and linguistic writings; all this took place in a recusant framework, funded by the counter-reformation, which thus imposed on it all the general *Leitmotiv* of identifying the heresy of Anglicanism with English state policy towards Ireland and its Catholics. What resulted was a cultural propaganda war which, on the Irish side, tended to aim for a refutation of the English slander on the Irish character and civilization.

Gaelic poets had since early Tudor times lashed out against the foe that threatened their culture and its social setting; now, however, such discourse spilled beyond the poetic medium into that of prose; and instead of adopting the congenial loftiness of one aristocrat (the poet) addressing himself to another one (the clan chieftain), the tone of such writings now became either scholarly or populist. This was a profound change, not to be performed overnight; and as the Gaelic recusants were gathering up steam, and to some extent were continuing bardic (e.g. grammatical) pursuits in their colleges, the first Irish recusant writings were produced by the more urban Old English exiles. A collaboration of sorts was at times entered into between Old English and Gaels, traditionally antagonistic, but now united by their common religion and their common exile. As it was, a distinction persisted in the fact that recusant Old English tended to become Jesuits, whereas the Gaelic exiles drifted mainly towards the Franciscan order. Corollary to this distinction was the fact that Old English recusants on the whole looked towards France as their Continental ally, Gaelic ones towards Spain.[5]

It was the Palesman/Jesuit Henry Fitzsimon (born in Dublin in 1566) who opened the long tradition of Irish counter-propaganda, and even in his early activities one can see a pattern which remained noticeable throughout the century: to attack English policy in Ireland as a combination of heretical persecution and insulting slander on the Irish fatherland. Fitzsimon had been imprisoned in Dublin in the years 1599–1604; in this period he had a dispute with the young student of divinity James Ussher and, more importantly, with John Rider, Protestant dean of St. Patrick's Cathedral. Rider had challenged Fitzsimon to prove certain Catholic teachings from Scripture, and Fitzsimon had answered in his manuscript treatise entitled 'Brief collections from the Scriptures' (1601). Rider rejoined with a printed pamphlet called A *friendly caveat to Ireland's Catholics,* whereupon Fitzsimon countered with another manuscript, leading, in turn, to Rider's printed *Rescript.* By then, Fitzsimon was freed from prison and spent the years 1604–30 on the Continent, where he found opportunity to have his answer to Rider's *Rescript* printed. It appeared in Rouen in 1608 under the title A *Catholic confutation of Mr. Rider's claim to antiquitie.*

Here as in nearly all later exile writings by Irish authors, it can be noticed that what looks like a purely theological discussion is in fact full of political import. Fitzsimon's 'dedicatorie epistle', addressed to 'the Catholickes of Ireland and of all Estates, and Degrees' is already a case in point. Part of its rhetoric consists of recalling to the readers 'the quondam dignitie of your now debased countrye' (par. 11, p. [viii]), and the defence of Catholicism against

Protestantism is thus, *ab ovo,* mixed with a defence of Ireland against England, more especially of the old Irish dignity against its modern debasement at English hands. Similar elements of national pride are employed in Fitzsimon's later *Justification and exposition of the divine sacrifice of the masse* (1611), which is also directed against Rider and which is also far less exclusively concerned with theological or religious matters than its title would seem to suggest. Of equal importance is the fact that such a defence against a religious-cum-national enemy is made by appealing to a *national* community of interests (transcending the divisions of 'estates' and 'degrees') defined in its *Catholicism.*

The same pattern remains in force in recusant writings of subsequent years. Whether it was the anonymous *Breve relacion de la presente persecucion in Irlanda,* that was printed 'por el Colegio Irlandes' in Sevilla in 1619, or Maurice Conry's denunciation of the Cromwellian persecution published in Innsbruck in 1659 as *Threnodia Hiberno-Catholica;* whether the author was the Old English Wexford-man French, bishop of Ferns, writing mainly against the role of Ormond and the royalists during and after the civil war, or the Franciscan Anthony Bruodine, scion of the bardic Mac Bruaideadha family, who listed Irish martyrs of English persecution in his *Propugnaculum Catholicae veritatis* (1669) – all these writings amalgamated their religious and their national feelings, saw English evil at work both in the political and in the religious persecution of their country; and both forms of persecution were denounced jointly.

Thus, from the 1620s onwards, religious solidarity between Old English and Gaels could unite them into an anti-English camp which could with some justice consider itself 'Irish' – as distinct from older, narrower categories – and give to its recusant stance a strong national dimension. The establishment of the Confederation of Kilkenny in the civil war climate of the 1640s was the first political expression of this process, in which religious solidarity between two population groups could lead to something like a national unity between them; one of the original rebels of 1641, Rory O'More, is accordingly quoted as saying, 'we are of the same religion, and the same nation; our interests and sufferings are the same'. The Confederation likewise laid it down that 'There shall be no difference between the ancient and mere Irish and the successors of English, moderne or ancient', such differences being superseded by the fact that both 'be professors of the holy church and maintainers of the country's liberties'; the Confederation's motto *Pro deo, pro rege, pro patria unanimis* is a further expression of religious unity leading to national co-operation.[6] In the frictions of the Confederation's polarization between royalist and ultramontane trends, this union was torn apart into its constituent parts – the Gaelic Franciscans and laity (though Old English clerics like French and Poncius were with them) on the whole taking the side of the papal nuncio Rinuccini, whereas the Old English Jesuits and secular priests (but also Walsh, Callaghan, Bellings) were more conciliatory to Ormond.

The more radical, less conciliatory stance of the Catholic Gaels motivated a highly interesting book by the Jesuit Cornelius O'Mahony, born in Co. Cork. It was published in 1645, a year of fair prospect to the Confederate cause, in

Lisbon – albeit disguised by an impressum stating Frankfurt to be the place of publication. It stands largely in the Irish recusant tradition and bears the title *Disputatio apologetica et manifestativa de iure regni Hiberniae Catholicis Hibernis adversos hæreticos Anglos.* O'Mahony argues with great casuistry that England never had any title to Ireland, and even if it did, it would now have forfeited its rights on the grounds of its heresy. The author himself indicates that his book is inspired by national-cum-religious feeling:

> * Nec Angli mirari debent quod ego Catholicus Hibernicus pro iure Catholicorum Hibernorum contra iniuriam haereticorum Anglorum pugnem. (p. 2)

The religious and national categories are consistently mentioned in combination. The book ends with a similarly conceived exhortation for the Confederate cause:

> ° Agite ergo Catholici Hiberni, & felicem finem imponite operi, quod incaepistis, & nolite timere haereticos adversarios, timete, & amate Deum, eius praecepta servate, & fidem defendite, & ipse vobis retribuet & immarcosibilem [*sic*] gloriae coronam, quam mihi, & vobis praestare dignetur. (p. 129)

Nevertheless, O'Mahony's book is written from a Gaelic rather than a Confederate point of view – so much so that the Rinuccinian party was gravely embarrassed with the book and, concerned for the misgivings it might cause among the Old English parties, went as far as banning it. O'Mahony's call to reinstate a sort of high-kingship – to choose an Irish, or more particularly a Gaelic king ('vernaculum seu naturalem Hibernum', p. 103) went directly against the Confederation's main claim to legitimacy, its loyalist support for Charles I, and, though it was in itself presumably an echo of old bardic rhetoric,[7] suggested a form of Gaelocentric nationalism whose time only came when Patrick Pearse arrived on the political scene. At this point in time, O'Mahony's argument was merely an indication how fragile the community of interests between Gaelic and Old English forces was.

The collapse of the Confederation brought with it a bitter aftermath of mutual recriminations between Rinuccinians and Ormondites, between Gaels and Old English, between Franciscans and Jesuits, clerics and laymen. A printed letter by a Franciscan called Paul King, which appeared as early as 1649, sparked off a chaotic and acrimonious debate that involved, on the Rinuccinian and anti-Ormondist side, John Poncius and Nicholas French, as well as the two authors of the large *Commentarius Rinuccinianus,* and, on the anti-Rinuccinian side, Richard Bellings and John Callaghan – the two being frequently confused as the authors of each other's works which bore similar titles. Even the later activities of Peter Walsh, one of the most important Irish historians of the

---

* Nor should the English marvel that I, an Irish Catholic, do battle for the right of the Catholic Irish against the injustice of the heretical English.

° Onwards, then, ye Catholic Irish, crown with success the work you have undertaken, and do not fear your heretical adversaries, but fear and love God, serve his precepts and defend the faith, and he shall reward you and may deign to vouchsafe all of us the undiminishing crown of glory.

century, stood to some extent under the shadow of this bitter debate, which for a while re-divided Old English and Gaelic Irish.[8]

Gaelic activities on the Continent tended to concentrate on theological propaganda, strengthening the anti-English cause primarily in its Catholic aspects. The anti-English nature of that cause remained, however, despite its religious packaging: for behind the title-pages announcing lives of the saints, catechisms, explanations of Christian doctrine or of the mass, a battle was fought for the sake of Gaelic national pride which continued well into the eighteenth century. The net result of this barrage of Gaelic-Catholic propaganda printed in exile was the recognition of Catholicism as the official religion of Irish nationality, and the recognition of the Gaelic past as the root of that nationality.

The English-Irish cultural confrontation tended to adopt a religious frame of reference owing to three separate factors: (a) the fact that sixteenth-century colonial attitudes tended to deny religious morality to the barbarian natives – a tendency reinforced by the fact that the first entry of English forces into Ireland had had papal sanction based on religious and moral arguments, and that the later split between reformed England and recusant Ireland could perpetuate this colonial denial of native piety; (b) the fact that, on the Irish side of the confrontation, English national centralization may often have been recognized primarily in its immediate religious impact – the enforcement of an Anglican reformation in Ireland; and (c) the fact that post-bardic activities on the Continent were performed in the context of (and funded by!) the counter-reformation.

However, the fact that English authors had invariably described the Gaelic Irish, not only as religious barbarians, but also as cultural ones, as a people without the least vestige of civility, was an important added grievance among Gaelic intellectuals. Hence, a dual purpose can be noticed in religious writings by Continental Gaelic scholars: to reassert Gaelic *civility* by pointing at the country's proud achievements in matters of *religion*. To the dual English taunt that Ireland had no civility and no true religion was opposed the dual Gaelic counter-claim that since the days of St. Patrick, Christian Ireland, Isle of Saints and Scholars, had given abundant proof to the contrary, and that, in the heroic steadfastness of the contemporary Irish Catholics under the scourge of heresy, it was continuing that proud tradition. Before turning to the former, historical argument, it may be useful to consider the latter, which applied the recusant stance to contemporary issues – i.e. the role of religious propaganda in the cultural confrontation with English Protestants.

Religious propaganda and the Irish language

Irish exiles on the Continent did much to aid the Catholic cause in Ireland against the influence of English heresy; their religious writings were populist in their approach and considered subversive by the Protestant authorities in Ireland. Unlike the theological works which were usually written in Latin, these works of religious propaganda for the 'home front' were mostly written in Irish; they included a number of Gaelic translations of pious works originally written in other languages. The Catalan *El Desseoso* was printed in an Irish version known alternatively as *Emanuel, Scáthán an chrábhaidh* or *Desiderius*[9] in Louvain as early as 1616; the translator was also the founder of the Irish college there, Flaithrí Ó Maolchonaire – later to become archbishop of Tuam, a well-known authority on St. Augustine with Jansenist leanings. This same man had earlier, in 1593, composed a Gaelic catechism after a Spanish original. Another man who, like Ó Maolchonaire, came from a family of high bardic standing, was Eochaidh Ó hEoghusa's brother Bonaventura O'Hussey, who wrote another catechism in the Louvain college where he lived – a source-text for nearly all later productions in this vein.[10] This catechism was published in 1611, and Bonaventura O'Hussey's metrical abridgement of Christian doctrine was also to remain influential. The theologian and poet Hugh Mac Caghwell (of whom more below) published his *Sgáthán shacramuinte na haithridhe,* indebted to O' Hussey, in 1618. Anthony Gernon, chaplain to queen Henrietta Maria, published *Parthás an anma* in 1645, and in the second half of the century a number of writings by St. Francis de Sales, Juan Eusebio Nieremberg, Angelo Elli and Thomas à Kempis were translated into Gaelic, though not printed,[11] largely within Ireland. On the Continent, the printed production of devotional works included Dowley's *Suim bhunadhasaigh an teagaisg Chriosdaidhe* of 1663, influenced by Gernon's book of 1645, as was Francis O'Molloy's *Lucerna fidelium* or *Lochrann na gcreimheach* of 1676, with Latin and Irish on facing pages. An earlier bilingual work (English-Irish) was the *Treatise of miracles* (1667) by the Jesuit Richard Archdekin. This tradition stretched into the eighteenth century: Dowley's catechism was reprinted in 1728 as an appendix to Hugh Mac Curtin's *Elements of the Irish language,* and as late as 1742 a *Teagasg Criosduidhe,* by Andrew Donlevy, was published in Paris. Within Ireland, a limited number of pious works managed to see the light of day notwithstanding the anti-Catholic laws: a Dublin priest, Cornelius Nary, published, in Dublin, his *Prayers and meditations* in 1705, his *Rules and godly instructions* in 1716, and *A catechism for the use of the parish* in 1718; and James Gallagher, Catholic bishop of Raphoe, living in hiding, could publish his *Irish sermons* (in Gaelic) in Dublin (1737).

The mere enumeration of all these books – and there were more – may indicate how very intensive the production of devotional works was. By far the most important effect of all this activity was that Irish was now reaching the printing press: the Gaelic fount at Louvain, later moved to Rome, was kept busy, and also used for non-religious material, such as the publication of a few poems by Bonaventura O'Hussey (*c.* 1615). And this in turn may indicate that, apart from the obvious religious intention of all these works, a certain wider interest, an enthusiasm for their linguistic medium, was also inherent in all this activity. The added linguistic dimension is the more understandable if it is remembered that the early generation of Gaelic monks in exile had by and large come from a bardic background, where a conscious cultivation and protection of the language had ever been operative. Bonaventura O'Hussey, for instance, did not limit himself to writing poetry and a catechism – he was also the author of a Gaelic grammar, continuing an old bardic grammatical tradition[12] and transplanting it into the modern Continental milieu. This grammar was to prove of seminal importance to all later activity in the field[13] and its influence is noticeable in, for instance, the manuscript *Brevis instructio in grammatica Hibernica,* written in Prague in 1659 by Anthony O'Connor. Earlier, in 1637, one Philip O'Clery had written a *Grammatica Hibernica* in the Franciscan college at Rome, including a list of archaic words. Michael O'Clery's dictionary of archaic Gaelic words was printed in Louvain after the compiler had returned from Ireland, in 1643; his *Foclóir nó sanasan nua* was dedicated to Baothghalach Mac Aedhagáin, representative of one of the foremost bardic families of Ireland. Another post-bardic influence in this linguistic endeavour was Tuileagna Ó Maolchonaire, who called himself 'seancha coitchenn Erenn' or 'historian general of Ireland', and who wrote a redaction of a prosody by Tadhg Óg Ó hUiginn in Madrid in 1659.[14]

It seems, then, that this linguistic activity was no less lively than the devotional one among these Gaelic authors. The links between the two are manifold, e.g. in the strong commitment to the Irish language that predominated in the Franciscan college at Rome, where the students were 'bound by rule to speak Irish, and an Irish book was to be read in the refectory during dinner and supper'.[15] An especially noteworthy example of the overlap between religious and linguistic zeal is a catechism that was published at Antwerp in 1639 by Theobald Stapleton; the author was chaplain to the regent of the Spanish Netherlands, Don Ferdinando, and like many others returned to Ireland during the Confederation. He died in the fall of Cashel (1647). His catechism was a bilingual production with Irish and Latin on facing pages, and it is his preface that is of especial interest here. In it, Stapleton gives as the motive for his little work that the uneducated Irish are cut off from instruction, especially since they know no other language than their native Gaelic:

> * miserum est tot videre Hibernos, qui aliam nullam praeter Hibernicam linguam norunt, orationem Dominicam, Symbolum Apostolorum, Praecepta Dei & Ecclesiae, & caetera, quae Christianus scire tenetur, corruptis ac indecoris linguae Lantinae [sic] verbis recitare audentes, nescientes quid dicunt . . . (p. [xiv])

But Stapleton goes further; he also formulates the general principle that it is no more than natural, and generally accepted, that a nation cleaves to its national language:

> ° nulla exstat natio in universo orbe quae suae Patriae linguam nativam scire, legere, aut scribere praeclarum esse, non existimet. (ibid.)

---

* It is a sad sight that so many Irish, who know no other language save Irish, can be heard to recite the Lord's Prayer, the Apostles' Creed, the Commandments of God and of the Church, and those others which it is a Christian's duty to know, in corrupt and unbecoming Latin speech, not knowing what they are saying. . .

° There is not a nation in the entire world which does not consider it eminently important to know, read or write the native language of the Fatherland.

The equation between 'natio' and 'patria' is an interesting one. The preface concludes with an exhortation that the Irish – and especially the upper classes and educated Irish – are to protect and foster their language, which, in the Gaelic corresponding to this passage, is emphatically expanded from 'nostra lingua & idioma' to 'ár dteanga ndúchais nadúrtha féin': our own natural native language:

> * Qua ratione consentaneum est, ut nos Hiberni nostram linguam & idioma retineamus, excolamus & extollamus, quae, quod ita iacet deserta, quasi in oblivionem iret, tribuendum vitio est linguae Hibernicae Authoribus atque Poëtis, qui eam verborum obscuriorum varietate offuscaverunt; nec culpa vacant plerique nostrae Patriae viri nobiles ac primarii, qui linguam suam (tametsi olim celebrem ac locupletem) respuentes, externas amplectuntur, in iisque addiscendis temporis iacturam faciunt, maternaque lingua (quae ab antiquitate, perfectione, atque elegantia maxime commendatur) paenitus eradicata, & exterminata est. (p. [xv])

In Stapleton, a novel, more populist attitude is beginning to manifest itself. Unlike his bardic predecessors, Stapleton is not concerned with the language as the medium of bardic culture and historical continuity, but also as a living social force. Hence his remarkable assessment of the language as a central support of native pride. These remarks were later interpreted as a kind of revivalism *avant la lettre;* but that may be an anachronism. Stapleton's real importance seems to me to lie in his attempt to rehabilitate the Irish language, to rescue it from the polarizing forces of pedantic archaisms and convolution of style among the lettered on the one hand, and, in its spoken form on the other hand, a degeneration and erosion towards a low-brow vernacular. The language is defended both as a cultural heritage, worthy of interest and fosterage, and as the medium of communication between, and instruction of, a large number of people.

A similar attitude motivated the most important grammatical production of the century: an Irish grammar in Latin, published by the *Congregatio de propaganda fide* in 1677; its author was Francis O'Molloy, whom I have mentioned as author of the bilingual pious work *Lucerna fidelium.* Though in itself indebted to earlier grammars (ultimately, again, leading back to Bonaventura O'Hussey), O'Molloy's grammar became the most widely accessible and authoritative compendium of the Irish language, and was of material benefit to those non-Gaelic scholars whose linguistic interest led them to a study of Gaelic. O'Molloy's outline of the purpose of his book again mentions the language, not only as a vehicle for social intercourse and political or religious instruction, but also as a cultural

---

* And for that reason it is fitting that we Irish hold on to, cultivate, and raise up our native language and speech, whose present neglect, nearly to the point of oblivion, is to be blamed on the bad style of literary and poetical Irishmen, who have obfuscated it under a welter of overly obscure words; nor are most of the leading and noble men of our Fatherland free from guilt, who, scorning its language (which yet was so celebrated and thriving of old), embrace foreign ones; in learning these they make a sacrifice of time while their mother tongue (which is commended by its antiquity, perfection and elegance all at once) lies nearly wholly uprooted and exterminated.

heritage, and a means of access to older documents – 'sic antiquissima Patriae monumenta':

> * Multorum iniuriâ . . . ortum habuit, quòd Catholicae Hibernorum Nationi, malleum inter, & incudem diu positae, ex quo praeli introductum est beneficium inhibitum fuerit, ne dum proprii Idiomatis studium; verùm etiam publicus, imò privatus (proh dolor!) passim usus, ut vel sic antiquissima Patriae monumenta, Sanctorum vitae, Religio, Ecclesiae traditiones, & memoria protractu temporis, sepulta penitùs iacerent, & aeternae tandem traderentur oblivioni: quo fit hodie ut rudiores in populo linguam, quam non noverant, audiant; decipiantur in dies, inque infinitos propemodum seducantur errores. Ego idcircò Idiota quidem, zelo tamen, quo debui, ductus, tanto volens occurrere damno, hoc funditus Opusculum composui, tùm doctis, tùm indoctis, Anglis, Scotis, Hibernis, aliisque quibuscunque ad praefatum Idioma discendum, legendum, scribendum, debitè pronunciandum, conservandumque. (p. [iii] ff.)

O'Molloy's grammar may be regarded as the flowering of the long linguistic activity of Continental Gaelic scholars, much of which did not reach the printing press.[16] A manuscript tradition in this field existed within Ireland, too, and grew in importance as the exile activity diminished, although a Gaelic dictionary (by bishop John O'Brien) was published in Paris as late as 1768. However, the activities of eighteenth-century Gaelic grammarians and lexicographers took place within the context of an Ascendancy Ireland, in a constant exchange of information and patronage with non-Gaelic linguists and antiquaries. It is their influence on such non-Gaelic scholars that is of primary importance in the present study; and the linguistic tradition after O'Molloy will therefore be discussed further below (pp. 281 ff).

To conclude, this linguistic activity can be seen as concomitant both to the intention of religious propaganda – a type of literacy project in order to facilitate Catholic religious instruction among the Gaelic Irish – and to the historical interests of the exiled scholars: a historical interest which, as we have seen, was gaining immediate political relevance as a point of debate between the detractors from, and the advocates of, Gaelic Ireland's cultural standards and achievements. The defence undertaken by the exiled scholars of their country's past glory was therefore largely of a historical, more particularly of a religious-historical, nature. Two main interconnected trends characterize much of this defence of Gaelic

---

* It has resulted from the injustice of many, that the Catholic Irish nation, placed between hammer and anvil, was denied every privilege, yes even the study of its own language: not only public, but also (oh woe!) the general private use; so that the so very ancient records of the fatherland, Lives of the Saints, Religion, Church traditions and the memory of a long time lie buried deep and are indeed delivered to eternal oblivion. And this results today in the fact that the untaught among the people hear a language they do not know. They make mistakes each day, and are seduced into almost numberless errors. For that reason, I (though but a layman in these matters, yet driven by an imperative zeal), wishing to set my face against so great a curse, have fully composed this little book, both for the educated and for the uneducated, English, Scottish, Irish, and all others, for the teaching, reading, writing, properly pronouncing and preserving of the aforesaid language.

civility and morality: the interest in the great schoolman John Duns Scotus, and the efforts to salvage the Irishness of the great Gaelic past from the Scottish embezzlement perpetrated by Thomas Dempster and others.

Gaelic learning and the counter-reformation

The colourful Scots adventurer/scholar Thomas Dempster had, in the opening years of the century, added the final insult to Irish injuries by publishing a number of works which asserted that most matters of Gaelic antiquity pertained to Scotland and not, as previously believed, to Ireland. After a number of early works, his *Scotia illustrior* of 1620, *Menologium Scotorum* of 1622 and *Historia ecclesiastica gentis Scotorum* of 1627 put Dempster's case in its final version; such views were supported as late as 1631 by David Camerarius' *De fortitudine, doctrina & pietate Scotorum.*

Gaelic scholars on both sides of the North Channel had always agreed on the point that the Scottish Highlands had been planted with Gaels from Ireland – in other words, that Ireland was the 'mother country' of the Scottish Gaels. This version had been accepted by the most important early modern Scottish historians, Boece and Buchanan. In this model, the Latin use of the geographical term *Scotia* (and its lexical companion, the national appellation *Scotus*) presented no difficulty: it referred to the Gaels at large, and to their country, and, unless otherwise specified, that meant the motherland of the *Scoti,* the insular Gaels: Ireland. Dempster, however, inverted the traditional model – with nothing much by way of argument, except the slim and misleading resemblance between the Latin *Scotia* and its later Germanic derivative 'Scotland' (in Gaelic, *Alba,* cf. Albany or Albion). As a result, this theory necessarily threw into doubt the nationality of the two most famous *Scoti* of history: John Scotus Erigena and John Duns Scotus. Nor did Dempster stop there: his national covetousness turned any saint or scholar who had ever, in medieval Latin, been labelled 'Scotus' (i.e. 'a Gael') into full-blooded Caledonians – including national Irish patron saints like St. Patrick and St. Brigid. In short, Dempster was robbing the 'Isle of Saints and Scholars' of its saints and scholars.

The debate on the origin of John Scotus Erigena and John Duns Scotus is problematic; little distinction seems to have been made between the evidence concerning either's nationality – although the (then obscure) ninth-century Erigena and the thirteenth-century Scottish *doctor subtilis* have little enough in common beyond their confusingly similar names. The arguments pointing at Duns' Scottish background, and those favouring Erigena's Irishness, were thus indiscriminately applied to a John Scotus whose name 'Duns', for instance, was considered by the pro-Irish camp to refer to the Northern Irish county Down, rather than to the village in Berwickshire. The great revival of Scotistic theology in the seventeenth century owed much to the efforts of Irish Franciscans – Mac Caghwell, who published commentaries to Duns, and above all Luke Wadding, principal of the Irish college at Rome. Wadding supervised (with Mac Caghwell) the edition of Duns's complete works (12 vols., Lyon 1629); he had earlier published his Πρεσβεια (1624) in support of the Immaculate Conception – a central point in Duns's theology, and one whose official recognition was advocated at the time by the Spanish Crown; when Wadding wrote his Πρεσβεια he was secretary to the Spanish ambassador at Rome. And in turn, the enthusiasm of the Irish Franciscans for the *doctor subtilis* may have owed as much to national zeal (in that they regarded Duns as their countryman) as to their preference for the fellow Franciscan Duns over the Dominican *doctor angelicus,* Aquinas. Wadding himself, for instance, was also a most eminent historian of the order of St. Francis, e.g. with his *Annales Minorum* which appeared in eight volumes between 1625 and 1634.

The Irish reaction to Dempster's claims was one of immediate outrage, and seems to have triggered off a long and intensive, as well as extensive, tradition of cultural self-defence. Even when Irish authors began to write against other traducers of Irish culture – e.g. Cambrensis – the reassertion of Ireland's claim to her saints and scholars remained the central line of argument. This, again, corresponded to the primarily religious turn that the cultural debate between England and Ireland was beginning to take.

Henry Fitzsimon had again foreshadowed later developments when he proudly reminded his readers of Ireland's erstwhile fame as *Insula Sanctorum,* as the senior part of *Scotia.* He supported this boast with a list of Irish saints called *Catalogus aliquorum* (or *praecipuorum) sanctorum Hiberniae,* which was to prove a valuable asset in the propaganda war. Published originally in Douai in 1615, it was reprinted in Liège and Antwerp in 1619 and 1621, and reappeared furthermore as a contribution to O'Sullevan Beare's *Compendium* of 1621 and in David Roth's *Hiberniae, sive antiquioris Scotiae vindiciae adversus immodestam parechasim Thomae Dempsteri, moderni Scoti, nuper editam,* of the same year. As this title may indicate, Roth was one of the more outspoken defenders of Ireland's glory. Like Fitzsimon, he had links with the Old English college at Douai; born in Kilkenny, he was to rise to the episcopacy of that diocese (Ossory). In that function he became highly influential in his old age, during the Confederation, in which he took a cautiously monarchist, rather than ultramontane, stance. Roth had earlier, in the years 1616–1619, published three volumes of *Analecta sacra* (the third one known as *De processu martyriali)* which stood in the tradition of political recusancy, denouncing the Reformation politics under Elizabeth and James I. More specifically against Dempster were his hagiography of St. Brigid, *Brigida Thaumaturga* (1620) and a work that appeared under the pseudonym 'Donatus Roirk', but that is generally ascribed to him: *Hibernia resurgens, sive refrigerium morsum serpentis antiqui* (1621); he also answered Scottish claims in an unpublished manuscript entitled *Hierographia sacrae insulae Hiberniae lineamenta adumbrata,* containing a 'decertatio apologetica adversus Conaeum, Camerarium, Demsterum'.[17]

Roth also collaborated with a third important writer in the Old English defence of Irish culture: not only with Fitzsimon, but also with Thomas Messingham, moderator of the Irish college at Paris. In 1624, Messingham published what is perhaps the single most important work in this tradition, the *Florilegium insulae sanctorum, seu vitae et acta sanctorum Hiberniae*. It contained hagiographical sketches by various hands, including Jocelin's life of St. Patrick and Roth's 'De nominibus Hiberniae tractatus', and became a generally recognized authoritative source for Irish ecclesiastical antiquity; thus it was used even by the staunchly Protestant archbishop of Armagh, James Ussher, who, by the way, was a no less inveterate opponent of Dempster and that man's Scottish pretensions. Messingham's main importance lies, however, in his collaboration with the Gaelic monastic activists on the Continent, whose writings were to become more and more frequent from the mid-1620s onwards.

Messingham had met three Irish Franciscans in Paris, two of whom were of a venerable stature in the world of Gaelic learning; they were Patrick Fleming, Hugh Ward (one of the scholarly Mac an Bhaird family of Tyrconnell, who was appointed professor of philosophy at the Irish college in Louvain) and Hugh Mac Caghwell, the aforementioned theologian, erstwhile tutor to the sons of Hugh O'Neill, and later to become archbishop of Armagh. Better known by his angelic nickname 'Mac Aingil', Mac Caghwell was also one of the most refined post-bardic poets in the Irish language; and he had already crossed swords with Dempster concerning the nationality of Duns Scotus.[18] The meeting of these Franciscans with Messingham in Paris in 1623 led to the idea (inspired, it seems, by Messingham) of joining forces for an ambitious hagiographical project: to settle Ireland's claim to the title *insula sanctorum et doctorum* once and for all by drawing up an encyclopedic compendium of all Irish saints. The initiators themselves did not live to see the results of their plans. Mac Caghwell was occupied by ecclesiastical matters and by his collaboration with Wadding on the edition of Scotus' works; he died in 1626; Patrick Fleming collected materials concerning St. Columba (published posthumously in 1667 as *Collectanea sacra*) but was murdered in 1631 shortly after his appointment as principal of the Franciscan college at Prague; Messingham's role dwindled after his contribution of the *Florilegium* in 1624, and with him the Old English participation in the project seems to have ceased.[19] Ward himself was in bad health and died in 1635, but he did write a life of St. Romuald, at the request of the archbishop of Mechlin. A posthumous republication of that work, edited by Thomas O'Sheerin in 1662, recalls even at that late date the basic anti-Dempsterian motivation of all this activity, for the sub-title states that in this work

> * ex Scriptoribus antiquis et novis, ac publicis instrumentis demonstratur Hibernia ad saeculum quindecimum Christianum vocatum Scotia, et Hiberni Scoti.

With the death of O'Sheerin in 1673, the hagiographical project seems to have reached its inconclusive end. It had, however, meanwhile led to remarkable results. Though Ward was in no position to conduct any strenuous research

---

* It is demonstrated from ancient and modern authors and from public archives that until the fifteenth century of the Christian era Ireland was called 'Scotia' and the Irish 'Scoti'.

himself, he had instigated other activities in the Louvain college where he taught; his supervision of hagiographical work there was continued after his death by his successor John Colgan. Previous to that, as early as 1626, Ward had already sent a 'fieldworker' to Ireland in order to collect data and manuscript materials. This fieldworker, a lay brother in the Franciscan order, hailed, like Ward himself, from a venerable bardic family of the North-West of Ireland: it was Michael O'Clery, who was to prove himself the most important and fecund Gaelic antiquarian of the century. In his person, the confluence of native scholarship and church sponsorship is exemplified as perhaps nowhere else.

It should be pointed out that a preoccupation with hagiographical collections was very much 'in the air' in the Spanish Netherlands at the time – the shape that O'Clery's labours were to take under the supervision of Colgan is strongly reminiscent of the first productions of the Bollandists, a group of Flemish Jesuits around Jean Bolland and Herbert Rosweyde who were just then starting their (still continuing, centuries-long) project to collect the lives of the saints. Bolland himself knew of the project of the Louvain Franciscans, and although this project was not originally inspired by Bollandist motives, the form that its results were to take (e.g. the phrasing of the titles of the two folios eventually published by Colgan, and the arrangement of the saints by the dates of their respective feast days) resembles that of Bollandist productions.

O'Clery's activities in Ireland consisted largely of copying older manuscripts and culling information from them. It is interesting to see how, as time went on (he returned to Louvain sometime between 1636 and 1642), his preoccupations gradually broadened from the strictly hagiographical to include more secular history. After the compilation of the 'Martyrology of Donegal' and his redaction of the pseudo-history *Leabhar Gabála,* he was from 1632 to 1636 in charge of an attempt to draw up the definitive chronicle of Gaelic Ireland, from the Creation to the seventeenth century. This chronicle, now known as the 'Annals of the Four Masters'[20] was presumably intended as a general historical introduction to the actual lives of the saints, whose publication was envisaged in six folios, the historical introduction being the first of these; this much can be assumed from the fact that one of the ecclesiastical approbations, that of the bishop of Elphin (the very Baothghalach Mac Aedhagáin to whom O'Clery was to dedicate his dictionary, cf. above, p. 261), took the form of an imprimatur: it authorized that the work 'in publicum lucem edatur' (AFM vol. 1, lxx). However, it should be kept in mind that the Annals were written in Gaelic and not in the language of the other two published volumes, Latin. Hence, it may be assumed that they were primarily intended as the basis on which to rear a Latin history or chronicle of Gaelic Ireland, to appear as the first volume of the series. As it was, the Annals were not printed until the mid-nineteenth century. The volumes that were actually published were the second and third of the intended six; they were edited by Colgan under the titles *Triadis thaumaturgae acta* in 1647, and *Acta sanctorum Hiberniae* in 1645. The former dealt with the three patron saints of Ireland, Patrick, Brigid and Columba, the latter with those other saints whose feast-days fell in the first three months of the calendar year. Both works' subtitles spell out Ireland's claim to the appellation of 'veteris et majoris Scotiae' and of 'Sanctorum insulae'. The final three volumes, containing the lives of the saints of the further nine calendar months, never saw the light of day.

Although the Louvain project only led to the publication of two, out of an intended six, volumes, its results were massive and respectable enough to deal a death-blow to Scottish pretensions, Dempster-style. It helped to redefine Gaelic national pride primarily in terms of its ecclesiastical and cultural history; and by giving rise to the monumental Annals of the Four Masters, it was important in placing its industry and resources in the service of secular Gaelic antiquity. Here as in counter-reformation writings, then, the link between the religious, anti-heretical, and a more general, cultural vindication of Ireland, comes to light. It also implied that Catholic, anti-English Ireland is equated increasingly with *Gaelic* Ireland: Old English recusancy is absorbed and swamped out by this general identification between Gaelic culture and Irish sanctity.

The Annals of the Four Masters, sparked off by the Louvain project, are, at the same time, the last and perhaps the greatest achievement of traditional bardic learning. All its sources belong to the medieval canon of chronicles and collections of myths/histories, the most modern source being the late sixteenth-century life of Red Hugh O'Donnell, *Beatha Aodha Ruaidh Uí Dhomhnaill*, by Michael O'Clery's kinsman Lughaidh – one of the foremost participants in that last flourish of bardic 'school' poetry, the Contention of the Bards. Owing to Lughaidh O'Cléirigh's biography of O'Donnell, the Annals, as they approach the seventeenth century, grow less terse, more discursive; but on the whole they restrict themselves to bald statements of fact, with little or no admixture of a controversialist nature. The facts themselves, in all their overwhelming multitude, stand as Gaelic Ireland's claim to a long and continuous historical tradition. Their frame of reference, their perspective, is exclusively Gaelic; so much so, that they were submitted for approval to two leading scholars of Gaelic Ireland, Flann Mac Aedhagáin and Conchobhar Mac Bruaideadha. It is symbolic, and perhaps a quite consciously intended symbolism, that these two authorities represented leading scholarly families, one (Mac Bruaideadha) Eberian, the other (Mac Aedhagáin) Eremonian, who had engaged in that bitter bardic Contention less than twenty years previously.[21] The Annals of the Four Masters were obviously intended as a monument to Gaeldom as a whole, transcending the bardic Eberian-Eremonian divide which in any case had become an anachronism in the seventeenth-century context.

The only direct reference to contemporary politics is to be found in the Annals' dedication. The patron of the compilers' activities was a small local nobleman, Fearghal Ó Gadhra. He had, in an Anglicization drive of James I, been given a Protestant education as ward of the Crown, and was one of those 'civil' Irish whose position was not crushed under English rule. Next to his chieftainship of the Uí Ghadhra (an altogether subordinate clan of the Luighne sept), he held the title of Lord of Magh-O-Ghara and Coolavin, and sat as one of the few Gaelic Irish in the Dublin parliament of 1634; he was later to support the Confederation of Kilkenny and its general, Eoghan Rua O'Neill.[22] Ó Gadhra, being of undisputed nobility both in the English and in the Gaelic frame of reference, was thus a suitable patron after the greater chieftains of the north-west, O'Donnell and Maguire, had been broken; all the same, O'Clery's praise of Ó Gadhra's long, illustrious ancestry has a defensive, nearly apologetic ring to it. To cap the irony of having to turn to an English-recognized, subordinate chieftain, the dedication of 1636 is dated as 'an taonmadh bliadhain decc do righe an Righ Carolus os Saxain, Frainc, & os Éirinn' (vol. 1, lxi): the eleventh year of the reign of king Charles over England, France and Ireland. This is counterbalanced, however, by O'Clery's eulogy to Ó Gadhra's munificence and moral support during the compilation of this great work. It is here that Ó Gadhra has shown his true Gaelic mettle, has proven himself a worthy scion of the Gaelic nobility. The difference, however, from similarly argued bardic poems to plucky chieftains like those of Í Bhroin lies in the fact that the motivation described here is not a personal or a clannish one, but one of Gaelic pride in general. O'Clery seems to attribute a professionally bardic concern (the continuation of the heritage) to a chieftain/patron, and does so in one of his very few passages that have a contemporary political slant:

> * As ní coitcheand soilleir fon uile domhan in gach ionadh i mbí uaisle no onoir in gach aimsir da ttainicc riamh diaidh i ndiaidh nach ffuil ní as glórmaire, & as airmittnighe onoraighe (ar adhbharaibh iomdha) ina fios seandachta na seanughdar, & eolas na naireach, & na nuasal ro bhádar ann isin aimsir reampo do thabhairt do chum solais ar dhaigh co mbeith aitheantas, & eolas ag gach druing i ndeadhaidh aroile cionnas do chaithsiot a sinnsir a ré & a naimsir, & cia haireatt ro battar i tticcearnas a nduithce, i ndignit, no i nonoir diaidh i ndiadh, & cred i an oidheadh fuairsiott. . . .
>
> Do bhraitheas ar bhar nonoir gur bhadbar truaighe, & nemhele, doghailsi, & dobroin libh, (do chum gloire dé & onora na hereann) a mhed do dheachattar sliocht Gaoidhil meic Niuil fo chiaigh & dorchadas, gan fios ecca na oidheadha Naoimh, na bannaoimhe Ardepscoip, Epscoip, na abbadh, na uasal graidh eccailsi oile, Righ, na Ruirigh, tighearna na toisicch, comhaimsir na coimhsineadh neich dibhsidhe fri aroile. (vol. 1, lv-lvi)

O'Clery's insistent use of *onóir*, 'honour', for what I here call 'Gaelic pride', is remarkable, and recalls the way in which earlier bardic poetry could employ

---

* It is a thing general and plain throughout the whole world, in every place where nobility or honour has prevailed in each successive period, that nothing is more glorious, more respectable, or more honourable (for many reasons), than to bring to light the knowledge of the antiquity of ancient authors, and a knowledge of the chieftains and nobles that existed in preceding times, in order that each successive generation might possess knowledge and information as to how their ancestors spent their time and life, how long they were successively in the lordship of their countries, in dignity or in honour, and what sort of death they met. . . .

I have calculated on your honour that it seemed to you a cause of pity and regret, grief and sorrow (for the glory of God and the honour of Ireland), how much the race of Gaedhal the son of Niul have gone under a cloud and darkness without a knowledge of the death or obit of saint or virgin, archbishop, bishop, abbot, or other noble dignitary of the Church, of king or prince, lord or chieftain (and) of the synchronism or connexion of the one with the other (ed.'s trl.)

related notions like *uaisle,* 'nobility', and *éineach,* 'honour': the quality in a chieftain that would cause him to protect the cultural heritage by extending patronage to poets and scholars, thus acquitting himself honourably of his own responsibility towards the Gaelic heritage. Later on, nationalistically oriented scholars took the above-quoted parenthetical phrase 'do chum gloire Dé agus onóra na hÉireann' (for the glory of God and the honour of Ireland) out of its context and willed it to apply, not to the motive behind Ó Gadhra's munificence but to O'Clery's own motivation in undertaking his historical labours; it could accordingly (and quite spuriously) become a kind of motto for nationalistically-motivated research into Ireland's past,[23] thus retrospectively attributing such attitudes to these seventeenth-century scholars. It will be noticed, however, that O'Clery's words seem to indicate that he regarded his Annals as an epitaph, a last monument to Gaelic glory, rather than as a weapon in a propagandist endeavour; and this sentiment, too, is in keeping with post-bardic poetic practice in the pessimistic years between the deaths of the exiled Ulster earls and the rising of 1641. In this sense, the Annals of the Four Masters, though initiated by, and written for, the more combative Louvain Franciscans, are also a product of post-bardic practice in the plantation-ridden Ulster where they were written.

Meanwhile, back on the Continent, Irish defence against English denigrations was (as we have seen) generally embedded in a less pessimistic, counter-refor-matory attitude, and tended to concentrate on the religious dimension of the conflict. However, a more secular trend can be found within this general context, one which is at pains to disprove the English attribution of barbarism and incivility, not only by pointing at Irish religiousness past and present, but also by elaborating upon the high antiquity and civilization of Gaelic culture as a whole, including its pre-Christian antiquity. This is an important line of argument in that, from the outset, the investigation of Irish antiquity (meaning, of necessity, Gaelic antiquity, thus once again stressing the equation between 'Ireland' and 'Gaelic Ireland') was undertaken with a national motivation: to vindicate the reputation of native culture against English defamations.

This type of cultural self-defence was only undertaken after the diaspora of Gaelic scholars across Continental Europe; until that time, their audience had consisted exclusively of their fellow-intellectuals and clan chieftains within Gaelic society, who were not in need of much historical argument to convince them of the antiquity of their heritage. Accordingly, this quite novel type of activity tended to address itself to a Continental readership, the jury, as it were, in the conflicting Gaelic-English claims.

An early instance is Peter Lombard, archbishop of Armagh. An ex-pupil of none other than William Camden, and a Doctor of Divinity from Louvain, he resided in Rome rather than in his precarious archiepiscopal see, and had an important voice in the Curia, which he used to defend the interests of the Catholic Irish, especially those of O'Neill, against Elizabeth. To this purpose he also wrote his *De regno Hiberniae sanctorum insulae commentarius,* later (1632) to be published in print. It was one of the first anti-English interpretations of the

Irish political situation to reach the European public, and in parts it is directly
concerned with the reputation of the country and the people: the twelfth chapter
treats 'De indigenarum, sive incolarum dispositionibus' (pp. 104–15), and aims
to correct the negative reports that had been spread concerning them. Lombard's
foremost objects of criticism in this chapter are Strabo, Solinus and Giraldus,
whom he denounces as being fantastic. At the same time, however, the actual
content of the generally current image of Ireland is hardly attacked at all – the
individual attributes are merely placed in a different, more flattering light.
Lombard concedes that the generality of the Irish are not highly cultivated, but
stresses the positive implications of the fact that they are 'inedia & laboris
tollerantes' (p. 107) – not quite a novel phrase, and indeed a commonplace until
well after baron Ronsele's time. Lombard likewise concurs with English reports
on Irish hatred towards England, but blames English policy rather than the native
disposition of the Irish for this (p. 109). Again, Irish laziness and sensuality are
also agreed upon: Lombard calls his countrymen

> * nimium otiositati, unde cum proclivior sit quorundam ex iis lapsus ad
> venerem & Bacchem. (p. 110)

– but he takes care to counterbalance that with dwelling on their hospitality, and
their musical and literary interests; and this, once again, is in full accordance with
the English view, although men like Derricke or Spenser complained of, rather
than praised, the authority of harpers and poets. And when Lombard calls the
Irish 'tenacissimi orthodoxae fidei' (pp. 112f.), he is describing in approving
terms what among English commentators was equally recognized, albeit under
the different heading of benighted stubbornness and superstition.

There is only one major divergence between the actual content (as opposed
to the valorization) of the characteristics attributed to the Irish: while the Irish
had in English reports always been represented as uneducated blockheads,
Lombard is explicit in stating that there is a long tradition of cultural achievements in Irish history. The educated Irish, he says, 'Scientias seu liberalis
disciplinas multum amant' (p. 112). The main refutation, then, in answering
English denigrations lies in the assertion of a native civilization; and this was
to become the pattern of Irish antiquarianism of the next two centuries: to
bolster national pride by juxtaposing English oppression with a past – a Gaelic
past – of high antiquity and great intellectual refinement.

The works of a young Gaelic nobleman who lived and worked in Spain are
also illustrative of this tendency to equate a defence of *Ireland*'s moral and cultural
reputation with a defence of the excellence of the *Gaelic* character. The author in
question, Philip O'Sullevan Beare, had been sent to Spain for his education, in the
opening years of the seventeenth century, and had been barred from returning to
Ireland by the defeat of Kinsale, where his family fought on the losing side. He
became an officer in the Spanish navy, and wrote controversial books in defence

---

* all too indolent, whence they are all the more prone to lapse into love-making and carousing.

of Ireland's reputation. One of these was an attack on Dempster (now lost) under the title *Tenebriomastix,* which was drawn on to some extent by later antiquaries like Lynch and O'Flaherty; a similar work, *Zoilomastix,* castigated Dempster, Camerarius and Stanyhurst. He contributed a life of St. Mochudda to Colgan's *Acta sanctorum* (p. 4) and in 1629 published his *Decas Patritiana,* a work in ten books on the life and works of St. Patrick, with a vehement appendix attacking the Protestant Irish church historian, archbishop Ussher of Armagh. This attack, entitled 'Archicornigeromastix', describes Ussher's character as bearish (a weak pun on Usserus, the prelate's Latinized name), as idiotic, etc. The strictly *ad hominem* character of the attack may be explained by the fact that O'Sullevan Beare might not have had much access to Ussher's works, these being heretical and thus proscribed in Spain. Apart from O'Sullevan Beare's characteristically sanguine personal attacks, he attempts to represent the bardic, Milesian, view of Irish antiquity (fol. 2v. ff.) and the high civilization attained by the ancient Gaels (fol. 14r.). The author's most influential and most interesting work, which deals more exclusively with matters historical, and which had appeared earlier (in 1622) was entitled *Historiae Catholicae Iberniae compendium.* As implied in its title, the work adopts a recusant stance. It intends to obtain Spanish sympathy for the anti-English cause by representing it as a battle of suffering Catholics against heresy; the author argues the larger strategic importance of the Irish anti-heretical fight by claiming 'Iberniam esse arcem, & propugnaculum, unde Haeretici possent debellari, & alia regna conservari' (fol. 10r.).

Part of this attempt to obtain Spanish sympathy is O'Sullevan Beare's rosy description of Irish culture and character. An important part of his *Compendium* is concerned 'De Hibernorum origine, nobilitate, & sermone' and 'De Ibernorum moribus, atque religione'. The Irish are described as

> * homines animo ingenuo, & liberali, in litteris, & armis vitae praesentis gloriam constituentes, servitutem, & opera mechanica exhorrentes, tractabiles, benigni, hospitales, alii in alios, & magis erga externos, & maxime comes . . . . Sicut sunt statura elegantes, ita corporis & animi robore praediti, aptissimi bello, frigoris, caloris, sitis, famis patientissimi: calamitate invicti, quamvis enim possessionibus, & bonis deturbentur, adversa fortuna premantur, aerumnarum cumulis obruti, ammo tamen erecto, & celso, vultu infracto, & ingente prosperioris cursus spe se loetos esse praeseferunt. (fol. 36v. f.)

* men of an ingenious and liberal disposition, who take honour in the scholarly and military side of their earthly life, who abhor servitude and mechanical labour, who are complaisant, benign, and hospitable to each other, and even more so to strangers, and most friendly. As they are of elegant build, so too they are of prodigious physical and intellectual vigour, highly skilled in warfare, and most patient of cold, heat, thirst and hunger: unvanquished in adversity, even if their very goods and possessions are despoiled, they are oppressed by bad fortune; are weighed down by a mound of troubles, but they show in their upright spirit, their proud and unbroken mien and their characteristic hope for an improvement in their prospects, that they are of good cheer.

Here, as in Lombard's description, the Irish counter-image echoes the initial English descriptions – with the one difference that the general tendency is here to praise rather than to derogate the Irish character. Only when the author attacks Stanyhurst's description does he elaborate on the intellectual aspects of the Irish, e.g. their veneration for literature and poets ('observantia erga litteras, & litteratas'); for the contention that 'Stanihursti librum de moribus, & rebus Hiberniae esse fide, & authoritate indignum' (title to chap. 1, Bk. 4) stands as a motto over the entire discussion of Gaelic culture.

The attack against Stanyhurst is the more remarkable in that he, too, was an Irishman – albeit a Palesman – and a Catholic; we have seen before how he was attacked around the same time by a more Protestant Palesman, Barnaby Rich, for being too sympathetic towards his Irish fellow-papists. It is a further illustration of how doubtful the position was of the recusant Old English, and how this position was to become nearly untenable in the conflagration of the Civil War. O'Sullevan Beare divides the population of Ireland in 'Iberni Ibernici' (i.e. the Gaels, in a tautological terminology later used by the 'Irish Irelanders', and a typical illustration of the tendency to call Gaelic Ireland the 'real' Ireland), whom he also calls 'veteres Iberni', and the 'Iberni Anglici' or 'novi Iberni' (fol. 34v. f.). The latter group are also called 'Anglo Ibernes' and seem to comprise recusant Old English as well as latter-day Protestant English settlers; both seem to be considered untrustworthy in that they are not Gaelic, and a setback in Hugh O'Neill's rebellion is largely blamed on non-Gaelic priests: 'maxima culpa in aliquot Anglo Ibernes sacerdotes iure transferenda est' (fol. 263r.). O'Sullevan Beare thus explicitly excludes non-Gaelic forces from the anti-English cause. This may be explicable to some extent from his traditional (bardic/genealogical) view of Irish history, in which all Gaels are one large cluster of relatives, all descended from that Míl who settled Ireland from Spain (thus, aptly, known as Míl Easpáine); and O'Sullevan Beare's book is permanently concerned with creating a sense of solidarity between 'Iberi' and 'Iberni'. The manichean division of humanity into Gael and Gall, Gael and Foreigner, Gael and non-Gael, is inherent in this genealogical view of history. It is also this implied manicheism which makes a non-Gaelic and yet anti-English stance unthinkable: to be a credible opponent of English interests, one must be Gaelic, or at least wholly identify with the Gaels. Thus, 'Ireland' (in the contrastive pair 'Ireland–England') could become fully identical with 'Gaelic Ireland': a Gaelic Ireland which all other Catholic groups were to subscribe to in the common decline of Catholic hopes after Cromwell. In the words of Edmund Curtis:

> Milesian or Old English, Danish or Norman, whatever their origin they have all accepted the Irish legend as against the English legend.[24]

This point has been elaborated pertinently by P.J. Corish:

> The explanation of why the groupings we call 'national' have formed in one way rather than another must be sought, then, in history, or, to follow Professor Curtis's nuance, in legend, meaning by legend the interpretation placed by the community on its history, its reaction to and rationalizing of past events.[25]

And it is here that the activities of the exiled Irish scholars gain their significance: in deploying Ireland's history (its Gaelic history) as a weapon in the propaganda war with English colonialist writers, they created that very 'legend' from their country's cultural traditions which could become the focus for a national allegiance rather than a tribal or a racial one like that of O'Sullevan Beare.

The main textbook of that national legend, a history practically worthless as history, but of the utmost importance as a focusing point for national feeling, was, curiously enough, written neither in exile nor by a Gael. It was *Foras feasa ar Éirinn*, written in the late 1620s by the Tipperary priest Geoffrey Keating. Keating (his name probably a corruption of Hiberno-Norman MacÉtienne, a French name with a Gaelic patronym) had been educated in France in the years 1605–1621, where he obtained a doctorate of divinity, and had written recusant and pious works in Irish. His prose-style in other works as well as in his poetic productions (his authorship of a good few poems traditionally attributed to him is now often, and not always with good reason, called into doubt) indicate that he had undergone the influence of the classical, bardic usage of the language.[26] It was, however, the more modern language of *Foras feasa ar Éirinn* that was to become the linguistic and stylistic lodestar of modern Irish prose, much like Luther's Bible translation had been for German. Keating's work was a controversial history, written as a counter-blow against detractors of Irish culture, and gained immense popularity in Gaelic-speaking Ireland. Literally hundreds of manuscript copies were made well into the nineteenth century, and it has been pointed out that this was probably the last important book in European literature whose influence and dissemination owed nothing to the printing press. It stands neatly at the divide between old bardic learning and contemporary controversy, attacking many Tudor historians, and drawing, among other sources, on Messingham's *Florilegium* of 1624; the list of names for the island of Ireland contributed to *Florilegium* by David Roth is gratefully made use of in Keating's claim to the appellation *Scotia* for Ireland – against Dempster, of course.[27] Its influence could spread to non-Gaelic circles – initially through Latin and English manuscript translations, until an English version was printed in 1723. In non-Gaelic circles, the book met with very little credit; Keating's work was read here as a straightforward history, rather than as a controversialist compendium of national myth, and taxed with credulity and indulgence in silly fables. It is interesting, however, that the vehemence with which it was attacked often overshot the mark; if Keating's history were only, in the words of one critic, 'for the most part, a heap of insipid, ill-digested Fables, and the rest but very indifferently handled',[28] why then should its English publication have called forth such strenuous objections?

> if another new Translation of the Fables above-mentioned be obtruded upon the world, for the sake of a little present Gain. I believe that every true and understanding Native will look upon it as an Injury to their Country, and explode it accordingly.[29]

The importance of Keating's book lay not in its historical accuracy, but rather in its capacity to capture the imagination, to feed an affective, an ideological rather than a scholarly interest in Irish antiquity. Keating's history straddles the divide between history and fiction: its source tradition, the bardic lore of the national heritage, antedated the distinction between the two, between reports concerning the ninth century AD, or those concerning the second millennium BC; both were integral parts of an inherited tradition, where history and mythology are as intermingled as in Homer or Hesiod. To concentrate on the historical accuracy of Keating would be equivalent to a refusal to recognize the importance of the *matière de Bretagne* in medieval literature because Geoffrey of Monmouth does not live up to modern historiographical standards. The importance of Keating's history lies in the fact that it made the native heritage textually accessible, through the copies made so laboriously and in such great number by near-destitute scribes, in a physical act of appropriation that was in itself a defiance of the insults added to the injury of subjection and expropriation. What Keating summed up was precisely that 'legend' mentioned by Curtis and by Corish; his work, though notoriously uncritical of its source-material, is as much and as little (non-)fictional as the Grimms' collection of German sagas and fairy tales; its inspiration value lay in the field of literature no less than in that of antiquarianism.

Keating himself saw his book primarily as a counter-attack against pro-English descriptions of Ireland. He sets out to disprove the narrow and misguided assertions of a number of authors: those enumerated by him include Cambrensis, Spenser, Stanyhurst, Camden, Moryson, Davies, Campion 'agus gach Nua-Ghall eile d'á scríobhann uirre [i.e. Ireland] ó shoin amach' ('and every other new foreigner who has written on Ireland from that time': vol. 1, 2ff.). Such a specific list implies that Keating had paid close attention to English attitudes, some of them expressed in unpublished and not easily accessible manuscripts, and that he makes them, in a way, the negative source material for his own history.

Keating's main objection against these writers is that they all ignore the better side of Irish life, and morbidly concentrate on its negative aspects; his well-known metaphor is that of a beetle, which on a beautiful spring day is interested only in finding dung (vol. 1, 4). This tallies with the prevalent post-bardic attitude outlined in the foregoing chapter, which criticized the new, post-Tudor dispensation most of all in its aspect of exploding ancient class distinctions between the Gaels and of submerging the ancient Gaelic aristocracy into an encroaching Gaelic peasantry. Keating thus continues:

> * ní cromadh ar shubhailcibh nó ar shoibheusaibh na n-uasal do Shean-Ghallaibh agus do Ghaedhealaibh do bhí ag áitiughadh Éireann re n-a linn do rinneadar, mar atá scríobhadh ar a gcródhacht agus ar a gcrábhadh, ar ar' thógbhadar do mhainistreachaibh . . . ar ar' bhronnadar do thear-

---

* they have displayed no inclination to treat of the virtues or good qualities of the nobles among the old foreigners and the native Irish who then dwelt in Ireland; such as to write on their valour and on their piety, on the number of abbeys they had founded . . . on the privileges they had granted to the learned professors of Ireland, and all the reverence they manifested

> mannaibh d'ollamhnaibh Éireann, agus ar gach cádhas d'á dtugsad do
> phearsannaihh agus do phreuláidibh eaglaise. . . ní haoin-nídh dhíobh so
> lorgairthear le croinicibh Nua-Ghall na haimsire seo, acht is eadh doghníd
> cromadh ar bheusaibh fodhaoine agus cailleach mbeag n-uiríseal, ar dtabhairt
> maith-ghníomh na n-uasal i ndearmad . . . (vol. 1, 4f.)

The rest of his extensive introduction is a detailed attack on those English
historians-detractors of his country, and concludes with his intention to con-
found these slanders by a version of Irish history that will give Gaelic greatness its
due:

> * Ní ar fhuath ná ar ghradh droinge ar bioth seach a chéile, ná ar fhuráileamh
> aonduine, ná do shúil re sochar d'fhaghbháil uaidh, chuirim rómham stáir na
> hÉireann do scríobhadh, acht do bhrígh gur mheasas ná'r bh'oircheas comh-
> onóraighe na hÉireann do chrích, agus comh-uaisle gach foirne d'ár áitigh í, do
> dhul i mbáthadh, gan luadh ná iomrádh do bheith orra: agus measaim gurab
> córaide mo theist do ghabháil ar Éireannchaibh ar an tuarasgbháil dobheirim, do
> bhrígh gurab ar Ghaedhealaibh is ro-mhó thráchtaim. Cibé lé n-ab mór a n-
> abraim riu, nach inmheasta go mbéarainn breath le báidh ag tabhairt iomad
> molta tar mar do thuilleadar orra, agus mé féin do Shean-Ghallaibh do réir
> bunadhasa . . . díommoltar an fhoireann leis gach Nua-Ghall-stáraidhe d'á
> scriobhann uirre, agus is leis sin do gríosadh mise do chum na stáire seo do
> scríobhadh ar Éireannchaibh, ar mhéid na truaighc do ghabh mé fa'n eugcóir
> fhollusaigh doghníthear orra leó. Dá dtugadaois, trá, a bhfír-theist féin ar
> Éireannchaibh, ni fheadar creud as nach cuirfidís i gcoimhmeas re haoin-
> chineadh 'san Éoraip iad i dtrí neithibh, mar atá, i ngaisgeamhlacht, i léighean-
> tacht, agus i n-a mbeith daingean i san gcreideamh Catoileaca. . . (vol. 1, 76f.)

It is remarkable how emphatic Keating, himself of Old English stock, is in
identifying with the Gaelic Irish rather than with the new English settlers. The
Gaels are called *Gaedhil, Sean-Ghaedhil* or (in his poetry) *Fíor-Ghaedhil*: Gaels,

towards churchmen and prelates . . . Nothing of all this is described in the works of the
present-day foreigners, but they take notice of the ways of inferiors and wretched little hags,
ignoring the worthy actions of the gentry (ed.'s trl.)

* It is not for hatred nor for love of any set of people beyond another, nor at the instigation of
anyone, nor with the expectation of obtaining profit from it, that I set forth to write the
history of Ireland, but because I deemed it was not fitting that a country so honourable as
Ireland, and races so noble as those who have inhabited it, should go into oblivion without
mention or narration being left of them: and I think that my estimate in the account I give
concerning the Irish ought the rather to be accepted, because it is of the Gaels I chiefly treat.
Whoever thinks it much I say for them, it is not to be considered that I should deliver
judgement through favour, giving them much praise beyond what they have deserved, being
myself of the old Gall as regards my origin. . . .

the race is dispraised by every new foreign historian who writes about it, and it is by that
I was incited to write this history concerning the Irish, owing to the extent of pity I felt at the
manifest injustice which is done to them by those writers. If only indeed they had given their
proper estimate to the Irish, I know not why they should not put them in comparison with
any nation in Europe in three things, namely, in valour, in learning, and in being steadfast in
the Catholic faith (ed.'s trl.)

Old Gaels or True Gaels. The manichean counterpart of that entity, *Goill*, meaning, indiscriminately, 'stranger', had, as we have seen, narrowed its reference down by Keating's time to apply mainly to people who had come to Ireland from England. Keating takes great pains to distinguish between those Old English who had come over in the middle ages, and had since then (like himself) become wholly Gaelicized, and those who had come over since Tudor times, supporting Crown policy and Protestantism. The former he calls *Sean-Ghoill* or 'Old Foreigners'; the other *Nua-Ghoill* or 'New Foreigners'; his own group, the *Sean-Ghoill*, are at all stages identified with the Gaels, and the *Nua-Ghoill* are their common enemies. Keating tends to call Gaels and Old English together *Éireannaigh*, 'Irishmen', an interesting appellation which replaces the racial/genealogical entities by a geographic one, derived from the land they jointly inhabit. It is indicative, however, of the type of old-fashioned mistrust that was also envinced by O'Sullevan Beare, that notwithstanding Keating's sense of solidarity with the Gaels, his research for *Foras feasa ar Éirinn* was hampered by the fact that a few Eremonian Gaelic families were reluctant to co-operate with this Gall from Eberian-dominated Munster.[30]

The Cromwellian aftermath

Most energies of ecclesiastical scholars during the 1640s were directed towards support of the Confederate cause rather than towards the pursuit of learning and the perusal of manuscripts. Men like Fitzsimon, French, and many others returned to Ireland; those who escaped from the Cromwellian persecution following the Confederacy's breakdown returned to the Continent during the Interregnum; I have touched on the recriminatory debate that was sparked off there.

The most important scholar of this immediately post-Cromwellian generation is perhaps John Lynch, archdeacon of Tuam; from the fall of Galway (1657) to his death in 1674 he lived in St. Malo, where he translated Keating into Latin, published contributions to the post-Confederate debate (*Alithinologia* and *Supplementum Alithinologiae*, taking a conciliatory stance towards the Old English Catholics), as well as a controversialist defence of Ireland's character and reputation. With Lynch, however, the immediate enemy is no longer Thomas Dempster but the older detractor, Giraldus Cambrensis. After O'Sullevan Beare, Keating and others had attacked Cambrensis in the context of their broader apologias for Ireland, Lynch was now the first to come to grips directly and exclusively wih the fountain-head of English detractions; his only predecessor in this endeavour had been the Old English Jesuit Stephen White, who had written an unpublished *Apologia pro Hibernia adversus Cambrensis calumnias* around 1615. White had taught and researched in Ingolstadt, Kassel and Schaffhausen and was a peripheral collaborator in the Louvain project, which he supplied with manuscript materials gleaned in German and Swiss monasteries and collected in unpublished treatises like his *De sanctis et antiquitate Hiberniae*;[31] he was even known to, and esteemed by, non-Catholic scholars like Ussher. White's attack against Cambrensis had been mainly *ad hominem,* employing his considerable casuistry to destroy the Welshman's credibility by accusing him of mendacious and even heretical tendencies.

Lynch's attack was published in 1662 under the title *Cambrensis Eversus, seu potius historica fides, in rebus Hibernicis, Giraldo Cambrensi abrogata.* Dempster still merits an 'aside'-chapter (the seventeenth), and Lynch had previously attacked Dempster in a letter to Jacques Boileau – brother to the poet, and a professor of history at the Sorbonne. Lynch's main target is, however, Cambrensis and all that he stands for: Ireland's past and present cultural achievements are strenuously defended against imputations of barbarity. The counter-image that Lynch presents is reminiscent of that of Keating, and foreshadows similar books by Walsh and O'Flaherty. It was, however, the first time that a more or less comprehensive representation of the bardic, Gaelic, view of Irish history was published in print, other than as a supportive argument in political or religious propaganda. Even greater importance lies perhaps in Lynch's conscious attempt to de-politicize the status of the Irish language. Its usage had traditionally been condemned by supporters of the English interest, and conversely, as has been indicated, been defended by scholars working in a counter-reformatory context as the natural medium for a specifically anti-English (and non-Protestant) culture. Lynch, however, attempts to represent the language a-politically:

> *   num Walli, quod Wallici sermonis cognitione praediti sunt, Angliae principis obsequium prestare detrectabant? Armoricos in Gallia, Vascones Cantabros in Hispania a suorum regum imperiis non desiscere videmus, quod sermone a suorum principum lingua diverso utuntur. Hiberni tamen si patrio idiomata tritum & pervagatum habuerint, an continuo perniciem sui principis capiti moliri dicentur? nec aliam video causam cur illi abolendae tam acriter insistatur. (p. 16)

A similar de-politicization of the language was arrived at a few decades later by Anglo-Irish Protestants, who were to use similar arguments. And it was only by such tacit agreement to cease to regard Gaelic as subversive, that its study could be undertaken on a wider scale in the Ascendancy Ireland of the eighteenth century. Lynch's moderate, neutral, deliberately a-political attitude was the first instance of this trend, which was to prove of vital importance to the Gaelic cultural revival in the late eighteenth century – a 'secondary' revival, within an Ascendancy context, whilst the native poetic tradition was in its final decline.

Lynch himself was an offshoot of an uninterrupted tradition of Gaelic, post-bardic scholarship: his mentor in his native Galway had been none other

---

*   For did the Welsh ever refuse to show obedience to the monarch of England by reason of the fact that they are steeped in the Welsh language? We don't see the Bretons in France or the Basques in Spain deny the authority of their kings because they happen to use a speech that differs from the language of their princes. Yet if the Irish have maintained their current and widespread ancestral speech, will they as an immediate result be said to hatch dangerous plots against their supreme prince? For I see no other reason who that language's abolition is insisted upon so vehemently.

than Duald Mac Firbis, who worked for Sir James Ware, who was himself a pupil of the great bardic Mac Aedhagáin family, and who was also one of the most important chroniclers, topographers and scribes of the mid-century.

One of Lynch's fellow-pupils under Mac Firbis came from Connemara: Roderic O'Flaherty, a man who, even more than Mac Firbis, embodies the final emergence of post-bardic, autonomously Gaelic scholarship into the context of established Anglo-Irish domination, into a society on the threshold of the Enlightenment. Chieftain of his clan, bardic scholar, he was to be plunged into the deepest destitution and, as a pauper, become the first Gaelic scholar to have his work published in London – within the realm rather than in exile. It is true that the publication of O'Flaherty's Latin *Ogygia* in 1685 (presumably sponsored by one of the Molyneux brothers who had entered into a correspondence with him[32]) had been preceded, three years earlier, by Peter Walsh's *Prospect of the state of Ireland*. But although Walsh was an Irish Franciscan, his whole-hearted support of the royalist cause and of Ormond had made him an outcast among clerical and Gaelic Irish, who, being by and large Rinuccinian themselves, saw his Ormondist stance as a betrayal of the Catholic cause, and who came close to hounding the hapless friar into Protestantism. The *Prospect* was published while Walsh was living in London, surrounded by the sympathy of moderate Protestants and royalists like Ormond; and in its characteristically conciliatory attempts at impartiality, it cannot count as a representative offshoot of the native 'Gaelic' tradition:

> I confess I have taken a quite contrary course to the late *British* Writers, in magnifying, so far as good Authority did warrant me, the *Ancient Irish Nation:* which they, a man would think, made it their business to lessen and vilifie all they could. But nevertheless, I doubt not, all judicious impartial men will acknowledg [sic], how much more it must redound to the honour of the *English Nation,* to have conquered an ancient, civil, warlike, brave People in the days of Yore, than such an obscure, barbarous, vile, hideous generation of men as partly the *Cambrian Author,* partly others that follow'd the pattern left by him represent those *Old* Inhabitants of *Ireland* in their time. (fol. c3r.)

In contrast to this, Roderic O'Flaherty's history is as unadulterated a representation of bardic mytho-antiquarianism as Keating's *Foras feasa ar Éirinn*; the main difference is that O'Flaherty has a new generation of anti-Irish authors to write against, such as Borlase (against whom he wrote, in 1682, his manuscript *Observations on Dr. Borlase's Reduction of Ireland*[33]) and Sir John Temple. At the same time, his *Ogygia* is an early illustration of the high hopes that Gaelic Catholic Ireland was vesting in James Stuart: it was well known that Charles II's brother was a convinced, practising Catholic, and bardic-learning was eagerly broadening the common basis by repeatedly pointing at the Scottish, hence Highland, hence Gaelic, hence originally Irish background of the Stuart dynasty. As we have seen, the short reign of James was to prove of immense importance in the development from a post-bardic Gaelic consciousness towards a nationally Gaelic one; but even while James was still duke of

York, O'Flaherty already placed his *Ogygia* under his patronage with a remarkable dedication which began:

> * Antiquissima majorum tuorum incunabula, Dux Invictissime, Hibernia Anti-quitatibus suis jam luce publica donandis vestrae Celsitudinis patrocinium demissime implorat . . . caput cinere conspersa, Lumbos cilicio succincta, capillis a vertice defluentibus, cum Lachrymis in maxillis eius: & passis manibus Librum porrigit, in quo scriptae *Lamentationes, carmen & vae* (Ezek. 2.10). (p. [iii])

King James's reign did not last long; and in the aftermath of its collapse, the affrighted Irish Protestants took care to stifle possible pro-Stuart convulsions by breaking the economic and social position of the Catholics. Thus, with a penal legislation stripping the majority of the population of elementary civil rights and robbing it of its economic foothold, what is now known as the 'Protestant Ascendancy' became secured. O'Flaherty himself sank into the anonymity of destitution and only once again, in 1709, came to be noticed – as living,

> very old, in a miserable condition at Park, some 3 hours west of Gallway, in Hiar or West-Connaught. I expected to have seen some old Irish manuscripts, but his ill fortune has stripp'd him of these as well as his other goods, so that he has nothing now left but some few of his own writing, and a few old rummish books of history printed.[34]

O'Flaherty's reference to lamentations and woe had proved to be all too prophetic; a friend and fellow scholar, Thady Roddy, commented around the same time on the sad decline of learning among the oppressed Gaels:

> within 20 yeares there lived three or four that could read and understand them [i.e. old MSS] all, but left none behinde absolutely perfect in all them books, by reason that they lost the estates they had to uphold their publique teaching, and that the nobility of the Irish line, who would encourage and support their posterity, lost all their estates too, so that the antiquaryes posterity were forced to follow husbandry, etc., to get their bread, for want of patrons to support them.[35]

While the native scholarly tradition was thus languishing, however, a non-native, non-Gaelic interest in its heritage seems at last to have been kindled. After the initial indications of interest of Sir James Ware, and of the Molyneux brothers who were in contact with O'Flaherty, Gaelic learning was to be given a new, final lease of life within the Protestant context of Ascendancy Ireland. That this should be so is in itself astounding, given the traditional religious and political enmity between these Gaelic scholars and the Protestant Anglo-Irish. A tortuous

---

> * Ireland, the most ancient cradle of your forefathers, O most victorious duke, in the publica-tion of her Antiquities implores most humbly your Grace's patronage . . . with ashes strewn on her head, her loins girded with a hair-shirt, her loosened hair hanging down her face, and with tears in her eyes: and in her outstretched hands she proffers a book in which are written *lamentations, mourning and woe* (Ezek. 2:10)

development leads from the cultural defence of Gaelic Ireland, across the European Continent, to its eventual impact on the Ascendancy, arousing even there some sympathetic interest in the Gaelic past, and ultimately a minor revival of Gaelic learning under the aegis of Ascendancy Ireland. In this development, an important role was played by the interest which linguists and antiquaries, both in Britain and on the Continent, began to take in the Celtic languages.

The spread and development of celtological interest

The Annals of the Four Masters, that impressive and fascinating encyclopedia of Gaelic historical lore, make sad reading. Compiled with immense labour as the definitive synopsis of an ousted, overthrown civilization, in a language that was known only to those who were themselves the victims of its collapse; its information inaccessible (both in a physical and in a linguistic sense) to those whom it aimed to inform; and characterized by a bardic, that is to say, a medieval view of prehistorical antiquity which was losing all credit in the modern spirit of the seventeenth century – the Annals seem in themselves an instance of the civilization's defeat that forms their subject. And yet, their eventual complete edition in print, by John O'Donovan with substantial help of Eugene O'Curry, more than two centuries later and under the auspices of an upper- to upper-middle-class, Protestant, Anglo-Irish society, could be instantly recognized as a triumph of national historiography, and bestow on the Annals the status of a 'national classic' which they enjoy to this day.

The fact that bardic antiquarianism[36] could survive the mortal decline of the social class whose hereditary profession it had been, and of the ethnic community whose cultural heritage it contained; the fact that it could survive the murder of men like Tadhg Mac Bruaideadha and Duald Mac Firbis, or the pauperization of Roderic O'Flaherty and Hugh MacCurtin; the fact, moreover, that its insights and models could eventually be transmitted to a different cultural and ethnic tradition in Irish life: all this is in itself an indication that Gaelic antiquarian interest was not wholly confined to the post-bardic Gaels whose decline and exile I have described. Again, this is in itself noteworthy, given the hermetic and exclusive nature of bardic learning as it was practised into the early seventeenth century. The appearance of a Hiberno-Norman name like Keating in the 1620s is indicative of the fact that some non-bardic scholars were beginning to share in bardic learning. It was this spread of antiquarian interest in Gaelic culture among non-Gaelic scholars that eventually proved to be the one condition for the salvage of that culture from social annihilation; more particularly, the slow growth of antiquarian interest among the new, English-oriented and Protestant upper class of Ireland, proved in the long run to be of material importance. How these Protestants, perennially in apprehension of native resentment and disaffection, in constant memory of the rebellion of 1641, could go beyond socioeconomic and religious divisions, and take a positive interest in Irish antiquity *as if it were their own:* this remarkable phenomenon, taking place at an accelerating pace throughout the eighteenth century, must be seen as the result of various, interconnected earlier developments. One of these is the tradition of a proselytizing use of the Irish language in certain Anglo-Irish Protestant circles; another, the gradual transmission of native learning to Continental linguists, who in turn prepared the spread of new linguistic and historical assessments of the Gaelic cultural heritage in the British Isles and in Europe. It was precisely what Gaelic scholars had from the outset hoped to achieve with their work: a subversion of the image of Gaelic barbarity and its replacement by one of Gaelic antiquity and civilization – though by what extraordinary vicissitudes, none of them could have foreseen.

Not immediately influential in this process, but important in undermining Protestant hostility towards the Irish language and its use, was a tradition of proselytization dating back to Elizabethan days. Elizabeth herself seems to have had a certain scholarly, general, interest in Irish: a manuscript grammar was made for her private use by a ward of the Crown, studying at Cambridge: Christopher Nugent, future baron of Delvin. He was scion of a Hiberno-Norman family that had become wholly Gaelicized[37] and met Elizabeth when she visited his place of study, Cambridge, in 1594. In the same year he compiled his little primer and alphabet, inscribed to the queen, and obviously in response to 'the desyer your Highness hath to understand the language of your people'.[38] In fact, Elizabeth had ordered a fount of Gaelic printing-type to be cut as early as 1570, which was sent to Ireland to facilitate the printing of an Irish translation of the Bible.[39] In 1573, the translation of the New Testament was begun by Nicholas Walsh and John Kearney, both connected with St. Patrick's Cathedral; it was finished by William Daniels, and printed in 1602. Meanwhile, Kearney had used the fount to print a Protestant catechism, *Aibidil gaoidheilge & caiticiosma*, published in 1571 and addressed to 'gac aon da mbhe fomanta do reacht Dia & na bannriogha sa righe seo' – 'everyone who would submit to the power of God and of the queen in this realm' (title page). It was the first book ever printed in Irish, to be followed by Daniels' version of the Book of Common Prayer in 1608. The Bible translation also had the co-operation of Nehemiah O'Donnellan, from 1595 archbishop of Tuam (and as such the predeccessor of William Daniels himself in that see), and, more importantly, of a bardic poet from Thomond: Maoilín Óg Mac Bruaideadha, who was at the time employed at Trinity College – a kinsman of the Tadhg Mac Bruaideadha who was shortly thereafter to instigate the Contention of the Bards, and, it seems, a Protestant like his O'Brien patrons, Gaels who still persisted in their bardic and clannish awareness, but active Protestants nevertheless, and co-operating with the English authorities.

The activities of Kearney and Daniels form the beginning of a long, if inter-mittent, Protestant interest in the Irish language. In the past, historians of Gaelic culture and literature[40] have treated these proselytizing activities with a marked lack of sympathy. The argument is encountered repeatedly that this corruption of the usage of Gaelic with Protestant religion only served to make the language odious or suspect to the Gaelic Irish, thus contributing to its decline – an interpretation not supported by any evidence I have seen, and dictated, one suspects, by the *a priori* notion that Protestantism and Gaelic culture must be mutually anathema, and that, wherever the former is at work, the latter must of necessity suffer. It is this *a priori* polarization between the concepts 'Gaelic' and 'Protestant' which has diverted much energy into ultimately insignificant questions as to whether Fearghal Ó Gadhra, patron of the Annals of the Four Masters, did or did not become a Protestant while studying at Trinity College, or whether or not archbishop Ussher converted to Catholicism on his death bed; it is also an attitude that leaves little room for an assessment of those 'marginal' figures like Maoilín Óg Mac Bruaideadha, Christopher Nugent or Fearghal Ó Gadhra, who, in not wholly belonging to either of the opposing camps, could make some minimal osmosis or intercourse between the two possible.

One of the most eminent victims of this inability to see any common ground between Gaelic culture and Protestant interest is archbishop Ussher of Armagh. He has been regarded for over a century as a bigoted persecutor of all things Gaelic or Catholic; though it is true that, as a churchman, Ussher was a staunch defender of the Protestant interest in Ireland, he was, however, far more enlightened as a historian, far more tolerant of 'the other side' than the later scholars who condemned him wholesale.[41] He could gratefully draw on the researches of Wadding, Messingham, Roth (whom he calls 'patriarum antiquitatum indagator diligentissimus'), the Jesuit Stephen White ('viro antiquitatum, non Hiberniae solum suae, sed aliarum etiam gentium scientissimo') and even his old debating opponent, the Jesuit Henry Fitzsimon.[42] Ussher's most recent biographer, R.B. Knox, elaborates on the prelate's 'respect for scholarship which jumped the ecclesiastical barriers' (p. 36) with an illustration taken from a letter sent to Luke Wadding in March 1629 by Thomas Strange, guardian of the Franciscan house in Dublin (where Michael O'Clery had a short while previously spent a few weeks copying manuscripts):

> [Strange] said that Ussher had made a great collection of ancient historical records and was willing to lend this collection to him; he also said that Ussher was willing to help Wadding in his antiquarian studies; indeed, said Strange, Ussher could give more help than all the kingdom besides. Further, a certain Didacus Gray also wrote to Wadding, saying that Ussher had received two volumes of Wadding's works and, despite his profession, could appreciate them better than could most others who 'are not so sensible of the common good of our Kingdom'. There is evidence that this contact with Wadding continued even after the outbreak of the Irish rebellion of 1641 when divisions became sharper than ever; in 1642 Don Jayme Nocera, the Pope's pseudonymous agent in Ireland, wrote to Wadding reminding him of a promise to procure a Greek manuscript for Ussher. (pp. 36f.)

Nor is this an isolated example. The Franciscan provincial of Ireland, Francis Matthews, or O'Mahony, sent many Lives of Irish saints to Louvain (presumably in aid of the hagiographical project) which he had copied from manuscripts in Ussher's possession.[43] Ussher even contributed (directly or indirectly) source material for Michael O'Clery's genealogical work, by lending the Book of Lecan, an important codex owned by him, to Connell Mageoghegan, who put either this manuscript, or else a copy of it which he had made for him, to the use of his guest O'Clery. It was Mageoghegan who testified, in O'Clery's Genealogy, as to its fidelity to its sources. Mageoghegan himself is noteworthy in that he was among the very first scholars who made Gaelic histories accessible to readers ignorant of the language: in 1627, he translated the Annals of Clonmacnoise (the Gaelic original of which has since disappeared) into English. This English version – the first English translation of a bardic history – was intended for the use of his kinsman Toirdhealbhach Mac Coghlain, though not without a barbed comment aimed at those Irish who 'neglect their Bookes, and choose rather to put their children to learne eng: than their own native language'.[44] Eventually it was Mac Coghlain, though obviously not himself a great master of Irish, who became the patron of O'Clery's *Genealogiae*.

The Protestant tradition proper was continued under Ussher's archiepiscopacy by William Bedell, bishop of Ardagh and Kilmore, and ex-provost of Trinity College, Dublin, where he had arranged lectures to be held in Irish. His dislike of ecclesiastical ostentatiousness, as well as his opposition to pluralities (i.e. the incumbency of a single man in various ecclesiastical positions, and his receiving the remuneration attendant on all of these) made him certain enemies, who attempted to represent him to Ussher as being dangerously prone to popish tendencies, e.g. in his usage of Irish. Bedell did indeed steer a conciliatory rather than an antagonistic course *vis-à-vis* the rural Catholics of his diocese. Part of this policy were his proselytizing activities, for which he made use of the Irish language: he published a small catechism with scriptural passages and prayers in 1631, with English and Irish on facing pages. It seems that Bedell became quite proficient in the language.[45]

Bedell is best known for his Irish translation of the Old Testament. It was a project which was known to, and, one presumes, condoned by Ussher,[46] and which Bedell pursued throughout the 1630s with the help of two native speakers, Murtagh King and James Nangle. When the work was ready for the press, the rebellion of 1641 broke out, and Bedell died a few months after; the well-known anecdote how he was respected, and buried with military honour, by the rebels (a Catholic priest exclaiming at the grave-side, 'Sit anima mea cum Bedello!') is an indication that Bedell's conciliatory and tolerant attitude had been highly prudent and clear-sighted, rather than the form of weakness which other Protestant clerics considered it to be. Such an attitude, of which isolated instances can be encountered throughout Charles I's reign, was made impossible in the polarization of the next decades – the shining exception being, of course, Ussher's protégé Sir James Ware, whose interests were, however, strictly antiquarian and non-religious.

Protestant preoccupation with the Irish language was continued at Trinity College by Robert Ussher – a nephew of the prelate, and Bedell's successor as provost. In the words of Maxwell:

Ussher is chiefly noted as having strengthened the national element in the College by promoting the study of Irish. He directed that a chapter of the Irish Testament should be read by a native scholar each day during dinner. The twelve most efficient were to do this, and continue till the others were able to do the same. This they must do within six months or forfeit their native's places.[47]

Such activities lapsed in the 1640s. In 1652, an Irish translation of *The foundation of Christian doctrine, gathered into six principles* (by the Protestant divine William Perkins) was published as *The Christian doctrine / An teagasg Criosttuidhe* by one Godfrey Daniels, who appended 'Brief and plain rules for the reading of the Irish tongue' (p. 83–9) and prefixed a dedication to the English House of Commons, breathing a strong Roundhead spirit. Meanwhile, Bedell's diocesan policy was continued by Thomas Price – previously archdeacon under Bedell, from 1660 bishop of Kildare, from 1667 archbishop of Cashel. He encouraged the ordination of Gaelic-speaking ministers and had services read in Irish in his cathedral.

In 1679, Narcissus Marsh, later to become archbishop of Dublin and eventually of Armagh, became provost of Trinity College. Here, he resumed Bedell's and Robert Ussher's emphasis on linguistic training for students of divinity; later, he was to see Bedell's Old Testament through the press, together with a re-publication of Daniels' New Testament. In this, he was materially supported by the great scientist Robert Boyle, who, being a strongly religious man, was involved in organizations like the Corporation for the Spread of the Gospel in New England, and whose linguistic interests made him learn Greek, Hebrew, Chaldean and Syrian.

Boyle had undertaken to have a new fount of Gaelic print cut in 1680; as a result, Daniels' New Testament could be re-published in 1681, Bedell's Old Testament following in 1685. An Irish grammar was also thought of, but the contacts between Marsh (in Dublin) and Boyle (in London) seem to have been unsatisfactory, and not enough support was found for this project.[48]

The proselytizing use of Irish continued into the eighteenth century. In 1703, the Lower House of Convocation in Ireland 'passed a resolution desiring the appointment in every parish of an Irish-speaking minister', and in 1710, Charles Lynegar was appointed a lecturer of Irish at Trinity College, where the language was to be taught 'to convert the natives and bring them over to the Established Church'.[49]

At the same time, John Richardson, a native of Armagh, alumnus of Trinity College, and chaplain to the duke of Ormond, resuscitated a proselytization drive based not only on Gaelic Bibles and prayer books (Richardson himself published an Irish version of the Book of Common Prayer in 1712, and his sermons were translated into Irish in 1711), but also on the system of orphanages and charter schools so strongly supported by the Walpolian archbishop of Armagh, Boulter. Richardson obtained the help of the London Society for Promoting Christian Knowledge, but official subsidies were later discontinued, because of disapproval of whatever bolstering effect apparently such activities might have on the status and position of the Irish language. The fact that such fears existed may in itself serve as a preliminary indication that these proselytizing Protestants (though certainly not ecumenically minded!) were less antagonistic towards the Gaelic population than the English authorities would like. Indeed, many representatives of the early Patriot tradition in Ascendancy Ireland supported these plans: archbishop King of Dublin, and, as late as the 1730s, bishop Berkeley.[50]

In 1713 appeared an anonymous pamphlet defending Irish-language prosely-tization against governmental mistrust by proclaiming *Preaching the gospel in Irish, not contrary to law*. Richardson himself defended his scheme in his *Proposal for the conversion of the popish natives of Ireland* (1711) and his *Short history of the attempts that have been made to convert the popish natives of Ireland* (1712, repr. 1714). These defences are of some interest and, one feels, significant in that they attack an Anglocentric attitude that had been at work since the law 28 of Henry VIII – the idea that the use of Irish was not to be condoned since it was a hindrance to complete Anglicization. Against this view, the more modern attitude (though still convinced of the need for a religious, i.e. Protestant Anglicization) attempts to extricate the language from this political entanglement. The Irish language is now no longer equated *per se* with anti-English subversiveness; and this new awareness (echoing the case that John Lynch had put fifty years earlier), this loss of political apprehension towards the alienness of native culture, was to form one of the most important pre-conditions for the later, secular interest in Gaelic culture among the Anglo-Irish. Thus, Richardson can say:

> Preaching the *Irish* Language is not an Encouragement of the *Irish* interest, any more, than preaching in *French* in *England,* is an Encouragement of the *French* Interest: For the *Irish* Papists, who can speak *English,* ever were, and still are as great Enemies to the *English* Interest, as the *Irish* Papists who cannot speak *English.* And I see no reason why the *Welsh* Language in *England,* and the *Irish* Language in *Scotland,* should not be as pernicious to the *British* Interest, as the *Irish* Language in *Ireland:* Wherefore it is very evident, that it is the Popish Religion, and not the Irish Language, that is repugnant to the *English* Interest in *Ireland*.[51]

And, again: 'the Irish Language, as such, hath nothing of Impiety, Heresie, or Immorality in it; and no Man, I presume, will be condemned at the Last Day for speaking Irish'.[52]

Lynegar's activities at Trinity College, followed by those of the more genteel Fellows like Dr. Raymond or Dr. Sullivan, gradually veered in a less religious, more secular direction, antiquarian in orientation. An early indication of this gradual secularization of the interest in Irish – or rather, this complementing of religious interest by a scientific interest – is the fact that the chemist and physicist Robert Boyle was a member of the Royal Society in London (founded in 1660), and that archbishop Marsh was to be one of the instigators of a scientific society in Dublin on the model of the Royal Society, namely the Dublin Philosophical Society, established in 1684. Among the other founding members were the Molyneux brothers, who at this time were already in contact with

Gaelic scholars in connection with a projected natural history of Ireland. Such societies, established for longer or shorter life-spans throughout the eighteenth century, were highly influential in the slow growth of a non-sectarian spirit among the more 'Enlightened' Dublin Anglo-Irish, and, from their sponsorship of Edward Lhuyd to the foundation of the Royal Irish Academy, often involved antiquarian pursuits.[53]

A common denominator of both the earlier, Protestant, and the later, antiquarian, tradition was their constant recourse to native scholars – the example that Sir James Ware had set with his employment of Duald Mac Firbis was followed by archbishop Marsh's employing amanuenses with bardic names like Ó hUiginn (Paul Higgins, ex-priest turned Protestant, tutor of Irish at Trinity College). The ex-Jesuit Andrew Sall, won over to Protestantism by archbishop Price of Cashel, helped in the publication of the Bible by Marsh and Boyle, and the latter had, in London, a highly critical proof-reader in the person of one O'Reilly.[54] Richardson had obtained linguistic and historical instruction from men with (again) bardic names like Philip Mac Brody and John O'Mulchonri. All these were men who, in lending support to Protestant propaganda, placed themselves outside the mainstream of the post-bardic Gaelic tradition, which was vigorously Catholic; in doing so, however, they created the middle ground needed for the transfer of information that eventually was to create a new, non-sectarian audience for the heritage guarded by that tradition. The extent to which the learned Gaelic tradition of the eighteenth century existed in a symbiosis of sorts with Ascendancy antiquarianism shall be examined in the next chapter; first, the beginnings of a non-proselytizing, antiquarian interest in Gaelic culture among Protestant Irishmen have to be accounted for.

Apart from the tradition of native and exiled bardic tradition, and the proselytizing efforts preparing some sort of Anglo-Irish audience for that tradition, a third historical factor plays into the origins of eighteenth-century antiquarian interests among the Anglo-Irish: that of early linguistics, pursued mainly on the Continent but having its main celtological impact with the work of the Welshman Edward Lhuyd.

Seventeenth-century Continental linguistics was, again, often dominated by an ultimately Protestant motivation. The mainspring behind most linguistic activity at this time was the basic Protestant objective of preparing translations of the Scriptures into the various vernaculars, in order to bring an unmediated understanding of the Bible to the common people. Concomitant to this was the establishment of an uncorrupted version of Old and New Testament; a great variety of comparative textual analyses of codices in a number of languages was undertaken. The study of hitherto alien, unfamiliar languages like Iranian, Chaldean, Coptic and Phoenician from the middle of the sixteenth century onwards gradually eroded the traditional linguistic model, in which all languages had broken away from Hebrew at the Tower of Babel; in the words of Daniel Droixhe,

> Grâce aux recherches d'érudits tels que Reinesius (1637), Bochart (1646), Raue (1648–50) et bientôt Ludolf, la reconnaissance, vers le milieu du XVIIe siècle, d'une unité sémitique suffisament étouffée permit ainsi d'envisager l'hébreu dans un cadre comparatif plus réaliste, peu favorable à ses attributs mythiques. A mesure que s'affirme son étroite union avec le punique ou l'éthiopien, comment pouvait se maintenir sa singularité de langue originelle et sacrée?[55]

The first tentative re-grouping of European languages, performed by Scaliger in his 'Diatriba de Europaeorum linguis' (published in *Opuscula varia,* 1610, and influential with early philologists like Ussher) grouped certain languages, such as Romance, or Germanic ones, together into related families. In this model, Irish and Welsh were considered unrelated individual entities, radically different, each constituting a separate, problematic one-member 'fringe'-family, like Basque or Finnish.

In the next decades, Flemish and Dutch scholars, especially around the university of Leyden, developed the concept of a nordic language group which was called 'Scytho-Celtic'. This development – beginning with Van der Mijl's *Lingua Belgica* of 1612[56] and *Germania antiqua* by Philip Cluverius of 1616, also had its participants further afield. The activities of Samuel Bochart, and his attempt to relate most European languages back to Phoenician, to some extent borrowed from the Scytho-Celtic model; and even in their flimsiness, his theories were influential in provoking the retorts of a far more perspicacious scholar, Marcus Boxhorn. Bochart's impact on the Irish scholarly tradition cannot be discounted: his Phoenician theories fitted in neatly with Gaelic myths concerning the history and early wanderings of their distant ancestors, and O'Flaherty's *Ogygia* echoed some of Bochart's ideas closely enough. Furthermore, Bochart's interpretation of the Carthaginian's speech in Plautus' *Poenulus,* as representing the Carthaginian (i.e. radically Phoenician) language in a distorted Roman ortho-graphy, was to become a rather popular idea among Irish scholars. Tadhg Ó Neachtain, in the early eighteenth century, also turned to *Poenulus'* verbal Rorschach test, and in it recognized Phoenicio-Gaelic roots; and Charles Vallancey later that century (one of the last and most quixotic advocates of the Phoenician model) resuscitated Ó Neachtain's interpretation.[57]

In the Anglo-Irish tradition, Bochart and other Continental scholars were more directly influential. Ussher called the Frenchman 'eruditissimus Bochartus', and corresponded on matters of Gaelic and oriental linguistics with outstanding Leyden scholars like Lodewijk De Dieu and, through De Dieu, Johann Elichmann.[58] The friendship between Bochart and Sir James Ware has been mentioned; and Ware discussed the possible links between Irish and Welsh, and between these and the 'Scytho-Celtic' languages, in his *De Hibernia et antiquitatibus eius* – the first time, that the possible appurtenance of Irish to other European languages was considered. Ware mentions various waves of Scytho-Celtic colonization in Ireland, and discusses at some length the question whether 'lingua Hibernorum veterum . . . eadem fuerit cum Britannica' (pp. 6 ff.). In this con-text, Ware also based himself on his contemporary Marcus Zuerius Boxhorn.

This Leyden scholar created the last condition necessary for a manifest proof of the European roots of the Irish language. Boxhorn, rightly called 'un des plus grands et des plus influents linguistes de l'âge classique'[59] had begun to posit 'Scytho-Celtic' as a possible mother language at the common root of Latin, Greek and the Germanic languages in his publication of 1647, *Bediedinghe van de tot noch toe onbekende afgodinne Nehalennia,* provoking a pamphlet containing *Vraaghen aan de Heer M.Z. van Boxhorn over de Bediedinghe,* and Boxhorn's *Antwoord op de Vraaghen.* Boxhorn avoided the then common confusion of Celts and Teutons, and when he had got hold of one of the earliest and best printed Welsh-Latin dictionaries (John Davies' *Antiquae linguae Britannicae dictionarium duplex* of 1632), he realized that a definite relationship between Welsh and his 'Scythic' languages could indeed be outlined. His recognition of Welsh as a European language – meaning nothing less than the overthrow of the marginality and the isolation in which the British languages had traditionally been placed, most recently by Scaliger – was published in the same year as Ware's *De Hibernia* (1654) and carried the title *Originum Gallicarum liber;* it contained a comparative Welsh-Latin dictionary derived from Davies.

As a result, a definitive proof of the relations between Welsh and Irish, already speculated on by Ware, would now suffice to establish the historical, philological importance of Ireland's obscure 'fringe' vernacular. The linguistic relations between the British languages and the other European languages were elaborated upon by Pezron in his *Antiquité de la nation et de la langue des Celtes* of 1703, which provoked more interest in the possible light that these 'Celts' might shed on early European history. The connection between Welsh and Irish was eventually made, first by the disreputable troublemaker John Toland, and then by Edward Lhuyd.

John Toland[60] was a native speaker of Irish, from the northern part of Co. Donegal. After his early conversion to Protestantism, he studied at Glasgow and Edinburgh, subsequently in Leyden. He visited Oxford (where Lhuyd was keeper of the newly founded Ashmolean Museum) in the years 1694–95. At that time he was preparing his *Christianity not mysterious* (1696), a founding text of English Deism, and he had already developed his unfortunate habit of loudly proclaiming his controversial views in coffee houses and other public places. Later, in 1718, Toland was to claim (in a letter to Molesworth) that it was he who had pointed out to Lhuyd the parallels between his native Irish and Lhuyd's native Welsh, that it was owing to his, Toland's, influence that

> the illustrious Mr. EDWARD LHUYD, late keeper of the *Museum* at Oxford, perceiv'd this affinity between the same [i.e. Welsh] words and the Irish, by the demonstration I gave him of the same in all said instances.[61]

Although Toland, who was then entering his life-long notoriety as a subversive, free-thinking, eccentric, is here speaking after Lhuyd's rise to fame with his *Archaeologia Britannica* of 1707 (throwing some doubt on his account on various counts), his version of events is supported by some external evidence.[62] Some remarks in Lhuyd's own correspondence of the period also corroborate the theory of Toland's influence, e.g. the mention that

> One Mr. Tholonne is lately come hither (but as yet I am not acquainted with him) with a design to write an Irish dictionary & a dissertation to prove Irish a colony of Gauls.[63]

It was, however, the painstaking fieldwork and assimilative critical spirit of Lhuyd that furnished Toland's throwaway speculation with scientifically valid proof. Lhuyd undertook the preparations for his *Archaeologia Britannica* in the late 1690s as a comprehensive project on the natural and cultural antiquities of the British Isles; the volume of 1707, subtitled 'Glossography', was intended as a first instalment, to be followed by researches on Lhuyd's other main speciality, fossils and archeological monuments. In all, four volumes were planned, but the subscribers, disappointed by the non-paleontological nature of the first volume, withdrew support.

Lhuyd travelled, in the years 1699–1701, from Scotland to Brittany via Ireland and Cornwall. He learned Gaelic and Cornish, and his main achievement was the recognition of the linguistic connection between the Gaelic and Brythonic languages.

It is interesting to see how this realization draws on all three traditions of Celtological interest outlined so far.[64] The Continental tradition of early linguistics (which had exerted its influence on British endeavours from Edward Brerewood's *Enquiries touching the diversity of languages and religions,* 1614 to Stephen Skinner's *Etymologicon linguae antiquae,* 1671) is assimilated by way of Vossius, Bochart, Boxhorn and Pezron (pp. 1, 267 and III following 312); Lhuyd likewise draws on Daniels' New Testament and Bedell's Old Testament as the most important sources for his Gaelic vocabulary (p. 311). More important in his relations with the early scientific tradition among the Anglo-Irish are perhaps his contacts with the Molyneux brothers, who were among his regular correspondents and who may have been the first to propose a 'Natural History of Ireland' to him as a suitable topic of research.[65] When Lhuyd (who, it should be kept in mind, was at that time known primarily as a fossil-expert and keeper of the Ashmolean) arrived in Dublin in August 1699, he was received by the Molyneux' recently-founded Dublin Philosophical Society, who provided him with access to the manuscripts in the library of Trinity College – manuscripts which, by the way, stemmed largely from archbishop Ussher's collection. It was also this Dublin Philosophical Society on which Lhuyd placed his hopes for the sales of his book in Ireland.[66] However, Lhuyd's most important sources were part of the native Gaelic tradition – though it is by no means unlikely that the Welshman's initial contact with Roderic O'Flaherty was brought about through Molyneux. Lhuyd travelled across Ireland in search of manuscripts and of linguistic or antiquarian information, and indeed collected a good many texts, many in the hand of Duald Mac Firbis:

> I have in divers parts of the kingdom picked up about 20 or 30 Irish manuscripts
> on parchment; but the ignorance of their criticks is such, that tho' I consulted the
> chiefest of them, as O'Flaherty (author of the *Ogygia*) and several others, they
> could scarce interpret one page of all my manuscripts; and this is occasioned by
> want of a Dictionary. . . .[67]

The *émigré* tradition is also drawn on: besides the Protestant Bible and Keating's
Foras feasa ar Éirinn, O'Molloy's grammar of 1677 and Michael O'Clery's printed
dictionary of 1642 are among Lhuyd's most important sources, and a knowledge
of Stapleton's catechism is likewise in evidence (p. I after 312). However,
Lhuyd's personal contacts with Thady Roddy and, especially, with Roderic
O'Flaherty are doubtless the most important of all;[68] O'Flaherty contributed a
laudatory Latin poem on Lhuyd, which was prefixed to the *Archaeologia*.

The result of all this synoptic, assimilative research was a comparative celtological work of extreme thoroughness. One must concur with Sir John Rhys's
estimate that Lhuyd was 'in many respects the greatest Celtic philologist the
world has ever seen':

> It is not too much to say that had Celtic philology walked in the ways of Edward
> Lhuyd, and not of such men as Dr. Pughe and Col. Vallancey, it would by this time
> [1896] have reached a higher ground than it has, and native scholars would have
> left no room for the meteoric appearance of Zeuss and of other Germans who have
> succeeded him in the same field of study.[69]

Archaeologia Britannica includes the first printed Gaelic dictionary since that of
O'Clery, the first printed Gaelic grammar since that of O'Molloy, a translation of
a Breton grammar, a Breton vocabulary, a supplement to John Davies' Welsh
dictionary and a grammar of Cornish. The work's main merit, however, resides
in its first two chapters, a 'comparative etymology' and a 'comparative vocabulary' of Welsh and Irish, establishing beyond all doubt the relations between
those two languages, and, hence, the appurtenance of Gaelic to the complex of
European languages.

The importance of Lhuyd's work was recognized almost immediately. His work
was greeted by native Gaelic poets in a number of odes, and its implications were
pointed out by none other than G.W. Leibniz. Leibniz' linguistic convictions are
problematic; he stood in the 'Scytho-Celtic' tradition which allowed him to
regard Breton as closely linked to German, and to place the Celts in a 'Scythic' or
'Japhetan' descent. He saw, however, the contradictions and limitations of this
model – a model resulting from speculative and often misguided, unscientific
etymologizations that could not adequately distinguish between cognates and
loanwords, and where even the flimsiest of resemblances could be adduced in
evidence as to one form of 'descent' or other. As a result, Leibniz' use of 'Scythic'
categories is uneasy and subject to change,[70] the newly recognized position of
Irish creating additional contradictions and complexities. The doubts and

hesitations that Leibniz expresses repeatedly when discussing these matters is thus a more admirable testimony to his linguistic insight – caught in the cul-de-sac of the Scytho-Celtic model – than the uncritical lucubrations and word-games of men like Pezron.

It is mainly Pezron, who is criticized in various detached linguistic writings by Leibniz, published as 'Celtica' in the posthumous *Collectanea etymologica* of 1717. 'Celtica' contains a 'Glossarii Celtici specimen', a further endeavour to provide etymological proof for the links between the Brythonic and Germanic languages. Leibniz is here already aware of Lhuyd's work, and mentions that his own etymological specimens would gain

> * si conferrentur tum indices Celtorum Vocabularium Pezroniani, tum vero novissimum de antiqua lingua Britannica opus in Anglia editum. (p. 177)

The implications of Lhuyd's discovery of the Irish-Welsh parentage are outlined further in Leibniz' conclusion, which takes the characteristic form of a gingerly expressed hypothesis indicating necessary future research:

> ° Postremo ad perficiendam vel certe valde promovendum *Literaturam Celticam,* diligentius *linguae Hiberniae* studium adiugendam censeo, ut Lloydius egregie facere coepit. Nam, ut alibi iam admonui quemadmodum Angli fueri colonia Saxorum, & Britanni emissio veterum Celtarum, Gallorum, Cimbrorum; ita Hiberni sunt propage antiquiorum Britannicae habitatorum, Colonis Celticis Cimbrisque nonnullis & ut sic dicam mediis, anteriorum. Itaque ut ex Anglicis linguae veterum Saxonorum & ex Cambricis veterum Gallorum; ita ex Hibernicis vetustiorum, adhuc Celtarum Germanorumve & ut generaliter dicam accolarum Oceani Britannici cismarinorum antiquitates illustrantur. Et, si ultra Hiberniam esset aliqua insula Celtici sermonis, eius filo in multo adhuc antiquiora duceremur. (pp. 153–4)

Later scholars (e.g. bishop O'Brien in his dictionary of 1768, and Richard McElligott in the *Transactions of the Gaelic Society* of Dublin of 1808) were to make grateful use of this vindication, by such an august hand, of their celto-logical interest. It was the ultimate argument against all those who sought to discredit a scholarly interest in what had been, until Lhuyd's time, the obscure vernacular of uncouth semi-barbarians, with a built-in subversive potential.

---

* if one could adduce, not only the material in Pezron's 'Vocabulary of the Celts', but the recent work that has come out in England on the ancient British language.

° Finally, in order to complete or to enhance the study of Celtic letters, I think that the Irish language must be more diligently studied, as Lhuyd has outstandingly undertaken. For, as I have elsewhere argued to which extent the English are a colony of the Saxons, and the Britons derive from the ancient Celts, Gauls and Cimbri; so, too, the Irish are an offshoot of the earlier inhabitants of Britain, anterior to the 'intermediary' Celtic and Cimbric colonies. Thus, much as the language of the old Saxons can be understood from the English, and that of the ancient Gauls from the Welsh, so too the Irish can throw light on the more remote pre-Celtic and pre-Germanic antiquities of the inhabitants of the Atlantic seaboard. And if there were to be another Celtic-speaking island beyond Ireland, that would in turn lead us into yet more ancient strata.

Later research was to continue in the ultimately fruitless Scytho-Celtic model, which, until its replacement by the sounder methods of Grimm and Bopp, was to degenerate into the fantastical speculations and etymological solecisms of men like Bullet and La Tour d'Auvergne in France, William Pughe in Britain and Charles Vallancey in Ireland. One may follow Sir John Rhys in deploring this later degeneration – but still, the ultimate importance of men like Vallancey may perhaps be as little dependent on his linguistic merits as Keating's is on his historiographical soundness.

The larger significance (surpassing the exclusively scientific, linguistic one) of Lhuyd's synthesis of various proto-celtological traditions is untainted by the fact that the field he opened was later to become the playground of puerile analogy-hunters like Vallancey; indeed, the very fact that a man like Vallancey – a British officer of Huguenot parents – could make a distinguished career as an antiquary and philologist in Ireland, within an Ascendancy context of spreading interest in Ireland's Gaelic past, cannot be seen in isolation from the similar opportunities thus provided for the more valuable activities of scholars like Charles O'Conor, Sylvester O'Halloran, J.C. Walker, Charlotte Brooke. And here, again, it may be less the historiographical than the ideological significance of such activities that matters. The interest generated in Irish antiquity and Gaelic culture was to prove highly significant for the development of an iconography on which a national ideology could draw. The legitimation of that interest, both in scholarly and in political terms, was made possible by Lhuyd's scientific reappraisal of the Irish language; Lhuyd's grand synthesis, uniting a variety of (often conflicting) source traditions, provided access to Gaelic antiquity for the first time to a larger non-Gaelic and not religiously motivated audience. As O'Flaherty, in his ode to Lhuyd, put it: 'Arbiter hinc veterem renovandi *Camber* honorem arripit'.[71]

THE DEVELOPMENT OF AN IRISH NATIONAL SELF-IMAGE IN THE EIGHTEENTH CENTURY

The Ascendancy's links with England and the beginnings of Patriotism

Lhuyd's *Archaeologia Britannica* appeared in the year that the parliamentary union of the kingdoms of England and Scotland into the United Kingdom of Great Britain was concluded. The reaction in Ireland – that is to say, in political, i.e. Protestant, Anglo-Irish circles – was one of spite. Unionism had been a rather popular political idea since the Protestant landlord class had taken hold of the reins of the country, after the overthrow of James II. It was plain to all Protestants that their claims to a sizeable portion of the land of Ireland (a claim of recent date, based on an ambiguous right of conquest, gained in circumstances of civil war, subject to contradictory jurisprudence and concerning a proportion of land far in excess of the actual Protestant share in Ireland's population) could only be made good by a repression of Catholic opposition, a repression that would need the active political support of England. The Anglo-Irish of the early eighteenth century saw themselves as Englishmen born in Ireland,[1] and never grew tired of proclaiming the fact. A popular toast of the time was 'English blood and Irish birth'. In the year that the Scottish-English union came into effect, Swift wrote his satirical 'Story of the injured lady', in which Ireland was a maiden betrayed by her lover (= England) who was now marrying a rival (= Scotland). Also in 1707, the Irish parliament voiced its desire for a union with England, and earlier, in 1703 (in which year Henry Maxwell had published the *Essay towards an union of Ireland with England*), a request had been sent by the Irish House of Commons to queen Anne, expressing their desire to enter into a parliamentary union with England. An influential figure behind these moves was the then lord chancellor, Sir Richard Cox; the bishop of Derry (later archbishop of Dublin), William King, had advocated a union in 1697;[2] but the project had been formed as early as 1672, when Sir William Petty had written his *Political anatomy of Ireland* containing a lengthy exposure of 'The inconveniences of the Not-Union' (pp. 32ff.) Petty's argument hinges on the fact that the Anglo-Irish, loyal upholders of the English, Protestant interest and themselves wholly English in background and outlook, should not labour under a constitutional system devised in earlier times to keep a restive country under control – with a parliament powerless to introduce its own bills except through the English Privy Council, and with an executive appointed from London rather than from Dublin. Indeed the clamour for a union, e.g. in the cases of Sir Richard Cox and Jonathan Swift, was largely motivated by the desire to gain some control (via a parliamentary representation in Westminster) over British policy regarding Ireland. Petty had already pointed out the iniquity and potential divisiveness of the situation:

> It is absurd, that Englishmen born, sent over into Ireland by commission of their own King, and there sacrificing their lives for the King's interest, and succeeding in his service, should therefore be accounted aliens, foreigners, and also enemies, such as were the Irish before Henry the Seventh's time. . . . It is absurd, that the inhabitants of Ireland, naturally and necessarily bound to obey their Sovereign, should not be permitted to know who, or what the same is, *i.e.* whether the Parliament of England, or that of Ireland; and in what cases the one, and in what the other. Which uncertainty is or may be made a pretence for any disobedience. (pp. 32–3)

Petty's warnings were all the more justified since the English parliament, in its mercantilist protectionism, tended to curb the Irish economy whenever it became flourishing enough to represent possible competition for native English industry. Anglo-Irish business was concentrated in the areas of agriculture and trade, and had the advantage of having cheap lands and cheap labour at its disposal. However, as early as 1663, an amendment to the Navigation Act of 1660 began to curb these advantages: Irish ships could no longer engage in direct colonial trade (15 Charles II *c.* 7); this measure, confirmed by 22–3 Charles II in 1670, neutralized the advantageous geographical position of the Irish harbours between Britain and its colonies, and was made even more restrictive in 1696 (7–8 William III *c.* 22), when all imports of colonial goods were ordered to take place through English ports. Furthermore, the Irish export of cattle and beef to England was suppressed by Acts of 1665 and 1680. Although Anglo-Irish economic interests were severely damaged by such acts, there was no constitutional channel open to those affected which would allow them to influence this legislative procedure.

The first sign that the English loyalty of the Anglo-Irish Protestants could come under stress for economic reasons, appeared in 1698. As a result of the restrictions on cattle exports, landlords had turned to sheep farming, and, as a sideline, a wool-manufacture was beginning to establish itself in Ireland. As it was, the exportation of wool from Britain or Ireland to the Continent had been prohibited for some time, and the colonial trade, too, had been closed to Irish export. Consequently, Irish woollens were exported mainly to England, which in turn threatened the local wool industry there.[3] The clamour for a suppression of Irish competition was heeded by Parliament, bills were brought up to this effect in 1698, and in 1699 were enacted as export restrictions on Irish woollen manufactures (10–11 William III, *c.* 5 and 10).

This blow to the Irish economy (which was to remain ailing and depressed for most of the eighty years that these trade restrictions were to remain in force) elicited in 1698 – as the woollen bill was being discussed in the House of Commons – the first political attack from a member of the Ascendancy against British policy. A pamphlet was published stating *The case of Ireland's being bound by acts of parliament in England;* its author was the correspondent of O'Flaherty and Lhuyd, founding member of the Dublin Philosophical Society, William Molyneux – who was also the translator of Descartes' *Méditations* into English, and a regular correspondent and friend of John Locke. He was a member (for Trinity College) of the Irish parliament.

Molyneux's argument in his *Case of Ireland* is mainly historical and juridical. It adduces historical precedents in evidence for the case that Ireland had, from the days of Henry II, been a separate kingdom, with its own parliament and legislative independence, united to England only through the person of the common monarch. Molyneux thus places the relation England-Ireland on the same footing as that between England and Scotland after Elizabeth (p. 79). He denies the difference resulting from the fact that Ireland, unlike Scotland, became linked to the English throne by conquest: even so, he argues, Ireland's parliament is not that of the conquered, but of the conquerors, dating back to the Cambro-Norman barons who came over as free subjects of Henry II, conquered Ireland for him and brought their parliamentary rights and privileges over with them:

> supposing Henry II. had *Right* to Invade this Island, and that he had been oppos'd therein by the Inhabitants, it was only the *Ancient Race* of the *Irish,* that could suffer by their Subjugation; the *English* and *Britains,* that came over and Conquer'd with him, retain'd all the Freedoms and Immunities of Free-born Subjects. (pp. 19–20)

A dilemma lurks at the bottom of this argument, however. Another of Molyneux's important points in his defence of Irish parliamentary rights is that the Anglo-Irish Protestants are wholly loyal to their king and to England, their mother country; the book's dedication to the king already asserts that 'Your Majesty has not in all Your Dominions a People more *United* and *Steady* to your Interest, than the *Protestants* of *Ireland*' (fol. a3 r.). This attitude in contemporary matters is irreconcilable to Molyneux's historical invocation of the medieval rights of the Old English: for those Old English who had established parliamentiary practice in Ireland had, by and large, remained Catholic and pro-Stuart, and had become united with their fellow-Catholic, Gaelic compatriots. Elsewhere (pp. 18–19), Molyneux argues that the Irish population had, since the conquest, amalgamated into one whole, on the basis of which the more recently arrived Protestant Anglo-Irish can claim to share in the political rights of the other Irishmen; but that, again, threatens the basis of Molyneux's identification of the Anglo-Irish, not with the other, unruly Irish, but rather with the English interest.

This dilemma is basic to the Anglo-Irish position, and from it follows the entire ambiguity of Anglo-Irish policy during the eighteenth century: the Ascendancy can claim the rights both of loyal English subjects (on the basis of their Protestantism and their role in guarding the Protestant, English interest in an unruly country) and of citizens of the Kingdom of Ireland, whose interests are at variance with those of Britain in matters of trade and industry.

The implication is momentous indeed. Occasionally, the Anglo-Irish Ascendancy asserted interests that contravened those of the constituents of the

British parliament. In the assertion of those interests, and in their vindication, the Anglo-Irish drew on a pre-Reformation Irish tradition of jurisprudence or political practice – i.e. a tradition that antedated their own presence in the Irish kingdom; that, again, is tantamount to saying that the Anglo-Irish could place themselves in the position of heirs to a tradition that was historically, *sua natura,* anti-English. It is from this infinitesimal shift, that the widening gap between Anglo-Irish and English interests could eventually lead to a growing identification with a *Gaelic* Ireland (which had meanwhile absorbed the remaining Catholic Old English).

Molyneux's own book stands out as the very beginning of this process, and itself furnishes an illustration of it: for Molyneux's own argument was not wholly new. It had been brought up in the pre-Rebellion Irish parliament of 1641, where it was defended with vigour and ability by the Old English, Catholic lawyer Patrick Darcy. Darcy was later to become one of the leading Ormondite politicians in the Confederation of Kilkenny, and it was under the Confederacy's auspices that Darcy's *Argument* was printed in 1643. In this respect, Molyneux's own book stands in an Old English, Catholic, anti-English tradition – though its author might have been aghast at the thought had he been told so. The point was made in one of the more level-headed critiques elicited by Molyneux's *Case of Ireland, An answer to Mr. Molyneux,* where the writer observed astutely that, going by Molyneux's argument, the Irish parliament should be filled with Old English – renegades, Jacobites, Gaelicized papists all. This rejoinder was only one instance of the indignation with which Molyneux's book was greeted in England[4] – including parliamentary condemnation. In Ireland, however, it was to be reprinted repeatedly in the next years – a fifth time, significantly, during the scandal around Wood's Halfpence. This divergence between the book's reception in England and in Ireland indicates that no complete concord existed between English and Anglo-Irish opinion; the strenuous protestations of loyalty on the part of the latter did not stifle their sense of grievance. It is to this background that the intensive demand for a parliamentary union must be seen: not only as an expression of loyalty, but equally as a redress of grievances. It is no coincidence that the most important supporter of a parliamentary union, Sir Richard Cox, was also the author of one of the few pamphlets surrounding the Woollen Act overtly taking Molyneux's side: *Some thoughts on the bill for prohibiting the exportation of woollen manufactures.* Here, he complains of the unfair treatment meted out to the Anglo-Irish,

> an unhappy Nation, who in the cause, and for the sake of *England* have lost their Fathers, their Children, their Brothers, their Relations. . . . . They are Englishmen sent over to conquer *Ireland,* your Countrymen, your Brothers, your Sons, your Relations, your Acquaintance; governed by the same King, the same Laws; of the same Religion, in the same Interest, and equally engaged in the common cause of Liberty. (p. 16)

One Sir Walter Harris had also contrasted loyalty with unfair treatment, in pointing out

> That it seems hard, that an English man, because he goes to inhabit in *Ireland,* or is sent thither to help to secure that Conquest to *England,* should therefore lose a great part of the Priviledge of an *English man,* and be treated as a Forreigner. (p. 36)

And in 1704, Cox went as far as to warn the earl of Nottingham, that, if this grievance were not redressed, loyalty must as a result suffer:

> if the English here feel themselves oppressed, they will return to their mother country, as many as are able; and the rest, prompted by indignation, necessity, or despair, will turn Scotch or Irish. There is no remedy so proper for both kingdoms, as some sort of union which would enrich and strengthen England, and establish the English interest here, and make it prosper.[5]

The real importance of Molyneux's *Case* transcends, however, the field of colonial relations with the mother country. It did not only address the rights of the Anglo-Irish as upholders of the English interest in Ireland, but also as members of a commonwealth. In fact, Molyneux's book may count as one of the first instances of the effect of Enlightenment thought on the British political scene. Apart from historical and juridical arguments, Molyneux also addresses the question of the relationship between an individual's reliance on, and his privileges under, government authority. Molyneux no longer sees government authority as the self-evident and inevitable concomitant of a social community of individuals (as Hobbes had done) but considers it in constant need of being justified through its serviceableness to that social community, to the common good. As a result, legislation does not derive its authority from the mere fact that it emanates from the government, but from the fact that it serves the public good entrusted to that government. Such proto-liberal axioms crop up time and again in Molyneux's argument; there are frequent shifts in perspective from British politics to general political theory:

> That *Ireland* should be bound by Acts of Parliament made in *England,* is against Reason, and the Common Rights of all Mankind. All men are by Nature in a State of Equality, in Respect of Jurisdiction or Dominion: this I take to be a Principle in it self so evident, that it stands in need of little Proof. (p. 150)

Equally frequently, 'Laws of Nature and Nations' are invoked in order to support one's right 'of being Subject *Only* to such Laws to which Men give their *Own Consent*'. This maxim is considered

> so inherent to all Mankind, and founded on such Immutable Laws of Nature and Reason, that 'tis not to be *Alien'd,* or *Given up,* by any Body of Men whatsoever. For the End of all Government and Laws being the Publick Good of the Common-wealth, in the Peace, Tranquillity and Ease of every Member therein; whatsoever Act is contrary to this End, is in it self void, and of no effect. (p. 123)

Passages like these clearly show the influence of Molyneux's ideological source: the second *Treatise on government* by his friend John Locke. It was Locke who had added the cautionary qualification 'and all this only for the Publick Good' to his definition of 'power';[6] it was Locke who had imposed on every law, as the condition 'which is absolutely necessary to its being a law',

> *the consent of the Society,* over whom no Body can have a power to make Laws, but by their own Consent, and by Authority received from them. (p. 374)

A number of Molyneux's more specific arguments (e.g. the basic human equality as exemplified in people's equal conditions at the moment of birth, or concerning the lawfulness of the right of conquest[7]) echo Locke's *Treatise* nearly verbatim. The most obvious discrepancy between the two is linked to the dilemma underlying Anglo-Irish political claims which I have outlined previously; whereas Locke gives a detailed discussion of the implications of the possibility 'that the Conquerors and Conquered never incorporate into one People, under the same Laws and Freedom' (chapter heading, p. 405), the problem is largely avoided by Molyneux.

Although Locke never openly admitted his authorship of the *Treatise* – not even in his letters to Molyneux[8] – and although the philosopher consequently never came to the support of his friend's *Case,* his influence on Anglo-Irish political thought was to remain a constant and increasingly influential force throughout the following century.[9]

Molyneux's *Case* proved its continuing topicality around 1719. One of the corollary questions in its argument had been whether the judicial authority of the English House of Lords could, in Irish cases, equal or possibly even surpass that of the Irish Upper House. In 1698, the question was topical because of a legal conflict involving a member of the spiritual nobility: archbishop King of Dublin. Another case in 1719, with both Houses of Lords asserting their superior authority in jurisdiction, led to the Declaratory Act of 1720 (6 George I c. 5), whereby the British parliament in so many words laid claim to the right to legislate for Ireland.

Meanwhile, the Irish economy was in a steady decline. After a devaluation of Irish money in 1701[10] and as a result of the trade restrictions (ineffectually counteracted by attempts to stimulate a domestic linen industry), the Irish economy began to stagnate; forced unemployment among the Gaelic Irish grew, and in turn contributed to an alarming increase in the number of beggars. Not only sluggish external trade, but also the fact that many landlords chose to live in England, thus spending their Irish incomes outside the country, was a steady drain on the financial resources of the kingdom, and a shortage of coin became noticeable. English policy did little to help: many official Irish posts were given to Englishmen (who resided little, or not at all, in the country), often as sinecures. Irish pensions – not subject to the scrutiny of the Westminster parliament – were convenient for 'discreet' purposes such as the upkeep of royal mistresses etc.

These developments provoked the reaction of men who were often inspired by Locke's political ideas, the precursors of the Patriots whose heyday came later that century. A terminological clarification may be in order here.

The words 'patriot' and 'patriotism' nowadays have a distinctly nationalistic connotation, referring to one's devotion to the honour and reputation of one's fatherland, to one's readiness to defend and enhance its honour and reputation. In present-day general usage, 'patriotism' is nothing more, or less, than a euphemistic, de-politicized, toned-down equivalent of 'nationalism'. This modern meaning did not inhere in the term in the early and middle eighteenth century. In those years, patriotism was rather a form of political philanthropy: a desire to contribute to the public benefit, to live up to one's responsibilities as a citizen by contributing actively to the improvement of society – of the *state*, as a political and economic entity, that is, not the affective *fatherland* which has since become the object of modern 'patriotic' feelings. Bishop Berkeley defined it succinctly in his *Maxims concerning patriotism* of 1750:

> A patriot is one who heartily wisheth the public prosperity, and doth not only wish, but also study and endeavour to promote it.[11]

This sense of civic responsibility often expressed itself in projects of general profit, aimed at improving public health, economy, agriculture, cultural life, etc. It also included a middle-class sense of distrust for aristocratic corruption, linked to a desire to promote virtue, especially in the exercise of public office. In this more libertarian sense, its ideas were propounded in Bolingbroke's essay *On the spirit of patriotism* and on *The idea of a patriot king*, published in 1749 but written in 1736–8. Here, Patriotism meets the liberalism of those 'Commonwealth-men' like Molesworth, who followed Locke's political ideas most radically.[12] This is the sense (the libertarian, anti-aristocratic connotation) which one can recognize in the *patriotisme* that was an alternative term for revolutionary zeal in post-1789 France, or in the lines of Scott,

> His was the patriot's burning thought,
> Of freedom's battle bravely fought.[13]

Similarly, under the stadholdership of William V, the bourgeois anti-Orangists of the United Provinces called themselves 'patriotten', in recognition of a liberalism that they shared with the early, moderate revolutionaries in France, the American founding fathers, and, indeed, the Irish Patriots around Grattan: one of public virtue and accountability, of opposition against corrupt power-politics and against neglect of the public good for private interest.[14]

Patriotism was, in the earlier decades of the eighteenth century, largely concerned with economic problems. One of the more important causes of the Irish recession was the stagnation of external trade and this was a matter which could be addressed without prejudice to Anglo-Irish loyalty towards England. Rather than blame unsatisfactory foreign trade on English restrictions on Irish exports, attention was paid to the large imports of what was considered luxurious extravagance; as early as 1673, Sir William Temple had written to the then lord lieutenant, Essex, on the necessity 'to introduce, as far as can be, a vein of parsimony throughout the country, in all things that are not perfectly the native growths and manufactures'.[15] Such sentiments were not contrary to the English interest; Temple could even go on in the same letter to announce – one is struck by the early date, and the great diplomat's foresight – that the Irish woollen industry 'seems not fit to be encouraged' (p. 14).

The idea of a drive towards the consumption of home goods only was espoused mainly by Temple's erstwhile secretary Swift, who remained a staunch defender of this autarkist attitude throughout his career. Characteristically, Swift is much more controversial than his more philanthropic fellow-Patriots. He was to write to Pope that he did not deserve the appellation of Patriot, since his motivation was not philanthropy, but rather his characteristic *saeva indignatio*:

> I do profess without affectation, that your kind opinion of me as a Patriot (since you call it so) is what I do not deserve; because what I do is owing to perfect rage and resentment, and the mortifying sight of slavery, folly, and baseness about me, among which I am forced to live.[16]

Accordingly, Swift's *Proposal for the universal use of Irish manufacture* is in fact an anti-English (or rather, anti-English-Whig-government) pamphlet, a proposal for the universal disuse of English manufacture; for its own subtitle already specifies the use of Irish goods as 'utterly rejecting and renouncing every thing wearable that comes from England'. The famous exhortation to 'burn every Thing that came from England, except their *People* and their *Coals*' was coined here.[17]

Swift's contemporaries were more cautious and less political, and always took care not to offend British feelings. How difficult this must have been is aptly illustrated by Samuel Madden's collection of *Reflections and Resolutions* aimed at Irish gentlemen, upon whom it tried to inculcate Patriot principles in the form of 'good resolutions'. These principles emphatically included solidarity with the English interest: 'We will ever sincerely wish for, consult, and promote the Happiness and Welfare of *Great Britain* as our common Parent' (p. 107); 'That we will be so true to ourselves as never to hurt the Trade or Interest of *Great Britain*' (p. 109). And yet – a resolution like the following strikes one as odd:

> We resolve, as we will never forget what we owe to *England*, so we will ever hope that she will remember what Benefit and Advantage she does, or may receive, by encouraging us. (p. 111)

This exhortation is clearly aimed at an English conscience; but it is disguised as a proposal for Anglo-Irish reflection, and the cramped attitude of an Anglo-Irish Patriot who does not dare to criticize un-Patriotic English protectionism is reflected in the cramped syntax which disguises an exhortation to England in reflexive terms, addressed at an Ireland that 'resolves to hope that England will remember'.

The cautiousness of early Patriots like Madden seems to have avoided critical political issues by concentrating on the desirability of import limitations, particularly concerning imports from the Catholic enemy, France or the Spanish

Netherlands. Most importantly, the import of claret (which must indeed have been sizeable[18]) was repeatedly denounced as extravagant and injurious to the country – one of the origins, perhaps, of the later image of the hard-drinking Irish squire. Flemish linen was decried on similar grounds. As early as 1691, the anonymous *Remarks on the affairs and trade of England and Ireland* (by Sir Walter Harris) denounced the importation of French wine and Flemish linen. Such restrictions on the importation (or rather, the consumption) of Continental goods was repeatedly represented as an alternative to anti-English grumblings against the effects of the Woollen Act. Thus, Berkeley's *Querist* asked

> Whether it would not be more prudent, to strike and exert ourselves in permitted branches of trade, than to fold our hands, and repine that we are not allowed the woollen?[19]

Similarly, Arthur Dobbs:

> And instead of being Splenatick or grumbling at any Restrictions put upon us by our Ancestors, let us endeavour to promote the enjoyment of what we have with pleasure and satisfaction; that we may all in our several spheres chearfully contribute to support the Power, Wealth, Fame and Commerce of the British Empire, of which *Ireland* is no inconsiderable member.[20]

With the exception of Swift's *démarche*, the use of Irish goods was to remain an issue without anti-British connotations, a pure ideal of public spirit in Ireland throughout the century. In 1703, 1705, and once again in 1707, the Irish House of Commons passed unanimously, that

> it would greatly conduce to the relief of the poor and the good of the kingdom, that the inhabitants thereof should use none other but the manufactures of this kingdom in their apparel and the furniture of their houses.[21]

– and well into the century, *soirées* could be held 'where the ladies and gentlemen will appear in fancied habits of Irish manufacture'.[22] Swift contributed a further pamphlet on the topic (*A proposal that all ladies should appear constantly in Irish manufacture,* 1729), and Richard Dickson's newspaper *The Dublin intelligence* was around the same time beginning its denunciation of the use of foreign silk. In 1735, the *Dublin evening post* reported that enraged Dublin weavers had rioted and taken to squirting aqua fortis on any gowns and petticoats made of India silk or calico. Samuel Madden's *Letter to the Dublin Society* of 1739 mentioned proudly on its title-page that it had been 'Printed on *Irish* Paper'.[23]

Another key issue, conveniently 'neutral' in political terms, was the improvement of agriculture. Arthur Dobbs,[24] member of the Irish parliament, drafted, in 1732, an important bill to this effect; earlier, the Irish commonwealth-man Molesworth, friend of Molyneux and of Toland, had published his *Considerations for the promoting of agriculture* (1723), as a result of which, Swift was to inscribe one of his Drapier's Letters to him. But the most important step in the improvement of agriculture was taken by Swift's (and Berkeley's) friend Thomas Prior,[25] who, in 1731, founded the Dublin Society, for the promotion of husbandry, manufacture, science and the useful arts. Other founding members were Dobbs and Madden. The later influence of this body (the present Royal Dublin Society, one of the first of its kind in Europe) is incalculable. It was, in a sense, also a continuation of the Dublin Philosophical Society, and was later to stand godfather to the fledgeling Royal Irish Academy; in this sense, on the institutional level, it reflects a development from early scientific rationalism via economic Patriotism to antiquarian and literary interest in early Ireland. The Dublin Society's members also included Sir Thomas Molyneux, William Molyneux's brother; affiliated with it, through his friendship with Prior, was the most important British philosopher between Locke and Hume, bishop George Berkeley, incumbent of an Irish diocese.[26] Berkeley's own contribution to the 'public good' was nothing less than a universal medicine. He presented his panacea, tar water (!), to the world in his *Siris* of 1744, and its use was vigorously promoted for a while by Prior (e.g. in his *Authentick narrative of the use of tar-water,* 1746). More important than tar water, and far more influential on Anglo-Irish attitudes, were the economic questions and theories that Berkeley fielded in *The Querist.*

The Querist was published in three parts in 1735, '36 and '37, edited by Madden and Prior. A revised edition appeared in 1750, and again in Berkeley's posthumous miscellanea of 1752. This economic tract utilizes a strange, but at that time not altogether unusual, form of argumentation: a long uninterrupted series of rhetorical questions (in all 895 in the first edition, 595 in that of 1750). Berkeley's management of this form gives it special power and elegance: in ever changing combinations, patterns of mutual allusion and illumination, permutations and juxtapositions, a number of basic problems in the Irish economy are scrutinized from ever changing angles of perspective. In a fugatic treatment that will drop a certain point and turn to another, then, later, bring it up again in a different context, the reader is pulled from question mark to question mark, hooked, as it were, by their rhetorical force, into the direction that Berkeley envisages – far more effectively so, than the 'push' of an assertive argumentation would have done. The following passage may give a brief inkling both of Berkeley's Socratic rhetoric and of his main concerns:

> Whether the number and welfare of the subjects be not the true strength of the crown?
> Whether in all public institutions there should not be an end proposed, which is to be the rule and limit of the means? Whether this end should not be the well-being of the whole? And whether, in order to this, the first step should not be to clothe and feed our people?
> Whether there be upon earth any Christian or civilized people so beggarly, wretched, and destitute as the common Irish?
> Whether, nevertheless, there is any other people whose wants may be more easily supplied from home?[27]

One of the central contentions of *The Querist* is already contained here: Ireland can solve its economic problems by itself, and does not need international trade expansion to that end. Berkeley, too, wants to limit the importation of luxury goods:

> Whether he whose luxury consumeth foreign products, and whose industry produceth nothing domestic to exchange for them, is not so far forth from injurious to his country? (Qu. 57)
> Whether those who drink foreign liquors, and deck themselves and their families with foreign ornament, are not so far forth to be reckoned absentees? (Qu. 104)

What is new in Berkeley's position, however, is the shift from Locke's notion of *property* as the basis of societal relations (and of economy) towards that of the *circulation of property* through society – an anticipation of Adam Smith's economic theories.[28] This brings Berkeley to condemn gold as a means of exchange: it has, he says, too much intrinsic value and will be hoarded rather than circulated. Paper money, worthless in itself, is more suitable as a means of exchange; and the establishment of a bank, too, would initiate a welcome trend: the emancipation of the abstract concept of credit into an independent vehicle for economic traffic. In Berkeley's view, Ireland's poverty is only the symptom of its economic disease; the disease itself is that of stagnation. After the decline of trade and of the woollen industry, not enough has been done by way of an alternative: instead, old grievances have been nourished in a potentially divisive defeatism:

> Whether our hankering after our own woollen trade be not the true and only reason which hath created a jealousy in England towards Ireland? And whether anything can hurt us more than such jealousy?
> Whether it be not the true interest of both nations to become one people? And whether either be sufficiently apprised of this?
> Whether the upper part of this people are not truly English, by blood, language, religion, manners, inclination, and interest?
> Whether we are not as much Englishmen as the children of the old Romans, born in Britain, were still Romans? (Qu. 89–92)
> Be the restraining of our trade well or ill advised in our neighbours, with respect to their own interest, yet whether it be not plainly ours to accommodate ourselves to it? (Qu. 136)

It is obvious that Berkeley's motives are not anti-English – on the contrary. Correspondingly, he speaks of the Gaelic Irish with some disdain and even distaste:

> Whether our natural Irish are not partly Spaniards and partly Tartars; and whether they do not bear signatures of their descent from both these nations, which is also confirmed by all their histories?
> Whether the Tartar progeny is not numerous in this land? And whether there is an idler occupation under the sun than to attend flocks and herds of cattle?
> Whether the wisdom of the State should not wrestle with this hereditary disposition of our Tartars, and with a high hand introduce agriculture? (Qu. 512–14)

> Whether our old native Irish are not the most indolent and supine people in Christendom?
>
> Whether they are yet civilized, and whether their habitations and furniture are not more sordid than those of the savage Americans?
>
> Whether it be not a sad circumstance to live among lazy beggars? And whether, on the other hand, it would not be delightful to live in a country swarming, like China, with busy people? (Qu. 357–9)

Such attitudes were not uncommon among the unionist, Protestant Anglo-Irish of the time. What, then, is the importance of *The Querist*?

A new element in Berkeley's argument opposes the disdain for the Gaelic population and the emphasis on Anglo-Irish unity with England: it is the realization that Ireland is a complete and discrete economic unit in which both the Gaelic and the Anglo-Irish population are implicated. Berkeley employs various metaphors for this economic community comprising Gaels and Anglo-Irish alike – such as, for instance, that of a family or of a tree:

> Whether to provide plentifully for the poor be not feeding the root, the substance whereof will shoot upwards into the branches, and cause the top to flourish? (Qu. 59)

Or, more prosaically:

> Whether a scheme for the welfare of this nation should not take in the whole inhabitants? And whether it be not a vain attempt, to project the flourishing of our Protestant gentry, exclusive of the bulk of our natives? (Qu. 255)

Berkeley's use of the term *nation* is striking here: with its added reference to 'the whole inhabitants' it embraces the 'natives' as well as 'the Protestant gentry'. Elsewhere, it is asked, 'Whether a nation might not be considered a family?' (Qu. 176). What is at work here is a sense of responsibility towards the well-being of the Gaelic population – a sense of responsibility, in which both Patriotic civic awareness and colonial paternalism (as exemplified in the metaphor of the family) are at work. The economic conflict with English interests thus began to involve a sense of economic unity with the non-English inhabitants of Ireland. This is a new development. After the selective responsibility of late seventeenth-century authors, who attributed all progress to English presence, all backwardness to Irish stubbornness, a more comprehensive view is now taken, based on a realization that economic laws function without regard for religious or social antagonisms. The change from the older to the more modern attitude can be followed within *The Querist* itself. At one point, Berkeley can pose the question,

> Whether the bulk of our Irish natives are not kept from thriving, by that cynical content in dirt and beggary which they possess to a degree beyond any other people in Christendom?[29]

– but then again, it can also happen that 'the nation' at large is represented as the victim of the reckless luxury of the upper class:

> Whether the vanity and the luxury of a few ought to stand in competition with the interests of a nation?
> Whether national wants ought not to be the rule of trade? And whether the most pressing wants of the majority ought not to be first considered? (Qu. 167–8)

Berkeley elsewhere specifies 'the most pressing wants of the majority' as 'the dirt, and famine, and nakedness of the bulk of our people' (Qu. 106). In this sense, Irish backwardness can be seen as the result, rather than the cause, of Irish economic woes, and contradict Berkeley's own facile reliance on a hypothetical 'cynical content in dirt and beggary'. Swift expressed this reappraisal of the traditional view quite forcefully around the same time: in a letter of 1732, he gives a 'traditional' view of Irish dirt and backwardness, which is wholly subverted by one last added comment towards the end:

> . . . . a bare face of nature, without house or plantations; filthy cabins, miserable, tattered, half-starved creatures, scarce in human shape; one insolent ignorant oppressive squire to be found in twenty miles riding; a parish church to be found only in a summer-day's journey, in comparison of which, an English farmer's barn is a cathedral; a bog of fifteen miles round; every meadow a slough, and every hill a mixture of rock, heath, and marsh; and every male and female, from the farmer, inclusive to the day-labourer, infallibly a thief, and consequently a beggar, which in this island are terms convertible. . . . There is not an acre of land in Ireland turned to half its advantage; yet it is better improved than the people: and all these evils are the effects of English tyranny: so your sons and grandchildren will find it to their sorrow.[30]

The implication is obvious: Patriotic thought is becoming more critical of the irresponsibility of the upper classes and the English interest than of the boorishness of the natives. One of the strongest expressions of this new criticism of the status quo was the mounting denunciation of absenteeism. In the 1690s, Sir Walter Harris could still praise the English residence of Anglo-Irish landlords as a reinforcement of unity between England and the Ascendancy; now, however, a less rosy view was taken. The drain of the absentees' incomes on the national economy was a keenly felt grievance; another one was that a middleman would move into the absentee's empty place, paying a wholesale rent to the landlord in England and subletting the land to the actual tenants. Sometimes the middleman's margin of profit would be substantial enough to warrant his own absenteeism, so that various interpositions of middlemen and sub-middlemen between landlord and tenant were the result – the latter having to provide for the sustenance of numerous superiors by way of what became known, aptly enough, as rackrents.

Absenteeism had already become a dirty word with Berkeley (Qu. 104), and was attacked especially by his and Swift's friend Prior, founder of the Dublin Society. Prior's *List of absentees of Ireland and an estimate of the yearly value of their estates and incomes spent abroad,* though hardly more than a table of names and figures, was nothing less than a denunciation. It was first printed in 1729, and often reprinted in updated versions during the entire eighteenth century. As late as 1793, a similar list appeared in the magazine *Anthologia Hibernica* (vol. 1, 213–20). Counter-measures were repeatedly proposed, e.g. a taxation on absentee incomes of four or even five shillings in the pound, i.e. twenty or twenty-five per cent,[31] obviously aiming at coercing absentees to return to Ireland, or indemnifying the country for their absence. This motive stands in marked contrast to Harris' integrationist view, and indicates that, in economic terms, the Anglo-Irish could begin to view England as a 'foreign' country – the use of the term 'abroad' in the title of Prior's list of absentees is remarkable.

An anti-English undertone is noticeable even more strongly in the opposition to a phenomenon parallel to absenteeism: the granting of Irish posts to English functionaries, often as a sinecure to be fulfilled by a *locum tenens* while the dignitary himself was, in fact, an absentee, spending his Irish income in England. What this opposition in fact amounted to was an incipient criticism of the entire basis of 'English interest' in Ireland – it may be for this reason that Prior's list was so disquieting to archbishop Boulter, Walpole's right hand in Ireland and as such the strongest champion of the English interest. A radical among churchmen, archbishop King of Dublin, had already attacked the English interest in the Church of Ireland, the granting of dignities to English rather than to Irish divines; it was perhaps owing to these attacks, and to King's well-known Patriot principles, that the archbishop of Dublin was never preferred to the see of Armagh and the primacy of all Ireland. Next to the more permanent fixture Boulter, the lord lieutenant of the moment was the main instrument of the English interest, and Patriots began to resent the way these dignitaries would only reside in Ireland for the minimum time needed to fulfill their duties – thus Swift remarked with ham-fisted sarcasm

> that the Lords Lieutenants, for several years past, have not thought this Kingdom *worthy the Honour of their Residence,* longer than was absolutely necessary for the King's Business; which consequently *wanted no Speed in the Dispatch.* (vol. 10, 56)

Swift, with his easily outraged sense of equity, was by far the most radical of the Anglo-Irish Patriots of this time, and must as such be regarded as the precursor of later developments: whereas most of the early eighteenth-century Anglo-Irish Patriots, whose names have been mentioned in the previous pages, voiced their cautious hopes and fears in the 1730s and 1740s, Swift's main activity lay in the 1720s, and was far more controversial than any of his immediate successors dared to be.

It is obviously impossible to deal adequately with one of the most eminent writers in English literature, and one of the most influential political writers in Irish history, within the framework of the present argument. I shall therefore limit my argument to that aspect of Swift which has a particular bearing on the development of Irish Patriot thought. Although Swift was too misanthropic a humanist, too staunch a believer in the old values of Anglican rationalism, to feel comfortable with the idealistic, progressive connotations in the appellation 'Patriot', he did share a number of grievances with Anglo-Irish Patriots. Like them, he felt that the Anglo-Irish devotion to the Protestant interest warranted a better treatment at the hands of the British government; witness his letter of 1726 to the earl of Peterborough, complaining,

> That all persons born in *Ireland* are called and treated as *Irishmen*, although their fathers and grandfathers were born in *England*; and their predecessors having been conquerors of *Ireland*, it is humbly conceived they ought to be on as good a foot as any subjects of *Britain*, according to the practice of all other nations, and particularly of the *Greeks* and *Romans*.[32]

Such sentiments had already reached their most demagogic public expression in Swift's finest hour as a political pamphleteer, the period (1724–5) of the Drapier's Letters. The following passage, which shows a use of rhetorical questions quite different from that of Berkeley, is famous:

> Were not the People of *Ireland* born as *free* as those of *England*? How have they forfeited their Freedom? Is not the *Parliament* as fair a *Representative* of the *People*, as that of *England*? And hath not their Privy Council as great, or a greater Share in the administration of publick Affairs? Are they not Subjects of the same King? Does not the same *Sun* shine over them? And have they not the same *God* for their Protector? Am I a *free-man* in *England*, and do I become a *Slave* in six Hours by crossing the Channel? (vol . 10, 31)

The Drapier's Letters were written during the affair of Wood's Halfpence – another instance, after the Woollen Act of 1698, of how Irish public opinion, Anglo-Irish public opinion even, could be disregarded by English authorities.[33] Swift was not alone in his outrage: his Drapier's Letters had been preceded by complaints from the commissioners of revenue and of the House of Commons; however, their sheer demagogic brilliance could revive flagging interest, and result in nationwide denunciations of the proposed coin, by guilds, city councils etc. During the same period, Molyneux's *Case of Ireland* was reprinted.

In fact, Swift's denial of the English government's right to go against the stated wishes of the Irish citizenry is closely enough related to Molyneux's *Case,* and the latter's influence is quite obvious in Swift's argument; for instance:

> Those who come over hither to us from *England,* and some *weak* people among ourselves, whenever, in Discourse, we make mention of *Liberty* and *Property,* shake their Heads, and tell us, that *Ireland* is a *depending Kingdom;* as if they would seem, by this Phrase, to intend, that the People of *Ireland* is in some State of Slavery or Dependence, different from those of *England:* Whereas, a *depending Kingdom is a modern Term of Art;* unknown, as I have heard, to all antient *Civilians,* and *Writers upon Government. . . .* For I declare, next under God, I *depend* only on the King my Sovereign, and on the Laws of my own Country, And I am so far from *depending* upon the people of *England,* that, if they should ever *rebel* against my

Sovereign, (which God forbid) I would be ready at the first Command from his Majesty to take Arms against them. . . .[34]

Swift even quotes 'the famous Mr. *Molyneaux*' in this context. Similarly, he could dedicate one of the Drapier's Letters to Molesworth, the veteran commonwealthman and personal friend of Molyneux. In this letter, Swift particularly endorses the

Writings of your Lordship, Mr. *Locke*, Mr. *Molineaux*, Colonel *Sidney*, and other dangerous Authors, who talk of *Liberty as a Blessing, to which the whole Race of Mankind hath an Original Title; whereof nothing but unlawful Force can divest them.* (vol. 10, 86)

There was, however, one important difference between the years 1725 and 1698: in the meantime (1720) the British parliament had in so many words arrogated the right to legislate for Ireland. Unlike Molyneux's arguments, Swift's were unmistakably at odds with the constitutional status quo; and if Molyneux's cautious reasoning was already frowned upon in the year 1698, it is no surprise to find that the British authorities under the then lord lieutenant, Carteret, were forced to act against the demagogical oratory of the dean. The image of 'unlawful force' hinted at in the preceding quote was applied unmistakably to English government policy; for Swift had contrasted the opposition of Molyneux and of 'several of the greatest Patriots and *best* Whigs in *England*' – 'as far as *Truth, Reason,* and *Justice* are capable of *opposing*' – with the brutal power politics of the British parliament:

but the Love and Torrent of Power prevailed. Indeed, the Arguments on both Sides were invincible. For in *Reason*, all *Government* without the Consent of the Governed, is the *very Definition of Slavery:* But in *Fact, Eleven Men well armed, will certainly subdue one single Man in his Shirt.* (vol. 10, 62–3)

In this way, the cause of the Anglo-Irish interest (as opposed to the English interest) becomes identified with the Patriot tradition of Locke's followers (stressing the necessary 'Consent of the *Governed*') and, hence, with the cause of Liberty itself. It is this libertarian notion in Patriot opposition, so important later for men like Charles Lucas and Henry Grattan, which was thus introduced for the first time by the dour, intolerant dean of St. Patrick's. Another Swiftian line of argument that announced important future developments is his opposition to the corruption of public government by private interests – for instance, his sarcastic 'refusal' to believe

that a Lord Lieutenant is to be dispatched over in great Haste, before the ordinary Time, and a Parliament summoned, by anticipating a Prorogation; merely to put an Hundred Thousand Pounds into the Pocket of a *Sharper,* by the ruin of a most loyal Kingdom (vol. 10, 57)

Such denunciations of the corruption caused by the policy of 'English interest' were to become central to Patriot opposition.

Swift's main achievement, however, is the fact that he could provoke such a scandal with his Drapier's Letters that the British government was forced to back down. This success – the first time in living memory that Anglo-Irish public opinion had been able to assert itself in defiance of British policy – made the Drapier's Letters a 'classic' with the liberal Irish reading public, and their anonymous author (whose identity was a public secret) a national hero. Nothing succeeds like success – and the fact that the Drapier managed to achieve his aim may have been all-important to his later influence.

Swift's assessment of the relationship Ascendancy–England is complemented by his view of the relationship Ascendancy–Ireland. The passage quoted above (p. 306) has already indicated that Swift, though he had little enough personal liking for the rude and plebeian Catholic natives, shared Berkeley's sense of responsibility for their welfare under the Ascendancy. The most eloquent expression of Swift's attitude in this point is, of course, his *Modest proposal*; and in the following (satirically inverted) 'denunciation' of remedies for Ireland's woes, one may perhaps suspect Swift's own opinions, which close on a note of compassion for the plight of the rural poor:

> *Therefore, let no man talk to me of other expedients:* Of taxing our Absentees at five Shillings a Pound: Of using neither Cloaths, nor Household Furniture except what is of our own Growth and Manufacture: Of utterly rejecting the Materials and Instruments that promote foreign Luxury: Of curing the Expensiveness of Pride, Vanity, Idleness, and Gaming in our Women: Of introducing a Vein of Parsimony, Prudence and Temperance: Of learning to love our Country, wherein we differ even from LAPLANDERS, and the Inhabitants of TOPINAMBOO: Of quitting our Animosities, and Factions; nor act any longer like the *Jews,* who were murdering one another at the very Moment their City was taken: Of being a little cautious not to sell our Country and Conscience for nothing: Of teaching Landlords to have, at least, one Degree of Mercy towards their Tenants. (vol. 12, 116)

Like the above-quoted letter to Brandreth, this was written well before the other Patriots were able to overcome their long-standing fears of Catholic perfidy. Swift was also one of the first to stop regarding Catholics with suspicion: in his *Queries relating to the sacramental test* of 1732 he wrote:

> For *Popery,* under the Circumstances it lies in this Kingdom; although it be offensive, and inconvenient enough, from the Consequences it hath to encrease the Rapine, Sloth and Ignorance, as well as Poverty of the Natives; it is not properly dangerous in that Sense, as some would have us take it; because it is universally hated by every Party of a different religious Profession. . . . The landed *Popish* Interest in England, far exceeds that among us, even in Proportion to the Wealth and Extent of each Kingdom. The little that remains here, is daily dropping into *Protestant* Hands, by Purchase or Descent. . . . The Papists are wholly disarmed. They have neither Courage, Leaders, Money, or Inclinations to rebel. (vol. 12, 258–9)

In fact, Swift seemed to regard the division between Protestants and Catholics as less important than the one between Irish interest and English interest; he arrived at this opinion, which was still avant-garde in the 1770s, as early as 1733, in his *Advice to the freemen of Dublin:*

> We consist of two Parties, I do not mean Popish and Protestant, High and Low Church, Episcopal and Sectarians, Whig and Tory; but of these English who happen to be born in this Kingdom, (whose Ancestors reduced the whole Nation under the Obedience of the *English* Crown,) and the Gentlemen sent from the other Side to possess most of the chief Employments here. . . . (vol. 13, 80)

Here lies Swift's most important contribution to the development of Irish Patriotism. These shifts from a Patriot sense of political integrity to a common Irish opposition to English interest were not immediately followed by the less radical Anglo-Irish – not, at least, until their anti-Catholic misgivings had been assuaged by the uneventful passing of the year 1745 in Ireland.

Not a ripple stirred in the overwhelmingly Jacobite Catholic majority of Ireland's famine-racked population, at the very time when the Young Pretender's armies were striking deep into English territory. This fact is in itself indicative of how effective the penal laws had been in breaking the political position of Catholicism in Ireland. With the battle of Culloden, the Stuart cause went into its terminal decline; and as the fears of Jacobite upheavals in Ireland diminished, so did Anglo-Irish fears of the Catholic population. The appellation 'enemies' for Catholic subjects, in widespread use between 1706 and 1733,[35] had already fallen into disuse, and a further relaxation can be noted after 1745. Indeed, Catholic writers themselves argued that the calm of 1745 ought to assuage the fearful memories of 1641; John Keogh was quick to point out, in his *Vindication of the antiquities of Ireland* (1748), that

> The very Roman Catholics of Ireland have proved themselves to be loyal subjects to the present Government; for there has been no rebellion or insurrection here since the late wars of Ireland, though since then three in Scotland.[36]

An instance of noticeable Protestant relaxation after 1745 is given by bishop Berkeley. While the rebellion of 1745 was raging in Scotland, he addressed a *Letter to the Roman Catholics of the diocese of Cloyne* which is an epitome of Ascendancy apprehensiveness, as well as an example of Protestant inability to sympathize with Catholic grievances. Berkeley addresses the victims of the penal laws in a tone both uneasy and schoolmasterish, and can even voice the obviously nonsensical contention

> that you have been treated with a truly Christian lenity under the present government; that your persons have been protected, and your properties secured by equal laws: and that it would be highly imprudent as well as ungrateful to forfeit these advantages, by making yourself tools to the ambitions of foreign princes, who fancy it expedient to raise disturbances among us at present, but, as soon as their own ends are served, will not fail to abandon you, as they have always done.[37]

Berkeley's relief after the passing of 1745 must indeed have been considerable, and seems to have contributed to a marked relaxation in his attitude towards Irish Catholics. As Leyburn has pointed out, the post-1745 edition of *The Querist* replaced the earlier expression 'Papists' by the more courteous 'Roman Catholics', and in 1749 Berkeley addressed a remarkably conciliatory open letter to the Catholic clergy, entitled *A word to the wise*.[38] Although even here Berkeley regards Irish 'antipathy to labour' (p. 438) as an axiomatic common-place, he feels it necessary to add:

> But whatever is said must be so taken as not to reflect on persons of rank and education, who are no way inferior to their neighbours; nor yet to include all even of the lowest sort, though it may well extend to the generality of those especially in the western and southern parts of the kingdom, where the British manners have less prevailed. (p. 439)

Thus, a national image is tempered and restricted in social terms until it loses practically all 'national' applicability, and comes to mean little more than that the uneducated rural Irish have not yet reaped the benefits of an education in 'British manners' – a nearly tautological redundancy. And what the bishop was pleased to call 'equal laws' in 1745 is now recognized as 'the discouragements attending those of your Communion', which 'do in some measure, damp industry and ambition in persons of a certain rank' (p. 442). Less radical than Swift, Berkeley sees no need to propose any change in this state of affairs; but, he adds with cheery resourcefulness, 'if it is impossible for our cottagers to be rich, yet it is certain they may be clean' (p. 445). Dobbs had gone further than that; he, like Berkeley, seeing the economic relatedness of Irish Catholics and Irish Ascendancy, had realized as early as 1731 that the agricultural stagnation was to a large extent born 'from the communalty's having no fixed property in their land, the want of which deprives them of a sufficient encouragement and industry'.[39] Later that century, that argument was to resurface persistently: to grant Catholics the possibility of land ownership would give them a vested interest in, and hence conciliate them to, the political status quo. Berkeley, however, though more conservative in his acceptance of penal restrictions, went further again in his *Word to the wise*: he recognizes the Catholics as an organic part of Irish society, with whom there should be co-operation, rather than as a distinct group which must be pacified somehow. The opening of his letter uses a tone that would have been unthinkable earlier, stressing the community of Protestants and Catholics in matters regarding the public good:

> Be not startled, Reverend Sirs, to find yourselves addressed by one of a different Communion. We are indeed (to our shame be it spoken) more inclined to hate for those articles wherein we differ, than to love one another for those wherein we agree. But, if we cannot extinguish, let us at least suspend our animosities, and, forgetting our religious feuds, consider ourselves in the amiable light of country-men and neighbours. Let us for once turn our eyes on those things in which we have a common interest. Why should disputes about faith interrupt the duties of

civil life? or the different roads we take to heaven prevent our taking the same steps on earth? Do we not inhabit the same spot of ground, breathe the same air, and live under the same government? Why, then, should we not conspire in one and the same design – to promote the common good of our country. (p. 437)

And again, at the end, Berkeley declares that he considers the Catholic clergy 'as my countrymen, as fellow-subjects, as professing belief in the same Christ' (p. 451); the clergy so addressed reacted in equally positive and courteous terms (pp. 451–2).

A similar shift is noticeable in the problematic and not always creditable figure of Henry Brooke, one of the more conspicuous literary Patriots of the mid-century. His drama *Gustavus Vasa* (1739), an attack on the threat posed to liberty by standing armies, and a *pièce-à-clef* against Walpole's nearly dictatorial powers, has gone down in theatre history owing to the fact that its production was banned by the lord chancellor. It was performed in Ireland with the additional sub-title 'The Patriot' (1741), and it is far from impossible that the Dublin audiences may have given the exertions of the Patriot Gustavus against the Danish oppression of his native Sweden a more 'international' interpretation than the lord chancellor: one that saw an analogy in the relationship between Denmark and Sweden, and that between England and Ireland.[40] Later in his career, Brooke defended the cause of the Patriot Charles Lucas, and on that occasion offered the following thoughts on the meaning of Patriotism:

> It is but lately, very lately, my Brethren, that the Word, PATRIOT, hath a Signification in *Ireland*; a Kingdom, whose Natives, of any Wealth or Consideration, were either worse than *Aliens* to their Country, by becoming *Absentees*, or yet *worse* than Absentees by their *Places* and *Dependencies* under foreign Influence. A Kingdom, whose Offices of *Trust* were turned into Matters of *Traffic*, whose *Funds* for public Utility, into prsvate [sic] *Barter* and *Jobb*; while with *Parties* in our *Parliaments*, *Factions* in our *Counties*, *Practice* on our *Juries*, &c. &c. &c. we were only so far uncorrupted, so far saved from *Venality*, as we were not judged of sufficient *Weight* to merit the *Temptation*.[41]

Later again, in the 1760s, Brooke was to write for the Patriot *Freeman's Journal*. At least until 1745, however, Brooke's Patriotism was accompanied by a strongly anti-Catholic attitude. During the rebellion of 1745, he wrote his alarmist *Farmer's Letters*, warning the Protestants of Ireland that the absolutist monarchists and craven Jacobite papists were poised to take over Ireland, to suppress liberty and the Protestant religion. He repeatedly reminds his readers of the 1641 rebellion, and compares 1641 and 1745 as follows:

> I observe that the *Papists* of this Kingdom, are particularly placid and peaceable, at this Season: But reflect whether we ought not to dread the heavier Storm, from so very still and sullen a Calm. They say to us, *had we lived in the Days of our Fathers, we would not have been Partakers with them, in their Oppressions and Massacres: But herein they confess themselves to be the Children of those Men,* by whom our Maidens were polluted, by whom our Matrons were left childless, [etc.][42]

After the continuing calm of the Catholic population, Brooke seems to have changed his mind. To be sure, he did not overnight become a warm advocate of Catholicism, but he did repudiate his vehement anti-Catholicism of 1745 in no uncertain terms:

> I most solemnly assure you, that when I wrote those letters I was in perfect love and charity with every Roman Catholic in the kingdom of Ireland. I knew that they were a depressed people. I had long pitied them as such. I was sensible that the laws, under which they suffered, had been enacted by our ancestors, when the impressions of hostility were fresh and warm, and when passion, if I may venture to say so, co-operated, in some measure, with utility and reason.[43]

Brooke later claimed that he was 'never anti-Catholic, but merely fearful that persecution had made Catholics disloyal'.[44] Around the same time, 1760, he was even willing to write in the employment of the Catholic Committee, a body founded by Charles O'Conor, John Curry and Thomas Wyse for anti-penal propaganda;[45] the result was Brooke's *The tryal of the Roman Catholics,* which attempted to deflate the myth of 1641, to make a case for the trustworthiness of Catholics and, hence, against the justification and the usefulness of the penal laws. All this was a far cry from his pre-1745 attitude.

However, though the placidity of Ireland in 1745 may have been a catalyst in this change, it was no doubt partly the result of wider developments. Irish Patriotism was close to the new scientific spirit that expressed itself in societies like the Dublin Philosophical Society, the Dublin Society, and the Physico-Historical Society which was founded in 1744 by Madden, Prior and others, 'to make inquiries into the natural and civil history of the kingdom'. The physician Sir Thomas Molyneux, a member, and William's brother, wrote an unpublished tract called *Some considerations on the taxes paid by Ireland to support the government* (1727) – obviously too 'hot' to be printed. All this Enlightenment threw a shadow of its own; in 1723, the grand lodge of Irish freemasonry was founded in Dublin, and even a man like bishop Berkeley indulged in neoplatonist interests: in *Siris* he refers back to Pico della Mirandola, Hermes Trismegistus and the 'corpus hermeticum', and he had plans for a hermetic society, whose members were not to reveal 'the secrets of the assembly' – whatever they may have been.[46] And John Toland, an opponent of revealed religion who argued that Christianity could be comprehended rationally, toyed with the idea of a (likewise hermetic) 'Socratic Society'.[47] At the same time, Toland attacked the declaratory act of 1720, not with any national, Irish arguments (for Toland repeatedly expressed a unionist attitude like that of Sir Richard Cox), but with the libertarian argument that this act would give the House of Lords a dangerous supremacy over the Commons.[48]

In this sense, political libertarian thought in the wake of Locke, scientific thought in the wake of Newton, and modern metaphysics ranging from freemasonry to Deism, could co-operate to diminish the absolute, all-engrossing importance that the Protestant-Catholic conflicts had had throughout the seventeenth century. In a similar process, the rise of Patriotism as a new political programme was to outflank the old polarity of Whig vs. Tory; though fed by Whiggish liberal principles, it opposed itself to the arbitrary nature of government policy and corruption that in Ireland was established by the long Whig supremacy under the first two Georges. These developments, taking their slow course in the decades when the Catholic population was unable to assert its claims in a manner that could disturb the complacency of the Protestant class, could thus create a certain relaxation (at least, a relaxation measured by the standards of Borlase and Story), which, without being spectacular in itself, was a transition from the prevalent No-Popery attitude of the 1690s to the national reconciliation of Grattanite Patriotism.

The Ascendancy and native antiquity

Gaelic Ireland of the eighteenth century has not unreasonably been called the 'Hidden' Ireland. The activities of the Continental Gaelic tradition were now beginning to die down, and under the political and social pressure of the penal laws, Gaelic society, Gaelic culture, and especially the Gaels' Catholic religion acquired an 'underground' character. Even so, the intellectual tradition that had gone into exile in the seventeenth century was continued in this penal 'sub-culture' of Ascendancy Ireland. The scholars, scribes and poets grew shabbier each year, but manuscripts continued to be copied and poems continued to be composed, and the sordidness of the present could only enhance, by way of contrast, the brilliance of the past.

Nevertheless, Gaelic culture was a moribund tradition, though it kept a tenacious existence until the ultimate death-blow of the great famine in the mid-nineteenth century. Whatever presence Gaelic culture safeguarded after the Famine was owing to a middle-class, Anglo-Irish interest; the heritage of the Gaelic cultural tradition was passed on through increasingly non-traditional or even non-Gaelic channels, through the mediation of the printing press commissioned by scholarly societies, through the employment provided by interested Anglo-Irish men of letters. If it had not been for this growing Anglo-Irish interest, and for middle-class, nineteenth-century revivalism, the poetry of Ó Rathaille or of Merriman might now be studied (if at all) only by a few specialized philologists, as specimens of a bygone literary tradition in a dead language.

The basis for this cultural osmosis of Gaelic culture into the Anglo-Irish classes was, in the main, laid in the eighteenth century – preceded only by the isolated instances of Ussher and Ware, announced by the unusual case of O'Flaherty and made viable by the work of Lhuyd. It may be imagined from the literature of the period – Story's History no less than Ó Bruadair's poems – how deep the antagonism between the two populations of Ireland was. The hostility of the Protestant Anglo-Irish was exemplified in the person of Sir Richard Cox, who had fled from Ireland during Tyrconnell's viceregency, had been a strong supporter of the revolution of 1688, and had, as lord chancellor, been one of the prime movers behind the penal laws of 1703–04. Cox was the author of essays with revealing titles like *An essay for the conversion of the Irish, showing that 'tis their duty to become Protestants* (1698). His *Hibernia Anglicana: or, the history of Ireland from the conquest thereof by the English to this present time* (1689–90) stands wholly in the anti-Catholic English tradition of the seventeenth century, and it is no surprise to see Cox castigate Keating, Walsh, O'Flaherty, O'Sullevan Beare and O'Mahony's *Disputatio apologetica* (fol. b r./v.; fol. c v.), or to find that words like 'silly', 'barbarous' and 'ridiculous' are frequent epithets when the author deals with Gaelic Ireland; and yet, a difference from Borlase, Shirley and Story lies in the fact that Cox, at least, is aware of the existence of authors like Keating, Walsh, O'Flaherty, etc. Cox may have stopped his ears – but at least a noise was beginning to reach the ears even of the lord chancellor.

As yet, however, that was no basis for communication, for the exchange of ideas; this, Hugh MacCurtin was to find to his cost. MacCurtin (Mac Cruitín, whom we have encountered as a poet) was probably the most eminent Gaelic scholar of the generation after O'Flaherty. He was of a family hereditarily linked to the O'Briens as historians, and as such succeeded to his cousin, the poet Ainnrias Mac Cruitín. He had followed lord Clare over to France after the defeat of James II, and there was tutor to the dauphin until his return to Ireland in 1714. After his return, he became the first scholar since O'Flaherty to continue the historical self-defence of Gaelic Ireland. In order to prove,

> that the Antient Irish before the coming of the English were no Way inferior to any People or Nation in the known World for Religion, Literature, Civility, Riches, Hospitality, Liberality, War-like Spirit &c. (pp. 286 f.)

and especially against Cox's *Hibernia Anglicana,* he published *A brief discourse in vindication of the antiquity of Ireland* in 1717. Apart from Walsh's book, this was the first Gaelic history in English, and apart from, again, Walsh's book and O'Flaherty's *Ogygia,* the first printed in the British Isles. It was the first, *tout court,* to be published in Ireland. Sir Richard Cox reacted by having the author clapped in jail – he happened to be Chief Justice at the time, as well as a historian. MacCurtin's rude introduction to the fact that Gaelic historiography in Ireland was more precarious than on the Continent did not, fortunately, deter him from further activities. Though he never managed to produce the continuation of his *Brief vindication,* announced at the end of that work (pp. 312 f.), he commenced a grammar of the Irish language even while still in prison.

Written in English, it was the first Gaelic grammar published since the one contained in Lhuyd's book – but this time, the author was prudent enough to publish it at Louvain, where it appeared in 1728 with, as an appendix, a reprint of Dowley's catechism of 1663. It was dedicated to one of the 'wild geese', Catholic Irish gentlemen in Continental military service: John Devenish, major-general of the Austrian army in the Netherlands.

Like the grammars of Stapleton and O'Molloy, that of MacCurtin aimed to bolster the Irish language, 'now in its decay and almost in darkness, even to the

Natives themselves' (p. 4). Nevertheless, his main interest (betraying his post-bardic, professionally scholarly background) is philological rather than popular; he disagrees with Lhuyd's proposals for a simplified orthography, since this would make older texts less accessible and etymologies more obscure (p. 8); for MacCurtin, the Irish language has its primary importance in providing access to, and vouchsafing continuity with, the past. For that reason, his grammar directs itself mainly at

> the studious and other ingenious Gentlemen, lovers of Antiquity; that by little labour they might learn, how it [i.e. the Irish language] abounds with such synonymous words and clear Epithets applicable to proper & Common Names, with the Arts & Sciences most brightly sett forth therein, which might induce such persons to bestow some pains & time to revive & improve it, and engage the curious to tast of the sweet streams of Oratory & poetry in the copious language of a long time neglected. (p. 4 f.)

Accordingly, the decay of the Irish language is to be deplored primarily as the decay of Ireland's link with its own past; this had also been the drift of some of MacCurtin's own poetry (cf. pp. 207–8 above); correspondingly, the conclusion of his grammar sums up a whole century of Continental grammars and histories motivated by national pride:

> It is certain, most of our Nobility and Gentry have abandon'd it, and disdain'd to Learn or speak the same these 200 years past. And I could heartily wish, such persons would look back and reflect on this matter; that they might see through the Glass of their own reason, how strange it seems to the world, that any people should scorn the Language, wherin the whole treasure of their own Antiquity and profound sciences lie in obscurity, so highly esteem'd by all Lovers of Knowledge in former Ages, that swarms of foreign Students from all parts of Europe flock'd into the Nation to taste of, and learn the Arts and sciences therein contained. (p. 7)

Four years after that, in 1732, MacCurtin published a dictionary in Paris which he and a priest named Begley (Ó Beaglaoich) had jointly composed; the preface to the work seems to appeal to a celtological interest:

> Of all the dead and living Languages none is more copious and elegant in the Expression, nor is any more harmonious and musical in the Pronunciation than the Irish, tho it has been declining these Five Hundred Years Past, along with the declining Condition of our Country. . . . Our Authors affirm it to be the old Scythian Language, and upon that account very well deserves to be rescued from Oblivion. (p. liii])

However, even here a more national motivation is not far off, for the authors continue with the observation:

> That a People so naturally ambitious of Honour and so universally covetous of Glory, as several generous *British* Historians described the Irish to be, can so

> strangely neglect cultivating and improving a language of some Thousands of Years
> standing may indeed seem very surprising. . . . (p. [iii])

And this leads, ultimately, to the same position as that of MacCurtin's poem 'A
uaisle Éireann áilne' (above, p. 207), and of his grammar:

> The Irish Gentry have therefore Opportunities enough, still left, for recovering and
> preserving their Mother-Language, and, consequently, are without the least Colour
> of Excuse if they shamefully continue to neglect it. (p . [iv])

Thus, the preface to this dictionary is in itself an example *in nuce* of how
celtological interest was to be absorbed by, rather than to distract from, the
cultural pride of Gaelic scholars. MacCurtin's work was to prove a valuable
source of information (alongside bishop O'Brien's dictionary of 1768) for later
Continental scholars like Pictet and Bopp.[49]

One of MacCurtin's better-known colleagues – indeed, a friend – was Tadhg
Ó Neachtain, who came from a bardic family from Connacht. His father Seán
was a well-known poet, and both had moved to Dublin where Tadhg eked out a
living as a schoolteacher in the Liberties of St. Patrick's Cathedral. He had also
compiled a dictionary, trilingually explaining Irish through English and Latin.
It was based on earlier work by the priest Francis Walsh, and a phrase on the
calligraphed title-page of the manuscript ('nunc autem illustrium quorundam
virorum Cura et Munificentia in Lucem editum',[50]) indicates that Ó Neachtain
had at one point hoped that his dictionary, like MacCurtin/Begley's, would be
published.

Ó Neachtain's main interest for the present study lies less in his dictionary, or
in the lives of the saints that he copied; it lies not even in the noteworthy fact that
he attempted to prove O'Flaherty's theory of the Phoenician roots of Irish by
reading the Carthaginian speech in *Poenulus* in Gaelic terms, thus echoing
Bochart;[51] but rather in an occasional poem from 1728, written in doggerel *deibhí*
to commemmorate the fact that no fewer than twenty-six Gaelic scholars were at
that time assembled in the capital. This poem, which contains names that each
individually have come down in history through the obscure and isolated
manuscripts of the penal age, is proof positive that the scholars enumerated here
formed indeed a cohesive tradition, that they were aware of each other's work,
and that between them they shared the conscious guardianship of a cultural
heritage. The glimpse that Ó Neachtain's poem thus offers us into the inner
practice of Gaelic scholarship puts nearly all the more important Gaelic men of
letters of the period – Ó Neachtain, MacCurtin, Walsh, Dermod O'Connor and
others – in a meaningful relationship to each other, as much as the surrealist
manifestos testify to the connection between some of the more important writers
and artists of twentieth-century French literature.[52]

Apart from Ó Neachtain senior, pride of place is given in this poem to clerical
scholars, among whom figures the grammarian and lexicographer Francis
Walsh. MacCurtin is mentioned further on, as is the translator of Keating's *Foras*

feasa ar Éirinn, Dermod O'Connor – although his personal relationship with Tadhg Ó Neachtain was less than cordial. O'Connor's translation of Keating's work into English was published in London in 1723, and elicited, as we have seen, strenuous denunciations – notwithstanding which it was reprinted a few years later in a more sumptuous edition. O'Connor dedicated his translation to the O'Brien earl of Inchiquin, who suitably combined Gaelic nobility, a title in the peerage and the Protestant religion. Although later scholars made it a habit of treating O'Connor's translation with contempt, it nevertheless marked an important development: Keating's history, directed towards Gaelic-speaking Irishmen, now became available to a larger English and Anglo-Irish audience, again under the aspect of a cultural self-defence against, as O'Connor put it,

> the Censures of illiterate and unjust Men, who insolently attempt to vilify and traduce the lineal Descendants of the great *Milesians* (a Martial, a Learned, and a Generous Race) as a Nation ignorant, meanspirited, and superstitious. (p. [iii]f.)

The fact that O'Connor should ask for Inchiquin's patronage is not just an instance of the common dedicatory practice of the time, given the severe attacks on his intended translation, and the fact that MacCurtin had been thrown in jail for a similar undertaking only six years previously. O'Connor's translation was reprinted in 1726 and 1732, then annotated by an Ascendancy scholar who co-operated with a few members of the 'Ó Neachtain circle': Dr. Raymond, a fellow of Trinity College. It was Raymond who let Ó Neachtain have the use of the Book of Ballymote, which he borrowed from the College library in 1719; he employed MacCurtin as a translator. A manuscript introduction to Irish history which he had written was used by Charles O'Conor and Ferdinando Warner.[53]

Other figures mentioned by Ó Neachtain are of equal importance in this traffic between the Gaelic 'sub-culture' and the Ascendancy. Contacts with Trinity College seem to have been especially fecund, mainly in the person of Charles Lynegar, the Cathal Ó Luinnín whom Ó Neachtain's poem mentions in ll. 49–52. Lynegar links the Ó Neachtain circle with the more proselytizing interest around Trinity: he was a lecturer of Irish there, in a post created by archbishop Marsh, and he is mentioned as such by John Richardson. His service to the Protestant cause (which also involved him in the redaction/transcription of an Irish grammar for one of the Trinity fellows) earned him a satire from the more staunchly principled Ó Neachtain.[54] Moreover, the Seán Ó Súilleabháin whom Ó Neachtain's poem mentions in ll. 25–28 was the scribe who had made a copy of the Louvain grammar for Lhuyd's Dublin bookseller Pepyat. Another character mentioned here is Dr. John Fergus, who earned Charles O'Conor's gratitude by having one of the two master copies of the Annals of the Four Masters re-bound, and who donated his large collection of books and manuscripts to the library of Trinity College; and yet a further link with the College was Aodh Ó Dalaigh, referred to by Ó Neachtain in ll. 73–76, who was in the employ of the law professor Francis Stoughton Sullivan, a Protestant Galwayman from a Gaelic family. Ó Dalaigh copied Irish myths and tales for Sullivan, and composed a phrasebook for him.[55]

But by far the most interesting mention among all these names is that of Cathal Ó Conchobhair, 'from the area of Cruacha' (ll. 61–64). This was a young student who would, later that century, become famous as 'the venerable O'Conor of Belanagar', the most influential Gaelic antiquarian of the eighteenth century. He was a lineal descendant of the last high-king of Ireland, Roderick O'Conor, whom Henry II had confirmed in his provincial kingship of Connacht,[56] and was just completing his early education in the capital, eighteen years old at the time. O'Conor is thus the last link in a tradition that, through the Ó Neachtain circle, stretched back to MacCurtin, thence to O'Flaherty, Mac Firbis and the Four Masters, into the mainstream of bardic learning; and it was O'Conor who, in his long career stretching through most of the century, could gain enough authority in Anglo-Irish circles to become one of the most, if not the most, important mediators of Gaelic learning to non-Gaelic audiences.

One last name to be gleaned from Ó Neachtain's poem is that of Hugh MacGauran, a rumbustious poet whose poem *Pléaráca na Ruarcach* was perhaps the first to gain literary fame in an English translation. An English version of this poem celebrating a feast given by an O'Rourke was made by none other than Jonathan Swift, presumably after a literal English prose version then versified by the dean into a rollicking tetrameter: 'O'Rourke's noble fare will ne'er be forgot,/ by those who were there or those who were not'.

This translation gains its interest in view of Swift's marked dislike for native culture, expressed in passages like the following:

> It would be a noble achievement to abolish the Irish language in this kingdom, so far at least as to oblige all the natives to speak only English on every occasion of business, in shops, markets, fairs, and other places of dealing. . . . This would, in a great measure, civilize the most barbarous among them, reconcile them to our customs, and reduce great numbers to the national religion, whatever kind may then happen to be established. The method is plain and simple, yet I could heartily wish some public thoughts were employed to reduce this uncultivated people from that idle, savage, beastly, thievish manner of life, in which they continue sunk to a degree, that it is almost impossible for a country gentleman to find a servant of human capacity, or the least tincture of natural honesty; or who does not live among his own tenants in continual fear of having his plantations destroyed, his cattle stolen, and his goods pilfered. (vol. 12, 89)

The contradiction may be explained by the fact that *Pléaráca na Ruarcach* was known as a song rather than a poem – and we have seen sufficient positive references to Irish music and to Irish songs to realize that it may have been *Pléaráca na Ruarcach*'s musical rather than literary charms which provided it with its initial popularity among an Anglo-Irish audience.[57]

The man responsible for the music of *Pléaráca na Ruarcach* was not MacGauran, but Carolan (Toirdhealbhach Ó Cearbhalláin), whose popularity in Anglo-Irish circles was by all accounts extraordinary. According to a nearly contemporary anecdote it was he who prompted or abetted Swift's English version.[58] The general popularity of Carolan's Irish airs is proved by the fact that they repeatedly appeared in print: as early as *c.* 1721, a collection of his music was printed in Dublin, and especially the 'hit' *Pléaráca na Ruarcach* was included in other collections published throughout the century. Even Beethoven, who admired Scottish folk music, arranged three airs by Carolan in his collection of Irish airs that appeared in Edinburgh in 1814–16.[59] It must even be surmised that the later enthusiasm among the Anglo-Irish for Irish harp music (witness the harp festivals in Granard in the 1780s, and in Belfast in 1793) stood to no small extent in the heritage of Carolan's initial fame. Irish music could the easier be relished since it was so intrinsically a-political – as long as it was instrumental, that is. Even so, a number of Carolan's pieces carry politically 'charged' titles like 'Squire Wood's lamentation on the refusal of his halfpence', 'Limerick's lamentation', 'Patrick Sarsfield' and 'Lament for Owen Roe O'Neill'.

What makes Carolan's occasional pieces, addressed to patrons and hospitable landlords, interesting is that they are by and large in Gaelic, despite the fact that their audience was Anglo-Irish on the whole. In the words of O'Sullivan:

> A point that has been hitherto insufficiently noticed is the mutual cordiality of the relations existing between Carolan and his patrons of English origins. Some of them were of only the second or third generation in the country but they must have been thoroughly familiar with Irish, for we can hardly suppose that songs would have been sung in their praise in a language that was unintelligible to them.[60]

It may be, then, that Gaelic culture, though socially crushed by the penal laws, was to some extent on the rebound; Ó Neachtain's poem and Carolan's success-ful career both indicate this. Without wanting to confuse the *post hoc* and the *propter hoc,* it is difficult not to think of Lhuyd's indirect influence here; and this possibility is supported by the appearance, in 1724, of *The Irish historical library* by bishop William Nicolson. This book contained the English translations of the Prefaces that Lhuyd had written in Welsh and in Irish for the corresponding parts of his *Archaeologia Britannica.* After Lhuyd's book, the work of bishop Nicolson is a first indication that matters Gaelic now began to be approached with some positive interest by British antiquaries.[61] Before Nicolson had been appointed bishop of Derry in 1718, he had published his *English historical library* in three parts (1696–99) and his *Scottish historical library* (1702). Nicolson's was the first Protestant book on Irish history printed in Dublin since Cox's *Hibernia Anglicana,* and the difference between them is astounding. Instead of damning the works of Keating, Walsh and O'Flaherty, as Cox had done, Nicolson makes them his chief sources for the description of pre-Norman Irish antiquity; and MacCurtin's *Brief vindication* now gains similar credit. Cox's defensive apprehension of things Gaelic is now superseded by genuine and unprejudiced interest; only the more strident anti-Protestantism of men like Cornelius O'Mahony (pp. 8 f.) is unacceptable to the bishop. It may be that Nicolson's more tolerant attitude was a consequence of his English background, which made him, perhaps, less a victim of the 'garrison'-mentality of those Anglo-Irish Protestants who had seen their world crumble during Tyrconnell's viceregency. But then again, even one of the more bigoted anti-Catholics in the Ascendancy, Walter Harris, could, in his antiquarian work, pay most un-bigoted attention to Ireland's ancient history.

It is obvious that Harris, a lawyer from Co. Laois, was no friend of the Catholic interest; for it was he who, when the Catholic activist Dr. John Curry had published an anonymous, pseudo-Protestant pamphlet expressing the need for tolerance towards the victims of the penal laws, wrote a withering counter-blast entitled *Fiction unmasked, or, an answer to a dialogue lately published by a popish physician* (1752), which all but disclosed Curry's identity. Curry tried to pick up the pieces with his anonymous rejoinder *Historical memoirs of the Irish rebellion in the year 1641* (1758) – for naturally the year 1641 loomed large in discussions concerning penal legislation. Curry's *Historical memoirs* contained a prefatory advertisement by Charles O'Conor which called Harris 'a mercenary and injudicious Compiler of historical Fragments' (p. ix) – but that seems a point of debating rhetoric rather than a fair or even sincerely-felt statement.

Harris had married a great-granddaughter of Sir James Ware, and subsequently began to re-edit his great-grandfather-in-law's works in an English translation. He undertook this work under the auspices of the Physico-Historical Society; Ware's works appeared between 1739 and 1746 with subscriptions from leading Patriots like Madden and Dobbs, from the Whiggish archbishop of Armagh, Boulter, from young Lawrence Parsons, later to become a Grattanite Patriot, from Sir Richard Cox the younger[62] and even from the ailing dean Swift. Harris' edition was more than just a translated republication; in many points, the editor had modernized and expanded appreciably, especially in his treatment of Irish language and literature, where Harris gives substantially more, and more, detailed information than Ware himself.[63] Harris is able to draw on the writings of O'Flaherty, O'Molloy and MacCurtin, attacks Scaliger for not seeing the familiarity between Welsh and Irish (vol. 2, 22) and shows the influence of Lhuyd by providing 'A comparative Table of some few Words among Thousands, shewing the Affinity between the *Irish* and *British* languages' (vol. 2, 26 ff.). From O'Flaherty and Keating, Harris culls the names of pre-Christian Gaelic authors (vol. 2, 23f.), and Ware's criticism of Cambrensis (cf. above p. 57) is expanded by a reference to Lynch's *Cambrensis eversus*. This is more remarkable in the light of Harris' strenuously pro-English attitude: the first volume was dedicated to archbishop Boulter, the penal laws are called 'wholesome Bills' (vol. 3, 220), Sir Richard Cox the elder is praised to the skies (vol. 3, 207–52) and Molyneux treated with a marked lack of sympathy. Yet, Harris' judgement of his Gaelic sources is far more balanced than one might have expected. Without sharing the blind faith of traditional Gaelic antiquaries, he can at the same time avoid the unmixed ridicule that was heaped on Gaelic lore by English historians, including the admired Cox, against whom he defends Keating and O'Flaherty (vol. 3, 106, 271). Harris' real achievement is perhaps the recognition that Gaelic traditional historical lore is at least as much a literary as a historical tradition:

> It should be considered, that the Compilers of the antient History of *Ireland* have drawn their Accounts from the Sonnets of the ancient Bards, and have (it must be confessed injudiciously) copied for Truth the Metaphors and Flights of those Poetic Madmen; from whence it had happened, that the later Writers of the antient History of *Ireland* (and the same may be said of other Countries) have copied into their Works such monstrous Fables as exceed all Credibility. . . (vol. 3, 106)

The implications of this view come to the fore more openly in a work that Harris wrote under his own flag rather than that of Sir James Ware. It was a miscellaneous collection in two volumes that he edited for the Physico-Historical Society under the title *Hibernica* (1747), and to the first volume of which he himself contributed an essay about 'the Defects in the Histories of Ireland, and Remedies proposed for the Amendment and Reformation thereof', in the form of an open letter to the chairman of the Physico-Historical Society, lord Newport.

It is a cause of discontent for Harris, that, since Strabo, historians (and even modern historians) of Ireland maintained the point that 'the People of Ireland are at this Day uncivilized, Rude, and Barbarous' (p. 135); he then goes on to ask:

> When such an odious Picture is drawn of us, who, my Lord, can refrain from a just Indignation? . . . But you know, my Lord, that these are groundless Aspersions, and the result of Ignorance and Malice. The Nobility and Gentry of this Kingdom are as Polite, well-bred, and humane, as those of other Nations; the Merchants and Traders as just and honest in their Dealings; and the bulk of the People not inferior to the Populace elsewhere. Doubtless Exceptions may be pointed out to these general Allegations; and what Country is free from such Exceptions? (p. 136)

That is not to say that Harris agrees with the uncritical adulation of a mythical past, in the style of Keating, which, as Harris puts it, is a remnant of older forms of myth-making, examples of which (Geoffrey of Monmouth, for instance) can be found in the annals of all European countries (p. 138). Such myths are literary embellishments of old tales; to take them as historical truths would be to misread the rhetorical figures of old poetry, to take hyperbole and metaphor literally (pp. 139f.). Now is the time, says Harris, to apply more modern historiographical insights to Irish history and to elucidate the Irish past by rational and level-headed inquiry.

All this is interesting, perhaps, as an early indication of Enlightenment attitudes to Irish history-writing – the more so, since it reflects what seems by then to have become a long-standing desire for a new, non-partizan history of Ireland: whilst bigoted works like Sir John Temple's *Irish rebellion* were reprinted with dreary regularity,[64] new initiatives seem to have been taken also – albeit with, for the nonce, little result. In 1707, the Dublin Philosophical Society made plans for a book on Ireland 'with divers Remarks on the Ancient State';[65] Dr. Raymond had plans for a History of Ireland, and had managed to obtain subscriptions from, among others, Inchiquin and Swift;[66] bishop Nicolson expressed the hope that his *Irish historical library* might be 'service to the compilers of a general History of Ireland' (subtitle); and Harris's theoretical observations certainly seem to continue this tradition of preparations for a future large-scale, modern history of Ireland. But what is more (and here lies, perhaps, Harris' deeper importance), this endeavour is represented as being inspired by Patriotic motives – for he continues the above-quoted passage as follows:

> Many intelligent Men have thought, that the adjusting the History of *Ireland* to a good Frame, the shewing the antient and modern State of it in true and proper Colours, together with the several Revolutions in property, Religion, and Government, would tend not only to the honour, but to the real Emolument of the Kingdom. . . . The Physico-Historical Society was erected with a view of removing these gross Misrepresentations, which have been handed down from early Ages concerning this Country, and are yet Continued. (p. 136)

This attitude, in turn, gains additional interest when it is noticed that Harris can feel 'indignation' at narrow-minded denigrations of Irish character and considers the correction of these a matter of 'honour', and conducive to the 'real Emolument of the Kingdom'. It may well be asked, why should he? As a member of the Ascendancy, Harris did not have to feel any concern at the judgements contained in older, pre-Cromwellian descriptions; we have seen how they always explicitly restricted their defamations to the mere, Gaelic Irish, and English-oriented authors like Stanyhurst, Rich and Cox had heartily contributed to this practice. Obviously, this is now changing. The notion of a common cause between Gaelic and Anglo-Irish, formulated on the economic plane by bishop Berkeley, is now taken to the historiographic level by Harris, the man who could draw simultaneously on Cox and MacCurtin.

What this in effect means is that the Anglo-Irish now begin to regard Ireland's Gaelic history as their own. The recognition of the pre-Anglo-Irish Gaelic past (that is to say, a past antedating the arrival of the Protestant settlers in Ireland) as the inheritance of the Anglo-Irish themselves had already been performed in a political and jurisprudential sense by Molyneux; this was now done in a cultural sense by Harris. This, again, means that all derogation of the Gaelic past can now begin to be regarded as a reflection, not only on the lineal heirs to that past – the native peasantry – but also on those Protestants who, with the support of the British crown, maintained their Ascendancy. In short: Protestant Patriotism was beginning to appropriate Gaelic culture as a legitimate point of interest.

And again that vague and ubiquitous dabbler Henry Brooke is another case in point.[67] Though Brooke belonged, unlike Harris, to the pro-Lucas radicals, his anti-Catholic attitude was (at least in the years discussed here, 1743–44) no less strong than Harris's. Yet, Brooke had earlier in life evinced interest in Irish, characteristically because of the fact that a Gaelic poet had addressed a flattering poem to him. He never mastered the language, though his interest may have stimulated that of his daughter, the far more important Charlotte Brooke. Be that as it may, in 1744 he had another fling at Gaelic culture, and published the prospectus for a work on ancient Irish history, planned to fill four volumes. It was given the following title:

The History of Ireland, From the Earliest Times; Wherein are set forth the Ancient and Extraordinary Customs, Manners, Religion, Politics, Conquests, and Revolutions, of that once Hospitable, Polite, and Martial Nation; interspersed with Traditionary Digressions, and the Private and Affecting Histories of the most celebrated of the Natives.[68]

The prospectus also contained a 'Preface Dedicatory to The Most Noble and Illustrious the several Descendants of the Milesian Line' – a fawning apostrophe to those whom he was to denounce in the following year as untrustworthy papists, descendants of the murderers of 1641 rather than of the 'Milesian Line'; Brooke was obviously trying to get subscriptions for his work, and played on Gaelic pride towards that end. Accordingly he promises to take 'the authentic historians and antiquarians of Ireland' (p. 180) into account for his work, and not to detract from 'the achievements and glory of your ancestors';

I shall advance nothing from tradition, which is not true in nature; nor from history, which is not so in fact; and I shall shew to the most prejudiced and incredulous, that your ancestors were deep in learning, pious in their religion, wise in their institutions, just in their laws, and continued, for many ages, the most generous and valiant people that lived upon the face of the earth. (p. 184)

It all sounded too good to be true, and indeed the reality was less edifying.

In 1743, one Robert Digby had attempted to cash in on the then current taste for exotic tales,[69] by publishing the prospectus for a volume of *Ogygian tales*. As it was, Digby did not have the historical or linguistic knowledge needed for such a project, and as a result Charles O'Conor was called upon to provide Gaelic historical and literary material suitable for the kind of tales that Digby had in mind. O'Conor gave manuscript materials to Digby which were then embezzled by Digby's cousin, Henry Brooke, who intended to use them for his History of Ireland.

Though Brooke's plans were therefore of a plagiaristic, not to say a fraudulent, nature, they furnish another illustration of the more positive interest among the Anglo-Irish for Gaelic antiquity. What is more, the specific case of Digby indicates the awareness that began to exist of the literary potential of Gaelic history.

Gaelic Ireland in Anglo-Irish literature before 1760

Digby had based his projected *Ogygian tales* on the popularity of other such exotic collections. He may have specifically been inspired by a volume that had appeared in 1716: Mrs. Sarah Butler's *Irish tales: or, instructive histories for the happy conduct of life,* which had been reprinted as late as 1734. This brief collection is probably the first example of what one might call 'Anglo-Irish fiction', written by a woman of Irish descent and birth,[70] and inspired by what she herself calls 'those many Transactions which made up the Lives of two of the most potent Monarchs of the *Milesian* Race, in that ancient Kingdom of Ireland' (p. [ix]). She gives a variety of historical source materials on which her tales are based, among which figure Gaelic antiquaries such as Keating (whom she read 'in his manuscript'), O'Flaherty and Peter Walsh (p. [xi]). Thus, the *Irish tales* may well be the first instance of post-bardic Gaelic antiquarianism influencing English literature. The author prefixed a remarkable preface on 'the Learning and Politeness of the Antient Irish', showing a first sign of the amelioration of the Gaelic image in Ascendancy circles:

> Some, upon what Grounds I know not, would needs have their [the characters'] manner and way of making Love . . . to be too passionate and elegant for the *Irish,* and contrary to the Humours, they alledge, of so Rude, and illiterate a People; when all the while they do not consider, that although they may seem so now, in the Circumstances they lie under, (having born the heavy Yoke of Bondage for so many Years, and have [sic] been Cow'd down in their Spirits) yet that once *Ireland* was esteem'd one of the Principal Nations in *Europe* for Piety and Learning. . . . (p. [x]–[xi])

The most substantial tale (or 'novel', as it is called) in this collection involves a love-story set to the background of the Battle of Clontarf, when Brian Ború broke the last organized Danish resistance to his supremacy. The same period in Gaelic history was used later by one William Phillips for a historical drama in blank verse, written for the Dublin stage.[71] It was called *Hibernia freed* (1722). Phillips' treatment of the aspirations of Gaelic Ireland is wholly sympathetic – which, considering the pre-Norman setting of the play, could present no awkwardness to contemporary political sensitivities. Phillips' play is concerned with the expulsion of the Vikings from Ireland by 'O'Brien King of Munster and O'Neill King of Ulster' (the former obviously modelled on Brian Ború), and is, interestingly, dedicated to one of the O'Brien family that had since the sixteenth century espoused the English, Protestant cause: Henry O'Brien, earl of Thomond; an additional method of uniting Gaelic interest in the play with loyal, pro-English credentials. In his dedication, the author states, as his motivation for the choice of subject-matter, that 'Love of my Country induced me to lay the Scene of a Play there' (p. 2). Even so, anachronistic eulogies on the benefits of English rule are put into the mouths of the Gaelic characters. The bard Eugenius, obviously gifted with prophetic foresight, foretells that a new invasion will follow that of the expelled Danes:

> Another Nation shall indeed succeed,
> But different far in manners from the *Dane.*
> (So Heav'n inspires and urges me to speak)
> Another Nation, famous through the World,
> For martial Deeds, for Strength and Skill in Arms,
> Belov'd and blest for their Humanity.
> Where Wealth abounds, and Liberty resides,
> Where Learning ever shall maintain her Seat,
> And Arts and Sciences shall flourish ever,
> Of gen'rous Minds and honourable Blood;

> Goodly the Men, the Women heav'nly fair,
> The happy Parents of a happy Race,
> They shall succeed, invited to our Aid,
> And mix their Blood with ours; one People grow,
> Polish our Manners, and improve our Minds. (p. 57)

Nor is that enough of a sop to English feeling. Even the glorious O'Brien, who has just performed the arduous task of expelling the Danes, reacts with wholly uncharacteristic, but (for an Anglo-Irish audience) most gratifying fatalism:

> Whatever Changes are decreed by Fate,
> Bear we with Patience, with a Will resign'd.
> Honour and Truth pursue, and firmly trust,
> Heav'n may at last prove kind, it will be Just. (p. 57)

Such pro-English anachronisms were needed even more in a play that was performed in Dublin's Smock Alley theatre, and printed in 1720. It was called *Rotherick O'Connor, king of Connaght: or, the distress'd princess,* and its author was Charles Shadwell, whom we have briefly encountered before (p. 113) as author of *The humours of the army.* In *Rotherick O'Connor,* which addresses the politically thorny topic of the Norman conquest of Ireland, Shadwell's sympathies are clearly on the Norman side: Rotherick is considered a tyrant, wholly under the sway of the play's main villain, the archbishop of Tuam. That prelate's name, 'Catholicus', is an obvious device for identifying the Gaelic part of Ireland with Roman Catholicism, as opposed to the conquering part – even though the play is set centuries before the Reformation, and Strongbow was as 'Catholic' as Catholicus himself. Another deliberate parallel to the more modern, Ascendancy, view of Gaelic Ireland (as expressed politically in the penal laws) can be found in Strongbow's statement that

> Deceitfulness is very deeply rooted
> In each Corner of this wretched Isle;
> Instead of Friendship, Charity and Love,
> You plunder, burn, and sacrifice each other,
> And strive, and fight, and gape for Revenge. (p. 236)

Shadwell's notion of the Gaelic view of the situation is projected into his two lovers, Eva and Regan. Eva is full of apprehension and nationally-inspired fears at the thought of Norman help against Rotherick's tyranny: when she hears of Strongbow's landing, she curses 'the Hour since first these Strangers came,/ They will enslave us soon' (p. 226); earlier on, she says to Regan:

> But when they have conquer'd all our Enemies,
> Perhaps they'll then attack my Father's Friends,
> And so, in Time, make Slaves of all this Island. (p. 223)

Regan's answer is a typical example of the mechanism whereby the 'English' outlook on the English-Irish confrontation seeks to justify itself by being put into an Irish mouth: the Gaelic hero cheerfully acknowledges that the English are clearly superior and that, hence, their presence can only improve Ireland – well, if the Irish say so themselves. . . .

> The Men are gallant Men, and make some Show
> Of Virtue, and compassionate, good Nature.
> Their Country seems more civiliz'd that [*sic*] ours;
> With Arts and Sciences they pollish all
> The rude, the wild ungovernable Crew.
> No petty Princes there, dare take up Arms,
> Or, by a lawless Force, pretend to Right:
> One mighty Monarch governs thro' the land;
> He takes advice, indeed, of those Men,
> Who are, by long Experience, made most wise:
> His constant study is his people's Care,
> They are his Servants, Children, and his Friends. (p. 223)

This description of England is obviously meant to flatter the allegiances of the audience, rather than to represent a Gaelic attitude; this is made quite clear by the anachronistic reference to the proud English legacy of parliamentary control over the monarch's policy, which, as the play is set before king John was forced to grant Magna Carta, cannot make sense within its own historical setting, but only to a contemporary audience.

Eva's rejoinder is no less interesting; her national pride refuses to acknowledge the superiority of those who are more advanced, and she voices the contrast between 'natural honesty' and 'artful dissemblings' which was to prove such an important factor in the idealization of the Stage Irishman in the following decades; at the same time, Shadwell takes care to avoid any reflection on Ireland's bravery from the fact that the Gaels are militarily the inferiors of the Normans' 'artful Engines'.

> *Eva. Regan*, your Zeal for Strangers knows no Bounds;
> You have forgot you were in *Ireland* born,
> Where pure Religion, by St. *Patrick* taught,
> Is still kept up with a becoming Zeal:
> Here we are govern'd by Nature's Dictates,
> Not by dissembling Art; which teaches Men
> To act quite opposite to what they think:
> Wisdom makes Hypocrites, Nature makes none.
> Perhaps with artful Engines made for War,
> These Strangers may strike Terror thro' the Field,
> And so affright my Father's Rebel Subjects,
> Who, conscious of the Injuries they have done,
> No doubt, in dread of him, will fly before them:

But when the *Hibernian* Spirit's rous'd,
These Strangers will not be such mighty Men. (p. 223)

And Regan is forced to concur

Your Pardon, fairest Princess. I ne'er meant,
By praising of these Strangers, to take off
Any Glory from the Heroes of my Country (pp. 223–4)

Shadwell's attitude towards his Gaelic Ireland is more complex than that of previous authors. Although his political sympathy lies with the forces that had tried (and were still trying) to subdue Ireland's Gaelic population, he does not view those Gaels as inferior or reprehensible; a sneaking admiration and, if not fascination, at least interest, becomes noticeable. This ambivalence is highlighted by his choice of a controversial topic which in itself contains the germ of all later confrontations.

Charles O'Conor, Patriot politics and the Gaelic past

All this growing literary interest in Gaelic Ireland necessarily entailed a new role, and created a new audience, for Gaelic antiquarianism; the 'co-operation' between Digby and O'Conor may count as an early example. Not that it was a very auspicious start for O'Conor's scholarly career! However, the painful imbroglio around the *Ogygian Tales* and Brooke's History of Ireland (neither of which ever saw the light of day) proves, if nothing else, that O'Conor's reputation as a Gaelic antiquary[72] had reached Anglo-Irish circles by 1743. Ten years later, his history of Ireland, continuing in the tradition of MacCurtin, was printed under the title *Dissertations on the antient history of Ireland: wherein an account is given of the origins, government, letters, sciences, religion, manners and customs of the antient inhabitants.* Though written in English, the book directed itself mainly towards 'the genuine *Scots* and *Irish*' of Ireland and Scotland, i.e. those descendants of the 'Milesian Line' whom Brooke had also pretended to cater for. Nevertheless, the book's controversial fame spread further and wider than any previous production in this vein had managed to do, and won even Dr. Johnson's positive interest. Johnson went as far as exhorting O'Conor to continue his antiquarian research and wrote him the following letter:

Sir, I have lately, by the favour of Mr. Faulkner, seen your account of Ireland, and cannot forbear to solicit a prosecution of your design. Sir William Temple complains that Ireland is less known than any other country, as to its ancient state. The natives have had little leisure, and little encouragement for enquiry; and strangers, not knowing the language, have had no ability. I have long wished that the Irish literature were cultivated. Ireland is known by tradition to have been once the seat of piety and learning; and surely it would be very acceptable to all those who are curious either in the original of nations, or the affinities of languages, to be further informed of the revolutions of a people so ancient, and once so illustrious.

What relation there is between the Welch and the Irish languages, or between the language of Ireland and that of Biscay, deserves enquiry. Of these provincial and unextended tongues, it seldom happens that more than one are understood by any one man; and, therefore, it seldom happens that a fair comparison can be made. I hope you will continue to cultivate this kind of learning, which has lain too long neglected, and which, if it be suffered to remain in oblivion for another century, may, perhaps, never be retrieved. As I wish well to all useful undertakings, I would not forbear to let you know how much you deserve, in my opinion, from all lovers of study, and how much pleasure your work has given to, Sir, Your most obliged, And most humble servant, Sam. Johnson.[73]

O'Conor's book, thus appreciated in the most august and conservative literary circles, follows traditional Milesian history, claiming Irish to be a close approximation of the language of Japhet and his descendants (p. 37), and accordingly holding it to resemble Hebrew (p. 50). Needless to say, O'Conor finds much to regret in the country's more recent history; but obviously the times were changing, for, unlike O'Flaherty's pessimistic, and MacCurtin's defensive attitude, O'Conor can express some optimism – an optimism that seems to be inspired by the rise of Patriot thought and ideals:

> it is certain that the untoward fortune of *Ireland,* for several Ages past, hath at length happily relented. The first Men of the Nation have distinguished themselves throughout Europe, by the Encouragement of every Art extensive of its Happiness and Reputation: They have expelled its evil genius, by weeding *Prejudice* from *Patriotism,* hateful Distinctions from the common Interest, and all Schemes of Engrossment from Liberty. (p. xxxix)

Generally, a new attitude of assertiveness may be noticed among Gaelic Catholics, epitomized by two associations founded in the 1750s. One of these seems to have had close links with the O'Reilly family and is known as *Cóimhthionól Gaedhilge;* little is known of it beside the fact that it was founded in the autumn of 1752. The aim of this society was to protect the declining Irish language, and its rules specified

> That no language be spoken in the Club Room, but the Irish Language, on a pain of one penny for every such offence . . . save only Doctor Taafe, or such other Members, who may not be able to convey their Sentiments in the Irish, without the help of the English, until better acquainted therewith; but subject nevertheless to receive Instructions on such occasions.

Its motivation may sufficiently appear from the preamble to these rules (which constitute the only monument the society has left behind):

> Whereas the Irish, the mother Tongue of this Nation, has been long neglected and discouraged by the introduction of strange Languages not so full or Expressive, and that the Natives, not only find themselves alone among all the nations of the earth, ignorant, for the most part, of the language of their forefathers, but suffer frequently

in their Trade, Business, and accomplishments; besides the shameful Charge against them by other Countries, of the most gross Levity, in being so easily lead, to abollish and render obsolete the sacred Repository of their Annals and Archives from the earliest times faithfully recorded, now nowhere to be met with, but in foreign Libraries, whilst they are busied in cultivating and improving the Histories and Chronicles of Moors, and other Barbarians at home, to the great Detriment and immortal Dishonour of their Posterity, Now, the following Subscribers, feeling the deep Wound their Country suffered and full of hopes, that one Day or other, so grievous a Loss might be repaired, think proper to enter into an Irish Club, to which they also invite all others, that shall think proper to joyn them, subject nevertheless to the annexed rules.[74]

The other foundation of the period, far more important and influential in the long run, was a lobby of Catholics, the anti-penal Catholic Committee; it set itself the goal of convincing the Ascendancy authorities and public opinion of the superfluity and counterproductivity of the penal laws, and was founded in 1759 by O'Conor, Curry and the Waterford lawyer Thomas Wyse. It was to remain active intermittently, and in changing guises, from that time until the Emancipation of 1828.

While O'Conor was welcoming the arrival of a Patriot spirit promising a fairer treatment for Gaelic Ireland, something similar happened on the other side of the penal divide – a divide which O'Conor, even before the formation of the Catholic Committee, strove, with numerous pamphlets, to see abolished. For example, the freemason and editor of the *Dublin Spy*, James Eyre Weeks, had published a school children's geography of Ireland in 1752 which evinced a highly positive attitude towards the Gaelic inhabitants of the country:

Q. What Character do *Impartial* Writers give of the *Irish?*
A. That they are a People famous throughout *Europe* for their peculiar Strength of Body, their Courage, and their Loyalty; and that they are almost ever Victorious in Battle, tho' against double their number of Enemies; so that the name of *Irish-Soldiers* carries Terror with it. Which occasioned the following Lines by a Modern author of Eminence, when speaking of the *Irish, viz.*
　　Hard fated Race! Brave! Generous! and True!
　　Tho' Exil'd in all Climes, in all Subdue.
Q. How do the Irish behave to Strangers?
A. With great Civility and Politeness; so that a foreign Gentleman, who resided some Time in *Ireland* said, that if the People of a certain neighbouring Nation would visit *Ireland* as often as the *Irish* visit them; then the inhabitants of that Nation would probably be more civil and polite, and the *Irish* might become Richer.[75]

The barb against 'a certain neighbouring Nation' may indicate Weeks's political opinions, and indeed the Patriot attitude animating the author is noticeable enough in the Preface, which claims inspiration from the 'Men of Interest, Learning and Fortune' who have associated themselves to advance the Welfare of their native Country, and have endeavoured with true Patriot Spirits, not only to reclaim the Soil of this Nation, but even to reform the very Inhabitants, by opening Channels to Improvement, and removing political Obstructions. . . . (p. iii)

The Patriot idea was gaining ground – not, perhaps, as an active political force, but as an ideal at least; and it was beginning to gain its first toehold in parliament. In 1753, the House of Commons went against an English recommendation in the allocation of funds from a revenue surplus; in 1759, Henry Flood entered parliament; and it is indicative of the change in public opinion that the unfounded rumour of a contemplated parliamentary union between Great Britain and Ireland could, in 1759, lead to 'the most dangerous riot Dublin had witnessed for decades'.[76]

The next year was to be a watershed, marked by the coronation of George III (the first reigning Hannover without a German accent and with Tory sympathies) and by the appearance of the first Ossianic 'translations' by Macpherson. Meanwhile, the stage had been set for what was to be, not just a relaxation, but even an active co-operation, between Irish Patriots and the historians of Gaelic antiquity.

The debate around the rebellion of 1641

As yet, Irish history was still the battlefield of partisan writers. Gaelic points of view had been presented from the early seventeenth century onwards, first to a Continental or to a Gaelic audience, then, beginning with O'Flaherty's *Ogygia*, also to an English and Anglo-Irish public. The 'English' view had been given mostly by Anglo-Irish authors, whose views were dominated by their antipathy towards Catholicism and by the reports of the Ulster rebellion in 1641. English historians tended to deal with Ireland as a side-issue, of importance only in its effects on British developments.

As has been pointed out, the rebellion of 1641 played a key role. Hume had reiterated the Protestant propaganda, and had vested it with the aura of his 'philosophical', non-partizan approach. This was all the more grievous to Irish Catholics since the memory of '1641' played a large role in contemporary politics. The Irish parliament commemorated the rebellion on each twenty-third of October, with religious services whose anti-Catholic sermons were usually published in print; the History that Sir John Temple had written on the period was reprinted frequently. Indeed, '1641' served largely as a paradigmatic example of the untrustworthiness and bloodthirst of Catholics, and, hence, as a cornerstone in the political thought of which the penal laws were the juridical expression.

It is no surprise, then, to find that Gaelic historical revisionism concentrated largely on the rebellion of 1641. Here was a key event in Irish history, an event with more immediate political relevance than any other previous to 1688, one on which depended the penal legislation as well as the low opinion in which the Catholic/Gaelic Irish were held by the Ascendancy. If one wished to ameliorate the Ascendancy's image of Gaelic Ireland – ultimately, it was to be hoped, leading to a relaxation of the penal laws – one had to start with 1641. Thus, the Ulster rebellion became, for a while, a bone of contention similar to what the 'Scotia' debate, *mutatis mutandis,* had been a hundred years previously. In the first half of the century, the Catholic cause was fought by one Hugh Reily. He published *Ireland's cause briefly stated* in 1720; later that century, when Catholic claims were heard with greater readiness, this work was reissued as *The impartial history of Ireland* (1754, 1787) and as *The genuine history of Ireland* – an interesting progression in phraseology.[77] From the 1740s onwards, the two main advocates of the Catholic view were Dr. John Curry (the medical profession being still open to Catholics under the penal laws) and Charles O'Conor, who co-operated on a number of anonymous pro-Catholic pamphlets during the 1740s and 1750s, aiming to sway Protestant opinion. To this end, they often went as far as posing as Protestants themselves, a pro-Catholic (or at least less anti-Catholic) stance being the more convincing if voiced by a respectable Protestant. How Curry fared in this stratagem, which was mercilessly exposed by Walter Harris, we have seen. O'Conor published his *The Protestant interest considered as to the operation of the popery laws* in 1757, and *The danger of popery to the present government examined* in 1761. Then, for a decade, his pamphleteering activities virtually ceased, and he seems to have resorted to another, and characteristic, way of getting his ideas across: that of 'ghosting' other writers.[78] A pattern had been set when he had provided Digby with material for the *Ogygian tales.* When Henry Brooke himself entered the employ of the Catholic Committee as a hack-writer in 1760, he echoed – without much originality on his part – the arguments of Curry and O'Conor, which were now, presumably, weightier since they went under the true Protestant, Patriot flag of the author of *Gustavus Vasa.* However, the pamphleteering approach seems to have fallen into disuse after the formation of the Catholic Committee in 1759, when O'Conor, Curry and Wyse obtained the cautious, extremely cautious, help of Catholic noblemen like Trimleston, Kenmare and Fingall. The Catholic Committee was to fight the cause of the penal victims with the methods of a political lobby, and concentrated on issuing addresses to incoming lords lieutenant, or on the occasion of George III's accession to the throne, replete with civic responsibility and abject loyalty.

Instead, the question of guilt or blame in the 1641 rebellion became a more strictly historical issue, and O'Conor, rather than undertaking to write his own History, contented himself by trying to 'steer' Protestant historians of Ireland into a more moderate evaluation of those events. Harris, the most eminent worker in this field, had been too manifestly anti-Catholic to be useful towards a revisionist version. He had died in 1761 but the generally-felt want of an authoritative History of Ireland, to complement Hume's History of England, and Robertson's History of Scotland, was still present. The Dublin Society bought the Harris papers in 1755; and in 1761, a Protestant historian from England resolved to follow in Harris's footsteps. His name was Ferdinando Warner, and he had published a successful Ecclesiastical History in 1756–7, during the research for which he had taken an interest in Irish history. Warner travelled to Ireland in 1761, where he obtained the support of the Dublin Society and the chance to consult their Harris papers; he also researched in other important manuscript depositories such as Marsh's Library and Trinity College. The Dublin Society went as far as proposing a state subsidy in the House of Commons, and a call for subscriptions appeared in the *Dublin Journal* in mid-1762. It turned out, however, that neither public nor private finance were forthcoming to a satisfactory degree.

Warner had got in touch with O'Conor (who, since the success of his *Dissertations,* was beginning to count as one of the foremost authorities in the field) as early as June 1761, with questions concerning the *Dissertations.* O'Conor accordingly began to furnish Warner with information and material, and, typically, with such material (e.g. Curry's *Historical memoirs*) as would counterbalance the Protestant information that the historian would obtain in Dublin. O'Conor wrote to Curry in the next year:

> I had a letter of a sheet and a half last week from Dr. Warner. He plied me with queries, objections, etc. I answered as well as I could. I had a political end in doing so, for he is great now with the Earl of Halifax [then lord lieutenant]. *E re nata,* I threw in artfully some things relating to our late disappointments, our present dispositions, etc. He wants your *Memoirs* greatly since he perused the *Review.*[79]

However, by now O'Conor was becoming aware that Warner's project might abort due to lack of financial support,[80] and as Warner was preparing his first volume of the *History of Ireland* for the press, O'Conor opened another front by writing an open letter to David Hume, 'on some misrepresentations in his history of Great Britain' – misrepresentations, of course, regarding '1641'. The letter eventually appeared in 1763, in the *Gentleman's Magazine.* Furthermore, a copy of Curry's *Historical memoirs* was sent to the Edinburgh philosopher, then staying in Paris, around the same time.[81] Hume's ear was reached either by O'Conor's open letter or by Curry's book, since he seems to have responded with a not unfriendly, though noncommittal answer. Meanwhile, Curry's *Memoirs* were brought, through the intercession of Edmund Burke, to Tobias Smollett's attention (Smollett having himself written a Tory counterpart to Hume's History) who gave it a very favourable notice in his *Critical Review.* All this may have contributed to the fact that Hume did, in fact, tone down his account of the 1641 rebellion in the revised 1770 edition of his History.[82]

Meanwhile, in 1763, the first volume of Ferdinando Warner's *History of Ireland* had appeared, and seems to have sold well, despite a negative review by Smollett. As it dealt only with pre-Norman Irish history, it did not address the thorny mid-seventeenth century; hence, there was little enough controversial matter in this book, ancient Irish history now being much less vehemently debated as an issue than previously.[83] Warner could thus, with some justice, don the cloak of the 'philosophical' historian, and dedicate his volume to none other than the king:

> Your native Country, permit me, GREAT SIR, to say, looks rather with an eye of pre-judice and contempt on that deserving province; – a province of far greater importance and utility to this nation, than almost all the other provinces together in the whole British empire: And when Your Majesty is informed that no general history, either edifying or impartial, of that great branch of your dominions is already extant, I flatter myself that the whole Work which I have undertaken will be agreeable to Your Majesty, and attract Your notice. (fol. a2 v. and f.)

Similarly, Warner could with some complacency repudiate Gaelic histories for their lack of reliability, English histories for their manifest *parti pris*, and both for being 'neither of them impartial' (p. iv). Warner sees his own work as a new departure. Here, he says, the reader will find

> nothing argued for with a partial affection to one country, or with a prejudice against the other; and nothing contained in any part of it, which deviates from the true and noblest end of history, the persuading mankind to wisdom, liberty, and religion. (p. xx)

But in actual practice, Warner's 'impartiality' seems at times rather a hybrid of, and at times a vacillation between, the Gaelic and the English attitudes. O'Conor saw through this '*astutia historica*', as he called it,[84] and indeed Warner's scattered references to contemporary Ireland read like an uncomfortable combination of a Patriot-style concern for the poor's living condition, with an old-fashioned dislike for Irish sordidness and dirt:

> above three parts in four of the mere Irish live in little huts or cabins, without chimneys, doors, or windows. Their principal diet is potatoes, and milk sweet and sour, thick and thin. . . . Notwithstanding the greater plenty of flesh, they seldom eat any, unless it be of the smaller animals; and they are yet so far from being civilized, especially in villages distant from cities, and where the English manners have not prevailed, that their habitations, furniture, and apparel are as sordid as those of the savages in America. Whether the laziness which is attributed to them – and very justly – is more derived from their ancestors, or their original constitutions, it is hard to say; but it is certain, that there is still among the native Irish a very strong and remarkable antipathy to all labour; and that most of them possess a cynical content in dirt and beggary, to a degree beyond all other people in Christendom. (p. 107 f.)

– The last phrase is, of course, taken literally from Berkeley's *Querist* (cf. p. 305, above); but even Berkeley had become more sympathetic after 1745.

Warner did not receive enough financial support to pursue his work; and this failure seems to have contributed little to his sympathy for the country whose history he had been investigating. The second volume seems to have been intended to take matters up to the time of Charles I,[85] and Warner used his preparatory research to publish, in 1768, a separate *History of the rebellion and civil war in Ireland*. Although the preface is remarkable for its ill-dissembled peevishness about the lack of support Warner experienced in Ireland, the author still adopts an impartial stance, even to the point of warning his fellow-Protestants that they might be shocked by his tolerance towards Catholic claims; and he also condemns the penal laws (pp. xx f.). Warner does not deny Catholic guilt in the rebellion, but reduces the quantity of the outrages.

Meanwhile, O'Conor had found another candidate for the philosophical laurels of Irish historiography: Thomas Leland, a fellow of Trinity College, Dublin, whose biography of Philip of Macedonia had won applause.[86] Exhorted by Burke and by O'Conor, Leland undertook the preparations for an ambitious, full-scale History of Ireland in 1769, a year after Warner had gathered up the pieces of his project into his History of the rebellion. Leland found more public support than Warner: he obtained manuscripts from Burke and lord Charlemont, and O'Conor, again, was an important source of information for the earlier periods. O'Conor's hopes for a fair, unbiased treatment of 1641 were so high that he even called on Curry to interrupt the publication of a history of the rebellion which that physician was then preparing, and to wait for Leland's more authoritative book. These hopes were shattered, though, when Leland's book finally did come off the press in 1771: instead of being, as was expected, balanced and tolerant, and more sensitive to Catholic grievances about Protestant partiality, Leland's account of 1641 came down firmly on the side of the Temples and Humes, giving all the gory detail contained in the traditional anti-Catholic histories, ultimately based on the questionable contemporary 'depositions' kept at Trinity College. Leland did pretend to some impartiality in a short self-justification, pointing out that it was 'difficult, if not impossible' to treat of these events 'without offending some, or all, of those discordant parties who have been habituated to view them through the medium of their passions and prepossessions' (vol. 3, 89) – but it seems that Leland found it more expedient to offend one conflicting party rather than the other. Be that as it may, the damage was done and the untrustworthiness of the Irish Gaels was once again 'proven' in history. Curry rushed a pamphlet into print attacking Leland's book, followed by his Historical and critical review of the civil wars in Ireland; Burke added his condemnation; but Hume, who had mitigated his treatment of the 1641 rebellion in the 1770 edition of his History of England, became harsher again in the revisions for the 1778 edition.[87]

Even more so than in Warner's case, Leland's superficial 'impartiality' is an uncomfortable vacillation between conflicting claims, rather than a transcendence of their conflict; a typical passage from Leland's History of Ireland concerning the ancient civilization of the Gaels may illustrate this tendency to 'split the difference':

> In a word, it appears from all their legal institutions yet discovered, that the Irish, in their state of greatest composure, were indeed by no means barbarous, but far from that perfect civility which their enthusiastic admirers describe as their peculiar characteristic. (vol. 1, xxxviii)

A few years later, Dr. Johnson wrote again to O'Conor, reiterating his request that O'Conor should continue the promising start he had made with his

Dissertations, which had been successfully reissued in 1766 (with additions attacking Macpherson, which must have been pleasing to the Scotsman's arch-enemy). Johnson wrote:

> I expected great discoveries in Irish antiquity, and large publications in the Irish language; but the world still remains as it was, doubtful and ignorant. What the Irish language is in itself, and to what languages it has affinity, are very interesting questions, which every man wishes to see resolved that has any philological or historical curiosity. Dr. Leland begins his history too late: the ages which demand an exact enquiry are those times (for such there were) when Ireland was the school of the west, the quiet habitation of sanctity and literature. If you could give a history, though imperfect, of the Irish nation, from its conversion to Christianity to the invasion from England, you would amplify knowledge with new views and new objects. Set about it, therefore, if you can: do what you can easily do without anxious exactness. Lay the foundation, and leave the superstructure to others.[88]

It seems that O'Conor resolved to follow Johnson's call. By the late 1770s, the Ascendancy's mistrust of the Irish Catholics had largely spent itself, and the more positive attitude as expressed by travellers like Bush was becoming a noticeable political force; by 1782, the first important relaxations of the penal laws took place. O'Conor began work on a History of Ireland of his own, which he never completed. Old and infirm, he repeatedly voiced fears throughout the 1780s, that he might not finish this great task. The end came when O'Conor was eighty-one years old. In the year of his death, 1791, the traveller Charles Topham Bowden visited him at Belanagar, and reported that O'Conor

> has been, for many years of his life, employed in collecting materials and writing a history of Ireland, which was anxiously wished for by the public: whom I am sorry to inform they are never to behold that interesting work, as he has committed it to the flames, from an apprehension that his bad state of health would not permit him to complete it agreeable to his wishes, or worthy the rank he has long supported in the literary world.[89]

Much had changed, however, between O'Conor's initial contacts with Warner and the year of his death – not only in the public opinion regarding '1641', which remained undecided, and gradually developed a wholesome indifference to the controversies surrounding the assignment of guilt, or the mathematical quantification of human suffering tabulated according to the religion of the victims; but also in the field to which Dr. Johnson had referred in his letter: that of Irish antiquity. After a cautious and partial recognition on the side of Anglo-Irish historians of Gaelic claims to antiquity, the matter had rested there for a few decades – until the old Dempsterian controversy awoke with a vengeance, and Macpherson's Ossian burst on the stage to champion the Caledonian cause.

The impact of Ossian

The story is known and need not be gone into in detail: how James Macpherson published his *Fragments of ancient poetry* in 1760, which purported to be remains from a great epic by a third-century bard, Ossian, son of Fingal; how this publication caused a tremendous excitement in scholarly circles, where it was thought that a northern Homer lay awaiting discovery; how Macpherson, after 'fieldwork' in the Highlands, published the long epic poems *Fingal* and *Temora* in the following years, thereby sparking off the most momentous critical debate in Britain since the 'battle of ancients and moderns'; how 'Ossian's' fame spread across Europe to overwhelm young Goethe, and Napoleon, and practically everyone else besides. It is one of the more colourful episodes of the pre-Romantic period of European literature.

But the impact of Ossian, and the importance of Macpherson in Ireland, especially in the more historiographical context, have a special interest in their Irish dimension. It should be realized that, first of all, Macpherson's Ossian did not tally with the version of Gaelic antiquity that had gained historiographical consensus since the days of O'Flaherty. Dempster's revisionist claims had been silenced by the massive reaction they provoked, and the notion that Scotland had been populated from Ireland was restored. The date of the Gaelic plantation of the Scottish Highlands was brought forward from mythical pre-Christian times to the fourth century AD by the church historians Lloyd and Stillingfleet, notwithstanding the attacks that this occasioned, most notably from the Scotsman Sir George Mackenzie, who objected to the fact that the Stuart family tree was being pruned of forty generations of royal ancestors.[90] Mackenzie took a Dempsterian line when he interpreted the medieval appellation *Scotia* as meaning Scotland – he even went as far as claiming that *Hibernia* also often meant 'Scotland' (p. 150 ff.). This, again, provoked Roderic O'Flaherty, whose *Ogygia* Mackenzie had tried to discredit, and who answered in his *The Ogygia vindicated against the objections of Sir George Mackenzie,* which was not, however, printed. The debate was settled for the nonce by the authoritative voice of the Scottish Jansenist priest Thomas Innes, who, in *A critical essay on the ancient inhabitants of the northern parts of Britain or Scotland* (1729), endorsed the view of Lloyd and Stillingfleet.

Some rivalry seems, however, to have persisted among the general public, if the following altercation between Scottish Sir Archibald MacSarcasm and Irish Sir Callaghan O'Brallaghan (in Macklin's comedy *Love à la mode* of 1759) may be taken as an indication:

> *Sir Archy:* Hut, hut, hut, awa, mon, hut awa, ye mun na say that; what the deevil, conseeder our faimilies i'th'North; why ye of Ireland, sir, are but a colony frae us, an oot cast! a mere oot cast, and as sic ye remain till this 'oor.
> *Sir Callaghan:* I beg your pardon, Sir Archy, that is the Scotch account, which, you know, never speaks truth, because it is always partial – but the Irish history, which must be the best, because it was written by an Irish poet of my own family, one Shemus Thurlough Shannaghan O'Brallaghan; and he says, in his chapter of genealogy, that the Scots are all Irishmen's bastards.[91]

It was this long-standing rivalry that was re-awakened by Macpherson's Ossian. Vital to Ossian's success was the idea that his poems were genuinely ancient, and actually written by a third-century Gaelic bard. Unfortunately, the historical consensus since Innes' day was that, in the third century, the Gaels had not yet set foot on Scottish soil. As a result, dauntless Macpherson decided to change history in Ossian's image. He accordingly wrote an introduction to his *Fingal* (1762) entitled 'A dissertation concerning the poems of Ossian' which presented a neat inversion of received opinion. 'The improbable and self-condemned tales of Keating and O'Flaherty', which treat of an *Irish* Oisín, son of Fionn mac Cumhail (the obvious originals of Ossian and Fingal) are swept aside as 'credulous and puerile to the last degree'; instead, Macpherson argues for the seniority of Scottish Gaels over the Irish ones, with flimsy arguments such as this:

> A Scotchman, tolerably conversant in his own language, understands an Irish com-position, from that derivative analogy which it has to the *Galic* of North Britain. An Irishman, on the other hand, without the aid of study, can never understand a com-position in the *Galic* tongue. This affords a proof, that the *Scotch Galic is* the most original, and, consequently, the language of a more ancient and unmixed people[92]

Similarly, Macpherson concludes from unspecified 'internal proofs'

> that the poems published under the name of Ossian, are not of Irish composition. The favourite chimaera, that Ireland is the mother-country of the Scots, is totally subverted and ruined. (p. 263)

What passes for Ossianic poetry in Ireland (says Macpherson), dealing with a 'Fingal' called 'Fion Mac Comnal' [*sic!*] could not be older than the fifteenth century: it is too rude and fabulous, too primitive to belong to the golden age of the great Caledonian Gaeldom (pp. 264–6).

Macpherson later argued this theory at greater length, in his *Introduction to the history of Great Britain and Ireland* (1771), where he develops the idea that Britain's original, *Gaelic* Celts were driven back by successive waves of Brythonic Celts com-ing from Belgium – first into Scotland, eventually from Scotland into Ireland.

Macpherson's views, and the reaction they provoked from various quarters, were to exert an important influence on the current image of the 'Celts' and, *a fortiori*, on that of the Irish Gaels.

British opinion was quite ambiguous on this point. The Enlightenment attitude, with its belief in the progress of civilization and the improvement of mankind, tended to view the 'primitive' tribes who had settled the British Isles in prehistoric times as rude, ignorant and savage. Hume's most negative reflection on the Irish Gaels had been his observation that they had stayed outside the pale of the Roman Empire, and had thus been unable to profit from the civilization that the Roman conquerors had planted between the Rhine and Hadrian's Wall. This view persisted in the works of other eighteenth-century historians such as Whitaker (who voiced it in his influential *History of Manchester,* 1771) and Pinkerton, who asserted that the Celts

> are savages, have been savages since the world began, and will be forever savages while a separate people; that is, while themselves and of unmixed blood.[93]

That statement was voiced in Pinkerton's *Dissertation on the origin and progress of the Scythians or Goths* – which is, for two reasons, significant. First, its title illustrates how the Celts were often identified with that other non-Romanized tribe, the transrhenian Germans,[94] thus compounding the opposition between north and south (current in the climatological debate on national characters) with that between primitive culture (or lack of it) and Latin civilization; second, it shows how current images of demographic groups could begin to draw on the genealogically-structured models (here, the Scytho-Celtic one) of historical linguistics, and on their vocabulary, to bring a biological, racial element into play: Pinkerton's correlation of 'savagery' and 'Celtic blood' is an indication of this process.

As may be expected from such attitudes, Hume, Whitaker and Pinkerton were to range themselves on the anti-Macpherson side in the critical debate around Ossian; but, as will be pointed out later, Hume and Pinkerton were, in a way, overcompensating for their earlier interest in the Caledonian bard.

At the same time, another attitude to the 'primitive' Celts or Gaels had come into being, one which showed a positive interest, fascination even, with Celtic antiquity. It should be stressed that this interest antedates the publication of Macpherson's *Fragments* in 1760, rather than being a result of it; and it can be observed in all non-English parts of the British Isles. In Scotland itself, Macpherson had been anticipated by a certain Jerome Stone, who had published 'an old tale, translated from the Irish' in the *Scots Magazine* for January 1756, under the title 'Albin and the daughter of May'; it had an introduction regretting the neglect into which Gaelic poetry and antiquity had fallen. In Ireland, the *Cóimhthionól Gaedhilge* had been established in Dublin in 1752; and one year earlier, a similar Welsh society, the *Cymmrodorion*, had been established in London. Antiquaries like Lewis Morris and Evan Evans were bringing out materials on Welsh antiquity, and influenced Gray's poem *The bard* of 1757 and Mason's verse tragedy *Caractacus* of 1759. On the Continent, Celtic antiquity was studied eagerly by august bodies like the *Académie des inscriptions*.[95] Macpherson's Ossian appeared, then, when some positive interest in matters Celtic was already beginning to spread, and was eagerly seized upon by men interested in non-classical antiquity and in search of a respectable figure-head. Primitivism in British literary criticism was becoming popular, and this process was, in turn, given a boost by Ossian's primitive magnificence and the fascination engendered by Macpherson's 'discovery'. The gloom and doom in Macpherson's relentlessly 'sublime' prose, which moves ponderously between the thunderous and the stodgy, was not very new either. Gray, he of the country church-yard, had ended his proto-Ossianic *The bard* with the figure of an aged, defeated sage on a nocturnal mountain-top, from which,

> headlong from the mountain's height
> Deep in the roaring tide he plunged to endless night.

Mason's *Caractacus* likewise celebrated the heroic defeat of a noble soul super-seded by a new, pragmatic, militaristic age, thus also foreshadowing the Ossianic image of Celts who 'went forth to battle, but always fell'. No-one was better suited than Ossian to reinforce and perpetuate these initial types. Situated in a mountainous area, usually under cover of darkness, Ossian embodies a new type of Gael: not the bumpkin-savage of traditional estimate, but a personality whose greatness is not that of civilization, but of instinct, including 'natural' values like magnanimity, bravery, lyricism and, especially, sublime melancholia. As Hugh Blair, professor of rhetoric at Edinburgh university and one of Ossian's most stalwart supporters, put it:

> Homer is a more chearful and sprightly poet than Ossian. You discern in him all the Greek vivacity, whereas Ossian uniformly maintains the gravity and solemnity of a Celtic hero. This too is in a great measure to be accounted for from the different situations in which they lived, partly personal, and partly national.[96]

Ossian is also a visionary. Last survivor of a dead generation, closer to the dead than to the living, a man belonging to the night, to the past; in a darkness which is nearly that of the grave, and in which his inner self is stirred by ghostly inspiration to a non-formalized prose-poetry, unpremeditated, Ossian repre-sents a notion of 'literary inspiration' that is based on ideas of liminality and a non-rational faculty of the poetic mind, closer indeed to the *aislingí* and *caointe* of Gaelic poetry than to the eighteenth-century English tradition of Pope and Dr. Johnson.

Primitivists gladly adopted this orphic poet, whom they called, in a significant term, an *original genius,* like Homer or Shakespeare: creating by sheer force of inspiration; untrammeled by petty classicist requirement of form; sublime rather than polished. A critic like William Duff, with his *Essay on original genius* and his *Critical observations on the most celebrated original geniuses in poetry* (1767 and 1770) is an example. Especially in the second essay, he is largely motivated by an overriding enthusiasm for Ossian, and attempts to elevate that Caledonian bard to the heights of Shakespeare and Homer (far surpassing Spenser, Milton, Ariosto and Tasso), comparing them to each other according to certain critical criteria. Duff's attempts are constantly threatened, however, by the fact that Ossian was largely created on the latter-day patterns of literary taste as they prevailed in eighteenth-century Britain. This inherent dilemma, which explains at the same time why Ossian was able to be successful as a literary vogue and unable to be successful as a forgery, was recognized by Hume: he saw in Ossian's 'insipid correctness' the tell-tale difference from originals like Homer or Shakespeare who catered less scrupulously to eighteenth-century taste. Duff, however, though baffled again and again by his own Ossianistic standards,[97] by the discrepancy between his Ossian-inspired primitivism and the latter-day construct that inspired it, fails to come face to face with this contradiction, and prefers to shift his critical standards as soon as they begin either to partake of, or to hint at, Ossian's falsity.

What this means is that the impact of Ossian became independent from his authenticity. Though it was the claim to genuineness that opened the door to success for Ossian, the success and influence of the son of Fingal long outlasted the dwindling credit which his only begetter, James Macpherson, had obtained for his implied claims to historicity. Macpherson had, in Ossian, advanced a case for the revision of early Gaelic history; and as such, as a *historical* personage, Ossian was invoked as a historical authority by, for instance, Thomas Warton – in his essay 'On the origin of romantic fiction in Europe' (1764, in volume 1 of the *History of English poetry*). By 1777, however, Ossian had become a merely *literary*, fictional character, a Nestor rather than a Homer, a type of masculine Muse-of-the-North, and his historical existence is as immaterial as that of his nine, female, Parnassian colleagues.[98] – And yet, well into the nineteenth century, Ossianic imitations, versifications, adaptations, remained a vigorous tradition in pre-Romantic and Romantic English literature. Though Ossian fell flat before the critical mind, he continued to hold sway over the imagination.

It was in such a manner that Ossian's success could lay the basis for a new image of the Celt and, by implication, of the Irish Gael: as one who was untaught, but yet not a savage or barbarian, whose native virtues were not stunted by art. Macpherson himself had contrasted Fingal's uprightness against Latin decadence in the following terms:

> If we have placed Fingal in his proper Period, we do honour to the manners of barbarous times. He exercised every manly virtue in Caledonia, while Heliogabalus disgraced human nature at Rome.[99]

And Macpherson's earliest and most zealous adept, Hugh Blair, favourably contrasted Ossian's Celtic magnanimity with the 'ferocious spirit' of real barbarians, the Germanic tribes, 'Goths and Teutons':

> We must not therefore imagine the Celtae to have been altogether a gross and rude nation. They possessed from very remote ages a formed system of discipline and manners, which appears to have had a deep and lasting influence. (p. 306)

This view, in turn, involves a recognition of the literary talent of the Celts: Blair himself put the case that

> the Celtic tribes clearly appear to have been addicted in so high a degree to poetry, and to have made it so much their study from the earliest times, as may remove our wonder at meeting with a vein of higher poetical refinement among them, than was at first sight to have been expected among nations, whom we are accustomed to call barbarous. (p. 309)

And this point (which had been the strenuously argued *demonstrandum* of so many Gaelic historians) was taken up by Ogilvie, in a feedback to Duff's primitivism:

That the inhabitants of the HEBRIDES have been distinguished from the earliest times, by a talent for poetic composition, and an exquisite feeling of its beauties, is a fact as well attested as it is that these of the contiguous coast of Scotland (the native land of Ossian) possessed both qualifications. It appears indeed from the history of mankind in all ages, that this feeling of poetic beauty is in some measure characteristical of the species. Hence it is, that the most admired productions in this art have appeared in the least cultivated ages.[100]

This same author, Ogilvie, also subscribed to the extra-sensory receptiveness of Celtic people, which was one of Ossian's built-in trademarks. Whether 'second sight' or orphic inspiration, this mystification of the Celt was to remain a forceful image well until Yeats's time.[101] Like Ossian's literary appeal, such notions could survive the defeat of the Ossianists in the debates that raged around Macpherson's pretended translations throughout the 1760s and 1770s.

It should be pointed out that this debate itself was often fought with arguments invoking stereotyped national characteristics. Macpherson had, it seems deliberately, called national pride into play when he contrasted Ossian's nordic nobility with the coeval decadence of imperial Rome; again, he argued against the Irish nationality of his hero-bard by playing on the traditional contempt for Irish lack of civility:

> it would be as ridiculous to think, that Milton's Paradise Lost could be wrote by a Scottish peasant, as to suppose, that the poems ascribed to Ossian were writ in Ireland. (p.264)

At first, this strategy seems to have been successful enough: it is remarkable that a disproportionately large part of the pro-Ossianists were Scottish (Blair, Home, Kames etc.). Among these were also, at least initially, Hume and Pinkerton, both Lowland Scots. Hume's pride in his Scottishness is well known and not far inferior to Dr. Johnson's English chauvinism; and Pinkerton went as far as concocting himself a production called 'Hardy-Kanute' which he passed off as an 'old' Scottish ballad. Pinkerton also included Ossianic verses in his *Rimes* of 1781, e.g. a poem called 'The harp of Ossian' and one 'in the Gaelic manner' called 'The vale of woe', with its characteristic beginning 'Heard ye not the raven scream?/ Saw ye not the sable stream?/ Heard ye not the bleak wind blow/ Adown the vale of woe?' (p. 206). As Macpherson lost credibility, however, Hume and Pinkerton both changed their minds. Hume wrote his perceptive, but unpublished, essay on the subject; Pinkerton struck the Ossianic poems from the second edition of his *Rimes* and began to voice the anti-Celtic attitudes which we have already encountered (above, p. 340). Both justified their shift by redefining their demographic status. Whereas they had supported the Scotsman Macpherson as his fellow-Scotsmen, they now attacked the Highlander Macpherson as Lowland Scots. Hume, who had called Macpherson a 'sensible, modest young Fellow, a very good Scholar' in 1761, called him, in 1762, 'full of Highland Prejudices. . . . He would have all the Nation divided into Clans, and these Clans to be allways fighting'.[102]

Hence, it will be obvious that the net result of the Ossianic debate was a loss of credit for the Macphersonian, pro-Highland side. Hume himself voiced his opinion to Boswell that

> if fifty bare – – d highlanders should say that *Fingal* was an ancient poem, he would not believe them. He said it was not to be believed that a people who were continually concerned to keep themselves from starving or from being hanged, should preserve in their memories a Poem in six books. (p. 418)

More interesting, however, is the fact that the pro-Irish side in the Ossianic debate was not implicated in this defeat of the Highland claims; that, on the contrary, the reputation of Irish-Gaelic antiquity was, if anything, enhanced by the whole debate. What Macpherson had dismissed as the uncivilized rudeness of Irish Ossianic materials could become a point in favour of the genuineness of those materials, once the anachronism of Macpherson's 'insipid correctness' was recognized. Hume, for one, reached the conclusion that

> The songs and traditions of the Senachies, the genuine poetry of the Irish, carry in their rudeness and absurdity the inseparable attendants of barbarism, a very different aspect from the correctness of Ossian, where the incidents, if you will pardon the antithesis, are the most unnatural, merely because they are natural.[103]

It can be concluded, therefore, that the Irish-Gaelic past, and those who defended its greatness and interest, could profit from the Ossianic debate on two counts: not only in the literary aspect, which was, as we have seen earlier, not implicated in Macpherson's eclipse, but also in the historical aspect; moreover, Irish antiquaries had from the beginning ranged themselves on the anti-Macpherson side when it came to the historical implications of his Ossian. This happened both within Ireland and among the last continuators of the tradition of Continental Gaelic scholarship.

As indicated above, Macpherson's claims for a Caledonian Ossian were, in a sense, a re-opening of the old Irish-Scottish debate that had raged for a century, from Dempster to Innes. When Macpherson's *Fragments* appeared in 1760, the Continental-Gaelic *émigré* tradition, which had carried the banner in the attack against Dempster 150 years previously, was in its final decline. It had been bolstered in the early eighteenth century by a large increase in the emigration of those Jacobite Irish to the Continental monarchies who followed callings (mainly military and clerical) for which there was no room under the penal laws. Though not as continuous or as concerted as the seventeenth-century tradition, a number of *émigré* works in praise of Gaelic greatness continued to be produced through two thirds of the eighteenth century.[104] The last flourish of this tradition occurred, as it happened, around 1760, the year in which Macpherson's *Fragments* were published: the priest James Mageoghegan published his three-volume *Histoire de l'Irlande ancienne et moderne* in the years 1758–62, and a large Irish-English dictionary, *Focalóir Gaoidhilge – Sax-Bhéarla,* appeared in Paris in 1768; its compiler was John O'Brien, bishop of Cloyne.

It was O'Brien, too, who was among the first scholars to attack Macpherson – for Macpherson had, like Dempster, perpetrated an embezzlement of Irish history by Scotticizing Oisín, his father Fionn mac Cumhail and his son Osgur into Ossian, Fingal and Oscar. The introduction to O'Brien's dictionary contained an attack on Macpherson to this effect; but even earlier, in 1764, O'Brien had anonymously published an essay in the *Journal des sçavans* pointing out Ossian's (Oisín's) Irish nationality. The *Journal des sçavans* had in the previous year, 1763, published a letter by an Irish physician living in Brussels, Terence Brady, which addressed the same point with references to Keating. Van Tieghem holds that this letter constitutes 'la première fois que l'Irlande fait entendre sa voix pour réclamer Ossian';[105] but that is only true for the Continental Irish tradition.

Within Ireland, the scandal had broken yet sooner. Even while *Fingal* was in the press (it appeared in December 1761 with the imprint 1762), the *Dublin journal* for the 1st of December carried the following pre-emptive advertisement:

> Speedily will be published, by a gentleman of this kingdom, who hath been, for some time past, employed in translating and writing historical notes to FINGAL, A POEM, Originally wrote in the Irish or Erse language. In the preface to which, the translator, who is a perfect master of the Irish tongue, will give an account of the manners and customs of the antient Irish or Scotch; and, therefore, most humbly intreats the public, to wait for his edition, which will appear in a short time, as he will set forth all the blunders and absurdities in the edition now printing in London, and shew the ignorance of the English translator, in his knowledge of Irish grammar, not understanding any part of that accidence.[106]

The capital of Ireland, being beyond the reach of English jurisdiction, was a centre for cheap reprints of English books. This advertisement was more, however, than the effort of an unscrupulous printer to cut into the market: the subordination of 'Erse' to 'Irish' and the reference to the superior competence of the Irish translator, as opposed to the 'ignorance' of his 'English' colleague, will have been noticed. The public knew what to expect, since Macpherson's *Fragments* had been published nearly two years previously.

Shortly afterwards, in 1762, Ferdinando Warner published an attack on Macpherson, entitled *Remarks on the history of Fingal*. Although the author was an Englishman and the pamphlet appeared in London, this attack must nevertheless be considered to be of Irish origin. Warner, who was then preparing his *History of Ireland*, stood in contact with Charles O'Conor. It appears from O'Conor's correspondence that Warner's original intention was to accept *Fingal* at face value, as the *bona fide* translation of a genuine original; O'Conor could remark to Curry that 'He [Warner] still has credulity enough to think the epic poem of *Fingal* a translation'; and he adds 'I endeavoured to cure him of his prejudice by arguments that I think are unanswerable till the original is produced, what I am very sure cannot be produced'. Warner's pamphlet, then, was little more than the result of O'Conor's own 'unanswerable arguments'.[107]

The next year, 1763, saw a letter appearing (signed by a certain 'Miso-Dolos') in the *Dublin magazine* headed 'The poems of Ossine, the son of Fionne Mac

Comhal, re-claimed'. The opening paragraph is of such interest that I quote it at length:

> The esteem which mankind conceives of nations in general, is always in proportion to the figure they have made in arts and arms. It is on this account that all civilized countries are eager to display their heroes, legislators, poets, and philosophers; and with justice, since every individual participates of the glory of their illustrious countrymen. Never was nation blessed with a more numerous race of heroes, law-givers, poets, and philosophers, than Ireland; and though the records of the country should be for ever lost, yet the testimonies of the greatest men in Europe will for ever secure them this glory. Scotland, which has for some ages figured in arms as well as arts, jealous of the glory of their neighbours, has endeavoured, under the name of Scotia, which Ireland retained in the middle ages, to arrogate to itself many illustrious Irish philosophers, &c. but their vanity has been justly exposed by several writers, particularly our great primate Usher, who, though not of Irish descent, yet thought the glory of his country worth contending for. But of all the instances of Caledonian plagiary, the lately published poem of FINGAL is the highest.[108]

The way in which the pseudonymous writer (who in fact was the physician Sylvester O'Halloran, later to become one of Ireland's leading antiquaries) places the Ossianic controversy in the tradition of earlier Scottish impostures, will be noticed; what is more interesting, however, is the fact that the ownership of Ossian/Oisín is explicitly a matter of national honour: Macpherson's kidnap of Oisín is an attack on what the opening words pregnantly call 'The esteem which mankind conceives' of Ireland – in other words, the image of Ireland abroad, which needs 'the figure . . . made in arts and arms' to absolve itself from the taint of inferiority or barbarism. This article is, then, a continuation of the long Gaelic tradition, both on the Continent and in Ireland, to 'display their heroes, legislators, poets, and philosophers'; however, in this later, eighteenth-century context, the author is no longer motivated by émigré jealousies and bardic/anti-English propagandism but by a 'love for his country' that is unaffected by, and takes place within, the close unity between the three British nations:

> The three nations are happily now one people; and had this gentleman candidly owned the truth, and not altered passages in the poem, to answer his own, or patron's purposes, he would have deserved the same applause with many other modern critics and translators; and would not put a gentleman, who, by inclination or study, had little intention to meddle on disquisitions of this nature; but whom his love for his country, for want of a better pen, induced to undertake, and search into the records of antiquity (p. 23).

What all this in fact means is that the Gaelic past is no longer just a Gaelic, but rather a national Irish concern. Accordingly, the anti-Macpherson cause was taken up also by Anglo-Irish authors. It is perhaps not too bold to assume that the provocation of Macpherson's Ossian, and the universal interest it generated, gave an important focus for a national defence of Ireland's Gaelic antiquity, an issue where even those who did not see eye to eye on other matters like the insurrection of 1641 could join forces: for none other than Thomas Leland published, in 1772, *An examination of the arguments contained in a late Introduction to the history of the antient Irish and Scots* attacking Macpherson.

The definitive convergence of the two Irish historiographical traditions – the Gaelic and the Anglo-Irish – was signalled in the same year, 1772, by the establishment of a 'Select Committee' within the Dublin Society, with the general aim

> to inquire into the antient state of arts and literature, and into the other antiquities of Ireland; to examine the several tracts and manuscripts in the possession of the Society which have not been published; and also all other tracts on those subjects of which the said Committee can obtain the perusal.[109]

This Select Committee was the brainchild of a staunch friend of O'Conor, Charles Vallancey; son of a Huguenot officer in His Majesty's army in Ireland, derided by many as a charlatan or at best a naive nitwit, Vallancey contributed few ideas of any value to the study of Gaelic antiquity, but much badly-needed enthusiasm, energy and social/religious respectability. He had founded the periodical *Collectanea de rebus Hibernicis* as a forum for Irish antiquarianism, and hoped, with the Select Committee, to found an institution in which antiquaries could co-operate. In fact, the Select Committee was to lay the basis (especially in its later avatar, the 'Hibernian Antiquarian Society', which existed from 1779 to 1783) for what indeed became an institution of paramount importance in this field, namely the Royal Irish Academy, which, in 1782, counted Vallancey among its founding members. Such activities all took place within the Ascendancy context, dominated by names like Campbell, Ledwich, Leland and Lord Moira. It was, however, the additional merit of Vallancey to open this world to his friend and mentor O'Conor, in whose wake younger Gaelic, Catholic scholars like Sylvester O'Halloran, and, later, Theophilus O'Flanagan could begin to function in close collaboration with Ascendancy Protestants.

The Select Committee furnishes the first instance of this convergence, and it does so under the shadow of the Ossianic debate. O'Conor, though a Catholic – and an activist for the Catholic cause – was invited to become a corresponding member of the committee; so were the Catholic archbishop of Dublin, Carpenter, and Sylvester O'Halloran, who had, since his letter in the *Dublin journal*, begun to move to the forefront of Irish antiquarianism.

The president of the committee was a Patriot member of parliament who had earlier supported Charles Lucas; one of those Protestant O'Briens to whom men like Dermod O'Connor and the playwright William Phillips had dedicated their writings earlier in the century: he was Sir Lucius O'Brien, who, in his invitation to O'Conor, showed the same national pride that had motivated O'Halloran's letter to the *Dublin journal* and where Gaelic and Patriot attitudes seem to meet:

> If our Researches shall turn out of any service to the Publick or of any Honour to Ireland; If by shewing that the Inhabitants if this Islands were at all Times Respectable & often the Masters & more often the Instructors of Brittain we can

> Convince our Neibours that, alltho Providence has at present given them superior strength, yet ought they not to treat the Irish as a Barbarous, or a Contemptible People.[110]

Significantly, the first activity of the Select Committee managed at the same time to address the Ossianic debate and to hark back to the work of an earlier historian, none other than Roderick O'Flaherty. O'Conor was entrusted with the task of publishing O'Flaherty's defence against the Scotsman George Mackenzie, the manuscript *The Ogygia vindicated* (cf. above, p. 338). It appeared in 1775 with an introduction by O'Conor 'on the origin and antiquities of the antient Scots of Ireland and Britain' (p. xxv–xlviii), and an appendix containing John Lynch's anti-Dempsterian letter to Boileau (pp. 281–99, cf. above, p. 278). In this manner, O'Conor intended to 'have the latter as well as the former hypotheses of the north British writing [i.e. those of Dempster and of Macpherson] demolished in one book and under the same cover'.[111] In this respect, *The Ogygia vindicated* followed in the footsteps of O'Conor's own *Dissertations* which, in its second edition of 1766, had contained appendices against Macpherson.

All this does not mean, of course, that henceforth a complete concord existed in the antiquarian endeavour of Gaelic and Anglo-Irish scholars: we have seen how Leland's *History* re-opened old wounds in its treatment of the 1641 rebellion, even at the time that he gave O'Conor his invitation to join the Select Committee with a 'My dear Charles'-letter. Sylvester O'Halloran reacted shortly thereafter to Leland's *History* with his *Ierne defended,* which contained, as its subtitle put it,

> a Candid Refutation of such passages in the Rev. Dr. Leland's and the Rev. Mr. Whitaker's Works, as seem to affect the Authenticity and Validity of Antient Irish History.

At the same time, Vallancey's credulous acceptance of the Gaelic claims to prehistoric civility began to invite attacks from the opposite quarter: his 'Phoenician' model, which shed its 'ex oriente lux' on the primeval Gaels, was opposed by fellow-antiquarians; bishop Percy, the compiler of the *Reliques of ancient English poetry,* was sceptical and complained that

> Vallancey is as hot tempered as he is *hot-headed*, and downright quarreled with me one evening at the [Dublin] Society, for presuming to question some of his wild reveries.[112]

Other men, like William Beauford, Edward Ledwich and Thomas Campbell, who, like Percy, took a more 'Nordic' and consequently less rose-tinted view of Gaelic antiquity[113] began to deride Vallancey's 'wild reveries' openly in the *Collectanea de rebus Hibernicis,* which consequently became less a forum for Irish antiquarianism than a bear-baiting ground. It has, moreover, been pointed out (not unreasonably so) that Ledwich and Beauford (and, one might add, Percy and Campbell) were involved in the established Church of Ireland; and that, hence, it is probably not irrelevant that many of their kind in Ireland regarded all attempts to glorify the ancient Irish as a challenge to the English conquest and subsequent domination.[114]

A few examples may be illustrative; Campbell's own *Philosophical survey of the south of Ireland*, for instance, repeatedly takes a unionist stance, and this at a time (1777) when the Patriots were gaining an increasing hold on public opinion, when the unionism of the early century had gone into a complete eclipse (pp. 334–5, 341–2, 350–1, 359–60). Again, Ledwich contrasted native barbarism with English-imported civility in the preface to his *Antiquities of Ireland*:

> When Hibernians compare their present with their former condition; their just and equal laws, with those that were uncertain and capricious; the happy security of peace with the miseries of barbarous manners, their hearts must overflow with gratitude to the Author of such blessings: nor will they deny their obligations to the fostering care of Britain, the happy instrument for conferring them. (p. [iv])

The attacks against Vallancey were, to say the least, merciless – though in some degree justified by the progressing absurdities that Vallancey obtruded on the public. They were, to no unimportant extent, attacks against the native, bardic-derived view of Gaelic antiquity, in which Vallancey could be endorsed by O'Conor; and similar theories were current in France, where men like Jean-Baptiste Bullet and La Tour d'Auvergne gained considerable prestige with them (O'Conor and Vallancey knew Bullet's work, and Bullet himself had read Vallancey's *Essay on the antiquity of the Irish language*[115]). Therefore, the quarrels in the 1770s and 1780s were not just a continuation of the old conflict between Gaelic Catholics and Protestant Anglo-Irish, but to a certain extent formed part of a larger European conflict raging with equal force in, and between, Britain and France, and signalling the last stage of the decay of the old Scytho-Celtic model, soon to be overthrown by the Indo-European one.

Such quarrels, then, are not in themselves a denial of the convergence between Gaelic and Anglo-Irish antiquarianism: for Ledwich, who derided Vallancey's naive enthusiasm, prepared the way for the next generation of Irish antiquarians with the second edition (1804) of his *Antiquities of Ireland*; and Campbell, who was, if anything, even more caustic concerning his older colleague, could advocate, not only a parliamentary union between Great Britain and Ireland, but also (and, be it said, with considerable eloquence) a repeal of the penal laws (p. 250 ff.). As it is, such unionist and pro-English scholars are outvoiced by the greater publicity which was given to their more Patriotically oriented colleagues; but unionist and Patriot alike were ultimately relying on the first-hand knowledge of the actual Gaelic tradition. Apart from O'Conor's case, we have come across the contacts that existed between antiquarians like Walker and McElligott, and a poet like An Mangaire Súgach (above, p. 252); one could also mention the fact that Sylvester O'Halloran had learned Irish, as a boy, from none other than Seán Clárach Mac Domhnaill.[116]

Patriotism and a national ideal

Around this time – the mid-1770s – the Patriots were beginning to gain ground in their parliamentary politics. Under Henry Flood they had been able to carve out their first toehold in the monolithic system of vote-buying and undertakers, of the periodic trade-off between the British-appointed lord lieutenant who had honours and pensions to bestow, and parliamentarians who had votes to give or withhold. The position of the 'undertakers', the go-betweens in this business of policy-making, had been outmanoeuvered largely under the viceregency of lord lieutenant Townshend during the 1760s; Townshend established the more direct control of the British executive over the Irish House of Commons, and a tighter 'management' of its votes. The non-mercenary behaviour of Patriot parliamentarians like Sir Lucius O'Brien, Luke Gardiner, Henry Flood and Hely Hutchinson was gaining increasing public applause; in 1768, the government could be forced to grant an important concession, the Octennial Bill, stipulating that elections (and, hence, a public reckoning – at least theoretically – of an M.P.'s behaviour) were to be held every eight years. Lord lieutenant Townshend resigned in 1772, and in 1775 Henry Grattan entered the House of Commons.

The successes of Grattan's early career were due not only to the changing political climate in Ireland or to his own political talent, but also to the international context. It was the time of the American war of independence, and the parallels between the American and the Irish Patriots were lost on no-one. Both considered themselves to labour under the duties of loyal citizens without being able to enjoy the concomitant privileges. The American motto 'no taxation without representation' was not too unfamiliar to the Irish Patriots who chafed at trade restrictions and at their constitutional impotence; in both cases, local interest was subordinated to British interests without any possibility of effective local opposition.

Hence, perhaps, some reluctance among the more progressive British politicians to alienate the Irish opposition as badly as they had done with their American colonists. This motive became even more important when France joined the American colonies in their fight against Britain (1778). The military strain on British forces precluded the now necessary strengthening of Irish garrisons, and a civil militia was raised to ward off possible French threats. The Volunteers, as they were called, were usually inspired by Patriot motives of public utility and civic duty, and, as a result, soon began to resemble a military 'wing' of the parliamentary Patriots. The demand for free trade was now made with thinly-veiled threats of armed force, and Hussey de Burgh's famous reference to the Cadmus legend is indeed an apt assessment of the situation at the time: 'England has sown her laws like dragon's teeth and they have sprung up armed men'. Free trade was thus exacted from the British government, with the result that the Irish economy took a sudden turn for the better – a politically useful feather in the Patriots' caps.

The constitutional issue was the next grievance to be redressed. Based on the early Tudor 'Poyning's Law' of 1495, cemented in the Declaratory Act of 1720, the constitutional system made the governing process unwieldy, excessively vulnerable to bribery, and humiliating to those who (like the Patriots) felt it to constitute a subordination of the Irish parliament to the British executive. Grattan seized the opportune moment (the short period when the 'New Whig' Rockingham was in power in Britain, between the 'Old Whig' North and the Tory Pitt) to put the constitutional issue to the test, and he managed to obtain the official repeal of the Declaratory Act from the British parliament.

The moment was greeted by Grattan with one of the more famous pieces of parliamentary eloquence in the English language. The beginning of his speech (which may not have been originally pronounced in the form in which it has reached us) may be worth quoting, not only for its eloquence, but for other reasons as well.

> I am now to address a free people: ages have passed away, and this is the first moment in which you could be distinguished by that appellation. I have spoken on the subject of your liberty so often, that I have nothing to add, and have only to admire by what heaven-directed steps you have proceeded until the whole faculty of the nation is braced up to the act of her own deliverance. I found Ireland on her knees, I watched over her with an eternal solicitude; I have traced her progress from injuries to arms, and from arms to liberty. Spirit of Swift! spirit of Molyneux! your genius has prevailed! Ireland is now a nation! in that new character I hail her! and bowing to her august presence, I say, *Esto perpetua*! She is no longer a wretched colony, returning thanks to her governor for his rapine, and to her king for his oppression; nor is she now a squabbling, fretful secretary, perplexing her little wits, and fixing her furious statutes with bigotry, sophistry, disability, and death, to transmit to posterity insignificance and war. Look to the rest of Europe, and contemplate yourself, and be satisfied. Holland lives on the memory of past achievement; Sweden has lost her liberty; England has sullied her great name by an attempt to enslave her colonies. You are the only people, – you, of the nations in Europe, are now the only people who excite admiration. . . .[117]

It may be said that this speech heralds not only the triumph, but also the end of Irish liberal Patriotism. Patriotism had traditionally (one might almost say: inherently) been an opposition force, a bad conscience to those who wielded power and were corrupted by it; now it was in the ascendant, and found all its major grievances redressed. It had been concerned with justice and political equity in Irish *society*; now all that was left to do for it was to turn to the greatness and admirability of an Irish *nation*. As Grattan's speech so clearly illustrates, the cause of 'liberty' is fought and won, and no longer an issue; and Grattan turns from that cause of the past, from the cause of Molyneux and Swift, to the pride with which Ireland may compare herself, as a nation, to other European nations. To be sure, Grattan's definition of 'nation' is primarily a socioeconomic, synchronic one and cannot be equated with the diachronically defined 'nation' (the nation as an inherited culture, as the expression of a 'national character' working through history) as used in later, nineteenth-century, decades. But at the same time, Grattan is venturing beyond the *strictly* socio-economic frame of reference of the earlier Patriots: national pride is now becoming noticeable as a politically meaningful sentiment. The fish has not yet evolved into a reptile – but it is growing lungs, and venturing, for a brief moment, on dry land.

'National pride' had been announcing its impact on political attitudes for a few decades prior to 1782. Traditionally a moral quality, as general and non-partizan as notions like 'filial piety', 'marital fidelity', 'brotherly love' or 'fear of God', it was presumed to be equally strongly represented in all virtuous persons, regardless of their position on the political spectrum; it was, hence, not a specifically political issue, any more than the fact that most politicians of the period were religious men should have made their country a theocracy. However, the Patriots began to claim a monopoly on 'virtuous politics': the virtue of not being open to bribes, the virtue of supporting the public good rather than private or party interests, and, indeed, the virtue of loving one's nation and taking pride in it – with the understanding, once again, that in this (pre-nationalistic) period, the usage of 'nation' did not imply all that it did later on.

National pride was thus becoming capable of governing a political attitude. The subject had been dealt with by the successful Swiss thinker Zimmermann, and parts of his essay *Vom Nationalstolze* (cf. p. 386, note 21) had appeared in an English translation in the *Hibernian magazine* for 1771 and 1772 (vol. 1, 422–4, vol. 2, 327–8). The notion had cropped up also in earlier Irish writings. The colourful mountebank, Paul Hiffernan, whose career can be read in the *Dictionary of national biography,* published, in 1754, a pamphlet advocating the use of Irish subject-matter for a national (Anglo-) Irish literature – a call, in fact, to create a literature distinguishing itself by its *couleur locale* from the 'mainstream' English literature; the pamphlet was entitled *The Hiberniad,* and advocated Ireland's literary potential with an 'apologetic Sketch, in Behalf of Its Natural Beauties, And Genius of its Inhabitants' (p. 3). This is an interesting combination of elements – we have seen how, in the travel descriptions of the following years, Ireland's 'natural beauties' and 'the genius of its inhabitants' rose in close conjunction with each other. And the same two features are what Hiffernan considers the basis of the main argument of his pamphlet, pointing at the national pride that the Irish should take in their country. Indeed the entire first part is dedicated to the proposition that 'Two Motives for *national Pride,* are (1) The Beauties of the Country; (2) The extraordinary Talents of its Natives' (p. 5).

There is an apt example of how widespread these joint 'Motives for *national Pride*' had become in the mid-1770s; it is the case of Richard Twiss. Twiss, a professional traveller living by his travel descriptions, visited Ireland in 1775 and published his *Tour in Ireland* in the following year; a French version appeared in *An VI*, 1798. Though in various instances indebted to Bush,[118] Twiss partakes in no way of the double enthusiasm for Ireland's scenery and its inhabitants that Bush stands for. Instead, he echoes the earlier estimates of Fynes Moryson and gives lengthy verbatim quotes from Lithgow (pp. 137–8, 152 ff., and cf. pp. 29–30). Unlike his contemporary travellers/writers, Twiss has little sympathy for the grievances underlying the agrarian agitations of the time, and dismisses most Irish antiquarianism as a 'heap of pedantic trash'. With this superciliousness, Twiss incurred the wrath of the Irish reading public. A certain Richard Lewis wrote a poem entitled A *defence of Ireland,* 'in Answer to the Partial and malicious Accounts given of it by Mr. Twiss' (subtitle); and William Preston ridiculed Twiss's self-congratulatory descriptions of his sex-appeal with pamphlets drawing on the description of his Spanish journey. Apparently, there were even chamber pots with Twiss's portrait on the inside.[119]

Earlier, even before Hiffernan's curious pamphlet, some Catholic writings had brought up a hint of national pride in their political arguments. John Keogh, in his *Vindication of the antiquities of Ireland* (1748), posited that 'not any affront or abuse is half so much resented as a national one'[120] – a remarkably early formulation of what later was to furnish Sir Lucius O'Trigger with a pretext for his quarrelsomeness (cf. above, p. 147). And only a few years later, in 1754, one Charles Forman gave another example of provoked national pride when he defended the Irish against the imputation of cowardice that 'A Free Briton' had levelled at them. He published a pamphlet called A *defence of the courage, honour, and loyalty of the Irish-nation. In answer to the scandalous reflections in the Free-Briton and others.* What lends Forman's pamphlet additional interest, is the fact that he can adduce Gaelic and Old English Catholics (the *émigré* 'wild geese') in evidence as examples of Irish bravery, and refer to Protestant Anglo-Irishmen (Molyneux, Congreve, Steele, Swift), when illustrating Irish wit and learning (pp. 68–9). It seems, then, as if national pride was beginning to transcend the basic social and ethnic divide of religion, of penal legislation. This transcendence was to increase in force. Grattan's speech, hailing the birth of an Irish nation, referred scornfully to the 'furious statutes' that were part of the shameful past – meaning thereby the penal laws which had to a large extent been repealed by the Patriots in the preceding year.

Liberal conciliatory attitudes had long found reason to detest the manifest unfairness and wanton divisiveness of Ireland's anti-Catholic legislation, and had repeatedly attacked it with the argument that it stood in the way of uniting the forces of the nation, that it perpetuated Protestant mistrust of the Catholic majority by keeping that majority disaffected with a status quo based on iniquity. It was this that had motivated Arthur Dobbs in his proposals for agricultural reform, it was this that had been used as an argument in favour of a law of 1771, enabling Catholics to lease certain lands for a maximum of sixty-one years. The case was made most forcefully by Edmund Burke, himself the son of a mixed marriage, supporter of the work of John Curry and of the Catholic Committee.[121] Burke held that the penal laws, in repressing the majority of the citizens, sinned against the basic (Lockean) legislative principles of 'equity and utility' (p. 27), in that they formed a dangerous, structural flaw in the very foundation of Irish society (cf. p. 69). The most telling phraseology was employed when he wrote to the Irish Patriot Sir Hercules Langrishe, and stated that the penal law 'divided the nation into two distinct bodies, without common interest, sympathy, or connexion'.[122]

The relief of the penal laws was therefore undertaken by the Patriots, not only as a work of charity or as a natural consequence of their Lockean liberalism, but also as an act of *national integration*. Ireland could not become a true nation, i.e. an organic whole, without Catholic relief from penal oppression. Some Patriot statements during the reading of Gardiner's Relief Bill of 1781 illustrate this. The Protestant bishop of Cloyne (thus far had Patriot ideals penetrated) denounced the penal laws as being 'against national union, against national unity and against nature'; and according to Grattan, Gardiner's bill was to decide 'whether we shall be a Protestant settlement or an Irish nation'.[123] Again, one can see the national concept becoming politically charged: this time, as a transcendence of the religious conflict. Gardiner's bill was passed; the 'furious' statutes belonged largely though not entirely to the past, and the Volunteers, when convened in Dungannon in 1782, resolved

> that we hold the right of private judgement in matters of religion to be equally sacred in others as in ourselves; that as men and as Irishmen, as Christians and as Protestants, we rejoice in the relaxation of the penal laws against our Roman Catholic fellow-subjects, and that we conceive the measure to be fraught with the happiest consequences to the union and the prosperity of the inhabitants of Ireland.[124]

But there was some naivety in all this well-meaning optimism. The penal laws were aimed essentially against the landed interest and political leverage of the Catholic population; and not all who passed Gardiner's relief bill were willing to jeopardize their own economic and social privileges by recognizing Catholic rights in all their consequences. A certain amount of 'double-think' was still at work: Catholics were not yet given the right to sit in parliament, and the 'national unification', spoken of so loftily by Grattan and the bishop of Cloyne, was in fact little more than a partial redress of the most flagrant disabilities imposed on the Catholic population. The actual economic and political division of Irish society was not remedied thereby, and this fact was recognized by non-Patriots on both ends of the political spectrum. The contention of Sir Hercules Langrishe, 'that the Roman Catholics should enjoy everything *under* the State, but should not be *the State itself*' withered under the clear gaze of Edmund Burke,[125] who elsewhere, in his letter to his son Richard, gave testimony to a far more radical notion of 'liberty' than the one employed by the Patriots:

> A liberty made up of penalties! a liberty made up of incapacities! a liberty made up of exclusion and proscription, continued for ages, of four fifths, perhaps, of the inhabitants of all ranks and fortunes! In what does such liberty differ from the description of the most shocking kind of servitude? But it will be said that in that country some people are free – why, this is the very description of despotism. *Partial freedom is privilege, and prerogative, and not liberty.* (undated, early 1790s; p. 346)

In a similar way, the Patriots' most able pro-English opponent, Fitzgibbon, threw cold water on their idealism, when he pointed out, in 1788:

> For give me leave to say, sir, that when we speak of the people of Ireland, it is a melancholy truth that we do not speak of the great body of the people. . . . Sir, the ancient nobility and gentry of this kingdom have been hardly treated. The Act by which most of us hold our estates was an Act of violence – an Act subverting the first principles of the Common Law in England and Ireland. I speak of the Act of Settlement. . . . So I trust gentlemen of the opposite benches will deem it worthy of consideration how far it may be prudent to pursue the successive claims of dignified and unequivocal independence made for Ireland by the right honourable gentleman [i.e. Grattan].

And on the other side of the political spectrum, Wolfe Tone expressed surprisingly similar ideas:

> A country so great a stranger to itself as Ireland, where North and South and East and West meet to wonder at each other, is not yet prepared for the adoption of one political faith. . . . Our provinces are ignorant of each other; our island is connected, we ourselves are insulated; and distinctions of rank and property and religious persuasion have hitherto been not merely lines of difference, but brazen walls of separation. We are separate nations, met and settled together, not mingled but convened – uncemented, like the image which Nebuchadnezzar saw, with a head of fine gold, legs of iron, feet of clay – parts that do not cleave to one another.[126]

Much like the Catholic Relief Act of 1782, the legislative independence won and hailed so eloquently by Grattan in the same year was hollow at the core. The Irish executive, foremost among them the lord lieutenant, was still appointed by the English government which thus kept a considerable leverage on Irish affairs, and could, in fact, outflank the independent but not very influential legislative in the management of the country. It was thus that a less tolerant war-time government like that of Pitt could effectively shunt the Irish parliament (or at least the Patriot party controlling parliament) onto a dead-end track, when the political exigencies of the time made it too troublesome an ally to deal with. The Patriot party was caught in its own moderation during the increasing political tensions of the 1790s. Trammelled by an un-cooperative English-appointed executive, it failed to procure complete emancipation for the Irish Catholics in 1793 – for indeed Grattan himself, and his allies, did have enough honesty to advocate the complete emancipation of Irish Catholics, tantamount to a death sentence for the Protestant Ascendancy – and became unable to maintain a viable policy between increasingly radical ideas fed by the French Revolution, and the increasingly apprehensive and reactionary British government at Westminster and in Dublin Castle. The war between Great Britain and France became more serious in the year that Louis XVI was executed, and made a secure British control over Ireland a strategic necessity. This point gained even more urgency in view of the fact that a new political group had risen to the left of the Patriots: the United Irishmen, inspired by the French rather than by the American Revolution and attacking even that vestige of political thought that the Patriots held sacred: the monarchy. In accordance with their national-cum-republican democratic ideals, the United Irishmen could take up the idea of a national transcendence of religious and social-economic divisions, and argue that idea out with more radical consistency than the Ascendancy Patriots. Tone himself, who could mix democratic ('What is our end? The rights of man in Ireland!') and national ideas ('The truth is, I hate the very name of England') in equal parts, had been secretary to the Dublin Catholic Committee in 1790, and published his appeal of behalf of the Irish Catholics in 1791; even as the Ulster United Irishmen were becoming increasingly radical republicans, they could assimilate the Catholic, agrarian 'Defenders', who stood in the tradition of the disaffected Whiteboys and other rural Catholic secret organizations, and who had provoked the foundation of a Protestant anti-body, the Orange Order. The United Irishmen also tried to get a grip on the Volunteers, but were thwarted by a government act outlawing all armed militias, including the Volunteers. Thus the Patriots lost their military wing. A polarization began to take shape, with the government and rural Protestants facing republicans (now going 'underground') and rural Catholics; in this polarization, little ground was left under the Patriots' feet. Conciliatory bills introduced in parliament by Grattan in 1795 and 1796 were rejected by a great majority, and martial law was imposed on the country.

When at last the festering agrarian riots, fanned by republican ideals and by the harsh behaviour of the British army in re-imposing law and order, swelled into the various insurrections of the year 1798, which were motivated also by the hope of help from republican France, the Patriot ideal of a conciliated Ireland with citizens working disinterestedly for the public good eventually died a painful death. The dissolution of the Irish parliament, and (a century after Sir Richard Cox) the parliamentary union with Great Britain in 1800, erased the very forum in which Irish Patriotism had unfolded its activities.

The notion of a national community of interests, transcending the religious divisions of the country, survived the death of parliamentary Patriotism, however. Starting with the jurisprudential arguments of Molyneux, then with the economic theories of Berkeley and with Swift's denunciation of English interference as the overriding enemy, the notion of ties linking both parts of the Irish population despite their socio-religious antagonism had gained wide currency in the heyday of Patriot thought, and was adopted even in the United Irishmen's republicanism. A national ideal of Ireland, embracing Protestant Anglo-Irish and Catholic Gaels alike, had come into being. A new word was even coined to describe this newly imagined nation: the neologism *Erin* came into vogue around this time to denote a country that embraced both its Gaelic antiquity and its Enlightenment Anglo-Irish elite. To be sure, this national ideal was not yet the same as that romantic notion of Ireland which was to develop after the Union.[127] The Enlightenment ideal celebrated the concord between two ethnic traditions by optimistically (and on the gratuitously symbolical plane rather than in economic or political practice) cancelling historical debts and enmities, whereas the romantic ideal (which governed the outlook of the Young Irelanders and later nationalists) cultivated historical myth and fed on the unredressed grievances which the past had bequeathed to the present. Be that as it may, the final quarter of the eighteenth century did see the beginnings of a historicization of the national ideal, a tendency to define the nation in terms of its past, its history, its myths. Here, then, did the final precondition for the rise of Irish romantic nationalism find its origin: in the coalescence of Patriot ideals and a discovery of the Irish past. In this convergence, not only a historical vision, but also a political iconography were worked out, which were to form the basis of the rhetoric and vocabulary of Irish romantic nationalism. The process of the rediscovery, indeed the reappropriation, of Ireland's Gaelic past, and its links with Patriot ideals, therefore deserves closer scrutiny.

The idealization of a national past

As early as in 1763, the fledgeling antiquarian Sylvester O'Halloran – by profession a physician, having studied medicine on the Continent – published the anti-Macpherson letter that I have quoted on p. 346; it will be remembered how he undertook his defence with reference to 'The esteem which mankind conceives of nations in general', an esteem which, as O'Halloran puts it, 'is always in proportion to the figure they have made in arts and arms'.

This motivation of antiquarianism was to become prevalent in the following decades, and is echoed no less strongly in the letter from Sir Lucius O'Brien to Charles O'Conor quoted on p. 347. Such attempts to defend the reputation of Ireland (not, as was the case with the seventeenth-century Continental recusants, of a Gaelic or a Catholic Ireland, but of an undifferentiated nation of that name) were, then, often undertaken in a spirit of Patriotic *amor Patriae,* as the cultural side of a two-pronged Irish resurgence of which parliamentary Patriotism was the political one. Besides the figure of Sir Lucius O'Brien, the case of Richard Twiss provides another telling example – for Lewis' *Defence of Ireland* against Twiss's supercilious dismissal of Irish achievements, contains, among much invective in heroic couplets, an appeal to Ireland's foremost antiquarian, Charles O'Conor. He, Lewis seems to indicate, is Ireland's most able champion in the national fight against calumny and disdain:

> When cowardly Scribblers, with infernal Rage,
> IRELAND traduce in each malignant Page,
> When base Assassins grasp th'envenom'd Dart,
> And try to stab HIBERNIA to the Heart,
> Why sleeps O'CONNOR? Why, with powerful Arm,
> Will he not straight such Murderers disarm?
> Rise! rise! – thy Country calls! – In soft Repose
> Indulge not, but chastise thy Foes:
> Let not, Oh! let not those thou lov'st complain,
> Nor hear thy Country ask thy Aid in vain. (p. 28)

Lewis's assessment of O'Conor's merits uses terms that are wholly Patriotic in their rhetoric: the 'learned and worthy Author' is called 'a true Friend to his Country, and to Mankind in general' (p. 28n.).

Sylvester O'Halloran was the harbinger of a younger generation of anti-quarians who were overtly national in their motivation. His *Introduction to the study of the history and antiquities of Ireland* opened with a telling self-explanation from the author:

> Having a natural reverence for the dignity and antiquity of my native country, strengthened by education, and confirmed by an intimate knowledge of its history, I could not, without the greatest pain and indignation, behold . . . almost all the writers of England and Scotland . . . representing the Irish nation as the most brutal and savage of mankind, destitute of arts, letters, and legislation. . . . (p. i)

O'Halloran follows in the footsteps of men like Keating and Lynch when he attacks the older calumnies of Cambrensis, but also more modern ones uttered by Macpherson and Hume (pp. 282ff., 337 ff.); the difference is, that O'Halloran does so from an Irish, rather than from a Gaelic or Catholic perspective. The constitutional basis of English domination is attacked in a manner reminiscent of Anglo-Irish Protestants like Swift or Lucas (pp. iii–iv, 245 ff.). O'Halloran pursued similar goals with his larger *General history of Ireland* of 1778, which dealt with the earlier Gaelic past, antedating English presence; it attempted to point out the fact that the Gaels had attained a high standard of civilization at that early date. O'Halloran's works present a confluence of the Gaelic and Anglo-Irish traditions of antiquarianism, and seem to be more concerned with a vindication of Ireland's national reputation than with the elucidation of past history. That endeavour was also taken up by a Protestant *History of Ireland,* whose author, William Crawford, was fired by Patriot zeal. It appeared shortly after Grattan's declaration of Irish parliamentary independence and concluded with a reference to this recent triumph:

> If the flame of patriotism which, for almost five years, has burned in the breasts of our people with so pure and so bright a lustre be not permitted to die, what a coincidence of circumstances diffuse a cheering light upon our prospect! Emancipated from foreign bondage; by the blessing of peace, our intercourse, with new advantages, opened with the several nations of Europe, with Africa, with the West Indies, with our brethren in America, who, after a glorious struggle, have, with us, attained the accomplishment of their wishes. (vol. 2, 387)

A full identification with an Ireland that is essentially Gaelic can be noticed in this Patriot history. Those English from whom the author himself descended, and to whom his less distant ancestors would have expressed undying loyalty, are here represented as imposing 'foreign bondage' on an indiscriminate first person plural which can trace its past back to a pre-Norman, Gaelic Ireland:

> The God of Nature has distinguished our country with a variety of the choicest blessings: A fruitful soil, a happy temperature of climate, and advantages most favourable to extensive commerce. In the virtues of her inhabitants his kindness has been as eminently displayed. But the hand of power has deeply injured us in respect

to a good which is one of the first constituents of human happiness. Our best inheritance, our dearest rights have been violated. You will rejoice in the favourable change which has lately taken place in our Situation. The Genius of Liberty has dispersed the darkness that governed our political horizon, and opened to us the brightest prospect that can be presented to a free people. (vol. 1, 1–2)

Such Protestant, Anglo-Irish antiquarians 'Gaelicized' their outlook on Ireland's history much as the Hiberno-Norman *sean-Ghall* Keating had done a century and a half before. The Gaelic past thus became a national past, in complete contrast to the earlier opinions of Anglo-Irish historians like Sir Richard Cox. As a result, the Patriot historians of the late eighteenth century could inscribe their endeavour in the tradition of Gaelic historiography (e.g. Keating and O'Flaherty) rather than in an Anglo-Irish one (e.g. Borlase, Cox). This implies also a retrospective recognition of the post-bardic, Gaelic ideal of men like Keating and O'Flaherty *as if they were forerunners* of their own Patriot ideals. Cases in point are furnished by the re-publication of older controversialist works with a new, Patriot intention. We have seen O'Conor's edition of O'Flaherty's *The Ogygia vindicated* in 1775, under the auspices of the Dublin Society's Select Committee, and with its addition of more topical, anti-Macpherson chapters. In 1793, the *Ogygia* itself was published in an English translation by James Hely, a Protestant divine and fellow of Trinity College, Dublin, who dedicated his translation to 'The Irish Nation', and concluded that dedication

by sincerely and most ardently wishing that the blessings of peace, plenty, unanimity and brotherly love, may for ever continue in the land; that your arts and manufactures may rapidly flourish and increase, to a degree of celebrity and perfection; that your real grievances may procure immediate redress, and that every corrupt and gross abuse may be chased from this once unpolluted isle; and that your commerce and trade, through all its various branches, may, unobstructed and unrestricted, extend to all parts of the globe! (p. xii)

Two years later, John Lynch's *Cambrensis eversus* (cf. above, p. 278) was published in translation as *Cambrensis refuted,* the translator being a young Gaelic antiquarian employed at Trinity College, Theophilus O'Flanagan (he had helped Hely with his translation of O'Flaherty, cf. there p. vi). O'Flanagan represents Lynch's intention with his *Cambrensis eversus* (highly anachronistically) as a

vindication of the national and constitutional independence of Ireland, against the outrageous calumny and opprobrius [sic] traduction of all unprincipled adversary writers, one of whom is particularly designated, the false and flimsy Giraldus Cambrensis. (p. iii)

The translator adds copious footnotes to Lynch's own discourse in order to 'bring it up to date,' as it were, to enhance its contemporary relevance. The main enemy here is a man born a century after Lynch, one who, though roughly six hundred years Cambrensis' junior is called 'One . . . of Giraldus's followers' – Edward Ledwich, the anti-Phoenician opponent of Vallancey and of his Gaelic fellow-antiquarians. O'Flanagan can subsume Giraldus and Ledwich under the common imputation that both have the intention

> to degrade the character of our nation, and to endeavour, by every possible calumny, to bring us into disgrace and disrepute not only with the generality of the enlightened world, but even with ourselves. (p. iii)

Such a reinterpretation of past attitudes in the light of modern, contemporary issues, indirectly derived from them, in a sense suspends the passage of time within history, and links past and present attitudes. It is by a process like this that a sense of consistency or continuity between past and present can be reinforced, that the historian comes to suppose, behind the transience of history, the existence and influence of certain 'timeless' principles – like, for instance, the ideal of a Gaelic Ireland struggling against foreign domination.

It has been said that a sense of nationality can exist only by the tacit agreement to overlook the factors (linguistic, religious, socio-economic, geographic) that divide that 'nation'. This willing suspension of social differentiation is perhaps equally important on the diachronic, historical scale: it can be said that a sense of nationality exists by the grace of a willingness to overlook the differences between the various stages of that 'nation's' past development, to overlook the differences between the 'nation's' present situation and its past – or better, the past that such a nation selects and appropriates as its own, by a willingness, again, to exclude those elements which do not fit into its present self-understanding. What is needed for a national ideology is what Dinneen called so aptly 'the unification of history', synoptically canonizing and unifying Brian Ború, the great earl Fitzgerald, Eoghan Rua Ó Néill, Swift, Tone and O'Connell as avatars of a single timeless principle while disregarding the differences that are greater between any two of these than between contemporaries like, for example, George Washington and Catherine the Great. It is thus that a nation can begin to imagine itself as a historical community as well as a social one.

If, in these years, Irish antiquarianism strove to grasp Ireland's Gaelic past, it is not surprising that it should also do so by turning to two of the more solid, continuous links with that past: the Irish language and the literature written in it. Both had always been considered as guarantees for historical continuity by the Gaelic antiquarians in the bardic and post-bardic tradition. Such a preoccupation was the more plausible in the late eighteenth century context since it was also pertinent to the debate around the originality (and, if so, around the kind of originality) of Macpherson's Ossian. Only isolated instances of Ascendancy preoccupation with Irish language and literature can be pointed out prior to 1760. The *éclat* of Macpherson's Ossian created, however, an interest as intensive as it was widespread, and was to give a sudden boost to the slow development of Celtic (or more specifically Gaelic) philology. Though a good few rank forgeries tried to cash in on current trends, much was also done that was of real value. Thomas Ford Hill, for instance, collected smaller Ossianic poems from oral traditions in the Highlands and published them with scrupulous honesty in the *Gentleman's magazine* for 1781 and 1782. These did much to save the Ossianic child from the Macphersonian bathwater. At the same time, the distribution of the Bible in Scottish Gaelic kindled a new grammatical interest in that language, leading to the publication of grammars and dictionaries which drew on, and in turn had a stimulating effect on, Irish linguists.[128] In this field, the influence of Charles Vallancey, though of doubtful value, was of overwhelming importance.

As I have indicated before, Vallancey's hare-brained theories were not his sole responsibility, but instances of the Scytho-Celtic model which in France was the dominant linguistic theory and which in Britain inspired men like Rowland Jones (*The origin of languages and nations, hierographically, etymologically, and topographically defined and fixed,* 1764) and James Parsons (*Remains of Japhet: being historical enquiries into the affinity and origin of the European languages,* 1767). Even the Scottish lexicographer and grammarian William Shaw, friend of Dr. Johnson and opponent of Macpherson, could call Gaelic 'the language of Japhet, spoken before the Deluge, and probably the Speech of Paradise'.[129] Vallancey himself took such speculations to rare heights of absurdity. He jauntily compared Irish (that is to say, such etymons as he could extort from that language, of which his mastery was less than perfect) not only with Phoenician, but also with Iranian, Hindi, Arabic, Algonquin, Japanese and Chinese – the Chinese sage 'Confulus' obviously being identical with the great Gaelic legislator Cenn Faelad. . . .[130] One may chuckle at such ideas nowadays, but it should be understood that, though Vallancey can be called foolish (as he has often been called), he cannot be called an eccentric (as he has no less often been called); his activities must be seen in their pre-Indo-Europeanist, pre-Darwinian context. Indeed, Vallancey's status is comparable to that of Macpherson: regardless of the spuriousness of these men's actual writings and theories, so manifest to one with posterior knowledge, their contemporary position was sufficiently controversial to inspire much work which was, and has remained, of undisputed value: that of Thomas Ford Hill and of Matthew Young, distilling Gaelic philology from Macpherson's base concoctions; that of J.C. Walker and Charlotte Brooke, whom Vallancey's misguided ramblings inspired to lay the foundation of Irish literary history.

Vallancey's stature in the world of Irish antiquarianism was, if not undisputed, eminent – witness his authoritative voice in the Dublin Society, in its Select Committee, in the Hibernian Antiquarian Society (1779–1783) and in the Royal Irish Academy; witness also the peeved remarks of opponents of no less repute than bishop Percy (cf. above p. 348). Witness, finally, the well-known bequest of Henry Flood.

The fact that such an eminent Patriot as Henry Flood should bequeath the proceeds of an estate to Trinity College in order to found a chair of Irish philology there is in itself a remarkable indication of the sympathy between Irish antiquarianism and Patriot political thought; no less remarkable is, however, the stipulation in Flood's bequest, that the College was to appoint,

> if he shall be then living, Colonel Charles Vallancey to be the first professor thereof
> . . . seeing that by his eminent and successful labours in the study and recovery
> of that language he well deserves to be so first appointed.[131]

Even though the foundation was successfully opposed by Flood's relatives, the
bequest allows of a few conclusions. First, that the study of the Irish language
was an endeavour which met with Patriot approval; second, that the type of
antiquarianism which met with Patriot approval was not the rationalist,
debunking, cynical type of English-interest men like Campbell or Ledwich, who
were in open breach with Vallancey, but the speculative, mystifying type à la
Vallancey, which claimed a spectacular illustriousness for Ireland's Gaelic past. It
is also a significant fact that an important argument in the litigation undertaken
by Flood's relatives was the contention that the bequest contravened the old
Anglocentric act 28 Henry VIII (cf. above, pp. 38–9); that the validity of the
bequest was defended by one who was a no less eminent Patriot than Flood
himself, Lawrence Parsons; and that Parson's *Observations on the bequest of Henry
Flood* included, as the subtitle put it, a *Defence of the ancient history of Ireland,*
involving a defence of Vallancey's scholarly achievements. The study of Gaelic,
Parsons pointed out in this pamphlet, would make older manuscripts accessible

> which would throw a considerable light upon a very early era in the history of the
> human race, as well as relieve this country from the most unjust charges of
> ignorance and barbarism, at a time when it was by far more enlightened and
> civilized than any of the adjacent nations. (pp. 25–6)

Parsons' pamphlet is particularly emphatic in highlighting Vallancey's masterly
Phoenicio-Gaelic interpretation of the Carthaginian's speech in Plautus' *Poenulus*
(pp. 38–9). And earlier, a budding poet had lauded Vallancey and the triumph
of political Patriotism in one breath. His poem contained Patriotic lines like
these:

> What glorious prospects burst upon my eyes!
> New Floods and Grattans in idea rise!
> Who born in freedom, shall in freedom die,
> Nor sell for gold, their portion of the sky.[132]

– and the same poem had earlier described in glowing terms how Vallancey was
to aid the Muse of Ireland in preparing new glory for Irish culture:

> And see to cherish what fair hope imparts
> *Vallancey* born to cultivate the arts;
> His generous labours too shall aid the verse
> No more to mourn, save o'er the patriot's hearse.
> Her heav'nly numbers, and the historian's prose,
> Once more shall triumph o'er our barb'rous foes;
> His manly reason, and her holy rage,

Shall pour fresh lustre on the Irish page
So much indebted to the learned *Lloyd,*
Who erst the power of Ignorance destroyed. . . . (p. 23)

The author of this effusion, which obviously understands by Irish culture that part of it elucidated by Lhuyd and Vallancey, personifies the incipient literary importance of Irish antiquarianism. His name was Charles Henry Wilson, and he published a (now rare) collection of *Select Irish poems translated into English* around 1782. Apart from the isolated instance of Swift's version of *Pléaráca na Ruarcach,* it was the first time that Irish poetry was presented to an English-speaking public. Wilson's work was followed in 1789 by the *Reliques of ancient Irish poetry* (its title obviously an analogy to the *Reliques* of bishop Percy) by Charlotte Brooke – daughter of Henry Brooke, acquaintance of Wilson (who later published recollections of Brooke *père, Brookiana,* 1814) and without doubt the most outstanding mediator of her time between Gaelic literature and an Ascendancy audience.

Charlotte Brooke lived a retired life largely taken up by her care of her increasingly senile father, and was left in reduced circumstances after his death. She had been encouraged in her early study of Irish by her father, and collected poetry from local Gaelic speakers. Her retiring disposition kept her from offering these poems, and her translations into English, to the public; only her friend Joseph Walker, himself an antiquary of merit, could induce her to furnish his *Historical memoirs of the Irish bards* of 1785 with some Gaelic poems and translations – credited only to an anonymous 'fair hand'. It was not until Walker's work had met with a positive reception, that he and bishop Percy could prevail on Brooke to publish her collection of translations from the Irish. Unlike Wilson's rare and brief collection, her *Reliques* met with general approval and popularity, necessitating a speedy second edition. Brooke is thus the first mediator of importance between the Irish-Gaelic and the Anglo-Irish literary traditions – and was astute enough to recognize the importance of her translations in this respect. What is more, she saw this introduction of the Gaelic literary heritage to an Anglo-Irish readership, not, like Macpherson or Gray, as an opportunity to capitalize on its exotic value, but rather, like Wilson, as a Patriot endeavour in the service of her country: hoping to instill some appreciation for native Gaelic culture among the lettered Irish, and, hence, to raise Ireland and its culture in the British estimate:

> I trust I am doing an acceptable service to my country, while I endeavour to rescue from oblivion a few of the invaluable reliques of her ancient genius. . . . . And will they [i.e. her countrymen] not be benefited, – will they not be gratified at the lustre reflected on them by ancestors so very different from what modern prejudice has been studious to represent them? But this is not all . – As yet, we are too little known to our noble neighbour of Britain; were we better acquainted, we should be better friends. The British muse is not yet informed that she has an elder sister in this isle; let us introduce them to each other!. . . . Let them entreat of Britain to cultivate a nearer acquaintance with her neighbouring isle. Let them conciliate for us her esteem, and her affection will follow of course. Let them tell

> her that the portion of her blood, which flows in our veins is rather ennobled than disgraced by the mingling tides that descended from our heroic ancestors. (pp. vii–viii)

This reference to the Gaelic blood flowing through Anglo-Irish veins is remarkable, and shows how close the (nationally *Irish*) identification between the Anglo-Irish Patriots and the Gaelic heritage of their country was becoming. Charlotte Brooke herself defines her own position as standing in the tradition of O'Conor, O'Halloran and Vallancey, and she pretends with unjustified self-effacement that her

> comparatively feeble hand aspires only (like the ladies of ancient Rome) to strew flowers in the paths of these laureled champions of my country. (p. iii)

Again, the national phraseology, reminding one of Lewis' poetic description of O'Conor as a champion of his country, is striking. Such a Patriot-inspired 'defence of one's country' is perhaps present in Brooke's own work in a subtly anti-Macphersonian touch. Much of the poetry, and even the book's Irish motto (*A Oisín, as binn linn do sgéala* – 'O Oisín, we are charmed by your stories') are Ossianic, implicitly asserting the Irish provenance of this theme; and unlike Macpherson, Brooke is pointedly 'respectable' in including the Gaelic originals of her translations, thereby putting their genuineness beyond all possible doubt.

Thirty-five years previously, Paul Hiffernan had advocated the creation of a programmatically 'Irish' literature in English by making use of *couleur locale* and the Irish national character; as it turned out, the Gaelic past was to be an equally, if not more, important mainspring of 'Irishness' in Anglo-Irish literature. There are a few plays from this period on old Irish topics (cf. below, pp. 368–72); but the mythical and literary Gaelic heritage that was to become such an important source of inspiration and material for authors like Davis, Mangan, Ferguson, Yeats and many, many others, may safely be said to have been approached first by Charlotte Brooke. In the second place should also be named Joseph Cooper Walker's *Historical memoirs of the Irish bards,* which, as I have indicated, was under considerable debt to Brooke's translations. Walker himself was probably the most active Patriotic antiquarian of the generation after O'Halloran, and to some extent he managed to transcend the bitter divisions that the attacks on Vallancey had created in Irish antiquarianism; he corresponded eagerly with men from both camps; with O'Conor and Vallancey – his most important mentors – but also with Pinkerton, Ledwich and Campbell. His *Historical memoirs of the Irish bards* stands next to Ledwich's own *Antiquities of Ireland* as the work that was to remain most influential into the following century; like Walker's smaller investigations, it evinces an overriding interest in the social realities of Gaelic antiquity (including matters of dress, weaponry, pastimes, horticulture etc.) which are a welcome change after the airy generalities of men like Vallancey and O'Halloran. Walker calls a broad spectrum of native sources into play – not only secondary ones like Keating, MacCurtin, O'Flaherty, Toland

and O'Conor (as well as Thomas Warton, Ledwich and Thomas Ford Hill), but also primary material ranging from immediately post-bardic poetry (Fearflatha Ó Gnímh, the Contention of the Bards) to Carolan. Again, a Patriot spirit suffuses Walker's work no less than that of Brooke or Wilson:

> Can that nation be deemed barbarous, in which learning shared the honours next to royalty? Warlike as the Irish were in those days, even arms were less respected amongst them than letters. – Read this, ye polished nations of the earth, and blush! (vol. 1, 8–9)

Even an overtly anti-English tone can be discerned:

> It was hinted to me by a friend, who perused my manuscript, that I dwell with too much energy on the oppressions of the English; treading, sometimes with a heavy step, on ashes not yet cold. But, however thankful for the hint, I cannot subscribe to his opinion. I have only related unexaggerated historic truths. (vol. 2, 3)

Charlotte Brooke's translations were divulged once more that century: in 1795. In that year a 'Gaelic Magazine' was published under the title *Bolg an tsolair* in Belfast – the first time that an English-language publication of Irish interest was to make use of an Irish title. This magazine, of which only the first issue was to be published, contained Ossianic poetry with Brooke's translations, and a grammar of Irish – the first that was intended to offer a learner's introduction to, rather than a linguist's analysis of, the language. Towards this end, some easy 'phrases and dialogues', selected biblical excerpts and prayers, and a vocabulary were also included. *Bolg an tsolair*'s intentions were actually revivalist in nature: 'the main design of the following work is nothing else than to recommend the Irish language to the notie [sic] of Irishmen' (p. iii), it is said; and further,

> At present, there are but few who can read, and fewer that can write the Irish characters; and it appears, that in a short time, there will be none found who will understand an Irish manuscript, so as to be able to transcribe or translate it. It is chiefly with a view to prevent in some measure the total neglect, and to diffuse the beauties of this ancient and once-admired language, that the following compilation is offered to the public. . . . (pp. viii–ix)

The political undercurrent in this publication is sufficiently illustrated by the fact that it was published by the office of the *Northern Star*, the United Irishmen's Belfast newspaper, in the very year that that organization went underground and Tone fled to France by way of Philadelphia. Other Gaelophile activists in United Irish circles included the organizers of the well-known harpers' festival of Belfast.[133]

The last Patriot antiquarian of the century to be noted here was Theophilus O'Flanagan, who has already been mentioned as the translator of Lynch's *Cambrensis eversus* (cf. above, pp. 359–60). O'Flanagan is a rather vague and contradictory character who published little work of his own, and who fell under a grave, though probably ill-founded, suspicion of having forged one of those few publications.[134] Most of his projects had to be interrupted due to lack of funding and public interest, e.g. his potentially very valuable translation of the Annals of Innisfallen; and his employment as an Irish language expert at Trinity College and at the Royal Irish Academy did not put its incumbent in the way of scholarly kudos. However, it becomes apparent on closer scrutiny of contemporary publications that O'Flanagan's unobtrusive influence spread widely through Irish antiquarianism: his help is acknowledged gratefully by Charlotte Brooke, by J.C. Walker and by James Hely, the translator of O'Flaherty's *Ogygia*.[135] Campbell mentioned, in 1787, the help of 'Mr. Flanigan, a student of Trinity College, and greatest adept he [the librarian there] knew of in the Irish language', and bishop Percy thought that 'the very ablest assistance in this kingdom' he could offer to Pinkerton was that of Campbell and O'Flanagan.[136]

I have already quoted parts of O'Flanagan's translation of Lynch to illustrate his professional/political stance. It might further be pointed out that O'Flanagan dedicated his translation to none other than Henry Grattan, and that, in his footnotes, he advocated the study of the Irish language as a national cause – witness his condemnation of its neglect:

> Even to know the language, or to be more than superficially acquainted with the ancient history of this country, has been long considered, by frippery folly and ostentatious nonsense, within the very realm, an ungenteel and inelegant accomplishment – a mark of what contracted ignorance calls *barbarism,* and the fatal characteristic on which bigoted prejudice fixes its merciless talons. . . . This is the *flattering* picture of our national spirit, pride, and independence! – We reject national distinction, without advancing national prosperity! (pp. 46–7 n.)

O'Flanagan acquires his true importance, however, in the next century. It was in 1807 that he founded the Gaelic Society of Dublin, whose first volume (the only one to appear) of *Transactions* he edited in the following year. These *Transactions* contained valuable translations from the Irish, again by O'Flanagan: the tale of Deirdre and a poem by Tadhg Mac Bruaideadha, for instance. As with most of his other ventures, the initial effort proved to be the last; but the Gaelic Society of Dublin stands at the beginning of a long series of similar societies that stretches through the nineteenth century from the Act of Union to the foundation of the Gaelic League. In this respect, then, O'Flanagan is perhaps the most important link between the Patriot, pre-Union antiquarianism of Brooke and Walker, and the nineteenth-century practice – one of the more important, manifest examples of a historiographical continuity stretching across the incisive division of the Act of Union, and highly illustrative of the development that was to turn Patriotic antiquarianism into cultural nationalism. Moreover, O'Flanagan was also the most important link after O'Conor and before O'Curry between this antiquarian practice and the living Gaelic tradition. Himself from a Gaelic background, he had close links with the great Gaelic lexicographer Peter O'Connell and with the scholarly O'Gorman family; and a fellow-member of the Gaelic Society, Richard McElligott from Limerick had, as we have seen, contacts with the poet Aindrias Mac Craith, 'an Mangaire Sugach' (cf. above, p. 252).

If the post-Vallancey generation of Irish antiquarians (Brooke, O'Flanagan, Walker) managed to give the reading public access to Gaelic culture, more specifically, to Gaelic literature, they also imposed their own viewpoint on the field that they made accessible. In much the same ways as historical writings interpreted the past from a point of view determined by contemporary discussions, political and otherwise, so did the early philologists impose Patriot, national or Ossianistic readings on their sources. Vallancey stands at the beginning of this tradition with his *Grammar of the Iberno-Celtic or Irish language* of 1773. Vallancey's chief aim was to vindicate Gaelic culture by vindicating the language in which it expressed itself and which, so he thought, was inherently expressive of its greatness. The grammar was dedicated to the Patriot Sir Lucius O'Brien, who was addressed as follows:

> Sir, the repeated indignities of late years cast on the history and antiquities of this once famed and learned island, by many writers of Great Britain, have involuntarily drawn forth the following work. The puerile excuse hitherto offered by the invidious critics, of the want of means to learn the language of the country, whose history they presumed to censure, must from henceforth be rejected. (unpaged)

Vallancey sees the Gaelic language as an adequate gauge by which to measure the Gaelic national character – an early and highly interesting link between the two notions:

> Where the language of any ancient nation is attainable, a criterion is discovered for distinguishing accurately, the more remarkable features in the national character. Should the dialect be found destitute in the general rules of grammatical construction, and concordance; barren of scientific terms; and grating in its cadence; we may without hesitation pronounce, that the speakers were a rude and barbarous nation. The case will be altered much, where we find a language masculine and nervous; harmonious in its articulation; copious in its phraseology; and replete with those abstract and technical terms, which no civilized people can want. We not only grant that the speakers were once a thinking and cultivated people; but we must confess that the language itself, is a species of historical inscription, more ancient, and more authentic also, as far as it goes, than any precarious hearsay of old foreign writers, strangers in general, to the natural, as well as the civil history of the remote countries they describe. (p. i)

Bolg an tsolair continued this idea, but concentrated on the more sentimental rather than on the cultural aspects of the Irish language:

> The Irish will be found by the unprejudiced ear, to excell in the harmony of its cadence; nor was ever any language fitter to express the feelings of the heart; nor need it to be wondered at, when we consider that their country was the seat of the muses, from times of the remotest antiquity, and that no nation ever encouraged poets and musicians, more than the ancient Irish. . . . (p. iv)

This is strangely reminiscent of the Ossianic image of the ancient Gaels, noble, sad and full of commendable feelings. Although Irish antiquarianism had so strenuously rejected Macpherson's historical claims, it had in fact fallen under the resounding spell of his booming prose. It is interesting to observe, for instance, how *genuine* translations from Irish Gaelic sources, like those of Charles Henry Wilson, stylistically showed very little difference indeed from Macpherson's forgeries. The following specimen – from Wilson, not Macpherson – may illustrate that both used very similar idioms:

> How solemn is the hour of night! when all things listen to the voice of love! Welcome ye awful shades, all-hail your placid gloom. But, hark! it is the lark that calls upon the morn? (p. 86)

And although Charlotte Brooke is less Ossianic in tone, her adherence to contemporary formal requirements of poetic language make her translations often read less like 'Reliques of ancient Irish poetry' than like the usual Patriot-inspired heroics. This, for example, in the beginning of her translation of *Rosc Goill mac Morna*:

> High-minded Gaul, whose daring soul
> Stoops not to our Chief's controul!
> Champion of the navy's pride!
> Mighty ruler of the tide!
> Rider of the stormy wave,
> Hostile nations to enslave!
>
> Shield of freedom's glorious boast!
> Head of her unconquer'd host ! (etc. pp. 165–6)

This style in fact closely resembles the way in which Patriot playwrights had begun to deal with the subject-matter of Gaelic antiquity – again, on the Dublin stage rather than in London.

Gaelic Ireland in Anglo-Irish literature after 1760

After Butler's collection of *Irish tales* (cf. above, p. 325) had posthumously been reprinted in 1735, no further active literary interest in Gaelic antiquity is evinced until well after Macpherson's *éclat* with his Ossian. When at last, in the 1770s, two more plays on Irish history were produced in Dublin, both, again, dealt with the Gaelic struggle against the Danes – as in Mrs. Butler's tales and Phillips' *Hibernia freed* (above, p. 326). The Ossianic and gothic 'graveyard'-influence is clearly noticeable in *The siege of Tamor* (1773) by Gorges Howard,[137] where it embellishes the play's historical interest:

> Such heav'nly strains our antient *Druids* us'd
> In their mysterious rites, what time, the moon,
> Night's awful empress, from her clouded throne
> Survey'd the nether world, and silence came

> Under the wings of night; that hallow'd hour,
> Amidst their consecrated groves were heard
> Harmonious numbers wild; the list'ning bard,
> Felt glowing more than human, and conceiv'd
> That all around was holy and inspir'd. (p. 38)

Elsewhere in the play, king Malsechlin's Ossianistic lament for his valiant but
dead sons ends on a more interesting note:

> Where are ye now, my sons? where, where my champions?
> My first-born *Connal* first in glory's field;
> *Cormac* and *Heber* of the forward spear,
> And *Dermod* of the massy shield? where *Donald*,
> Whose voice was foremost in the charge to battle?
> *Donoch* the rock, and Conary the roe,
> And *Maony* that shot upon the prey
> As with an eagle's wing? alas! alas!
> As some old rock, of ev'ry branch despoil'd,
> Upon the blasted heath, how have you left me
> Naked to the storm? yet thanks, gracious heav'n!
> Fighting for freedom, they have nobly perish'd,
> And liberty sheds tears upon their graves – (pp. 13–14)

This ideal of valour consecrated by the cause of liberty is a new one and places
the drama firmly in a Patriot context. Malsechlin is the ideal of a 'Patriot king' in
the tradition of Bolingbroke, and can thus, when citizens wish to see him, reply:

> Admit them straight. The ears, the hearts of kings
> Be ever free and open to their people.
> The power heav'n gives us, is to guard their rights,
> Redress their wrongs, and make subjection happy. (p. 20)

Such lines were obviously 'playing to the gallery' no less than the loyal pro-English
effusions of the Irishmen on the contemporary London stage were – but it is
equally obvious that the Dublin gallery must by this time have differed substantially from London audiences when it came to their idea of 'sentiments that
deserve applause'. Another instance of Patriot, rather than loyalist, claptrap is:

> O! may th'almighty arm at once o'erwhelm
> This spacious isle beneath the circling main,
> Its name and its memorial quite efface,
> And sink it from the annals of the world,
> Ere the last remnant of her free-born sons
> Stretch forth their willing necks to vile subjection! (p. 12)

Whatever applause such lines may have drawn from the Dublin audience must
be interpreted as that audience's recognition of itself in the line 'the last remnant
of her free-born sons'. The Dublin audiences thus affectively identify with the

Milesian Gaels, and in this fact lies a basic difference from the London audiences whom Stage Irishmen served to confirm in their Englishness. Indeed one might interpret this fact as a central pre-condition for the development of a programmatically 'Irish' literature in English, as demanded by Hiffernan and heralded by the literary mediation of Brooke. The literature written in Ireland in the English language differed from 'mainstream' English literature (in contemporary drama exemplified by tragedies like *Douglas* and *Jane Shore*) largely on the basis of a sense of national identity (both among the authors and among the public) that was Gaelic rather than English in reference. Howard's play dates from 1773; so that, again, one can see that such national identities or (self-)identifications occur earlier, if anything, in a literary than in a discursive (e.g. historiographical) or political context. Howard's play was indeed seen as a specimen of a *nationally* Irish literature; this can be gathered from its Prologue, by a certain Mr. Peter Seguin, which is interesting and obscure enough to be quoted here in full. It regrets that, though Irish life and Irish history are no less abundant in edifying occurrences than that of Greece, Rome or Britain, thus far no native literature has taken inspiration from it, none has dared to celebrate Ireland or Irish themes in verse. It then welcomes Howard's attempt, and implores the audience's sympathy for the lofty patriotic motives and speeches of the play's characters. A nascent, programmatically 'Irish' literature in English is thus, from the outset, governed by Patriotic, political motives:

> The *Grecian* first, and next the *Roman* name,
> Had long monopoliz'd the trump of fame:
> At length, *Britannia* caught the lofty sound,
> And heroes, lovers, patriots rose around.
>
> To us alone, the niggard fates refuse
> The honours of the far-recording muse;
> Although, *Hibernia's* patriots might presume
> To rival those of *Sparta* and of *Rome;*
> Although, her heroes were as bold in fight,
> Her swains as faithful, and her nymphs as bright.
> Here too, of yore, stupendous deeds were done,
> High conquests enterpriz'd, high honours won.
> To the famed facts ten thousand harps were strung,
> And what our sires achiev'd, their poets sung:
> The circling nations listen'd and admir'd,
> But, with the closing age, the tale expir'd;
> For here, alas! we boast no *Homer* born,
> No *Shakespeare* rose, an intellectual morn
> To lift our fame perennial and sublime,
> Above the dearth of death, and tooth of time;
> While gothic fires attack'd us [!] as their prey,
> And, with our records, swept our name away.

But lo! a bard, a native bard, at last
Treads back the travels of ten ages past;
Plunging the gulph of long-involving night
Tears up the tale of virtue to the light,
And gives the living glory to your sight.

O shame! not now to feel, not now to melt
At woes, that whilom your fam'd country felt;
Let your swol'n breasts, with kindred ardours glow!
Let your swol'n eyes, with kindred passion flow!
So shall the treasure, that alone endures,
And all the world of ancient times – be yours!

Behold a royal, lovely, trembling maid!
Timid, yet fix'd; determin'd, though dismay'd;
Advent'rous, by a feeble arm, to gain
What mighty hosts had enterpriz'd in vain;
Advent'rous, by one daring stroke, to save
Her sire, her fame, her country, from the grave!

Now, mankind bow, the deed with wonder view,
And give her bright'ning sex the glory due.
Oh be her merits on yourselves imprest!
Take, take her patriot spirit to your breast,
With all that can ennoble or refine,
And lift the soul from human to divine;
Till rising in your worth this isle shall prove
The nurse of valour, and the land of love. (pp. iii–iv)

Howard's play was followed in the following year, 1774, by Francis Dobbs's *The patriot king; or, Irish chief*. Its interest and its political stance, closely resembling Howard's, appear from the title. Significantly, the play was rejected by the main London theatres, Covent Garden and Drury Lane, before it was performed in Dublin's Smock Alley (p. 8).

Dobbs's main intention seems to have been to show that not all Irish stage characters need be comical in the Stage Irish tradition. The prologue blames the traditional representations of 'Teague' for being plebeian, clownish, and unrealistic as well as undignified:

Full oft hath honest Teague been here display'd;
And many a roar have *Irish* blunders made:
The bull, the brogue, are now so common grown;
That one would almost swear they were – your own.
But lo! to-night, what you ne'er saw before,
A tragic hero from *Hibernia's* shore;
Who speaks as you do, both of men and things;
And talks heroics, just like other kings.
. . . . . .

To hold forth Nature, once the Stage was meant:
'Tis strangely alter'd from its first intent.
Were we by it to judge *Ierne's* sons,
They are all honest – but they are all clowns.

. . . . . .

So many lines without an *Irish* howl,
Without by *Jasus,* or *upon my shoul:*
'Tis strange indeed – nor can I hope belief,
When I declare myself, the IRISH CHIEF. (p. 9)

The historical backdrop here is the resistance of the heroic Ceallachan, king of Munster, against the Danish king Sitric of Dublin, played out in lofty blank verse full of Patriot virtue. Thus, when Ceallachan and a small band of soldiers are surrounded:

Ceall.   Oh! for a thousand of my Dalgais now! –
           But say, my gen'rous friends, how beats each heart?
           Doth glory nerve each valiant warrior's arm?
           Will ye ignobly live, or bravely die?
All.   We scorn ignoble life – we'll bravely die. –
Ceall. draws his sword Then, thus I hurl defiance at the foe.
           What are ten thousand slaves opposed to men
           Who fight for freedom, and for glory burn! (p. 33)

Again, the Gaelic cause is identified with the libertarian, Patriot one. Accordingly, Ceallachan's defiance when taken prisoner fits its historical setting less than the theatrical occasion:

Think's thou . . . I could resign
A loyal nation to tyrannic sway?
Had you e'er felt the flame of patriot fire,

Whose purifying blaze ennobles man,
And banishes each base, each selfish thought,
Far from the breast wherein it deigns to dwell. . . . (etc., p. 41)

Not only Charlotte Brooke's translations, but also her very own poem *Máon* – an epic poem based on a historical subject – imposes this Patriot sentiment and rhetoric on Ireland's Gaelic past, as the following excerpt may indicate:

Yet think me not, tho' true to love,
So dead to virtuous fame,
To prize a selfish joy above
The patriot's hallowed flame.
O Erin! that I hold thee dear,
This arm shall soon attest;
For now revenge – revenge draws near,
In death and terrors drest! (p. 359)

This brings us back to antiquarian practice; Brooke's example illustrates how easily the tone of such contemporary literary conventions was (and, indeed, understandably so) imposed on the perception of historical materials. It is, then, no wonder to find J.C. Walker represent the Gaelic bards as being uniformly motivated by patriotic feelings – so much so, that the oft-asserted melancholy nature of Irish music is attributed by Walker to the bards' sympathetic inability to raise their oppressed, troubled voices to major, rather than minor thirds, whilst their country lay weighed down under foreign rule!

> Thus we see that music maintained its ground in this country even after the invasion of the English. But its style suffered a change: for the sprightly Phrygian, 'to which,' says Gelden, 'the Irish were wholly inclined,' gave way to the grave Doric, or soft Lydian measure. Such was the nice sensibility of the Bards, such was their tender affection for their country, that the subjection to which the kingdom was reduced, affected them with the heaviest sadness. Sinking beneath the weight of sympathetic sorrow, they became a prey to melancholy. Hence the plaintiveness of their music. (vol. 1, 181)

Moreover, Walker's Patriotic view of the Irish bards and their literature leaves room for a few sentimental touches:

> But perhaps the melancholy spirit which breathes through the poetry and music of the Irish, may be attributed to another cause; a cause which operated anterior and subsequent to, the invasion of the English. We mean the remarkable susceptibility of the Irish of the passion of love. . . . (vol. 1, 185)

Once again, the main source for the idea that there was such a thing as a 'remarkable susceptibility of the Irish of the passion of love' seems to be the London stage, where gallant Milesian officers were forever stealing kisses from swooning chambermaids. Amorousness as a Gaelic-held self-image seems far less widespread than as an English imputation.

1798 and its aftermath

All this starry-eyed fascination with Ireland's Gaelic roots was rudely interrupted in the year 1798, when the amorous gentle Irish rose in open revolt. Both the United Irish republicans in Ulster and the disaffected rural Catholics in Wexford repudiated the link with Great Britain in a rather less academic or scholarly fashion than O'Flanagan and Walker had done. The pro-British forces in Ireland reacted horror-struck, and a studiously anti-Gaelic, pro-British vein of historiography reasserted itself, bolstered by the influential republication of Ledwich's *Antiquities of Ireland* in 1804.[138] The so-called *Impartial narrative* of the rebellion, by one John Jones, expressed in its preface the naive hope that it might suggest 'useful reflections' to the reader:

The surviving Loyalist will rejoice in the triumph of *Law* and the restoration of *order*. The surviving Rebel will repent of his folly, and enjoy the comforts which Law and Order distribute. (part I, p. vi)

And Patrick Duigenan's *Impartial history of the late rebellion in Ireland* followed the same tack, as did John Graham, who dedicated his *Annals of Ireland* to 'the Protestants of the united empire of Great Britain and Ireland' (p. [iii]). Such men and, most notably, the eccentric Sir Richard Musgrave, continued the older anti-Patriot tradition which had now come into the ascendant; they, too, tended to draw daring comparisons between past and present, and could see the risings of 1641 and 1798 as motivated by the same basic treacherousness of the papist Irish, the 1798 one being made possible by the culpable laxity or even connivance of irresponsible and unprincipled Patriots.

Writers from a Patriot background argued in similar, though inverted terms. They inverted the question of guilt and put the blame for all political upheavals at England's door, accusing it, if not of downright provocation in order to obtain the pretext for a constitutional union, at least of an oppressive and alienating policy causing needless disaffection; surviving sympathizers and members of the United Irishmen (such as Carey, MacNeven and Dennis Taaffe) in effect took much the same stance, holding that English policy left no choice but armed resistance. Catholic emancipationists also dwelt on the injustice meted out to the Catholic population, and strove to prove the political reliability of the Catholics by showing their meekness in the face of this adversity – thus, for instance, bishop Doyle. Each of these groups defended the role of his particular party (Patriot, democrat/republican, Catholic), each of them blamed England instead and extended ready sympathy to other parties whom England had accused of treasonable activity. In the process, new national saints were canonized as worthy successors of Molyneux and Swift: the Patriots Flood, Grattan and John Philpot Curran, the United Irishmen lord Edward Fitzgerald (particularly after the biography by Thomas Moore) and, a little later, Wolfe Tone and Robert Emmet.

The antiquarians themselves, shaken, kept a low profile. They tried to dissociate their anti-English sympathy for matters Gaelic from the violent revolts of 1798; the following fragment of a letter from J.C. Walker to Pinkerton may illustrate how:

> Vallancey must, as you suppose, be hurt at the conduct of those whose champion he has been. However, he has this consolation: the rebellion began amongst, and was for a considerable time confined to, the descendants of the English and other nations that settled in the counties of Dublin, Wicklow, and Wexford. I do not believe it would be possible to find one hundred or even fifty people in those three counties who understand or speak the Irish language. Latterly, indeed the Milesians have rallied round the standard of the rebellion.[139]

Indeed, men like J.C. Walker (whose *Historical memoirs of the Irish bards* was republished in 1804, and thus laid, alongside Ledwich's *Antiquities of Ireland,* the basis for nineteenth-century antiquarianism) continued their activities after the union – but with a scrupulous repudiation of any political intent or interest.

The best example here is Theophilus O'Flanagan, who, though firmly rooted in late eighteenth-century, Patriot attitudes, at the same time initiated the institutionalized form of antiquarian/cultural endeavour that stretched through the entire nineteenth century to culminate in Douglas Hyde's Gaelic League. O'Flanagan's Gaelic Society of Dublin, whose *Transactions* appeared in 1808, still followed in the footsteps of Vallancey, and used every opportunity to denounce Edward Ledwich, Vallancey's old adversary, as the 'Anti-Antiquary of Ireland', whose writings are 'deliberately designed and barefaced falsehoods' (p. 227). The advertisement to these Transactions can be seen to continue an established Patriot outlook:

> The Society recommends itself to every liberal, patriotic, and enlightened Mind; an opportunity is now, at length, offered to the Learned of Ireland, to retrieve their Character among the Nations of Europe, and shew that their History and Antiquities are not fitted to be consigned to eternal oblivion; the Plan, if pursued with spirit and perseverance, will redound much to the Honor of Ireland. (p. ix)

However, even though the motive for this endeavour is ostensibly nationally inspired, it was henceforth to take pains to deny any political tinge. This tendency seems to have established itself as an immediate reaction to the revolts of 1798; for even in March, 1800, J.C. Walker wrote to Pinkerton:

> A few years ago, '*Memoirs of the Life and Writings of the late Charles O'Conor*' were printed in Dublin, which, when ready for publication, it was thought prudent to suppress. The work, it is true, contains some curious historical facts, and some interesting particulars of the ancient Irish families; but it breathes the spirit of bigotry, broaches dangerous doctrines, and reflects with acrimony on the English settlers, and the Irish parliament, &c. Through the kindness of a friend, I am indulged with the use of this publication for a few days. I have already run my eye through it, and found honorable mention of you, and some severe attacks on Ledwich and Campbell.[140]

The dismay and surprise with which the violence of 1798 was greeted strikes one as remarkably naive. As we have seen in our survey of eighteenth-century Gaelic poetry, *aislingí* throughout the century (and indeed well into the nineteenth century) never tired of foretelling the overthrow of the Protestant landlords and their injustice; Irish Jacobitism remained a fundamentally insurrectionary ideal throughout the century to the point of being able to combine, on that score alone, with the United Irishmen's Jacobin republicanism. The fact that Anglo-Irish antiquaries were unaware of this severe disaffection is a measure of their starry-eyed view of matters Irish, which appears to have owed more to the conventions of the London sentimental comedy than to the activities of Whiteboys and other real-life peasants.

Peasant disaffection provides the most important factor of historical continuity across the centennial divide. Agrarian unrest continued well into the nineteenth century, feeding into the Rockite disturbances of the 1820s (which generated their amount of rebellious broadsheet ballads and 'prophecies' foretelling, in time-hallowed fashion, the ruination of the Protestants). This continuous tension apart, the years 1798–1800 mark an incisive change in cultural practice and political thought. In the newly sectarian climate, the optimistic and philanthropic ideals of Patriotism foundered. The Patriot ideal of Ireland, with a benevolent Ascendancy paternalistically conciliating the native Catholics, withered in the growing hostilities of the Napoleonic decades; what is more, Patriotism lost its vital political platform: an Irish parliament. Antiquarianism became politically incorrect and was quietly abandoned, as the *Transactions of the Royal Irish Academy* for these years show; what is more, developments in linguistics and archeology elsewhere were paving the way for the arrival of a new scholarly paradigm, that of the Indo-European model of ethnic and linguistic relations, which left no room for Orientalizing theories in the post-Keating or Vallancey mode.[141s]

The national ideal which survived most effectively into the nineteenth century was not the conciliatory, paternalist Patriot model but rather the insurrectionary separatist one. The Jacobin, democratic, republican ideals of the United Irishmen bequeathed much rhetoric and imagery to the nineteenth-century imagination, and in this respect coincided with the heritage of anti-English and anti-Penal resistance which had suffused the poetry and prose of the native literary tradition. The *Irish melodies* of Thomas Moore and the *Irish minstrelsy* of James Hardiman were to carry this dual, radical anti-English tendency into the new climate of romanticism.[142]

In all these new manifestations of Ireland's national conflict, one trend had however been firmly fixed in the course of the eighteenth century, and was to remain an operative force in later ideological developments: the implicit notion that Ireland was fundamentally a Gaelic country, that the true Ireland looked back to a Gaelic past, and that the presence of English-derived culture within the Irish shores was a matter of cultural adulteration. Irish nationalists, though usually belonging to an urban, English-speaking middle class or upper middle class, were to refer to native, Gaelic culture and to native, Gaelic antiquity in the first person, as something to identify with, while seeing England as an alien, foreign country. (And much as in the eighteenth century, this process took place by and large over the heads of the native peasantry, whose main concern was livelihood rather than nationhood.) The adoption and central canonization of a Gaelic cultural affiliation and a Gaelic-oriented historical self-awareness had been a slow and complex process, finally accomplished in the later eighteenth century; it was to remain central to the Anglo-Irish sense of national identity henceforth. In the various ethnic and cultural images and identity-constructs of Irishness which had been formulated over the centuries, the one which had finally gained pride of place was that of a fundamental, essential and intransigent non-Englishness.

CONCLUSION

When Irish nationalism took shape as a separatist ideology in the nineteenth century, it came to rely increasingly on the principle that Ireland, as a country, had a separate cultural individuality, un-English and un-British, and that as such Ireland could not be merged into a United Kingdom. The cultural individuality that played such an important role in the national self-definition of Ireland was a collective self-image of relatively recent vintage; it invoked the Gaelic roots of the country, the Catholicism and the folkways of the peasantry, the Protestantism and benevolent sense of Irish affiliation of the upper classes. Crucially, Ireland was seen as a country where social divisions coincided with ethnic and religious differences, but where, ideally, both halves of the population could subscribe to a joint territorial identity (the island of Ireland) and a joint sense that this territory was heir to a radically non-English cultural antiquity. This national ideal perpetuated an Enlightenment, Patriot attitude which had witnessed, in the second half of the eighteenth century, the adoption of a Dublin-centred, Irish sense of political loyalty, a corresponding ideal of non-sectarian intra-Irish solidarity and benevolence between elite and peasantry, Catholic and Protestant, and a non-English, Gaelic-oriented sense of cultural tradition and inheritance.

In the foregoing pages, I have attempted to outline how this optimistic Irish ideal, this national self-image, could have emerged from a history of colonial enmity, dispossession, oppression, religious intolerance and ethnic hatred. The history and mutual interaction between the conflicting parties in the Irish confrontation is a long, fascinating record in the annals of European prejudice and clashing cultures. The estimate that native Irish, English visitors and an English-imported settler class formed of each other and of themselves has wound its course over many painful centuries, in relative isolation from European upheavals such as the political transformations of the late Middle Ages, Thirty Years War, the wars of Louis XIV, the rivalry between absolutism and democratic thought, the French Revolution, the Napoleonic conquests and subsequent upheavals. Subject mainly to its own, inner dynamics with relatively little outside interference, the English-Irish confrontation offers a clear example of the various types and modes of interaction that can take shape in the imagery of cultural confrontation.

There is, to begin with, the process of 'othering', the exoticization of Irish society and culture in describing and evaluating it wholly in the ethnocentrist terms and standards of English culture. From Giraldus Cambrensis onwards, Irish society is described predominantly in those aspects wherein it is different from England; and in many cases this exoticization is discursively heightened for rhetorical purposes. The default value in such a process is one of denigration: the differentness of Ireland is by the same token a sign of inferiority, barbarism, savagery, since the standards of true civility and true humanity are aprioristically arrogated for the author's home culture. To the extent that the ideal self-image of English authors appears to invoke the ideals of continence, reasonableness, mature control over one's emotions and similar character traits traditionally ascribed to mature masculinity, Ireland will be characterized by a lack of such qualities: a lack of rational control over the emotions, a lack of cultural restraint on physical appetites, a lack of self-discipline and moral equilibrium. Like small children or otherwise immature (or even pathological) personalities, Irish society according to English representations seems to lack what Freud would call a super-ego. Occasionally, some commentators will point out that one should compare like with like, and that the contrast between the upper classes of the two countries, or between their respective peasant populations, is in fact less stark than certain descriptions would suggest; later again, in the context of Enlightenment appreciation of the primitive, the authentic and the exotic, a more positive valorization (or even a sentimentalization) of Irish otherness becomes noticeable. The immaturity, violence and bestiality of the Irish can be reinterpreted into a charming, natural, naive childlikeness, a direct emotionality and spontaneity of affect unspoiled by the insipid conventions of genteel social life.

However, the ethnocentrist denigration and the primitivist sentimentalization of the English image of Ireland are both of them variations on a single attitude: that of exoticism, of reducing Irish life to those aspects which are foregrounded as 'typical' and remarkable because of their divergence from English-based norms and expectations. In both cases, Ireland counts as the counterpart to mature, continent and self-controlled reasonableness. It is even possible for these two modalities of divergence to be conflated: if at one point the Irish count as violent fighters, and at another time they count as sentimental, ballad-singing dreamers, those two opposites, rather than cancelling each other out or invalidating each other, can be merged into a dualistic image: the Irish can then be seen as people who, untrammeled by rational restraint, veer in their emotions between sentimentality and violence. The ambiguousness of the reputation becomes a reputation of ambiguousness.

Moreover, there is a historically constant, invariant tendency for cultural differences to be evaluated against an implicit time-scale: the state of society as a stage of development. Ireland, to the extent that its cultural praxis differs from England, is 'backward', resembles the English past more than the English present, resembles a childish rather than a mature adult personality, is less far advanced in the march of progress. Ireland reflects an earlier, more primitive stage in the development of human character or society. Again, that can be formulated either as a negative criticism (Ireland is retarded, savage and underdeveloped) or as a sentimental appreciation (Ireland is in a more natural state, its emotionality and fantasy unadulterated by the specious innovations and degenerate fashions of civil society). In both cases, Ireland is considered to have a stronger element of 'pastness' in its cultural profile: its lifestyle is either old fashioned or else more traditional, historical developments and modernization processes have passed it by or have as yet failed to take full effect there. If the past is a foreign country, and if places like Ireland are, from the English point of view, a foreign country, then places like Ireland will be seen to have a privileged link with the past and a corresponding lack of modernity. That attitude has remained fundamentally constant from Giraldus's days to the present.

The dynamics of negative or positive valorization in this exoticist Irish image are in themselves noteworthy. To be sure, there appears to be a long-term development from crude ethnocentrism and denigration towards a more appreciative and culturally relativist attitude, but that development is by no means straightforward or linear. Two factors are at work influencing the positive or negative valorization of Ireland in English-centred discourse. One of these is directly political, the other is more autonomously a matter of discursive poetics and conventions. To begin with, there is the obvious tendency for images to deteriorate and to become more negative in times of political tension and enmity. Whenever Ireland offers active resistance and an active threat to English supremacy, English representations will veer to the register of war propaganda and will activate the most negative elements in the stock-in-trade of Irish commonplaces: savagery, dishonesty, laziness, lack of hygiene; conversely, periods of relative stability will witness a relative amelioration of the Irish as harmless, quaint, amusing. A cyclical pattern seems noticeable with periods of crisis and negative representations around 1600, 1640–1650, 1680–1690 and 1798 while the intervening periods of comparative stability (the 1620s and 1630s, 1660–1680, and 1710–1795) witness a gradual relaxation and amelioration of Irish representations.

But there seems to be an autonomously discursive dynamics at work as well. The amelioration of the Irish image in the course of the eighteenth century is to a great extent a spill-over from other literary domains, such as a growing appreciation for sublime landscapes and a sentimental revaluation of non-aristocratic ('honest', 'humble' and 'artless') virtues. This last development in particular is remarkable. Generally, literary characterization of Irish personages in fictional texts seems to follow the trends and patterns of representations set in non-fictional discourse: history-writing or political reflection. Irish literary personages seem to be characterized according to the general political attitudes vis-à-vis Ireland current at the time. Interestingly, the sentimentalization of the Stage Irishman, which takes place around the mid-eighteenth century, appears motivated by a different dynamics, namely an innovatory poetical desire to go against the hackneyed and threadbare clichés of a previous generation. Playwrights seems to play with the expectations of their audience, to give refreshingly unusual treatment to overdetermined stock characters, and to do so in the context of a sentimental appreciation of child like virtues such as spontaneity, honesty and simplicity. This development takes place in relative independence from the wider context of political and historical evaluations and representations of Ireland that were doing the rounds at the time; if anything, the literary treatment of Irish character is in itself a trend-setting development, which moves in advance of tendencies in other, non-fictional genres. Going by the chronology of publication, travel descriptions of the 1770s and 1780s give sentimental representations *in response to* sentimentalized stage characterizations, rather than vice versa. This is an indication that national characterization is to some significant extent a construct fashioned according to discursive poetics and genre conventions, and that the development of such literary imagery is not just a passive response to real-life situations. In this case at least, the relations between empirical reality and literary representation are clearly counter-mimetic. Art does not imitate life, but real-life attitudes follow in the footsteps of artistic license and literary models.

The situation summarized here was, in fact, highly impervious to real-life input. For one thing, the characterization of the native Irish was utterly heedless of the attitudes and self-image of the native Irish themselves. Although native material (song and music especially) did come to meet with a certain amount of aesthetic appreciation, it was always received in its 'otherness', its exoticism, its incomprehensibility. The textual content of poetry and balladry was reduced to 'gramachrees and lango-lees', mere phatic cyphers of alienness and difference, with no attention to the outlooks, attitudes and aspirations that might have been expressed in such material. The native Irish and the English image of them were in fact badly at cross-purposes. The English audience willed itself into a sentimental appreciation of Irish characters, and accordingly vested the Irish with all sorts of commendable feelings, including pro-British political loyalty, and cheerful submission to their destiny. But in reality, the predominant native Irish attitude (though politically incapacitated, paralysed under a repressive political and economic system, and weighed down by impoverishment to the point of frequent famine) was one of outraged grievance and ardent, messianic hope for a revolutionary overthrow of the status quo. The 1798 rebellion was, to be sure, inspired by metropolitan, democratic and even Jacobin values, and largely carried by an Ulster dissenting background rather than taking shape in the neat binary opposition between Anglo-Irish elite and native Gaels; even so, it could attract much peasant involvement because it appealed to a revolutionary Jacobite disaffection, which had been kept alive in *aisling* poetry throughout the century. This native tradition of never-relinquished hope for a redress of grievances had been strenuously maintained and volubly expressed in a steady stream of balladry and poetry, without anything of this transpiring to the sentimental English theatre audiences and travel writers. It is for this reason, perhaps, that the 1798 rebellion came as such a shock to the sentimental optimism of Enlightenment Patriots.

The native attitude had undergone a remarkable transformation; it had started out from a courtly-aristocratic mentality with more archaic elements, such as had been prevalent in the middle ages and expressed in bardic school poetry. In that attitude, class counted for more than nationality, and the civility of letters was seen as a courtly, noble medium of understanding which took shape in relative isolation from political or territorial conflicts. Next to this courtly-aristocratic self-image of the learned classes, the dominant political factor in the medieval Gaelic outlook was a genealogical one, which traced collective identities in terms of family relationships and descent. The bardic poetry of the middle ages offers a fascinating, though painful record of this remarkable world-view coming face to face with a colonial hegemonism and a centralized state ideology as fostered by the Tudors. To the terms of Tudor expansionism, the discourse of the politically decentralized bardic society could oppose no similar terms of politically unified pan-Irish ('nationwide') resistance, except in the metaphorical terms of a mythical high-kingship of Tara. Rather, the opposition urged by bardic poetry is one of cultural politics, enjoining political leaders to honour native custom and to resist and harrow 'the foreigners' (an invariably amorphous, vaguely-defined category). After the defeat of the last resisting native leaders, poets appear at a loss as to their role in a Gaelic society bereft of its aristocratic aegis.

A more effective common organizing focus for pan-Irish anti-English resistance was offered in the field of religion. The conflict between the native Irish and the English crown quickly became coterminous with the conflict between Reformation and Recusant, Protestant and Catholic; accordingly, it comes as no surprise to see most of the native intelligentsia in the seventeenth century associated in one way or another with the Catholic church and with the Counter-Reformation. The self-identification in terms of religion offered a common ground between aristocratic poet and humble peasant, Old English and Gaelic Irish; although some poets throughout the seventeenth century continue to express old-fashioned aristocratic intransigence and disdain for the native boors and foreign oppressors alike, a common dispossession is faced by all Catholic Irish after 1690. Poets of the eighteenth century begin to voice an outlook and sense of collective identity based on the shared factors of stubborn religious loyalty, social oppression and economic dispossesion, and a hankering after the true king in exile; in the course of that century, the idea that Irish language itself presents a common factor of cultural complicity gains in importance. Eighteenth-century poetry bespeaks a common awareness of a dispossessed Catholic underclass, defining itself in its cultural distinctiveness and hoping for redress from a messianic foreign intervention. This Gaelic-Catholic-Jacobite political self-image remains constant and highly forceful but does not spread beyond the hermetic underclass in question; it does not influence middle-class or Anglo-Irish attitudes and will eventually die out with the obliteration of the underclass in question, through famine, emigration and Anglicization in the nineteenth century. However, their stance was to be rediscovered, adapted and internalized by the revivalists and Pearsian nationalists of the early twentieth century.

One (politically less inflammatory) element of native culture did spread beyond the confines of its society of origin: its historical consciousness. English or English-oriented scholars from the early to mid-seventeenth began to take an antiquarian interest in Ireland's antiquity, and came to rely more and more on native sources made available to them by native intermediaries. Increasingly, native scholars and antiquaries began to reach a non-native audience, be it through the publications printed on the continent or through direct association with non-native scholars. The dissemination of a native historical outlook, invoking the mythographical and pseudohistorical traditions of medieval vintage, provided a constant challenge and provocation to antiquarian theorists throughout Europe, and especially in the British Isles; most importantly, this historical outlook exercised, in the course of the eighteenth century, a centrally important influence on the sense of identity of the Anglo-Irish settler class.

The Anglo-Irish upper middle class, gentry and nobility saw itself originally as a body of English nationals upholding English standards in an otherwise savage foreign country. Ireland was perceived as a threatening terrain filled with barely-contained political enmity, to be kept under control by firm repression and with the support of the English crown. This political garrison mentality relaxed somewhat after 1745. That fateful year, with its Jacobite campaign in Scotland, passed uneventfully in Ireland, where the native population was effectively kept from rising by penal legislation, economic deprivation and a lack of rallying leadership. The peaceful passing of 1745 in Ireland seems to have made the Anglo-Irish elite somewhat more susceptible to a positive interest in native culture; but that development should also be seen in the context of the worsening relations between the Anglo-Irish economic interests (where the Anglo-Irish found themselves facing an accumulating list of grievances in their economic and constitutional relations with Britain) and the general climate of budding primitivism.

Antiquarian publishing activities within Ireland, in an Ascendancy context, on the topic of Irish antiquity increase, slowly at first (1725–1760) and sharply from 1760 onwards. In these publications, the treatment of Irish antiquity prior to the English conquest tends (despite some more reluctant voices) to adopt the point of view of native sources, as communicated by native intellectuals. What is more, these Gaelic roots of the country become endorsed increasingly as the country's common, 'national' past, a mainspring to which not only the natives can affiliate themselves, but also the Anglo-Irish. Crucially, then, the Anglo-Irish self-image, while still oriented towards English values in their estimate of cultural and political relations in contemporary society, abandons an English-derived historical consciousess and grafts itself onto a native, Gaelic-oriented view of the country's ancient history. By the late eighteenth century, Anglo-Irish Patriots see themselves as successors to the ancient Gaels rather than as descendants of the English colonists. It was a stance which was to be intensified rather than subdued by the Union.

This hybrid position illustrates an interesting possible dynamics which can take shape in cross-cultural stereotyping: the dynamics of adoption and exchange rather than mutual polarization and 'othering'. Not only is there the process of mutual opposition such as we have seen it at work between two countries who are presented as their mutual counterparts; it is also possible for a sense of identity to 'cross the line' and to be adopted and internalized by the opposing party in the confrontation. A well-known pattern is of course that development in which a minoritarian culture interiorizes an outside estimate and reputation, and begins 'to see ourselves as others see us'. The Anglo-Irish self-image of the late eighteenth century works slightly differently, in that here the change takes place in a dominant culture and amongst a social group that is dominant in internal politics and subaltern *vis-à-vis* Britain. The Anglo-Irish position emerges from the imaginary fusion between two contradictory and hostile cultural traditions. The Anglo-Irish national self-image partakes of both Gaelic- and English-oriented viewpoints and merges them into an intermediary Irish hybrid. This development took place alongside the continuing polarity between English and Gaelic mutual stereotyping.

In order to trace this intriguing process, it is necessary to study the tenuous and conflict-ridden interface between Ireland's two conflicting cultures. Within Irish society, those two cultural camps, native and English, while being implacably opposed to each other, did not exist in mutual isolation. There was always a hybrid middle ground where the black-and-white contrast could become complicated or blurred. Hiberno-Norman barons could 'go native'; some native chiefs like the O'Briens could make common cause with the Crown; some native scholars would turn Protestant, some Protestants like bishop Bedell would risk opprobrium by taking a positive interest in their Catholic, Gaelic-speaking countrymen; in the world of learning, enmities between Catholic and Protestant, native and settler could be temporarily suspended and some information and lore could be exchanged. It was always around such intermediary figures that an interesting, tenuous tradition of cultural hybridization tended to take shape. This process was ultimately to make an 'Irish' sense of national identity possible, which inspired political life from the late eighteenth century onwards, and which in the nineteenth century was to become the very cornerstone of cultural and (later) political nationalism.

NOTES

Introduction

1 Dyserinck's methodological ideas on the aims and competences of Comparative Literature are expressed most comprehensively in Dyserinck 1981. Cf. also the earlier article Dyserinck 1966, or the studies of Dyserinck's former student M.S. Fischer (1979, 1981, 1983). Outside Aachen, the imagological work of the Parisian comparatist D.-H. Pageaux deserves mention (e.g. Pageaux 1981).

2 Dyserinck 1982. The term 'l'étranger tel qu'on le voit' was used first in Guyard 1951 (heading to chapter eight).

3 Regarding the terminology and its development, cf. Dyserinck 1982 p. 40n.

4 Popper 1979, esp. pp. 152–61. Cf. also Dyserinck 1982 pp. 37–8.

5 Cf. Foucault 1969, especially in the interpretation of E. Marc Lipiansky 1979 pp. 13–14.

6 Generally Dyserinck 1982.

7 Foucault 1969 pp. 32–3.

8 Accordingly, I will only in isolated instances have occasion to refer, in the following pages, to the less discursive documents which are the sources of the historian proper: census or election returns, gazetteers, state papers, diplomatic despatches or calendar rolls.

9 Cf. Leerssen 1996.

10 Cf. Dyserinck 1981, p. 129.

11 The following terminological clarifications are in order. By 'Ireland' is here meant the entire island; 'Irish' are all inhabitants of that island; 'native Irish' or 'Gaels' are those inhabitants of Ireland whose ancestors were settled in Ireland prior to 1169; their language is called Gaelic, Irish-Gaelic or Irish. Settlers who came over to Ireland from England before the Reformation are known as the 'Old English'; I will here use the term 'Hiberno-Norman' (an analogy to Anglo-Norman or Cambro-Norman) for those Norman barons who invaded Ireland after having occupied English or Welsh lands only for the period between the reigns of William the Conqueror and king John. (These families, of whom those of Butler, Fitzgerald and De Burgo will figure most prominently in the following pages, are usually called 'Anglo-Norman' in other works on the subject, or else considered as part of the 'Old English'.) In the present phraseology, the Old English consist more particularly of citydwellers and commoners.

The 'Anglo-Irish' are those settlers who came over from England after the Reformation, and who upheld the English interest and the Protestant religion in late seventeenth-century Ireland. One must be careful not to confuse this demographic usage of the term 'Anglo-Irish' with its literary usage, regarding which cf. the following footnote.

12 By 'Anglo-Irish' literature is meant literature written in the English language by authors of Irish background, often on matters Irish. This usage is quite distinct from the similar demographic term 'Anglo-Irish', denoting the Protestant upper-middle and upper classes, settled in Ireland, of English extraction. Thus,

authors like Yeats, Synge, O'Casey and Patrick Kavanagh all wrote in the literary tradition known as 'Anglo-Irish literature'; but only the first two of these four could be called 'Anglo-Irish' as to their social background.

13 Cf. Dyserinck 1964 and 1964–5, and Leerssen 1993.

The Idea of Nationality

1 Cf. generally Kohn 1945 and 1965, Koppelmann 1956, Popper 1945 (esp. vol. 2, chapter 12: 'Hegel and the new tribalism', pp. 25–76), Renan 1887; De Deugd 1970; Dyserinck 1981 and 1982.

2 I use the term 'demographic group' as a neutral term for any given collection of individuals. As for the priority of the willingness to, over the criteria used for, national self-definition, cf. Renan 1887, who, while exploding all deterministic use of 'national' criteria, defines a nation as 'un plébiscite de tous les jours' (p. 307).

3 Kedourie 1960 p. 9.

4 Koppelmann 1956 passim, e.g. p. 24.

5 Burke 1881 p. 354.

6 Benveniste 1969 vol. 1, 367 fl. Further references in the text.

7 The affirmative proposition 'Spaniards are monogamous' should, strictly speaking, be considered particularly rather than universally affirmative. There are, presumably, cases on record of Spanish bigamists. However, this proposition should be read as a common-parlance shorthand version of 'Spanish marital customs do not allow or condone bi- or polygamy'. In this sense the proposition may safely be considered universally affirmative – as far as everyday language can be made to fit the rules of formal logic.

The logical ambiguity between propositions like 'Spaniards are M' (-ortal or -onogamous? universally or particularly affirmative?) is not without its own implicit imagological interest. Koppelmann 1956 speaks of the tendency that

> durch den Gebrauch des Plurals mit dem bestimmten Artikel gemeinsame Eigenschaften, kollektive Verantwortlichkeit, oder Einigkeit vorgetäuscht werden: Die Katholiken sind so oder so – Die Deutschen haben dies oder das getan – Die Juden dürfen nicht . . . . – Die Indonesier verlangen. . ., usw. Der Sprecher würde in den meisten Fällen zögern, deutlich zu sagen: 'alle Katholiken', 'alle Juden' (infolge der Unvollkommenheit der Sprache, wo der Plural mit dem bestimmten Artikel entweder auf eine soeben genannte beschränkte Zahl von Individuen hinweist oder – wenn solch eine Gruppe nicht erwähnt worden ist – auf die Gesamtheit, wobei aber diese Gesamtheit so flüchtig und beiläufig bezeichnet wird, dass der Sprecher übertreibt und verallgemeinert, ohne es zu merken; die Nachlässigkeit des Ausdrucks führt zur Verfalschung des Gedanken. (p. 21)

8 Cf. generally Kedourie 1960, pp. 13–15.

9 Nicholls 1972 pp. 21–5.

10 Sieyès 1970 p. 126.

11 *Encyclopédie* 1777 s.v.

12 *Encyclopaedia Britannica* 1771 s.v.

13 Hume 1964 vol. 3, 248.

14 Cf. Stanzel 1987.

15 Hume 1964 vol. 4, 68. Cf. below, pp. 63–4.

16 Mossner 1980 p. 281. The essay is in Hume 1964 vol. 3; page references in the text.

17 Cf. generally Kliger 1952.

18 Johnson 1958 ff. vol. 2, 36–7.

19 'A comparative view of races and nations', in Goldsmith 1966 vol. 3, 66–86.

20 Hume to Edward Gibbon, 18 March 1776, in Hume 1932 vol. 2, 311. On the links between travel descriptions and the concept of national characters cf. Hayman 1971–2.

21 There are some indications, especially in German and Swiss authors of the later eighteenth century, to the effect that national characters took their place alongside the older Theophrastic or Hippocratic humours and temperaments as a new temperamental division of mankind. Thus, for instance, the early, 'vorkritische' Kant, who attempted, in his continuation of Burke's aesthetics entitled *Beobachtungen über das Gefühl des Schönen und Erhabenen,* a comparative psychological typology of aesthetic susceptibility, and did so by various different contrastive and comparative categorizations. At one point he proceeds along the division of humanity into sexes, and compares male and female attitudes and dispositions in aesthetic matters; at another point he calls the old temperamental humours into play and treats of the aesthetic dimension of choleric, sanguine, phlegmatic and melancholic characters; and yet another sub-section treats 'Von den National-charactern, in so fern sie auf dem unterschiedlichen Gefühle des Erhabenen und Schönen beruhen': of national characters, to the extent in which they are based on the different perception of the sublime and the beautiful. Kant thus employs both the temperamental and the national division of humanity as possible paradigms for a comparative aesthetic philosophy.

Something similar can be observed in two influential Swiss authors: Johann Georg Zimmermann and Johann Caspar Lavater, both of whom were well known in Britain. Zimmermann was the author of a seminal essay 'Von dem Nationalstolze', on national pride, which appeared first in 1758, and later, in thoroughly revised editions, in 1760 and 1768 (an English translation appeared in 1771). Here, the national pride which the political system of one's country may inspire is partly governed by the old temperamental humours; for such politically-motivated national pride, says Zimmermann, is 'nach den Temperamenten, der Denkungsart, und den Absichten des Menschen verschieden. Ein wilder, ungestümer, und unruhiger Kopf findet sich in der Demokratie glücklich; ein stiller, vernünftiger und tugendhafter Mensch in der Aristocratie; ein biegsamer, ehrgeitziger, aber nach den Umständen sich selber überwindender Geist, in der Monarchie.' (1760 ed. p. 156)

In fact, Zimmermann only intended his essay on national pride as a psychological, rather than a moral or political, treatise, comparable to his more famous essay on solitude, 'Von der Einsamkeit'. Accordingly, the preface to the second edition of 1760 places both 'Von dem Nationalstolze' and 'Von der Einsamkeit' in a context of temperamental interest:

'Ich denke seit vielen Jahren an ein Werk von den Temperamenten, und las, in der Unschuld meines Herzens, die Werke der Staatsmänner, damit ich besser von den Temperamenten schreibe. Der Nationalstolz und ein noch nicht gedrucktes, dem Geist und dem Herzen gewiedmetes Werk von der Einsamkeit, sind nur beyläufige Folgen der Untersuchungen dieses weit sich verbreitenden, tief in der Natur der Dinge liegenden, und noch wenig gekennten Vorwurfs'. (pp. v–vi)

Lavater attempted yet another typological division of humanity, one defined by facial traits as expressive of psychological predisposition; and he strove to fit his typology into the other, pre-existing modes of division, discussing cranial and facial features in relation to the different temperaments, to the different sexes as well as to the different nationalities (e.g. by calling racial features into play). Cf. Lavater 1789–98, e.g. vol. 3, 93–127.

22 For example Hayman 1971–2.

Ireland in English Representations

1 Giraldus Cambrensis, *Expugnatio Hibernica,* A.B. Scott ed., p. 146.

2 Cf. ibid. Scott's introduction, p. xxvii: 'It may well be . . . that the word *barbarus* did not have such a pejorative connotation in the Middle Ages, as it now has for us. Perhaps it should be translated as "uncouth," or even "outlandish".'

3 Giraldus Cambrensis, *Topographia Hibernica,* in *Opera* (1867) vol. 5; Lib. 3, cap. 29. Subsequent references to the *Topographia* are given in the text.

4 For a fuller discussion, see Leerssen 1995.

5 William of Newburgh (Rolls Series, ed. Hamilton) states that Ireland 'populos habet moribus incultos et barbaros, legum et disciplinae fere ignaros, in agriculturam desides, et ideo lacte magis quam pane viventes' (p. 159).

6 Quoted by Chotzen 1934, p. 8, who gives a comprehensive discussion of these terminological matters. Also, generally, Leerssen 1995.

7 Thus phrased in one of the Kilkenny Statutes themselves, in the redaction of Curtis & McDowell 1943, p. 55.

8 A statute had been issued in 1331 by Edward II admitting certain 'nativi' expressly to English law – an indication that this was a special measure super-seding, in this particular instance, the general rule. Other statutes regulating the cultural and legal relationship between English subjects and Irish enemies were, to give a few fifteenth-century examples: 'An act that he that will be taken for an Englishman shall not use a beard upon his upper lip alone: the offender shall be taken as an Irish enemy' (26 Henry VI c. 4:1447); 'An act that the Irishmen dwelling in the counties of Dublin, Myeth, Urriel, and Kildare, shall go apparrelled like Englishmen, and wear their beards after the English manner, swear allegiance, and take English surname' (5 Edward IV c. 3:1465).

The Statutes of Kilkenny were repeatedly re-enacted or confirmed, e.g. 10 Henry VII (1495). Cf. generally *The statutes at large.*

9 Canny 1976 p. 33.

10 Cf. Bradshaw's reference to Sir James Ware's interpretation in Bradshaw 1979 p. 266f.

11 *The statutes at large,* vol. 1, p. 119f.

12 Although Ireland cannot be called simply a 'colony' like, for instance, the Spanish colonies in the New World or the Dutch colonies in the East Indies, Tudor policy in Ireland was certainly inspired by colonialist attitudes, and often looked towards Spanish policy in America for inspiration (cf. Canny 1973 and Quinn 1958). The status of Ireland as a kingdom, with a parliament (albeit one excluding, on various counts, native representation) is the main difference between Ireland and a colony proper. But in other respects (the expropriation of the land, its distribution among immigrant settlers, the social establishment of

these settlers as a new ruling class, the submission of the native population both in social and economic terms, their employment as providers of cheap labour, the subordination of the country's internal economic interests to those of the 'mother country') Ireland did have the character of a colony. Plantation policy even in its nomenclature had a colonial connotation – the English colonies in North America were also known as *plantations*. And although slavery as such was not established in Ireland, the actual position of the labouring population in rural areas, especially under the penal laws of the eighteenth century, was one of complete social and economic dependence on the landlord, and lacking most elementary civic privileges. Isolated instances of slave deportations, e.g. to the West Indies, occurred during the Cromwellian settlement.

13 Elizabeth to Essex as quoted in Canny 1973 p. 581.

14 Cf. Canny 1975.

15 Stanyhurst 1577 fol. 28r. and ff.; Cf. Canny 1973, and Canny 1976 p. 123.

16 Camden later also edited Giraldus Cambrensis' description of Ireland, in his *Anglica, Hibernica, Normannica, Cambrica, a veteribus scriptibus* (Frankfurt, 1602).

17 The relationship between Camden's and Good's respective authorship is problematic. It is not clear whether Good wrote his description originally in Latin or in English. Camden's incorporation of the description in the first, Latin edition of *Britannia* may therefore have been either a Latinization of an English original, or an edited version of Good's own Latin; Camden says he gives Good's text 'suis ipsius verbis, ordine vero nostro' (p. 597). Hence, the later English edition of *Britannia* may have given Good's description (a) in the English translation of a Latin original; (b1) in Good's own English, though edited by Camden; or (b2) in an English retro-translation of an earlier Latin translation based on Good's original English. Hence, again, the difficulty in assessing whether, and to which extent, the description as printed in the English edition gives Camden's or Good's opinions, and how far these coincided or diverged. Cf. generally Gottfried 1943. It may be of interest to note that archbishop Ussher wrote to Camden as follows, when the latter was presumably preparing the English edition of 1610:

> I would wish, that the little treatise De Moribus Hibernorum which you told me was written by Good, the Jesuit, should be printed entirely without any altera-tion, and that in his own name, for so it will be better taken by our countrymen, and the envy wholly derived from you unto him, to whom it more properly belongeth. (Ussher to Camden, 30 Oct. 1606, in Ussher 1847–64 vol. 15, 7).

18 Carew MSS 1,400, as quoted by Maxwell 1923 p. 169

19 Cf. Curtis & McDowell 1943 item 23, pp. 119–20; of 22 stated aims, the first six concern church matters.

20 Quoted Quiggin 1911 p. 20.

21 Bodley's description (in Falkiner 1904, pp. 326–44) contains little more than the details of carousings etc.

22 In Harington 1801 vol. 1, 176f.

23 Harington ed. Macray (1879) p. 9f.

24 Harington's translation (ed. McNulty 1972) X 79, p. 119. By 'peerless piece' is meant the maiden who is about to be sacrificed à la Andromeda to a sea-monster, until Ruggier does the Perseus by her. Cf. also *Anthologia Hibernica* I (1793) 42, 191.

25 This and the following excerpts are taken from an unpublished part of Moryson's *Itinerary*, edited by Hughes in 1903 under the title *Shakespeare's Europe*. Further

references to *Shakespeare's Europe will* be given by page number in the text; references to Moryson's own *Itinerary* will be so specified and given in the text, the page number referring to the fourth volume.

26 Dineley ed. Graves (1870) p. 17f.

27 L.P. Curtis 1971 gives a comprehensive analysis of Victorian caricatures of Irishmen.

28 Cf. Stanzel 1987.

29 In Falkiner 1904 p. 356.

30 p. 1f. This excerpt is lifted from a 'sentence' that occupies three pages and meanders tortuously through a jungle of parentheses and syntactical non-sequiturs; hence the ungrammatical redaction of this quotation.

31 Some 500 of these, from the period 1642–49, are in the collection of the National Library of Ireland, all of them dealing with the Irish civil war; this figure indicates a production rate of about one to two each week. I have seen no reason to analyse their contents in detail here.

32 Most authoritative bibliographies, including the catalogue of the British Museum, the National Union catalogue, and Wing's short-title catalogue all give the anonymous author 'J.S.' as the playwright James Shirley – even though the book deals with the revolution of 1688 and James Shirley died in 1666. John Shirley (fl. 1680–1702), author of *Ecclesiastical history epitomiz'd* and *The triumph of wit* (1707), seems a more likely candidate.

33 In Clarendon 1849 vol. 7, 19. Further reference in the text.

34 In Murray 1912 p. 217. Murray spells the baron's name 'Rousele', which is presumably a misspelling in or of the MS. For the spelling adopted here, cf. Hist. MSS Comm, N.S. vol. 8 Ormonde papers, where mention is made of this obscure nobleman.

35 Robertson 1800 vol. 1, v.

36 *Works* vol. 4, 68; also quoted Mossner 1980 p. 301. Cf. generally Braudy 1970.

37 Gibbon, *Memoirs of my life,* as quoted in Braudy 1970 p. 31.

38 Hume 1823 vol. 5, 504. This passage is in a note to his treatment of Mary queen of Scots.

39 For Smith's criticism, compare Hume's letter to Smith, 9 Jan. 1775, in *Letters* ed. Greig vol. 1, 216f. Charles O'Conor's efforts to correct Hume's interpretation of '1641' will be discussed in the final chapter. None other than Edmund Burke, whose aesthetic theories concerning the sublime and the beautiful had won Hume's admiration, attacked, at a personal meeting between the two men, the Scottish philosopher's description as being misguided and misleading (cf. Mossner 1980 p. 394). Burke, like O'Conor, attempted to sponsor a 'philosophical' history of Ireland, on the model of Hume's history of England, and Robertson's history of Scotland; cf. Love 1961 and 1962 (a), and here, p. 336.

40 'John Dunton's letters', in MacLysaght 1950 pp. 326, 331, 355, 376. Further references to these letters will be given in the text, specified as 'MacLysaght'. References in the text to Dunton's own *Dublin scuffle* will be so specified.

41 Suppressed by MacLysaght but given in Bliss 1979 p. 133ff.

42 Cf. Hussey 1967 p. 7, Manwaring 1925 p. 6f.

43 Cf. Monk 1935 and Wood 1972.

44 Cf. Wood 1972 chapter 5, p. 169ff.

45 Quoted Manwaring 1925 p. 5 and Monk 1935 p. 210.

46 Cf. Manwaring 1925 p. 167f.

47 Preface to the Dutch translation, *Het merkwaardig Ierland* (Harlingen 1769) p. 11.

48 Cf. Bush 1769 p. 15ff.; Twiss 1775 p. 8 ff.; Young 1780 vol. 2 pt. 2 p. 108ff.

49 Young 1780 vol. 1 p. 152f. Burke was among the supporters of Young's Irish survey (vol. 1, xxvii), and later also helped Bowden with letters of introduction (Bowden 1791 p. 237).

50 Th. Campbell 1777 p. 290f.

51 Goldsmith 1966 vol. 3, 25.

The Fictional Irishman in English Literature

1 The most useful of these was Bartley 1954. Also Duggan 1937 and Truninger 1976. For non-dramatic fictional Irishmen: Mezger 1929, O'Brien 1977.

2 Of course these observations apply to prose fiction as well, cf. Genette's reference to reactions to *La princesse de Clèves*.

In this context, *selection* (as a mimetic device) means basically the author's inclusion of the meaningful and exclusion of the meaningless; as such, it legitimizes the tacit presupposition of the audience that, conversely, a given piece of fiction 'makes sense' within its own chosen frame of reference, and that its constituent plot elements 'make sense' in relation to the whole. In this respect, the principle of 'selection' in its formal implications and as employed in the present discussion of traditional (!) fiction may serve as an individual example from actual literary practice in support of the more abstract, general principle of 'mimesis as selection' elucidated by De Deugd 1973, esp. pp. 719–24.

3 Genette 1969 p. 73. *La Poétique* of Jules de La Mesnardière (1640; the quote by Genette is on p. 125) contains much of imagological interest, e.g. pp. 34, 38–9, where he discusses the 'vraisemblance' of characters as typified in their 'national' traits.

4 For example: Thomas Dekker, in his non-dramatic works which pretend to acquaint the innocent reader with the perfidies, dangers, tricks and other diverting aspects of low life, gives the following 'character'-vignette of an Irish pedlar:

an Irish toyle is a sturdy vagabond, who scorning to take paines that may make him sweat, stalks onely up and downe the country with a wallet at his backe, in which he carries laces, pinnes, points and such like, and under cullor of selling such wares, both passeth too and fro quietly, and so commits many villanies as it were by warrant. (Dekker 1886 vol. 3, 104–5)

Other such Theophrastic characters of Irishmen were written by Richard Flecknoe and (as late as 1703) by Ned Ward, in his *London Spy*.

Further references by Dekker to Irishmen similarly point out certain characteristics as matters of commonly held opinion, often in side-remarks smacking of a proverbial quality: souls stripped by Charon are 'more bare than Irish beggars' (vol. 3, 119). In a typically contrastive passage, national weaknesses are enumerated among which figure 'The *Irish* mans disease (*lazynes*)', 'the *Dutch*mans weakenesse (in not *Bearing* drinke)' and 'the *Italians* evill spirit that haunts him (*Lust*)'. Interesting is also his synoptic listing of various languages:

There was no *Spaniard* (in that Age) to brave his enemy in the Rich and Lofty *Castilian*: no *Romaine* Orator to plead in the *Rhetoricall* and *Fluent Latine*: no *Italian* to court his Mistris in the sweete and Amorous *Thuscane*: no *French-man* to parley in the full and stately phrase of *Orleans*: no *Germaine* to thunder out the high and ratling *Duch*: the unfruitfull crabbed *Irish*, and the voluble significant *Welch*, were not then so much as spoken of: the quick *Scottish Dialect* (sister to the *English*) had not then a tongue, neither were the stringes of the English speech (in those times) untyed' (vol. 3, 188).

Such parenthetical references to what are considered proverbial characteristics abound and shall not be noted further here.

5 There are a few pieces, from the later eighteenth century, which are specifically concerned with the disruption of the relationship between stage and theatre-audience, e.g. Samuel Foote's zany comedies or George Colman's preludes. In Foote's *The orators* and in Colman's *The manager in distress* the action is interrupted by an *Irish* character beginning to speechify from the pit or from a box.

6 It should be noted that this mode of accommodation had been foreshadowed in earlier instances; cf. for instance the political idealism implied in the presence of the Irish rivers at the wedding of Thames and Medway, in Spenser's *Faerie Queene* bk. 7, canto 6, st. 55.

7 Jonson 1925–52 vol. 7, 397–405. Further references in the text.

8 Shakespeare 1954 p. 414. (fol. 78 r. of the Histories).

9 Bartley 1954, pp. 16–17; Duggan 1937 p. 191; Truninger 1976 p. 26.

10 Dekker 153–61 vol. 4, 343.

11 Bartley 1954, p. 104

12 Both spellings are given in the printed text. Although one must be cautious not to read too much into the names of fictional characters, the 'diabolical' connotation may safely be taken as intentional – cf. other programmatic names of the period, such as 'Careless', 'Shacklehead', 'Misopapas'.

13 Sir Edward, whom the *dramatis personae* characterizes as a 'worthy Hospitable true English Gentleman, of good understanding, and honest Principles' (p. 104).

14 Cf. Dryden 1958 vol. 4 p. 1921, where this passage is quoted.

15 His strength seems to have consisted in the mimicking of unusual forms of speech. In Crowne's *City politiques*, he played the lawyer Bartolino, who speaks with a lisp. In Otway's *The cheats of Scapin* (where he was cast in the title role) he imitates the Welsh, Lancashire, and Irish accents as well as nautical slang. Leigh also played Teg in *The committee*.

16 An echo of O'Divelly appears in *The memoirs of captain Carleton*, where a certain Murtough Brennan, a priest from Kilkenny resident in Spain, attempts to debauch a young woman during confessional.

17 Nicoll 1921 p. 224.

18 Cf. Truninger 1976 p. 32.

19 Cf. Duggan 1937 p. 205, and the article on Cumberland in the *Dictionary of national biography*.

20 Ch. Williams 1822 vol. 1, 93 and 99.

21 Vol. 2, 309–12. Cf. Mezger 1929 p. 114.

22 Bartley 1954 p. 164.

23 Smollett 1901 vol. 12, 161–2. Further references in the text.

24 Huntington library, Larpent MS no. 274. Read on microcard.

25 For a fuller terminological discussion, see p. 300 above and Leerssen 1996, pp. 14–27.

26 Swift 1965–74 vol. 11, 135–6.

27 Churchill 1956 p. 18.

28 By George Colman is here meant the elder of the two. Colman's treatment of Stage Irish characters is more traditional, less positive. In Colman's plays, a 'good' Irishman is an Anglicized one. Thus, in *The Oxonians in town* the Irish Oxonian Knowall reflects:

> National reflections are always mean and scandalous: but it is owing to such men as these that so much undeserved scandal has been thrown on our country: a country, which has always produced men as remarkable for honour and genius as any in the world. A few mean wretches, who are acknowledged rogues and vagabonds there, are no sooner landed here, than they commence fine gentlemen and persons of honour. (p. 3)

Colman defended himself against the imputation of national bigotry, not only by giving such carefully balanced lines to Knowall, but also by dedicating the piece to a leading Irish Patriot politician, Hely Hutchinson.

> The pretence for this determined condemnation of the piece was, that it contained not only personal, but even national, reflections. The author has the greatest abhorrence of both . . . so far from intending to cast an illiberal reflection on the Irish nation, it was evidently his main design to vindicate the gentlemen of that country from the reproach deservedly incurred by worthless adventurers and outcasts. . . [The author] is so conscious of the purity of his own intentions, which he doubts not will appear on the perusal of the piece, that he has ventured to inscribe it to one of the most eminent characters of that kingdom. p. [v]

29 Quoted in Bartley 1954 p. 174. Further references in the text.

30 A lack of knowledge of Irish may have played tricks on the sentimentalization of the 'Lango-lee'. Bartley 1954 p. 176–7 indicates that *leangolaidhe* may have been a bawdy term, and that the songs in which it would have a recurring position would be far from sentimental in character.

31 For the sake of completeness, it should be indicated that a few plays are also in evidence where the Irish and the French Stage characters form a compound. In Frederick Reynold's comedy *Notoriety*, the valet Blunder O'Whack has acquired a few French mannerisms after a sojourn there. 'Mon Dieu! you dirty blackguard . . . by the red nose of St. Patrick, I am toute nouveau' (p. 8). And in Isaac Jackman's *The divorce* there is a scene in which an amiable Irish wooer of rich elderly ladies is taken for a Frenchman, and teaches his sweetheart Irish as if it were French. (p. 23).

32 Boulton 1768 p . 20.

33 For a synopsis of the complicated plot cf. Duggan 1937 pp. 312–3.

34 Bartley 1954 p 191.

35 Quoted in the editor's introduction, Sheridan 1973 vol. I, 35ff. References to other press notices (quoted from Price's survey in his introduction) in the text.

36 For a listing of these alterations cf. Bartley 1954 p. 183.

37 Cf. Bartley 1954 p. 312.

38 Some later, eighteenth-century plays still show echoes of this convention. In Oulton's *Botheration* a switch of identities between a frank Irish footman and a grouchy physician is used to make the doctor see that he treats servants with less courtesy than is their due. In David Garrick's *The Irish widow* an Irishwoman impersonates her own Irishness. The gentle young widow hams up her Irish traits to a caricatural degree in order to baulk an unwelcome suitor (vol. 2, 1634). Cf. also the loose disguise of Harriet as Captain O' Fire-away, in Holcroft's *Seduction*.

Gaelic Poetry and the Idea of Irish Nationality

1 Regarding the terminology 'bard'/'poet' (*file*), cf. Murphy 1940. Generally, the following observations on the social and professional position of the poet, on his poetry
   and on the Gaelic clan structures within which he worked, are largely indebted to
   TD (Knott's introduction), IBP (Bergin's introduction), Byrne 1973, Carney 1967,
   Dunne 1980, Knott 1960, Mac Cana 1982, Nicholls 1972, Ó hÓgáin 1982.

2 Notions like that of the *tuath* are problematic and tend to oscillate between a
   territorial and a genealogical pole; they underwent a shift during and after the
   Viking invasion which is described by Binchy as follows:

   > From the [earlier, J.L.] tracts themselves a reasonably clear picture emerges of the
   > various kin-groups, together with the rights and liabilities of each group. But
   > already by the time of the earliest glossators the picture has become blurred,
   > while the later jurists are hopelessly at sea in their attempts to interpret the word
   > *fine* in the text. From their confused and contradictory explanations we can
   > deduce that the rigid pattern of the old kin organization had given way to an
   > amorphous mass of persons claiming descent from a common ancestor, the
   > *slíocht* of later documents. In this post-Norse development we have, as MacNeill
   > has already suggested, the origin of the so-called 'Celtic clan' – an institution
   > which, to my mind, has been strangely distorted by anthropologists to fit their
   > own theories. (Binchy 1962 p. 132)

   Despite these problematic implications of the terms at hand, it is still
   justified, I think, to define the *tuath* (at least in the context of the later middle
   ages) as a 'clan territory' – meaning by this the territory under a sovereign clan
   chief and inhabited by his relatives and by families subservient to him.

   This, of course, raises the terminological difficulties inherent to the term 'clan' –
   difficulties also hinted at by Binchy. Again, I think that later, post-Norman practice,
   with its genealogical organization of society according to the claimed 'descent from a
   common ancestor', allows us to make use of the term despite its misleading connotations when applied to an earlier stage of Irish history. In this I follow Nicholls'
   defence of the term's usage, calling to mind also the facts as highlighted by Nicholls,
   namely that *tuath* would be rendered as 'country' or 'patria' in English/Latin texts of
   the period, and that a terminology like *natio* or 'nation' in such texts must accordingly be the rendition of something like 'clan'. Cf. Nicholls 1972 pp. 8–9, 22–3.

3 Mac Cana 1982 p. 206. Cf. generally Byrne 1973.

4 Carney 1967 p. 11.

5 Cf. BMCat vol. 1, 628.

6 Ed. McKenna, *Irish monthly* 49 (1919) 455.

7 Others being *aonaigh*, 'assemblies' like that of Tailteann, held by the king of Tara
   (who was later considered to have been *ex officio* high-king of Ireland). Cf. for
   instance Tadhg Óg Ó hUiginn's encomium on Toirdhealbhach Ó Domhnaill
   (1380). AithDD vol. I, 78, as quoted here in footnote 15 below. Cf. also the
   fragment by Sean Mór Ó Clumhain quoted here on p. 160.

8 For example the title of the eighteenth-century song 'Ar Éirinn ni 'neosfainn cé
   hí': 'Not for Ireland (i.e., not for anything in the world) would I say who she is'.

9 Mac Cana 1982 p. 216.

10 In accordance with widespread editorial practice, I use the capitalized term
    'Foreigners' to translate that usage of *gall/Gall, goill/Goill* (capitalization in Gaelic

MSS, as in non-Gaelic ones, being erratic, but mostly capitalized in printed editions) which refers in particular to Hiberno-Norman or Old English 'strangers', thus acquiring the flavour of a straightforward demographic denomination.

11 Prophecies of this kind can be traced back, as a genre, to Viking times. Thus the arrival of the Vikings is 'foretold' in the tenth-century *Immram Snédgusa ocus Maic Riagla*. For general observations on this highly important genre in Irish literature, the best source is still O'Curry 1861, pp. 382–434.

12 Conversely, a poet could, in an elegiac context, bewail the fact that the prophecy has been robbed of its imminent fulfillment since the hope-inspiring chieftain whose death is the subject of the elegy is now no longer alive. Cf. for example the anonymous elegy on Maolmórdha Ó Raghallaigh (†1636) in Carney 1950 pp. 63–71.

13 N. Williams 1980 p. 64.

14 Dunne 1980 p. 13.

15 For instance, the poems by Mac Con Midhe and Ó Clumhain quoted on pp. 160–1. The former advances the royal claims of Aodh Ó Domhnaill (†1337), the latter urges the rights of Tadhg Ó Conchobhair (†1374). In both poems, the removal of the Foreigners is merely a precondition for the ultimate goal: the high-kingship. Likewise, Tadhg Óg Ó hUiginn advanced the claims of Toirdhealbhach Ó Domhnaill in an inaugural encomium (1380) that linked the high-kingship with the expulsion of the *Goill*:

> Sgrios Gall do Ghort Laoghaire
> do nocht Flann an fáidhfhile
> da dtógbha trí haonaighe
> rí gun Fhódla d'áiridhe. (AithDD vol. 1, 78)

('Flann, the prophet-poet foretold that the Goill will be banished from Laoghaire's Field when the king destined for Fódla restores the three Assemblies', ed.'s trl.)

Tadhg Óg develops a similar argument in his ode to Niall Óg Ó Néill (†1403), cf. AithhDD vol. I, 55.

16 The poet was at liberty to compose odes to whomever he chose, apart from his professional duties to the chieftain whose *ollamh* he was. This situation may be compared to that of a nobleman's chaplain, who was equally at liberty to administer the sacraments to others, should the occasion call for it. Sometimes the poet would add an extra stanza for his personal protector even in poems addressed to others – much like a chaplain remembering his patron in his prayers – obviously without impeaching the credibility of the extraordinary regard he affects to feel for the poem's main subject.

17 N. Williams 1980 pp. 70–2.

18 Apart from the ode to Ó Raghallaigh which is dealt with in the text, one could mention Tuathal Ó hUiginn's ode to Tomhaltach Óg Mac Diarmuda of Mágh Luirg, which also contains barbed references to the shameful slavery of Connacht under Foreign sway: AithDD vol. 1, 127.

19 The earlier Viking intrusion had had a similar, though obviously transitory effect. Binchy has observed that the Vikings had represented a first threat of 'otherness' which, as he rightly points out, 'lies at the basis of nationalism' – or, at least, of a national awareness (cf. Mac Cana 1982 p. 109) .

Again, Donncha Ó Corráin endeavours to push the origins of national awareness in pre-Norman Ireland back as far as the seventh century, when the Irish 'had developed a sense of identity and "otherness"' (the question is begged: 'other' than who?) 'and had begun to create an elaborate origin-legend embracing all the tribes and dynasties of the country.' Interestingly enough, Ó Corráin then goes on to explain this sense of national co-appurtenance as the product 'of a mandarin class of monastic and secular scholars whose privileged position in society allowed them to transcend all local and tribal boundaries.' (Ó Corráin 1978 p. 35).

A strong factor to stimulate a pre-Norman pan-Gaelic awareness was, of course, the rise of the Í Néill, and the historiographical and mythographical revisionism that was perpetrated to support their dynastic claims. In this development, however, the Vikings represented an interruption rather than an acceleration, and the real origins of a pan-Gaelic outlook at the roots of later national thought must be sought in post-Norman times.

20 N. Williams 1980 p. 124.

21 For instance: he addresses Tadhg Ó Conchobhair with the line 'I n-urchomhair Gall do ghein/Ó Conchobhair dan cam dair', 'Ó Conchobhair whom oak salutes was born to fight Goill'; he calls Ó Conchobhair Ciarraidhe 'Rí Iarmhumhan airgneach Ghall', 'West Munster's king, the harrier of the Goill'; and he reminds Énrí Ó Néill that his great ancestor Niall Glundubh 'Riar Ghall ní ghabhadh do láimh', 'submitted not to serve the Goill' (in Niall Glundubh's case: the Vikings rather than the Hiberno-Normans). Cf. AithDD vol. 1, 14, 29, 66, and the corresponding translations by the ed. in vol. 2.

22 Cf. N. Williams 1980, ed's note on p. 303.

23 This view should be limited to Munster and Connacht. Around the Pale, the Old English presence was too massive to be accommodated or absorbed by Gaelic ways, principally because of the inherent foreignness of urban life (though in the fifteenth century the Irish language began to make headway even in the Pale). Be that as it may, the Old English of the Pale cannot be identified with the Hiberno-Normans.

24 Cf. Nicholls 1972 pp. 16–17.

25 Mac Niocaill 1963 p. 18. My translation follows the editor's tentative reading of the somewhat obscure first line of the stanza quoted here (cf. his note, p. 53). Further page references to this poem will be given in the text.

26 For Keating's usage, cf. p. 276–7. It should be mentioned that the term *Éireannaigh* is quite distinct from the older term *fir Érenn*, 'the men of Éire'. To begin with, it is possible that mythological connotations were at work in this older term, and that *fir Érenn* were 'the men of (the tribal goddess) Ériu' much as *Tuatha Dé Danann* were 'the tribes of the godess Danu'. Be that as it may, the term *fir Érenn* is generally used when referring to a pre-Norman context, within which it narrowly signifies the Gaels with even the possible exclusion of the Ulaid; as such it reinforces the idea that *fir Érenn* were Gaels, all Gaels and nothing but Gaels. Furthermore, the later term *Éireannaigh* implies a neat inversion of the relationship between land and inhabitants: compare *fir Érenn*, 'men of Éire', with Gearóid's *tír na nÉireannach*, 'land of the Irishmen'.

27 ibid. For the emendation, see Ó Cuív in *Éigse*, 11 (1965): 153.

28 Cf. his striking poems on the rivers of Ireland, Mac Niocaill 1963 pp. 23–5 and 42–3.

29 Edited by McKenna, *Irish monthly* 47 (1919) 509–14. References in the text.

30 Compare Tadhg Óg's ode to Neachtan Ó Domhnaill of 1439 with his poem to Uaitéar Mac Uilliam Íochtair (Walter Fitzwilliam Burke, the 'Lower Fitzwilliam', †1440), AithDD vol. 1, 93–6 and 145–51.

31 In the language of the time, even the geographical term Connacht would have a primarily genealogical meaning: '(territory of) the descendants of Conn'.

32 Carney 1945 p. 20.

33 Cf. ed.'s note, vol. 2, 263.

34 Edited by McKenna in *Studies* 37 (1948) 219–25.

35 O'Conor's irritation is the more understandable since the Burkes had occupied the ancestral territory of the O'Conor kings of Connacht, whose direct descendant he himself was. But even Tadhg Dall's editor, Eleanor Knott, finds the poem's 'political cynicism . . . somewhat astounding at first sight'; and her only excuse for Tadhg Dall is that his claims for Mac Uilliam were not meant seriously; cf. her note, TD vol. 1, xlvii–xlviii. Such criticism fails, however, to take into account that this apparently 'treasonable' poem contains, as a P.S., a complimentary stanza to Tadhg Dall's main patron, Conn Ó Domhnaill, and in fact only repeats the view of earlier Ó hUiginn bards like Tuathal (cf. here, p. 175) or Tadhg Óg, who wrote, *c.* 1445, that Éire belonged 'ag an tí bhus treise / gé bheith rí budh deise dhí': 'to the strongest, even though there exist a king who would suit her better' (AithDD vol. 1, 111; vol. 2, 66)

36 E.g. Domhnall Ó Cobhthaigh's poem to An Calbhach Ó Conchobhair Fhailghe, beginning 'T'aire riot, a mheic Mhurchaidh', 'O son of Murchadh, take heed'. Edited by McKenna, *Studies* 37 (1948) 484.

37 It seems a rather common diplomatic device, however, to represent the weakness of an individual clan or chieftain as the symptom or even the root cause of a similar weakness afflicting all of Gaeldom: in this manner, the poet can spare the listeners' feelings and even distill some flattery out of an awkward situation. Cf. for instance the poems addressed to the Connacht chieftain Tomás Mag Shamhradhain, who was a prisoner of the Í Chonchobhair in 1338–9. (These poems are in McKenna 1947 p. 183 ff.) Especially noteworthy is the poem by Aonghus Ó hEoghusa, which describes Mag Shamhradhain's inglorious captivity as symbolic of the way in which intra-Gaelic enmity enfeebles their common cause:

> Millte Eri dimthnud Ghaidheal
> ni gael sidha an seol do niad
> ai fhich ga cursun a caemhduch
> dursun nach frith daenghuth iad.

'Éire is ruined by rivalry among Gaoidhil; not mutual love in peace is their policy; their anger keeps them apart; sad they cannot agree!' (McKenna 1947 pp. 190 and 362) The poet can eventually twist this point even to the extent of deducing Mag Shamhradhain's suitability for the high-kingship from it . . . (p. 194)

38 In the version published previously, *Studies* 26 (1937) 123 ff.

39 There are a number of bardic poems which seem to refer to the presence of Foreigners mainly in terms of their convenience in providing raid-victims and booty. A poem like that by Seithfin Mór to An Calbhach Ó Conchobhair Fhailghe (a different person than his namesake mentioned in footnote 36 above), the text of which is given in IBP p. 154ff., can be mentioned as an example. It describes a raid on the Pale that largely tallies with descriptions that were given, from the victims' point of view, by men like John Derricke.

40 Cf. Canny 1976 pp. 33–4.

41 Edited by Ó Cuív, *Éigse* 15 (1973–4) 261–76. Further references in the text.

42 Ed.'s trl., but with my emendation italicized. Ó Cuív translated *Béarla* here as 'English speech'; the emendation 'Irish law' follows a suggestion to that effect by

James Carney, who feels that *Béarla* (lit. 'language') here stands for *Béarla Féine* (cf. Ó Cuív's reference to Carney's suggestion, p. 267).

Ó Cuív gives numerous examples of *béarla* in the later, narrower meaning 'English', but only one of these antedates the seventeenth century. And even this sole example (from 1567, which is still well after the probable date of composition of this poem) occurs in a context where a specification as 'gaillbhéarla' occurs in the preceding phrase. This specification '*gaillbhéarla*', 'the foreign speech' seems to have been *de rigueur* when using *béarla* to refer to the English language prior to 1600 – that, at least, is what Ó Cuív's own examples seem to indicate (pp. 275–6). Thus these examples do not in themselves constitute cogent proof for Ó Cuív's reading of *béarla* as 'English', which he has reiterated in NHI vol. 3.

Ó Cuív's reconciliation of the incongruities implied by his 'English' reading of *béarla* seems to me, with all the deference that befits a non-specialist, far less convincing than the reading suggested by Carney. Cf. generally pp. 266–7. It can, by the way, be pointed out that Eochaidh Ó hEoghusa uses a parallel expression when he describes the state of alienation of Enniskillen Castle which had become occupied by Foreigners: 'Gá ttám ní tuigthí an fadsa/comhrádh aithnidh umadsa' (IBP p. 130); ed. translates on p. 271: 'In short, all that time no familiar speech was understood around thee').

This sentiment – cultural alienation epitomized by a change of speech, by the abeyance of the usual mode of intercourse – would be diametrically opposite to the other poet's *fúbún* if *béarla* were to mean 'English'; on the other hand, the two would tally completely if *Béarla* were an ellipsis for *béarla féine*.

Another possible ellipsis implied in the poem's use of *béarla* was suggested to me by Professor Doris Edel: namely, that the term could stand for *béarla na bhfilí*. This emendation seems the most sensible of all, fitting the context of this individual poem as well as the bardic sensibility as expressed in other poems of these and subsequent years. I have adopted her suggestion here.

43 Ed. MacAirt 1944 pp. 31–2, which contains all the poems addressed to Ó Broin chieftains discussed in the following pages. The translation is that of Paul Walsh, in Walsh 1933 pp. 189–90.

44 Ed. MacAirt 1944 pp. 20–3. One of these instances is the adjectival form *anuasal*, 'very noble', p. 22. These poems to the Ó Bhroin have been analysed ingeniously by Bradshaw 1978. A more restrained and perhaps more convincing reading was subsequently offered by Dunne 1930. Further references to MacAirt 1944 in the text.

45 For a similar example from a different part of Ireland, see Tadhg Dall Ó hUiginn's ode to Cian Ó hEadhra, from the mid-sixteenth century (ed. MacKenna 1951 pp. 14–15).

46 Another example: Eoghan Rua Mac an Bhaird (or possibly his kinsman Fearghal Óg) foretells to Aodh Ó Domhnaill the restoration of the Gaelic order in the following terms:

> Biaidh roi-neart ag dáimh fá dheoigh,
> biaidh gach oireacht na náit féin,
> biaidh ana ar adhbha gach naoimh,
> gabhla an chraoibh da chur a gcéill.

'The poets will be powerful at last, each clan shall be in its proper place, there shall prosperity on the abode of every saint: the branching of the trees is evidence of it.' Ó Raghallaigh 1930 pp. 298 and 405.

47 Ó Raghallaigh 1930 pp. 206–8.
48 Edited by Knott in *Ériu* 8 (1915) 192–5. Knott, like O'Grady, takes the 'mac Marcuis' to be a mere patronym rather than a family name, and they identify the poet as a Mág Craith. But cf. O'Rahilly in *Proceedings of the Royal Irish Academy* vol. 36 section 'C', 105–6 and n.
49 Ó Raghallaigh 1930 p. 204.
50 Repeatedly edited, the best edition being Knott's, in *Celtica* 5 (1960) 161–71.
51 Edited by Padraig Breatnach, *Éigse* 17 (1977–9) 169–80.
52 Ó Concheanainn 1973–4. Page references in the text.
53 Mac Erlean 1910–7 vol. 3, 64 and ff.
54 IBP pp. 41–2. Similarly in another poem by Fearghal Óg to Flaithrí Ó Maolchonaire:
    Do choilleas onóir mh'anma
    's mo bhuar's mo lucht leanamhna
    's mo dhúthchas gidh dál pudhair
    i gclár chlúm-chas Chonchubhair.
    'I have lost the glory of my name, my stock, my servants, my country – sad story though it be – in the tangled-foliaged Plain of Conchobhar.' (edited/ translated by McKenna, *Irish monthly* 48 (1920) 51–4.)
55 Edited N. Williams 1981. Page references in the text.
56 In T. O'Rahilly 1927 pp. 141–7.
57 D'éag a huaisle's a hoireacht
    gan toidheacht aice ón oilbhéim,
    dá lamhadh sinn a mhaoidheamh,
    d'fhine Gaoidheal is oilchéim
    'That owing to the death of her nobility and her courts she cannot recover from the stigma, if we dared to proclaim it, it is an infamy to the race of the Gael' (from 'Beannacht ar anmain Éireann', in IBP p. 117 with ed.'s trl.)
    Or again:
    Tug fógra dhámh an domhain
    is col d'fhagháil d'ealadhain
    fuil chrannda dá cora i gcion
    's na fola arda íseal.

    A fhir scaoilte na scéal sean
    'gá mbí seanchas mac Míleadh,
    ní ham scéal do scaoileadh dheid
    tréan Gaoidheal an tan tairneig.
    'The outlawry of all poets and the ruin of learning set decrepit blood in honour and made high races low. Thou teller of ancient stories who hast the lore of Mil's sons, to-day, the Gaoidhil's power being gone, is no time to tell thy tales.' (From 'Táirnig éigse fhuinn Gaoidheal', in NDh vol. 1, p. 2; also edited by McKenna, *Irish monthly* 57 (1929), whence the translation (p. 166).
58 Edited by McKenna, *Irish monthly* 48 (1920) 314–8. The MacDonnells hailed originally from the Hebrides which had long been a Viking kingdom; they were held to descend from Viking stock. Hence the terminology.
59 Whatever common Gaelic concord might have existed, must have come under severe strain when the Thomond poet Tadhg Mac Bruaideadha attempted a revision of the Eberian–Eremonian enmity. The Eberian Mac Bruaideadha poets,

a relatively new name in the field of bardic literature, had been party to the Anglicization of their patrons, the O'Briens who were created earls of Thomond. The Maoilín Óg Mac Bruaideadha who collaborated with the Protestant translation of the Bible into Irish (cf. here, p. 282) had earlier practically blackmailed his patron, Conchobhair Ó Briain, third earl of Thomond, into munificence, partly by threatening to denounce O'Brien's adherence to Gaelic customs to the English authorities (Cf. the poem 'Bráthar don bhás an doidhbhreas' – poverty is unto death a brother – in O'Rahilly 1927 p. 41–4).

Maoilin Óg's nephew Tadhg had suffered from the Tyrone rebellion when O'Donnell's forces had moved through Thomond and robbed him of his cattle. In this war, the O'Briens were active supporters of the English forces under Carew.

Nearly twenty years later, after the death of O'Neill in Rome, Tadhg must have thought that the Eremonian preponderance in the Gaelic order (emphasized by the fact that it was the Eremonian north-west which had succumbed last to English pressure, which had been praised longest by the poets) was going into eclipse, and that the time had come for a new school of bardic learning, Eberian, safeguarded by active co-operation with the English authorities.

Tadhg accordingly celebrated the ascendancy of a new, modern, Eberian tradition over the old one which, to his mind, was exemplified in the semi-legendary Torna, poet to Conn of the Hundred Battles (Eremonian, ancestor of the 'Connachta'). He wrote a revisionist poem attacking Torna, and thereby rubbed salt into the wounds of the plantation-ridden, Eremonian North, which was mourning rather than criticizing ancient bardic learning. There, Tadhg's behaviour was considered a flagrant breach of bardic etiquette; an acrimonious debate was thus sparked off which took place under the heading of the Eremonian vs. Eberian dichotomy, but which may in fact have been rather a 'querelle des anciens et des modernes', bardic style. This controversy is now known as the 'Contention of the Bards', the corpus of which has been edited by McKenna 1918. Taking place during the implementation of the Ulster plantations, even such an academic debate as this, concerning the relative merits of Torna and of his latter-day detractor, generated an inordinate amount of energy – another indication that what mattered most to these poets was not, perhaps, their nationality, but rather their professional ethos and their social status, or their guardianship of the Gaelic genealogies and clan-lore. For a fuller discussion, see Leerssen 1994.

60 Williams 1981 p. 2. Cf. also Leerssen 1995.

61 Cf. Stern 1899 p. 339.

62 Mac Airt 1944 p. 178.

63 Edited by Gillies, Éigse, 13 (1969–70) 203–10.

64 p. 205. Monadh was a mythological Fomorian whose evil eye blighted the fields of Éire – a strong contrast to the lawful ruler's fertilizing effect on his territory. It may be pointed out that the Fomoire as a transmarine band of monster-wizards had in earlier centuries been the literary sublimation of the Viking raiders; cf. Binchy as quoted by Mac Cana 1982 pp. 207–8.

65 Tadhg Dall Ó hUiginn, for example, can call the Foreigners sonorous names like 'droing fiochmhair foirneartmhair', 'brón duaibhsigh dheinshuighidh', 'danair loma léirchreachaigh': wrathful tyrannical band, surly impatient band, ravenous, destructive barbarians; TD vol. 1, 109 and 112. Such epithets could be used of enemies of any nationality whatsoever.

66 Mac Giolla Eáin 1900 p. 17.

67 O'Molloy 1677 pp. 276–9. The translation is by Dr. A. Titley, St. Patrick's College, Drumcondra, to whom I am greatly indebted.

68 Walsh 1933 p. 90. The poet was one Diarmuid Mac Muireadhaigh. Further references in the text.

69 Ó Flannghaile 1924 pp. 40–3.

70 Ní Shéaghdha 1961 ff., fasc. 2, 59. Moreover, a revivalist language programme propagated in the *Gaelic Journal* (vol. 18 (1908) 13–18) carried the title 'Treigidh bhur dtrom-shuan!', taken from this same poem.

71 Mac Domhnaill 1955 p. 15.

72 Ó Buachalla 1983 p. 77. Ó Buachalla's quotation is from British Museum MS Egerton 146, p. 93.

73 As per note 67.

74 Cf. also J.T. Gilbert 'The Irish Vision at Rome', appendix XXIV to *A contemporary history of affairs in Ireland from 1641 to 1652* (ed. Gilbert: Dublin, 1866) vol. 3, 190–6.

75 Generally Ó Tuama 1964–6. For an example, cf. Mac Giolla Eáin 1900 p. 68.

76 Dunne 1980 pp. 17–18 .

77 Ó Buachalla 1983 p. 78. His quotation is the closing line of the vision-woman's prayer in *An Síogaí Rómhánach,* cf. here p. 218.

78 Murphy 1939–40 and Ó Tuama 1960.

79 Cf. Carney 1967 p. 20. Other examples can be found in BMCat vol. 1, 476 ff; Ó Raghallaigh 1930 p. 278; TD vol. 1, 7 and 41 ff.

80 'Seanabhean Criomhthain, Chuinn is Fheilim, / bean tsiuil ce dubhach dise ar ndenamh' (5PP p. 51): She who of old was Criomhthann's, Conn's and Fedlimid's is now a tramp, albeit aggrieved by what has been done.

81 Cf. T. O'Rahilly in *Ériu* 14 (1943) 19.

82 Cf. Mac Giolla Eáin 1900 pp. 67–70.

83 T. O'Rahilly 1925 p. 4.

84 'Lá dá rabhas ar maidin go fánach', in Mac Giolla Eáin 1900 pp. 38–43.

85 Mac Erlean 1910–17 vol. 1, 18. All references to Ó Bruadair's poetry will follow MacErlean's edition and will be given in the text by volume and page.

86 Dinneen 1902 p. 26–8.

87 N. Williams 1981 p. 42. The enumeration of Gaelic-aristocratic names is striking and corresponds to the enumeration of English names in other invective Gaelic poetry, which is thus satirically inverted. The character in *Pairlement Chloinne Tomáis* presented as the author of this poem is called Sir Domhnall Ó Pluburnain – a combination of a ludicrous, and obviously plebeian name (anglice something like 'Blubberham') with an English knighthood. Thus, from the opposite side of the confrontation, something similar is achieved to that English stage practice of the eighteenth century which gave ludicrous names to Irish characters like 'Sir Sturdy O'Tremor' – yet another indication of the symmetries that are apt to crop up at both ends of the national polarity.

88 Ó Buachalla 1983 p. 80.

89 Dunne 1980 p. 22.

90 Cf. the similar usage of 'Teague' or 'Teg' in contemporary English drama; though the 'typical' Irish name nowadays seems to be 'Paddy' or 'Mick', 'Teigue' is still used among Belfast Protestants as a nickname for Irish Catholics.

91 Mac Cárthaigh's poetry has been edited by Tadhg Ó Donnchadha; I quote here, however, from MacErlean's edition and translation of the poem, MacErlean 1910–17 vol. 3, 96–8.

92 Mac Erlean 1910–17 vol. 3, 104–6.

93 p. 134. The editor glosses 'Carolus' as Charles I or II. It might also refer to the Burke family, who claimed descent from Charlemagne.

94 Dunne 1980 p. 25.

95 Cf. Dunne's own note on p. 26.

96 Dinneen/O'Donoghue 1911 p. 6. All following references to Ó Rathaille's poetry will be to this edition and will be given in the text. As regards the present quotation: I have tacitly suppressed the embarrassing rash of exclamation marks which the editors thought fit to attach to every single line of this poem – a piece of editorial impudence that distorts the tone of the original, as well as the punctuation practice of Ó Rathaille's time, and which turns the elegiac poet into a Gaelic League soap-box orator.

97 Ó Tuama 1978.

98 Cf. for instance similar descriptions in Ó Rathaille's 'Do shiulaigh mise an Mhumhain mhín' and in the anonymous lament for Kilcash.

99 Ó Rathaille uses, in 'Cabhair ní ghairfead', the image of his being heir to an ancestral tradition of poetic patronage and loyalty stretching back into pre-Christian antiquity. Ó Rathaille's stubborn pride thus echoes the similarly stubborn and proud refusal of Oisín to enter Paradise (at the behest of St. Patrick, or so the story goes) if it meant forfeiting the company of Fionn and the Fianna who, being pagans, were in hell; for the phrase 'Oisín d'éis na bhFian', 'Oisín after the Fianna' had become a common-place symbol for the dispossessed bardic poets after the collapse of the clan system. Cf. Ó Bruadair's use of the phrase, MacErlean 1910–17 vol. 1, 16.

100 p. 100. For the emendation, see T.F. O'Rahilly, *Celtica*, 1 no. 2 (1950): 328–9.

101 Cf. generally Ó hÓgáin 1982.

102 NDh vol. 2, 41–2. The version given by Ó Fiaich 1973 (pp. 132–4) has slight differences in phraseology.

103 As quoted by Ó Gallchóir 1971 pp. 7–8. More instances of a similar nature are in Ó hÓgáin 1982.

104 Another indication of the poet's new acceptance of his social ties can be seen in the explicit link between *Tadhg*, 'the' Irishman, *tusa*, the poem's reader/listener, and the poet himself, *mise*, into a single group with one common interest:

Is deimhin dá dtigeadh tar uisce chughainn maithibh Éireann

Fé mheadhair i gcumas chum siosma cogadh a dhéanamh,

Go mbeadh Tadhg is tusa agus mise in arm gléasta

Ag roinnt na tiubaiste ar an bhfuirinn seo an ghalla-Bhéarla!

('Surely if the nobles of Ireland were to return to us over the water, joyously in power, to suppress all schism or strife, then Tadhg and you and myself would, equipped in arms, be inflicting sorrow on that crowd of the foreign English language!') This is from a poem by Diarmaid Ó Suilleabháin, edited Ó Foghludha 1938 (a) p. 42. A poet like Seán Ó Tuama 'an Ghrinn' does use scornful references to the offspring of Mór Bhuí and Liobar (as in *Pairlement Chloinne Tomáis*), but he does so in order to describe an attitude rather than a class.

One of the most interesting examples for the approximation between poetic self-awareness and social concerns is contained in a curious poem by Aindrias

Mac Craith, better known as *An Mangaire Súgach,* 'the jolly peddler', with its sudden shift from the penultimate to the last stanza.

Mo bhroid, mo dhoigh, mo scíos guirt,
Mo sceimhle, mo ghoin, mo ghádh,
Mo loit do loisc mo chroidhe ionnam
Ár saoithe 's ar sliocht ar fán;
Gan chion gan chuid gan oidhreacht,
Gan feidhm cirt gan cothrom stáit
Is tuirc is duirc is daoithe
Go buidheanmhar is bodacháin.

Dearcaim le dhuil cúilfhionn is meallaim maighdean,
An canna go húr diúgaim is dram le hintinn,
Gach drannaire dúr ná humhlann bainim rinnce as,
'S an Mangaire Súgach siúd mar chaitheann a aimsir.
(Ó Foghludha 1952 p. 196. 'O slavery, pang, bitter grief, O wound afflicting my heart inside me: that our worthies and our kindred are in exile; without their due, without property, without patrimony, without exercise of their right, without their due position, and reckless ruffians and churls thriving by the droves.

'I behold with desire the blond woman, I beguile the maiden, I quaff my tankard, my drink, afresh and with gusto, I make each obstinate snarler who is not deferential to me 'dance' – that is how this Jolly Peddler spends his time.')

105 O'Daly (1884) p. 6. The excerpt given here is quoted from Ó Foghludha 1933 (a) p. 36.
106 Ó Muirgheasa 1926 vol. 1, 7–10. The English stanzas were written in collaboration with one John Short.
107 Ó Fiaich 1973 p. 111.
108 Ó Foghludha 1918 (b) p. 53 ff. Dinneen 1906 p. 17.
109 Ó Buachalla 1975 p. 95.
110 Dinneen/O'Donoghue 1911 p. 258–61.
111 Ó Foghludha 1952 p. 215–16.
112 Ó Foghludha 1933 (b) p. 106. Further references in the text.
113 Examples from the closing years of the eighteenth century can be found in the poems of Diarmaid Ó Crochúir, cf. Ó Donnchú 1931 pp. 78–80.
114 Of course, one must take into account the typical 'Court'-organization of Munster poetry, and the fact that Munster poets often engaged in a question-and-answer game, conducting discussions, as it were, through the medium of poetry. Thus, for instance, Donncha Ó Súilliobháin's cynical answer to the *aisling* of his brother Conchubhar; or the transmigration of the formulaic 'An tan do bhiodair Gaoidhil in Éirinn beó', 'the time when the Gaels were alive in Ireland', from Diarmaid Ó Súilleabháin to Conchubhar Ó Rioghbhardáin, cf. Ó Foghludha 1938 (a) pp. 17–19.

Even so, parallels remain that are not quite as obviously mutual quotations, for instance between the friends Seán Ó Tuama 'an Ghrinn' and Aindrias Mac Craith, 'An Mangaire Sugach': for example, lines like Ó Tuama's 'Tiocfaid le chéile saor-shliocht gheal-Chuinn, / Néill is Art ghroidhe is Fháilbhe', 'together will come the noble descendants of bright Conn, of Niall, and Art the sturdy and of Failbhe', and An Mangaire's 'Dá dtagaidís na sáir-fhir tar sáile dár saoradh / Sliocht Airt is Chuinn is Fháilbhe is an fanach ná déarfainn', 'If the noblemen would come over the sea to liberate us, the descendants of Art and of Conn and of Failbhe and the wanderer whom I won't name' Ó Foghludha 1952 pp. 99 & 194.

115 Dinneen 1901 p. 121.

116 Ó Tuama 1960.

117 Cf. O'Daly (1884) pp. 69, 143; Ní Ógáin 1921 vol. 2, 31–3 & 44–5; Ó Foghludha 1952 pp. 118–20 for Ó Tuama's *aisling* of *Móirín Ní Chuilleanáin* beginning 'Im' aonar seal ag rodaidheacht'.

118 Ní Ógáin 1921 vol. 1, 65; vol. 2, 49–50.

119 NDh vol. 2, 79 and 5.

120 Dating from *c.* 1828: BMCat vol. 1, 691. O'Grady remarks that this song would have been written during Wellington's second ministry (1834–5). But nearly all the earlier entries in the MS he describes here (BM Add. 27, 946) are dated 1825 (nrs. 3. 7, 9, 14) or 1828 (note to nr. 12, BMCat vol. 1, 669). It would therefore seem more likely (and compatible with such internal evidence as I have been able to gather from O'Grady's presentation of the facts) that this song dates from the time of Wellington's first ministry, before Wellington introduced the Catholic Relief Bill – i.e. the first half of 1828. But of course I am basing this conjecture on O'Grady's own description of the MS, not having been able to consult the original myself.

121 Croker 1824 pp. 329–30.

122 Cullen 1969 pp. 18–19.

123 Ó Donnchú 1931 p. 64.

124 Another instance of formulaic phrases crossing the linguistic divide is the line 'And Paddy dear, and did you hear the news that's going round', known from famous political songs like 'The rising of the moon', but also attested in Liam Dall Ó hIfearnáin's poem beginning 'A Phádraig na n-arann, ar gcluin tú na gartha' (O Foghludha 1939 p. 58, and his note).

125 Fenton n.d. pp. 95–6.

126 Ó Muirgheasa 1933 p. 152.

127 Zimmermann 1967 p. 30.

128 Dinneen 1906 p. 130; Ó Foghludha 1952 pp. 203–4.

129 Pageaux 1981 p. 176.

130 Dinneen 1901 p. xxx.

131 Dinneen 1902 p. 26. His translation is in the first edition of the poems of Aogán Ó Rathaille (1903) p. 259.

132 To be sure, this polarity was (and still is) often treated in religious terms; but then again, religious divisions were in no way peculiar to the Gaelic-English conflict at that period and fixed on the parties concerned only such standard traits as Catholics all over Europe affixed on all Protestants, and vice versa.

133 Royal Irish Academy MS 24 O 55.

The Vindication of Irish Civility in the Seventeenth Century

1 Curtis & McDowell 1943 p. 55. Quite a few of the terms employed here are loanwords from Gaelic, e.g. fferdanes fr. *fir dána*, 'men of learning', skelaghes fr. *scealaí*, 'storyteller, newsmonger', clarsaghers fr. *clairseóir*, 'harper'.

2 This and the foregoing regulation as quoted in Walsh 1933 pp. 186–7. Walsh's italics.

3 Walsh 1933 p. 186. For further contemporary documents along the same lines, cf. T. O'Rahilly in *Proceedings of the RIA* vol. 36C p. 94, and Ó Cuív in NHI vol. 3 pp. 520–1.

4 Data from Tourneur 1905 p. 59; Bellesheim 1890–91 vol. 2 pp. 217–23, 315–20, 359–62; Spelman 1886 pp. 356–7.

5 Cf. generally Clarke 1978, and Boyce 1982 p. 63.

6 Cf. Boyce 1982 p. 81.

7 O'Malley may have been thinking of Eoghan Rua Ó Néill, general of the Confederates, who, as Hugh O'Neill's nephew, could be considered a direct continuation of the great Í Néill lineage. As we have seen, elegies on Eoghan Rua's death employ the bardic rhetorical figure of Ireland's 'widowhood' implying, retrospectively, Eoghan Rua's suitability for the high-kingship. Thus, O'Malley furnishes us, at the same time, with an example how utterly inadmisible such ideas were as soon as they left the formulaic context of poetry.

8 Cf. generally Corish 1954.

9 All these three titles are part of the original, long-winded title-page.

10 Cf. Anselm Ó Fachtna, 'Cúig teagaisg Chríostaidhe de'n seachtmhadh aois déag: compráid' in O'Brien 1944 p. 188ff.; Ó Maonaigh 1962; T. Ó Cléirigh 1936 pp. 30–1.

11 O'Maonaigh 1962 p. 189n.; BMCat vol. 1 591, vol. 2 594; *Gaelic Journal* 11 (1900) 10.

12 For this older tradition cf. Osborn Bergin's edition of 'Irish grammatical tracts' in supplements to *Ériu* 8 (1915), 9 (1921), 10 (1926–28) and 14 (1946), and Lambert McKenna's edition of *Bardic syntactical tracts* (Dublin: Dublin Institute for Advanced Learning, 1944).

13 Cf. *Graiméir* 1968, and P. MacAodhagain, 'Rudimenta grammaticae Hibernicae', in O'Brien 1944 pp. 238–42.

14 This Tadhg Óg was a son of Tadhg Dall, not the great fourteenth-century poet; cf. TD vol. 1, xxxii. Tuileagna Ó Maolchonaire had attacked the accuracy of the AFM, but his kinsman Ferfeasa Ó Maolchonaire, one of the compilers, replied to his accusations on O'Clery's behalf. Cf. O'Clery et al. 1918, pp. 131–8.

15 Hyde 1967 pp. 617–18.

16 Cf. Ó Maonaigh 1862 p. 193; BMCat vol. 1 160; TCDCat 372, RIACat p. 468.

17 O'Hanlon (1875) vol. 1 xxxvi–xxxvii.

18 Cf. Dempster 1627 pp. 229 & 686.

19 An exception was a *Life of the glorious bishop St. Patrick, St. Brigid and St. Columb, patrons of Ireland*, by Robert Rochfort. It was published at St. Omer in 1625; the author lectured at the Franciscan college of Louvain. Cf. O'Hanlon (1875) vol. 1 xliv, Jennings 1936 pp. 37–8.

20 The title is a misnomer. The chronicle's own title is *Annála rioghachta Éireann,* or 'Annals of the kingdom of Ireland'. The appellation 'Four Masters' stems from John Colgan (introduction to Colgan 1645, fol. b3 v.), who names, apart from Michael Ó Cléirigh, his collaborators Cucoigriche Ó Cléirigh, Cucoigcriche Ó Duibhgheannáin and Ferfeasa Ó Maolchonaire – as well as a fifth man on the team, Conaire Ó Cléirigh. The later editor of the Annals, John O'Donovan, ousted Ó Duibhgheannáin from the 'Four' Masters and includes Conaire Ó Cléirigh in his place, so as to make up the number. To complicate matters even further, one Muiris Ó Maolchonaire was, for a short while, a sixth 'master'. The motive for Colgan's problematic appellation is given by O'Donovan as follows: 'Quattuor Magistri had been long previously applied by the medical writers of the middle ages to the four masters of the medical sciences . . . this circumstance probably suggested to Colgan the appellation he has given to

the compilers of these Annals' (AFM vol. 1 xix). Brendan Jennings O.F.M. has this to add: '[Colgan] was probably influenced by another similar title, well known to every Franciscan, a commentary on the rule of St. Francis, the Expositio Quattuor Magistrorum, or Exposition of the Four Masters' (Jennings 1936 p. 125).

21 Cf. above, pp. 398–9 note 59.

22 Cf. Fearghus Bairéad, 'Muintir Gadhra', in O'Brien 1944 pp. 45–64; O'Donovan's note in AFM vol. 1 lvii; Jennings 1936.

23 The phrase was used repeatedly as a motto to books dealing with Irish culture or history, as a national variation on the pious Catholic 'AMDG'. It was also the legend on a postage stamp issued by the Irish Free State in 1943, in commemoration of the quartercentenary of Ó Cléirigh's death; a reproduction is given in O'Brien 1944.

24 E. Curtis 1950 p. 222.

25 Corish 1968 p. 2.

26 Bergin's introduction to his edition of Keating 1931 points out that Keating avoids the preposition *chum* or *do chum*, which (says Bergin) was discordant to a bardic sense of style – although it is often used in Michael O'Clery's prose, which is yet far less popular in its appeal than Keating's. Another indication of bardic influence is Keating's indulgence in 'runs' of alliterative epithets .

27 Cf. Keating 1902–14 vol. 2, 374rf., and Cronin 1943–4 p. 263ff.

28 Thomas O'Sullevane, in his prefatory 'Dissertation' to the Memoirs of Lord Clanrickarde, 1722. This dissertation is best known for its valuable information regarding ancient bardic practice in Ireland. The excerpt quoted here is also quoted in Ó Cuív 1958–61 p. 264.

29 Quoted Ó Cuív 1958–61 p. 269.

30 Cf. De Blácam 1929 p. 240. The report of Keating's fruitless appeal to some Eremonian families is first given in Mageoghegan 1758–62.

31 O'Hanlon (1875) vol. 1 xxxix.

32 Cf. Vance 1981 p. 219. Molyneux had entered into correspondence with a number of Gaelic scholars, including Thady Roddy in the early 1680s. Cf. A. De Valera 1978 p. 17. The importance of Molyneux within the Ascendancy context will be outlined in the next chapter.

33 O'Flaherty 1846 pp. 431–4

34 Molyneux 1846 p. 171.

35 Roddy 1846 p. 123.

36 By 'antiquarianism', I mean the pre-nineteenth century investigation (largely uncritical, often speculative) of the past, mainly in its cultural (religious, literary, linguistic . . .) aspects. It is now superseded by archeology and history proper.

37 This was presumably why Delvin was made a ward of the Crown. His brother William (Uilliam Mac Barúin Dealbhna) was one of the most refined poets in the Irish language in his time, and a friend of Bonaventura O'Hussey. Cf. Ó Tuathail 1940, Murphy 1948, IBP 36, and Iske 1978.

38 Cf. the reproduction in Iske 1978, fig. 2.

39 For the following, cf. generally Abbott 1913 and Ó Cuív in NHI vol. 3, 511.

40 This applies most of all to those Irish historians from the late nineteenth and early twentieth centuries linked to the Gaelic League: e.g. Desmond Ryan, Aodh de Blácam, Daniel Corkery. In recent years, much valuable work has been done on proselytization through Irish, especially on the early nineteenth-century 'Irish society': De Brún 1983-92, Bowen 1978. Work remains to be done,

however (notwithstanding Brian Ó Cuív's contribution to NHI vol. 3) on the seventeenth and eighteenth centuries in this tradition.

41 This condemnation was, ironically enough, based on a misinterpretation by Ussher's worthy Protestant biographer C.R. Elrington of an ambiguous phrase in one of Ussher's letters to Bedell (cf. Ussher 1847–64 vol. 1, 118 and vol. 15, 473). See William O'Sullivan's correction of Elrington, more than a century later, in *Irish Historical Studies* 16, 12 (Sept. 1968) 215–19.

42 Cf. Ussher 1847–64, vol. 4, 123 and 425; vol. 5, 309n.; vol. 6, 230, 284, 372, 425, 461, etc.

43 Jennings 1936 p. 81.

44 Mageoghegan 1896 p. 8.
    45Cf. Schuckburgh 1902 p. 133.

46 Cf. Bedell to Ussher, 30 July 1628, where Bedell's Irish-speaking amanuensis Murtagh King is discussed, and the archbishop is asked to procure for Bedell an Irish translation of the psalms, made earlier by Nehemiah O'Donnellan, Protestant archbishop of Tuam (Schuckburgh 1902 p. 296). Ussher may even have recommended King to Bedell (Schuckburgh 1902 pp. 131–2), and Bedell invoked Ussher's help when King's position was threatened by intrigue (Bedell to Strafford, quoted Schuckburgh 1902 p. 142; cf. also Harris 1739–47 vol. 3, 237).

47 C. Maxwell 1946 p. 36.

48 Cf. the correspondence between Marsh and Boyle, Marsh's Library, Dublin, MS Z4.4.8.

49 C. Maxwell 1946 p. 89.

50 Cf. *The Querist,* nos. 260–4 in the numeration of 1750. (Berkeley 1901 vol. 4).

51 J. Richardson 1711 pp. 94–5.

52 J. Richardson 1713 p. 118.

53 Cf. generally Hoppen 1964–5.

54 Correspondence between Marsh and Boyle, Marsh's Library, Dublin, MS Z4.4.8.

55 Droixhe 1978, p. 40. This excellent survey of seventeenth- and eighteenth-century linguistics was the source of much information used in the present argument. More specifically celtologically oriented are Bonfante 1956 and Tourneur 1905. None of these three, however, trace these developments with reference to the Anglo-Irish dimension as personified in Ussher and Ware, or exemplified in Lhuyd's influence in Ireland.

56 Both Droixhe and Bonfante place Van der Mijl firmly in the earlier Flemish linguistics school – an interpretation possibly prompted by the title of his work on the Netherlandic language, *Lingua Belgica,* so similar to the name of the kingdom established in 1830. In fact, Van der Mijl was born in Dordrecht and published in Leyden.

57 Cf. Hardiman 1831 vol. 1 xxvi, De Valera 1978 p. 232.

58 Ussher 1847–64 vol. 16, 13 and 25.

59 Droixhe 1978 p. 47.

60 Cf. generally Toland 1702 and 1726, and Simms 1968–9.

61 Toland 1726 p. 31 .

62 Cf. Simms 1968–9 p. 307n.

63 Lhuyd to Aubrey, 9 Jan. 1694, quoted Gunther 1945 p. 217.

64 These 'three traditions' (Gaelic, Anglo-Irish, Continental) are, of course, interconnected; figures like Ussher and Ware straddle the latter two of these three,

and the Anglo-Irish tradition was constantly nourished by native expertise. A typical example of such cross-currents is the development that leads from an anonymous manuscript grammar compiled in Louvain in 1669 to Lhuyd, via a copy made by the Dublin scribe Seán Ó Súilleabháin for the bookseller Jeremiah Pepyat – who was the Dublin outlet for the *Archaeologia Britannica*. Cf. Lhuyd 1707 p. 299.

65 Gunther 1945 pp. 256 and 258.
66 Gunther 1945 pp. 29 and 258, J. Campbell 1960 pp. 225–6.
67 Lhuyd to Tancred Robinson, 25 August 1700, quoted Gunther 1945, p. 431.
68 A. & W. O'Sullivan 1962 p. 63, Campbell 1960 pp. 225–6.
69 Quoted Gunther 1945 p. 51.
70 Cf. Bonfante 1956 p. 25n., Droixhe 1978 p. 132ff.
71 Lhuyd 1707 fol. d v.

The Development of an Irish National Self-Image in the Eighteenth Century

1 Swift called Molyneux 'an *English* Gentleman born here' (i.e. in Ireland). Swift 1939–68, vol. 10, 62.
2 Lecky 1892 vol. 1, 144.
3 Cf. generally Kearney 1959.
4 Cf. *Answer* 1698, Atwood 1698, Cary 1698.
5 Cox to Nottingham, 13 Febr. 1704, quoted Froude 1895 vol. 1, 303–4.
6 Locke 1960 p. 136. Subsequent references to the *Treatise on government* will be given in the text by page number.
7 Molyneux 1720 p. 18 ff. 150–1, and Locke 1960 p. 287, 404–5. Cf. also Laslett's introduction to Locke 1960, p. 14.
8 Locke 1976 ff., vol. 6, 348ff., 366ff.: Molyneux to Locke, 15 Mar. 1698, and Locke's answer, 6 Apr. 1698.
9 Regarding which, cf. Dunn 1969.
10 See Johnston 1970 p. 36ff.
11 In Berkeley 1901, vol. 4, 562.
12 Cf. generally Robbins 1959.
13 Scott, 'The Lord of the Isles', 3, 27; in Scott 1926 p. 437. This and Berkeley's use of the word 'Patriot' are quoted by the Oxford English Dictionary *s.v.*, which entry offers an interesting spectrum of seventeenth- and eighteenth-century connotations now largely overshadowed by the more nationalistic denotation.
14 For a fuller discussion on the nature of Enlightenment Patriotism, see Leerssen 1988 and Leerssen 1996, pp. 14–27.
15 W. Temple 1770 vol. 3, 11.
16 Swift to Pope, 1 June 1728, in Swift 1963–5 vol. 3, 289.
17 Swift 1965–75 vol. 10, 17. With all the necessary caution of the political pamphleteer, Swift only ventures this slogan as the report of a report, 'a pleasant Observation of some Body's', quoted to him by the – conveniently deceased – archbishop of Tuam. Swift's own ambiguous commentary on the 'pleasant observation' was rephrased between the 1720 and the 1735 edition of this pamphlet. That Swift's caution – including his anonymity – was no affectation, is

proved by the fact that the authorities seized on the pamphlet as being subversive, and involved the publisher/printer in a court-case marked by gross misdemeanour of the presiding judge, Whitshed, who solemnly asserted 'that the Author's Design was to bring in the Pretender' (vol. 10, 137) – an indication of Whig sensitivity to political criticism. For Swift's reaction see vol. 3, 3, 82, 89, 109, 137. Further references to the Drapier's Letters will be in the text.

18 Lecky 1892 vol. 1, 287–8.

19 Qu. 73 in the numeration of the 1750 edition; in Berkeley 1901 vol. 4, pp. 428–9.

20 A. Dobbs 1729–31 vol. 2, 16.

21 Quoted Lecky 1892, vol. 1, 181.

22 Quoted from an invitation of 1769 by Gilbert 1854 vol. 1, 80. C. Maxwell 1937 mentions similar occasions in prestigious places like Dublin Castle and Leinster House in the years 1779 and 1788; further examples from an earlier date (1729–30) are in Munter 1967 pp. 153–4.

23 Cf. Munter 1967 p. 154, and James 1973 p. 207.

24 Regarding Dobbs, cf. generally Clarke 1958.

25 Cf. generally Clarke 1951.

26 Regarding Berkeley and Ireland, cf. Hone 1934, Hone/Rossi 1931, Johnston 1970.

27 Qu. 130–133 in the numeration of the 1750 edition, Berkeley 1901 vol. 4, 434. Further references to *The Querist* will be given in the text by query-number, following the 1750 numeration.

28 The influence of Berkeley's theories is felt directly in Prior's *Essay to encourage and extend the linen-manufacture* (1749), which opens with the axiom that 'The Wealth of Every Country ariseth from the Labour and Industry of the Inhabitants' (p. 3).

29 Arthur Dobbs could, in his Essay on the trade and improvement of Ireland (1729-31), take a similarly complacent view. Irish beggars, he chose to believe, are impostors, they are not really indigent at all; many of them are small farmers, and 'when they have sown their Corn, planted their Potatoes and cut their Turf for Firing, do either hire out their Cows or send them to the Mountains, then shut up their Doors and go a begging the whole Summer until Harvest, with their Wives and Children, in the most tatter'd and moving Condition they can appear in . . .' (vol. 2, 47). This view seems to have been dictated to some extent (though seasonal migration was not uncommon) by wishful thinking, a refusal to look the overwhelming problem of Irish beggary (and its underlying root cause, forced unemployment) straight in the face.

30 Swift to Brandreth, 30 June 1732, in Swift 1963–65 vol. 4, 34.

31 Cf. Boulter to Walpole, quoted in Clarke 1958 pp. 329–30, and Swift 1939–68 vol. 10, 116.

32 Swift to Peterborough, 28 Apr. 1726, in Swift 1963–65, vol. 3, 132.

33 For a detailed description of the affair around Wood's Halfpence, and of the role that the successive Drapier's Letters played in its progress, cf. Herbert Davis' introduction to his edition of Swift 1965–75, vol. 10, ix–xxxi.

34 vol. 10, 62. Swift's comment is doubly ironic in inverting the Whiggish mistrust of possible Stuart sympathies amongst their Irish opponents and, in doing so, reminding them of the doubtful constitutionality of the revolution of 1688, the basis of Whig supremacy.

35 Lecky 1892, vol. 1, 166.

36 Quoted A. De Valera 1978 p. 92.

37 Berkeley 1901 vol. 4, 433.

38 Leyburn 1937–8. *A word to the wise* is in Berkeley 1901 vol. 4, 541–57. References will be given in the text by page number.

39 A. Dobbs 1729–31 vol. 2, 81.

40 Later that century, Charles O'Conor D.D. was to write in the biography of his grandfather, Charles O'Conor of Belanagar: 'There are so many passages in Gustavus, which seem to refer to the natives of Ireland, that we might say of this tragedy – *mutato nomine de te fabula narratur* (Ch. O'Conor D.D. n.d. p. 392n.).

41 H. Brooke 1749, letter 1, p. 4.

42 H. Brooke 1745, letter 2, p. 8.

43 Quoted in Wilson 1804 p. 187–8.

44 Quoted from a 1760 reprint of the *Farmer's Letters* in James 1973 p. 235n.

45 Brooke was paid for this work, and often seems to have expressed his commendable sentiments out of not altogether disinterested motives. Cf. James 1973 p. 214, Gilbert 1854 vol. 3, 336–7.

46 Cf. Hone/Rossi 1931 p. 21.

47 Cf. Hazard 1935 vol. 2, 43–4.

48 Toland 1720 p. 23.

49 Cf. Leerssen 1996, p. 91.

50 Marsh's library, Dublin, MS 3.1.13. For Walsh's grammar and dictionary cf. De Brún 1972 item 25, p. 64; *Graiméir* 1968 pp. xv–xvi.

51 Cf. Tourneur 1905 p. 79; Droixhe 1978 p. 39; RIACat p. 1764; BMCat vol. 2, 98ff.

52 Ed. T. O'Rahilly 1912–13. References to Ó Neachtain's poem will be given by line number in the text.

53 RIACat p. 1614–15; O'Conor to O'Halloran, January 1769, in O'Conor 1980 vol. I, 257; A. De Valera 1978 pp. 24–5; Warner 1762, introduction.

54 Cf. Quin 1939, Risk 1966.

55 Lloyd 1912–13, cf. BMCat vol. 1, 262, 499n. and vol. 2, 97.

56 Hence Ó Neachtain's description of young Charles' home area as 'Cruacha'. The actual homestead of the O'Conor family was Belanagar, a few miles from the actual Cruacha or Croghan. Ó Neachtain's circumlocution was not, however, dictated wholly by the exigencies of the *deibhí*-metre which he used in such a ramshackle fashion; for since the mythical days of Ailill and Medb, Cruacha had been the seat of the kings of Connacht, to whom Charles could trace back his descent. Ó Neachtain, as member of a Connacht family, would have been especially sensible of this point.

57 In this context it might be noted that Keating's translator Dermod O'Connor was also active musically. He contributed Irish airs to a volume of *Aria di Camera, being a choice collection of Scotch, Irish and Welsh airs* (London 1727).

58 Cf. Warburton et al., 1818 vol. 2, 903n.; D. O'Sullivan 1958 vol. 1, 83f.

59 Cf. D. O'Sullivan 1958.

60 D. O'Sullivan 1958 vol. 1, 45. It should be pointed out, however, that Henry Brooke, for one, started to learn Irish only after a Gaelic poet had addressed a poem of praise to him; not all those who were eulogized in Gaelic must therefore necessarily have been cognizant of the language.

61 Another, later instance is Thomas Tanner's *Bibliotheca Britannica-Hibernica* (1718) which included sketches of early Irish scholars gleaned from Ware, Messingham and Colgan (cf. pp. 2, 10, 12, 192) – implicitly endorsing the claims that such authors had made for the civility of Irish antiquity.

62 This was a grandson of the lord chancellor Sir Richard Cox. He is mainly known as the opponent of the Patriot Charles Lucas, but at the same time he belonged to the more progressive landlords, who modernized the management of their estates under the influence of the Dublin Society's exhortations. Cf. Clarke 1951 pp. 343–4.

63 Compare, for example, Ware 1654 p. 6ff. with Harris 1739–47 vol. 2, 18ff.

64 In 1713, 1716, 1724, 1746, 1766. Borlase's *History* reappeared in 1743. Cf. A. De Valera 1978 pp. 42–4.

65 A. De Valera 1978 pp. 19–20.

66 A. De Valera 1978 pp. 24–25.

67 John Toland might also be mentioned in this respect. Strenuous anti-Catholic, he was no less interested in Gaelic history. He outlined a plan for a history of Gaelic antiquity in a series of letters to Molesworth (published posthumously in 1726). Toland speaks with all the combined authority of a Protestant and of a native son, and vindicates the Gaelic past, even from a Protestant point of view, against those writers who were misguided by the Gaels' more recent shabbiness. Toland 1726 p. 5 ff.

68 Quoted Wilson 1804 p. 173. Further references in the text.

69 Cf. the following quotation, from an unspecified source, in Gilbert 1854 vol. 3, 334:

> 'The rapid sale of several works, published with the title of Tales, as the Arabian, Persian, and Peruvian, induced Digby to give his intended work, whatever it might be, that airy name: and the natives of this kingdom, at home and abroad, went so much on Milesianism, that nothing could be devised happier for a frontispiece than the sound of "Ogygian Tales".'

Digby's project might also have been inspired by Mrs. Butler's *Irish Tales*.

70 She may, or may not, have been the widow of a Williamite officer. One Sarah Butler, whose husband, captain James Butler, had been killed at the battle of Aughrim and who had lost her children and her house at the hands of Jacobite irregulars, had been given a pension by king William; when that pension ceased on William's death, she found herself debt-encumbered in England, with two grandchildren. Hist. MSS Comm, Portland MSS VIII, pp. 323 and 345 mentions two petitions for relief by this Mrs. Sarah Butler, dated December 1704 and December 1706, both from the Marshalsea debtors' prison, explaining her plight and stating her desire to 'return to her own country'. The Mrs. Sarah Butler who had written the *Irish Tales* had died by the time her book was reprinted in 1735; cf. Charles Guldon's preface to the 1735 edition.

71 A few plays had been written previously, which aimed at the Dublin stage rather than at that of London. The earliest one is presumably James Shirley's *St. Patrick for Ireland* (1641), which was written when that playwright was manager of the Werburgh Street theatre that had been set up under the viceregency of Strafford. With it, Shirley hoped to attract larger audiences to the flagging venture by presenting a topic of local interest in an impressive production full of the latest stage trappings.

A few dramatic pamphlets, such as Richard Burkhead's allegorical *Tragedie of Cola's furie*, on the Confederate war, or Michelburne's description of the siege of Derry (1705), can also be found and are likewise geared towards an Irish audience.

Finally, a few comedies were produced in Dublin which, though in no way dissimilar to their English counterparts, make use of (or rather, references to) a

Dublin setting: Richard Head's *Hic et ubique* (1663), William Phillips' *St. Stephen's Green* (1700) and some comedies by Charles Shadwell.

72 Most biographical information on O'Conor has been gathered from O'Conor, S.J., 1930 and 1949; Love 1961, 1962 (a), 1962–3; Ward/Ward 1979; De Valera 1978, and O'Conor's own letters, edited by Ward/Ward 1980 (hereafter referred to as *Letters*).

73 Johnson to O'Conor, 9 Apr. 1757; in Boswell 1934 vol. 1, 321–2.

74 O'Reilly MS no. 6 (Trinity College, Dublin, but read on microfilm in the National Library of Ireland, Dublin). Also Carney 1959 pp. 21–2.

75 Weeks 1752 p. 69. This is the third edition; earlier editions seem to be no longer extant. Though Weeks does not specify whether the 'Irish' he mentions are Gaelic or Anglo-Irish (which is in itself a novelty), the images he draws on are those traditionally applied to the Gaelic Irish. Especially the remark on the cosmopolitan bravery of Irish soldiers seems inspired by the 'wild geese'.

76 James 1973 p. 260.

77 Cf. A. De Valera 1978, p. 43.

78 O'Conor published an isolated pamphlet by himself (though, as usual, anonymous) between 1761 and 1771: *A vindication of Lord Taaffe's civil principles*. It was written in defence of the *Observations on affairs in Ireland from the settlement in 1691, to the present time*, published in 1766 by viscount Taaffe, an Irish Catholic nobleman living in exile in Austria. This work was based on materials gathered for Taaffe by O'Conor; cf. O'Conor to Taaffe, 14 June 1766, *Letters* vol. 1, 200–1. O'Conor took to the pen again in 1771 when he published his *Observations on the popery laws*; here as in his pamphlets of the mid-century, he posed as a moderate Protestant. The identity of the author became known, however, much to the mortification of O'Conor, and this made further anonymous impersonations of this kind impossible (cf. Love 1962–3 pp. 9–10).

79 O'Conor to Curry, 21 July 1763, *Letters* vol. 1, 135. The memoirs are Curry's *Historical memoirs*, the *Review* is the *Critical review*, which had given favourable notice to Curry's work. Cf. editors' note, *Letters* vol. 1, 133.

80 O'Conor to Curry, 13 November 1762, *Letters* vol. 1, 148.

81 Cf. Berman 1976 pp. 103–4.

82 Cf. Berman 1976 p. 107.

83 One point where Warner and O'Conor did not see eye to eye concerned the introduction of Christianity in Ireland. Warner took a Protestant, i.e. non-Roman, non-papal line. Apart from that, O'Conor felt that Warner 'has the merit of casting our antiquities into a good historical mould': O'Conor to Curry, 23 July 1763, *Letters* vol. 1, 164.

84 O'Conor to Curry, 19 August 1763, *Letters* vol. 1,172

85 O'Conor to Curry, 2 December 1766, *Letters* vol. 1, 210. Here, O'Conor, in discussing Warner's stagnation, apprehends that 'it is not for him that it was reserved to write *The History of Ireland During the Reign of Charles I*'.

86 The following outline on Leland's history is largely indebted to Love 1962 (a) and Love 1962–3.

87 Berman 1976 points out that Hume, after toning down his description of the 1641 rebellion in the revised edition of 1770 of his History, became harsher again in the edition of 1778. Berman himself suspects that Hume 'came to think that O'Conor and Curry were overstating their claim' (p. 107); I would like to

suggest that Leland's History, which appeared in 1771, may have contributed to this 'backlash' on Hume's part.

88 Johnson to O'Conor, 19 May 1777, in Boswell 1934 vol. 3,112.

89 Bowden 1791, pp. 218–19.

90 Mackenzie 1685.

91 Macklin 1968 p. 59.

92 Macpherson 1773 vol. 2, 262–3. It is obvious that such logic can allow one to 'prove' the 'descent' of Italian from Spanish – or vice versa – provided one is sufficiently careful in selecting suitable 'representative' native speakers. Macpherson himself is known to have had a less than adequate knowledge of either form of Gaelic, and can only quote the few Irish excerpts he gives in Scottish orthography – not, it will be agreed, a point in favour of his 'proof' of Scottish-Gaelic superior comprehension. Another minor indicator might be mentioned: a printing error, occasioned no doubt by the similarity between 'f' and 'long s' (*fruth* instead of *sruth* 'stream/current' of water) was allowed to stand uncorrected in all editions of Macpherson's dissertation on Ossian sighted by me that were printed during his lifetime. Cf. Macpherson 1773 vol. 2, 266.

93 Quoted by Snyder 1919–20, p. 723.

94 Cf. Goldsmith's review of a work entitled *Remains of the mythology and poetry of the Celtes, particularly of Scandinavia*, in Goldsmith 1966 vol. 1, 5ff. This equation, inherent in the Scytho-Celtic model, was also made in Nicolson 1724, which compares Gaelic bards and Scandinavian skalds and draws on Snorri Sturlusson's *Heims kringla*.

95 Cf. generally Viallaneix/Ehrard 1982.

96 Blair in Macpherson 1773 vol. 2, 327. Further references in the text.

97 Monk 1935 points out that 'it is amusing to see how grudgingly Duff grants Homer superiority in sublimity over Ossian on one page, only to throw the whole matter into doubt on the next' (p. 132).

98 Cf. Ogilvie 1777 p. 2 and his note on p. xv.

99 Macpherson 1773 vol. 2, 231.

100 Ogilvie 1777 p. 58n.

101 Cf. Bromwich 1965; Kelleher 1950; Shaw 1934.

102 Quoted Mossner 1980 p. 415.

103 Hume 1964 vol. 3, 420.

104 William O'Kelly, a professor at Vienna, published in that city a *Historica descriptio Hiberniae, seu majoris Scotiae, insulae sanctorum* (which phraseology may sound familiar) in 1703. In 1705, Matthew Kennedy, a lawyer, had reasserted Irish-Gaelic claims to the roots of the Stuart dynasty in his *Chronological, genealogical and historical dissertation on the royal family of the Stuarts* (cf. A. De Valera 1978 p. 40); Also in Paris appeared *c.* 1720 a heroic Jacobite poem by the physician Demetrius Mac Enroe, entitled *Calamus Hibernicus;* and the abbé A.N. O'Kenny followed suit with an almanack of 1739, called *Sommaire de l'isle des saints.* To this tradition belong also MacCurtin's grammar of 1728, his and Conor Begley's dictionary of 1732, and a partial reprint of Bruodine's *Propugnaculum Catholicae veritatis* of 1669 (cf. above, p. 257) under the title *Descriptio regni Hiberniae* (Rome, 1721).

105 Van Tieghem 1917 vol . I, 163.

106 Quoted in Macpherson 1773, vol. 2, 268n.

107 O'Conor to Curry, 4 June 1762, *Letters* vol. 1,133 and cf. editors' note on p. 134.

108 *Dublin magazine*, January 1763, pp. 21–2. Further page references in the text.

109 Minutes of the Dublin Society, 17 May 1772. Quoted in Gilbert 1854, vol. 3, 222.

110 O'Brien to O'Conor, 26 May 1772. Quoted O'Conor, S.J., 1949 p. 331.

111 O'Conor to Curry, 25 March 1772. *Letters* vol. 2, 13.

112 Percy to Pinkerton, 11 February 1786. In Pinkerton 1830 vol. 1, 113.

113 Probably under the influence of the views prevalent in England, where their most eminent spokesman was Whitaker. Cf. A. De Valera 1978, p. 147.

114 Love 1962 (a), p. 184.

115 Cf. A. De Valera 1978 p. 227, 233; O'Conor to Curry, 28 August and 15 September 1764 (*Letters* vol. 1, 184 and 186); O'Conor to Vallancey, 25 September 1773, *Letters* vol. 2, 48 and editors' note on p. 49.

116 O'Halloran 1772 p. 162.

117 Grattan 1822 vol. 1, 123.

118 Cf. his description of Sackville Street, of two-wheeled carts, of peat. Twiss 1776 pp. 28, 29, 34; also p. 85.

119 Preston 1776 (b) pp. 9–10; Luckombe 1780 pp. 39–40. The very word 'twiss', so eminently suited in its assonantial evocativeness, could even come to denote 'a chamberpot', cf. *Lexicon* 1971 s.v.

120 Quote A. De Valera 1978 p. 91.

121 It was Burke who found a London publisher for Curry's *Historical memoirs*, and who had drawn up an address on behalf of the Catholic Committee in 1764. Cf.Curry to Burke, 8 June 1765, in Burke 1958–78 vol. I, 201–3 and n. References in the text are to Burke 1881.

122 Burke 1856 vol. 6, 22.

123 Quoted in McDowell 1979 p. 191 and Lecky 1892 vol. 2, 313.

124 Quoted in Lecky 1892 vol. 2, 284.

125 Burke to Langrishe, 3 January 1792 (this letter was published in the same year), in Burke 1881, pp. 206–78. Further references in the text.

126 Fitzgibbon as quoted by Froude 1895 vol. 2, 553; Tone as quoted by Froude 1895 vol. 3, 12–13.

127 For a comparison, see Leerssen 1996, pp. 19–24.

128 Stewart 1801 was based on O'Molloy, bishop John O'Brien and Vallancey (pp. 4–5); Shaw 1778 drew on O'Molloy, Mac Curtin and Vallancey (p. xiii).

129 Shaw 1780 p. [vi].

130 *Collectanea de rebus Hibernicis* vol. 5 (1790) 140.

131 Quoted in Parsons 1795 p. 14. Further references in the text.

132 Wilson n.d. p. 25. Further references in the text.

133 Cf. generally McDowell 1979 p. 369 ff.

134 This refers to O'Flanagan's account of an Ogham inscription in Co. Clare, published in the first volume of the *Transaction of the Royal Irish Academy* (1787: section c, p. I ff. Cf also *Archaeologia* 7 (1785) 276–85). O'Flanagan's fanciful reading of this inscription was obviously misguided; however, the imputation that he had forgotten the inscription itself seems to overshoot the mark and has been ably refuted by Samuel Ferguson's vigorous defence in the *Proceedings of the Royal Irish Academy*, 2nd series, vol. 1, 160ff., 265ff., 315ff. Notwithstanding Ferguson's cogent arguments against the idea that O'Flanagan was a *mala fide* forger, some of the mud still sticks and prevents the antiquary from Co. Clare from being recognized, as is his due, as being equal in importance to Walker and Ledwich. On O'Flanagan, see also Leerssen 1996 p. 246 n. 18.

135 'Had I not been favoured with the aid of Mr. Theophilus O'Flanagan, of Trinity College, Dublin, I should often have had reason to regret, that my knowledge of the Irish language is so very confined' (Walker 1786, preface). 'I must confess (and I am proud I can do it with heart-felt gratitude) that I stand highly indebted to Theophilus O'Flanagan. Esq. of Trinity College, for his attention, aid and friendship in the prosecution of this work' (Hely 1793 p. xi). And cf. also Ch. Brooke 1789 p. ix.

136 Campbell to Percy, 27 February 1787; Percy to Pinkerton, 28 February 1787. Pinkerton 1830 vol. 1, 144 and 147 .

137 The author had at one point corresponded with O'Conor and had worked, as an attorney, for the Catholic Committee (cf. O'Conor to Curry, 22 January 1763, *Letters* vol. 1, 152; O'Conor to Howard, 4 July 1763, *Letters* vol. 1, 160–1). Cf. also Gilbert 1854 vol. 2, 44–8.

138 For Irish historiographical practice in the early nineteenth century cf. generally MacCartney 1957.

139 Walker to Pinkerton, 31 October 1798. Pinkerton 1830, vol. 2, 37.

140 Walker to Pinkerton, March 1800. Pinkerton 1830, vol. 2, 137-8. The reference is to Charles O'Conor, D.D., n.d., of which the preface is dated 11 March 1796; a footnote on p. 226, however, appears to refer to the United Irish uprising.

141 See generally Leerssen 1996.

142 See generally Thuente 1994.

BIBLIOGRAPHY

NOTE:
– Titles of English books and plays from the seventeenth and eighteenth centuries have been entered in their shortened forms as given by: A.W. Pollard et al., *A short-title catalogue of books printed in England, Scotland & Ireland and of English books printed abroad, 1475–1640* (second ed., 2 vols., London: The Bibliographical Society, 1976); Donald Wing, *Short-title catalogue of books printed in England, Scotland, Ireland, Wales, and British America and of English books printed in other countries 1641–1700* (second ed., 3 vols., New York: Modern Language Association, 1972); and G. William Bergquist, *Three centuries of English and American plays: a checklist* (New York: Readex, 1963).
– The names of putative authors are given in brackets.
– Entries marked with an asterisk have been read on microfilm or microcard.
– Capitalization in titles has been rationalized throughout.
– 'Mc-' is alphabetized as 'Mac-'.

Abbott, T.K. 'On the history of the Irish bible'. *Hermathena* 17 (1913) 29–50.
* *The abdicated prince: or, the adventures of four years.* London 1690.
Alspach, Russell K. *Irish poetry from the English invasion to 1798.* 2nd edition. Philadelphia: University of Pennsylvania Press, 1959.
An answer to Mr. Molyneux. London 1698.
Anthologia Hibernica. Collections of science, belles-lettres and history. 4 vols. Dublin 1793–4.
Ariosto, Lodovico, *Orlando Furioso.* Eds. Santorre Debenedetti & Cesare Segre. Bologna: Commissione peri testi di lingua, 1960.
——. *Orlando Furioso, in English heroical verse* (tr. Sir John Harington) (1591). Ed. R. McNulty. Oxford: Clarendon, 1972.
*(Atwood, William). *The history and reasons of the dependency of Ireland.* London 1698.
Bartley, J.O. *Teague, Shenkin and Sawney. Being an historical study of the earliest Irish, Welsh and Scottish characters in English plays.* Cork: Cork U.P., 1954.
Beaumont, Francis, and John Fletcher. *Works.* Ed. A. Waller. 10 vols. Cambridge University Press, 1905–12.
Beckett, James C. *The Anglo-Irish tradition.* London: Faber, 1976.
Bellesheim, Alphons. *Geschichte der katholischen Kirche in Irland von der Einführung des Christenthums bis auf die Gegenwart.* 3 vols. Mainz 1890–91.
Benveniste, Emile. *Le vocabulaire des institutions indo-européenes.* 2 vols. Paris: Les éditions de minuit, 1969.
Berkeley, George. *Works.* Ed. A.C. Fraser. 4 vols. Oxford: Clarendon, 1901.

Berman, David. 'David Hume on the 1641 rebellion in Ireland'. *Studies* 65 (1976) 101–112.

Binchy, D.A. 'The passing of the old order'. *Proceedings of the international congress of Celtic studies, held in Dublin, 6–10 July, 1959.* Dublin: Dublin Institute for Advanced Studies, 1962, 119–132.

Bliss, Alan. *Spoken English in Ireland. Twenty-seven representative texts.* Dublin: Dolmen, 1979.

Blome, Richard. *Britannica: or, a geographical description.* London 1673.

The bloody duke: or, the adventures for a crown. London 1690.

Bochart, Samuel. *Opera omnia, hoc est Phaleg, Chanaan, et Hiërozoicon.* Eds. J. Leusden & P. de Villemandy. Lugduni Batavorum/Trajecti ad Rhenum (Leyden/Utrecht) 1692.

Bogg-witticisms: or, Dear Joy's common-places. n.pl., n.d. (*c.* 1700?).

Bolg an tsolair: or, Gaelic magazine. Belfast 1795.

Bolg a tsolair. A m-Beal-fears'de (Belfast), 1837.

Bolingbroke, Henry St. John, lord. *Letters on the spirit of patriotism and on the idea of a patriot king.* Ed. A. Hassall. Oxford: Clarendon, 1917.

Bonfante, Giuliano. 'A contribution to the history of celtology'. *Celtica* 3 (1956) 17–34.

Borde, Andrew. *The fyrst boke of the introduction of knowledge.* (1552). Facs. repr. London 1814.

Borlase, Edmund. *A history of the execrable Irish rebellion.* London 1680.

Boswell, James. *The life of Samuel Johnson, LL. D.* Eds. G. Birkbeck Hill & L.F. Powell. 6 vols. Oxford: Clarendon, 1934.

*(Boulton, Thomas). *The sailor's farewell: or, the guinea outfit.* Second edition. Liverpool n.d.

Bouvier, Auguste. *J.G. Zimmermann 1728–1795.* Thesis: Université de Genève: Kundig, 1925.

Bowden, Charles Topham. *A tour through Ireland.* Dublin 1791.

Bowen, Desmond. *The Protestant crusade in Ireland, 1800–1870. A study of Protestant-Catholic relations between the Act of Union and disestablishment.* Dublin: Gill & Macmillan, 1978.

Boxhorn, Marcus Zuerius. *Originum Gallicarum liber.* Amstelodami 1654.

Boyce, D.G. *Nationalism in Ireland.* London & Canberra: Croom Helm; Dublin: Gill & Macmillan, 1982.

Bradshaw, Brendan. *The Irish constitutional revolution of the sixteenth century.* Cambridge University Press, 1979.

Bradshaw, Brendan. 'Native reaction to the westward enterprise: a case-study in Gaelic ideology'. In: K.R. Andrews et al. (eds.). *The westward enterprise. English activities in Ireland, the Atlantic, and America 1480–1650.* Liverpool: Liverpool U.P., 1978, 65–80.

Braudy, Leo. *Narrative form in history and fiction.* Princeton, N.J.: Princeton U.P., 1976.

Breatnach, R.A. 'Two eighteenth-century scholars: J.C. Walker and Charlotte Brooke'. *Studia Hibernica* 5 (1965) 88–97.

Brereton, William. 'Travels in Holland the United Provinces England Scotland and Ireland MDCXXXIV-MDCXXXV' (ed. Edward Hawkins for the Chetham Society). *Remains historical & literary connected with the palatine counties of Lancaster and Chester* vol. 1(1844).

*Breval, John Durant. *Play is the plot*. London 1718.

Breve relacion de la presente persecucion de Irlanda. Sevilla 1619.

Bromwich, Rachel. *Matthew Arnold and Celtic literature. A retrospect 1865–1965*. Oxford: Clarendon, 1965.

Brooke, Charlotte. *Reliques of Irish poetry: consisting of heroic poems, odes, elegies, and songs, translated into English verse*. Dublin 1789.

*Brooke, Henry. *A collection of pieces*. 4 vols. London 1778.

——. *Farmer's letters* (nos. 1–6, 'to the Protestants of Ireland'). Dublin 1745.

——. *Farmer's letters* (nos. 1–10, 'to the Free-men/Citizens/Electors of Dublin') Dublin 1749.

——. *The spirit of party*. 3 parts. Dublin 1753.

——. *The tryal of the Roman Catholics*. 3rd ed. Dublin 1762.

Bruodinus, Antonius. *Propugnaculum catholicae veritatis, libris x. constructum, in duasque partes divisum*. Pragae, 1669.

——. *Descriptio regni Hiberniae, sanctorum insulae, et de prima origine miseriorum & motuum in Anglia, Scotia, et Hibernia, regnante Carolo primo rege*. Romae 1721.

Burke, Edmund. *Correspondence*. Ed. Thomas W. Copeland. 10 vols. Cambridge U.P.; Chicago: University of Chicago Press, 1958–78.

——. *Letters, speeches and tracts on Irish affairs*. Ed. M. Arnold. London 1881.

——. *Works*. 6 vols. London 1856.

*Burkhead, Henry. *A tragedy of Cola's furie, or Lirenda's miserie*. Kilkenny 1645.

Bush, John. *Hibernia curiosa. A letter from a gentleman in Dublin, to his friend at Dover in Kent, giving a general view of the manners, customs, dispositions, &c., of the inhabitants of Ireland*. London 1769.

——. *Het merkwaardig Ierland*. Harlingen 1769.

Butler, Sarah. *Irish tales: or, instructive histories for the happy conduct of life*. London/ Dublin 1735.

Byrne, Francis John. *Irish kings and high-kings*. New York: St. Martin's Press, 1973.

C..., S. 'A discourse of the present state of Ireland' (1614). In: John Lodge (ed.) *Desiderata curiosa Hibernica, or a select collection of state papers*. (2 vols. Dublin 1772) vol. 1, 430–440.

Camden, William. *Britannia sive florentissimorum regnorum Angliae, Scotiae, Hiberniae chorographica descriptio*. London 1586.

*——. *Britain, or a chorographicall description of England, Scotland, and Ireland*. Tr. Ph. Holland. London 1610.

Campbell, J.L. 'The tour of Edward Lhuyd in Ireland in 1699 and 1700'. *Celtica* 5 (1960) 218–228.

Campbell, Thomas. *A philosophical survey of the south of Ireland, in a series of letters to John Wilkinson M.D.* London 1777.

——. *Strictures on the ecclesiastical and literary history of Ireland from the most ancient times till the introduction of the Roman ritual, and the establishment of papal supremacy, by Henry II king of England.* Dublin 1789.

Campion, Edmund. *Two bokes of the histories of Ireland* (ed. A.F. Vossen). Assen: Van Gorcum, 1963.

Canny, Nicholas P. *The Elizabethan conquest of Ireland: a pattern established 1565–76.* Hassocks, Sussex: Harvester Press, 1976.

——. *The formation of the Old English elite in Ireland.* (O'Donnell lecture, 1974) Dublin: National University of Ireland, 1975.

——. 'The ideology of English colonization: from Ireland to America'. *William and Mary Quarterly* 30 (1973) 575–598.

Carey, Mathew. *Vindiciae Hiberniae: or, Ireland vindicated. An attempt to develop and expose a few of the multifarious errors and falsehoods respecting Ireland.* Philadelphia 1819.

Carleton, George. *The memoirs of an English officer, who serv'd in the Dutch War in 1672, to the Peace of Utrecht, in 1713* (1728). In: *The novels and miscellaneous works of Daniel De Foe,* vol. 2, 255–464. London 1889.

Carney, James. *A genealogical history of the O'Reillys, written in the eighteenth century by Eoghan Ó Raghallaigh.* Cavan: Cumann sheanchais Bhreifne, 1959.

——. *The Irish bardic poet. A study in the relationship of poet & patron as exemplified in the persons of the poet Eochaidh Ó hEoghusa and his various patrons, mainly members of the Maguire family of Fermanagh.* Dublin: Dolmen, 1967.

——. (ed.) *Poems on the Butlers of Ormond, Cahir, and Dunboyne* (A.D. 1400–1650). Dublin: Dublin Institute for Advanced Studies, 1945.

——. (ed.) *Poems on the O'Reillys.* Dublin: Dublin Institute for Advanced Studies, 1950.

Carolan, Turlough. *A collection of the most celebrated Irish tunes.* Dublin n.d. (*c.* 1726).

*Cary, John. *A vindication of the parliament.* London 1698.

(Cecil, Edward, viscount Wimbledon). *The government of Ireland under the honourable governor Sir John Perrot.* London 1626.

Centlivre, Susannah. *Works.* 3 vols. London 1761.

The champion: containing a series of papers, humourous, moral, political, and critical. 2 vols. London 1741.

Chetwood, William Rufus. *A tour through Ireland in several entertaining letters.* Dublin 1946.

Chotzen, Th.M. 'De "Wilde Yr" bij Vondel en elders'. *Tijdschrift voor Nederlandsche taal-en letterkunde* 53 (1934) 1–18.

Churchill, Charles. *Poetical works.* Ed. D. Grant. Oxford: Clarendon, 1956.

*Churchyard, Thomas. *A scourge for rebels, wherin are many notable services.* London 1584.

Clarendon, Edward Hyde, earl. *The history of the rebellion and civil wars in England, together with an historical view of the affairs of Ireland.* 7 vols. Oxford 1849.

Clarke, Aidan. 'Colonial identity in seventeenth-century Ireland'. In: *Nationality and the pursuit of national independence.* Ed. T.W. Moody. Belfast: Appletree press, 1978, 57–71.

Clarke, Desmond. 'Thomas Prior, 1681–1751, founder of the Royal Dublin Society'. *Studies* 40 (1951) 334–344.

———. *Arthur Dobbs Esquire, 1689–1765.* London: Bodley Head, 1958.

*Cobb, James. *Ramah Droog.* London 1800.

*Cockings, George. *The conquest of Canada.* London 1766.

*Coffey, Charles. *The beggar's wedding.* Dublin 1729.

Colgan, John (ed.) *Acta sanctorum veteris et majoris Scotiae, seu Hiberniae sanctorum insulae . . . Tomus primus, qui de sacris Hiberniae antiquitatibus est tertius.* Lovanii 1645.

———. *Triadis thaumaturgae seu divorum Patricii Columbae et Brigidae, trium veteris et maioris Scotiae, seu Hiberniae sanctorum insulae acta.* Lovanii 1647.

Collectanea de rebus Hibernicis. 6 vols. Dublin 1770–1804.

Colman, George. *The Oxonians in town.* London 1770.

(Conry, Maurice) 'F.M. Morisonus'. *Threnodia Hiberno-Catholica, sive planctus universalis totius cleri et populi regni Hiberniae* (1659). *Archivum Hibernicum* 13 (1947) 67–101.

Corish, P.J. 'John Callaghan and the controversies among the Irish in Paris 1648–1654'. *Irish theological quarterly* 21 (1954) 35–50.

———. 'The origins of Catholic nationalism'. In: id. (ed.) *A history of Irish Catholicism*, vol. 3, ch. 8. Dublin/Sydney: Gill, 1968.

Corkery, Daniel. *The hidden Ireland. A study of Gaelic Munster in the eighteenth century* (1924). Repr. Dublin: Gill & Macmillan, 1967.

Cox, Richard. *Hibernia Anglicana.* 2 vols. London 1689–90.

———. *Some thoughts on the bill depending.* Dublin 1698.

Crawford, William. *A history of Ireland. From the earliest period, to the present time.* 2 vols. Strabane, 1783.

Croker, Th. Crofton. *Researches in the south of Ireland, illustrative of the scenery, architectural remains, and the manners and superstitions of the peasantry.* London 1824.

Cronin, Anne. 'Sources of Keating's "Foras feasa ar Éirinn"'. *Éigse* 4 (1943–4) 234–278, 5 (1945–7) 122–135.

*Cross, J.C. *British fortitude, and Hibernian friendship: or, an escape from France.* London 1794.

Crowne, John. *City politques* (1683). Ed. J.H. Wilson. Lincoln, Nebr: University of Nebraska Press, 1967.

Cullen, Louis M. 'The hidden Ireland: re-assessment of a concept'. *Studia Hibernica* 9 (1969) 7–48.

Cumberland, Richard. *The West Indian. A comedy.* London 1771.

———. *The natural son. A comedy.* London 1792.

*——. *The note of hand: or, a trip to Newmarket*. London 1774.

(Curry, John, & Charles O'Conor). *Historical memoirs of the Irish rebellion in the year 1641, in a letter to Walter Harris, Esq*. London 1758.

(Curry, John). *A brief account from the most authentic Protestant writers of the causes, motives and mischiefs of the Irish rebellion on the 23rd day of October 1641*. Dublin 1752.

——. *Occasional remarks on certain passages in Dr. Leland's History of Ireland relative to the Irish rebellion in 1641*. London 1773.

——. *An historical and critical review of the civil wars in ireland, with the state of the Irish Catholics*. Repr. Dublin 1793.

Curtis, Edmund. *A history of Ireland*. 6th edition. London: Methuen, 1950.

Curtis, Edmund & R.B. McDowell (eds.). *Irish historical documents 1172–1922*. London: Methuen, 1943.

Curtis, Lewis Perry. *Apes and angels. The Irishman in Victorian caricature*. Washington: Smithsonian institution, 1971.

*Darcy, Patrick. *An argument delivered*. 2nd edition. Dublin 1764.

Davies, Sir John. *A discoverie of the true causes why Ireland was never subdued until his majesties raigne*. London 1612.

De Blácam, Aodh. *Gaelic literature surveyed*. Dublin: Talbot Press, 1929.

De Brún, Pádraig. *Catalogue of Irish manuscripts in King's Inns library, Dublin*. Dublin: Dublin Institute for Advanced Studies, 1972.

——. 'The Irish Society's Bible teachers, 1818–27'. *Éigse* 19, 2 (1983) 281–322; 20 (1984): 34–92; 21 (1986): 72–149; 22 (1987): 54–106; 24 (1990): 71–120; 25 (1991): 113–149; 26 (1992): 131–172.

Dekker, Thomas. *Dramatic works*. Ed. F. Bowers. 4 vols. Cambridge: Cambridge U.P., 1953–61.

——. *Non-dramatic works*. Ed. A.B. Grosart. 5 vols. n.pl. 1886.

Dempster, Thomas. *Historia ecclesiastica gentis Scotorum lib. XIX*. Bononiae (Bologna) 1621.

*Dennis, John. *A plot, and no plot*. London n.d. (1697).

Derrick, Samuel. *Letters written from Leverpoole, Chester, Corke, the lake of Killarney*. 2 vols. Dublin 1767.

*Derricke, John. *The image of Irelande, with a discoverie of wood karne*. London 1581.

Deugd, Cornelis de. 'Mimesis. Het mimetisch karakter van de literatuur'. *Nieuw Vlaams tijdschrift*, October 1973, 710–732.

——. *Nationalisme en wetenschap*. Inaugural lecture, Vrije Universiteit Amsterdam, 1 May 1970. n.pl. [Amsterdam, Vrije Universiteit], n.d. [1970].

De Valera, Ann. *Antiquarian and historical investigations in Ireland in the eighteenth century*. M.A. thesis, University College, Dublin, 1978.

*Dibdin, Charles. *Harvest-home*. London 1787.

Dineley, Thomas. *Observations in a voyage through the kingdom of Ireland* (1681). Ed. James Graves et al. Dublin 1870.

Dinneen, P.S. (ed.). *Amhráin Eoghain Ruaidh Uí Shúilleabháin*. Baile Átha Cliath: Connradh na Gaedhilge, 1901.

———. *Dánta Phiarais Feiritéir*. Baile Átha Cliath: An Gúm, 1934.

———. *Dánta Shéafraidh Uí Dhonnchadha an Ghleanna*. Baile Átha Cliath: Connradh na Gaedhilge, 1902.

———. *Filidhe na Máighe nó amhráin Sheáin Uí Thuama & Aindriais Mhic Craith*. Baile Átha Cliath: Connradh na Gaedhilge, 1906.

———. *Foclóir Gaedhilge agus Béarla. An Irish-English dictionary*. New edition. Dublin: Irish Texts Society, 1927.

Dinneen, P.S. & T. O'Donoghue (eds.). *Dánta Aodhagáin Uí Rathaille. The poems of Egan O'Rahilly*. 2nd edition. London: Irish Texts Society, 1911.

Dix, Ernest, & S. Ua Casaide. *List of books, pamphlets, &c., printed wholly, or partly, in Irish, from the earliest period to 1820*. Dublin: Cló-Chumann, 1905.

Dobbs, Arthur. *An essay on the trade and improvement of Ireland*. 2 vols. Dublin 1729–31.

Dobbs, Francis. *The patriot king: or Irish chief*. London 1774.

*Dodd, J.S. *Gallic gratitude: or, the Frenchman in India*. London 1779.

Douglas, David C. *English scholars 1660–1730*. 2nd edition. London: Eyre & Spottiswoode, 1951.

Droixhe, Daniel. *La linguistique et l'appel de l'histoire (1600–1800). Rationalisme et revolutions positivistes*. Genève: Droz, 1978.

Dryden, John. *Poems*. Ed. J. Kinsley. 4 vols. Oxford: Clarendon, 1958.

Duff, William. *Critical observation on the writings of the most celebrated original geniuses in poetry*. 1770. Repr. New York: Delmar, 1973.

———. *An essay on original genius and its various modes of exertion in philosophy and the fine arts, particularly in poetry*. 1767. Repr. Gainesville, Fla.: Scholars' facsimiles and reprints, 1964.

Duggan, G.C. *The Stage Irishman. A history of the Irish play and stage characters from the earliest times*. Dublin/Cork: Talbot, 1937.

Duigenan, Patrick. *An impartial history of the late rebellion*. New ed. London, n.d. (1802).

Dun, John M. *The political thought of John Locke: a historical account of the argument of the 'Two treatises of government'*. London: Cambridge U.P., 1969.

Dunne, T.J. 'The Gaelic response to conquest and colonisation: the evidence of the poetry'. *Studia Hibernica* 20 (1980) 7–30.

Duns Scotus, Johannes. *Opera omnia*. Ed. Luke Wadding et al. 12 vols. (1639) Repr. Hildesheim: Olms, 1968–69.

Dunton, John. *The Dublin scuffle*. London 1699.

Dymmok, John. 'A treatice of Ireland' (ed. R. Butler for the Irish Archaeological Society). *Tracts relating to Ireland* 2 (1842) pt. 1.

Dyserinck, Hugo. 'De fransschrijvende Vlaamse auteurs van 1880 in de spiegel der Franse en Duitse literaire kritiek'. *Spiegel der letteren* 8 (1964–5) 9–30.

———. *Komparatistik: eine Einführung*. Aachener Beiträge zur Komparatistik, vol. 1. 2nd edition. Bonn: Bouvier, 1981.

———. 'Komparatistische Imagologie jenseits von "Werkimmanenz" und "Werktranszendenz"'. *Synthesis* 9 (1982) 27–40.

——. 'La pensée nationale chez les auteurs flamands d'expression française de la génération de 1880'. *Actes du IVe congrès de l'Association internationale de littérature comparée*. (Fribourg 1964). The Hague/Paris: Mouton, 1966.

——. 'Die Quellen der Négritude-Theorie als Gegenstand komparatistischer Imagologie'. *Komparatistische Hefte* 1 (1980) 31–40.

——. 'Zum Problem der "images" und "mirages" und ihrer Untersuchung im Rahmen der Vergleichenden Literaturwissenschaft'. *Arcadia* 1 (1966) 107–20.

Eachard, Laurence. *An exact description of Ireland*. London 1691.

Edwards, R. Dudley (ed.). 'The minute-book of the Catholic Committee 1773–92'. *Archivium Hibernicum* 9 (1942) 1–172.

Encyclopaedia Britannica: or, a dictionary of arts and sciences, compiled upon a new plan. 3 vols. Edinburgh 1771.

Encyclopédie, ou dictionnaire raisonné des sciences, des arts et des métiers. Ed. Denis Diderot et al. Troisième édition. Genève 1777.

Falkiner, C. Lytton. *Illustrations of Irish history and topography, mainly of the seventeenth century*. London: Longmans, 1904.

——. *The famous historye of the life and death of captaine Thomas Stukeley*. (1605) Repr.: Malone Society, 1975.

Farquhar, George. *The stage-coach* (1704). London 1715.

——. *Dramatic works*. Ed. A.C. Ewald. 2 vols. London 1892.

Fenton, James (ed.) *Amhráin Thomáis Ruaidh .i. the songs of Tomás Ruaidh O'Sullivan the Iveragh poet (1785–1848)*. Dublin: Gill, 1914.

Ferguson, Samuel. 'On the Ogham-inscribed stone on Callan Mountain, Co. Clare'. *Proceedings of the Royal Irish Academy*, 2nd ser. 1 160ff., 265ff., 315ff.

Field, Nathan. *Plays*. Ed. W. Peery. Austin, Texas: University of Texas Press, 1950.

Fielding, Henry. *The history of Tom Jones, a foundlings*. Eds. F. Bowers & M.C. Battestin. 2 vols. Oxford: Clarendon, 1974.

Fischer, Manfred S. 'Komparatistische Imagologie. Für eine interdisziplinäre Erforschung national-imagotyper Systeme'. *Zeitschrift für Sozialpsychologie* 10 (1979) 30–44.

——. 'Literarische Seinsweise und politische Funktion nationalbezogener Images. Ein Beitrag zur Theorie der komparatistischen Imagologie'. *Neohelicon* 10 (1983) 251–74.

——. *Nationale Images als Gegenstand Vergleichender Literaturgeschichte. Untersuchungen zur Entstehung der komparatistischen Imagologie*. Aachener Beiträge zur Komparatistik, vol. 6. Bonn: Bouvier, 1981.

Fitzsimon, Henry. *A Catholike confutation of M. John Riders clayme of antiquitie, and a caulming comfort against his Caveat*. Roan (i.e. Douai) 1608. Repr. Ilkley/London: Scolar Press, 1974.

——. The justification and exposition of the divine sacrifice of the masse, and of all rites and ceremonies therto belonging. (Douai) 1611.

The folly of priest-craft. London 1690.

Foote, Samuel. *Dramatic works*. 4 vols. London 1788.

——. The trial of Samuel Foote, Esq. for a libel on Peter Paragraph. In: *The wandering patentee* (ed. Tate Wilkinson). York 1795, 251–260.

Forman, Charles. *A defence of the courage, honour, and loyalty of the Irish-nation. In answer to the scandalous reflections in the Free-Briton and others.* Dublin 1754.

Foucault, Michel. *L'archéologie du savoir.* Paris: Gallimard, 1969.

*(French, Nicholas). *A narrative of the earl of Clarendon's settlement and sale of Ireland.* (Louvain) 1668.

*——. *The unkinde deserter of loyall men and true friends.* n.pl. 1676.

Froude, James Anthony. *The English in Ireland in the eighteenth century.* 3 vols. London 1895.

Garrick, David. *Plays.* Eds. H.W. Pedicord & F.L. Bergmann, vol. 2. Carbondale & Edwardville: Southern Illinois University Press, 1980.

Genette, Gérard. *Figures II. Essais.* Paris: Seuil, 1969.

Gilbert, John T. *A history of the city of Dublin.* 3 vols. Dublin 1854.

Giraldus Cambrensis. *Topographia Hibernica et expugnatio Hibernica.* (*Opera*, vol. 5) Ed. James F. Dimock (Rolls Series). London 1867.

——. *Expugnatio Hibernica. The conquest of Ireland.* Eds./trls. A.B. Scott & F.X. Martin. (A New History of Ireland: ancillary publications, vol. 3) Dublin: Royal Irish Academy, 1978.

Goldsmith, Oliver. *Collected works.* Ed. A. Friedman. 5 vols. Oxford: Clarendon, 1966.

Goodwin, Albert. *The friends of liberty. The English democratic movement in the age of the French revolution.* Cambridge, Mass: Harvard U.P., 1979.

Gordon, James. *History of the rebellion in Ireland.* London/Dublin 1803.

Gottfried, Rudolf B. 'The early development of the section on Ireland in Camden's "Britannia"'. *ELH* 10 (1943) 117–130.

Graham, John. *Annals of Ireland, ecclesiastical, civil and military.* London 1819.

Graiméir Ghaeilge na mBrathar Mionúr. (Ed. Parthalán Mac Aogáin) Baile Átha Cliath: Dublin Institute for Advanced Studies, 1968.

Grattan, Henry. *Speeches in the Irish and in the imperial parliament.* Edited by his son. 4 vols. London 1822.

*(Griffith, Elizabeth). *The platonic wife.* London 1765.

*(Griffith, Richard). *Variety.* London 1782.

Gunther, Raymond W.Th. *Early science in Oxford.* Vol. 14: The life and letters of Edward Lhuyd. Oxford: For the subscribers, 1945.

Guyard, Marius-Francois. *La littérature comparée.* Que sais-je?, vol. 499. Paris: Presses universitaires de France, 1951.

Hardiman, James (ed./trl.) *Irish minstrelsy, or bardic remains of Ireland; with English poetical translations.* 2 vols. London 1831.

Harington, John. *A short view of the state of Ireland.* Ed. W. D. Macray. Oxford/London 1879.

Harington, John. et al. *Nugae antiquae: being a miscellaneous collection of original papers in prose and verse.* Ed. H. Harington, re-ed. Th. Park. 2 vols. London 1804.

Harris, Walter. *Remarks on the affairs and trade of England and Ireland.* London 1691.

Harris, Walter (ed.). *Hibernica, or, some antient pieces relating to Ireland*. 2 vols. Dublin 1747–50.

——. *The whole works of Sir James Ware concerning Ireland*. 3 vols. Dublin 1739–46.

——. *Fiction unmasked: or, an answer to a dialogue published by a popish physician*. Dublin 1752.

Hayman, John. 'Notions on national characters in the eighteenth century'. *Huntingdon library quarterly* 35 (1971–2) 1–17.

Haynes, . . . *Certaine principall matters concerning the state of Ireland*. Ed. E. Hogan as 'Haynes' observations of the state of ireland in 1600'. *Irish ecclesiastical record*, 3rd ser., vol. 8 (1887) 1112–1122, and vol. 9 (1888) 54–66, 160–174.

Hazard, Paul. *La crise de la conscience européenne (1680–1715)*. 3 vols. Paris: Boivin, 1935.

*Head, Richard. *Hic et ubique: or, the humours of Dublin*. London 1663.

Hely, J. (trl.). *Ogygia, or, a chronological account of Irish events by Roderic O'Flaherty*. 2 vols. Dublin 1793.

Hennessy, William (ed.). *The book of Fenagh*. 2 vols. Repr. Dublin: Stationery office, 1939.

(Hiffernan, Paul). *The Hiberniad*. Dublin 1754.

Higden, Ralph. *Polychronicon Ranulphi Higden*. Ed. Ch. Babington (Rolls Series). 8 vols. London 1865.

Hill, Thomas Ford. *Antient Erse poems, collected among the Scottish Highlands, in order to illustrate the Ossian of Mr. Macpherson*. Repr. Edinburgh 1878.

Historical manuscripts commission. *Calendar of the manuscripts of the marquis of Ormonde, K.P., preserved at Kilkenny Castle*. N.S. vol. 8. London: HMSO, 1920.

*Holcroft, Thomas. *The school for arrogance*. London 1791.

*——. *Seduction*. 3rd ed. London 1787.

*Holman, Joseph George. *What a blunder!* London 1800.

Hone, Joseph M. 'Berkeley and Swift as national economists'. *Studies* 23 (1934) 421–432.

Hone, J.M. & M.M. Rossi. *Bishop Berkeley. His life, writings and philosophy*. London: Faber & Faber, 1931.

Hoppen, K. Theodore. 'The Dublin Philosophical Society and the new learning in Ireland'. *Irish historical studies* 14 (1964–5) 99–118.

*Howard, Gorges Edmond. *The siege of Tamor*. Dublin 1773.

*Howard, Sir Robert. *The committee*. London 1665.

Hume, David. *The philosophical works*. Ed. Th. H. Green & Th. H. Grose. 4 vols. (1882). Reprint Aalen: Scientia, 1964.

——. *The history of England from the invasion of Julius Caesar to the revolution of 1688*. 8 vols. London 1823.

——. *Letters*. Ed. J.Y.T. Greig. 2 vols. Oxford: Clarendon, 1932.

*Hurlstone, Thomas. *Just in time*. London n.d. (1792).

Hussey, Christopher. *The picturesque. Studies in a point of view*. London & New York: Putnam, 1927.

Hyde, Douglas. *A literary history of Ireland, from earliest times to the present day.* New edition (ed. B. Ó Cuív). London: Benn, 1967.

Innes, C.L. 'Through the looking glass: African and Irish nationalist writing'. *African literature today* 9 (1978) 10–24.

Innes, Thomas. *A critical essay on the ancient inhabitants of the northern parts of Britain, or Scotland.* New ed. Edinburgh 1879.

Í Sheanacháin, Máire bn. 'Theophilus Ó Flannagáin'. *Galvia* 3 (1956) 19–29.

Iske, Basil. *The green cockatrice.* Dublin: Meath Archaeological and Historical Society, 1978.

*Jackman, Isaac. *The divorce.* London 1781.

*——. The Milesian. 2nd ed. London 1777.

James, Francis G. *Ireland in the empire 1688–1770. A history of Ireland from the Williamite wars to the eve of the American revolution.* Cambridge, Mass.: Harvard U.P., 1973.

Jennings, Brendan. *Michael O Cleirigh, chief of the Four Masters, and his associates.* Dublin/Cork: Talbot, 1936.

——. 'The Irish Franciscans in Prague'. *Studies* 28 (1939) 210–222.

Johnson, Samuel. *Works* ('The Yale edition'). Eds. H.W. Liebert et al. New Haven: Yale U.P.; London: Oxford U.P., 1958 – ᶜin progress).

Johnston, Joseph. *Bishop Berkeley's Querist in historical perspective.* Dundalk: Dundalgan Press, 1970.

Jones, John. *An impartial narrative of the most important engagements which took place between his majesty's forces and the rebels, during the Irish rebellion, 1798.* 2 parts. Dublin 1799.

Jones, Rowland. *The origin of language and nations, hieroglyfically, etymologically and topographically defined and fixed.* Repr. Menston (Yorkshire): Scolar, 1972.

Jonson, Ben. *Works.* Ed. C.H. Herford et al. 11 vols. Oxford: Clarendon, 1925–52.

Kearney, H.F. 'The economic background to English mercantilism, 1695–1700'. *Economic history review*, 2nd ser. 11 (1959) 484–496.

Keating, Geoffrey. *Eochair sciath an aifrinn. An explanatory defence of the mass written in irish early in the seventeenth century.* Dublin 1898.

——. Trí bior-ghaoithe an bháis. The three shafts of death. 2nd edition: ed. Osborn Bergin. Dublin: Royal Irish Academy, 1931.

——. Forus feasa ar Éitinn. The history of Ireland. Ed./trl. D. Comyn & P.S. Dinneen. London: Irish Texts Society, 1902–14.

Kedourie, Elie. *Nationalism.* Revised edition. New York: Praeger, 1960.

Kelleher, John V. 'Matthew Arnold and the Celtic revival'. In: H. Levin (ed.). *Perspectives in criticism.* Harvard studies in comparative literature, vol. 20. Cambridge, Mass.: Harvard U.P., 1950, 197–221.

Kelly, Hugh. *The school for wives.* London 1792.

Kelly, R.J. 'The Irish Franciscans in Prague (1629–1786): their literary labours'. *Journal of the Royal Society of Antiquaries of Ireland* 52 (1922) 169–174.

Kliger, Samuel. *The Goths in England. A study in seventeenth and eighteenth century thought.* Cambridge, Mass.: Harvard U.P., 1952.

*Knight, Thomas. *The honest thieves*. London 1979.

Knott, Eleanor. *Irish classical poetry, commonly called bardic poetry*. 2nd edition. Dublin: At the sign of the three candles, 1960.

———. 'An Irish seventeenth-century translation of the Rule of St. Claire'. *Ériu* 15 (1948) 1–187.

Knox, R. Buick. *James Ussher archbishop of Armagh*. Cardiff: University of Wales press, 1967.

Kohn, Hans. *The idea of nationalism: a study in its origins and background*. New York: Macmillan, 1945.

———. *Nationalism – its meaning and history*. 2nd edition. Princeton, N.J.: Van Nostrand, 1965.

Koppelmann, H.L. *Nation, Sprache und Nationalismus*. Leiden: Sijthoff, 1956.

La Mesnardière, Jules de. *La Poëtique*. Paris 1640, repr. Genève: Slatkine, 1972.

The late revolution: or, the happy change. London 1690.

Lavater, Johann Caspar. *Essays on physiognomy: designed to promote the knowledge and love of mankind*. Tr. H. Hunter. 3 vols. in 5. London 1789–91.

Lecky, William E.H. *A history of Ireland in the eighteenth century*. 5 vols. London 1892.

Ledwich, Edward. *Antiquities of Ireland*. 2nd ed. Dublin 1804.

Leerssen, Joep. 'Archbishop Ussher and Gaelic Culture'. *Studia Hibernica* 22–23 (1982–83), 12–22.

———. 'Anglo-Irish Patriotism and its European Context: Notes towards a Reassessment'. *Eighteenth-Century Ireland*, 3 (1988), 7–24.

———. 'Literatuur op de landkaart: Taal, territorium en culturele identiteit'. *Forum der Letteren* 34 (1993), 16–28.

———. *The Contention of the Bards (Iomarbhágh na bhFileadh) and its Place in Irish Political and literary History*. London: Irish Texts Society, 1994.

———. 'Wildness, Wilderness, and Ireland: Medieval and Early-Modern Patterns in the Demarcation of Civility'. *Journal of the History of Ideas* 56 (1995), 25–39.

———. *Remembrance and imagination: Patterns in the historical and literary representation of Ireland in the nineteenth century*. Cork University Press, 1996.

Leibniz, Gottfried Wilhelm. *Collectanea etymologica, illustrationi linguarum veteris Celticae Germanicae, Gallicae, aliarumque inservientia*. Ed. J.G. Eckart. (1717). Repr. Hildesheim: Olms, 1970.

Leland, Thomas. *An examination of the arguments contained in a late Introduction to the history of the antient Irish and Scots*. Dublin 1772.

———. *The history of Ireland from the invasion of Henry II with a preliminary discourse on the ancient state of that kingdom*. 3 vols. Dublin 1773.

Lennon, Colm. *Richard Stanihurst the Dubliner, 1547–1618*. Blackrock, Co. Dublin: Irish Academic press, 1981.

Lewis, Richard. *A defence of Ireland. A poem in answer to the partial and malicious accounts given of it by Mr. Twiss, and other writers*. Dublin 1776.

Lexicon Balatronicum. A dictionary of buckish slang, university wit and pickpocket eloquence. London 1811, repr. Northfield, Ill.: Digest, 1971.

Leyburn, Ellen. 'Bishop Berkeley: The Querist'. *Proceedings of the Royal Irish Academy* 44 (1937–8). Section C, 75–98.

Lhuyd, Edward. *Archaeologia Britannica, giving some account additional to what has hitherto been publish'd, of the languages, histories and customs of the original inhabitants of Great Britain.* Oxford 1707.

Lipiansky, Edmond Marc. *L'âme francaise ou le national-libéralisme. Analyse d'une représentation sociale.* Paris: Anthropos, 1979.

Lithgow, William. *The totall discourse, of the rare adventures, of long nineteene yeares travayles.* London 1632

Lloyd, J.H. 'Mid eighteenth-century conversation'. *Gadelica* 1 (1912–13) 19–31.

Locke, John. *Correspondence.* Ed. E.S. de Beer. 8 vols. Oxford: Clarendon, 1976 – (in progress).

——. *Two treaties of government.* Ed. P. Laslett. Cambridge: Cambridge U.P., 1960.

Lombard, Peter. *De regno Hiberniae sanctorum insulae commentarius.* Lovanii 1632.

Love, Walter D. 'Edmund Burke and an Irish historiographical controversy'. *History and theory* 2 (1962) 180–198. (a)

——. 'Edmund Burke, Charles Vallancey and the Sebright manuscripts'. *Hermathena* 95 (July 1961) 21–35.

——. 'Charles O'Conor of Belanagare and Thomas Leland's "philosophical" history of Ireland'. *Irish historical studies* 13 (1962–3) 1–25.

——. 'The Hibernian Antiquarian Society: a forgotten predecessor to the Royal Irish Academy'. *Studies* 51 (1962) 419–431. (b)

Loveday, John. *Diary of a tour in 1732 through parts of England, Wales, Ireland and Scotland.* Edinburgh 1890.

(Luckombe, Philip) *A tour through Ireland. Wherein the present state of that kingdom is considered.* Dublin 1780.

Lynam, E.W. 'The Irish character in print 1571–1923'. *The library* 4th ser. 4, 34 (1 March 1924) 286–325.

Lynch, John. *De praesulibus Hiberniae, potissimis Catholoicae religionis in Hiberniae serendae, propagandae, et conservandae authoribus.* Ed. J.F. O'Doherty, 2 vols. Dublin: Oifig an tSoláthair, 1944.

——. *Cambrensis eversus, seu potius historica fides in rebus Hibernicis Giraldo Cambrensi abrogata.* n.pl. 1662.

Mac Airt, Seán (ed.). *Leabhar Branach. The book of the O'Byrnes.* Dublin: Dublin Institute for Advanced Studies, 1944.

Mac Cana, Proinsias. 'Notes on the early Irish concept of unity'. In: M.P. Hederman & P. Kearney (eds.), *The crane bag book of Irish studies.* Dublin: Blackwater press, 1982, 205–219.

MacCartney, Donald. 'The writing of history in Ireland 1800–30'. *Irish historical studies* 10, 40 (September 1957) 347–362.

Mac Curtin, Hugh. *A brief discourse in vindication of the antiquity of Ireland: collected out of many authentick Irish histories and chronicles, and out of foreign learned authors.* Dublin 1717.

———. *The elements of the Irish language, grammatically explained in English*. Louvain 1728.

Mac Domhnaill, an tAth Séamus (ed.). *Dánta is amhráin Sheáin Uí Ghadhra*. Baile Átha Cliath: Oifig an tSoláthair, 1955.

MacDonagh, Oliver. *States of mind. A study of Anglo-Irish conflict 1780–1980*. London: George Allen & Unwin, 1983.

McDowell, Robert B. *Ireland in the age of imperialism and revolution 1760–1801*. Oxford: Clarendon, 1979.

———. *Irish public opinion 1750–1800*. London: Faber & Faber, 1944.

Mac Erlean, John C. (ed.). *Duanaire Dháibhidh Uí Bhruadair. The poems of David Ó Bruadair*. 3 vols. London: Irish Texts Society, 1910–17.

MacFirbis, Duald. 'The annals of Ireland translated from the Irish for Sir James Ware in the year 1666' (ed. John O'Donovan). *Miscellany of the Irish Archaeological Society* 1 (1846) 198–302.

———. *The genealogies, tribes, and customs of Hy-Fiachrach, commonly called O'Dowda's country* (ed. John O'Donovan). Dublin 1844.

———. *Annals of Ireland. Three fragments, copied from ancient sources*. Ed. John O'Donovan. Dublin 1860.

Mac Giolla Eáin, E.C. (ed). *Dánta amhráin is caointe Sheathrúin Céitinn*. Baile Átha Cliath: Connradh na Gaedhilge, 1900.

McKenna, Lambert (ed.). *The book of Magauran. Leabhar Méig Shamhradáin*. Dublin: Dublin Institute for Advanced Studies, 1947.

———. *The book of O'Hara, Leabhar Í Eadhra*. Dublin: Dublin Institute for Advanced Studies, 1951.

———. *Iomarbhágh na bhfileadh. The contention of the bards*. 2 vols. London: Irish Texts Society, 1918.

*Mackenzie, George. *A defence of the antiquity of the royal line of Scotland*. Edinburgh 1685.

Macklin, Charles. *Four comedies*. Ed. J.O. Bartley. London: Sidgwick & Jackson; Hamden, Conn.: Archon, 1968.

MacLysaght, E. *Irish life in the seventeenth century*. 2nd edition. Cork: Cork U.P.; Oxford: Blackwell, 1950.

Mac Niacoill, Gearóid (ed.). 'Duanaire Ghearóid Iarla'. *Studia Hibernica* 3 (1963) 7–59.

Macpherson, James. *An introduction to the history of Great Britain and Ireland*. London 1771.

———. *The poems of Ossian*. 4th ed. 2 vols. London 1773.

*Macready, William. *The bank note, or, lessons for ladies*. London 1795.

*———. *The Irishman in London: or, the happy African*. London 1763.

(Madden, Samuel.) *Reflections and resolutions proper for the gentlemen of Ireland*. Dublin 1738.

———. *A letter to the Dublin Society for the improving of their funds*. Dublin 1739.

Madden, P.J. 'Printing in Irish'. *An leabharlann* Sept. 1954, 9–20.

Mageoghegan, Connell (trl.). *The annals of Clonnmacnoise*. Ed. D. Murphy. Dublin 1896.

Mageoghegan, James. *Histoire de l'Irlande ancienne et moderne, tirée des monuments les plus authentiques.* 3 vols. Paris 1758–62.

Manwaring, Elizabeth. *Italian landscape in XVIII century England. A study chiefly of the influence of Claude Lorrain and Salvator Rosa on English taste.* New York: Oxford U.P. 1925.

Maxwell, Constantia. *Dublin under the Georges 1714–1830.* New ed. London/Dublin: Harrap, 1937.

——. *A history of Trinity College, Dublin 1592–1892.* Dublin: Dublin University Press, 1946.

——. *Irish history from contemporary sources (1509–1610).* London: George Allen & Unwin, 1923.

(Maxwell, Henry.) *An essay upon an union of Ireland with England.* London 1703.

Mela, Pomponius. *De chororgraphia libri tres.* Ed. C. Frick. Leipzig 1880.

* Mendez, Moses. *The double disappointment.* London 1760.

Messingham, Thomas. *Florilegium insulae sanctorum seu vitae et actae sanctorum Hiberniae: quibus accesserunt non vulgaria monumenta.* Parisiis 1624.

Mezger, Fritz. *Der Ire in der englischen Literatur bis zum Anfang des 19. Jahrhunderts.* Palaestra 169. Leipzig: Mayer & Müller, 1929.

Middleton, Thomas. *Works.* Ed. A.H. Bullen. Repr. New York: AMS, 1964.

Miège, Guy. *The present state of Great Britain and Ireland.* 3rd edition. London 1715.

Millett, Benignus. *The Irish Franciscans, 1651–1665.* Roma: Gregorian U.P., 1964.

——. 'Survival and reorganization 1650–95'. In: *A history of Irish Catholicism* (ed. P.J. Corish) vol. 3, ch. 7. Dublin/Sydney: Gill, 1968.

Molesworth, Robert. *Some considerations for the promoting of agriculture and employing the poor.* Dublin 1723.

(Molloy, Charles) *The half-pay officers.* Repr. London: Cornmarket press, 1969.

Molyneux, Thomas. 'Journey to Connaught, April, 1709'. Ed. A. Smith. *Miscellany of the Irish Archaeological Society* 1 (1846) 161–178.

Molyneux, William. *The case of Ireland's being bound.* (1698). Repr. London 1720.

Monk, Samuel H. *The sublime: a study of critical theories in XVIII-century England.* New York: Modern Language Association of America, 1935.

Moore, Thomas. *The life and death of lord Edward Fitzgerald.* 2 vols. London 1831.

Morden, Robert. *Geography rectified.* London 1680.

Morgan, Prys. 'Boxhorn, Leibniz, and the Welsh'. *Studia Celtica* 8/9 (1973–4) 220–228.

Moryson, Fynes. *An itinerary written by Fynes Moryson Gent.* (1617) Repr. Glasgow: James MacLehose, 1907–08.

——. *Shakespeare's Europe: the fourth part of Fynes Moryson's Itinerary.* Ed. Ch. Hughes. London: Sherratt & Hughes, 1903.

Mossner, Ernest Campbell. *The life of David Hume.* 2nd edition. Oxford: Clarendon, 1980.

*(Mottley, John) *The craftsman.* London 1728.

Munter, Robert. *The history of the Irish newspaper, 1685–1760*. London: Cambridge U.P., 1967.

Murphy, Gerald. 'Bards and filidh'. *Éigse* 2 (1940–1) 200–7.

——. 'Notes on aisling poetry'. *Éigse* 1 (1939–40) 40–50.

——. 'Poems of exile by Uilliam mac Barúin Dealbhna'. *Eigse* 6 (1948) 8–15.

Murray, Robert H. (ed.). *The journal of John Stevens*. Oxford: Clarendon, 1912.

Nalson, John. *An impartial collection of the great affairs of state*. 2 vols. London 1682–83.

Nicholls, Kenneth. *Gaelic and gaelicised Ireland in the middle ages*. Gill history of Ireland, vol. 4. Dublin: Gill and Macmillan, 1972.

Nicoll, Allardyce. 'Political plays of the restoration'. *Modern language review* 16 (1921) 224–242.

Nicolson, William. *The Irish historical library. Pointing at most of the authors and records in print or in manuscript, which may be servicable to the compilers of a general history of Ireland*. Dublin 1724.

Ní Ógáin, Róis (ed.) *Duanaire Gaedhilge*. 2 vols. Baile Átha Cliath: Comhlucht Oideachais na hÉireann, n.d.

Ní Shéaghdha, Nessa. *Catalogue of Irish manuscripts in the National Library of Ireland*. Dublin: Dublin Institute for Advanced Studies, 1961 – (in progress).

Ó Beaglaoich, Conchobhar & Aodh Mac Cruitín. *The English Irish dictionary*. A bPairis, 1732.

O'Brien, George. 'The fictional Irishman 1665–1850'. *Studies* 66 (1977) 319–329.

O'Brien, John, *Focalóir Gaoidhilge – Sax-Bhéarla: or, an Irish-English dictionary*. (Paris) 1768.

O'Brien, Paul. *A practical grammar of the Irish language*. Dublin 1809.

O'Brien, Sylvester (ed.). *Measgra in gcuimhne Mhíchíl Uí Chlérigh. Miscellany of historical and linguistic studies in honour of Brother Micheal Ó Cléirigh, chief of the Four Masters, 1643–1943*. Assisi press, 1944.

*(O'Brien, William). *The duel*. London 1772.

Ó Buachalla, Breandán (ed.). *Cathal Buí: amhráin*. Carraig Dubh (Co. Dublin): Clóchomhar, 1975.

——. *I mBéal Feirste cois cuain*. Baile Átha Cliath: Clóchomhar, 1968.

——. 'An mheisiasacht agus an aisling'. In P. de Brún et al. (eds.). *Folia Gadelica*. (Festschrift for R.A. Breatnach). Cork: Cork U.P. 1983, 72–87.

Ó Cléirigh, Tomás. *Aodh Mac Aingil agus an scoil nua-Ghaedhilge i Lobháin*. Baile Átha Cliath: Oifig an tSoláthair, 1936.

O'Clery, Michael. 'Foclóir nó sanasan nua'. Ed. A.W. K. Miller. *Revue Celtique* 4 (1879–80) 349–428, 5 (1881–83) 1–69.

——. *The martyrology of Donegal. A calendar of the saints of Ireland*. Eds. J. H. Todd & W. Reeves. Dublin, 1864.

—— et al. *Genealogiae regum et sanctorum Hiberniae*. Ed. P. Walsh. Maynooth: St. Patrick's College Record Society, 1918.

Ó Concheanainn, Tomás. 'A feature of the poetry of Fearghal Óg Mac an Bhaird'. *Éigse* 15 (1973–74) 235–251.

O'Connor, Dermod (trl.). *The general history of Ireland* (by Geoffrey Keating). Dublin 1723.

O'Conor, Charles. *The case of the Roman Catholics of Ireland, wherein the principles and conduct of that party are fully explained and vindicated.* Dublin 1755.

——. *A cottager's remarks on the Farmer's Spirit of party.* Dublin 1754.

——. *Dissertations on the antient history of Ireland.* 2nd ed. Dublin 1766.

——. *Seasonable thoughts relating to our civil and ecclesiastical constitution.* Dublin 1753.

——. *A vindication of lord Taaffe's civil principles.* Dublin 1768.

——. *Letters.* Eds. C.C. & R.E. Ward. 2 vols. Ann Arbor, Mich.: Irish American Cultural Institute/University Microfilms, 1980.

* O'Conor, Charles, D.D. *Memoirs of the life and writings of the late Charles O'Conor.* Dublin, n.d.

* O'Connor, Charles, S.J. *The early life of Charles O'Conor (1710–1791) of Belanagare and the beginning of the Catholic revival in Ireland in the eighteenth century.* Unpublished typescript (dated 1930) in the National Library of Ireland.

——. 'Charles O'Conor of Belanagare. An Irish scholar's education'. *Studies* 23 (1934) 124–143, 455-469.

——. 'Origins of the Royal Irish Academy'. *Studies* 38 (1949) 325–337.

Ó Corráin, Donncha. 'Nationality and kingship in pre-Norman Ireland'. In: *Nationality and the pursuit of national independence* (ed. T.W. Moody). Belfast: Appletree press, 1978, 1–35.

Ó Cuív, Brian. 'An eighteenth-century account of Keating and his "Foras feasa ar Éirinn"'. *Éigse* 9 (1958-61) 264–269.

O'Curry, Eugene. *Lectures on the manuscript materials of ancient Irish history,* Dublin 1861.

O'Daly, John (ed.). *The poets and poetry of Munster.* 4th edition. Dublin n.d. (1884).

Ó Donnchú, Donncha (ed.). *Filíocht Mháire Bhuidhe Ní Laoghaire.* Baile Átha Cliath: An Gúm, 1931.

Ó Fiaich, Tomás (ed.). *Art Mac Cumhaigh: dánta.* Baile Átha Cliath: Clóchomhar, 1973.

O'Flaherty, Roderic. *A chorographical description of West or H-Iar Connaught.* Ed. J. Hardiman. Dublin 1846.

——. *Ogygia; seu, rerum Hibernicorum chronologia.* Londini 1685.

——. *The Ogygia vindicated against the objections of Sir G. Mackenzie.* Ed. Charles O'Conor. Dublin 1775.

Ó Flannghaile, Tomás (ed.). *Duanaire na macaomh. A selection of Irish poetry for schools and colleges.* Dublin: Gill, 1924.

Ó Foghludha, Risteárd (ed.). *Ar bruach na Coille Muaire. Liam Dall Ó hIfearnáin cct.* Baile Átha Cliath: Oifig an tSoláthair, 1939.

——. *Cois na Ruachtaighe: Clann tSúilleabháin Chaoil cct.* Baile Átha Cliath: Oifig an tSoláthair, 1938. (a)

——. *Donnchadh Ruadh Mac Conmara (1715–1810).* Baile Átha Cliath: An Gúm, 1933. (a)

——. *Éigse na Máighe .i. Seán Ó Tuama an Ghrinn, Aindrias Mac Craith - An Mangaire Súgach*. Baile Átha Cliath: Oifig an tSoláthair, 1952.

——. *Eoghan an Mhéirín cct*. Baile Átha Cliath: Oifig an tSoláthair, 1938. (b)

——. *Seán Clárach 1691–1754: a shaothar fileata agus scéal a bheathadh*. Baile Átha Chiath: Oifig an tSoláthair, 1933. (b)

Ó Gallchóir, . . . (ed.). *Séamas Dall Mac Cuarta; dánta*. Baile Átha Cliath: Clóchomhar, 1971.

Ogilvie, John. *Rona, a poem in seven books*. London 1777.

O'Halloran, Sylvester. *A general history of Ireland, from the earliest accounts to the close of the twelfth century*. 2 vols. London 1778.

——. *An introduction to the study of the history and antiquities of Ireland: In which the assertions of Mr. Hume and other writers are occasionally considered*. London/Dublin 1772.

O'Hanlon, John. *Lives of the Irish saints, compiled from calendars, martyrologies, and various sources related to the ancient church history of Ireland*. 3 vols. Dublin etc. n.d. (1873).

Ó hÓgáin, Dáithí. *An file. Staidéar ar osnadúrthacht na filíochta sa traidisiún Gaelach*. Baile Átha Cliath: Oifig an tSoláthair, 1982.

*O'Hussey, Bonaventura. *An teagasg Críosdaidhe ann so*. (Louvain) n.d.

*——. *Dan do rinne an Brathar Bocht dórd S. Proinsias B. Ó Héodhasa*. (Louvain) n.d.

*O'Keeffe, John. *Dramatic works*. 4 vols. London 1798.

*——. *Fontainbleau, or, our way in France*. Dublin 1790.

*——. *The she-gallant: or, square-toes outwitted*. London 1767.

*——. *The world in a village*. London n.d. (1793).

(O'Mahony, Cornelius). *Disputatio apologetica de iure regni Hiberniae pro Catholicis Hibernis adveros haereticos Anglos*. (Lisbon) 1645.

Ó Maolchonaire, Flaithrí (tr.) *Desiderius, otherwise called Sgáthán an chrábhaidh*. Ed. T.F. O'Rahilly. Dublin: Dublin Institute for Advanced Studies, 1955.

Ó Maonaigh, Cainneach. 'Scribhneóirí Gaeilge an seachtú haois déag'. *Studia Hibernica* 2 (1962) 182–208.

O'Molloy, Franciscus. *Lucerna fidelium, seu fasciculus decerptus ab authoribus magis versatis, qui tractarunt de doctrina Christiana*. Romae 1676.

——. *Grammatica Latino-Hibernica compendiata*. Romae 1677.

Ó Muirgheasa, Énrí (ed.). *Amhráin Airt Mhic Chubhthaigh agus amhráin eile*. 2nd edition. 2 vols. Dún Dealgan: Preas Dhún Dealgan, 1926.

——. *Amhráin na Midhe*. Cuid a haon. Baile Átha Cliath/Corcaigh: Comhlucht Oideachais na hÉireann, n.d. (1933).

Ó Néill, Séamus. 'The hidden Ulster'. *Studies* 55 (1966) 60–66.

Ó Raghallaigh, Tomás. *Duanta Eoghain Ruaidh Mhic an Bhaird*. Gaillimh: Ó Gormáin, 1930.

O'Rahilly, T.F. (ed.). *Burdúin bheaga. Pithy Irish quatrains*. Dublin etc.: Browne & Nolan, 1925.

——. 'Irish scholars in Dublin in the early eighteenth century'. *Gadelica* 1 (1912–13) 156–162.

——. *Measgra dánta*. Dublin/Cork: Cork U.P., 1927.

——. 'On the origin of the names "Érainn" and "Ériu"'. *Ériu* 14, 1 (1943) 7–28.

O'Reilly, Edward. *Sanas Gaoidhilge – Sags-bhearla, an Irish-English dictionary*. Dublin 1817.

O'Sullevan Beare, Philip. *Historiae Catholicae Iberniae compendium*. Ulyssipone (Lisbon) 1621.

——. *Patritiana decas, sive libri decem, quibus de diva Patricii vita, rebusque gestis: de religionis Ibernicae casibus, de Anglohaereticae ecclesiae sectis, accurate agitur*. Matriti 1629.

O'Sullivan, A., & W. O'Sullivan. 'Edward Lhuyd's collection of Irish manuscripts'. *Transactions of the hon. society of Cymmrodorion*, session 1962, 57–71.

O'Sullivan, Donal. *Carolan. The life, times and music of an Irish harper*. 2 vols. London: Routledge & Kegan Paul, 1958.

Ó Tuama, Seán. *Filí faoi sceimhle: Seán Ó Ríordáin agus Aogán Ó Rathaille*. Baile Átha Cliath: Oifig an tSoláthair, 1978.

——. *An grá in amhráin na ndaoine*. Baile Átha Cliath: Clóchomhar, 1960.

——. 'Téamaí iasachta i bhfilíocht pholatiúil na Gaeilge (1600–1800)'. *Éigse* 11 (1964–66) 201–213.

Ó Tuathail, Éamonn, 'Nugentiana'. *Éigse* 2 (1940) 4–14.

Otway, Thomas. *Works*. Ed. Montague Summers. 3 vols. London: Nonesuch press, 1926–7.

*Oulton, Walley Chamberlain. *Botheration: or, a ten year's blunder*. London 1798.

Pageaux, Daniel-Henri. 'Une perspective d'études en littérature comparée: l'imagerie culturelle'. *Synthesis* 8 (1981) 169–85.

Parsons, James. *Remains of Japhet: being historical enquires into the affinity and origin of the European languages*. London 1767.

Parsons, Lawrence. *Observations on the bequest of Henry Flood, Esq. to Trinity College, Dublin. With a defence of the ancient history of Ireland*. Dublin 1795.

Payne, Robert. *A briefe description of Ireland: made in this yeare 1589*. Repr. Amsterdam: Theatrum Orbis Terrarum; New York: Da Capo Press, 1973.

*Pearce, William. *Netley Abbey*. London 1794.

Petty, William, *The political anatomy of Ireland*. London 1691.

Pezron, Paul Yves. *Antiquité de la nation et de la langue des Celtes autrement appelez Gaulois*. Paris 1703.

*Phillips, William. *Hibernia freed*. London 1722.

*Pilon, F. *The siege of Gibraltar*. London 1780.

Pinkerton, John. *Literary correspondence*. 2 vols. Londn 1830.

——. *Rimes*. 2nd ed. London 1782.

Plomer, Henry R. 'Dermod O'Connor and Keating's history'. *Irish book lover* 3, 8 (March 1912) 125–127 and 155.

Pococke, Richard. *Pococke's tour in Ireland in 1752*. Ed. G.T. Stokes. Dublin/London 1891.

Popper, Karl R. *Objective knowledge: an evolutionary approach*. Revised edition. Oxford: Claredon, 1979.

——. *The open society and its enemies.* 2 vols. London: Routledge, 1945.

*Powell, George, *A very good wife.* London 1693.

Preaching the gospel in Irish, not contrary to law; but enjoyned expressly by several statues and canons now in force in this kingdom, as well as by the word of God. Dublin 1713.

(Preston, William). *An heroic epistle from Donna Teresa Pinna y Ruiz, of Murcia, to Richard Twiss, Esq; F. R. S.* Dublin 1776. (a)

——. *An heroic answer, from Richard Twiss, Esq. F. R. S. at Rotterdam, to Donna Teresa Pinna y Ruiz, of Murcia.* Dublin 1776. (b).

(Prior, Thomas). *A list of the absentees of Ireland, and the yearly value of their estates and incomes spent abroad. With observations on the present state and condition of that kingdom.* Dublin 1729.

——. *Observations on coin in general, with some proposals for regulating the value of coin in Ireland.* Dublin 1729.

——. *An essay to encourage an extend the linen-manufacture in Ireland, by praemiums and other means.* Dublin 1749.

Quin, Cosslett. 'A manuscript written in 1709 by Charles Lynegar for John Hall, vice-provost of Trinity College, Dublin'. *Hermathena* 53 (May 1939) 127–137.

Quinn, David Beers. 'Ireland and sixteenth century European expansion'. *Historical studies* 1 (1958) 20–32.

——. *The Elizabethans and the Irish.* Itaca, N.Y.: Cornell U.P. 1966.

Renan, Ernest. 'Qu'est-ce qu'une nation?' In: Id. *Discours et conférences.* Paris 1887, 277–310.

*Reynolds, Frederic. *Notoriety.* London 1793.

Rich, Barnaby. 'Remembrances concerning the state of Ireland, 14th Aug. 1612'. Ed. C. Litton Falkiner *Proceedings of the Royal Irish Academy* 26 (1906) 125–142.

——. *A catholicke conference between Syr Tady Mac. Mareall and Patricke Plaine.* London 1612.

——. *A new description of Ireland: wherein is described the disposition of the Irish.* London 1610.

——. *A short survey of Ireland.* London 1069 (i.e. 1609).

——. *A true and kind excuse written in defence of that booke, intituled, A new description of Irlande.* London 1612.

Richardson, John. *A catechism to which are appended brief and plain rules for reading the Irish language.* London n.d.

——. (trl.). *Seanmora ar na priom phocibh na creideamh; Sermons upon the principal points of religion.* London 1711.

—— . (trl.). *The church catechism explain'd: Caitecism na heaglaise minighthe.* (By John Lewis) London 1712.

——. *A short history of the attempts that have been made to convert the popish natives of Ireland to the establish'd religion: with a proposal for their conversion.* 2nd ed. Dublin 1713.

Richardson, Samuel. *The history of Sir Charles Grandison*. Ed. Jocelyn Harris. 3 vols. London: Oxford U.P. 1972.

Risk, M.H. 'Charles Lynegar, professor of the Irish language, 1712'. *Hermathena* 102 (1966) 16–25.

Robbins, Caroline. *The eighteenth-century commonwealthman. Studies in the transmission, development and circumstance of English liberal thought from the restoration of Charles II until the war with the Thirteen Colonies.* Cambridge, Mass.: Harvard U.P., 1959.

Roddy, Thady. 'Autograph letter of Thady O'Roddy'. Ed. J.H. Todd. *Miscellany of the Irish Archeological Society* 1 (1846) 112–125.

(Roth, David). *Hibernia resurgens, sive refrigerium antidotale. Adversus morsum serpentis antiqui, in quo modeste discutitur, immodesta parechasis T. Dempsteri a Muresck Scoti de repressis mendicabulis. Et Hibernia sancti sui vindicantur; ac bona fide asseruntur.* Rothomagi (Rouen) 1621.

*The royal flight: or, the conquest of Ireland. London 1690.

*The royal voyage: or, the Irish expedition. London 1690.

Saunders, Thomas Bailey. *The life and letters of James Macpherson, containing a particular account of his famous quarrel with Dr. Johnson, and a sketch of the origin and influence of the Ossianic poems.* London 1894.

Schuckburgh, Evelyn S. (ed.). *Two biographies of William Bedell, bishop of Kilmore, with a selection of his letters and an unpublished treatise.* Cambridge: At the University Press, 1902.

Scott, Walter. *Poetical works.* Ed. J. Logie Robertson. London: Oxford U.P. & Humphrey Milford, 1926.

**Shadwell, Charles. *Five new plays*. London 1720.

**——. *The humours of the army*. London 1713.

Shadwell, Thomas. *Complete works.* Ed. Montague Summers. 6 vols. London: Fortune Press, 1926–7.

Shakespeare, William. *Comedies, histories & tragedies.* Facs. ed. New Haven, Mass.: Yale U.P., 1954.

Shaw, Francis, 'The Celtic twilight'. *Studies* 23 (1934) 25–41, 260–278.

Shaw, William. *An analysis of the Galic language.* 2nd ed. Edinburgh 1778.

——. *A Galic and English dictionary.* London 1780.

Sheridan, Richard Brinsley. *Dramatic works.* Ed. Cecil Price. 2 vols. Oxford: Clarendon, 1973.

**(Sheridan, Thomas). *The brave Irishman*. Edinburgh 1755.

Shirley, John. *The true and impartial history and wars.* London 1691.

Sieyès, Emmanuel. *Qu'est-ce que le tiers état?* Ed. Robert Zapperi. Genève: Droz, 1970.

Simms, J.G. 'Ireland in the age of Swift'. In: Roger McHugh & Philip Edwards (eds.). *Jonathan Swift 1667–1967: a Dublin tercenary tribute.* Dublin 1967, 157–175.

——. 'John Toland (1670–1722), a Donegal heretic'. *Irish historical studies* 16 (1968–9) 304–320.

Sir John Oldcastle (1600). Repr.: Malone Society, 1908.

Smith, John. *Galic antiquities, consisting of a history of the druids, a dissertation on the authenticity of the poems of Ossian: and a collection of ancient poems, translated from Galic of Ullin, Ossian, Orran. &c.* Edinburgh 1780.

——. *Sean dana; le Oisian, Ulann, &c.* Edinburgh 1787.

Smollett, Tobias. *Works.* 12 vols. Westminster: Constable; New York: Scribner, 1901.

——. *The adventures of Roderick Random.* Ed. P.-G. Boucké. Oxford etc.: Oxford U.P. 1979.

Snyder, Edward D. *The Celtic revival in English literature 1760–1800.* Cambridge, Mass.: Harvard U.P., 1923.

——. 'The Wild Irish: a study of some English satires'. *Modern philology* 17 (1919–20) 687–725.

Solinus, C. Iulius. *Polyhistor, ex antiquis codicibus restitutus.* Ed. E. Vinetus. Pictavis (i.e. Poitiers)1554.

The South-Briton: a comedy of five acts. London 1774.

The spectator. Ed. G.G. Smith. 8 vols. London 1897.

Spelman, J.P. 'The Irish in Belgium'. *Irish ecclesiastical record.* 3rd. ser. 6 (1885) 791–801; 7 (1886) 350–357, 437–444, 641–649, 732–742, 1100–1106; 9 (1888) 16–21.

Spenser, Edmund. *The faerie queene.* Ed. J.C. Smith. 2 vols. Oxford: Clarendon, 1909.

——. *A view of the present state of Ireland.* Ed. W.L. Renwick. London: Scolartis press, 1934.

Stafford, Thomas. *Pacata Hibernia. Ireland appeased and reduced.* London 1633.

Stanyhurst, Richard, *De rebus in Hibernia gestis libri quattuor.* Antverpiae 1584.

——. 'A treatise contayning a playne and perfect description of Irelande'. In: Raphael Holinshed. *The firste volume of the chronicles of Englande, Scotlande, and Irelande.* London 1577.

Stanzel, Wolfgang. 'Das Nationalitätenschema in der Literatur und seine Entstehung zu Beginn der Neuzeit', in *Erstarrtes Denken. Studien zu Klischee, Stereotyp und Vorurteil in englischsprachiger Literatur.* Ed. G. Blaicher. Tübingen: Narr, 1987, 84–97.

Stapleton, Theobald. *Catechismus, seu doctrina Christiana Latino-Hibernica, per modum dialogi inter magistrum et discipulum.* Bruxellis, 1639.

The statutes at large, passed in the parliaments held in Ireland. 13 vols. Dublin 1786.

Stern, L. Chr. 'Die ossianischen Heldenlieder'. *Zeitschrift für vergleichende Litteraturgeschichte* N.F. 8 (1895) 51–86, 143–74.

——. 'Über eine Sammlung irischer Gedichte in Kopenhagen'. *Zeitschrift für Celtische Philologie* 2 (1899) 323–372.

Stewart, Alexander. *Elements of Galic grammar.* Edinburgh 1801.

Story, George. *A true and impartial history of the most material occurrences in the kingdom of Ireland.* London 1691.

——. *A continuation of the impartial history.* London 1693.

Strabo. *Geography*. Ed./trl. H.L. Jones. 8 vols. London: Heinemann; New York: Putnam, 1917–32

Swift, Jonathan. *Correspondence*. Ed. H. Williams. 5 vols. Oxford: Clarendon, 1963–65.

——. *Prose writings*. Ed. H. Davis. 16 vols. Oxford: Basil Blackwell, 1965–75.

Tanner, Thomas. *Bibliotheca Britannico-Hibernica, sive de scriptoribus, qui in Anglia, Scotia et Hibernia ad saeculi XVII initium floruerunt*. Londini 1748.

Temple, John. *The Irish rebellion*. London 1646.

Temple, William. 'An essay upon the advancement of trade in Ireland'. In: *The works of Sir William Temple* (4 vols., London 1770) vol. 3, 5–31.

Thuente, Mary Helen. *The harp re-strung. The United Irishmen and the rise of Irish literary nationalism*. Syracuse University Press, 1994.

Toland, John. *Vindicius liberius: or, Mr. Toland's defence of himself against the late lower house of convocation and others*. London 1702.

——. *Reasons offer'd to the honourable house of commons why the bill sent to them shou'd not pass into a law*. London 1720.

——. *A collection of several pieces now first published*. 2 vols. London 1726.

Tourneur, Victor. *Esquisse d'une histoire des études celtiques*. Liége: Faculté de philosophie et lettres, 1905.

Transactions of the Gaelic Society of Dublin. Dublin 1808.

Transactions of the Iberno-Celtic Society. Dublin 1820.

Transactions of the Ossianic Society. 6 vols. Dublin 1855–61.

Truninger, Anneliese. *Paddy and the Paycock. A study of the Stage Irishman from Shakespeare to O'Casey*. Bern: Francke, 1976.

Turner, John P. (ed.). *A critical edition of James Shirley's 'St Patrick for Ireland'*. New York & London: Garland, 1979.

Twiss, Richard. *A tour in Ireland in 1775*. London 1776.

Ussher, James. *The whole works*. Ed. C.R. Elrington. 16 vols. Dublin 1847–64.

Vallancey, Charles. *A grammar of the Iberno-Celtic or Irish language*. Dublin 1773.

Vance, Norman. 'Celts, Carthaginians and constitutions: Anglo-Irish literary relations, 1780–1820'. *Irish historial studies* 22, 87 (March 1981) 216–238.

Van Tieghem, Paul. *Ossian en France*. 2 vols. Paris: F. Rieder, 1917.

*Vaughan, Thomas. *The hotel: or, the double valet*. London 1766.

Viallaneix, Paul, & Jean Ehrard (eds.). *Nos ancêtres les Gaulois. Actes du colloque international de Clermont-Ferrand*. Clermond-Ferrand: Faculté des lettres et sciences humaines de l'Université de Clermont-Ferrand II, 1982.

* (Waldron, Francis Godolphin). *The maid of Kent*. London 1778.

Walker, Joseph Cooper. *Historical memoirs of the Irish bards*. London 1786.

Walsh, Paul. *Gleanings from Irish manuscripts*. 2nd edition. Dublin: At the sign of the three candles, 1933.

——. *Irish men of learning*. Ed. Colm Ó Lochlainn. Dublin: At the sign of the three candles, 1947.

Walsh, Peter. *A prospect of the state of Ireland*. London 1682.

Warburton, John et al. *History of the city of Dublin from the earliest accounts to the present time: containing its annals, antiquities, ecclesiastical history and charters.* 2 vols. London 1818.

Ward, Edward. *Works.* 2 vols. London 1703.

Ward, R., & C.C. Ward. 'The Catholic pamplets of Charles O'Conor (1710–1791)'. *Studies* 68 (1979) 259–264.

Ware, James. *De Hibernia et antiquitatibus eius disquisitiones.* Londini 1705.

——. *The antiquites and history of Ireland.* London 1705.

A warning for faire women (1599). Facs. reprint: Tudor Facsimile Texts, 1912.

Warner, Ferdinando. *The history of Ireland.* London 1763.

——. *The history of the rebellion and civil-war in Ireland.* 2nd ed. London 1768.

Warton, Thomas. *The history of English poetry, from the close of the eleventh to the commencement of the eighteenth century.* 4 vols. London 1774–81.

Weeks, James Eyre. *A new geography of Ireland.* 3rd ed. Dublin 1752.

Whitaker, John. *The genuine history of the Britons asserted in a full and candid refutation of Mr. Macpherson's Introduction.* London 1771.

White, Stephen. *Apologia pro Hibernia adversus Cambri calumnias. Sive fabularum et famosorum libellorum Silvestri Giraldi Cambrensis sub vocabulis topographiae, sive de mirabilibus Hiberniae, et historiae vaticinalis, sive expugnationis eiusdem insulae refutatio.* Ed. M. Kelly Dublinii, 1849.

William of Malmesbury. *Willelmi Malmesbiriensis monachi De gestis regum Anglorum.* Ed. W. Stubbs. (Rolls Series). 2 vols. London 1889.

William of Newburgh. *Historia rerum Anglicarum.* Ed. H.C. Hamilton: Publications of the English historical society. Repr. Vaduz 1964.

Williams, Charles Hanbury. *Works.* 3 vols. London 1822.

Williams, N.J.A. (ed.). *Pairlement Chloinne Tomáis.* Dublin: Dublin Institute for Advanced Studies, 1981.

——. *The poems of Giolla Brighde Mac Con Midhe.* Dublin: Irish Texts Society, 1980.

*(Wilson, Charles Henry), *Brookiana.* 2 vols. London 1804.

——. *Select Irish poems, translated into English,* n.pl. (Dublin?), n.d.

Wood, Theodore E.B. *The word 'Sublime' and its context 1650–1760.* The Hague/Paris: Mouton, 1972.

Young, Arthur. *A tour in Ireland, with general observations on the present state of that Kingdom.* 2 vols. Dublin 1780.

Zimmermann, Georges-Denis. *Songs of Irish rebellion. Political street ballads and rebel songs 1780–1900.* Hatboro, Pa.: Folklore Associates, 1967.

Zimmermann, Johann Georg. *Von dem Nationalstolze.* 2nd and 4th editions. Zürich 1760, 1768.

INDEX